W9-CGN-586

Engineering Economics
for Capital
Investment Analysis

Engineering Economics
for Capital
Investment Analysis

TUNG AU

Professor of Civil Engineering and Public Policy
Carnegie Institute of Technology
Carnegie-Mellon University

THOMAS P. AU

William Larimer Mellon Fellow
Graduate School of Industrial Administration
Carnegie-Mellon University

ALLYN AND BACON, INC.
Boston   London   Sydney   Toronto

This book is part of the
ALLYN AND BACON SERIES IN ENGINEERING
Consulting Editor: Frank Kreith
University of Colorado

Library of Congress Cataloging in Publication Data

Au, Tung, 1923–
    Engineering economics for capital investment analysis.

    (Allyn and Bacon series in engineering)
    Includes index.
    1. Capital investments—Evaluation. 2. Engineering
economy.   I. Au, Thomas P., 1957–   .   II. Title.
III. Series.
HG4028.C4A9   1983   658.1'52   82-22604
ISBN 0-205-07911-3
ISBN 0-205-07965-2 (International ed.)

Printed in the United States of America

10 9 8 7 6 5 4 3 2 1   88 87 86 85 84 83

CONTENTS

v

Chapter 4   Computation of Rates of Return

Chapter 5   The Economic Feasibility of Independent Projects

Chapter 6   The Comparison of Mutually Exclusive Proposals

Chapter 7   The Benefit-Cost Ratio Method

Chapter 8   The Internal Rate of Return Method

Chapter 9   Capital Rationing

Chapter 10   Estimation of Costs and Benefits

Chapter 11   Depreciation and Corporate Taxation

Chapter 12 Analysis of Before-Tax and After-Tax Cash Flows

Chapter 13 Price Level Changes

Chapter 14 Financial Statements

Chapter 15 Uncertainty and Risk

Chapter 16 Capital Investment Decisions in Private Firms

Chapter 17 Resource Allocation Decisions for Public Projects

PREFACE

The objective of this book is to present the basic concepts and the analytical techniques for the economic evaluation of engineering projects in both the public and private sectors. It covers the subject in sufficient detail to develop a thorough understanding of the decision-making process in capital investment planning with a minimum amount of descriptive material on the decision environment of the public or private institutions. It emphasizes the application of analytical techniques to a great variety of problems that may confront engineers and managers who are concerned with capital budgeting.

As an introductory text on engineering economic analysis, the book concentrates on the principles that provide a solid foundation in the pursuit of more advanced topics such as benefit-cost analysis and financial management. It is self-contained in offering a proper perspective that is essential to the understanding of capital investment decisions. One of the most important features of this book is the separation of the profit measures of investment decisions from the methods of analysis. Hence, the criteria for the acceptance of independent projects and for the selection of mutually exclusive projects are clearly defined before the various methods of analysis are introduced.

The general approach of this book is to begin with analytical techniques based on simplifying assumptions and to relax these restrictions gradually in order to introduce the more complicated elements reflecting professional practices. Although the net present value method is recognized as the most direct and unambiguous basis in the evaluation of capital projects, the benefit-cost ratio method and the internal rate of return method are also treated thoroughly because of their extensive uses in the public and private sectors, respectively. The implications of capital rationing in economic evaluations are also discussed. A serious examination of various critical issues is undertaken in order to dispel the misconceptions surrounding such problems.

In addition to the traditional coverage of cost and revenue functions in production, depreciation of capital assets, and corporation taxation, this book provides an unusually thorough treatise on the effects of price level changes on economic evaluation, including the variations of differential price change rates of labor, material, and energy costs. It contains a chapter on the basic features of financial statements pertinent to decision makers who are not well versed in managerial accounting.

xiii

The topic of uncertainty and risk in the economic evaluation of capital projects is explored, including the treatment of diversifiable and nondiversifiable risks. Such a discussion provides the basic understanding of the selection of the minimum attractive rate of return for capital investments in the private and public sectors. Finally, the problems associated with both the capital investment decisions in the private firms and the resource allocation decisions for public projects are examined.

This book has provided more than sufficient material for a one-semester course so that the instructor may exercise some discretion in the selection of topics for coverage. It is entirely possible to use the text for a two-quarter or two-semester sequence to deal with the subject more thoroughly, depending on the level at which the course is taught. The first six chapters contain the fundamental principles for which the student must gain a high degree of proficiency, while the subsequent chapters can be treated selectively with various degrees of emphasis in order to satisfy the preference of the instructor.

This book represents a joint undertaking of the authors to capture the forefront of development in engineering economic analysis. Chapters 1 through 9 and Chapter 17 were written by the first author and Chapters 11, 12, and 14 by the second author. Chapters 10, 13, 15, and 16 were written jointly. However, the manuscript has been checked by both for continuity and consistency.

We wish to express special thanks to Dr. Chris T. Hendrickson and Dr. Martin Wohl for their criticisms and suggestions in the development of the manuscript of this book. We also wish to express our appreciation to many others whose works have been cited in the appropriate references. While we are indebted to their contributions that have improved our own efforts, we are solely responsible for any possible errors or omissions.

It is our sincere hope that this book offers new insights into an old subject and may stimulate the interest of practitioners as well as students who are interested in economic evaluation of capital investment projects. The opinions expressed in this book are our own views and not necessarily those of the university or its colleges with which we are affiliated in our respective capacities.

T.A.
T.P.A.

Engineering Economics
for Capital
Investment Analysis

1

INTRODUCTION

1.1 Engineering Project Development

Engineering facilities and products are constructed or manufactured to meet human or societal needs and desires. An engineering facility or product is made up of many diverse components serving a common purpose and is often referred to as an engineering system. The entire process of planning, design, construction, operation, and maintenance of engineering systems, such as interstate highways or industrial plants, entails many important and often complex decisions. Both technological and economic considerations are essential in undertaking any new project requiring modern technology and involving a heavy commitment of resources.

The initiation of a new project follows the perception of human needs and desires in the society. An engineering system developed to satisfy such needs must pass tests of technological and economic feasibility under the prevailing institutional, social, and political conditions. First, an engineering system must be proved technologically feasible before anyone will commit resources to build it. Obviously, it would be a waste of time, effort, and resources to try to build a perpetual motion machine. Second, even if an engineering project is technologically feasible, it may not be worth building if the cost is prohibitively high compared to the benefit derived from the project. Because the advancement of technology is dynamic, the cost of a new system can be greatly reduced through continual technological improvements, and the cost relative to benefit may change rapidly. Furthermore, old technologies often become obsolete economically as well as technologically with the passage of time. Generally, economic consideration of an engineering project is based on the expected financial return on the investment. However, other institutional, social, and political forces as well as technological developments will tend to influence and modify the economic considerations. Thus, the goal of promoting economic efficiency is often tempered by other goals such as social equity, quality of life, or preservation of the environment.

Apart from the bare minimum requirements for human survival, societal needs are often based not on the demand in a competitive market, but on value judgments.

What are considered needs in one society may be considered luxuries in another. Hence goals and constraints as well as needs and requirements are value-laden. For example, in some developing countries, the emphasis on improving the national welfare through increasing economical efficiency is so great that the only hindrances to an engineering project are technological and economic constraints. Goals such as comfortable working conditions, health and safety standards, and environmental quality, while desirable in themselves, are often compromised in the interest of technological developments. In developed countries, such actions will be seriously challenged by the general public as well as those whose personal lives and fortunes are affected.

In the private sector, the failure of a new venture to satisfy perceived needs and desires will result in a loss on the investment and its ultimate disappearance from the marketplace. In the public sector, however, the failure of a new project to meet the societal needs is less evident since public welfare cannot be conveniently measured, and the project may turn out to be a liability that cannot easily be disposed of. Hence, in the development of an engineering project, it is important to assess its benefits and costs before making a choice. Although the motives in the initiation of a project are different in private and public sectors, there are enough similarities in the approaches for assessing the merit of a project that are applicable to both. Consequently, we shall examine the basic principles that will guide us to make better choices in the development of engineering projects.

1.2 The Decision-Making Process

In general, the decision-making process for engineering project development includes the following basic steps:

1. Defining the problem
2. Establishing objectives and criteria
3. Generating alternative plans and designs
4. Evaluation and choice
5. Implementation and control

Although these steps are often carried out in sequential order, backtracking and iteration are necessary when more detailed investigation in a subsequent step leads to new insight and results in modification of actions taken in previous steps. Thus, the delineation of this sequence and the grouping of actions for various steps are not rigid or unalterable.

Before developing a definitive statement of a problem, we must first recognize and understand the environment in which the problem exists. This environment includes the available technology, economic requirements, and social values of the time and locale, among other factors. Then and only then can we set realistic goals and constraints for initiating a new engineering project. It is important to distinguish the causes, rather than the symptoms, of a problem that we wish to solve. For example, if the problem is the high cost of energy, we should strive to find and develop new energy sources or make more efficient use of available energy. To introduce price controls alone would not only fail to solve the problem but would aggravate the problem by maintaining an artificially high demand for scarce energy. In order to avoid self-deception, we must collect information related to the problem and examine the issues to determine which factors or parameters are most relevant. It is important to realize that in defining a problem, the decision maker has injected his or her value judgment into the perception of the environment, including a propensity or aversion to taking risks in the face of uncertainty. He or she must also exercise value judgments in assessing the "needs" and "requirements" according to the prevalent trend of the society which is forever changing at a rapid pace. Thus, when we formulate the problem in a rational framework for analysis, we must recognize the limitations of our knowledge and understanding of the situation.

Since the goals of a proposed project are often broadly stated, they must be translated into specific objectives and operational criteria that can be measured in specific terms. It is important to note the hierarchical nature of the decision making in an organization. The goals at the highest level are reiterated as specific objectives and operational criteria as guideposts for setting goals at the next lower level. For example, a company may have several divisions that operate independently but must follow goals that are compatible with those of the company. Each division, in turn, may consist of several departments that must work toward a common goal. Depending on the major function of an organization, the information flows through various levels of the hierarchy in influencing the goals, objectives, and criteria may vary considerably.

The generation of alternative plans to meet the criteria for a proposed project involves the inductive process of synthesizing various solutions to the problem. The activities in synthesis are often described as an art rather than a science and are regarded as more akin to creativity than to knowledge, or to judgment than to methodology. The decision maker attempts to anticipate the consequences of various solutions and to make trade-offs among such factors as safety, economy, and aesthetics. The decision maker must search extensively and select judiciously among numerous possible alternative plans those that are most promising for further consideration.

Moreover, the technological and economical feasibility of each of the promising alternative plans must be scrutinized, and the infeasible ones are thus eliminated. In general, the conceptual models of proposed alternative engineering systems are analyzed and evaluated with regard to the characteristics of the relevant parameters and variables, and, if necessary, are modified and developed to optimize their performance with respect to cost. Useful as the quantitative relationships between performance and cost are in making a choice between alternative plans, they are not necessarily the only basis for comparison since they often do not include intangible factors, such as aesthetics, and social benefits and costs that cannot be readily quantified. In the final analysis, the decision must be based on the qualitative evaluation of intangible factors as well as on the quantitative evaluation of quantifiable parameters.

After a choice is made, the implementation of the proposed project can commence upon the commitment of adequate resources. In the process of implementation, it is necessary to exercise control to ensure that the project is carried out as planned and to provide feedback to the decision maker if adjustments in the original plan are necessary. For example, in the case of constructed facilities, not only must the detailed plans of the facilities be faithfully executed during the construction, but also the operating and maintenance procedures for the completed facilities must be followed.

This description of the decision-making process is intended to illustrate the complexity of many problems confronting a decision maker. There are, of course, different degrees of complexity in the problems at different levels of the hierarchy within an organization, or at different times or locales. In the final analysis, a decision about initiating an engineering project must be based on as complete a consideration of all relevant factors as the decision maker can comprehend and on as detailed an analysis of the problem as the benefit from the analysis can justify its cost.

1.3 Resource Allocation Decisions for Public Projects

A commitment to a public engineering project usually represents the allocation of a substantial amount of societal resources for some expected social benefits. It is difficult to measure social benefits against social costs, much less express the social value as a function of technological performance. For example, when the United States decided to land a person on the moon, technological feasibility was the major consideration; there was no attempt to evaluate its social benefits in terms of national pride and the uplift of the human spirit, although the latter must have been weighed in the decision. Even in allocation of resources to civilian projects, the consideration of social benefits and social costs is far from simple.

One of the difficulties in project evaluation is that the stated goals for such projects are often broad and evasive. For example, one of the historic pieces of legislation involving the government in large-scale civilian projects, the Flood Control Act passed by the U. S. Congress in 1936, states in part:[1]

> ... the Federal Government should improve or participate in the improvement of navigable waters or their tributaries, including watersheds thereof, for flood control purposes if the benefits to *whomsoever they may accrue* are in excess of the

[1] See *United States Code* (Washington, DC: Government Printing Office, 1940), p. 2964.

estimated costs, and if the lives and social security of people are otherwise adversely affected. [Italics added]

The difficulties in implementing this national goal were succinctly pointed out by Marglin:[2]

> The prime objective of public water resource development is often stated as the maximization of national welfare. That this is a goal to be desired, few would question; that it cannot be translated directly into operational criteria for system design, few would deny. Translation would require not only agreement on a definition for the deceptively simple phrase national welfare, but also some assurance that the defined concept is measurable.
>
> One possibility is to define national welfare as national income. The objective of system design then becomes maximization of the contribution of the system to national income. This definition is measurable, but it has implications for the meaning of national welfare that make us unwilling to accept it as a complete expression of the broad objective. Identifying national welfare with the size of the national income not only excludes non-economic dimensions of welfare but also implies that society is totally indifferent as to the recipient of the income generated by river-development systems, or that a desirable distribution of gains will be made by measure unrelated to the manner in which the system is designed.

Depending on the nature of a public project, one of the following specific objectives is often suggested:

1. Maximization of national income
2. Maintaining a balance between income generation and distribution
3. Encouraging regional development and environmental quality improvement

For each of these objectives, the proposed plans for the project will be considerably different. Obviously, how the problem is defined affects the ultimate solution of the problem.

While it is not possible to examine all relevant factors at this stage, a simplified example is introduced to illustrate some aspects of the decision-making process.

Example 1.1

Towns *A* and *B* are located near each other in the tributaries of a river basin as shown in Fig. 1.1. Over a number of years Town *A* experienced water shortages in dry seasons, and Town *B* was subjected to flooding at times when the snow accumulated on the mountains in the watershed melted too suddenly. The people in both towns are discussing their problems and suggesting that water conservation and

---

[2] See Ref. [1.1], p. 17, for a more complete discussion following this statement.

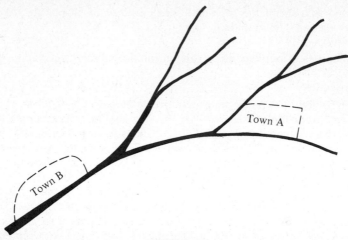

FIGURE 1.1

flood control projects should be undertaken individually or jointly to improve their situations. How can they achieve their goals?

Traditionally, the responsibility for maintenance and improvement of navigable rivers has been delegated to the U. S. Army Corps of Engineers. However, the Corps of Engineers cannot initiate any project unless it is authorized to do so by the U. S. Congress. Consequently, the problem must first be brought to the attention of the congress members representing the districts in which the towns are located. If the problems are deemed sufficiently important to warrant intervention by the federal government, a bill must be passed by the Congress to authorize a feasibility study of initiating a project or projects to alleviate the problems.

After receiving an authorization from the Congress, the Corps of Engineers will then go through an entire planning process. It will communicate with the local people and assess their needs, and then define the objectives of the project or projects within the context of the national goal. Next, alternative plans will be studied. For example, a small dam may be built to provide a reservoir near Town *A* and a dike may be built near Town *B* to prevent flooding. On the other hand, a larger dam may be built near the confluent just upstream from Town *B* so that it may alleviate both the problems of water shortages in Town *A* and of flooding in Town *B*. However, as a part of the authorized feasibility study, the Corps of Engineers may also investigate the opportunity to create recreational areas for swimming and boating near the reservoir. Hence, specific objectives of the project must be clearly defined. Should the Congress authorize a study to solve only the pressing local problems at the lowest cost? Should it expand the project to benefit more people in the region even though greater expenditures may also be incurred, as in the case of creating recreational areas? Who will be benefited the most and who will have to make the most sacrifices in making the project possible? How should benefits and costs, particularly social benefits and costs, be identified and measured?

Local citizens have increasingly demanded direct participation in this phase of decision making pertaining to value judgments, particularly in times of changing values. Consequently, communications with various segments of the communities are important in developing the criteria for judging the merits of alternative plans. After the consequences of each plan in terms of benefits and costs are determined, the alternative plans then can be evaluated on the basis of the same set of criteria. Finally, the recommendations of the Corps of Engineers will be reported to the Congress, which will select the best plan, if any, according to its collective judgment, and make the necessary appropriations for constructing the project.

It should be noted that in planning, designing, and constructing a public project, the professional staff only makes decisions at the level of its professional competence. It must assess the technological problems in site selection and project construction, the economic efficiency in terms of monetary gains and losses, or the environmental impacts of alternative plans. However, the ultimate decision of what to build or whether to build at all rests with public officials who often view a decision as an attempt to resolve conflicts and interests of various groups affected by the decision.

1.4 Capital Investment Decisions in Private Ventures

Although business enterprises are organized with profit motives, the goals of a private corporation may also be vague. In large corporations, most stockholders can effectively exercise their powers only to the extent of selling their stock when they lose confidence in the management. Consequently, the officers of the corporation will set goals that may include prestige, security, power, and continuity of the organization.

However, the most common specific objectives guiding the transactions of a corporation are:

1. Maximizing profits
2. Maintaining its market position
3. Stabilizing company structure with respect to assets and liabilities
4. Maximizing sales

Usually, these objectives are pursued within the constraints of government regulations and tax laws. Before making a substantial commitment of resources to a new venture, the dominant factors that may affect the marketing of the product must be considered.

For example, the use of solar energy for home heating and cooling may become a viable alternative if the costs of conventional fuels are expected to rise steadily. Even so, private investors are still cautious in embarking on new ventures in the solar energy field without some form of government commitment and tax incentives. Thus, the recent federal legislation on solar energy development enacted by the U. S. Congress represents only a first step to bring the developing technology into the marketplace. It will increase the prospects of making profits and decrease the degree of risks for private ventures.

Generally, all ventures involve taking risks. Executives of private corporations who authorize major investment in physical plant expansion must base their decisions on future outcomes that are far from certain. What will be the trends of technology? Will the supply of natural resources including energy and materials be adequate? Will the governmental regulations and tax policies become more restrictive? What will be the social values that may influence the manufacturing process of a new product as well as its market demand? However, long-range forecasting is inherently difficult. It is never advisable to extrapolate the trends of the next few years into the next few decades. Attempts to discern the general direction of social changes are generally more fruitful in long-range investment planning. No company wants to tie up all its assets in some marginally productive enterprises while missing more profitable investment opportunities.

While the relevant factors influencing the commitment of resources for private investment can be very complex, an example is given to illustrate some aspects of the decision-making process.

Example 1.2

A company which manufactures home heating and cooling equipment (furnaces, air conditioners, etc.) would like very much to develop a new product line of units that can utilize solar energy if necessary. Because of the anticipated shortage of conventional fuels, the company feels that there will be a demand for such units in the near future. How does the company go about making a decision?

First, the company collects relevant information regarding the technology of producing solar energy for home heating or cooling. Next it determines which type of equipment is most suitable for the intended purpose. It is found that there are no technological barriers for home heating and cooling with solar energy, at least as a supplementary source of energy for new construction. The significant obstacles to widespread use of solar energy are high initial costs, lack of support from utility companies, rigid building code requirements, no guarantee of sun rights, and uncertainty of public acceptance. Consequently, the company wants to determine if the lastest technology avaliable may possibly remove some of these obstacles.

In a quick review of the climatic conditions in the United States, it appears that in most regions, solar energy can best be used as supplementary energy source for home heating and cooling. Even though recent research reports indicate that new solar cells for converting a high proportion of sunlight to electricity are technologically feasible, the company does not feel that its own capabilities and resources should be diverted to a product line which is completely unrelated to its current activities. Instead, it is interested only in the development of capacities for producing solar panels and accessories that collect, store, and supply solar energy to supplement conventional fuels. Thus, the company concentrates its initial investigation on the types of solar panels and accessories that are necessary and determines whether some available in the market are compatible with its own existing equipment and whether they are cost-effective.

However, the company must also look at the broader picture of home construction which provides supplementary solar energy. Usually, the additional construction cost of outfitting a home for solar heating and cooling is substantial. Even if the long-run cost of using solar energy is lower, it is necessary for the home builders to make arrangements to finance the additional costs for home construction and for the purchase of the solar panels and accessories for solar heating and cooling. In addition, the company is concerned about the lack of national standards governing products for solar home heating and cooling. Consequently, manufacturers must tailor their products to the most stringent local standards currently in force, which will increase the cost of production and thus reduce the potential sales volume. All things considered, the company regards this potential investment opportunity as rather risky at this time and decides to postpone introducing this new product line.

1.5   The Role of Engineering Economic Analysis

Technological developments for satisfying societal needs have been accepted as a way of life since the Industrial Revolution. Technological considerations establishing the relationship between the expected performance of a new development and the required investment of societal resources are a traditional part of all engineering planning and design. Thus, the planning and design of an engineering facility or product entails a variety of activities such as preliminary investigation, feasibility studies, detailed analyses, and careful specification of the process of construction or manufacturing.

A broad view of engineering was incorporated in 1828 by the Institution of Civil Engineers (London) in its charter which defined engineering as "the art of directing the great sources of power in nature for the use and convenience of man."[3] Hence, the responsibility of engineers was linked to the management and allocation of resources within the context of nature, people, and technology. With the subsequent rapid expansion of technologies, engineers were very much preoccupied with technological development and gave scant attention to the impact of technology on

---

[3] See the description in "The Institution—Its Origin and Progress," *Journal of Institution of Civil Engineers* (London), **1** (1935), 4.

human beings and nature. The danger of concentrating on the development of "the great sources of power in nature" to the neglect of "the use and convenience of man" was recognized by people of vision as forewarned in 1887 by Wellington:[4]

> ... the distorted pre-eminence given by engineers, and by those who teach them and employ them to the pettiest details of *how* to build the separate works which make a railway, to the neglect of the larger questions of where to build and when to build, and whether to build them at all, has in it something at once astounding and discouraging.

In the evaluation of the overall worth of an engineering project, many issues must be considered. With the possible exception of technological and economic considerations, it is generally not possible to quantify the relevant factors in the decision-making process. Consequently, more attention has been given to economic analysis of engineering projects than other considerations besides technological investigation. However, this emphasis on economic analysis should not detract from the qualitative evaluation of other relevant factors in reaching the final decision.

The purpose of engineering economic analysis is therefore to provide a basic understanding of the probable answers from an economic viewpoint to the questions of what to build, where to build, and when to build, or whether to build at all. As an introduction, it deals primarily with concepts and methods of analysis related to the study of economic efficiency of engineering projects in terms of their benefits over cost to the society. Other factors influencing decisions in engineering project investments are discussed only briefly. Since the evaluation of such investments based on economic analysis must be reconciled with other considerations, each problem must ultimately be dealt with in the context of its real environment. However, engineering economic analysis is an important first step toward broadening the decision maker's perspective, enabling her or him to understand the consequences of decisions with greater insight and confidence.

1.6   Summary and Study Guide

In this chapter, we have highlighted the decision-making process in the development of engineering projects. We have also examined briefly the application of such a process within the context of developing public projects and private ventures. Although the economic efficiency of such projects in terms of their benefits over costs to the society has been emphasized, it has been pointed out that other factors, such as equitable distribution of income, stabilization of the economy, and preservation of the quality of life valued by the society, also play a significant role in the decision-making process. All these objectives must be pursued within the existing political and institutional constraints.

---

[4] See Ref. [1.2], p. 7.

While acknowledging various social and political concerns in the development and selection of engineering projects, the primary objective of this book is to provide a systematic treatment of the principles of economic analysis leading to the acceptance and selection of economically efficient projects for investment. In subsequent chapters, the concepts and methods of analysis will be discussed in depth, but the institutional environments associated with the application of these concepts and methods will receive only cursory reference. Since most activities related to engineering construction or manufacturing processes as well as the transactions in business and financial worlds are too complex for detailed description in an introductory course in engineering economic analysis, the examples used in this text are often simplified models of reality, focusing the attention only on the specific topics under consideration. The students are expected to grasp firmly the basic principles of making investment decisions and acquire the proficiency in applying these principles correctly.

REFERENCES

1.1 Marglin, S. A., "Objectives of Water Resource Development: A General Statement," *Design of Water Resource Systems* (A. Maass et al., contributors). Cambridge, MA: Harvard University Press, 1962.

1.2 Wellington, A. M., *The Economic Theory of Railroad Location*, 6th ed. New York: John Wiley and Sons, 1906.

PROBLEMS

P1.1 In the 1960s and 1970s, many older cities in the United States were encouraged and heavily subsidized by the federal government to redevelop or renew the blighted urban areas. The results were mixed. If you were given the opportunity to advise the Congress for a new legislation for the redevelopment of the blighted urban areas now, what would you consider as the major objectives of the program?

P1.2 In recent years, many industries have considered using robots to take over some of the jobs now performed by human workers. If you were a production manager responsible for making a decision of introducing robots in your own plant, what would be the most important factors that would influence your decision?

CHAPTER

2

BASIC CONCEPTS

OF CAPITAL INVESTMENT

2.1 The Nature of Investment

Investment may be defined as the commitment of resources to some economic activity in anticipation of greater returns or benefits in the future. Thus, investment clearly implies foregoing consumption now with the expectation of more consumption at a later time. In a strict economic sense, investment takes place only when natural resources are converted into capital assets such as the plant and equipment. Thus, an investment occurs when a user of capital, such as a private corporation or a public agency, takes the savings resulting from foregoing present consumption out of the capital or financial market and spends them on the acquisition of new assets.

In the private sector, savings may flow into investments through the creation of equity or debt. *Equity* refers to the value of the stock of a corporation, and new assets may be added either by issuing new shares of stocks or by ploughing back corporate earnings. *Debt* may be incurred either by taking loans from banks or by issuing bonds to the public which are redeemed at a later date. Individual savings are channeled into investments through intermediary financial institutions which provide a market mechanism to establish the relative values of various investment opportunities. For example, when a person deposits his or her personal savings in a bank, no real investment is made until someone borrows the money from the bank and spends it for home building, plant expansion, and similar activities.

In the public sector, present consumption may be deferred involuntarily through taxation by the government for the purpose of investment. The investments in public projects may also be financed by public debt in order to achieve socially desired goals. In either case, the market mechanism for capital formation is replaced by the compulsory action of the government.

Investment in new capital assets, whether in the private or public sector, is referred to as *capital investment*. An investment project of this nature requires a long-term commitment of resources with returns to be realized over the life of the

12

physical asset. The purpose of an economic evaluation of an investment in a capital project is to determine whether the long-run benefits will outweigh the long-run costs. What constitutes a satisfactory return depends on investor attitudes and on the resources available. On the other hand, the commitment of savings into investment through various means provided by financial institutions is referred to as *financial investment*.

It is therefore important to distinguish between an economic evaluation of a project and a feasibility study of its financing. The former refers to an analysis to determine whether a capital investment is economically worthwhile, assuming that the resources are available. The latter refers to an investigation to find the means of obtaining necessary funds to acquire a specified capital asset. These two types of analysis are different and they will be treated separately.

Example 2.1

Mr. Wilbur recently bought 100 shares of existing stock of Michigan Mining Company in the stock market. In a strict economic sense, is this purchase a new investment?

Mr. Wilbur merely acquired the ownership of the shares that were relinquished by someone else. The purchase is a financial investment and not a capital investment. In a strict economic sense, it is not a new investment.

Example 2.2

The Manor County Sanitary Authority plans to construct a new sewage treatment plant which will cost $5 million. It has engaged the professional services of a consultant to investigate the possibility of raising the money for construction through issuing public bonds. After a careful analysis of the bond market, the consultant recommends an annual interest rate of 6% for the bonds in order to attract enough buyers. Is this analysis an economic evaluation?

The consultant has analyzed the feasibility of financing the construction by borrowing. It has nothing to do with the question of whether the project is worthwhile in terms of future returns of the proposed investment. Therefore, this analysis is not an economic evaluation.

2.2   Time Preference

Although we are primarily interested in the analysis of capital investments in a strict economic sense, it is often easier to illustrate the basic principles by using simple examples in personal financial transactions familiar to most people. We shall therefore discuss the time preference of investors in the context of financial investment.

The time period to which an investor wishes to look ahead is called the *planning horizon.* When she or he plans to make an investment, she or he is interested in the return that will produce the greatest satisfaction for her or him. The time preference between consumption in different periods is measured by the *rate of time preference.* For example, if an investor is indifferent regarding either the prospect of receiving $100 now or receiving $110 a year later, he or she is said to have a rate of time preference of 10% per year. In general, if an investor has a rate of time preference of i per time period, then he or she is indifferent toward either the prospect of consuming P units now or consuming $P(1 + i)$ units at the end of the period. Conversely, the rate of time preference i, by which a return of $P(1 + i)$ at the end of the period is discounted to present value P, is called the *discount rate.*

For a person of limited means, the most obvious way to save for future consumption is to deposit the money in a savings account. The interest rate offered for savings accounts by a bank must be at least as high as the rate of time preference of this person if she or he decides to commit her or his money to a savings account. Then, the interest rate offered by the bank may be regarded as the *minimum attractive rate of return* of the investor. In reality, the situation is far more complex than this simplified explanation. For example, the investor may prefer depositing the money in a savings account over other investment opportunities because it is risk-free, it can easily be liquidated, or it is simply more convenient. In general, the minimum attractive rate of return of an investor depends on a number of factors. If a sum of money is committed to a particular investment, the same sum cannot be invested in other opportunities to earn a return. The cost of foregoing other investment opportunities is called the *opportunity cost* and can be expressed in terms of the rate that the best foregone opportunity will earn. By saving or borrowing against future returns, an investor will be able to select the pattern of consumption that he or she enjoys most by making proper choices of investment and financing.

2.3   A Simplified View of Market Economy

An important aspect of economics that concerns the evaluation of capital investment is the study of the allocation of scarce resources among alternative uses. The allocation process is said to be *economically efficient* when the total amount of benefits received by members of society from the consumption of all commodities is maximized under the prevailing income distribution. In a production and exchange economy, the economic efficiency is dependent on the following premises:

1. The objective of production is the satisfaction of individual wants so that the goods and services desired by the members of society are produced.
2. An interconnected market system sets the prices of goods and services according to individual preferences and productive technology.

The actual functioning of a production and exchange economy is extremely complex, and the possibilities of market failure will not be considered here. However, it is possible to examine a highly simplified view of the market system in order to understand the role of the financial institutions as intermediaries for production and exchange. The demand of investment capital can be described by a *demand curve or schedule* which represents the relationship between the interest rate for borrowing and the amount of capital demanded. Similarly, the supply of investment capital can be described by a *supply curve or schedule* which represents the relationship between the interest rate for lending and the amount of capital supplied. These curves are shown in Fig. 2.1. The willingness of the users of capital to borrow at certain interest rates depends on the rate of productivity in their potential uses of the capital. As the interest rate for borrowing decreases, more users of capital are willing to borrow and thus the aggregate demand for capital increases. Conversely, the willingness of the suppliers of capital to lend at certain interest rates depends on their rates of time preference. As the interest rate for lending increases, more suppliers of capital are willing to lend and thus the aggregate supply of capital increases. Since the users of capital must bid for what they want and the suppliers of capital will try to maximize their satisfaction, the equilibrium of supply and demand is reached when the amount of capital supplied and the amount demanded are equal. Hence, under the conditions of perfect competition, the point of equilibrium must be at the intersection of the supply and demand curves in Fig. 2.1. The interest rate corresponding to the point of equilibrium in a perfectly competitive market is referred to as the *market interest rate*.

In a perfectly competitive market, an investor can borrow or lend freely at the

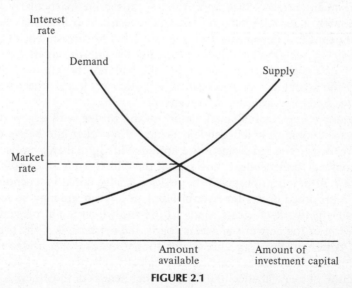

FIGURE 2.1

market interest rate. However, he or she will borrow only if investment opportunities exist that will earn a higher return than the market interest rate. Similarly, she or he will loan the money to others only if she or he cannot receive a greater satisfaction in her or his time preference than the market interest rate. Hence, the market interest rate may be regarded as the minimum attractive rate of return for an investor.

In reality, the market is imperfect and different interest rates may exist because of transaction costs in borrowing and lending. For example, an investor may not be able to find willing lenders for worthwhile projects if he or she is already heavily committed to other projects, or a lender may impose a higher interest rate for financing projects involving greater risks for fear of the bankruptcy of the investor. Such conditions which prevent the free flow of investment capital are referred to as *capital rationing*. When a budget limit or constraint for spending is imposed by an investor, the situation is referred to as *internal capital rationing*; when different interest rates for lending or borrowing are specified by the lenders, the situation is referred to as *external capital rationing*. These conditions may cause complications in economic evaluation. Nevertheless, they can be taken into consideration in the analysis.

2.4   The Classification of Investment Projects

Before undertaking a new capital investment, an extensive search is usually made to spot potential investment opportunities. It is important to recognize the characteristics of investment projects that appear to be attractive, particularly their interrelationships with other potential projects. An investment project may be economically independent of or dependent on other projects. An investment project is said to be *economically independent* if it is technically feasible to undertake this project alone and if its expected profit or net benefit will not be affected favorably or adversely by the acceptance or rejection of any other projects; otherwise an investment project is said to be *economically dependent*.

For example, replacing a small, deteriorating bridge with a new one may be regarded as an economically independent project if no other alternative or supporting actions related to the replacement are anticipated. In reality, a project is seldom totally economically independent; however, if the effects from other possibilities are small, then for all practical purposes the project is considered independent. On the other hand, a proposed bridge for river crossing at a given site may be economically dependent on a network of access roads to the site which is not presently in existence, since without the network of access roads, the net benefit of the bridge cannot be realized. Alternatively, if an underwater tunnel instead of a bridge is proposed near the same site, then neither one is economically independent of the other since the construction of one will affect the expected net benefit of the other.

When two projects are dependent on each other, they may either *complement* each other or *substitute* for each other to some degree. For example, a proposed bridge and a proposed network of access roads complement each other. Suppose that the network of access roads can serve the community near the bridge site regardless of the acceptance or rejection of the bridge proposal, but the bridge will be inaccessible without the road network. Then the proposed network of access roads is said to be the *prerequisite* of the proposed bridge. On the other hand, a proposed bridge and a proposed underwater tunnel near the same site of the river crossing may have a substituting effect for each other for lack of sufficient traffic volume to justify the construction of both. In fact, if the construction of one makes it technically infeasible to construct the other or if the net benefit expected from one proposed project will be completely eliminated by the acceptance of the other, then they are said to be *mutually exclusive.*

In economic evaluation, we arrange the potential projects in the form of a set of investment proposals so that they are not economically interdependent. If the investment proposals are independent, we can analyze each proposal on its own merit since its net benefit will not be affected by the acceptance or rejection of other proposals. If all investment proposals are mutually exclusive, the acceptance of one investment will automatically lead to the rejection of all others. Hence, we can rank the merits of various investment proposals and select the best among them.

To appreciate the importance of preparing independent or mutually exclusive investment proposals for evaluation, we need to understand the decision structure of the organization which will finance the investment. In most organizations, the funds available for investment are limited by the management. All capital investment proposals above a certain spending level are subject to review and approval by higher levels of management. If the set of investment proposals submitted for review and approval contains some dependent projects with complementary effect but only one of them is selected, the net benefit expected of the selected project cannot be realized because of the rejection of the remaining dependent projects. On the other hand, if the set of investment projects consists of some dependent projects with substituting effects and more than one of them is selected, the net benefit of each of the selected projects will be adversely affected by the acceptance of dependent projects. By presenting investment proposals as a set of projects that are not interdependent, we can make the appropriate choice according to the specified criteria of selection. This approach is applicable whether the decision is made by the person who conducts the analysis or by higher levels of management in the organization.[1]

2.5   The Cash Flow Profile of an Investment Proposal

An investment proposal can be described by the amount and timing of expected costs and benefits in the planning horizon. Here, the terms *benefits* and *costs* are

[1] See Ref. [2.1] for further discussion.

used in a broad sense to denote receipts and disbursements, respectively. The term *net benefit* is usually associated with public projects encompassing all social benefits less costs, while the term *profit* is used to denote receipts less disbursements in the private sector. Generally, the costs refer to the expected outlays and benefits to the expected proceeds over the life of an investment. When the outlays are paid in cash at market prices and the proceeds are also received in cash at market prices, an investment proposal can be represented by a stream of cash disbursements and receipts over time. For example, in the acquisition of a new machine, the typical costs are determined by the cash disbursements for the initial purchase price and the annual expenditure for operating and maintenance. The salvage value of the machine, which represents its market price at the time when it is disposed of, may be regarded either as a benefit or as a *negative* cost. The benefits may be measured by the cash value of the amount of labor saved. The investment proposal will thus be converted into a series of cash flows.

The stream of disbursements and receipts for an investment proposal over the planning horizon is said to be the *cash flow profile* of the investment. For private corporations, the cash flows may be estimated from expected *gross revenues* and *expenses*. Since some of the cash receipts are subject to taxation, the series of cash flows representing each investment alternative refers to after-tax values. In public investment projects, estimated benefits include only those that are quantifiable in monetary terms, and estimated costs represent the price to the society for obtaining the desired benefits. The series of the cash flows representing such an investment alternative refers to the before-tax values since government agencies are tax-exempt.

Although the amount and timing of the cash flows associated with each investment proposal can only be estimated in advance, they are generally assumed to be known with certainty for analysis. In reality, the future is uncertain, and various factors affecting the cash flows, such as inflation, change in tax rate, etc., must also be considered in making an investment. It is sufficient to point out at this time that an investment proposal can be appropriately represented by its cash flows at regular time periods, say years. Then, the cash flow at each time period is said to have a time value corresponding to the timing of its receipt or disbursement. The subject of the time value of money will be treated in detail in Chapter 3.

Example 2.3

Office copying equipment that costs $6,000 now is expected to be kept for 5 years. At the end of 5 years, it will have a salvage value of $800. The annual operating and maintenance cost is $1,000 per year, and the annual benefit generated by the equipment is $3,000 per year. Assuming that the receipts and disbursements are made at the end of the year, except the initial cost which is paid at present (end of year 0), describe this investment proposal in terms of its cash flows.

The series of cash flows describing this investment proposal may be represen-

Table 2.1

Cash Flows of the Investment

Year	Annual Cost	Annual Benefit	Annual Net Benefit
0	$6,000	$ 0	− $6,000
1	1,000	3,000	+ 2,000
2	1,000	3,000	+ 2,000
3	1,000	3,000	+ 2,000
4	1,000	3,000	+ 2,000
5	1,000	3,800	+ 2,800

ted by the annual net benefits, i.e., annual benefits in excess of annual costs as shown in Table 2.1. Note that at the end of year 5, the annual benefit is $3,800 because the salvage value of $800 is regarded as a benefit such that $3,000 + 800 = 3,800$.

Example 2.4

Suppose that the salvage value of $800 in Example 2.3 is treated as a negative cost instead of an additional benefit. What is the cash flow at the end of year 5?

In this case, the cost will be $1,000 + (−800) = 200$ and the benefit will be 3,000 at the end of year 5. Hence, the net benefit for the year will be $3,000 − 200 = 2,800$, which is the same as that in Example 2.3.

2.6   Measures of Profit Potential

The profit potential of an investment can be measured in a number of ways. Basically, an investor wants to know how good the return on his or her investment is at the end of the planning horizon *relative* to what might have been received from the best opportunity foregone in the same time period. Hence, *the measure of the profit potential is invariably tied to the minimum attractive rate of return of the investor* since possible alternative uses of his or her resources cannot be ignored.

Before discussing the time value of cash flows and the rate of return of investments which will be treated in detail in Chapters 3 and 4, respectively, we shall consider here only the simplest situation of a single sum P at the beginning of a *single* time period and a single sum F at the end of this period. If i is the *interest rate* for this period, then the amount F is related to the amount P in this cash flow profile as follows:

$$F = P + Pi = P(1 + i) \tag{2.1}$$

in which Pi represents the interest accrued during this period. Conversely,

$$P = F(1 + i)^{-1} \qquad (2.2)$$

where i is sometimes referred to as the *discount rate* because the present sum P may be regarded as a discounted value of the future sum F. Furthermore, the interest rate or discount rate i may be obtained as follows:

$$i = \frac{F - P}{P} \qquad (2.3)$$

Suppose that an investor invests a sum P_0 in a proposed project now and expects to receive a sum F_1 a year later and that the minimum attractive rate of return of the investor is i^*. Then, by letting $i = i^*$ in Eq. (2.1), we find F^* at the end of 1 year as follows:

$$F^* = P_0(1 + i^*)$$

where F^* is the amount that the investor could have obtained by investing in the best opportunity foregone. The difference between F_1 and F^* is referred to as the *net future value* (NFV), i.e.,

$$\text{NFV} = F_1 - P_0(1 + i^*) \qquad (2.4)$$

A positive NFV indicates the net benefit that the investor would have gained at the end of 1 year by having invested in the proposed project instead of investing in the best opportunity foregone, and a negative NFV indicates a net loss. Hence, the net future value is a direct measure of the profit potential of the proposed project. Alternately, we can obtain the discounted value P^* from F_1 by letting $i = i^*$ in Eq. (2.2) as follows:

$$P^* = F_1(1 + i^*)^{-1}$$

The difference between P^* and P_0 is referred to as the *net present value* (NPV), i.e.,

$$\text{NPV} = F_1(1 + i^*)^{-1} - P_0 \qquad (2.5)$$

A positive NPV also means that the proposed project will yield a higher return than the best opportunity foregone, and a negative NPV means otherwise, but the amount represented by NPV requires further explanation. That is, the net present value represents the amount that will yield the net future value in Eq. (2.4) if it is left to accrue interest at the minimum attractive rate of return. From Eqs. (2.5) and

(2.4), we note

$$(NPV)(1 + i^*) = [F_1(1 + i^*)^{-1} - P_0](1 + i^*)$$
$$= F_1 - P_0(1 + i^*) = NFV$$

In other words, the net present value refers to the *equivalent* net benefit at the present time if the net future value is discounted to the present at the specified minimum attractive rate of return. Since we relate more directly to the values of goods and services at present than those in the future, the net present value is a convenient measure of profit potential of the proposed project in spite of the fact that its meaning is derived from that of the net future value.

Another possible measure of profit potential of a proposed project is the return on the investment expressed as the percentage of the original amount invested, which is referred to as the *rate of return*. Thus, the rate of return i' for 1 year from an investment P_0 which yields an amount F_1 at the end of the year is

$$i' = \frac{F_1 - P_0}{P_0} \tag{2.6}$$

More specifically, the quantity i' represents the rate of return from investing in the proposed project and is sometimes referred to as the *internal rate of return*. However, it does not indicate whether the proposed project is worthwhile unless a proper comparison is made with the minimum attractive rate of return for the best opportunity foregone. A detailed discussion of the rate of return must be deferred until Chapter 4 because this concept requires careful interpretation. It is sufficient to point out at this time that from the viewpoint of an investor, the *overall rate of return* over the entire planning horizon may or may not be the same as the internal rate of return of a proposed project.

Generally, the cash flow profile of an investment project over the planning horizon may consist of cash disbursements and receipts at different points in time. Under such circumstances, the net present value of the discounted cash flows based on the minimum attractive rate of return will provide an unambiguous measure of the net benefit from the viewpoint of an investor. (It goes without saying that the net future value can serve the same purpose.) On the other hand, the term *rate of return* can be ambiguous unless carefully qualified when the internal rate of return of a proposed project is different from the overall rate of return of the investor. These measures of profit potential can be illustrated by some simple examples.

Example 2.5

The City of Blacksboro owns a vacant lot and has agreed to sell it to a builder a year later for development. In the interim period, the city can spend $1,000 for improving the ground and rent it to a parking lot operator for a rent of $1,210 to be paid at the end of the year. The city requires a minimum attractive rate of return of 10% per annum. What is the profit potential in investing $1,000 to improve the vacant lot?

The net benefit of the proposed project at the end of the year is represented by the net future value, which can be obtained from Eq. (2.4) as follows:

$$NFV = 1,210 - 1,000(1 + 0.10) = \$110$$

Thus, the city will gain an amount of $110 at the end of the year by investing $1,000 in the parking lot improvement rather than by investing it in the best opportunity foregone which would yield a return at the minimum attractive rate of return at 10%.

Alternatively, the net present value of the proposed project can be obtained from Eq. (2.5):

$$NPV = 1,210(1 + 0.10)^{-1} - 1,000 = \$100$$

This means that the city will gain an equivalent of $100 at present which can be invested at a minimum attractive rate of return of 10% to obtain a future value of $110 at the end of 1 year.

Finally, the rate of return of the proposed project can be obtained from Eq. (2.6):

$$i' = \frac{1,210 - 1,000}{1,000} = 0.21 = 21\%$$

The rate of return of 21% is clearly higher than the minimum attractive rate of return of 10%. Hence, the project is worthwhile in comparison with the best opportunity foregone.

Example 2.6

Suppose that you have $10,000 in a savings account which pays interest at an annual rate of 5%. Because of a sudden surge in the market interest rates for U.S. Treasury notes and the certificates of deposit offered by commercial banks, you are confronted with two unusual opportunities. The U.S. Treasury note quoted at an annual interest rate of 14% requires an immediate payment of $8,771.93 with a total return in the amount of $10,000 at maturity 1 year later. On the other hand, a certificate of deposit quoted at an annual interest rate of 13.5% requires an immediate payment of $10,000 with a total return of $11,350 in principal and interest 1 year later. Assume that you cannot borrow more money and you can only deposit the money in the bank if you do not purchase either the U.S. Treasury note or certificate of deposit. What is the total return on the $10,000 at the end of 1 year as a result of making either of these investments?

This example specifies a budget constraint of $10,000. The minimum attractive rate of return is 5%, which is the interest rate from the savings account.

In buying the U.S. Treasury note, you invest $8,771.93 now at 14%, but $10,000 - 8,771.93 = 1,228.07$ will be left in the savings account. Therefore, at the end of 1 year, we have

$$(8,771.93)(1 + 0.14) = \$10,000$$

$$(1,228.07)(1 + 0.05) = \$1,289.47$$

Hence, the total return is $10,000 + 1,289.47 = \$11,289.47$. The total return from the certificate of deposit is simply $(10,000)(1 + 0.135) = \$11,350$.

The profit potential for buying the U.S. Treasury note as expressed in the net future value is

$$NFV = 11,289.47 - (10,000)(1 + 0.05) = \$789.47$$

and that for buying the certificate of deposit is

$$NFV = 11,350.00 - (10,000)(1 + 0.05) = \$850.00$$

In other words, by buying the U.S. Treasury note instead of leaving all $10,000 in the bank, you will be $789.47 ahead at the end of 1 year; but by buying the certificate of deposit instead of leaving the $10,000 in the bank, you will be $850.00 ahead at the end of 1 year. Consequently, the purchase of the certificate of deposit yields a higher net future value than that of the U.S. Treasury note.

Using the net present value as a measure of the profit potential, we can find for the former

$$NPV = (11,289.47)(1 + 0.05)^{-1} - 10,000 = \$751.88$$

and for the latter

$$NPV = (11,350)(1 + 0.05)^{-1} - 10,000 = \$809.52$$

These values also indicate that the purchase of the certificate of deposit is preferable. Note that if each of these present sums is deposited at the bank to accrue an annual interest of 5%, you will obtain at the end of the year the following:

$$(751.88)(1 + 0.05) = \$789.47$$

$$(809.52)(1 + 0.05) = \$850.00$$

This example also shows that the internal rate of return of an investment proposal per se is not necessarily the same as the overall rate of return to the investor. Note that the internal rate of return of the U.S. Treasury note is 14% and the internal rate of return of the certificate of deposit is 13.5%. However, the overall rate of return from the purchase of the U.S. Treasury note is

$$i° = \frac{11,289.47 - 10,000}{10,000} = 0.1289 = 12.89\%$$

For the certificate of deposit, the overall rate of return is simply 13.5%. Hence, the certificate of deposit is preferable in spite of the fact that the U.S. Treasury note has a higher internal rate of return.

2.7   Criteria for Investment Decisions

Among the objectives of an organization engaged in economic activity, that of maximizing the profit potential is by far the most important from the standpoint of economic analysis. The operating criteria for this objective can be applied to independent projects and mutually exclusive projects. However, these criteria are affected by the presence of capital rationing.

If an organization can obtain additional funds or invest its excess funds in the capital market at a market interest rate, then the investment decision criterion for accepting noncompeting or independent investment proposals is to accept each independent project that produces an overall net benefit or profit. Under the same conditions, the investment decision criterion for selecting the best project among a set of mutually exclusive alternatives is to select the project with the highest overall net benefit or profit. When capital rationing is imposed for whatever reasons, each problem must be treated on the basis of additional information available.

Let N denote the net benefit or profit of an investment, B denote the total benefit realized, and C denote the total cost incurred, all of which are based on the same point in time. Since the total benefit B and total cost C are commonly expressed in the present values, the decision criterion for accepting an independent project without capital rationing is that the net present value N must be nonnegative. That is,

$$N = B - C \geq 0 \tag{2.7}$$

For mutually exclusive proposals, the objective is to maximize profit potential by accepting only the best of all proposals. Then, the decision criterion for profit maximization without capital rationing is to select the alternative with the highest nonnegative net present value. That is, if B, C, and N are again expressed in present values, the criterion becomes

$$\text{Maximize} \quad N = B - C \tag{2.8}$$

In some situations in which the level of performance of a project is specified, the objective is to select the proposal that requires the lowest cost. For example, after a target for productivity improvement is set and expressed in terms of the number of labor-hours saved through the acquisition of a new machine, the management will seek a machine of minimum cost that can meet this target. Then, the criterion is reduced to the selection of the alternative that requires the minimum total cost. That is,

$$\text{Minimize } C \quad \text{for } B = \text{constant} \tag{2.9}$$

On the other hand, there are situations in which a specific amount is allocated for the cost of a project with the expectation that the proposal selected will be the most effective alternative for the cost incurred. Then the criterion becomes the selection of the alternative that yields the maximum total benefit. Thus,

$$\text{Maximize } B \quad \text{for } C = \text{constant} \tag{2.10}$$

Since these decision criteria reflect different underlying objectives and other pertinent factors, they should be applied judiciously. The criterion represented by Eq. (2.7) will be examined in detail in Chapter 5, and those represented by Eqs. (2.8) through (2.10) will be discussed in Chapter 6.

Example 2.7

Suppose that the proposal for improving the vacant parking lot in Example 2.5 is one of two mutually exclusive alternatives with cash flow profiles shown below:

Year	Alternative 1	Alternative 2
0	− $1,000	− $1,480
1	+ $1,210	+ $1,760

The city is free to borrow or lend at a market interest of 10% per annum. Which alternative should be selected?

Using a minimum attractive rate of return of 10%, we can compute for the two alternatives:

1. $\text{NPV} = -1,000 + \dfrac{1,210}{1 + 0.10} = \$100$

2. $\text{NPV} = -1,480 + \dfrac{1,760}{1 + 0.10} = \$120$

On the basis of the decision criterion of maximizing net benefit, alternative 2 should be selected.

Example 2.8

If the city imposes a budget limitation of $1,200 for the improvement project in Example 2.7, which alternative should be selected?

The computation of the net present values for the alternatives in Example 2.6 remains unchanged. However, since the city is unwilling or unable to raise an amount beyond $1,200, only alternative 1 can be selected.

2.8   Summary and Study Guide

In this chapter, we have defined the problem of capital investment and established the objectives and criteria for investment decisions. Since the problem is inherently complex, simplifying assumptions have been introduced in problem formulation. Some of these assumptions can be removed as additional concepts are delineated and more sophisticated methods of analysis are introduced in subsequent chapters.

In order to emphasize the basic concepts, we have specifically assumed the following conditions:

1. A rate of time preference exists at which an individual is indifferent between consumption and investment.
2. Individual savings are channeled into productive uses through the financial markets, and the equilibrium of supply and demand is reached when the amount of capital supplied and the amount demanded are equal.
3. In a perfectly competitive market, an investor can borrow or lend freely at the market rate, which may be regarded as the minimum attractive rate of return for an investor.
4. The cash flows over the planning horizon can be accurately estimated from market prices.
5. There are no price level changes, i.e., no inflation or deflation.
6. The cash flows either are nontaxable in the case of a public agency, or represent the after-tax values in the case of private corporations.
7. Risk and uncertainty can be ignored.
8. The foremost objective in economic evaluation is to maximize the profit potential.

Using simple examples, we have considered the use of the net present value of discounted cash flows for an investment as the most direct measure of its profit potential, although the mechanics of computing the net present value for an investment represented by a stream of cash disbursements and receipts for more than one time period are not discussed until Chapter 3. It has been pointed out that the rate of return to an investor is a subtle concept that generally requires careful interpretation, and its detailed explanation must be deferred until Chapter 4. In any case, the measure of the profit potential is invariably tied to the minimum attractive rate of return one way or the other.

In the economic evaluation of investment proposals, we must differentiate independent projects from the mutually exclusive projects. We have examined the criteria for accepting independent projects and for selecting the best project among the mutually exclusive proposals. Although we have not discussed capital rationing in detail, it has been pointed out that the conditions of internal capital rationing or external capital rationing must be dealt with according to the available information.

It cannot be overemphasized that the economic evaluation of investment proposals is based on certain generally accepted assumptions. Once the assumptions have been agreed upon, economic evaluation provides an objective and consistent approach for making the most appropriate choice. As changes in these assumptions become warranted, they can be systematically incorporated in the decision-making process. Thus the capital investment decision may be viewed as the logical result of a consensus process, in which the critical evaluation of acceptable assumptions is at least as important as the reliance on the sophisticated methods of analysis. Consequently, the results and conclusions of any analysis based on these assumptions must be subjected to review which should take into consideration the basis and assumptions of the analysis.

REFERENCES

2.1 Bierman, H., Jr., and S. Smidt, *The Capital Budget Decision*, 4th ed. New York: Macmillan, 1975.

2.2 McKean, R. N., *Efficiency in Government through Systems Analysis*. New York: John Wiley and Sons, 1958.

PROBLEMS

P2.1 A government bond with a face value of $1,000 which is redeemable in full value at the end of 10 years contains 20 coupons for periodic interest payments of $60 each redeemable semiannually. The market price of the bond fluctuates with the market interest rates. At the time this bond is issued, its market price is $950, although the government guarantees that it will be repaid at its face value plus periodic interest. If an investor buys this bond now, describe the cash flow profile of his investment over 20 time periods of 6 months each, i.e., the cash flows at $t = 0$, at each period from $t = 1$ to $t = 19$, and at $t = 20$.

P2.2 An industrial bond with a face value of $10,000 is sold in the bond market for $9,800. This bond bears an annual interest at 8% of its face value payable at the end of each year, and it can be redeemed for the full amount of $10,000 at the end of 25 years. If an investor buys this bond at the market price, describe the cash flow profile of the investment over the 25-year period, i.e., the cash flows at the end of each year from year 1 through year 24, and at the end of year 25.

P2.3 Rodney Jackson has $100 in a savings account in the bank which pays 5% interest per year. If he leaves the money in the savings account for 2 years, the interest accrued in the first year will automatically be added to his principal at the end of the first year. Suppose that he is now offered an opportunity to invest this $100 in a project for 2 years and is promised a return of $10 at the end of the first year and $110 at the end of the second year. Compare the amounts at the end of 2 years if (1) he leaves this $100 in the savings account, and (2) he invests this $100 in the project and deposits the return of $10 at the end of the first year in the savings account.

P2.4 Betty Alexander has $100 in a savings account in the bank which pays 6% interest per year. If she leaves the money in the savings account for 2 years, the interest accrued in the first year will automatically be added to her principal at the end of the first year. Suppose that she is now offered an opportunity to invest $50 now and $50 a year later and is promised a return of $120 at the end of 2 years. Compare the amounts at the end of 2 years if (1) she leaves the $100 in the bank, and (2) she takes out the amount necessary for investing in the project when it is needed.

P2.5 A manufacturer of a new line of heavy equipment has made projections on the annual production costs and sales revenues at various levels of production. These costs and revenues are discounted to present values shown below. Determine the level of production (number of units produced) which will maximize the profit. Show computation.

Number of Units Produced	Production Costs in Million Dollars	Sales Revenues in Million Dollars
1,000	2	6
2,000	4	9
3,000	6	12
4,000	12	15
5,000	20	18

P2.6 A parcel of urban land may have four possible different uses. The costs and benefits associated with development for such uses (expressed in present values in millions of dollars) are given below. Which alternative should be selected? Show computation.

Alternative use	Benefits	Costs
1. Parking lot	4	1
2. Children's playground	10	5
3. Public park with band shelter	14	7
4. Public library	16	12

P2.7 Zappan Company is considering two advertising plans to improve its profits for the coming year. The first calls for an expenditure of $1,000 in newspaper advertisements now and is expected to increase the sales revenues by $1,500 at the end of 1 year. The second calls for an expenditure of $3,000 in television advertisements now and is expected to boost the sales revenues by $5,000 at the end of the year. The company uses a minimum attractive rate of return of 15% per year for such expenditures. Determine which plan should be used (a) if there is no budget constraint, and (b) if the advertising budget is limited to $2,000.

P2.8 Mr. Thorndike has $28,000 in a savings account which pays an annual interest rate of 5%. He plans to improve the income from this fund by investing either in U.S. Treasury notes or certificates of deposit. Each U.S. Treasury note has a face value of $10,000 at maturity 1 year later and is currently sold at a discount rate of 13%. Each certificate of deposit costs $10,000 now and is promised an annual interest rate of 12.5%. Assuming that Mr. Thorndike cannot borrow more money but can always deposit his money in the savings account, what is the overall rate of return on his $28,000 at the end of 1 year as a result of making either one of these two investments? Using the net present value as a measure of profit potential, which investment is better?

P2.9 Ms. Jordan has $12,000 in a savings account which pays an annual interest of 6%. She plans to purchase a U.S. Treasury note which has a face value of $10,000 at maturity 1 year later and is currently sold at a discount rate of 13.5%. Assuming that she cannot borrow more money but can always deposit her money in the savings account, what is the overall rate of return on her $12,000 at the end of 1 year if she decides to buy the U.S. Treasury note?

P2.10 Sandiana Amusement Park is considering two mutually exclusive alternatives in improving its facilities for the next season. The cash flow profiles for these alternatives are given below. The minimum attractive rate of return per year is 20%. Which alternative should be selected?

Year	Alternative 1	Alternative 2
0	$-$12,000	$-$15,000
1	$+$15,000	$+$20,000

3

COMPOUND INTEREST
FORUMULAS AND OPERATIONS

3.1 Time Value of Money

Before discussing the essential features of engineering economic analysis, it is necessary to acquire a basic understanding of the time value of money. This concept is most easily understood when it is presented in the context of transactions in the financial world.

The same amount of money spent or received at different times has different values because opportunities are available to invest the money in various enterprises to produce a return over a period of time. For this reason, financial institutions are willing to pay interest on deposits because they can lend the money to the investors. Based on the specified interest rate, deposits or investments will accumulate interest over time. As a result, the future value of a present amount of money will be larger than the existing amount because of the accumulated interest; conversely, the present value of a future amount of money to be received some time later would be smaller than the indicated amount after making a discount for interest that could have been accumulated if the money were available at present. Hence, the interest rate plays a significant role in determining the time value of money.

If an amount of money is deposited in a bank, interest accrues at regular time intervals. Each time interval represents an *interest period* at the end of which the earned interest on the original amount will be calculated according to a specified interest rate. The interest accrued in a single interest period is referred to as *simple interest*. If the earned interest is not withdrawn at the end of an interest period and is automatically redeposited with the original sum in the next interest period, the interest thus accrued is referred to as *compound interest*.

In business transactions, the interest period may be a month, a quarter, or a year. For example, the interest charge for the purchase of a household appliance on credit may be compounded monthly, while the interest accrued from a savings account in a bank may be compounded quarterly. Unless otherwise stated, practically all current transactions are based on compound interest; however, the length of the interest period for compounding as well as the interest rate per period must be specified for individual transactions. When the length of the interest period is finite, the compounding operation is referred to as *discrete compounding*. As will be explained later, when the length of the interest period is infinitesimally small, the compounding operation is called *continuous compounding*.

Thus, the *interest rate* may be interpreted as the rate at which money increases in value from present to future. Conversely, the *discount rate* refers to the rate by which the value of money is discounted from future to present. This basic concept of the time value of money is illustrated by simple examples.

Example 3.1

Jefferson University has recently received a bequest of $1 million to establish a trust for providing annual scholarships in perpetuity. The trust fund is deposited in a bank that pays 7% interest per annum, and only the annual interest will be spent for the designated purpose. What is the annual amount that is available for scholarships?

Since the interest will be withdrawn at the end of the interest period, the simple interest per annum is

$$(\$1,000,000)(0.07) = \$70,000$$

Note that at the end of each year, the trust fund remains intact after the interest is withdrawn from the bank. Thus, $70,000 is available annually for scholarships in perpetuity.

Example 3.2

A sum of $1,000 is invested in a 2-year savings certificate that pays 8% interest per year compounded annually. What is the total amount to be received at the end of 2 years?

The principal and interest at the end of each year for the 2 years are as follows:

$$\text{End of year 1} \quad 1,000 + (1,000)(0.08) = 1,080.00$$

$$\text{End of year 2} \quad 1,080 + (1,080)(0.08) = 1,166.40$$

Hence, the total amount to be received at the end of two years is $1,166.40.

Example 3.3

A manufacturer expects to receive $20,200 one month after the shipment of goods to a retailer. The manufacturer needs the cash and has arranged with a bank for a loan of $20,000 upon the shipment of goods on the condition that the bank will collect all of the $20,200 from the retailer a month later. What is the monthly interest rate charged by the bank?

Since there is only one interest period, the interest rate per month is

$$\frac{20,200 - 20,000}{20,000} = 0.01 = 1\%$$

This is also the discount rate by which the future sum of $20,200 is discounted to a present value of $20,000.

3.2   Equivalence of Cash Flows

A series of cash flows over time may be depicted by a horizontal axis having an origin denoting the present time and a scale denoting interest periods of equal time intervals. The receipts and disbursements are regarded as positive and negative cash flows, respectively. To simplify the computation of interest, it is assumed that receipts and disbursements are made only at the dividing points of the interest periods. For a transaction whose cash flows cover n interest periods, these points are denoted by $t = 0, 1, 2, \ldots, n$, with $t = 0$ representing the present time. Hence, net receipts (i.e., receipts less disbursements) in all periods will accumulate compound interest at the specified interest rate per period and over the specified number of interest periods.

A single sum or a series of cash flows can be represented by an equivalent single sum at a selected point in time. It has already been noted in Example 3.3 that a future sum of $20,200 to be received a month from now is equivalent to a present value of $20,000 if the monthly interest rate is 1%. The present time is selected as the point of reference because in this example, the manufacturer needs the money now and wants to know the equivalent present value of the amount to be received later. In contrast, a person who contributes annually to a retirement fund is more concerned with the equivalent future sum of money that he will receive at the time of his retirement. Similarly, a single sum or a series of cash flows may also be represented by a series of cash flows at a set of selected points in time. For example, if a person buys a car on credit, she would be interested in knowing the size of monthly payment since this information is more useful to her in estimating her ability to pay from her monthly salary than the amount she owes at the time of purchase. In general, the magnitude of a specified cash flow equivalence depends on the interest rate, the number of interest periods, and the magnitudes and timing of receipts and disbursements in the cash flows. The most common forms of equivalence are *present value* (at point $t = 0$), *future value* (at point $t = n$), and *uniform series* (at each of the n points from $t = 1$ to $t = n$).

It is convenient to visualize a series of cash flows as being generated either by lending or borrowing. Generally, receipts are denoted as positive cash flows and disbursements as negative cash flows and can be represented schematically by upward and downward arrows, respectively, in a diagram. For example, if a present sum P is loaned out at a specified interest rate for n periods, and an equivalent future sum F is repaid at time $t = n$, then the cash flows for this lending situation can be depicted by the diagram in part (a) of Fig. 3.1; a similar borrowing situation is shown in part (b) of Fig. 3.1. The *net present value* of a series of cash flows refers to the equivalence of a single sum of money to be received or disbursed at $t = 0$ if all future receipts and disbursements over time are properly discounted to the present time and then summed algebraically. On the other hand, the *net future value* of a series of cash flows refers to the equivalence of a single sum of money to be received or disbursed at some future time $t = n$ if all receipts and disbursements over time are properly compounded to that future point in time and summed algebraically. If the cash flow consists only of a series of disbursements or a series of receipts, there will be no change of sign in the cash flows. Then, the net present value and the net future value of a cash flow can simply be referred to as *present value* and *future value*, respectively.

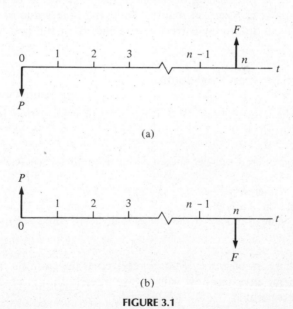

(a)

(b)

FIGURE 3.1

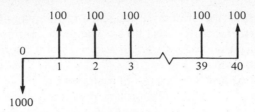

FIGURE 3.2

Example 3-4

A home builder estimates that by adding better insulation, installed at an initial cost of $1,000, to an average three-bedroom house the owner can save $100 of heating fuel cost per year over the next 40 years. He therefore claims that the total gross saving to the owner over the useful life of the house (40 years) is $4,000 and the total net saving is $3,000. Is this claim valid?

Since the saving of heating fuel cost per year is $100, the builder claims that the total saving over the next 40 years is 40 × $100 = $4,000. After subtracting the initial cost of $1,000 in installing additional insulation material, the net saving over 40 years is $3,000. The cash flows for this problem are shown in Fig. 3.2. However, unless the interest rate for money is zero, a saving of $100 a year from now does not have the same value of $100 available now; nor does the saving of $100 in any subsequent year. The real saving depends on the time value of money since the interest rate is usually not zero in reality. Thus, the time value of money must be considered in order to obtain the correct equivalence of cash flows.

3.3 Relationship Between Single Sums

Let us consider the simplest case of a single sum of money that is being invested now for a future return. Let

i = percentage interest rate per interest period, expressed as decimals in computation
n = number of interest periods
P = a present sum of money
F = a future sum of money at the end of n interest periods starting from the present

What should be the sum of money F to be received at the end of n interest periods if a single sum P being invested now will receive interest that is compounded at the end of each interest period?

The interest accrued in any interest period is the product of the amount at the beginning of an interest period and the interest rate per period. Then, the amount of money at the end of each interest period is equal to the sum of the amount of money at the beginning of that period and the interest accrued in that period. Hence, we can determine the amount of money accumulated progressively at the end of each interst period through compounding as shown in Table 3.1. Note that in each period, the amount of money at the end of the period is obtained by adding the amount at the beginning of the period and the interest for the period, e.g., $P + iP = P(1 + i)$. Thus, the future value F of a single present sum P with interest rate i compounded over n interest periods is given by

$$F = P(1 + i)^n \tag{3.1}$$

Conversely, we may wish to find a single sum of money P which at present is equivalent to a single sum to be received at the end of n interest periods for a discount rate i per period. For computational purposes, we shall use the terms discount rate and interest rate interchangeably. In this case, because the amount of money at the beginning of each period is computed backward by subtracting the interest for the period from the amount at the end of that period, the net effect is to discount or reduce the future sum F to its present value P. By transposing P and F in Eq. (3.1),

$$P = \frac{F}{(1 + i)^n} = F(1 + i)^{-n} \tag{3.2}$$

In Eq. (3.1), the factor $(1 + i)^n$ has the effect of increasing the magnitude of the present sum P through compounding and is referred to as the *compound amount factor*; whereas in Eq. (3.2), the factor $(1 + i)^{-n}$ has the effect of discounting the magnitude of the future sum F and is referred to as the *discount amount factor*.

Table 3.1

Compound Interest for a Single Sum

Period	Amount at Beginning of Period	Interest for the Period	Amount at End of Period
1	P	iP	$P(1 + i)$
2	$P(1 + i)$	$iP(1 + i)$	$P(1 + i)^2$
3	$P(1 + i)^2$	$iP(1 + i)^2$	$P(1 + i)^3$
...	....	....	....
n	$P(1 + i)^{n-1}$	$iP(1 + i)^{n-1}$	$P(1 + i)^n$

Example 3.5

Gretchen Boyd borrows $1,000 for 4 years and agrees to pay 5% interest per year compounded annually. What is the total amount that she will repay the debt at the end of 4 years?

Since $P = \$1,000$, $i = 5\%$, and $n = 4$, we get from Eq. (3.1)

$$F = (1,000)(1 + 0.05)^4 = \$1,215.51$$

Example 3.6

Andrew Burke wants to put aside a sum of money in the bank now so that he can have $1,000 available 2 years from now. If the bank pays 1.5% interest per quarter (every three months) compounded quarterly, what is the amount P that he should deposit now?

Since $F = \$1,000$, $i = 1.5\%$, $n = (2)(4) = 8$, we get from Eq. (3.2)

$$P = (1,000)(1 + 0.015)^{-8} = \$887.71$$

3.4   Decomposition and Superposition of Cash Flows

In dealing with a series of cash flows, we can treat each sum separately in determining its equivalence and then obtain the combined effects of all sums on the final result. This operation is referred to as the *decomposition* and *superposition* of cash flows. Although the numerical computation is often tedious, it can be greatly facilitated by using a programmable pocket calculator. As will be explained later, compound interest tables are also available as aids for numerical computation.

In general, we attempt to *decompose* the cash flows into a number of single sums whose values are converted to equivalent amounts at the *same point in time* and then to *superimpose* the individual equivalent amounts to obtain the composite results. This principle of decomposition and superposition can be applied to obtain the net present value or net future value of any series of cash flows, provided the interest rate per period and the number of interest periods associated with receipts or disbursements are known.

Let us consider a series of disbursements $P_1, P_2, \ldots, P_n$ at time $t = 1, 2, \ldots, n$ as shown in part (a) of Fig. 3.3. We can treat each of these disbursements P_t separately in determining its equivalent future value f_t at time $t = n$ as shown in

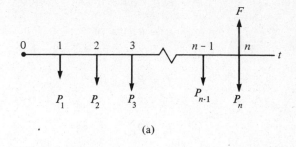

(a)

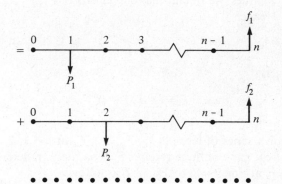

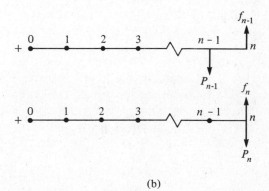

(b)

FIGURE 3.3

part (b) of Fig. 3.3. Then, according to Eq. (3.1),

$$f_1 = P_1(1 + i)^{n-1}$$

$$f_2 = P_2(1 + i)^{n-2}$$

. . . .

$$f_t = P_t(1 + i)^{n-t}$$

. . . .

$$f_n = P_n$$

By summing these values, we obtain the total effects of P_1, P_2, ..., P_n on the future value F at $t = n$. Hence,

$$F = f_1 + f_2 + \cdots + f_n$$

or

$$F = \sum_{t=1}^{n} P_t(1 + i)^{n-t} \tag{3.3}$$

Similarly, for a series of receipts F_1, F_2, ..., F_n at $t = 1, 2, ..., n$ as shown in Fig. 3.4, we can treat each of these receipts F_t separately in determining its equivalent present value p_t at time $t = 0$ by Eq. (3.2) as follows:

$$p_1 = F_1(1 + i)^{-1}$$

$$p_2 = F_2(1 + i)^{-2}$$

. . . .

$$p_t = F_t(1 + i)^{-t}$$

. . . .

$$p_n = F_n(1 + i)^{-n}$$

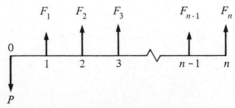

FIGURE 3.4

By summing these values, we obtain the total effects of $F_1, F_2, \ldots, F_n$ on the present value P at $t = 0$. Hence,

$$P = p_1 + p_2 + \cdots + p_n$$

or

$$P = \sum_{t=1}^{n} F_t(1 + i)^{-t} \qquad (3.4)$$

For the general case of a series of mixed positive and negative cash flows, the same principle may be applied. Let $A_0, A_1, A_2, \ldots, A_n$ be the cash flows at $t = 0, 1, 2, \ldots, n$ which are designated as positive for receipts and negative for disbursements. Then, the net future value (NFV) of the series at $t = n$ is given by

$$NFV = \sum_{t=0}^{n} A_t(1 + i)^{n-t} \qquad (3.5)$$

Similarly, the net present value (NPV) of the series at $t = 0$ is given by

$$NPV = \sum_{t=0}^{n} A_t(1 + i)^{-t} \qquad (3.6)$$

The derivations of Eqs. (3.5) and (3.6) are analogous to those of Eqs. (3.3) and (3.4). However, since A_t (for $t = 0, 1, 2, \ldots, n$) may be positive, negative, or zero, the summation must be carried out algebraically.

Example 3.7

Rhoda Gould is planning a trip to Europe 3 years from next January. She intends to deposit her savings of \$1,000 in a bank at the end of this year and expects to deposit another \$500 at the end of next year. If the bank pays 5% interest per year compounded annually, how much money can she expect to be available to her at the time of her departure?

The cash flow for this problem is depicted in Fig. 3.5 in which $P_0 = \$1,000$ and

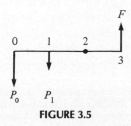

FIGURE 3.5

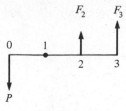

FIGURE 3.6

$P_1 = \$500$. The amount available at $t = 3$ is

$$F = P_0(1 + i)^3 + P_1(1 + i)^2$$
$$= (1,000)(1 + 0.05)^3 + (500)(1 + 0.05)^2$$
$$= 1,157.63 + 551.25 = \$1,708.88$$

Example 3.8

Ron Alexander arranged to buy a used car from a friend through a deferred payment plan. He is allowed to possess the car immediately, but he must pay $500 two months from now and another $500 three months from now, which include interest charges of 1% per month compounded monthly. What is the equivalent of these payments if he can afford to make a single payment now?

The cash flow for this problem is depicted in Fig. 3.6 in which $F_2 = F_3 = \$500$ at $t = 2$ and $t = 3$, respectively. The equivalent single present sum is given by

$$P = F_2(1 + i)^{-2} + F_3(1 + i)^{-3}$$
$$= (500)(1 + 0.01)^{-2} + (500)(1 + 0.01)^{-3}$$
$$= 490.15 + 485.30 = \$975.45$$

3.5   Uniform Series of Cash Flows

In many situations, the cash flows consist of a uniform series of disbursements or receipts continuing for a number of interest periods. For example, we may deposit an amount U at the end of each interest period in order to accumulate a single sum F at the end of n interest periods as shown in Fig. 3.7, or we may invest a single sum P now with the expectation of receiving an amount U at the end of each interest period continuing for n interest periods as indicated in Fig. 3.8. In each case, the disbursements or receipts U in the uniform series *are assumed to be made at the ends of interest periods.*[1] The assumption that disbursements and receipts are made only

---

[1] The notation U is used to denote the amount at the end of each interest period for a *uniform* series with U at period $t = 1, 2, \ldots, n$. This is a departure from the traditional use of the notation A for this purpose because in this book the notation A is used to denote net *annual* cash flow. The advantage of this new notation becomes obvious in Section 5.6 (Chapter 5).

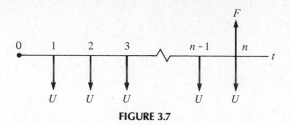

FIGURE 3.7

at the ends of interest periods is adopted in order to simplify the derivations of compound interest formulas for uniform series and is generally accepted in conventional practice. The point $t = 0$ representing the present time may be regarded as the end of a fictitious period 0.

Referring to Fig. 3.7, the future value F of the uniform series may be obtained by first converting each of the U values at $t = 1, 2, \ldots, n$ to a future value at $t = n$ and then superimposing these values to obtain F. Thus, for U at $t = 1$, its future value at $t = n$ is $U(1 + i)^{n-1}$, and the process of finding the future value equivalence of each U is continued until the last U at $t = n$. Then,

$$F = U(1 + i)^{n-1} + U(1 + i)^{n-2} + \cdots + U(1 + i) + U$$

This equation represents a geometric progression whose sum F can be easily obtained in a simple form. Factoring out U and multiplying both sides of the equation by $(1 + i)$, we get in two successive steps

$$F = U[(1 + i)^{n-1} + (1 + i)^{n-2} + \cdots + (1 + i) + 1]$$

$$(1 + i)F = U[(1 + i)^n + (1 + i)^{n-1} + \cdots + (1 + i)^2 + (1 + i)]$$

Subtracting the first from the second equation above,

$$iF = U[(1 + i)^n - 1]$$

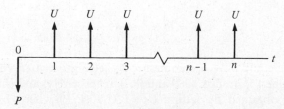

FIGURE 3.8

Consequently,

$$F = U\left[\frac{(1 + i)^n - 1}{i}\right] \qquad (3.7)$$

or, expressing U in terms of F,

$$U = F\left[\frac{i}{(1 + i)^n - 1}\right] \qquad (3.8)$$

Similarly, referring to Fig. 3.8, the present value P of the uniform series may be obtained by superposition. Thus, for U at $t = 1$, its present value is $U(1 + i)^{-1}$; for U at $t = 2$, its present value is $U(1 + i)^{-2}$, and the process of finding the present value equivalence of U is continued until the present value of U at $t = n$ is found to be $U(1 + i)^{-n}$. Then,

$$P = U(1 + i)^{-1} + U(1 + i)^{-2} + \cdots + U(1 + i)^{-(n-1)} + U(1 + i)^{-n}$$

This equation also represents a geometric progression whose sum P can be easily obtained in a simple form. Factoring out U and multiplying the equation by $(1 + i)$, we get in two successive steps

$$P = U[(1 + i)^{-1} + (1 + i)^{-2} + \cdots + (1 + i)^{-(n-1)} + (1 + i)^{-n}]$$

$$(1 + i)P = U[1 + (1 + i)^{-1} + \cdots + (1 + i)^{-(n-2)} + (1 + i)^{-(n-1)}]$$

Subtracting the first from the second equation above,

$$iP = U[1 - (1 + i)^{-n}]$$

Consequently, by carrying out the algebraic operations, we get

$$P = U\left[\frac{1 - (1 + i)^{-n}}{i}\right] = U\left[\frac{(1 + i)^n - 1}{i(1 + i)^n}\right] \qquad (3.9)$$

or, expressing U in terms of P,

$$U = P\left[\frac{i(1 + i)^n}{(1 + i)^n - 1}\right] \qquad (3.10)$$

Note that Eq. (3.9) could have been obtained by letting $P = U(P/F)(F/U)$ where P/F and F/U are obtained from Eqs. (3.2) and (3.7), respectively, and similarly, Eq. (3.10) could have been obtained by letting $U = P(U/F)(F/P)$ where U/F and F/P are obtained from Eqs. (3.8) and (3.1), respectively.

The uniform series in Fig. 3.7 is typical of the situation where we try to build up a future fund by depositing uniform payments over a number of interest periods. Hence the factor $[(1 + i)^n - 1]/i$ in Eq. (3.7) is referred to as the *compound uniform series factor*, while its reciprocal $i/[(1 + i)^n - 1]$ in Eq. (3.8) is called the *sinking fund factor*. On the other hand, the uniform series in Fig. 3.8 is typical of the situation where we attempt to recover an initial capital investment by receiving uniform repayments over a number of interest periods. Hence the factor $[(1 + i)^n - 1]/i(1 + i)^n$ in Eq. (3.9) is referred to as the *discount uniform series factor*, while its reciprocal $i(1 + i)^n/[(1 + i)^n - 1]$ in Eq. (3.10) is called the *capital recovery factor*. These factors are applicable only to uniform series involving end-of-period payments continuing for n interest periods.

The relationships between various factors can be seen from Eqs. (3.1), (3.2), (3.7), (3.8), (3.9), and (3.10). For example, the factors in Eqs. (3.8) and (3.10) are the respective reciprocals of those in Eqs. (3.7) and (3.9). Also, the factors in Eqs. (3.8) and (3.10) are related as follows:

$$\left[\frac{i}{(1 + i)^n - 1} \right] + i = \left[\frac{i(1 + i)^n}{(1 + i)^n - 1} \right] \tag{3.11}$$

Consequently, we can always derive appropriate relationships from these equations.

Example 3.9

An excavation contractor decided 7 years ago to put aside an amount U annually to build up a sinking fund to replace a piece of equipment by the end of 7 years. He encountered a run of financial difficulties and was not able to make deposits at the end of the third and fourth years, as shown in Fig. 3.9. Before deciding how much money should be added to the fund at the end of the seventh year in order to purchase the equipment, he wants to find out the value at this time equivalent to all previous payments that have accrued interests at a rate i compounded annually.

Since the payments in Fig. 3.9 do not constitute a uniform series, we can treat each payment U as a single sum and compute the value F at $t = 7$ by superposition. Thus,

$$F = U(1 + i)^6 + U(1 + i)^5 + U(1 + i)^2 + U(1 + i)$$

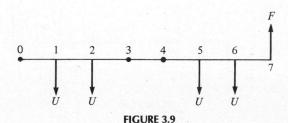

FIGURE 3.9

Alternately, we may regard the payments as a uniform series for 7 years, except that payments at $t = 3$, $t = 4$, and $t = 7$ are to be deleted as single sums. Then, by applying Eq. (3.6) at $t = 7$ for the uniform series, we obtain the future value of the cash flow as:

$$F = U\left[\frac{(1 + i)^7 - 1}{i}\right] - U(1 + i)^4 - U(1 + i)^3 - U$$

The results of both approaches are equivalent.

Example 3.10

John Benjamin wishes to deposit a sum of money in the bank on the tenth birthday of his daughter Mary for the purpose of financing her college education. She is to receive an amount U on her seventeenth, eighteenth, nineteenth, and twentieth birthdays, as shown in Fig. 3.10. If the bank pays interest at a rate i compounded annually, determine the single sum that he should deposit in the bank when his daughter reaches ten years old.

For the problem, in Fig. 3.10, we can theoretically choose the day of Mary's birth as the origin of the time axis and her age as the chronological time scale. In that case, we will make reference to $t = 0$ for all payments. Thus, the sum of money to be deposited at $t = 10$ is related to other payments as follows:

$$P(1 + i)^{-10} = U[(1 + i)^{-17} + (1 + i)^{-18} + (1 + i)^{-19} + (1 + i)^{-20}]$$

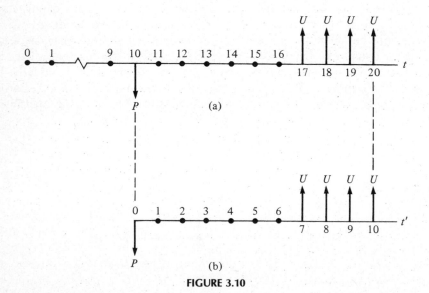

FIGURE 3.10

or, multiplying through by $(1 + i)^{10}$,

$$P = U[(1 + i)^{-7} + (1 + i)^{-8} + (1 + i)^{-9} + (1 + i)^{-10}]$$

However, the computation can be simplified if we select a new time scale t' such that $t' = t - 10$. In other words, the origin $t' = 0$ is located at $t = 10$, and other points in time for payments become $t' = 7, 8, 9,$ and 10. In this case, the sum of money P at $t' = 0$ is the present value which is identical to the expression for P in the last equation.

Alternately, we can treat the problem as the difference between two uniform series: the first with uniform payments U from $t = 11$ to $t = 20$ (i.e., $t' = 1$ through 10) and the second with uniform payments U from $t = 11$ to $t = 16$ (i.e., $t' = 1$ through 6). The sum P is given by applying Eq. (3.9) to the two uniform series:

$$P = U\left[\frac{(1 + i)^{10} - 1}{i(1 + i)^{10}}\right] - U\left[\frac{(1 + i)^{6} - 1}{i(1 + i)^{6}}\right] = U\left[\frac{(1 + i)^{4} - 1}{i(1 + i)^{10}}\right]$$

It should be noted that this result is quite different from that of

$$P_6 = U\left[\frac{(1 + i)^{4} - 1}{i(1 + i)^{4}}\right]$$

where P_6 is a single sum at $t' = 6$, which is equivalent to the uniform series of payments U from $t' = 7$ through 10. However, it is not the answer to the question because we are interested in the sum P at $t' = 0$. Carrying out the conversion to $t' = 0$, we get

$$P = P_6(1 + i)^{-6} = U\left[\frac{(1 + i)^{4} - 1}{i(1 + i)^{10}}\right]$$

This result is the same as that previously obtained by considering the difference of two uniform series.

3.6 Functional Notation and Compound Interest Tables

The use of the compound interest formulas derived in this chapter is often tedious. Therefore, a functional notation is introduced to simplify our reference to such formulas. The numerical computation can easily be carried out with the aid of a pocket calculator. However, compound interest tables listing various factors in these formulas for a wide range of combinations of interest rates and interest periods are readily available. Appendix A shows a set of discrete compound interest tables to facilitate the computation.

The various factors for the compound interest formulas in Eqs. (3.1), (3.2), (3.7), (3.8), (3.9), and (3.10) are expressed in the functional notation as follows:[2]

(a) Compound amount factor

$$\frac{F}{P} = (1 + i)^n = (F \mid P, i, n) \tag{3.12}$$

(b) Discount amount factor

$$\frac{P}{F} = \frac{1}{(1 + i)^n} = (P \mid F, i, n) \tag{3.13}$$

(c) Compound uniform series factor

$$\frac{F}{U} = \frac{(1 + i)^n - 1}{i} = (F \mid U, i, n) \tag{3.14}$$

(d) Sinking fund factor

$$\frac{U}{F} = \frac{i}{(1 + i)^n - 1} = (U \mid F, i, n) \tag{3.15}$$

(e) Discount uniform series factor

$$\frac{P}{U} = \frac{(1 + i)^n - 1}{i(1 + i)^n} = (P \mid U, i, n) \tag{3.16}$$

(f) Capital recovery factor

$$\frac{U}{P} = \frac{i(1 + i)^n}{(1 + i)^n - 1} = (U \mid P, i, n) \tag{3.17}$$

In (a), the notation $(F \mid P, i, n)$ reads "to find F, given $P = 1$, for the specified i and n." In other words, if the present sum P is \$1, the compound amount factor $(F \mid P, i, n)$ yields the dollar value of the future sum F for the specified values of i and n. This value F is listed for each i value in a separate table and for each n value in a column under the heading $(F \mid P, i, n)$. Thus, for any given value of P that is different from

---

[2] The term *compound amount factor* is traditionally referred to as *single payment compound amount factor*, the term *discount amount factor* referred to as *single payment present worth factor*, the term *compound uniform series factor* referred to as *uniform series compound amount factor*, and the term *discount uniform series factor* referred to as *uniform series present worth factor*. The terminology used in this book has simplified the designation of these factors.

$1, we can obtain F by multiplying this factor by that value of P. Similarly, in (b), the notation $(P|F, i, n)$ reads "to find P, given $F = 1$, for the specified i and n." If the future sum F is $1, this discount amount factor $(P|F, i, n)$ yields the present sum P for the specified values of i and n. This explanation of the functional notation applies to the compound interest factors in the remaining formulas. The use of these tables for numerical computation will be further explained in the examples.

Example 3.11

In Example 3.4, compute the present value P of the uniform series with $U = \$100$ continuing over $n = 40$ years if the annual interest rate i is (a) 8%, and (b) 10%.

(a) For $i = 8\%$, we can formulate the problem in terms of the functional notation as follows:

$$P = U(P|U, i, n) = (100)(P|U, 8\%, 40)$$

In the compound interest tables in Appendix A, we look for the page with interest rate $i = 8\%$. On that page, we search for the column heading $(P|U, i, n)$ and read downward for a number on a line corresponding to $n = 40$. The number 11.9246 is the discount uniform series factor $(P|U, 8\%, 40)$. Hence,

$$P = (100)(11.9246) = \$1,192.46$$

(b) For $i = 10\%$, we can find $(P|U, 10\%, 40) = 9.7791$ from another page with interest rate $i = 10\%$. Thus,

$$P = (100)(P|U, 8\%, 40) = (100)(9.7791) = \$977.91$$

Example 3-12

The Dutch merchant Peter Minuit bought the island of Manhattan in New York from the Manhattos Indians in 1626 for $24. Assuming that he could have deposited $24 in a bank in Holland that would pay compound interest at an annual interest rate of 6%, what would the value of his investment be in 1976?

This problem as depicted in Fig. 3.11 can be formulated in functional notation and solved by using a pocket calculator as follows:

$$F = P(F|P, i, n) = (24)(F|P, 6\%, 350) = \$17.2688 \times 10^9$$

In the table for $i = 6\%$ in Appendix A, the value of n goes up to 100, and we cannot find the compound amount factor $(F|P, 6\%, 350)$. However, from Fig. 3.11, we note that we can find the future value F_{100} at $t = 100$. Using F_{100} as present value, we

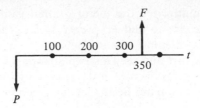

FIGURE 3.11

can find the future value F_{200} at $t = 200$, etc. Hence,

$$F_{100} = P(F\mid P, 6\%, 100)$$

$$F_{200} = F_{100}(F\mid P, 6\%, 100)$$

$$F_{300} = F_{200}(F\mid P, 6\%, 100)$$

$$F_{350} = F_{300}(F\mid P, 6\%, 50)$$

From the table for $i = 6\%$ in Appendix A, $(F\mid P, 6\%, 100) = 339.3021$ and $(F\mid P, 6\%, 50) = 18.4202$. Hence, for $F = F_{350}$,

$$
\begin{aligned}
F &= P(F\mid P, 6\%, 100)^3(F\mid P, 6\%, 50) \\
&= (24)(339.3021)^3(18.4202) \\
&= \$17.2689 \times 10^9
\end{aligned}
$$

The significant figures have been rounded off in the computation.

Example 3-13

In Example 3-9, let $U = \$1,000$ and $i = 8\%$, and determine the amount F at the end of 7 years.

   If we treat each payment as a single sum, the problem can be expressed in functional notation as follows:

$$
\begin{aligned}
F &= (1,000)(F\mid P, 8\%, 6) + (1,000)(F\mid P, 8\%, 5) + (1,000)(F\mid P, 8\%, 2) \\
&\quad + (1,000)(F\mid P, 8\%, 1)
\end{aligned}
$$

The compound amount factors can be found from the table for $i = 8\%$ in Appendix A. Then,

$$
\begin{aligned}
F &= (1,000)(1.5869 + 1.4693 + 1.1664 + 1.080) \\
&= (1,000)(5.3026) = \$5,302.60
\end{aligned}
$$

Alternately, if we regard the payments as a uniform series for 7 years and subtract those not included in the problem, the solution becomes:

$$F = (1{,}000)(F \mid U, 8\%, 7) - (1{,}000)(F \mid P, 8\%, 4)$$
$$- (1{,}000)(F \mid P, 8\%, 3) - 1000$$
$$= (1{,}000)(8.9228 - 1.3605 - 1.2597 - 1)$$
$$= (1{,}000)(5.3026) = \$5{,}302.60$$

Example 3-14

In Example 3-10, let $U = \$4{,}000$ and $i = 6\%$, and determine the amount P to be deposited on Mary's tenth birthday.

If we treat each payment as a single sum, the problem can be expressed in functional notation as follows:

$$P = (4{,}000)[(P \mid F, 6\%, 7) + (P \mid F, 6\%, 8) + (P \mid F, 6\%, 9)$$
$$+ (P \mid F, 6\%, 10)]$$
$$= (4{,}000)(0.6651 + 0.6274 + 0.5919 + 0.5584)$$
$$= (4{,}000)(2.4428) = \$9{,}771.20$$

Alternately, we can treat the problem as the difference between two uniform series: the first continuing for 10 years from the time of making the deposit and the second continuing for 6 years from the same time. Thus

$$P = (4{,}000)(P \mid U, 6\%, 10) - (4{,}000)(P \mid U, 6\%, 6)$$
$$= (4{,}000)(7.3601 - 4.9173)$$
$$= (4{,}000)(2.4428) = \$9{,}771.20$$

If we treat the payments as a uniform series from the seventh through tenth years, the solution becomes

$$P_6 = (4{,}000)(P \mid U, 6\%, 4)$$

and

$$P = P_6(P \mid F, 6\%, 6)$$
$$= (4{,}000)(P \mid U, 6\%, 4)(P \mid F, 6\%, 6)$$
$$= (4{,}000)(3.4651)(0.7050) = \$9{,}771.58$$

Example 3-15

A power company is considering the installation of antipollution equipment in an old coal-based generating plant that is expected to be used for another 10 years. If antipollution equipment is not installed immediately, more expensive low-sulfur coal

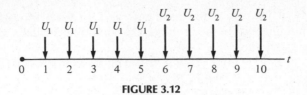

FIGURE 3.12

must be used in order to meet the new air-quality standards, and even more expensive fuel must be used 5 years from now as the air-quality standards become more stringent. It is estimated that by installing the antipollution equipment, the saving of fuel cost will be $U_1 = \$15,000$ per year in the first 5 years and $U_2 = 20,000$ in the second 5 years. Determine the present value of the annual savings in the next 10 years if the annual interest rate is 10%.

The cash flow for this problem is depicted in Fig. 3.12. We can treat it as the difference between two uniform series: the first with $U = U_2 = 20,000$ continuing from $t = 1$ through $t = 10$, and the second with $U = U_2 - U_1 = 5,000$ from $t = 1$ through $t = 5$. Thus,

$$P = (20,000)(P \mid U, 10\%, 10) - (5,000)(P \mid U, 10\%, 5)$$
$$= (20,000)(6.1446) - (5,000)(3.7908)$$
$$= 122,892 - 18,954 = \$103,938$$

If we try to treat the problem as the superposition of two uniform series not having the same starting point in time, the computation of the present value will be less direct. For example, we may consider the first series with $U = U_1 = 15,000$ continuing from $t = 1$ through $t = 10$, and the second with $U = U_2 - U_1 = 5,000$ from $t = 6$ through $t = 10$. Then

$$P = (15,000)(P \mid U, 10\%, 10) + (5,000)(P \mid U, 10\%, 5)(P \mid F, 10\%, 5)$$
$$= (15,000)(6.1445) + (5,000)(3.7908)(0.6209)$$
$$= 92,175 + 11,769 = \$103,937$$

We can also treat the problem as the superposition of two other uniform series: the first with $U_1 = 15,000$ continuing from $t = 1$ through $t = 5$, and the second with $U_2 = 20,000$ continuing from $t = 6$ through $t = 10$. Then

$$P = (15,000)(P \mid U, 10\%, 5) + (20,000)(P \mid U, 10\%, 5)(P \mid F, 10\%, 5)$$
$$= (15,000)(3.7908) + (20,000)(3.7908)(0.6209)$$
$$= 56,862 + 47,074 = \$103,936$$

3.7   Cash Flows in Linear Gradients

In some situations, the cash flow profile may follow the form of a linearly increasing or decreasing gradient as the disbursements or receipts change linearly over time.

For example, the maintenance cost of equipment may increase annually according to a linear gradient, or the savings in the operating cost of a physical plant after remodeling may decrease annually according to a linear gradient. Consequently, it is convenient to develop special formulas for finding the equivalence of cash flows in linear gradients.

Let us consider the case of a cash flow in the form of a linear gradient with increasing increments as shown in Fig. 3.13. The receipts at $t_1, t_2, \ldots, t_n$ are, respectively, L_1; $L_2 = L_1 + G$; $L_3 = L_1 + 2G, \ldots, L_{n-1} = L_1 + (n-2)G$; and $L_n = L_1 + (n-1)G$, where L_1 is the constant portion of receipts in each period while G is a constant increment such that $L_1, L_2, \ldots, L_n$ is an arithmetic progression. Consequently, the linear gradient of part (a) in Fig. 3.13 may be decomposed into two components as represented by parts (b) and (c) of the figure. Part (b) is a uniform

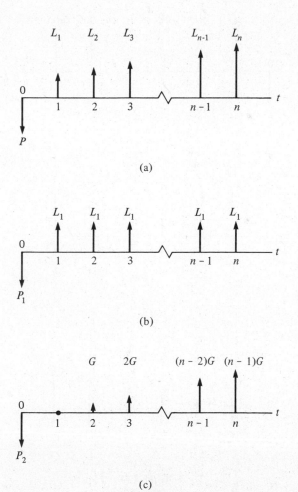

(a)

(b)

(c)

FIGURE 3.13

series whose present value P_1 can be obtained from Eq. (3.9). Part (c) shows a basic linear gradient whose present value P_2 can be determined as later shown in Eq. (3.18). Then the present value of the linear gradient is $P = P_1 + P_2$.

A basic linear gradient is a special case of the linear gradient having an initial point of zero value at $t = 1$ and a constant increment of G at each succeeding point in time until the value reaches $(n - 1)G$ at $t = n$ as shown in part (a) of Fig. 3.14. The present value P of the basic linear gradient is given by

$$P = \frac{G}{(1 + i)^2} + \frac{2G}{(1 + i)^3} + \cdots + \frac{(n - 2)G}{(1 + i)^{n-1}} + \frac{(n - 1)G}{(1 + i)^n}$$

Factoring out G and multiplying both sides of the equation by $(1 + i)$, we get in two

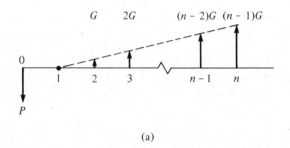

(a)

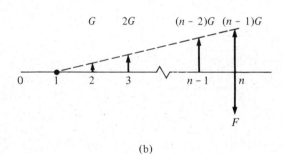

(b)

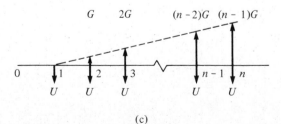

(c)

FIGURE 3.14

successive steps

$$P = G\left[\frac{1}{(1+i)^2} + \frac{2}{(1+i)^3} + \cdots + \frac{n-2}{(1+i)^{n-1}} + \frac{(n-1)}{(1+i)^n}\right]$$

$$(1+i)P = G\left[\frac{1}{(1+i)} + \frac{2}{(1+i)^2} + \cdots + \frac{n-2}{(1+i)^{n-2}} + \frac{n-1}{(1+i)^{n-1}}\right]$$

Subtracting the first from the second equation above

$$iP = G\left[\frac{1}{(1+i)} + \frac{1}{(1+i)^2} + \cdots + \frac{1}{(1+i)^{n-1}} - \frac{(n-1)}{(1+i)^n}\right]$$

or

$$P = \frac{G}{i}\left[\frac{1}{(1+i)} + \frac{1}{(1+i)^2} + \cdots + \frac{1}{(1+i)^{n-1}} + \frac{1}{(1+i)^n}\right] - \frac{nG}{i(1+i)^n}$$

The expression in the brackets on the right-hand side of the above equation is the present value of a uniform series with $U = 1$, and its sum can be obtained by Eq. (3.9). Hence,

$$P = \frac{G}{i}\left[\frac{(1+i)^n - 1}{i(1+i)^n}\right] - \frac{nG}{i(1+i)^n}$$

$$= G\left[\frac{(1+i)^n - 1 - ni}{i^2(1+i)^n}\right] \tag{3.18}$$

Again, introducing the functional notation, the *discount gradient factor* is defined as

$$\frac{P}{G} = \left[\frac{(1+i)^n - 1 - ni}{i^2(1+i)^n}\right] = (P\,|\,G, i, n) \tag{3.19}$$

We can also derive directly the future value F. However, this is unnecessary since we can make use of the relationship in Eq. (3.1). Hence, the equivalent F in part (b) of Fig. 3.14 is obtained as

$$F = P(1+i)^n = G\left[\frac{(1+i)^n - 1 - ni}{i^2}\right]$$

and the *compound gradient factor* is defined as

$$\frac{F}{G} = \left[\frac{(1+i)^n - 1 - ni}{i^2}\right] = (F\,|\,G, i, n) \tag{3.20}$$

Similarly, from Eq. (3-10), the equivalent uniform series U in part (c) of Fig. 3.14 is obtained as

$$U = P\left[\frac{i(1 + i)^n}{(1 + i)^n - 1}\right] = G\left[\frac{(1 + i)^n - 1 - ni}{i(1 + i)^n - i}\right]$$

and the *uniform series gradient factor* is defined as

$$\frac{U}{G} = \left[\frac{(1 + i)^n - 1 - ni}{i(1 + i)^n - i}\right] = (U \mid G, i, n) \tag{3.21}$$

The reciprocals of these relationships, i.e., G/P, G/F, and G/U, can easily be obtained if desired.

In the case of a cash flow in the form of a basic linear gradient with constantly decreasing increments, the formulas represented by Eqs. (3.19), (3.20), and (3.21) are still applicable except that G will be negative instead of being positive. Thus, the cash flow equivalence of such a basic linear gradient is also negative.

The expressions in functional notation for various compound interest factors in Eqs. (3.19), (3.20), and (3.21) can also be tabulated in numerical computation for convenience. However, only one factor $(P \mid G, i, n)$ is listed in the appendix, and the functional notation for this factor reads "to find P, given $G = 1$, for the specified i and n." The relationships between other compound interest factors and this factor can be obtained as follows:

1. Discount gradient factor

$$\frac{P}{G} = (P \mid G, i, n) \tag{3.22}$$

2. Compound gradient factor

$$\frac{F}{G} = (F \mid G, i, n) = (F \mid P, i, n)(P \mid G, i, n) \tag{3.23}$$

3. Uniform series gradient factor

$$\frac{U}{G} = (U \mid G, i, n) = (U \mid P, i, n)(P \mid G, i, n) \tag{3.24}$$

Example 3.16

The maintenance cost for a new school bus is expected to be $1,500 in the first year and $300 more for each additional year (i.e., $1,800 in the second year, and $2,100 in the third year, etc.) until the bus is disposed of at the end of 10 years. If the annual compound interest rate is 6%, determine the equivalent present value of the maintenance costs.

The problem can be decomposed into a uniform series with $U = \$1,500$ and a basic linear gradient with $G = \$300$. Thus,

$$
\begin{aligned}
P &= (1,500)(P\,|\,U,\ 6\%,\ 10) + (300)(P\,|\,G,\ 6\%,\ 10) \\
&= (1,500)(7.3601) + (300)(29.6023) \\
&= 11,040 + 8,881 = \$19,921
\end{aligned}
$$

Example 3.17

A piece of solid waste disposal equipment was purchased for the purpose of reducing operating costs. In the first year of operation, the savings were $38,000 with $6,000 less savings in each succeeding year (i.e., $32,000 in the second year, $26,000 in the third year) until the equipment was retired after 5 years of service. If the annual interest rate was 12%, determine a single equivalent sum of the savings at the time the equipment was retired.

The problem can be decomposed into a uniform series with $U = \$38,000$ and a basic linear gradient with $G = -\$6,000$. Hence,

$$
\begin{aligned}
F &= (38,000)(F\,|\,U,\ 12\%,\ 5) - (6,000)(P\,|\,G,\ 12\%,\ 5)(F\,|\,P,\ 12\%,\ 5) \\
&= (38,000)(6.3528) - (6,000)(6.3970)(1.7623) \\
&= 241,406 - 67,641 = 173,765
\end{aligned}
$$

Example 3-18

A new office duplicating machine is expected to generate a stream of annual benefits in dollars for the next 9 years, as shown in part (a) of Fig. 3.15. If the annual discount rate is 8%, determine the present value of the cash flows.

The cash flows can be decomposed into two streams as shown in parts (b) and (c) of Fig. 3.15. That is, $U_1 = 600$ for $t = 1, 2, 3$, and 4; $U_2 = 200$ for $t = 5, 6, 7, 8$, and 9; and $G = -100$ for $n = 4$. Then, the present value is given by

$$
\begin{aligned}
P &= (600)(P\,|\,U,\ 8\%,\ 4) + (200)(P\,|\,U,\ 8\%,\ 5)(P\,|\,F,\ 8\%,\ 4) \\
&\quad - (100)(P\,|\,G,\ 8\%,\ 4)
\end{aligned}
$$

Alternately, it can be obtained by

$$
P = (200)(P\,|\,U,\ 8\%,\ 9) + (400)(P\,|\,U,\ 8\%,\ 4) - (100)(P\,|\,G,\ 8\%,\ 4)
$$

In either case, we obtain $P = \$2,109$.

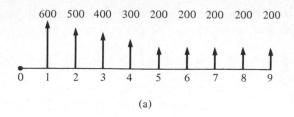

(a)

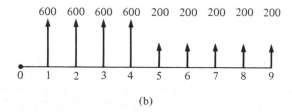

(b)

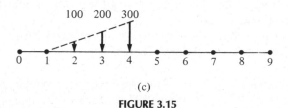

(c)

FIGURE 3.15

3.8   Nominal and Effective Interest Rates

In previous sections, we have emphasized compound interest at an interest rate per period for a number of interest periods. In engineering economic analysis, a year is usually used as an interest period since investments in engineering projects are of long duration and a calendar year is a convenient period for accounting and tax computation. However, financial institutions that provide opportunities for making deposits and loans often offer more than one interest period per year in compounding the interest. Consequently, we introduce the terms *nominal interest rate* and *effective interest rate* to describe more precisely the *annual interest rate* for such situations.

If a financial institution offers more than one interest period per year in compounding the interest, it usually quotes a *nominal annual interest rate*, which is the annual interest rate *neglecting the effect of any compounding during the year*. However, it pays its depositors on the basis of an *effective annual interest rate*, *considering the effect of all compounding during the year*. For example, a nominal annual interest rate of 8% compounded semiannually means that the interest rate per period is 8%/2 = 4% for each of the 6-month periods during the year. Then the interest for a sum of \$1 accrued at the end of the year is

$$\left(1 + \frac{0.08}{2}\right)^2 - 1 = 0.0816$$

Thus, the effective annual interest rate is 8.16%. Similarly, a nominal annual interest rate of 8% compounded quarterly means that the interest rate per period is $8\%/4 = 2\%$ for each of the 3-month periods during the year. Hence, the effective annual interest rate is

$$\left(1 + \frac{0.08}{4}\right)^4 - 1 = 0.0824 = 8.24\%$$

Let r be the nominal interest rate per year and s be the number of interest periods per year. Then, the interest rate per interest period is r/s. The effective interest rate i_e is defined as the annual interest accrued by depositing \$1 at a nominal interest rate r compounded over s interest periods during the year. Thus,

$$i_e = \left(1 + \frac{r}{s}\right)^s - 1 \tag{3.25}$$

For the special case where $s = 1$, i.e., one interest period per year with $r/s = r$, Eq. (3.25) reduces to $i_e = r$. That is, the effective annual interest rate is identical to the nominal annual interest rate.

If a sum P is deposited to accrue interest for n years, the future sum at the end of n years is

$$F = P(1 + i_e)^n$$

Noting the value of $(1 + i_e)$ obtained from Eq. (3.25), we get

$$F = P\left(1 + \frac{r}{s}\right)^{sn} \tag{3.26}$$

Some financial institutions offer a large number of interest periods per year, such as $s = 365$ for daily compounding. As the number of interest periods s becomes very large, the interest rate per interest period r/s becomes very small. If s approaches infinity and r/s approaches zero as a limit, the limiting condition is equivalent to continuous compounding. Thus,

$$F = \lim_{s \to \infty} P\left(1 + \frac{r}{s}\right)^{sn} \tag{3.27}$$

The limit in Eq. (3.27) can be evaluated by first noting the limit of the following expression through binomial expansion, which results in an infinite series:

$$\lim_{x \to \infty} \left(1 + \frac{1}{x}\right)^x = 1 + 1 + \frac{1}{2!} + \frac{1}{3!} + \cdots$$
$$= 2.71828 \cdots = e$$

Let $r/s = 1/x$; then $s = rx$ and $sn = rxn$. Furthermore, $s \to \infty$ as $x \to \infty$. Then, Eq. (3.27) can be expressed in the form

$$F = \lim_{x \to \infty} \left[P\left(1 + \frac{1}{x}\right)^{rxn} \right]$$
$$= P\left[\lim_{x \to \infty} \left(1 + \frac{1}{x}\right)^x \right]^{rn} = Pe^{rn}$$

Hence, for continuous compounding, we have

$$F = Pe^{rn} \tag{3.28}$$

and

$$P = Fe^{-rn} \tag{3.29}$$

The factors e^{rn} and e^{-rn} in Eqs. (3.28) and (3.29) are listed in the table of basic factors for continuous compounding in Appendix B.

For $n = 1$, Eq. (3.28) yields the sum of principal and interest at the end of the first year. Then, the *effective annual interest rate* for continuous compounding is obtained from $(F - P)/P$ as follows:

$$i_e = (Pe^r - P)\frac{1}{P} = e^r - 1 \tag{3.30}$$

Consequently, we can always compute the effective annual interest rate if we know the nominal annual interest rate and the number of interest periods per year, including an infinite number of periods corresponding to continuous compounding.

Example 3.19

Peoples State Bank advertises a nominal annual interest rate of 6% compounded semiannually, and Consolidated Savings and Loans Association advertises a nominal annual interest rate of 6% compounded continuously. What are their effective annual interest rates?

For Peoples State Bank, $r = 6\%$ and $s = 2$. Then, the effective annual interest rate is obtained from Eq. (3.26) as follows:

$$i_e = \left(1 + \frac{0.06}{2}\right)^2 - 1 = 0.0609 = 6.09\%$$

For Consolidated Savings and Loans Association $r = 6\%$ and $n = 1$, or $rn = 0.06$ for entry to Table B1 in Appendix B for continuous compounding. From Eq. (3.30),

$$i_e = e^{0.06} - 1 = 1.0618 - 1 = 0.0618 = 6.18\%$$

3.9   Continuous Compounding Interest Formulas

With the availability of automatic data processing, the use of continuous compounding in computing interest has become more common. For every given nominal annual interest rate, it is easy to compute the corresponding effective annual interest rate from continuous compounding by Eq. (3.30). However, in engineering economic analysis, the receipts and disbursements are often assumed to occur only at the end of the time periods $t = 0, 1, 2, \ldots, n$, where each time period is 1 year. Therefore, we can introduce a new functional notation and compound interest tables based on continuous compounding at the nominal annual interest rate r.

The compound interest factors resulting from continuous compounding of single sums of money can readily be derived from Eqs. (3.28) and (3.29). We shall define a new functional notation for these factors as follows:

$$\frac{F}{P} = e^{rn} = (F \mid P, r, n)_c \tag{3.31}$$

$$\frac{P}{F} = e^{-rn} = (P \mid F, r, n)_c \tag{3.32}$$

where r is the nominal annual interest rate and n is the number of years. The subscript c outside the parenthesis denotes continuous compounding.

For the uniform series shown in Fig. 3.7, we see that the future value F at $t = n$ due to continuous compounding is given by

$$F = Ue^{r(n-1)} + Ue^{r(n-2)} + \cdots + Ue^r + U$$

Factoring out U and multiplying both sides by e^r, we get in two successive steps

$$F = U[e^{r(n-1)} + e^{r(n-2)} + \cdots + e^r + 1]$$

$$e^r F = U[e^{rn} + e^{r(n-1)} + \cdots + e^{2r} + e^r]$$

Subtracting the first from the second equation above,

$$(e^r - 1)F = U(e^{rn} - 1)$$

or

$$F = U\left(\frac{e^{rn} - 1}{e^r - 1}\right) \tag{3.33}$$

Similarly, for uniform series in Fig. 3.8, we see that the present value at $t = 0$ due to continuous compounding is given by

$$P = Ue^{-r} + Ue^{-2r} + \cdots + Ue^{-(n-1)r} + Ue^{-nr}$$

Factoring out U and multiplying both sides by e^r, we get in two successive steps

$$P = U[e^{-r} + e^{-2r} + \cdots + e^{-(n-1)r} + e^{-nr}]$$

$$e^r P = U[1 + e^{-r} + \cdots + e^{-(n-2)r} + e^{-(n-1)r}]$$

Subtracting the first from the second equation above,

$$(e^r - 1)P = U(1 - e^{-nr})$$

or

$$P = U\left(\frac{1 - e^{-nr}}{e^r - 1}\right) \tag{3.34}$$

Using the new functional notation, the compound interest factors resulting from continuous compounding of a uniform series are obtained from Eqs. (3.33) and (3.34) as follows:

$$\frac{F}{U} = \frac{e^{rn} - 1}{e^r - 1} = (F\,|\,U, r, n)_c \tag{3.35}$$

$$\frac{U}{F} = \frac{e^r - 1}{e^{rn} - 1} = (U\,|\,F, r, n)_c \tag{3.36}$$

$$\frac{P}{U} = \frac{1 - e^{-nr}}{e^r - 1} = (P \mid U, r, n)_c \tag{3.37}$$

$$\frac{U}{P} = \frac{e^r - 1}{1 - e^{-nr}} = (U \mid P, r, n)_c \tag{3.38}$$

For the basic gradient in part (a) of Fig. 3.14, we use superposition to obtain

$$P = G[e^{-2r} + 2e^{-3r} + \cdots + (n-2)e^{-(n-1)r} + (n-1)e^{-nr}]$$

Multiplying by e^r

$$e^r P = G[e^{-r} + 2e^{-2r} + \cdots + (n-2)e^{-(n-2)r} + (n-1)e^{-(n-1)r}]$$

Subtracting from the last equation the previous one,

$$(e^r - 1)P = G[e^{-r} + e^{-2r} + \cdots + e^{-(n-1)r} + e^{-nr} - ne^{-nr}]$$

Noting the relationship in Eq. (3.34), we get

$$(e^r - 1)P = G\left(\frac{1 - e^{-nr}}{e^r - 1} - ne^{-nr}\right)$$

or

$$\frac{P}{G} = \frac{1}{(e^r - 1)}\left(\frac{1 - e^{-rn}}{e^r - 1} - ne^{-rn}\right) \tag{3.39}$$

Hence

$$\frac{F}{G} = \left(\frac{F}{P}\right)\left(\frac{P}{G}\right) = \frac{e^{rn}}{(e^r - 1)}\left(\frac{1 - e^{-rn}}{e^r - 1} - ne^{-rn}\right) \tag{3.40}$$

and

$$\frac{U}{G} = \left(\frac{U}{P}\right)\left(\frac{P}{G}\right) = \frac{1}{1 - e^{-nr}}\left(\frac{1 - e^{-rn}}{e^r - 1} - ne^{-rn}\right) \tag{3.41}$$

Using the new functional notation, the above three equations are denoted by

$$\frac{P}{G} = (P \mid G, r, n)_c \tag{3.42}$$

$$\frac{F}{G} = (F \mid G, r, n)_c \tag{3.43}$$

$$\frac{U}{G} = (U \mid G, r, n)_c \tag{3.44}$$

It should be noted that Eqs. (3.33) through (3.41) involve the quotient of the differences of two numbers with the same order of magnitude. Consequently, many significant figures must be carried out in order to obtain accurate values for various factors in the continuous compound interest tables that are given in Appendix C.

Example 3.20

If the nominal annual interest rate is 10% compounded continuously for Example 3.15 while all other quantities remain unchanged, determine the present value of the annual savings in the next 10 years.

Using the same approach but a different set of values for $r = 10\%$ from the continuous compound interest tables in Appendix C, we get

$$\begin{aligned} P &= (20,000)(P \mid U, 10\%, 10)_c - (5,000)(P \mid U, 10\%, 5)_c \\ &= (20,000)(6.0104) - (5,000)(3.7412) \\ &= 120,208 - 18,706 = 101,502 \end{aligned}$$

Note that because of a higher effective annual interest rate due to continuous compounding, the present value obtained in this problem is smaller than that in Example 3.15.

3.10 Summary and Study Guide

In this chapter, we have examined the concept of the time value of money and the equivalence of cash flows. We have discussed the principle of decomposition and superposition of cash flows which is the foundation for computing the net present value or the net future value of a cash flow profile.

Discrete compound interest formulas have been derived for converting present sums, future sums, uniform series, and linear gradients to specified points in time. While these special cases have wide applications, the derivations should not obscure the basic principle in treating the general cash flow profile which may consist of positive, negative, or zero flows at different interest periods. For ease of reference, a functional notation has been introduced. The students are encouraged to conceptualize the problems in the functional notation before carrying out the numerical computation.

We have also covered the concepts of nominal interest rate and effective interest rate, leading to the idea of continuous compounding. Continuous compound interest formulas were then derived. However, we have considered only discrete cash flows, i.e., cash flows received or disbursed at the end of finite interest periods, even though the interest for such cash flows may be compounded discretely or continuously. We have not considered cash flows that are received or disbursed continuously over time since such coverage will divert the primary focus of our attention on the equivalence of cash flows. Similarly, it is possible to derive additional formulas for computing the present value or future value of cash flows in nonlinear gradients and other special cases. However, such formulas are rather cumbersome in application and have not been included.

Although the formulas for computing the compound interest factors are generally cumbersome, the numerical computation can be carried out with the aid of a pocket calculator, and in some cases, a programmable calculator. The tables in the appendices also help to reduce the amount of numerical computation.

REFERENCES

3.1 Barish, N. N., and S. Kaplan, *Economic Analysis for Engineering and Managerial Decision Making*, 2nd ed. New York: McGraw-Hill, 1978.

3.2 DeGarmo, E. P., *Engineering Economy*, 6th ed. New York: Macmillan, 1979.

3.3 Grant, E. L., W. G. Ireson, and R. S. Leavenworth, *Principles of Engineering Economy*, 6th ed. New York: John Wiley & Sons, 1976.

3.4 Newnan, D.G., *Engineering Economic Analysis*, rev. ed. San Jose, CA: Engineering Press, 1980.

3.5 Riggs, J. L., *Engineering Economy*. New York, McGraw-Hill, 1977.

3.6 Smith, G. W., *Engineering Economy: Analysis of Capital Expenditures*, 3rd ed. Ames, IA: Iowa State University Press, 1979.

3.7 Tarquin, A. J., and L. T. Blank, *Engineering Economy*. New York: McGraw-Hill, 1976.

3.8 Taylor, G. A., *Managerial and Engineering Economy*, 3rd ed. New York: D. Van Nostrand, 1975.

3.9 Thuesen, H. G., W. J. Fabrycky, and G. J. Thuesen, *Engineering Economy*, 5th ed. Englewood Cliffs, NJ: Prentice-Hall, 1977.

3.10 White, J. A., M. H. Agee, and K. E. Case, *Principles of Engineering Economic Analysis*. New York: John Wiley & Sons, 1977.

PROBLEMS

P3.1 In considering a 5-year budget for remodeling a testing laboratory, it is expected that $10,000 each will be spent at the end of the first and third years, but no money will be spent at the end of the second and fourth years. How much money can be spent at the end of the fifth year if an initial sum of $25,000 for this purpose is deposited in a bank that pays an interest of 6% compounded annually?

P3.2 The Public Works Department of a city plans to repave some of the city streets in its 6-year budget. The plan calls for the expenditures of $20,000 at the end of the first year, $10,000 each at the end of the second and third year, and $12,000 each at the end of the fourth, fifth, and sixth year. If the annual discount rate is 6%, what is the present value of the expenditures?

P3.3 Eight years ago, Mr. Williams decided to set aside $2,000 at the end of each year in the bank in anticipation of his need to buy a new truck in the future. He was able to do so in all 8 years except at the end of the third and fifth years when he ran into financial difficulties. Having just deposited $2,000 at the end of the eighth year in a bank where the money has accrued interest at 6% per annum, he found a new truck priced at $15,000. Has he sufficient money in the bank to purchase it?

P3.4 An issue of 6-year U.S. savings bonds has a face value of $100 at maturity. If the annual interest rate is 6% per year, how much should a bond be sold for when it is issued?

P3.5 A company invests $5,000 in a new machine that is expected to produce a return of $1,000 per year for the next 10 years. At a 10% annual interest rate, is the investment worthwhile?

P3.6 A solar heating system for residential buildings is advertised for $3,000 cash. The company marketing the system offers a deferred payment plan so that the first payment will be made at the end of 2 years and subsequent payments of the same amount will be paid every 6 months until the end of 5 years, i.e., seven equal payments. If the nominal interest rate is 8% compounded semiannually, what should be the amount of each payment so that the deferred payment plan will be equivalent to the $3,000 cash payment now?

P3.7 Mr. and Mrs. Payne would like to buy a $40,000 home with a down payment of $10,000 and a 20-year mortgage on the rest. If they are allowed to make uniform end-of-year payments at 8% annual interest, what will be the annual payment over a 20-year period?

P3.8 A contractor expects to receive $2,000 per year during the next 10 years, except the end of the second and the sixth year. What is the present value of these receipts at 9% annual interest?

P3.9 The annual maintenance cost on a piece of construction equipment is $200 for each of the first 3 years, with an increase of $50 more in each subsequent year (i.e., $250 for the fourth year, $300 for the fifth year, etc.) until the end of the seventh year, when the equipment will be disposed of. At 6% annual interest, what is the equivalent sum of the maintenance costs at the end of the seventh year?

P3.10 An engineer's starting annual salary is $16,000. For the next 10 years, he expects

3/16

Toby:

I would appreciate you
comments when you have time
to view this book

Steve

a $2,000 raise each year. What is the present value of his expected earnings in the next 10 years if the annual interest rate is 6%?

P3.11 Ms. McDonald bought a car for $6,000 and agreed to pay for it in 24 equal end-of-month payments at 1% monthly interest. Immediately after making the sixth payment, she wants to pay the balance due in a single sum. What should the final single payment be if there is no penalty for making the extra payment?

P3.12 Mr. Goodman has just reached his fifty-fifth birthday and wants to save $800 per year at 7% annual interest for 10 years until his sixty-fifth birthday. If he plans to spend this money in five equal amounts to be withdrawn on his sixty-sixth, sixty-seventh, sixty-eighth, sixty-ninth, and seventieth birthdays, what will be the amount in each withdrawal?

P3.13 The annual maintenance cost of a nuclear power plant is expected to be $300,000 for the first year and to decline $30,000 each subsequent year until it reaches $150,000 in the sixth year, beyond which the annual maintenance cost will remain uniform at $150,000. If the useful life of the power plant is 40 years and the maintenance costs are end-of-year charges, what is the present value of these charges at a 10% annual interest rate?

P3.14 A small construction firm entered into a 10-year contract with a quarry for gravel supply with an agreement to pay $50,000 immediately plus $10,000 per year beginning with the end of the sixth year and ending with the end of the contract period. Because of substantial profits at the end of the fourth year, the firm requested that it be allowed to pay off the rest of the contract with a lump sum. Both the firm and the quarry agreed to an interest rate of 7% compounded annually. What should this lump sum be?

P3.15 A new telephone system is being installed in a business office with an expectation of reduction in staff. The annual savings will be $40,000 in the first year, with $5,000 less savings in each subsequent year (i.e., $35,000 savings in the second year, $30,000 in the third year) until the equipment is retired after 6 years of service. At a 6% annual interest rate, determine the equivalent sum of the savings at the time the equipment is retired.

P3.16 A person borrows $6,000 at 6% compounded annually and wishes to pay back the loan with annual payments over a 5-year period. It is agreed that the annual payments will decrease by $300 per year. That is, the payment in the second year is to be $300 less than that in the first year, the payment in the third year is to be $300 less than that in the second year, etc. What should be the payment at the end of the first year?

P3.17 Martha Donohue expects to receive an annual bonus from her employer and wishes to deposit it in an account that pays interest at a rate of 8% compounded annually. Her bonus in the first 4 years is to be $2,000 per year and will be increased at a rate of 6% per year from the fifth to the seventh year. What will be the accumulated amount in the account after she deposits the last bonus at the end of the seventh year?

P3.18 An entrepreneur in a new engineering venture attempts to borrow $10,000 for 5 years with no repayment for 5 years. Babcock National Bank offers him the loan at a nominal interest rate of 12% compounded semiannually, and Kensington State Bank makes an offer at a nominal annual interest rate of 11% compounded continuously. What will be the repayment at the end of 5 years from each of these offers?

P3.19 The First National Bank offers 8% interest compounded quarterly for 8-year savings certificates. The Wilkin City Bank offers 7.5% interest compounded continuously for the same type of certificate. What are the values of the certificates from the two banks after 8 years if the initial value of each is $1,000?

P3.20 A Savings and Loan Association advertises a nominal interest rate of 7% compounded continuously for an 8-year savings certificate. (a) What is the effective annual interest rate? (b) What is the total interest at the end of 8 years for a certificate of $1,000 at the time of purchase?

P3.21 Jim Wilson deposited $100 in a savings account 10 years ago. For the first 5 years, the bank offered a nominal interest rate of 6% compounded semiannually, and for the last 5 years, it offered a nominal interest rate of 8% compounded quarterly. How much was in the account at the end of 10 years?

P3.22 A bank is offering an interest rate of 0.5% per month for its savings account and is considering a switch to continuous compounding at a nominal annual interest rate of 6.25%. What are the effective annual interest rates before and after the switching?

P3.23 A bill sent to a customer by the City Water Authority contains the following information: "Pay $3.60 on or before the due date of January 23, or $3.78 after the due date. The last date of acceptance for $3.78 without additional penalty is March 23." If you intend either to pay $3.60 on January 23 or $3.78 on March 23, what is the effective annual interest rate by choosing the late payment date?

P3.24 If the nominal annual interest rate is 6% compounded continuously for Problem P3.9 while all other quantities remain unchanged, determine the equivalent sum at the end of the seventh year.

P3.25 If the nominal annual interest rate is 10% compounded continuously for Problem P3.13 while all other quantities remain unchanged, determine the present value of the charges.

P3.26 If the nominal annual interest rate is 8% compounded continuously for Problem P3.17 while all other quantities remain unchanged, determine the equivalent sum of the savings at the time the equipment is retired.

4

COMPUTATION OF
RATES OF RETURN

4.1 Computation of Unknown Interest Rate

In each of the compound interest formulas derived in Chapter 3, only one unknown is to be determined from the other quantities given. So far, we have not dealt with the problem of computing the unknown interest rate i while all other quantities in the formula are given, because such computation can be quite tedious.

Let us consider first the simplest case involving a single present sum P (at $t = 0$) and a single future sum F (at $t = n$) as represented by Eq. (3.12) or (3.13), i.e.,

$$\frac{F}{P} = (1 + i)^n \quad \text{or} \quad \frac{P}{F} = \frac{1}{(1 + i)^n}$$

Solving for the interest rate i, we obtain

$$i = \sqrt[n]{\frac{F}{P}} - 1 \tag{4.1}$$

The interest rate i is conventionally defined as a positive quantity. If $F/P > 1$, Eq. (4.1) yields a unique positive real number for i. The interest rate i at which a single sum P will be accumulated to a single sum F over n interest periods is referred to as the *rate of return*.

It is important to note that Eq. (4.1) represents a special case in which the value of i can be obtained by taking the nth root of F/P. For other compound interest formulas in Chapter 3, which involve either a series of receipts or a series of disbursements, the solution of i is not nearly as simple. For example, from Eqs. (3.14) and (3.16), we obtain, respectively,

$$\left(\frac{F}{U}\right)i = (1 + i)^n - 1 \tag{4.2}$$

and

$$\left(\frac{P}{U}\right)i(1 + i)^n = (1 + i)^n - 1 \tag{4.3}$$

The solution of i from either Eq. (4.2) or Eq. (4.3) requires the solution of an algebraic equation involving the nth power of i. Thus, the computation of the unknown interest rates generally can be quite tedious.

For the group of compound interest formulas in Eqs. (3.12) through (3.17) corresponding to the six sets of cash flows in Fig. 4.1, a positive interest rate i exists when $F > P$, $F > nU$, and $P < nU$. For a specified value of n, we can find the numerical values of the compound interest factors for a range of values of i from the

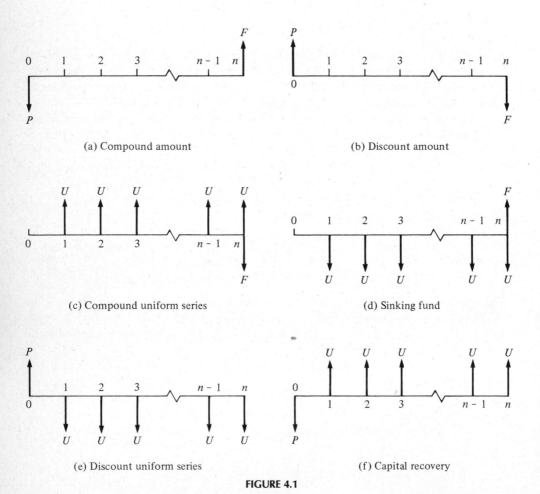

(a) Compound amount   (b) Discount amount

(c) Compound uniform series   (d) Sinking fund

(e) Discount uniform series   (f) Capital recovery

FIGURE 4.1

discrete compound interest tables in Appendix A, and plot such factors versus the interest rate i in a graph as shown schematically in Fig. 4.2. It can be seen that the compound interest factors represented by Eqs. (3.12) through (3.17) are monotonically increasing or decreasing functions of the interest rate i. Consequently, the computation of the unknown interest rate from any of these formulas is reduced to seeking the particular value of i which satisfies the corresponding formula.

Using the discrete compound interest tables in Appendix A, it is possible to

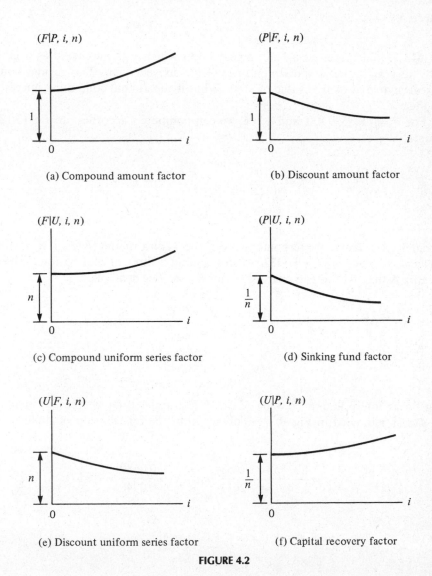

$(F|P, i, n)$

1

0   i

(a) Compound amount factor

$(P|F, i, n)$

1

0   i

(b) Discount amount factor

$(F|U, i, n)$

n

0   i

(c) Compound uniform series factor

$(P|U, i, n)$

$\frac{1}{n}$

0   i

(d) Sinking fund factor

$(U|F, i, n)$

n

0   i

(e) Discount uniform series factor

$(U|P, i, n)$

$\frac{1}{n}$

0   i

(f) Capital recovery factor

FIGURE 4.2

compute the approximate value of i by linear interpolation of values for a factor corresponding to the formula under consideration. The accuracy of the interpolation depends on the interval of i values used. This method of interpolation for computing the unknown interest rate i can best be illustrated by examples. A more general approach in the formulation and solution of the unknown interest rate from a series of cash flows representing an investment will be discussed in later sections.

Example 4.1

Tony MacDonald received a U.S. savings bond which was purchased as a gift for him by his grandfather at a discount price of $75 six years ago. This savings bond is now redeemable at its face value of $100. What is the annual compound interest for the bond?

For $P = 75$, $F = 100$, and $n = 6$, we can compute i according to Eq. (3.12) as follows:

$$i = \sqrt[6]{\frac{100}{75}} - 1 = \sqrt[6]{1.3333} - 1$$

$$= 1.409 - 1 = 0.049 = 4.9\%$$

Alternately, we can use interpolation from the values of the $(F|P, i, n)$ factor in Appendix A. Since $F/P = 1.3333$, we try to find values of i in various tables in Appendix A that lead to F/P near 1.3333 for $n = 6$. For example,

Trial i	$(F|P, i, 6)$
3%	1.1941
4%	1.2653
5%	1.3401

Using linear interpolation between 4% and 5%, and letting $x\%$ be the increment from 4% as indicated in Fig. 4.3, we obtain from the relationship of similar triangles,

$$\frac{x}{5 - 4} = \frac{1.3333 - 1.2653}{1.3401 - 1.2653} \quad \text{or} \quad x = \frac{0.0680}{0.0748} = 0.91$$

Hence,

$$i = 4 + x = 4 + 0.91 = 4.91\%$$

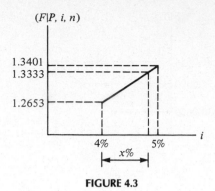

FIGURE 4.3

Example 4.2

A bank solicits customers who will deposit \$1,000 at the end of each year for 20 years with the promise of a return of \$35,000 at the end of 20 years. What is the annual compound interest rate that the bank is offering?

The equivalence of the uniform payments $U = \$1,000$ is known to be a return $F = \$35,000$ for $n = 20$. For $F/U = 35$, we try to find values of i from various tables in Appendix A that lead to F/U near 35 for $n = 20$. For example,

Trial i	$(F\,|\,U, i, 20)$
4%	29.7781
5%	33.0659
6%	36.7856

Using linear interpolation between 5% and 6%, and letting $x\%$ be the increment from 5%, as shown in Fig. 4.4, we get

$$\frac{x}{6-5} = \frac{35.0 - 33.0659}{36.7856 - 33.0659} \quad \text{or} \quad x = \frac{1.934}{3.7197} = 0.52$$

Hence,

$$i = 5 + x = 5 + 0.52 = 5.52\%$$

Example 4.3

An insurance company offers an annuity policy to retired persons that requires an immediate payment of \$40,000 in return for a guaranteed annual income of \$2,500

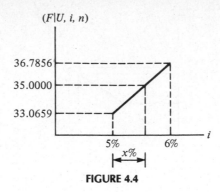

FIGURE 4.4

for the next 30 years. What is the annual compound interest rate that the insurance company offers to pay in this policy?

In this problem, the present sum paid is $P = \$40,000$ and the annual receipt $U = \$2,500$ in a uniform series continuing for $n = 30$ years. For $P/U = 16$, we try to find values of i from various tables in Appendix A that lead to P/U near 16. For example,

Trial i	$(P\,|\,U, i, 30)$
3%	19.6004
4%	17.2920
5%	15.3725

Using linear interpolation between 4% and 5%, and letting $x\%$ be the increment from 4% as indicated in Fig. 4.5, we get

$$\frac{x}{5-4} = \frac{16.0 - 17.292}{15.3725 - 17.292} \quad \text{or} \quad x = \frac{-1.292}{-1.9195} = 0.67$$

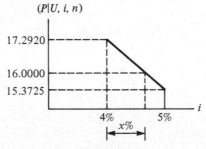

FIGURE 4.5

Hence

$$i = 4 + x = 4 + 0.67 = 4.67\%$$

4.2   The Internal Rate of Return for Simple Cases

It is convenient to regard the problem of finding unknown interest rates for the simple cases cited in Fig. 4.1 in the context of lending and borrowing. Cases (a), (d), and (f) in Fig. 4.1 each represent a typical lending situation where one or more periods of disbursements are followed by one or more periods of receipts, whereas cases (b), (c), and (e) each represent a typical borrowing situation where one or more periods of receipts are followed by one or more periods of disbursements. The investment and financing aspects of a project correspond to the lending and borrowing situations, respectively.

For either a lending or borrowing situation, we can find the equivalence of the cash flows discounted or compounded to a specified reference point in time. For example, we can select time $t = 0$ and discount the cash flows to net present values (NPV) at a discount rate i. If the net present values corresponding to different values of i are plotted on a graph, the general shapes of the curve representing the lending and borrowing situations are found to be those shown in parts (a) and (b) of Fig. 4.6, respectively. We need to examine only one of the situations in detail since borrowing represents the reverse of lending and differs by a negative sign in the cash flows. The discount rate i' which sets the net present value of a series of cash flows equal to zero is called the *internal rate of return* (IRR). If we select a future time $t = n$ as a reference point, we can compound the cash flows to net future value (NFV) at an interest rate i. The general shapes of the NFV versus i curve representing lending and borrowing situations are shown in Fig. 4.7, in which the discount rate i' is the IRR.

The plotting of the NPV versus i curve (or the NFV versus i curve) is accomplished by assigning a range of values for i starting from $i = 0$ and by computing the NPV (or the NFV) corresponding to each i. Since the internal rate of return which sets the net *present* value of a series of cash flows equal to zero will also set the net *future* value of the same series equal to zero, we can obtain the internal rate of return for a series of cash flows from either NPV = 0 or NFV = 0. The positive real root of the equation resulting from NPV = 0 or NFV = 0 can be obtained algebraically, even though the solution may be complicated when n is large.

If the equation resulting from NPV = 0 or NFV = 0 contains only one compound interest factor having i as the unknown, as in the simple cases of lending or borrowing, the internal rate of return can be obtained by linear interpolation from the discrete compound interest tables in Appendix A. For each of the six cases in

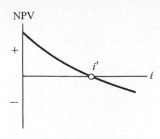

(a) Typical lending
or investment

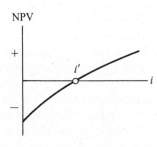

(b) Typical borrowing
or financing

FIGURE 4.6

Fig. 4.1, we can express the net present values in functional notation as follows:

1. Compound single amount $(F > P)$

$$\text{NPV} = -P + F(P \mid F, i, n) \tag{4.4}$$

2. Discount single amount $(P < F)$

$$\text{NPV} = +P - F(P \mid F, i, n) \tag{4.5}$$

3. Compound uniform series $(nU < F)$

$$\text{NPV} = +U(P \mid U, i, n) - F(P \mid F, i, n) \tag{4.6}$$

4. Sinking fund $(F > nU)$

$$\text{NPV} = -U(P \mid U, i, n) + F(P \mid F, i, n) \tag{4.7}$$

5. Discount uniform series $(P < nU)$

$$\text{NPV} = +P - U(P \mid U, i, n) \tag{4.8}$$

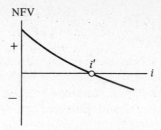

(a) Typical lending
or investment

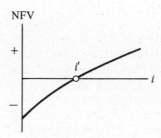

(b) Typical borrowing
or financing

FIGURE 4.7

6. Capital recovery $(nU > P)$

$$\text{NPV} = +U(P\,|\,U, i, n) - P \qquad (4.9)$$

For NPV = 0, Eqs. (4.4) through (4.9) reduce to the compound interest factors in Eqs. (3.12) through (3.17) if we note the mathematical relationships among these factors, e.g.,

$$(F\,|\,P, i, n) = \frac{1}{(P\,|\,F, i, n)} \qquad (4.10)$$

$$(F\,|\,U, i, n) = \frac{(P\,|\,U, i, n)}{(P\,|\,F, i, n)} \qquad (4.11)$$

$$(P\,|\,U, i, n) = \frac{(F\,|\,U, i, n)}{(F\,|\,P, i, n)} \qquad (4.12)$$

$$(U\,|\,F, i, n) = \frac{(P\,|\,F, i, n)}{(P\,|\,U, i, n)} \qquad (4.13)$$

$$(U\,|\,P,\,i,\,n) = \frac{(F\,|\,P,\,i,\,n)}{(F\,|\,U,\,i,\,n)} \tag{4.14}$$

The net future values of these six cases can be similarly obtained.

Consequently, the unknown interest rate for each of these special cases can be obtained as discussed in Section 4.1, and the interest rate thus obtained is the internal rate of return of the investment. Furthermore, for the case of a single sum P invested at $t = 0$ and a single sum F returned at $t = n$, the internal rate of return is the same as the rate of return as defined in Section 4.1.

Example 4.4

An investment proposal of 1-year duration indicates that a cost of \$1,000 will be incurred at the beginning and a benefit of \$1,210 will accrue a year later. Plot a NPV versus i graph for annual discount rates of 0%, 5%, 10%, 15%, 20%, and 25%. Also plot NFV versus i for the same range of annual discount rates.

For this problem, there is only one interest period with a negative cash flow of $-1,000$ at $t = 0$ and a positive cash flow at $t = 1$. Hence,

$$\text{NPV} = -1,000 + (1,210)(1 + i)^{-1}$$

$$\text{NFV} = -(1,000)(1 + i) + 1,210$$

The values of NPV and NFV for the range of given i are tabulated as follows:

i	0%	5%	10%	15%	20%	25%
NPV	210	152	100	52	8	-32
NFV	210	160	110	60	10	-40

For NPV $= 0$, we obtain

$$1,000 = \frac{1,210}{(1 + i)}$$

$$(1 + i) = \frac{1,210}{1,000} = 1.21$$

$$i = 1.21 - 1 = 0.21 = 21\%$$

And for NFV $= 0$, we also get $i = 21\%$. Consequently, the internal rate of return is 21%, whether we obtain it by setting NPV $= 0$ or NFV $= 0$. The plots of NPV versus i and of NFV versus i are shown, respectively, in parts (a) and (b) of Fig. 4.8.

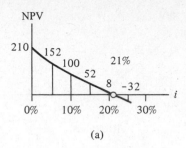

(a)

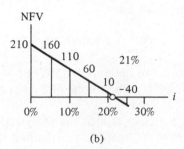

(b)

FIGURE 4.8

Example 4.5

An investment proposal for the duration of 2 years indicates that a cost of $1,000 will be incurred in the beginning and a benefit of $600 will result at the end of each of the first and second year. Plot a NPV versus i graph for annual discount rates of 0%, 5%, 10%, 20%, and 25%. Also find the internal rate of return.

From the given cash flows over two interest periods, we get

$$NPV = -1,000 + 600(1 + i)^{-1} + 600(1 + i)^{-2}$$

The values of NPV for the range of given i are tabulated as follows:

i	0%	5%	10%	15%	20%	25%
NPV	200	116	41	−25	−83	−136

For NPV = 0, we get

$$-1,000(1 + i)^2 + 600(1 + i) + 600 = 0$$

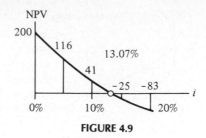

FIGURE 4.9

Expanding and collecting terms, we have

$$-1,000i^2 - 1,400i + 200 = 0$$

Solving the quadratic equation, we obtain $i = 0.1307$ or -1.5307. Taking the positive root only, we have $i = 13.07\%$. The results of the net present values are plotted in Fig. 4.9.

It can be seen that for n greater than 2, the analytical solution of the algebraic equation is complicated. However, the effort of finding the real roots of such an algebraic equation can be reduced with the aid of a programmable pocket calculator or by the use of the method of interpolation from interest tables. For this problem, for example, we can rewrite the equation in the form

$$\text{NPV} = -1,000 + 600(P\,|\,U, i, 2) = 0$$

or

$$(P\,|\,U, i, 2) = \frac{1,000}{600} = 1.6667$$

We try several values of i from the discrete compound interest tables in Appendix A that lead to $P\,|\,U$ near 1.6667 for $n = 2$. For example,

Trial i	$(P\,|\,U, i, 2)$
10%	1.7355
12%	1.6901
15%	1.6257

Using linear interpolation between 12% and 15%, we get

$$i = 12\% + (15\% - 12\%)\frac{1.6901 - 1.6667}{1.6901 - 1.6257} = 12\% + 1.09\% = 13.09\%$$

4.3   The Internal Rate of Return for the General Case

We shall now consider the general case of an n-period cash flow profile A_0, A_1, A_2, ..., A_n, each of which may be positive or negative, constituting a mixed lending and borrowing situation over the entire time span. When the net present value of the cash flows is summed algebraically, we obtain

$$\text{NPV} = A_0 + A_1(1 + i)^{-1} + A_2(1 + i)^{-2} + \cdots + A_n(1 + i)^{-n} \tag{4.15}$$

The internal rate of return (IRR) for an investment represented by the series of cash flows A_0, A_1, A_2, ..., A_n is defined as the discount rate which sets the net present value of this series of cash flows equal to zero. Thus, the IRR can be obtained by finding the value(s) of i in the algebraic equation

$$A_0 + A_1(1 + i)^{-1} + A_2(1 + i)^{-2} + \cdots + A_n(1 + i)^{-n} = 0 \tag{4.16}$$

The numerical solution of Eq. (4.16) can be simplified by letting $x = 1 + i$ and multiplying through by x^n. Then,

$$A_0 x^n + A_1 x^{n-1} + \cdots + A_{n-2} x^2 + A_{n-1} x + A_n = 0 \tag{4.17}$$

The algebraic function of the left-hand side of this equation can be abbreviated as

$$f(x) = A_0 x^n + A_1 x^{n-1} + \cdots + A_{n-1} x^2 + A_n \tag{4.18}$$

The function $f(x)$ is said to have a *change of sign* if the coefficients of two successive terms in $f(x)$ have opposite signs. Powers of x having zero coefficients are not counted. Then, according to the Descartes rule of signs, the number of positive real roots in Eq. (4.17) cannot exceed the number of changes in sign in $f(x)$.

It is theoretically possible that there is no positive real root for $f(x) = 0$, regardless of the number of sign changes. In general, if there is only one sign change in $f(x)$, there will be a positive real root for $f(x) = 0$. However, if there are two or more sign changes in $f(x)$, there may be 0, 1, 2, ..., c positive real roots for $f(x) = 0$ where c is the actual number of sign changes.

Since $x = 1 + i$, we can obtain the value of $i = x - 1$ corresponding to every positive real root of $f(x) = 0$. That is

$$i = x - 1 = \begin{cases} \text{Positive} & \text{for } x > 1 \\ 0 & \text{for } x = 1 \\ \text{Negative} & \text{for } x < 1 \end{cases} \tag{4.19}$$

Hence for every positive root x, i can be either positive or zero because a negative value of i is not admissible as an internal rate of return. Consequently, the number of nonnegative values of the internal rate of return i for a cash flow profile of A_0, $A_1, \ldots, A_n$ also cannot exceed the number of sign changes in the sequence, not counting the periods with zero cash flow, if any, in the sequence.

The solution of Eq. (4.17) representing NPV $= 0$ for the general case of mixed positive and negative cash flows is generally quite complicated when n is large. Numerical methods for solving an algebraic equation expressed in descending powers of the variable are readily available, although the solution procedure is often lengthy and requires the trial and error approach. The computational effort can be reduced with the aid of a programmable pocket calculator or by interpolations from the tables in Appendix A.

In finding an approximate numerical solution of Eq. (4.17) by trial and error, we can try a range of values of x until we find all possible positive real roots of x that will lead to $f(x) = 0$. Let x_1 and x_2 be two successive values of x in a trial. If $f(x_1)$ and $f(x_2)$ are of opposite signs (one positive and the other negative), then a positive real root exists between x_1 and x_2 as shown in Fig. 4.10. Conversely, if

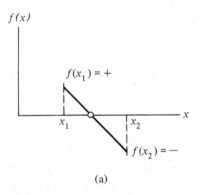

(a)

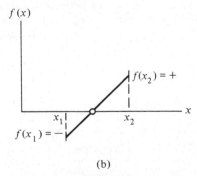

(b)

FIGURE 4.10

$f(x_1)$ and $f(x_2)$ have the same sign, there may be none or an even number of positive real roots between x_1 and x_2 as shown in Fig. 4.11. Therefore, care must be taken so that the unsearched interval between any two values of x will be sufficiently small if there are multiple sign changes if $f(x) = 0$. With the aid of a programmable pocket calculator, we can find the smallest positive real root if we start the trial solution from $x = 0$. When two or more positive real roots exist, each root may be obtained successively from the remaining equation after the smallest one has been found and factored out. Finally, the values of i corresponding to positive values of x found in Eq. (4.17) can be obtained from Eq. (4.19).

The approximate numerical solution of Eq. (4.17) may also be obtained by trial solution with the aid of the discrete compound interest tables in Appendix A. Again, it is important to observe the number of sign changes in the equation and to check for possible multiple positive roots when the conditions warrant. For the purpose of interpolation, it is more convenient to express the net present value of a series of mixed cash flows in the following form:

$$\text{NPV} = \sum_{t=0}^{t=n} A_t(1 + i)^{-t} = \sum_{t=0}^{t=n} A_t(P \,|\, F, i, t) \tag{4.20}$$

We can try a range of values of i in Eq. (4.20) until we find all possible nonnegative

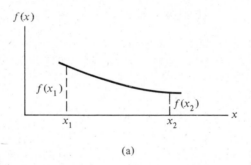

(a)

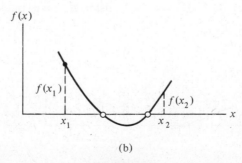

(b)

FIGURE 4.11

value(s) of i that will lead to NPV $= 0$. It should be pointed out again that we can easily miss some positive values of i if we choose too large an interval of i in the search of the multiple values of i. The detailed procedure for obtaining nonnegative value(s) of i by trial solution in combination with the method of linear interpolation will be illustrated by examples.

Example 4.6

A cash flow profile with two interest periods consists of $A_0 = +1,000$, $A_1 = -2,500$, and $A_2 = +1,540$. Find the internal rate of return per interest period.

First, we find the net present value of the cash flow profile and set it equal to zero. Thus,

$$NPV = 1,000 - (2,500)(1 + i)^{-1} + (1,540)(1 + i)^{-2} = 0$$

Letting $x = 1 + i$ and multiplying through with x^2, we get

$$1,000x^2 - 2,500x + 1,540 = 0$$

For this simple quadratic equation, we recognize that

$$(10)(10x - 11)(10x - 14) = 0$$

Hence $x = 1.1$ and $x = 1.4$. Then from $i = x - 1$, we get $i = 0.1 = 10\%$ and $i = 0.4 = 40\%$. A plot of NPV versus i is shown in Fig. 4.12 in which the internal rates of return are seen to be 10% and 40%. The meaning of multiple values of IRR will be explained later.

Example 4.7

A cash flow profile with three interest periods consists of $A_0 = -1,000$, $A_1 = +3,700$, $A_2 = -4,540$ and $A_3 = +1,848$. Verify that the internal rate(s) of return per interest period are 10%, 20%, and 40%, using the analytical approach.

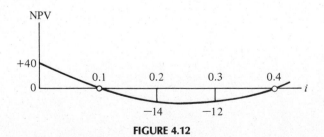

FIGURE 4.12

We find the net present value of the cash flow profile and set it equal to zero. Thus,

$$NPV = -1{,}000 + (3{,}700)(1 + i)^{-1} - (4{,}540)(1 + i)^{-2} + (1{,}848)(1 + i)^{-3} = 0$$

By letting $x = 1 + i$ and multiplying through by x^3 we get

$$-1{,}000x^3 + 3{,}700x^2 - 4{,}540x + 1{,}848 = 0$$

Generally, the analytical solution of a cubic equation is lengthy. However, for this problem, the results are already given, i.e., $i = 0.1$, 0.2, and 0.4. Consequently, we need to verify the analytical solution by factoring, i.e.,

$$(10x - 11)(10x - 12)(10x - 14) = 0$$

which indeed leads to the given results of $i = 10\%$, 20%, and 40%.

Example 4.8

Find the numerical values of the internal rate(s) of return for the cash flow profile in Example 4.7, using the trial and error approach.

From the previous example, it is seen that for $NPV = 0$ we have

$$f(x) = -1{,}000x^3 + 3{,}700x^2 - 4{,}540x + 1{,}848 = 0$$

Since there are three sign changes in $f(x)$, there may be up to three positive real roots. Suppose that we try a set of values $x = 0$, $x = 1$, and $x = 1.3$. We find that

$$f(0) = +1{,}848$$

$$f(1) = -1{,}000 + 3{,}700 - 4{,}540 + 1{,}848 = +8$$

$$f(1.3) = -2{,}197 + 6{,}253 - 5{,}902 + 1{,}848 = +2$$

We may infer that there is no positive real root between $x = 0$ and $x = 1$, or between $x = 1$ and $x = 1.3$. While the former conclusion turns out to be correct, the latter is not. There is no way to verify this fact other than to try smaller intervals of x between $x = 1$ and $x = 1.3$. Let us try a number of values between $x = 1$ and $x = 1.5$ and compute the corresponding values of $f(x)$ as follows:

$$x = 1 \qquad f(1) = +8$$

$$x = 1.1 \qquad f(1.1) = \quad 0$$

$$x = 1.15 \qquad f(1.15) = -1$$

$$x = 1.2 \qquad f(1.2) = \quad 0$$

$$x = 1.3 \qquad f(1.3) = +2$$

$$x = 1.4 \qquad f(1.4) = \quad 0$$

$$x = 1.5 \qquad f(1.5) = -12$$

From these results, we can conclude that there are three positive real roots, $x = 1.1$, $x = 1.2$, and $x = 1.4$ as shown in Fig. 4.13. The corresponding values of the internal rate of return obtained from $i = x - 1$ are $i = 0.1 = 10\%$, $i = 0.2 = 20\%$, and $i = 0.4 = 40\%$.

Example 4.9

The Maxwell Manufacturing Company plans to invest \$77,000 in an energy-saving device with the expectation of receiving benefits for the next 5 years in the amounts of \$38,000, \$32,000, \$26,000, \$20,000, and \$14,000 at the end of first, second, third, fourth, and fifth years, respectively. What is the internal rate of return for investing in this device?

This series of cash flows has only one sign change since the cash flow at $t = 0$ is negative and all other cash flows at $t = 1, 2, ..., 5$ are positive. We expect only one positive real root of i, which can be obtained by using the method of linear interpolation. Since the benefits can be represented by a uniform series with $U = \$38,000$ and a basic gradient with $G = -\$6,000$ for $n = 5$, then the net present

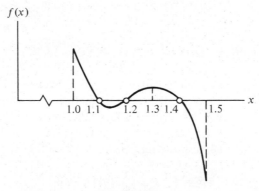

FIGURE 4.13

value of the cash flows in $1,000 is

$$\text{NPV} = -77 + (38)(P\,|\,U, i, 5) - (6)(P\,|\,G, i, 5)$$

We can try various values of i until we find out which one sets the NPV equal to zero. We shall observe the change of the NPV as the value of i is increased until we note a change of NPV either from positive to negative, or vice versa. The accuracy of the result of linear interpolation depends, of course, on the interval of i. For example, if we try $i = 20\%$, we can find the values of $(P\,|\,U, 20\%, 5)$ and $(P\,|\,G, 20\%, 5)$ from Appendix A and compute NPV from the above equation. The results of the computation for $i = 20\%, 25\%$, and 30% are summarized as follows:

Trial i	$(P\,|\,U, i, 5)$	$(P\,|\,G, i, 5)$	NPV in $1,000
20%	2.9906	4.9061	$-77 + 113.643 - 29.437 = +7.206$
25%	2.6893	4.2035	$-77 + 102.193 - 25.221 = -0.028$
30%	2.4356	3.6297	$-77 + 92.553 - 27.778 = -6.225$

Using linear interpolation of NPV between $i = 20\%$ and $i = 25\%$, and letting $x\%$ be the increment from 25% as shown in Fig. 4.14, we get

$$\frac{x}{25 - 20} = \frac{7.206}{7.206 + 0.028} \qquad x = (5)\frac{7.206}{7.234} = 4.98$$

Hence, the internal rate of return is

$$i = 20 + x = 20 + 4.98 = 24.98\% \text{ (close to 25\%)}$$

   In general, when the series of cash flows cannot be represented by a combination of the uniform series and the basic gradient, we can use Eq. (4.20) expressed

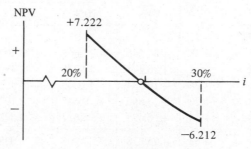

FIGURE 4.14

in the functional notation:

$$\text{NPV} = \sum_{t=0}^{t=n} A_t(P \,|\, F, i, t)$$

For this particular problem, the NPV (in $1,000) is

$$\text{NPV} = -77 + (38)(P\,|\,F, i, 1) + (32)(P\,|\,F, i, 2) + (26)(P\,|\,F, i, 3)$$
$$+ (20)(P\,|\,F, i, 4) + (14)(P\,|\,F, i, 5)$$

For each trial value of i, we can find the compound interest factors in the above equation from the tables in Appendix A. The resulting terms for each trial value of i are given in the vertical columns in Table 4.1, with the NPV in the bottom line.

It can be seen that the net present values for $i = 20\%$, 25%, and 30% are slightly different from those obtained previously due to truncation of digits in the tables. Nevertheless, the internal rate of return remains close to 25%.

Example 4.10

The Chapman Construction Company has been engaged by a foreign government to build an oil refinery. The cash flows (in millions of dollars) in the 5-year period of construction are $+18$, $+10$, -40, -60, $+30$, and $+50$, for $t = 0, 1, 2, \ldots, 5$, respectively. Find the internal rate of return from the construction of the refinery.

Since this series of cash flows has two sign changes, we expect to find at most

Table 4.1

Computation of Internal Rate of Return by Trial

Year t	Cash Flow A_t	$A_t(P\,|\,F, i, t)$				
		0%	10%	20%	25%	30%
0	−77	−77	−77	−77	−77	−77
1	+38	+38	+34.546	+31.665	+30.400	+29.230
2	+32	+32	+26.445	+22.221	+20.480	+18.934
3	+26	+26	+19.534	+15.046	+13.312	+11.835
4	+20	+20	+13.660	+9.646	+8.192	+7.002
5	+14	+14	+8.693	+5.627	+4.588	+3.770
NPV		+53	+25.878	+7.205	−0.028	−6.229

Table 4.2

Computation of Internal Rate of Return by Trial

Year t	Cash Flow A_t	$A_t(P\|F, i, t)$					
		0%	10%	20%	30%	40%	50%
0	+18	+18	+18	+18	+18	+18	+18
1	+10	+10	+9.091	+8.333	+7.692	+7.143	+6.667
2	−40	−40	−33.056	−27.776	−23.668	−20.408	−17.776
3	−60	−60	−45.078	−34.722	−27.312	−21.864	−17.778
4	+30	+30	+20.490	+14.469	+10.503	+7.809	+5.925
5	+50	+50	+31.045	+20.095	+13.465	+9.295	+6.585
NPV		+8	+0.492	−1.601	−1.320	−0.025	+1.623

two positive real roots of i. The net present value of the cash flow in millions of dollars is:

$$\text{NPV} = +18 + (10)(P\|F, i, 1) - (40)(P\|F, i, 2) - (60)(P\|F, i, 3) \\ + (30)(P\|F, i, 4) + (50)(P\|F, i, 5)$$

Not knowing what the values of these roots may be, we try a range of values $i = 0\%, 10\%, 20\%, 30\%, 40\%,$ and 50%. The results of the computation are given in Table 4.2.

The results indicate that one positive real root of i lies between 10% and 20% and the other between 40% and 50% as shown in Fig. 4.15.

Using linear interpolation, we get

$$i = 10\% + (20\% - 10\%) \frac{0.492}{0.492 + 1.601} = 12.35\%$$

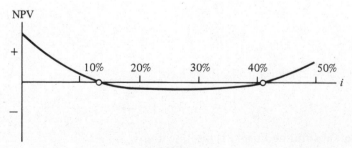

FIGURE 4.15

and

$$i = 40\% + (50\% - 40\%) \frac{0.025}{0.025 + 1.623} = 40.15\%$$

Since each of these two values of i satisfies the equation NPV $= 0$, both are mathematically correct solutions of the internal rate of return.

4.4   An Alternate Definition of Internal Rate of Return

The internal rate of return of an investment may also be defined as the interest rate earned on the unrecovered balance of an investment such that the unrecovered balance at the end of the life of the investment will be zero. In order to prove this statement, let us introduce the following notation:

i = the interest rate earned on the unrecovered balance for each time period
A_t = the cash flow at the end of period t (positive for a receipt and negative for a disbursement)
R_t = the unrecovered balance or cumulative surplus at the end of period t (positive for a cumulative surplus and negative for an unrecovered balance)
I_t = the interest accrued during period t on R_{t-1} (positive for interest earned from the cumulative surplus and negative for interest charged for the unrecovered balance)
Q_t = the amount of unrecovered balance that is reduced or the amount of cumulative surplus that is increased during period t (positive for a net increase and negative for a net decrease)

Then, the following relationships exist for $t = 1, 2, 3, \ldots, n$

$$I_t = R_{t-1}i \tag{4.21}$$

$$Q_t = A_t + I_t \tag{4.22}$$

$$R_t = R_{t-1} + Q_t \tag{4.23}$$

Substituting Eq. (4.22) into Eq. (4.23), we have

$$R_t = R_{t-1} + A_t + I_t$$

Furthermore, substituting Eq. (4.21) into the above, we get

$$R_t = A_t + R_{t-1}(1 + i) \tag{4.24}$$

Initially, $R_0 = A_0$ since the unrecovered balance at $t = 0$ is the amount invested at that point in time. Hence, according to Eqs. (4.21) through (4.23), we have for $t = 1$

$$I_1 = R_0 i = A_0 i$$

$$Q_1 = A_1 + I_1$$

$$R_1 = R_0 + Q_1 = A_0 + Q_1$$

We can obtain similar quantities for subsequent periods $t = 2, 3, \ldots, n$. Note that Eq. (4.24) provides a recursive relationship for $t = 1, 2, \ldots, n$ as follows:

$$R_1 = A_1 + R_0(1 + i) = A_1 + A_0(1 + i)$$

$$R_2 = A_2 + R_1(1 + i) = A_2 + A_1(1 + i) + A_0(1 + i)^2$$

$$\cdots\cdots\cdots\cdots\cdots\cdots\cdots\cdots\cdots\cdots\cdots\cdots\cdots\cdots\cdots\cdots\cdots\cdots\cdots\cdots$$

$$R_t = A_t + R_{t-1}(1 + i) = A_t + A_{t-1}(1 + i) + \cdots + A_1(1 + i)^{t-1} + A_0(1 + i)^t$$

Thus, for $t = n$,

$$R_n = A_n + A_{n-1}(1 + i) + \cdots + A_1(1 + i)^{n-1} + A_0(1 + i)^n \qquad (4.25)$$

Note that this value of R_n is the same as the net future value (NFV) of the cash flows $A_0, A_1, \ldots, A_n$ compounded to $t = n$ at an interest rate i. If i is the internal rate of return on an investment with a cash flow profile $A_0, A_1, \ldots, A_n$, then by the definition introduced in previous sections, NFV $= 0$. Then, R_n must also be zero, and the alternative definition introduced in this section also holds true. Hence, the internal rate of return of an investment project may be regarded as a measure of the rate of return of the unrecovered funds during the periods when the funds are in use.

Example 4.11

Verify that, for the investment in Example 4.9, the unrecovered balance at the end of 5 years is zero if $i = 25\%$ is the internal rate of return.

The year-by-year unrecovered balance has been computed by using Eqs. (4.21) through (4.23), and the results are tabulated in Table 4.3. Because $i = 25\%$ has been obtained by linear interpolation, it introduces small numerical errors in the values of R_t. Consequently, at $t = 5$, $R_t = -0.087$ instead of zero.

Table 4.3

Year-by-Year Unrecovered Balance for Example 4.9

t	A_t	R_{t-1}	I_t	Q_t	R_t
0	-77	—	—	—	-77
1	$+38$	-77	-19.250	$+18.750$	-58.250
2	$+32$	-58.250	-14.563	$+17.437$	-40.813
3	$+26$	-40.813	-10.203	$+15.797$	-25.016
4	$+20$	-25.016	-6.254	$+13.746$	-11.270
5	$+14$	-11.270	-2.818	$+11.183$	-0.087

Example 4.12

Verify that, for the investment in Example 4.10, the unrecovered balance at the end of 5 years is zero if (a) $i = 12.35\%$ or (b) $i = 40.15\%$, each of which represents an internal rate of return.

The cash flow profile consists of mixed cash flows with two sign changes. For each of the two internal rates of return $i = 12.35\%$ and $i = 40.15\%$, the year-by-year unrecovered balances are computed as shown in Table 4.4. In both cases, R_t at $t = 5$ is approximately zero.

Example 4.13

A government bond of $1,000 denomination redeemable at full value in 15 years with an annual interest rate of 4% payable at the end of each year was originally sold at its face value. Since the issuance of this bond 10 years ago, the market interest rates have gone up steadily. After collecting the interest at the end of 10 years, this $1,000 bond can sell only for $700 in the market. If a holder of this bond wants to sell at this price, what is the internal rate of return for his investment? If the buyer keeps the bond to maturity, what is the internal rate of return for the buyer?

The annual interest from the bond is based on 4% of the face value of $1,000 and is $40 irrespective of the market price. If a holder of this bond keeps it until maturity, the cash flow profile of the investment will be as shown in part (a) of Fig. 4.16, and the internal rate of return for the investment will be 4%.

If the holder of this bond sells it at $700 after 10 years, the cash flow profile of the investment will be as shown in part (b) of Fig. 4.16, and the internal rate of return of the investment can be obtained as follows:

$$NPV = -1,000 + (40)(P \mid U, i, 10) + (700)(P \mid F, i, 10) = 0$$

Table 4.4

Year-by-Year Unrecovered Balance for Example 4.10

(a) Internal Rate of Return = 12.35%

t	A_t	R_{t-1}	I_t	Q_t	R_t
0	+18	—	—	—	+18
1	+10	+18	+2.223	+12.223	+30.223
2	−40	+30.223	+3.733	−36.267	− 6.044
3	−60	− 6.044	−0.746	−60.746	−66.790
4	+30	−66.790	−8.249	+21.751	−45.039
5	+50	−45.039	−5.562	+44.438	− 0.601

(b) Internal Rate of Return = 40.15%

t	A_t	R_{t-1}	I_t	Q_t	R_t
0	+18	—	—	—	+18
1	+10	+18	+ 7.227	+17.227	+35.227
2	−40	+35.227	+14.144	−25.856	+ 9.371
3	−60	+ 9.371	+ 3.762	−56.238	−46.867
4	+30	−46.867	−18.817	+11.183	−35.684
5	+50	−35.684	−14.327	+35.673	− 0.011

We try the following values of i to obtain the compound interest factors in the tables in Appendix A.

i	$(P \mid U, i, 10)$	$(P \mid F, i, 10)$	NPV
1%	9.4713	0.9053	+12.56
2%	8.9826	0.8203	−66.49

Using linear interpolation between 1% and 2%, we find

$$i = 1\% + (2\% - 1\%) \; \frac{12.56}{12.56 + 66.49} = 1.16\%$$

For the buyer, the cash flow profile of the investment will be as shown in part (c) of Fig. 4.16 and the rate of return of the investment can be obtained as follows:

$$\text{NPV} = -700 + (40)(P \mid U, i, 5) + (1,000)(P \mid F, i, 5) = 0$$

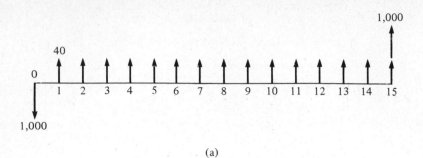

(a)

(b)

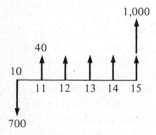

(c)

FIGURE 4.16

We try the following values of *i* to obtain the compound interest factors in the tables in Appendix A.

i	$(P\,|\,U, i, 5)$	$(P\,|\,F, i, 5)$	NPV
10%	3.7908	0.6209	+71.53
12%	3.6048	0.5674	+11.59
15%	3.3522	0.4972	−68.71

Using linear interpolation between 12% and 15%, we find

$$i = 12\% + (15\% - 12\%)\ \frac{11.59}{11.59 + 68.71} = 12.43\%$$

4.5   Principal and Interest Payments in Borrowing

For borrowing or in financing investment projects, it is often important to distinguish the portion of each repayment that is interest and the portion that is left for reducing the principal amount borrowed, and it is also important to know the principal amount remaining to be paid after each payment. If no payment is made at a subsequent period, the interest accrued on the previously unpaid principal amount will be accumulated to produce a larger principal amount remaining to be paid. If additional borrowing takes place, not only is the interest accrued on the previously unpaid principal amount but the newly borrowed amount will also be accumulated to the principal amount remaining to be paid.

The principle of computing principal and interest payments in borrowing is analogous to that for lending since borrowing represents the reverse of lending and differs only by a negative sign in the cash flows. In the case of borrowing, let us adopt the following notation:

$i =$ the specified interest rate per time period for borrowing

$A_t =$ the cash flow at the end of period t (positive for a receipt from loan and negative for payment of principal and/or interest)

$R_t =$ the principal amount of loan remaining at the end of period t (positive for an unpaid balance and negative for an overpayment beyond the principal and interest owed)

$I_t =$ the interest accrued during period t on R_{t-1} (positive for interest on an unpaid balance and negative for interest on an overpayment)

$Q_t =$ the amount to be added to the unpaid balance or the amount to be used to reduce the unpaid balance on loan during period t (positive for a net increase and negative for a net decrease)

Then, the relationships in Eqs. (4.21) through (4.25) are applicable to the computation of principal and interest payments in borrowing. If the borrowing spreads over a time span of n interest periods, the unpaid balance at the termination of the loan, i.e., R_n must be zero. Consequently, we conclude that NFV = 0 since R_n in Eq. (4.25) is identical to the expression for the net future value. We note that the condition of repayments of principal and interest also sets NPV = 0.

For a given interest rate i, the amount of interest paid for each of the n periods over the entire time span of a loan is given by Eq. (4.21) as $I_1 = R_0\,i$, $I_2 = R_1\,i$, ...,

$I_n = R_{n-1}i$. Hence, the total amount of interest paid in n periods is given by

$$\sum_{t=1}^{n} I_t = i \sum_{t=0}^{n-1} R_t \tag{4.26}$$

The value of $\Sigma\, I_t$ or $\Sigma\, R_t$ in Eq. (4.26) indicates the extent of the use of money for a loan arrangement.

For the special cases in Section 4.2, the equations for computing principal and interest payments can be considerably simplified. For example, in the case of a loan to be repaid in uniform series, i.e., $A_0 = P$ and $A_1 = A_2 = \cdots = A_n = -U$, Eq. (4.25) becomes

$$R_n = -U[1 + (1 + i) + (1 + i)^2 + \cdots + (1 + i)^{n-1}] + P(1 + i)^n$$

Hence,

$$R_n = -U\left[\frac{(1 + i)^n - 1}{i}\right] + P(1 + i)^n$$

At the end of period t, we have

$$R_t = -U\left[\frac{(1 + i)^t - 1}{i}\right] + P(1 + i)^t$$

In functional notation,

$$R_t = -U(F\,|\,U, i, t) + P(F\,|\,P, i, t) \tag{4.27}$$

This is the principal amount remaining to be paid at the end of period t for a borrowed amount P with a uniform series of repayment of U. It is the same as the remaining balance at the beginning of period $(t + 1)$, i.e., using t as the beginning point until the end of period n for $(n - t)$ periods,

$$R_t = U(P\,|\,U, i, n - t) \tag{4.27a}$$

Example 4.14

Gerald Heins borrows $200 from a finance company at 10% per annum with the understanding that he will pay back $115.24 each at the end of the first and second year. Determine the principal amount and interest in each payment, and the principal amount remaining to be paid at the end of each year.

Since the interest rate is known to be 10%, we can verify that NPV = 0 and

NFV = 0. Thus,

$$\text{NPV} = 200 - (115.24)(P \mid U, 10\%, 2)$$
$$= 200 - (115.24)(1.7355) = 0$$

and

$$\text{NFV} = (200)(F \mid P, 10\%, 2) - (115.24)(F \mid U, 10\%, 2)$$
$$= (200)(1.2100) - (115.24)(2.1000) = 0$$

Using the general relationships in Eqs. (4.21) through (4.23), we get

At $t = 0$

$$R_0 = A_0 = 200$$

At $t = 1$

$$A_1 = -115.24$$

$$I_1 = R_0 i = (200)(10\%) = 20$$

$$Q_1 = A_1 + I_1 = -115.24 + 20 = -95.24$$

$$R_1 = R_0 + Q_t = 200 - 95.24 = 104.76$$

At $t = 2$

$$A_2 = -115.24$$

$$I_2 = R_1 i = (104.76)(10\%) = 10.48$$

$$Q_2 = A_2 + I_2 = -115.24 + 10.48 = -104.76$$

$$R_2 = R_1 + Q_2 = 104.76 - 104.76 = 0$$

For this particular problem involving a uniform series, we could have obtained R_1 and R_2 directly from Eq. (4.27). Thus,

$$R_1 = (-115.24)(F \mid U, 10\%, 1) + (200)(F \mid P, 10\%, 1)$$
$$= (-115.24)(1.0000) + (200)(1.1000) = 104.76$$

$$R_2 = (-115.24)(F \mid U, 10\%, 2) + (200)(F \mid P, 10\%, 2)$$
$$= (-115.24)(2.1000) + (200)(1.2100) = 0$$

Thus, at the end of the first year, $20 is for the interest and $95.24 is for the principal amount, making a total of $115.24. At the end of the second year, $10.48 is for the interest and $104.76 is for the principal amount, again making a total of $115.24.

Example 4.15

Determine the year-by-year interest and principal amount for each of the loan arrangements represented by the following cash flow profiles. The borrowing interest rate is known to be 8% per annum for all cases.

(a) A loan of $10,000 to be repaid with a single sum of $14,693 at the end of 5 years

(b) A loan of $10,000 with a series of repayment of $2,505 per year for the next 5 years

(c) A series of loans of $2,505 each year beginning at the end of the first year for 5 years, to be repaid with a single sum of $14,693 at the end of 5 years

These three cases are identified respectively as (a) discount amount problem, (b) discount uniform series problem, and (c) compound uniform series problem. The computation can be carried out by using Eqs. (4.21) through (4.23), and the results are tabulated in Table 4.5.

The extent of the use of money for each of the loan arrangements is represented by part (a), (b), or (c) in Fig. 4.17. The area under each step function (expressed in the unit of dollar-years) is a measure of the term ΣR_t in Eq. (4.26).

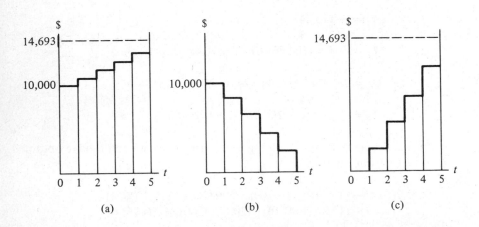

(a)   (b)   (c)

FIGURE 4.17

Table 4.5

Computation of Year-by-Year Unrecovered Balance

(a) Discount Amount Problem

t	A_t	R_{t-1}	I_t	Q_t	R_t
0	+ 10,000	—	—	—	+ 10,000
1	0	+ 10,000	+ 800	+ 800	+ 10,800
2	0	+ 10,800	+ 864	+ 864	+ 11,664
3	0	+ 11,664	+ 933	+ 933	+ 12,597
4	0	+ 12,597	+ 1,008	+ 1,008	+ 13,605
5	− 14,693	+ 13,605	+ 1,088	+ 1,088	0

(b) Discount Uniform Series Problem

t	A_t	R_{t-1}	I_t	Q_t	R_t
0	+ 10,000	—	—	—	+ 10,000
1	− 2,505	+ 10,000	+ 800	− 1,705	+ 8,295
2	− 2,505	+ 8,295	+ 664	− 1,841	+ 6,454
3	− 2,505	+ 6,454	+ 516	− 1,989	+ 4,465
4	− 2,505	+ 4,465	+ 357	− 2,148	+ 2,317
5	− 2,505	+ 2,317	+ 185	− 2,319	− 2

(c) Compound Uniform Series Problem

t	A_t	R_{t-1}	I_t	Q_t	R_t
0	—	—	—	—	—
1	+ 2,505	—	—	—	+ 2,505
2	+ 2,505	+ 2,505	+ 200	+ 2,705	+ 5,210
3	+ 2,505	+ 5,210	+ 417	+ 2,922	+ 8,132
4	+ 2,505	+ 8,132	+ 651	+ 3,156	+ 11,288
5	+ 2,505 } − 14,693 }	+ 11,288	+ 903	− 11,285	+ 3

4.6   The External Rate of Return for Reinvestment

In most investment situations, one or more periods of disbursements are followed by one or more periods of receipts. When the receipts earned prior to the end of an investment project are not needed for the project any more, such receipts may be consumed or invested elsewhere. The rate of return from investments other than the project under consideration is referred to as the *external rate of return* (ERR).

Of all investment situations, the simple case of investing a single sum at the beginning and receiving a single sum in return at the end of the time span is the only case that cannot possibly be affected by an external rate of return. For other situations, an external rate of return is either implicitly or explicitly specified for reinvesting the early period receipts. Consequently, the external rate of return is sometimes referred to as the *reinvestment rate*.

For the general case of mixed positive and negative cash flows over the entire time span, interim funding (or borrowing) as well as reinvestment (or lending) may take place. Therefore, from the viewpoint of an investor, it is necessary to establish a *reinvestment policy* for investing all returns paid back before the completion of the project and a *financing policy* for building up sufficient amounts needed for investment in later periods of the project. The necessity for such policies will be explained in the next section.

In the computation of the internal rate of return, it has been implicitly assumed that the ERR for reinvestment and financing is identical to the internal rate of return (IRR). Such tacit assumptions can be demonstrated by Examples 4.11 and 4.12. In Example 4.11, the net future value of the cash flow profile based on an external rate of return i is given by

$$NFV = -(77)(F \,|\, P, i, 5) + (38)(F \,|\, U, i, 5) - (6)(F \,|\, G, i, 5)$$

If ERR $=$ IRR, i.e., $i = 25\%$, then, from the definition of the internal rate of return, NFV $= 0$. Under such circumstances, it implies that the company will find other investment opportunities which yield 25% for reinvesting the receipts paid back to the company before the end of 5 years. In reality, the company may not be able to do so, and the assumption of ERR $=$ IRR may therefore be invalid.

In Example 4.12, the net future value of the cash flow profile based on an external rate of return i is

$$NFV = (18)(F \,|\, P, i, 5) + (10)(F \,|\, P, i, 4) - (40)(F \,|\, P, i, 3)$$
$$- (60)(F \,|\, P, i, 2) + (30)(F \,|\, P, i, 1) + 50$$

If ERR $=$ IRR, then, from the definition of the internal rate of return, either $i = 12.35\%$ or $i = 40.15\%$ will set NFV $= 0$. In reality, the external rate of return cannot be both 12.35% and 40.15%. Consequently, the assumption of ERR $=$ IRR is clearly invalid for this example.

The crux of the problem to be recognized is that from the viewpoint of an investor, the internal rate of return is the rate of return over the entire life of the investment *if and only if* the external rate of return for reinvestment of early returns is identical to the internal rate of return. Depending on the particular circumstances confronting an investor, the external rate of return may or may not be the same as the internal rate of return. Hence, the internal rate of return of an investment project is not necessarily a valid measure of the profit potential to the investor.

Example 4.16

The cash flow profiles of two investment projects are given as follows: (a) Invest an amount of $10,000 now and receive a return of $14,693 only at the end of 5 years, and (b) invest an amount of $10,000 now and receive a yearly amount of $2,505 for the next 5 years. Find the future value of the receipts from the investment project at the end of 5 years under the following different circumstances:

1. The external rate of return per year is identical to the internal rate of return of the project
2. The minimum attractive rate of return (MARR) per year for reinvestment is 6%
3. The investor intends to consume any return as soon as it is paid back from the project

For both investment proposals, the internal rate of return is found to be 8%. However, for case (a), the future value of the receipt at the end of 5 years is simply $F = \$14,693$ for all circumstances since there is no money for reinvestment or consumption until the end of 5 years.

For case (b), each of the situations presents a different future value F_e of the *receipts* at the end of 5 years:

1. For ERR = IRR = 8%,

$$F_e = (2,505)(F \mid U, 8\%, 5) = (2,505)(5.8666) = 14.696$$

2. For ERR = MARR = 6%,

$$F_e = (2,505)(F \mid U, 6\%, 5) = (2,505)(5.6371) = 14,121$$

3. Nothing will be left if all returns are consumed immediately.

4.7   The Overall Rate of Return to the Investor

Investors are primarily interested in the expansion of their fortune over a time span to which they wish to look ahead. The total amount accumulated at the end of the life of a capital project is influenced by the financing of the outlays at various time periods and the reinvestment of the returns prior to the end of the life of the project. If all net outlays over the planning horizon are discounted at the ERR = MARR to an equivalent present sum P_e at the beginning and all net returns are compounded at the ERR = MARR to an equivalent future sum F_e at the end, then the overall rate of return to the investor is defined as the interest rate which compounds the equivalent present sum P_e to the equivalent future sum F_e at the end of the planning horizon.

For the special case of investing a single sum P at $t = 0$ and receiving a single sum F in return at the end of the time span, the internal rate of return for an investment project is the rate of return per period *throughout the duration of the project* and therefore is its *overall rate of return*. That is, by setting NPV = 0 for this cash flow profile, we have

$$-P + F\,(P\,|\,F,\,i^\circ,\,n) = 0$$

Then, the overall rate of return i° can be obtained from the compound interest factor

$$(P\,|\,F,\,i^\circ,\,n) = \frac{P}{F} \tag{4.28}$$

For all other cases, the internal rate of return is the same as the true rate of return only if the external rate of return is identical to the internal rate of return. However, it is generally unrealistic to assume that ERR = IRR; instead, it is more likely that the external rate of return should be based on the reinvestment rate that is realizable by the investor. Consequently, a reinvestment policy and a financing policy are generally necessary for the computation of the overall rate of return.

Let us consider the typical investment case with a disbursement P at $t = 0$ and a series of receipts A_t at the subsequent periods $t = 1, 2, \ldots, n$. We must know whether the early-year receipts before $t = n$ are to be reinvested and if so at what rate. In the absence of special reasons, it is reasonable to assume that all early year receipts will be reinvested until $t = n$ at the external rate of return in the financial market or the minimum attractive rate of return of the investor. We can find the equivalent future value F_e of the early year receipts A_t. That is,

$$F_e = \sum_{t=1}^{n} A_t(1 + i)^{n-t} \tag{4.29}$$

where i is the reinvestment rate specified. Then, the overall rate of return i° can be determined from Eq. (4.28) in which F is replaced by F_e obtained by Eq. (4.29).

On the other hand, if we have a series of disbursements A_t for $t = 1, 2, \ldots, (n - 1)$ in early years and only one receipt F at $t = n$, it can be assumed that, for an ongoing organization, an equivalent sum P_e is available at $t = 0$, which accrues interest at a specified external rate of return such that it will provide the amounts A_t for $t = 1, 2, \ldots, (n - 1)$ as needed. That is,

$$P_e = \sum_{t=0}^{n-1} A_t(1 + i)^{-t} \tag{4.30}$$

where i is the specified external rate of return. Then, the overall rate of return $i°$ can be determined from Eq. (4.28) in which P is replaced by P_e obtained by Eq. (4.30).

For the general case of a project with mixed positive and negative cash flows, the overall rate of return (ORR) will be affected by the reinvestment and financing policies unless specified policies are adopted in defining the ORR. In order to be consistent with the computation of net present values and net future values, we adopt the reinvestment policy that all net returns (positive cash flows) in the cash flow profile will be compounded at the external rate of return in the market until the end of the planning horizon, and all net outlays (negative cash flows) will be discounted at the external rate of return in the market to the present. Then, the interest rate that compounds an equivalent initial sum P_e at the beginning to an equivalent final sum F_e at the end of the planning horizon is defined as the overall rate of return for the case with mixed cash flows.

It is important to emphasize that the overall rate of return depends on the time span to which an investor wishes to look ahead and on the external rate of return that is realizable by the investor if early year returns or later year outlays are involved. Hence, the overall rate of return reflects the profit potential of a project from the viewpoint of the investor. The consequences of adopting different reinvestment and financing policies will be discussed in Chapter 9.

Example 4.17

An organization is making an investment plan over the next 5 years. The minimum attractive rate of return for its investments is specified to be 6%. The two investment projects in Example 4.16 are found to have an internal rate of return 8%. The early year returns from each project are expected to be reinvested at the minimum attractive rate of return specified by the organization. What is the profit potential of each project for the organization as measured by the overall rate of return over 5 years?

For case (a), the overall rate of return is the same as the internal rate of return, which is found to be 8%.

For case (b), we can find an equivalent future value F_e at time $t = n$ for the receipts reinvested at 6%, i.e.,

$$F_e = (2{,}505)(F \mid U, 6\%, 5) = (2{,}505)(5.6371) = 14{,}121$$

Since $P = 10,000$ at $t = 0$, the overall rate of return $i°$ may be obtained from Eq. (4.28). Thus,

$$(P \mid F, i°, 5) = \frac{10,000}{14,121} = 0.7082$$

By the method of linear interpolation from the tables in Appendix A, $i°$ is found to be 7.15%. Note that the overall rate of return to the investor is lower than the internal rate of return for the project because the reinvestment rate of 6% for the early year returns is less than IRR = 8%.

Example 4.18

An investment project requires a series of disbursement of \$2,505 each year at the end of years 1, 2, 3, 4, and 5, with an expected return of \$14,693 at the end of 5 years. Determine the overall rate of return for the 5-year period if the external rate of return is 6%.

Since an equivalent sum P_e is available at $t = 0$ and is invested at 6% in order to provide the amounts for later disbursements, we have

$$P_e = (2,505)(P \mid U, 6\%, 5) = (2,505)(4.2124) = 10,552$$

Since $F = 14,693$ at $t = 5$, we have from Eq. (4.28)

$$(P \mid F, i°, 5) = \frac{10,552}{14,693} = 0.7182$$

By the method of interpolation from the tables in Appendix A, $i°$ is found to be 6.85%.

Example 4.19

For the cash flows in Example 4.10, determine the overall rate of return if the external rate of return is 8%.

Following the definition of the ORR for projects with mixed positive and negative cash flows, we obtain for P_e and F_e in \$ million as follows:

$$P_e = -(40)(P \mid F, 8\%, 2) - (60)(P \mid F, 8\%, 3)$$
$$= -34.292 - 47.628 = -81.92$$

$$F_e = (18)(F \mid P, 8\%, 5) + (10)(F \mid P, 8\%, 4) + (30)(F \mid P, 8\%, 1) + 50$$
$$= 26.447 + 13.605 + 32.400 + 50 = 122.452$$

By setting NPV $= 0$ for the time stream with P_e at $t = 0$ and F_e at $t = 5$, we get

$$-81.92 + (122.452)(P\,|\,F, i°, 5) = 0$$

or

$$(P\,|\,F, i°, 5) = \frac{81.92}{122.452} = 0.6690$$

By interpolation from the tables in Appendix A, we find $i° = 8.38\%$.

4.8   The Meaning of Various Rates of Return

We have introduced up to this point a variety of definitions related to the rate of return, including IRR, ERR, MARR, and ORR. It is therefore appropriate to recapitulate the meaning of each of them.

In a strict sense, the term *rate of return* refers to the interest rate per period when a single sum is invested at the beginning and a single sum is received at the end of the planning horizon. In a broad sense, it denotes the interest rate per period associated with investing or financing and may refer to IRR or ORR under different contexts. To avoid ambiguity, it is desirable to be specific whenever possible.

The *internal rate of return* (IRR) measures the merit of an investment project as represented by its cash flow profile if a unique value of IRR exists. It is independent of the MARR of an investor and by itself does not reflect whether or not the investment is good from the viewpoint of the investor. When multiple values of IRR occur, none of these values provides a measure of the merit of an investment. The *external rate of return* (ERR) refers to the *reinvestment rate* for any fund not needed for the specific project under consideration during any period of the planning horizon.

The *minimum attractive rate of return* (MARR) is defined as the cost of foregoing other investment opportunities and is expressed as the discount rate that the best foregone opportunity will earn. Based on the MARR, an investor will be able to make investment and financing choices which will maximize the profit. Under normal circumstances, the MARR will be used as the ERR or reinvestment rate for early returns not needed in the specific project under consideration.

The *overall rate of return* (ORR) represents the rate of return to the investor over the planning horizon which takes into account the MARR of the investor in reinvesting early-period returns and in financing later-period outlays when such actions become necessary.

4.9   Summary and Study Guide

In this chapter, we have discussed the mechanics of computing unknown interest rates from a series of cash flows. We have also examined the meaning of internal rate of return, external rate of return, and the overall rate of return.

The discount rate which sets the net present values of a series of cash flows equal to zero is called the internal rate of return (IRR). The computational procedures can be summarized as follows:

1. If the equation resulting from NPV = 0 has only one sign change in the cash flows and contains only one compound interest factor having i as the unknown, the internal rate of return can be obtained directly by linear interpolation from the discrete compound interest tables in Appendix A.
2. If the equation resulting from NPV = 0 has only one sign change in the cash flows but contains more than one compound interest factor having i as the unknown, the internal rate of return can be obtained by trial solution with the aid of the tables in Appendix A.
3. If the equation resulting from NPV = 0 has two or more sign changes in the cash flows, we must search for the possibility of multiple internal rates of return. There is no guarantee that a trial solution will yield all possible values.
4. In all cases, the calculation can be carried out on a programmable pocket calculator instead of relying on linear interpolation from the tables in Appendix A.

Since the discount rate which sets NPV = 0 also sets NFV = 0, the internal rate of return can alternately be defined as the interest rate earned on the unrecovered investment such that the unrecovered amount equals zero at the end of the planning horizon. Using a similar definition for the interest for borrowing instead of investing, we can find the portion of each repayment for a loan that is interest and the portion that is left for reducing the principal amount borrowed. When an investment produces returns before the end of planning horizon, the early period returns are reinvested elsewhere at the external rate of return (ERR), which is also referred to as the reinvestment rate.

The computation of internal rate of return is important and useful for the following cases:

1. The investment of a single sum at the beginning and the return of a single sum at the end of the planning horizon
2. An investment involving early period returns but having only one sign change in the cash flows *and* a reinvestment rate equal to the IRR
3. The investment involving outlays in several periods but having only one sign change in the cash flows *and* an interest rate for financing equal to the IRR

For the above cases, the internal rate of return is the overall rate of return over the entire planning horizon. However, it is generally unrealistic to set the reinvestment rate or the interest rate for financing equal to the IRR since such rates are dependent on the market interest rate while IRR is not. The internal rates of return do not represent the overall rates of return of other types of investment projects and therefore are not essential in the economic evaluation of such projects. These cases include:

1. The cash flow profile of the investment consists of only one sign change, but the reinvestment rate for early period returns is not set equal to the IRR.
2. The cash flow profile of the investment consists of mixed inflows and outflows, whether it leads to multiple values of IRR or not, as long as the reinvestment rate is not set equal to IRR.

Hence, the difficulties in finding the IRR for some cases should not be regarded as a stumbling block for computing the ORR.

The overall rate of return over the entire planning horizon can be used as a measure of profit potential to the investor. It is based on the following assumptions on the reinvestment and financing policies:

1. For an investment involving a single payment at the beginning and a single sum in return at the end, the IRR is the overall rate of return. No reinvestment or financing policy need be assumed.
2. For an investment involving a single payment at the beginning and some early period returns before the end of the planning horizon, the reinvestment rate for the early period returns is assumed to be the same as the MARR.
3. For an investment involving several payments in early periods and a single sum in return at the end of the planning horizon, it is assumed that a single sum available at the beginning, if compounded at the MARR, will provide all subsequent payments.
4. For an investment with mixed inflows and outflows over the planning horizon, it is assumed that all net returns in the cash flow profile will be compounded at the MARR until the end of the planning horizon and all net outlays will be discounted at the MARR to the beginning.

REFERENCES

4.1 Arrow, K. J., and D. Levhari, "Uniqueness of the Internal Rate of Return with Variable Life of Investment," *Journal of Economics*, **79** (September 1969), 560–566.

4.2 Lorie, J., and L. J. Salvage, "Three Problems in Capital Rationing," *Journal of Business*, **28** (1955), 229–239.

4.3 Newnan, D. G., *Engineering Economic Analysis*, rev. ed., San Jose, CA: Engineering Press, Inc., 1980, pp. 128–138.

PROBLEMS

P4.1 An investment project requiring $20,000 cash now is expected to produce an income of $3,000 per year over a period of 10 years. What is the annual internal rate of return on the project?

P4.2 An investment consists of a uniform series of 9 payments of $1,000 each at the end of the first year through the end of the ninth year. At the end of 10 years, an amount of $14,193 will be paid to the investor. What is the annual internal rate of return on the investment?

P4.3 Ms. Brennen has secured a loan of $6,000 with an agreement to pay back $800 at the end of the first year, and $300 more at each subsequent year, i.e, $1,100 at the end of the second year, $1,400 at the end of the third year, etc., for a period of 5 years. Determine the annual internal rate of return for the loan.

P4.4 A government office is installing a new telephone system at a cost of $120,000 with an expectation of reducing the staff for answering the telephone. The annual savings will be $40,000 the first year, with $5,000 savings less in each subsequent year until the equipment is retired after 6 years, i.e., the annual savings will be $35,000 the second year, $30,000 the third year, etc. The equipment will have no salvage value at the end of 6 years. Find the annual internal rate of return of the investment.

P4.5 Mr. Eberhart invested $10,000 in a venture from which he received no return in the first 5 years, and an amount of $4,000 each at the end of the sixth through the end of the tenth year. What was the annual internal rate of return of the venture?

P4.6 The cash flow profile of an operation for 2 years is as follows: $A_0 = -1,000$, $A_1 = +3,000$, and $A_2 = -2,160$. Find the annual internal rate(s) of return by solving the algebraic equation resulting from setting the net present value of the cash flow profile equal to zero.

P4.7 The cash flow profile of an investment project for 3 years shows that $A_0 = -1,000$, $A_1 = +3,700$, $A_2 = -4,520$, and $A_3 = +1,820$. Verify that the annual internal rates of return for this cash profile are $i = 0\%$, $i = 30\%$, and $i = 40\%$ by substituting each value of i into the equation NPV $= 0$.

P4.8 The cash flow profile of an investment project for 4 years shows that $A_0 = +10,000$, $A_1 = -50,000$, $A_2 = +93,500$, $A_3 = -77,500$, and $A_4 = +24,024$. Verify that the internal rates of return of this cash profile are $i = 10\%$, $i = 20\%$, $i = 30\%$, and $i = 40\%$ by substituting each value of i into the equation NPV $= 0$.

P4.9 A city issues a new 20-year bond for the construction of a sewage system. Each unit for sale has a face value of $1,000 and pays 6% of its face value as annual interest at the end of the year. Ten years after Mr. Stone bought a unit at $1,000, the market value of each unit was dropped to $900. Mr. Stone decided to sell it to Ms. Sand at that price after collecting the interest at the end of 10 years. What is the internal rate of return for Ms. Sand if she keeps the bond for the remaining 10 years?

Problems

107

P4.10 Mr. Jackson purchased a 30-year bond having a face value of $1,000 and bearing interest of 5% payable annually for a price of $960. Twenty years later, after collecting the annual interest for that year, he sold the bond at a price of $720. What is the actual annual interest rate on Mr. Jackson's investment? If the new buyer intends to keep the bond until maturity at the end of the thirtieth year, what is the actual annual interest rate for the new buyer?

P4.11 A turnpike authority plans to finance a bridge project through the sale of bonds. It issues a 30-year bond with a total amount having a face value of $5,000,000 bearing interest of 5% payable annually. However, at the bond market, the authority can sell the bonds for only $4,800,000. What is the actual annual interest rate that the authority must pay for the fund it receives?

P4.12 Lisa Sampson borrows $9,000 with an agreement to pay back $3,367 per year in the next 3 years. Determine the actual interest rate for the loan. Find also the year-by-year principal and interest payments for the loan.

P4.13 Joe Brennen borrows $5,500 with an agreement to pay back $800 at the end of the first year, and $300 more at each subsequent year, i.e., $1,100 at the end of the second year, $1,400 at the end of the third year, etc., for a period of five years. Determine the actual annual interest rate for the loan. Find also the year-by-year principal and interest payments for the loan.

P4.14 Determine the year-by-year unrecovered balance for each of the following two cash flow profiles, both of which have an internal rate of return of 10% per year.

(a) A loan of $20,000 with no return other than a single sum of $29,282 at the end of 4 years.
(b) A loan of $20,000 with a series of repayment of $6,310 per year for the next 4 years.

P4.15 Find the annual overall rate of return over 5 years for an investment of $10,000 with a uniform annual return of $4,000 for 5 years. Use MARR = 20%.

P4.16 Find the annual overall rate of return over 4 years for an investment of $20,000 with a uniform annual return of $6,310 for 4 years if the MARR for the investor is 8%.

P4.17 The Canfield Coal Company is considering a strip-mining project which has a cash flow profile in the 5 years of its operation: $A_0 = -38.3$, $A_1 = A_2 = A_3 = A_4 = +28$, and $A_5 = -80$ where the cash flows are expressed in terms of millions of dollars.

(a) Determine the internal rates of return for the project.
(b) Determine the overall rate of return if MARR = 20%.

P4.18 Repeat Problem P4.17 if the cash flow profile is found to be as follows: $A_0 = -57.1$, $A_1 = +18$, $A_2 = +68$, $A_3 = +88$, $A_4 = -2$, and $A_5 = -130$. The MARR remains at 20%.

5

THE ECONOMIC
FEASIBILITY OF
INDEPENDENT PROJECTS

5.1 Basic Principles of Economic Evaluation

A prelude to an economic evaluation of investment proposals is the generation of promising proposals for consideration. For the purpose of analysis, such proposals may be classified either as independent or mutually exclusive. Consider, for example, an oil company which plans to build five new refineries in different parts of the United States. The production and marketing operations of each of these new plants are expected to be independent of those of other plants. Then, these proposed new refineries may be regarded as independent projects. On the other hand, if five alternate designs of a refinery reflecting different scales of operation are considered for construction at a given site, then these proposed alternatives are mutually exclusive.

The basic concepts of economic evaluation have already been introduced in Chapter 2. After having discussed the necessary computational techniques in Chapters 3 and 4, we can examine more closely these concepts and the underlying assumptions. In this chapter, we shall consider the evaluation of independent proposals to determine whether they are economically feasible. Essentially, we judge whether *each* independent proposal is superior or equal to the *null alternative*, which is defined as an alternative having no benefit and no cost over the entire planning horizon. If each of the independent proposals is feasible, then all of them are acceptable.

In the evaluation of mutually exclusive proposals, we must rank the merits of all proposals and select only the best one, provided that it is economically feasible. It does not make sense economically to select the best among all mutually exclusive alternatives when even the best is not good enough. It is implicit in the evaluation of mutually exclusive proposals that the best alternative must be judged directly or indirectly to be equal or superior to the null alternative. Consequently, the concept of judging the economic feasibility of an independent proposal is equally applicable to each individual alternative in a set of mutually exclusive proposals. Thus, this chapter also serves as a prerequisite for the analysis of mutually exclusive alternatives. The methods of ranking mutually exclusive proposals for the purpose of selecting the best alternative will be treated separately in Chapter 6.

A systematic approach for economic evaluation of independent projects involves the following steps:

1. Generate a set of investment projects for consideration
2. Establish the planning horizon for economic study
3. Develop the cash flow profile for each project
4. Specify the minimum attractive rate of return
5. Examine the objectives and profit measures
6. Establish the criterion for accepting or rejecting a proposal
7. Perform sensitivity analysis
8. Accept or reject a proposal on the basis of the established criterion

This same approach is applicable to the economical evaluation of mutually exclusive proposals except that the details of application will be different from those for evaluating independent proposals and that only the best among all mutually exclusive alternatives will be selected.

It is important to emphasize that many assumptions and policies, some implicit and some explicit, are introduced in economic evaluations by the decision maker. For example, the generation of a set of investment projects for consideration out of an infinite number of possibilities is a matter of judgment. The planning horizon reflects the time span over which the investor wishes to look ahead. The cash flow profile of an investment project represents the forecast of the benefits and costs over the planning horizon.

One of the most important factors that affects the measure of the profit potential to an investor is the minimum attractive rate of return (MARR). The determination of the MARR by an organization is based on the policy decisions at the top management level and is not the prerogative of the person who performs the economic evaluation. Similarly, whether or not to impose capital rationing in budgeting for investment projects is also a high-level policy decision. Some of the investment and financing policies are not stated explicitly because they are implied in the procedures of analysis specified by the organization; others must be given explicitly in order to ensure their implementation in the analysis.

Because of organizational preferences and policies, we must differentiate the intrinsic merit of an investment project from its profit potential to an investor. Although the quality of an investment project is important, its effects on different investors may not be the same. Since economic evaluation is a decision-making process to accept or reject investment projects from the viewpoint of an investor, the use of different measures of merit is often motivated by different objectives. There-fore, we ought to examine various steps in detail in order to highlight the rationale for the systematic approach to economic evaluation.

5.2   The Planning Horizon

The period of time to which an investor wishes to look ahead is called the *planning horizon.* Since the future is uncertain, the period of time selected is limited by our ability to forecast. Hence, the planning horizon may be regarded as the foreseeable future during which some reasonable estimates can be made. The factors that influence the selection of the planning horizon include, but are not limited to, the objectives of the organization, the tax status of the organization, the nature of the investment proposals, and technological obsolescence. Several common approaches have been used and are summarized as follows:

1. The planning horizon reflects the period of intended use of the capital.
2. The planning horizon represents the period of intended use of a facility in which the investment is made.
3. The planning horizon is assumed to be infinite if the facility is to be used indefinitely.
4. The planning horizon is set equal to a period of time that allows coincidence of the expiration of several facilities which have different useful lives.

We shall examine these approaches in the context of economic analysis under different conditions.

Consider, for example, a private firm which is in the process of making a long-range plan for capital investment. The management wishes to look as far ahead as possible, but at the same time recognizes that the costs and benefits of various proposals cannot be estimated with any degree of accuracy beyond a certain time period. Consequently, it may choose arbitrarily a planning horizon, say 20 years. If the useful life of a facility is shorter than 20 years, a replacement facility may or may not be necessary for the remaining years, depending on the nature of the facility. On the other hand, if the useful life of a facility is longer than 20 years, then the salvage value of the facility at the end of 20 years must be included in the analysis.

The term *useful life* of a facility refers to the period of time during which the physical condition of the facility, as well as its economic value, continues to be acceptable. For example, an office building may still be structurally sound after 40 years of service; however, if it costs more to remodel the building than to demolish it and construct a new one to provide the level of service and convenience required, then the building is no longer acceptable for economic reasons. In that case, the useful life is regarded to be 40 years because the effects of benefits and costs after 40 years will be negligible. In the economic evaluation of a major investment project having a long useful life, it is often convenient to take the useful life of the facility as the planning horizon, which is also referred to as the *life cycle* of the investment project.

There are situations in which a facility is intended to be used indefinitely. For example, in planning a new sewage system or other types of infrastructure for a city, the facility is expected to be in use as long as it can perform the intended function. Recognizing that the effect of benefits and costs in the distant future will be negligible due to discounting, the planning horizon for such facilities may be regarded as infinite.

Another example is the consideration of a group of independent projects by an organization which attempts to use a consistent standard in selecting those which are economically feasible. Suppose that each of these projects is independent of the others and they do not have the same useful life. A consistent standard must be established by imposing the same planning horizon for all projects while properly taking into consideration all costs and benefits within the planning horizon. One possibility is to set the planning horizon at the expiration of all projects, i.e., equal to the least common multiple of useful lives of all projects. However, this approach is often unrealistic, although it may be applicable to some special situations. In any case, it is important to choose a planning horizon within which the investment proposals can be realistically represented.

Example 5.1

An owner of two existing commercial buildings is considering the possibility of retrofitting them for energy conservation. Both buildings are otherwise in good condition and are expected to last for another 30 years. Preliminary investigations indicate that technologically a solar energy system with 25 years of useful life is most suitable for building no. 1, and a heat recovery system with 18 years of useful life is most suitable for building no. 2. What planning horizon should be used for the economic analysis of these two projects?

Let the period of intended use of the buildings after retrofitting for energy conservation be $N_0 = 30$ years. Let the useful life of the solar energy system proposed for building no. 1 be denoted by $N_1 = 25$ years, and the useful life of the heat recovery system proposed for building no. 2 be denoted by $N_2 = 18$ years. The owner apparently has not found a suitable alternative energy conservation system with a useful life of 30 years to cover the entire period of intended use of the buildings, and she does not expect to do anything else to retrofit the buildings again when the usefulness of the proposed systems expires.

Since the proposed systems for the two separate buildings are independent projects, we can examine the economic feasibility of these projects separately and determine if each of them is acceptable. The owner of the buildings is interested in

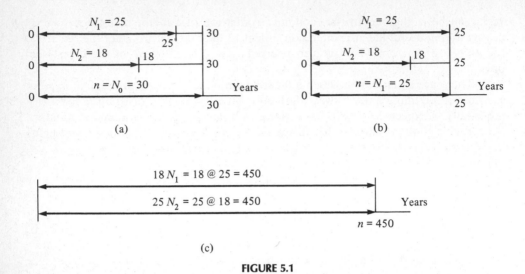

(a)

(b)

(c)

FIGURE 5.1

the profit potential of both projects in the foreseeable future. It is therefore possible to adopt a common planning horizon for these two projects in spite of the fact that they have different useful lives. For example, we may choose a planning horizon of $n = N_0 = 30$ years or $n = N_1 = 25$ years, as shown in parts (a) and (b) of Fig. 5.1, respectively. In both cases, it is implied that the net return from each project in any year will be reinvested at a specified rate of return until the end of the planning horizon. Theoretically, we may also choose a planning horizon of $n = N_2 = 18$ years, provided that the salvage value of the solar energy system at the end of 18 years can be realistically determined. The practical difficulty in determining the salvage value is that the solar system is a valuable asset as long as it remains in service in the building for 7 more years but may be worthless in the market once it is taken out of the building.

The use of the least common multiple of $N_1 = 25$ years and $N_2 = 18$ years will lead to $n = (25)(18) = 450$ years as indicated in part (c) of Fig. 5.1. The use of the least common multiple factor as the planning horizon tacitly assumes that each of the two energy conservation systems will be replaced with a system identical to the original one when its useful life expires. It ignores the fact that the buildings themselves will become obsolete after 30 years and neither system will actually be replaced. Consequently, the use of the least common multiple factor of the useful lives of these projects is incorrect for this case.

5.3   Cash Flow Profiles

In the evaluation of investment projects, the proposals are represented by their cash flow profiles over the planning horizon. To simplify the economic analysis, it is assumed that each interest period corresponds to 1 year, and the cash flows are accrued in a lump sum at the end of each year. For a project whose expected life is n years, the cash flows can occur in a time stream with n equal interest periods. The points dividing the interest periods are denoted as $t = 0, 1, 2, \ldots, n$, with $t = 0$ representing the present time.

In many engineering projects, large initial outlays for construction will occur in the early periods, followed by periods of smaller expenditures for operation and maintenance as well as proceeds from the investment. However, this is not necessarily a normal pattern. For some investments, such as strip mining or mineral extraction, heavy outlays may be required at the end of the projects to restore the sites to environmentally acceptable conditions. For highways and mass transit systems, heavy outlays for reconstruction or rolling stock replacement may be required intermittently. Consequently, the benefits and costs of each project over the planning horizon should be carefully estimated. The separate cash flow profiles of benefits and costs of an investment are referred to as the *time streams of benefits and costs*, respectively.

Let $B_{t,x}$ be the annual benefit at the end of year t for an investment project x, where $x = 1, 2, \ldots$ denotes projects no. 1, no. 2, etc., respectively. Then, a series of values $B_{t,x}$ (for $t = 0, 1, 2, \ldots, n$) represents a time stream of benefits over a planning horizon of n years. Let $C_{t,x}$ be the annual cost at the end of year t for the same investment project x. Then, a series of values $C_{t,x}$ (for $t = 0, 1, 2, \ldots, n$) represents a time stream of costs over the planning horizon. Cash receipts accrued and cash disbursements incurred are the most obvious forms of benefits and costs, respectively; however, benefits and costs may also be measured indirectly by *imputed* prices. For example, in purchasing a new machine to reduce the labor in a manufacturing process, benefits may be estimated by the savings from the reduction of labor costs. On the other hand, the salvage value of the machine, which represents its estimated market value at the time of disposal minus the cost of disposal, may be treated as a benefit to be realized at the time of disposal. Therefore, the actual benefits and costs of an investment proposal should be carefully assessed in establishing the cash flow profile of a project.

The *net annual cash flow* is defined as the annual benefit in excess of the annual cost. Let $A_{t,x}$ be the net annual cash flow at the end of year t for an investment project x. Then, for $t = 0, 1, \ldots, n$

$$A_{t,x} = B_{t,x} - C_{t,x} \tag{5.1}$$

The value of $A_{t,x}$ is positive if $B_{t,x} > C_{t,x}$ and is negative if $B_{t,x} < C_{t,x}$. A series of values $A_{t,x}$ (for $t = 0, 1, 2, \ldots, n$) represents a time stream of net annual benefits or costs over a planning horizon of n years.

In the economic evaluation of an investment proposal, we measure the profit potential of this proposal against a baseline of no gain and no loss. We define this baseline as the *null alternative*, which will be denoted by $x = 0$ such that $B_{t,0} = 0$, $C_{t,0} = 0$, and $A_{t,0} = 0$ for all values of t. For example, in considering a construction project that will provide a new service, we can measure its profit potential against the prospect of doing nothing; then the status quo alternative is identical to the null alternative. However, if we consider a new project to replace an existing facility already providing a service, the status quo alternative may represent a money-losing proposition which is quite different from the null alternative. Even the abandonment of an existing facility does not necessarily lead to a null alternative since it is possible that the defunct facility must be removed as required by law or local ordinance. Then the removal cost must be included in the abandonment alternative.

The costs incurred through the life cycle of a physical asset generally include the initial acquisition costs, the subsequent operation and maintenance costs, and the cost of disposal at the end of the life cycle. In planning capital investment projects, we are only interested in *present* and *future* costs. *Past costs* refer to the expenditures already spent on an existing project. Unrecoverable past costs are called *sunk costs* and must not be included in the analysis of future investments.

The problem of treating sunk costs properly is very important in economic evaluation. Consider, for example, a transit authority which had spent $1 million in constructing a tunnel for a new transit line when the work was abandoned 4 years ago because of strong public opposition. Finally a compromise is reached and the project will be revived. Should the $1 million already spent affect the economic feasibility of the revised proposal which will include this tunnel? The answer depends to some degree on the circumstances. If the tunnel cannot be put to any other use except for the transit line, the $1 million already spent represents a sunk cost and should not be included in the economic evaluation of the revised proposal. However, if the $1 million had been spent in the acquisition of land which could be sold to recover part of the original cost, then the sunk cost would be the difference between the original cost and the current market value of the land previously acquired for the project.

The benefits derived from the physical asset throughout the planning horizon may be quantified directly or indirectly. Some benefits, such as rents for an office building or fuel cost savings from energy conservation schemes, are explicitly expressed in monetary values; others, such as the reduction of travel time due to a new transit facility or the water recreation opportunities from a flood control project, are far more difficult to measure or express in terms of money.

In evaluating the economic feasibility of an independent project, it is necessary and essential to consider the absolute benefits and the absolute costs of the project. Then, the measure of profit potential obtained from such time streams of benefits and costs is the true measure of the net benefit. Relative benefits and relative costs (between two projects or among several projects) are not by themselves sufficient for analyzing the economic feasibility of independent projects.

5.4 The Minimum Attractive Rate of Return

The minimum attractive rate of return (MARR) may be defined as the cost of foregoing other investment opportunities, which is referred to as the *opportunity cost.* The opportunity cost reflects the interest that can be earned from the best opportunity foregone. Basically, if the resources of an organization are committed to a proposed project, the same resources cannot be invested in other opportunities. An organization may acquire the necessary funds for a proposed project by using its working capital, liquidating some of its assets, issuing new stocks, selling long-term bonds, or borrowing from banks. Other investment opportunities foregone may include not only capital investment projects, but also financial investments which may be characterized as lending, i.e., depositing money in banks or money market funds, purchasing certificates of deposit, acquiring stock of other companies, etc. When there are other investment opportunities that will yield returns equal to the MARR, we should invest in a proposed project only if it will earn a return at least as large as the MARR.

Different approaches have been used by private firms and public agencies to establish the MARR, and no one single approach is indisputably superior. A detailed discussion of this subject will be postponed until Chapters 16 and 17. In general, the MARR specified by the top management in a private firm reflects the *opportunity cost of capital* of the firm, the market interest rates for lending and borrowing, and the risks associated with investment opportunities. It is sometimes referred to as the *hurdle rate* for capital investments. For public projects, the MARR is specified by a government agency, such as the Office of Management and Budget or the Congress of the United States, which is authorized by law to act in the public interest. The MARR thus specified reflects social and economic welfare considerations and is referred to as the *social rate of discount.* Hence, the specification of the MARR is not the prerogative of the person who performs the economic evaluation.

Regardless how the MARR is determined by an organization, the MARR specified for the economic evaluation of investment proposals is critically important in determining whether any investment proposal is worthwhile *from the standpoint of the organization.* Since the MARR of an organization often cannot be measured accurately, it is advisable to use several values of the MARR in assessing the profit potential of an investment proposal so that we can appraise how sensitive the profit potential is to the variation of the MARR.

5.5   Net Future Values and Net Present Values

A capital investment involves the commitment of resources now in anticipation of greater returns in the future. An organization that undertakes a capital project is obviously interested in knowing what return this project will produce at the end of the planning horizon. Hence, the *net future value* of the cash flow profile of the investment compounded at the specified MARR at the end of the planning horizon is a *direct measure* of the profit potential.

For a given series of net cash flows $A_{t,x}$ for a project x over a planning horizon of n years (for $t = 0, 1, 2, \ldots, n$), and a given value of MARR $= i$, the net future value of the series at $t = n$ is given by

$$\text{NFV}_x = \sum_{t=0}^{n} A_{t,x}(1 + i)^{n-t} = \sum_{t=0}^{n} A_{t,x}(F \mid P, i, n - t) \tag{5.2}$$

It is important to note that the NFV_x is dependent on the planning horizon n as well as the MARR $= i$. Since the useful life N_x of a capital project x may be different from the planning horizon n, we must ascertain whether a replacement is necessary when the project expires before the end of the planning horizon. If there is no replacement, the total return at the end of the life of a project will be reinvested at the MARR until the end of the planning horizon; otherwise, the net cash flows of the replacement should be included to cover those years after the expiration of the original project. All these possible situations can be covered by Eq. (5.2) since the net cash flows $A_{t,x}$ may be zero, negative, or positive for some years t as the case may be.

Since the cash flow profile of an investment proposal can be represented by its equivalence at any specified reference point in time, the net present value of a series of cash flows $A_{t,x}$ (for $t = 0, 1, \ldots, n$) for project x can be obtained as follows:

$$\text{NPV}_x = \sum_{t=0}^{n} A_{t,x}(1 + i)^{-t} = \sum_{t=0}^{n} A_{t,x}(P \mid F, i, t) \tag{5.3}$$

It can easily be shown that

$$\text{NFV}_x = \text{NPV}_x(F \mid P, i, n)$$

or

$$\text{NPV}_x = \text{NFV}_x(P \mid F, i, n)$$

The net present value is often preferred as a profit measure of a project because its value is not affected by the planning horizon *as long as* the planning horizon is greater than or equal to the useful life of the project *and* there is no replacement when the project expires. However, the assumptions used in the computation of the net *future* value of a project are also implicit in the computation of the net *present* value. Consequently, if $\text{NFV}_x \geq 0$, it follows that $\text{NPV}_x \geq 0$, and vice versa.

Example 5.2

The cash flow profiles for the solar energy system ($x = 1$) and the heat recovery system ($x = 2$) in Example 5.1 are given in Table 5.1. The MARR is specified to be 10%. Compute the net present value and the net future value of each project over a planning horizon of 30 years.

Table 5.1

Cash Flow Profiles for the Energy Conservation Projects

	x = 1			x = 2		
t	$B_{t,1}$	$C_{t,1}$	$A_{t,1}$	$B_{t,2}$	$C_{t,2}$	$A_{t,2}$
0	0	100,000	− 100,000	0	80,000	− 80,000
1–18 (each)	12,000	0	+ 12,000	11,000	0	+ 11,000
19–25 (each)	12,000	0	+ 12,000	0	0	0

We note in Example 5.1 that although the period of intended use of both buildings is 30 years, it is not practical to retrofit any other energy-conserving system in either building when the usefulness of the current proposed projects expires. Consequently, the net present value of each of the independent projects remains the same as long as the planning horizon is set equal to or greater than 25 years since $B_{t,x}$ and $C_{t,x}$ for both $x = 1$ and $x = 2$ are zero for t greater than 25. That is, for a project x with a useful life of $N_x \le n$, we have from Eq. (5.3)

$$\text{NPV}_x = \sum_{t=0}^{N_x} A_{t,x}(P \,|\, F, i, t)$$

Thus, at MARR = 10%

$$[\text{NPV}_1]_{10\%} = -100,000 + (12,000)(P \,|\, U, 10\%, 25)$$
$$= -100,000 + (12,000)(9.0770) = +8,924$$

$$[\text{NPV}_2]_{10\%} = -80,000 + (11,000)(P \,|\, U, 10\%, 18)$$
$$= -80,000 + (11,000)(8.2014) = +10,215$$

Obviously, the net future value of a project depends on the specific future point in time, which is used to indicate the future value. Hence, the planning horizon must be specified explicitly if the net future value at the end of n years is desired. Furthermore, in the absence of special circumstances, it is reasonable to use the MARR as the reinvestment rate for benefits received before the end of the planning horizon. Thus, for $n = 30$, we obtain from the cash flow profiles of the two projects the net future values as follows:

$$[\text{NFV}_1]_{10\%} = -(100,000)(F \,|\, P, 10\%, 30) + (12,000)(F \,|\, U, 10\%, 25)(F \,|\, P, 10\%, 5)$$
$$= -(100,000)(17.4494) + (12,000)(98.3470)(1.6105)$$
$$= -1,744,940 + 1,900,656 = +155,716$$

$$[NFV_2]_{10\%} = -(80,000)(F\,|\,P,\ 10\%,\ 30) + (11,000)(F\,|\,U,\ 10\%,\ 18)(F\,|\,P,\ 10\%,\ 12)$$
$$= -(80,000)(17.4494) + (11,000)(45.5992)(3.1384)$$
$$= -1,395,952 + 1,574,194 = +178,242$$

These results can be obtained readily from the net present values if they are computed first. Thus,

$$[NFV_1]_{10\%} = (NPV_1)(F\,|\,P,\ 10\%,\ 30)$$
$$= (+8,924)(17.4494) = +155,718$$

$$[NFV_2]_{10\%} = (NPV_2)(F\,|\,P,\ 10\%,\ 30)$$
$$= (+10,215)(17.4494) = +178,246$$

5.6   Net Equivalent Uniform Annual Values

The net equivalent uniform annual value refers to a *uniform* series over n years whose net present value is the same as that of a series of net cash flows $A_{t,x}$ for $t = 0$, $1, 2, \ldots, n$ representing project x. If the net present value of project x is denoted by NPV_x, then the net equivalent uniform annual value (NUV) for project x is given by

$$NUV_x = NPV_x(U\,|\,P,\ i,\ n) \tag{5.4a}$$

or

$$NPV_x = NUV_x(P\,|\,U,\ i,\ n) \tag{5.4b}$$

Let us elaborate further on the meaning of the term *net equivalent uniform annual value*, which should not be confused with some related terms.[1] When a series of *net annual cash flows* $A_{t,x}$ (for $t = 0, 1, 2, \ldots, n$) is used to represent the cash flow profile of project x, the value of $A_{t,x}$ can be positive, negative, or zero for any given t. The net present value of this series may be designated as NPV_x. The net equivalent uniform annual value (NUV) of project x simply refers to a uniform series whose annual value is NUV_x in the years $t = 1, 2, \ldots, n$ such that its net present value equals NPV_x. Note that for a uniform series, the cash flow at $t = 0$ is zero. Thus, the series of cash flows $A_0 = -P$, $A_1 = A_2 = \cdots = A_n = U$ is *not* a uniform series, although the series $A_0 = 0$, $A_1 = A_2 = \cdots = A_n = U$ is. Furthermore, let BPV_x be the present value of a time stream of benefits $B_{t,x}$ (for $t = 0, 1, 2, \ldots, n$) of project x. Then, the *equivalent uniform annual value of benefits* (BUV) of project x refers to a uniform series whose annual value is BUV_x in the years $t = 1, 2, \ldots, n$ such that its

[1] To avoid confusion, the notation U has been used to represent the *uniform* cash flows in the functional notation for the compound interest factors involving the uniform series, while the notation A has been used to denote net *annual* cash flow.

present value is the same as BPV_x. Similarly, let CPV_x be the present value of a time stream of costs $C_{t,x}$ (for $t = 0, 1, 2, \ldots, n$) of project x. Then, the *equivalent uniform annual value of costs* (CUV) of project x refers to a uniform series whose annual value is CUV_x in the years $t = 1, 2, \ldots, n$ such that its present value is the same as CPV_x. Thus,

$$BUV_x = BPV_x(U \mid P, i, n) \tag{5.5a}$$

and

$$CUV_x = CPV_x(U \mid P, i, n) \tag{5.5b}$$

It should be emphasized that the net equivalent uniform annual value of a series of cash flows is based on a specific planning horizon and a specified MARR. Consequently, the same assumptions used in the computation of the net future value or net present values also prevail.

Example 5.3

Find the net equivalent uniform annual values of the two projects in Example 5.2 for a planning horizon of 30 years as these facilities will not be replaced upon expiration.

For MARR = 10%, the NUV_x for these two projects over the planning horizon of 30 years are obtained as follows:

$$[NUV_1]_{10\%} = (NPV_1)(U \mid P, 10\%, 30)$$
$$= (+8,924)(0.1061) = +947$$

$$[NUV_2]_{10\%} = (NPV_2)(U \mid P, 10\%, 30)$$
$$= (+10,215)(0.1061) = +1,084$$

5.7   The NPV-MARR Graph

Since the minimum attractive rate of return is so crucially important in the computation of the net present value and yet so difficult to pinpoint exactly, it is advisable to compute the net present value of a proposal for several values of the MARR. The sensitivity of the net present value with respect to the MARR can be illustrated by a graph of NPV versus MARR. If a broad range of the MARR is included, such a graph will often show the internal rate(s) of return as well as the variation of the net present value in this range of the MARR. Thus, the NPV-MARR graph also provides some insight into the computation of the internal rate(s) of return of an investment proposal since the IRR(s) occurs at NPV = 0.

Example 5.4

A strip-mining operation requires an initial cost of $545,000 which will yield an annual net income of $150,000 from mining for the next 8 years. However, at the end of 8 years, an amount of $150,000 will be required to restore the landscape for environmental protection according to the law, and this amount negates all the income from mining for the year. Is this operation economically sound at MARR = 10%? Also, check the economic feasibility of this project at MARR = 5% and MARR = 15%. Plot the NPV versus MARR graph for MARR = 0% to 30%.

Let the proposed operation be designated as $x = 1$ (as opposed to $x = 0$ for the null alternative). The net present values of this operation in thousands of dollars is given by

$$NPV_1 = -545 + (150)(P|U, i, 7) + 0$$

For MARR = 0%, 5%, 10%, and 15%, we obtain

$$[NPV_1]_{0\%} = -545 + (150)(7) = +505$$

$$[NPV_1]_{5\%} = -545 + (150)(5.7864) = +323.0$$

$$[NPV_1]_{10\%} = -545 + (150)(4.8684) = +185.3$$

$$[NPV_1]_{15\%} = -545 + (150)(4.1604) = +79.1$$

It is obvious that this operation is economically sound for the values of MARR computed. Thus, even if the MARR varies from the specified values of 10% by $\pm 5\%$, it will not affect the merit of accepting this proposal. The NPV versus MARR graph is shown in Fig. 5.2.

Example 5.5

Suppose that the strip-mining operation requires an initial cost of $340,000 which will yield an annual net income of $150,000 from mining for the next 8 years. At the end of the eighth year, the cost of restoring the landscape for environmental protection is $980,000, resulting in a net cost of $830,000 after deducting the net income of $150,000 for the year. Plot the NPV versus MARR graph for MARR = 0% to 30%. Is this operation economically feasible at MARR = 10%?

The net present value of this operation (designated as $x = 1$) is given in thousands of dollars as follows:

$$NPV_1 = -340 + (150)(P|U, i, 7) - (830)(P|F, i, 8)$$

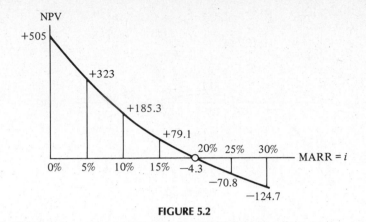

FIGURE 5.2

For $i = 0\%$, 5%, 10%, 15%, 20%, 25%, and 30%, the net present values can be tabulated in Table 5.2.

The NPV versus MARR graph is shown in Fig. 5.3. Note that the cash profile for this operation has two sign changes, leading to two values for the internal rate of return (at 9.6% and 22.9%, approximately). At MARR = 10%, NPV = 3 is positive. However, not only is this positive value very small, but it is very sensitive to the change in the MARR. Consequently, we should seek additional information beyond the results of economic evaluation and exercise subjective judgment to make the final decision.

Example 5.6

Suppose that the cost for restoring the landscape in Example 5.5 is reduced to $860,000 at the end of the eighth year, resulting in a net cost of $710,000 after deducting the net income of $150,000 for the year. Plot the NPV versus MARR graph for MARR = 0% to 30%. Is this operation economically feasible at MARR = 10%?

Table 5.2

Net Present Value at the Specified MARR

i	0%	5%	10%	15%	20%	25%	30%
-340	$-$ 340	-340	-340	-340	-340	-340	-340
$+150(P\|U, i, 7)$	$+1,050$	$+868$	$+730$	624	$+541$	$+474$	$+420$
$-830(P\|F, i, 8)$	$-$ 830	-562	-387	-271	-193	-139	102
NPV_1	$-$ 120	$-$ 34	$+$ 3	$+$ 13	$+$ 8	5	$-$ 22

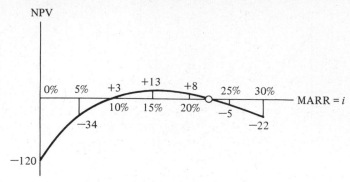

FIGURE 5.3

The net present value of this operation (designated as $x = 1$) is given in thousands of dollars as follows:

$$\text{NPV}_1 = -340 + (150)(P \,|\, U, i, 7) - (710)(P \,|\, F, i, 8)$$

For $i = 0\%$, 5%, 10%, 15%, 20%, 25%, and 30%, the net present values can be tabulated in Table 5.3.

The NPV versus MARR graph is shown in Fig. 5.4. Note that the cash profile for this operation has two sign changes, leading to two values for the internal rate of return (at 0% and approximately 28.4%). However, since the NPV at MARR $= 10\%$ is positive, and remains so even for a fairly large deviation from the MARR ($\pm 5\%$), the proposed operation is economically feasible and is not affected by the presence of two values of the internal rate of return.

5.8   The Net Present Value Criterion

The economic feasibility of an independent project can be determined directly by computing the net present value of the cash flow profile representing the proposed

Table 5.3

Net Present Value at the Specified MARR

i	0%	5%	10%	15%	20%	25%	30%
-340	$-\ 340$	-340	-340	-340	-340	-340	-340
$+150(P\,|\,U, i, 7)$	$+1{,}050$	$+868$	$+730$	624	$+541$	$+474$	$+420$
$-710(P\,|\,F, i, 8)$	$-\ 710$	-481	-331	-232	-165	-119	$-\ 87$
NPV_1	0	$+\ 47$	$+\ 59$	$+\ 52$	$+\ 36$	$+\ 15$	$-\ 7$

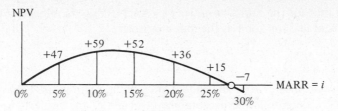

FIGURE 5.4

project. If this net present value is greater than or equal to zero, the proposed project is economically feasible; otherwise it is not feasible. This method of analysis is referred to as the *net present value method.*

Let BPV_x be the present value of benefits of a project x and CPV_x be the present value of costs of the project x. Also let NPV_x be the net present value of the project x. Then, for $MARR = i$ over a planning horizon of n years,

$$BPV_x = \sum_{t=0}^{n} B_{t,x}(1 + i)^{-t} = \sum_{t=0}^{n} B_{t,x}(P\,|\,F, i, t) \qquad (5.6)$$

$$CPV_x = \sum_{t=0}^{n} C_{t,x}(1 + i)^{-t} = \sum_{t=0}^{n} C_{t,x}(P\,|\,F, i, t) \qquad (5.7)$$

Then,

$$NPV_x = BPV_x - CPV_x \qquad (5.8)$$

or

$$NPV_x = \sum_{t=0}^{n} (B_{t,x} - C_{t,x})(P\,|\,F, i, t) \qquad (5.9)$$

In view of Eq. (5.1), the last equation can be replaced by Eq. (5.2), i.e.,

$$NPV_x = \sum_{t=0}^{n} A_{t,x}(1 + i)^{-t} = \sum_{t=0}^{n} A_{t,x}(P\,|\,F, i, t)$$

In general, $B_{t,x}$ and $C_{t,x}$ vary from year to year, i.e., for different values of t. If they can be expressed in uniform series or linear gradient under special conditions, the formulas in Chapter 3 can be used to simplify the computation.

If there is no budget constraint, then all independent projects having net present value greater than or equal to zero are acceptable. Thus, the criterion for accepting an independent project x is

$$NPV_x \geq 0 \qquad (5.10)$$

It is implicit that for the null alternative $(x = 0)$, $NPV_0 = 0$. Hence, the project x is superior to or at least as good as the null alternative.

Example 5.7

The cash flow profiles of six independent projects are shown in Table 5.4. Using a MARR of 20%, determine the acceptability of each of the projects on the basis of the net present value criterion for accepting independent projects.

Using $i = 20\%$, we can compute NPV_x for $x = 1, 2, \ldots, 6$ from Eq. (5.9). Then, the acceptability of each project can be determined from Eq. (5.10). Thus,

$$[NPV_1]_{20\%} = -77 + (235)(P\,|\,F,\,20\%,\,5)$$
$$= -77 + 94.4 = +17.4$$

$$[NPV_2]_{20\%} = -77 + (38)(P\,|\,U,\,20\%,\,5) - (6)(P\,|\,G,\,20\%,\,5)$$
$$= -77 + 113.6 - 29.4 = +7.2$$

$$[NPV_3]_{20\%} = -75.3 + (28)(P\,|\,U,\,20\%,\,5)$$
$$= -75.3 + 83.7 = +8.4$$

$$[NPV_4]_{20\%} = -(28)(P\,|\,U,\,20\%,\,4) + (201.9)(P\,|\,F,\,20\%,\,5)$$
$$= -72.5 + 81.1 = +8.6$$

$$[NPV_5]_{20\%} = -39.9 + (28)(P\,|\,U,\,20\%,\,4) - (80)(P\,|\,F,\,20\%,\,5)$$
$$= -39.9 + 72.5 - 32.2 = +0.4$$

$$[NPV_6]_{20\%} = +18 + (10)(P\,|\,F,\,20\%,\,1) - 40(P\,|\,F,\,20\%,\,2)$$
$$-(60)(P\,|\,F,\,20\%,\,3) + (30)(P\,|\,F,\,20\%,\,4) + 50(P\,|\,F,\,20\%,\,5)$$
$$= +18 + 8.3 - 27.8 - 34.7 + 14.5 + 20.1 = -1.6$$

Hence, the first five projects are acceptable, but the last project should be rejected.

Table 5.4

Cash Flow Profiles of Six Independent Projects (in $ million)

t	$A_{t,1}$	$A_{t,2}$	$A_{t,3}$	$A_{t,4}$	$A_{t,5}$	$A_{t,6}$
0	− 77.0	−77.0	−75.3	0	− 39.9	+18.0
1	0	+38.0	+28.0	− 28.0	+28.0	+10.0
2	0	+32.0	+28.0	− 28.0	+28.0	−40.0
3	0	+26.0	+28.0	− 28.0	+28.0	−60.0
4	0	+20.0	+28.0	− 28.0	+28.0	+30.0
5	+235.0	+14.0	+28.0	+201.9	−80.0	+50.0

5.9   The Benefit-Cost Ratio

The *benefit-cost ratio* may be defined as the ratio of the discounted benefits to the discounted costs with reference to the same point in time, i.e., the discounted benefits per unit of discounted costs. It is sometimes referred to as the *savings-to-investment ratio* when the benefits are derived from the reduction of undesirable effects.

Using the present as a point of reference, we can compute the present values of benefits and costs for a project x according to Eqs. (5.6) and (5.7), respectively. Then, the benefit cost ratio of the project x is given by

$$\frac{B_x}{C_x} = \frac{\mathrm{BPV}_x}{\mathrm{CPV}_x} = \frac{\sum\limits_{t=0}^{n} B_{x,t}(P\,|\,F, i, t)}{\sum\limits_{t=0}^{n} C_{x,t}(P\,|\,F, i, t)} \tag{5.11}$$

In view of Eq. (5.8), the net present value criterion in Eq. (5.10) can be expressed as

$$\mathrm{BPV}_x - \mathrm{CPV}_x \geq 0 \quad \text{or} \quad \mathrm{BPV}_x \geq \mathrm{CPV}_x$$

Consequently, the criterion for accepting an *independent* project on the basis of the benefit-cost ratio is

$$\frac{B_x}{C_x} = \frac{\mathrm{BPV}_x}{\mathrm{CPV}_x} \geq 1 \tag{5.12}$$

A word of caution should be added about the use of Eq. (5.11). In the course of assessing benefits and costs, some items may exist that can be interpreted either as additional benefits or reduced costs. For example, the salvage value of a physical asset may be interpreted either as a *positive* benefit or a *negative* cost at the time of disposal. However, the former interpretation will add an amount to the numerator and the latter will subtract the same amount from the denominator from Eq. (5.11). Hence, the value B_x/C_x is not as unambiguous a measure of the profit potential as the value NPV_x.

The application of the benefit-cost ratio criterion will be discussed in detail in Chapter 7. It is sufficient to point out here that while the criterion in Eq. (5.12) is applicable to the evaluation of the acceptability of an independent project, it is not necessarily an accurate measure of the profit potential of the project.

Example 5.8

Compute the benefit-cost ratios for the six independent projects in Example 5.7, using a MARR of 20%.

The present value of benefits BPV_x and the present value of costs CPV_x for each of the projects $x = 1, 2, \ldots, 3$ can be obtained from Eqs. (5.5) and (5.6), respectively. Then, the ratios are computed according to Eq. (5.11):

1. For $x = 1$,

$$[CPV_1]_{20\%} = 77$$

$$[BPV_1]_{20\%} = (235)(P\,|\,F, 20\%, 5) = 94.44$$

$$\frac{B_1}{C_1} = \frac{94.44}{77} = 1.23$$

2. For $x = 2$,

$$[CPV_2]_{20\%} = 77$$

$$[BPV_2]_{20\%} = (38)(P\,|\,U, 20\%, 5) - (6)(P\,|\,G, 20\%, 5) = 84.22$$

$$\frac{B_2}{C_2} = \frac{84.22}{77} = 1.09$$

3. For $x = 3$,

$$[CPV_3]_{20\%} = 75.3$$

$$[BPV_3]_{20\%} = (28)(P\,|\,U, 20\%, 5) = 83.75$$

$$\frac{B_3}{C_3} = \frac{83.75}{75.3} = 1.11$$

4. For $x = 4$,

$$[CPV_4]_{20\%} = (28)(P\,|\,U, 20\%, 4) = 72.49$$

$$[BPV_4]_{20\%} = (201.9)(P\,|\,F, 20\%, 5) - 81.14$$

$$\frac{B_4}{C_4} = \frac{81.14}{72.49} = 1.12$$

5. For $x = 5$,

$$[CPV_5]_{20\%} = 39.9 + 80(P\,|\,F, 20\%, 4) = 72.05$$

$$[BPV_5]_{20\%} = 28(P\,|\,U, 20\%, 5) = 72.49$$

$$\frac{B_5}{C_5} = \frac{72.49}{72.05} = 1.01$$

6. For $x = 6$,

$$[\text{CPV}_6]_{20\%} = 40(P\,|\,F, 20\%, 2) + 60(P\,|\,F, 20\%, 3) = 62.50$$

$$[\text{BPV}_6]_{20\%} = 18 + 10(P\,|\,F, 20\%, 1) + 30(P\,|\,F, 20\%, 4) + 50(P\,|\,F, 20\%, 5)$$
$$= 60.90$$

$$\frac{B_6}{C_6} = \frac{60.90}{62.50} = 0.97$$

5.10   The Internal Rate of Return

The *internal rate of return* (IRR) refers to the discount rate(s) at which the net present value of the cash flow profile representing a proposed project is zero. As stated in Chapter 4, the IRR is an indicator of the merit of a project as represented by its cash flow profile if a unique value of IRR exists. However, it is independent of the MARR of an investor and by itself does not reflect whether or not the investment is worthwhile from the viewpoint of the investor.

If there is only one sign change in the cash flow profile representing a project proposal, a unique value of the IRR is assured. In that case, the criterion for accepting an *independent* project can be established on the basis of the IRR. Let the IRR of the cash flow profile for project x be i'_x, and let the MARR specified by a firm be denoted by i^*. When there is only one positive IRR, the internal rate of return criterion for accepting project x is

$$i^* \le i'_x \tag{5.13}$$

The application of the internal rate of return criterion will be discussed in detail in Chapter 8. It is sufficient to emphasize here that the criterion in Eq. (5.13) is applicable only to independent projects whose cash flow profile has one sign change. Furthermore, the IRR does not take into consideration the differences in capital intensities at various time periods of the planning horizon, nor does it generally reflect the reinvestment rate of any early year returns. Hence, it is not necessarily an accurate measure of the profit potential of the project.

Example 5.9

Using a MARR of 20%, determine the acceptability of each of the independent projects in Example 5.7 on the basis of the internal rate of return criterion as represented by Eq. (5.13).

There is only one sign change in the cash flow profiles of projects $x = 1$ through $x = 4$, and for each case, IRR is found to be 25%, using the computation procedures discussed in Chapter 4. Since 20% < 25%, each of these four projects is acceptable according to Eq. (5.13).

There are two sign changes in the cash flow profiles of projects $x = 5$ and $x = 6$, and for each case, two values of IRR are found. Hence, Eq. (5.13) is not applicable for determining the acceptability of these two projects.

5.11 The Overall Rate of Return

The overall rate of return represents the rate of return to the investor over the planning horizon which takes into account the specified MARR in reinvesting early year returns and in financing later period outlays when such actions are necessary. It is a measure of the profit potential of an investment project which is consistent with other direct measures such as net present value or net future value. As explained in Chapter 4, the ORR can be computed first by discounting all net outlays at the specified MARR to present and by compounding all net returns at the MARR to the end of the planning horizon. Then, the interest rate which compounds an equivalent initial sum P_e to an equivalent final sum F_e at the end of the planning horizon is referred to as the ORR.

Let the ORR for project x over a planning horizon of n years be denoted as i_x^0 and let the MARR specified by a firm be denoted by i^*. Then, the criterion for accepting project x based on the ORR is

$$i^* \le i_x^0 \tag{5.14}$$

Although the computation of the ORR is not as straightforward as that for the NFV or the NPV, the criterion represented by Eq. (5.14) is based on the same assumptions as those for the NFV and the NPV.

Example 5.10

Compute the overall rates of return for the six independent projects in Example 5.7, using a MARR of 20%.

For $x = 1$, there is only a single sum $P = 77$ at $t = 0$ and a single sum $F = 235$ at $n = 5$. Hence, for NPV $= 0$,

$$-77 + 235(P \mid F, i_1^0, 5) = 0$$

or

$$(P \mid F, i_1^0, 5) = \frac{77}{235} = 0.3277$$

From the tables in Appendix A, we find $i_1^0 = 25\%$.

For $x = 2$, 3, and 4, NPV $= 0$ leads to the following equations involving i_2^0, i_3^0, and i_4^0 respectively:

$$-77 + [(38)(F \mid U, 20\%, 5) - (6)(F \mid G, 20\%, 5)](P \mid F, i_2^0, 5) = 0$$

$$-75.3 + (28)(F \mid U, 20\%, 5)(P \mid F, i_3^0, 5) = 0$$

$$-(28)(P \mid U, 20\%, 4) + (201.9)(P \mid F, i_4^0, 5) = 0$$

By interpolation from the tables in Appendix A, we find $i_2^0 = 22.3\%$, $i_3^0 = 22.7\%$, and $i_4^0 = 22.8\%$.

For $x = 5$, we compute first P_e and F_e as follows:

$$P_e = 39.9 + (80)(P \mid F, 20\%, 5) = 72.1$$

$$F_e = (28)(F \mid U, 20\%, 5) - 28 = 180.4$$

Hence, for NPV $= 0$,

$$-72.1 + (180.4)(P \mid F, i_5^0, 5) = 0$$

from which we obtain $i_5^0 = 20.1\%$. Similarly, for $x = 6$,

$$P_e = (40)(P \mid F, 20\%, 2) + (60)(P \mid F, 20\%, 3) = 62.5$$

$$F_e = (18)(F \mid P, 20\%, 5) + (10)(F \mid P, 20\%, 4) + (30)(F \mid P, 20\%, 1) + 50 = 151.5$$

Then, for NPV $= 0$,

$$-62.5 + 151.5(P \mid F, i_6^0, 5) = 0$$

from which we get $i_6^0 = 18.5\%$.

5.12   The Payback Period

The *payback period* refers to the length of time within which all benefits received from an investment can repay all costs incurred. For simple investment situations, it is a measure of how fast the initial outlay is repaid, but it is not a measure of profit potential. Using the net annual cash flows $A_{t,x}$ (for $t = 0, 1, 2, \ldots, n$) representing project x, the payback period (PBP$_x$) refers to the smallest positive integer q such that

$$\sum_{t=0}^{q} A_{t,x} \geq 0 \tag{5.15}$$

For the simplest case in which $A_{0,x} = -C_{0,x}$ for $t = 0$ and $A_{t,x} = \bar{B}_x$ for $t = 1$ to $t = n$, i.e., $C_{0,x}$ is the initial cost and $\bar{B}_x$ is the uniform annual benefit from project x, the PBP$_x$ is the smallest positive integer q such that

$$q \geq \frac{C_{0,x}}{\bar{B}_x} \qquad (5.16)$$

For a mixed series of cash flows over the planning horizon, the term payback period is undefined and meaningless.

The payback period can at best be used as a secondary measure, given that the primary measure of profit potential of the project is satisfied. At worst, it may be misleading as an indicator of merit.

Example 5.11

Find the payback period for each of the six independent projects in Example 5.7.

The payback period can be obtained according to Eq. (5.15) for each of the projects with only one sign change in the cash flow profile.

1. For $x = 1$, PBP$_1$ is found to be 5 years because

$$\sum_{t=0}^{4} A_{t,1} = -77 + 0 = -77 \quad (<0)$$

$$\sum_{t=0}^{5} A_{t,1} = -77 + 235 = 158 \quad (>0)$$

2. For $x = 2$, PBP$_2$ is found to be 3 years because

$$\sum_{t=0}^{2} A_{t,2} = -77 + 38 + 32 = -7 \quad (<0)$$

$$\sum_{t=0}^{3} A_{t,2} = -77 + 38 + 32 + 26 = 19 \quad (>0)$$

3. For $x = 3$, PBP$_3$ is found to be 3 years because

$$\sum_{t=0}^{2} A_{t,3} = -75.3 + (2)(28) = -19.3 \quad (<0)$$

$$\sum_{t=0}^{3} A_{t,3} = -75.3 + (3)(28) = 8.7 \quad (>0)$$

4. For $x = 4$, PBP_4 is found to be 5 years because

$$\sum_{t=0}^{4} A_{t,4} = -(4)(28) = -112 \quad (<0)$$

$$\sum_{t=0}^{5} A_{t,4} = -(4)(28) + 201.9 = +89.9 \quad (>0)$$

For $x = 5$ and $x = 6$, the payback period is undefined since mixed cash flows are involved in each project.

5.13 The Decision-Making Structure

Although this chapter is primarily devoted to the economic evaluation of independent projects, it is important to recognize the decision-making structure in an organization in order to understand the delineation and classification of investment projects. In a large organization, a specialist may be assigned the task of making a preliminary screening of potential investment opportunities as independent projects without the full knowledge of the investment and financing policies of the organization. The manager at the middle management level is likely to be responsible in making capital investment choices among mutually exclusive proposals on the basis of the full range of organizational policies and recommending them to the top-level management for approval. The top management and the board of directors may approve individual investment proposals one at a time. Knowing that each individual proposal has been scrutinized and chosen for submission by the middle management, the board of directors may judge the merit of a proposal on the basis of the track record of the manager who recommends the proposal instead of the supporting economic analysis. At most, they may use the least time-consuming secondary measure, i.e., the payback period, to make a quick check on the proposals.[2]

Once this decision structure in an organization is understood, it is easy to explain the popularity of some measures of merit and methods of analysis that are demonstrably incorrect and/or inconsistent with respect to the objective of profit maximization. A method of analysis is sometimes preferred by a decision maker because it produces the desired measure as its by-product. In other words, various members of an organization involved in the decision-making process may use different measures of merit and/or methods of analysis commensurate with the degree of sophistication desired at different management levels.

From the viewpoint of profit maximization for the organization, the logical

---

[2] For a first-hand observation of decision making on capital investments in the boardrooms of large corporations, see Ref. [5.1].

approach is to consider the profit potential as the primary measure of merit of investment proposals and to adopt the most reliable and unambiguous method of analysis for their evaluation. Supplementary or secondary measures of merit desired by the decision makers at different management levels of an organization can be computed in a straightforward manner independent of the method of analysis. For that purpose, the net present value of the cash flow profile provides the most reliable and unambiguous measure of the profit potential of an investment proposal, whether it is applied to evaluate the acceptability of independent projects or to rank mutually exclusive projects. Some other measures of merit discussed in this chapter cannot be applied without modification to the evaluation of mutually exclusive projects. Consequently, the net present value is emphasized both as a profit measure and a decision criterion throughout this book.

After a project has been selected on the basis of the net present value criterion, any supplementary measure desired may be computed according to the procedures developed in Chapter 4 and in this chapter. Among the supplementary measures, the overall rate of return discussed in Section 4.7 is attractive to an investor because it is expressed as the percentage of return over the entire planning horizon and it takes into account the MARR specified by the investor for reinvesting and financing.

It should be emphasized that we have so far considered only the economic evaluation of independent projects without capital rationing and have cursorily mentioned the analysis of mutually exclusive projects which will be examined in Chapter 6. The applications of the benefit-cost ratio criterion and the internal rate of return criterion without capital rationing will be treated in detail in Chapters 7 and 8, respectively. The effects of capital rationing on economic evaluation of capital projects will be considered in Chapter 9.

Example 5.12

Compare the measures of merit for the six independent projects in Example 5.7. Use three values of $i = 0\%$, 8%, and 20% for the MARR in computing the net present value, the benefit-cost ratio, and the overall rate of return. Use the reinvestment policy and the financing policy described in Section 4.7 in computing the overall rate of return.

Since the computation of these measures has been described previously, only the results are tabulated in Table 5.5.

The values of NPV, ORR, and B/C for projects $x = 1, 2, \ldots, 6$ have been computed using three different values of MARR. It is interesting to note that the acceptability based on the NPV criterion also leads to acceptance of the same project based on the other two measures.

On the other hand, the internal rate of return indicates the first four projects ($x = 1, 2, 3, 4$) are equally meritorious in spite of the differences in their capital

Table 5.5

Comparison of Measures of Merit for Six Independent Projects

Project		$x = 1$	$x = 2$	$x = 3$	$x = 4$	$x = 5$	$x = 6$
NPV	$i = 0\%$	$+158.0$	$+53.0$	$+64.7$	$+89.9$	-7.9	$+8.0$
(\$ million)	$i = 8\%$	$+82.9$	$+30.5$	$+36.5$	$+44.7$	-1.6	$+1.4$
	$i = 20\%$	$+17.4$	$+7.2$	$+8.4$	$+8.6$	$+0.4$	-1.6
ORR	$i = 0\%$	25.0%	11.1%	13.3%	12.5%	<0%	1.6%
	$i = 8\%$	25.0%	15.5%	16.9%	16.9%	7.0%	8.4%
	$i = 20\%$	25.0%	22.3%	22.7%	22.8%	20.1%	18.5%
B/C	$i = 0\%$	3.05	1.69	1.86	1.80	0.93	1.08
	$i = 8\%$	2.08	1.40	1.48	1.48	0.98	1.02
	$i = 20\%$	1.23	1.09	1.11	1.12	1.01	0.97
IRR		25.0%	25.0%	25.0%	25.0%	9.4% and 25.0%	12.3% and 40.2%
PBP (years)		5	3	3	5	—	—

intensities at various time periods of the planning horizon. Furthermore, it fails to provide meaningful information for decision making in the case of projects $x = 5$ and $x = 6$ when multiple values of IRR exist.

The payback period provides no indication on the profit potential of a project even when it can be applied as a measure of the liquidity of the cash flow profiles for the first four projects. For the last two cases involving mixed cash flows, it cannot be applied to obtain meaningful results.

5.14   Sensitivity Analysis of Net Present Values

Since the net present value of an investment project as represented by Eq. (5.8) or Eq. (5.9) is the primary measure in determining the economic feasibility of the project, it is important to examine how sensitive the NPV may be within the ranges of its parameters which include i, t, $B_{x,t}$, and $C_{x,t}$. For the sake of simplification, we shall consider only the variation of one variable at a time.

We have already emphasized the sensitivity of the net present value with respect to MARR $= i$ in Section 5.5. It can be seen from Eq. (5.9) that the net present value is also sensitive to the timing of future costs and benefits. Because of the nature of the discount amount factor $(P|F, i, t)$, costs incurred and benefits received far in the future (those with large t values) are less significant than those near the present. Furthermore, the larger the MARR (the value of i in the factor), the less significant will be the effects of costs and benefits in the future years.

The variation in the estimation of annual benefits $B_{x,t}$ and annual costs $C_{x,t}$ may also affect the net present value to the extent that the acceptability of an investment project may be in jeopardy. The underestimation of the costs or the overestimation of the benefits may result in the acceptance of a project which is not worthwhile, while the underestimation of the benefits or the overestimation of the costs may result in the rejection of an otherwise worthwhile project.

Example 5.13

Find the present value of $10,000 to be received at year t, for $t = 1, 20, 40, 60, 80$, and 100 years, if the discount rate is $i = 4\%, 7\%$, and 10%. Plot the results of present value versus time in years.

The present value can be obtained by multiplying $10,000 by the discount amount factor $(P|F, i, t)$. The results (rounded to the nearest even dollar) are tabulated below and plotted in Fig. 5.5.

	$t = 1$	$t = 20$	$t = 40$	$t = 60$	$t = 80$	$t = 100$
$i = 4\%$	9,615	4,564	2,083	951	434	198
$i = 7\%$	9,346	2,584	668	173	45	12
$i = 10\%$	9,091	1,486	221	33	5	1

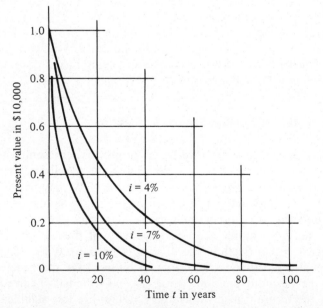

FIGURE 5.5

Example 5.14

A motel chain considers building a 300-unit motel in a new location. A planning horizon of 12 years and a MARR of 15% are used for evaluation. The initial cost of the building is $3.6 million including the land, and the terminal value at the end of 12 years is estimated to be $1.2 million including the land. The furnishings for the motel cost $1.2 million and last 4 years with no salvage value, and replacements will be made at 4-year intervals at the same cost. The annual operating and maintenance costs are estimated to be $600,000. The average rate per unit is anticipated to be $20 per day, and the motel is expected to be open year-round including weekends and holidays. Evaluate the economic feasibility of this project on the basis of average daily occupancy rates of 60%, 75%, and 90%.

The present value of the cost stream (in millions of dollars) over the planning horizon of 12 years is given by

$$CVP = 3.6 + 1.2[1 + (P|F, 15\%, 4) + (P|F, 15\%, 8)] \\ - 1.2(P|F, 15\%, 12) + 0.6(P|U, 15\%, 12) \\ = 8.907$$

The equivalent uniform annual value of the costs is

$$CUV = (8.907)(U|P, 15\%, 12) \\ = 1.643$$

The annual revenues or benefits based on full occupancy for 365 days are found to be

$$(300)(20)(365) = \$2,190,000$$

Hence, the net equivalent uniform annual values (in millions of dollars) corresponding to different occupancy rates are as follows:

$$60\% \text{ rate, NUV} = (0.60)(2.190) - 1.643 = -0.329$$

$$75\% \text{ rate, NUV} = (0.75)(2.190) - 1.643 = 0$$

$$90\% \text{ rate, NUV} = (0.90)(2.190) - 1.643 = +0.328$$

Thus, the investment will break even at the 75% occupancy rate.

5.15 Summary and Study Guide

This chapter has presented the basic principles of economic evaluation which are applicable to the evaluation of independent projects or mutually exclusive proposals, although the detail of application to these two categories of projects may be slightly different. In this chapter, we have examined some important concepts in determining whether the independent projects under consideration are economically feasible. It also serves as a prerequisite for the analysis of mutually exclusive alternatives in the next chapter.

We have emphasized the importance of the minimum attractive rate of return specified by an organization in determining the profit potential of investment proposals. Since the MARR is so crucial in the computation of the net present value and yet so difficult to pinpoint exactly, it is advisable to compute the net present value of an investment proposal for several values of the MARR.

We have also examined the objectives of investment decisions and their influence on the choice of measures of merit of an investment proposal. Once the decision process in an organization is understood, it is easy to explain the popularity of some measures of merit which are incorrect and/or inconsistent with respect to the objective of profit maximization. Consequently, the net present value criterion is presented as the basis for the most direct method of analysis. Supplementary or secondary measures, such as the benefit-cost ratio, the overall rate of return, the internal rate of return, and the payback period, which may be desired by the decision makers at different levels of an organization, can be computed in a straightforward manner.

The comparison of the measures of merit for six independent projects with substantially different cash flow profiles is shown in Table 5.5. This table gives a summary of the agreements and disagreements of these measures in the evaluation of these projects.

Since the net present value of an investment project is the primary measure in determining the economic feasibility of the project, it is important to examine its sensitivity with respect to the MARR, the timing of future costs and benefits themselves. The NPV-MARR graph and other considerations have been suggested for the sensitivity analysis.

REFERENCES

5.1 Cyert, R. M., M. H. DeGroot, and C. A. Holt, "Capital Allocation within a Firm," *Behavioral Science*, **24**(1979), 286–295.

5.2 Simon, H. A., *Organization Behavior*, 3rd ed. New York: The Free Press, 1976.

5.3 White, J. A., M. H. Agee, and K. E. Case, *Principles of Engineering Economic Analysis*. New York: John Wiley & Sons, 1977.

PROBLEMS

P5.1 A company is making a capital investment plan for the next 6 years and a project with a useful life of 6 years is under consideration. The cash flow profile of a proposed project requires an initial cost of $10,000 and a series of uniform annual net benefit of $3,000 over the 6-year period. Determine the net present value, the net future value at the end of 6 years, and the net equivalent uniform annual value of this project if the specified MARR is 12%.

P5.2 A public agency is planning a capital budget for the next 6 years. A proposed project of 4-years' duration has the following net annual cash flows: $A_0 = -\$10,000$, $A_1 = A_2 = A_3 = +\$6,000$ and $A_4 = +\$8,000$. Using a MARR of 12%, determine the net future value at the end of the 6-year period and the net equivalent annual value over the 6-year period for this project.

P5.3 Plot the NPV-MARR graph for the project in Problem P5.1, using the values of MARR of 0%, 5%, 10%, 15%, 20%, and 25%. Determine the internal rate of return and the overall rate of return of the project over the 6-year period.

P5.4 Plot the NPV-MARR graph for the project in Problem P5.2, using the values of MARR of 0%, 10%, 20%, 30%, 40%, and 50%. Determine the internal rate of return and the overall rate of return of the project over the 6-year period.

P5.5 The cash flow profile of an investment project of 5-years duration is as follows: $A_0 = -\$1,000$, $A_1 = +\$400$, $A_2 = +\$600$, $A_3 = \$0$, $A_4 = -\$200$, and $A_5 = +\$800$. Using a MARR of 8%, determine the net equivalent uniform annual value of this project.

P5.6 An investment of $90,000 in automatic equipment at present is expected to save $15,000 per year in the next 5 years and $10,000 per year from the sixth through the tenth year. Using a MARR of 8%, determine whether this investment is worthwhile. Also find the overall rate of return of this investment over the 10-year period.

P5.7 The Samluck Company purchases a hydraulic press which is expected to generate a net revenue of $8,000 per year over the next 8 years. The purchase price is $50,000 with a salvage value of $5,000 at the end of 8 years. The company borrows $30,000 from the bank at 6% interest compounded annually, and the loan is to be repaid with equal annual payments including interest over a 5-year period. The remaining $20,000 is taken from the internal funds of the firm which has a MARR of 8%. Is the purchase worthwhile?

P5.8 The Fulton Company plans to purchase a compressor which is expected to produce a savings of $5,000 per year over the next 10 years. The purchase price is $40,000 with no salvage value at the end. The company borrows $25,000 from the bank at 8% interest compounded annually, and the loan is to be repaid with equal annual payments including interest over a 6-year period beginning from the end of the first year. The MARR specified by the firm is 10%. Is the purchase worthwhile?

P5.9 For the six independent projects in Table 5.4 of this chapter, find the net present values of their cash flow profiles, using a MARR of 8%.

P5.10 For the six independent projects in Table 5.4 of this chapter, find the net equivalent uniform annual value of their cash flow profiles, using a MARR of 8%.

P5.11 For the six independent projects in Table 5.4 of the chapter, find the benefit-cost ratios from their cash flow profiles, using a MARR of 8%.

P5.12 A taxicab company plans to replace a retired cab with a new vehicle which is expected to be driven 30,000 miles per year and to have a useful life of 3 years. The new vehicle costs $9,000 with a salvage value of $1,000 at the end of 3 years. The annual operating and maintenance cost of the vehicle is $20,000, excluding the fuel cost. The fuel consumption of the vehicle averages 15 miles per gallon and the fuel cost averages $1.40 per gallon. Using a MARR of 15%, determine the annual revenue from operating the vehicle in order to break even if average fuel cost is (a) $1.40 per gallon as estimated, (b) 20% higher, and (c) 50% higher.

P5.13 A firm is considering two independent investment proposals, each requiring an initial expenditure of $10,000 but offering different benefits in the next 5 years. Proposal no. 1 yields $2,000 per year in the first 2 years and $3,000 per year in the last 3 years. Proposal no. 2 yields $2,700 in each of the 5 years. Using a MARR of 10%, should any of these proposals be accepted?

P5.14 The installation of a new pipeline for transporting crude oil between two locations requires an initial cost of $10 million. The useful life of the pipeline is 40 years with no salvage value at the end of its useful life. The net revenues generated by the pipeline per year depend on volume of crude oil transported. Assume that the expectation is to transport 150 million barrels per year in the first 5 years, 200 million barrels per year in the following 25 years, and 100 million barrels per year in the last 10 years. The net revenue for transporting each million barrels through the pipeline is $6,000. The MARR is specified to be 10%. Determine whether the pipeline project is worthwhile if the transport volume is (a) 100% as expected, (b) 90% of the expectation, and (c) 110% of the expectation.

P5-15 A precision inspection instrument is purchased for $80,000. The operating and maintenance costs are $5,000 for the first year, and increase by $500 each year from the previous year thereafter. The revenues produced by the machine are estimated to be $15,000 in the first year and increase by $1,500 from the previous year each year thereafter. The machine is expected to have a useful life of 10 years with a salvage value of $10,000 at the end of 10 years. Using a MARR of 12%, determine whether the purchase is worthwhile.

6

COMPARISON OF
MUTUALLY EXCLUSIVE
PROPOSALS

6.1 The Generation of Mutually
Exclusive Alternatives

In the search for capital investment opportunities, we often encounter potential projects that are not independent of each other. If two or more projects are complementary to each other, then they should be grouped together as a single alternative so that they will be accepted or rejected as a group. On the other hand, if two or more projects have a substituting effect on each other, they should be set apart or in different groups so that the acceptance of one will not lead to the acceptance of the others. Furthermore, several independent projects may also be combined as a single proposal for comparison with other proposals. Thus, we can generate a number of feasible mutually exclusive proposals through the proper grouping of potential investment projects.

Consider, for example, the potential flood control measures for a town located on the bank of a river as shown in Fig. 6.1. These potential measures include a dam at site A, B, or C and a dike at site D. Each of these measures provides a different level of protection because they are designed for different flood intensities. These potential measures may be regarded as mutually exclusive if each of them can satisfy the minimum level of protection desired. On the other hand, it is possible that some combination of these measures may provide a higher level of protection which is more desirable. For example, a small dam at site A and a dike at site D, which will complement each other, may provide approximately the same level of protection as a large dam at site C. In that case, the combination of a dam at A and a dike at D is also a suitable alternative in a set of mutually exclusive proposals.

Very often, the mutually exclusive alternatives are conceived as possible variations in the size of a facility. For example, given a specific site for the construction

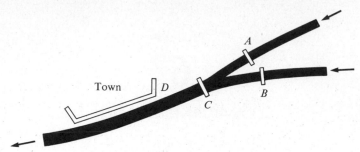

FIGURE 6.1

of an office building, we may wish to compare several designs of different heights or of different base dimensions.

It is understood that the best proposal among a set of mutually exclusive alternatives must be superior or equal to the null alternative to be acceptable. Furthermore, if the alternative of maintaining the status quo or abandoning an existing facility is different from the null alternative, it should be considered along with other mutually exclusive alternatives. If this is not done, there is the inherent danger of either accepting a new proposal when the status quo alternative is in fact better, or retaining an existing facility which is no longer economically feasible.

6.2   Direct Approaches for Comparison

The net present value method offers a direct approach for comparing the profit potentials of mutually exclusive alternatives. The net present value method for evaluating the economic feasibility of an independent project has been explained in detail in Section 5.6. The same principle may be applied to the evaluation of the economic feasibility of each of a set of mutually exclusive alternatives. In addition, we must rank the merits of all mutually exclusive proposals and select only the one that has the maximum nonnegative net present value.

Let NPV_x be the net present value of the project x for $MARR = i$ over a planning horizon of n years. It is implicit that for the null alternative $(x = 0)$, $NPV_0 = 0$. Then, for a set of m mutually exclusive proposals, $(x = 1, 2, \ldots, m)$, the criterion for selecting a particular proposal j is that it has the maximum net present value among those projects which are economically feasible. That is,

$$NPV_j = \operatorname*{Max}_{x \in m} NPV_x \tag{6.1}$$

provided that

$$NPV_j \geq 0$$

Since all mutually exclusive alternatives for comparison must be evaluated at a specified MARR $= i$ over the same planning horizon of n years, we can also compare the net future value or the net equivalent uniform annual value of these alternatives. Thus, the criterion for accepting a particular project j on the basis of the net future values at the end of n years is

$$\text{NFV}_j = \underset{x \in m}{\text{Max NFV}_x} \qquad (\text{NFV}_j \geq 0) \tag{6.2}$$

Similarly, the criterion based on the net equivalent uniform annual value is

$$\text{NUV}_j = \underset{x \in m}{\text{Max NUV}_x} \qquad (\text{NUV}_j \geq 0) \tag{6.3}$$

The direct approaches using Eq. (6.1), (6.2), or (6.3) are straightforward, and the results thus obtained are unambiguous regardless of the number of possible values for the internal rate of return. To avoid repetitions, further discussion of the direct approaches will be devoted primarily to the net present value method, although the same principles may also be applied to the net future value or the net equivalent uniform annual value.

Example 6.1

The cash flow profiles in Table 6.1 represent the expected annual net costs and benefits of three mutually exclusive alternatives in the selection of a drilling machine. The first alternative ($x = 1$) is the purchase of a new machine that is expected to last 6 years. The second alternative ($x = 2$) is a new machine advertised for lease purchase over a 6-year period with a two-tier payment schedule for the first and second 3-year periods. The third alternative ($x = 3$) is to continue the use of the existing machine which requires a major overhaul now as well as additional maintenance in the next few years. The annual benefits and costs of these alternatives have been netted to obtain the cash flow profiles as shown. The MARR is specified to be 12%. Determine which of the three alternatives should be selected, using (1)

Table 6.1

Cash Flow Profiles for the Drilling Machines

t	$A_{t,1}$	$A_{t,2}$	$A_{t,3}$
0	$-10,000$	$-10,000$	$-1,500$
1–3 (each)	3,000	6,000	1,000
4–6 (cach)	3,000	0	1,000

the net present value criterion, (2) the net future value criterion, and (3) the net equivalent uniform annual value criterion.

Using the net present value criterion, we can compare NPV_x for $x = 1, 2, 3$:

$$[\text{NPV}_1]_{12\%} = -10{,}000 + (3{,}000)(P \mid U, 12\%, 6)$$
$$= -10{,}000 + (3{,}000)(4.1114) = 2334$$

$$[\text{NPV}_2]_{12\%} = -10{,}000 + (6{,}000)(P \mid U, 12\%, 3)$$
$$= -10{,}000 + (6{,}000)(2.4018) = 4411$$

$$[\text{NPV}_3]_{12\%} = -1{,}500 + (1{,}000)(P \mid U, 12\%, 6)$$
$$= -1{,}500 + (1{,}000)(4.1114) = 2611$$

Since all net present values are positive and NPV_2 is the largest, the second alternative should be selected.

Using the net future value criterion, we can compare NFV_x for $x = 1, 2, 3$:

$$[\text{NFV}_1]_{12\%} = -(10{,}000)(F \mid P, 12\%, 6) + (3{,}000)(F \mid U, 12\%, 6)$$
$$= -(10{,}000)(1.9738) + (3{,}000)(8.1152) = 4608$$

$$[\text{NFV}_2]_{12\%} = -(10{,}000)(F \mid P, 12\%, 6) + (6{,}000)(F \mid U, 12\%, 3)(F \mid P, 12\%, 3)$$
$$= -(10{,}000)(1.9738) + (6{,}000)(3.3744)(1.4049) = 8706$$

$$[\text{NFV}_3]_{12\%} = -(1{,}500)(F \mid P, 12\%, 6) + (1{,}000)(F \mid U, 12\%, 6)$$
$$= -(1{,}500)(1.9738) + (1{,}000)(8.1152) = 5155$$

Since NFV_2 is largest, the second alternative should be selected.

Similarly, using the net equivalent uniform annual value, we can compute NUV_x for $x = 1, 2, 3$ from the corresponding net present values NPV_x as follows:

$$[\text{NUV}_1]_{12\%} = (2{,}334)(U \mid P, 12\%, 6) = (2{,}334)(0.2432) = 568$$

$$[\text{NUV}_2]_{12\%} = (4{,}411)(U \mid P, 12\%, 6) = (4{,}411)(0.2432) = 1{,}073$$

$$[\text{NUV}_3]_{12\%} = (2{,}611)(U \mid P, 12\%, 6) = (2{,}611)(0.2432) = 635$$

Obviously, the second alternative should be selected.

6.3 The NPV-MARR Graph for Mutually Exclusive Alternatives

Since the minimum attractive rate of return is crucially important in the computation of the net present value but difficult to pinpoint exactly, it is advisable to

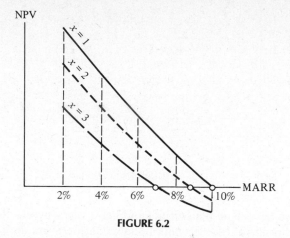

FIGURE 6.2

compute NPV_x of all alternatives ($x = 1, 2, \ldots, m$) for several values of **MARR**. By plotting a graph of NPV versus MARR, the sensitivity of the ranking of the alternatives based on the net present values can be observed.

For alternative investment proposals in which one or more periods of disbursements are followed by one or more periods of receipts, the NPV-MARR graph may be represented schematically by either Fig. 6.2 or Fig. 6.3. In Fig. 6.2, the ranking of the mutually exclusive alternatives is not affected by the change in MARR, while in Fig. 6.3, the ranking of the alternatives changes at different ranges of MARR values. In the former case, the curves for various alternatives do not intersect with each other; in the latter case, the intersections of the curves represent the demarcations of change in the ranking of the alternatives.

When one or more of the alternative investment proposals consist of cash flow

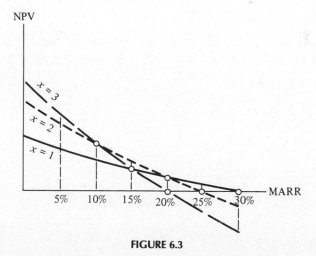

FIGURE 6.3

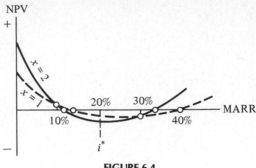

FIGURE 6.4

profiles with mixed periods of net receipts and net disbursements, the ranking of the alternatives in the range of MARR values under consideration may still be observed from the NPV-MARR graph. When the value of MARR is specified, the ranking of the alternatives can be made by computing the net present values of the alternatives at the specified MARR, regardless whether or not some of the alternatives may have multiple internal rates of return. Two possible examples are shown schematically in Figs. 6.4 and 6.5 in which the specified MARR is denoted by i^*.

If the net present values of a set of mutually exclusive alternatives are computed at several values of MARR, the sensitivity of the net present values with this range of values of MARR can be observed. Then, the alternatives can be ranked on the basis of the net present values and the best alternative can be determined. It is important to emphasize that the absolute values of benefits and costs should be used in computing the net present values in order to make sure that the best alternative is nonnegative. If this practice is followed, then the net present value method always leads to an unambiguous choice among a set of mutually exclusive alternatives.

Example 6.2

Three plans have been proposed for a small commercial building at a leased site. The building is expected to have a useful life of 40 years and no salvage value at the

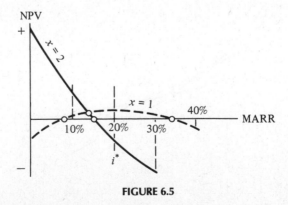

FIGURE 6.5

Table 6.2

Cost and Benefit Streams (in $1,000) for Example 6.2

t	x = 1		x = 2		x = 3	
	$C_{t,1}$	$B_{t,1}$	$C_{t,2}$	$B_{t,2}$	$C_{t,3}$	$B_{t,3}$
0	200	0	250	0	300	0
1–40 (each)	40	63	30	52	55	77

Table 6.3

Net Present Values (in $1,000) for Example 6.2

i	NPV_1	NPV_2	NPV_3
4%	255.234	185.442	135.442
6%	146.065	81.019	31.019
8%	74.266	12.341	−37.659

end of the period. The initial construction costs, the annual maintenance costs, and the annual benefits of the three mutually exclusive plans are shown in Table 6.2. If MARR is specified to be 6%, rank these alternatives on the basis of their net present values. Repeat the computation for MARR = 4% and 8%.

For each alternative x, the uniform annual costs $C_{t,x}$ and the uniform annual benefits $B_{t,x}$ (for $t = 1, 2, \ldots, 40$) may be represented by $\bar{C}_x$ and $\bar{B}_x$, respectively. Then, the net present value of alternative x is given by

$$NPV_x = -C_{0,x} + (\bar{B}_x - \bar{C}_x)(P \mid U, i, 40)$$

The results of the computation for $i = 4\%$, 6%, and 8% are listed in Table 6.3. A NPV-MARR graph for the range of MARR from 0% to 10% is also shown in Fig. 6.2. For all three values of MARR, $x = 1$ is the best, $x = 2$ is the second, and $x = 3$ is the last.

Example 6.3

The cash flow profiles of three mutually exclusive alternatives (values in dollars) are given below:

t	$A_{t,1}$	$A_{t,2}$	$A_{t,3}$
0	−1,000	−2,000	−3.000
1	+1,300	+2,500	+3,600

Table 6.4

Net Present Values (in $1,000)
for Example 6.3

i	NPV_1	NPV_2	NPV_3
0%	300	500	600
5%	238	381	429
10%	182	273	273
15%	131	174	131
20%	83	83	0
25%	40	0	−120
30%	0	−77	−231

Compute the net present values of these alternatives at 5% intervals from $i = 0\%$ to $i = 30\%$. Plot a NPV-MARR graph for this range of MARR.

The net present values of these alternatives with 1-year's duration can easily be computed.

$$NPV_1 = -1,000 + (1,300)(P|F, i, 1)$$

$$NPV_2 = -2,000 + (2,500)(P|F, i, 1)$$

$$NPV_3 = -3,000 + (3,600)(P|F, i, 1)$$

The values based on $i = 0\%$ to $i = 30\%$ at 5% intervals have been computed and tabulated in Table 6.4. The results have also been plotted in the NPV-MARR graph in Fig. 6.3.

It is interesting to note that alternatives $x = 2$ and $x = 3$ intersect at $i = 10\%$, alternatives $x = 1$ and $x = 3$ at $i = 15\%$, and alternatives $x = 1$ and $x = 2$ at $i = 20\%$, as indicated by the net present values in Table 6.3. Consequently, the ranks of the alternatives at various intervals of MARR from 0% to 30% are observed from Fig. 6.3 as follows:

Range of i	Best	Second	Last
0%–10%	$x = 3$	$x = 2$	$x = 1$
10%–15%	$x = 2$	$x = 3$	$x = 1$
15%–20%	$x = 2$	$x = 1$	$x = 3$
20%–25%	$x = 1$	$x = 2$	Negative
25%–30%	$x = 1$	Negative	Negative

6.4 Relationship Between Incremental Net Present Value and Incremental Internal Rate of Return

The underlying principle of economic evaluation is to maximize the profit potential as measured by the discounted net benefit, such as the net present value. When the net present value criterion is used for selecting the best proposal from a set of mutually exclusive alternatives, all that is necessary is to compute the net present values of all alternatives at the specified MARR and select the one which has the maximum nonnegative value.

However, in evaluating the sensitivity of the net present values of mutually exclusive alternatives, we want to know the conditions under which the curves representing different alternatives will or will not intersect with each other; and if they do intersect, we want to find the points of intersection. We can address these issues by examining systematically each pair of alternatives in a set of mutually exclusive alternatives.

Let projects x and y be a pair of mutually exclusive alternatives, and $A_{t,x}$ and $A_{t,y}$ be their respective cash flow profiles for $t = 0, 1, 2, \ldots, n$. Also, let the incremental cash flow profile of x over y be

$$\Delta A_{t,x-y} = A_{t,x} - A_{t,y} \tag{6.4}$$

and the incremental net present value (INPV) of x over y be

$$\Delta NPV_{x-y} = NPV_x - NPV_y \tag{6.5}$$

In general, $A_{t,x}$ and $A_{t,y}$ are either given directly or netted from the annual benefits and costs according to Eq. (5.1). Then, from Eq. (5.2),

$$NPV_x = \sum_{t=0}^{n} A_{t,x}(1 + i)^{-t}$$

and

$$NPV_y = \sum_{t=0}^{n} A_{t,y}(1 + i)^{-t}$$

Hence,

$$\Delta NPV_{x-y} = \sum_{t=0}^{n} \Delta A_{t,x-y}(1 + i)^{-t} \tag{6.6}$$

The internal rate of return i_{x-y} resulting from the incremental cash flow profile x over y is the value of i which sets $\Delta NPV_{x-y} = 0$. This value $i = i_{x-y}$, which is referred to as the *incremental internal rate of return* (IIRR) of x over y, is obtained by solving for *i* in the algebraic equation

$$\sum_{t=0}^{n} \Delta A_{t,x-y}(1 + i)^{-t} = 0 \tag{6.7}$$

Since the left-hand side of Eq. (6.7) is a polynomial of *i* to the *n*th power, its solution may be obtained in accordance with the discussion in Section 4.3 of Chapter 4. The value(s) of i_{x-y} thus obtained will be the intersection(s) of the curves representing NPV_x and NPV_y as functions of *i*.

Let us consider first the simple cases in which there is only one sign change in the incremental cash flow profile $A_{t,x-y}$ for $t = 0, 1, 2, \ldots, n$. Then, there exists only one positive real root for Eq. (6.7). It is convenient to order *x* and *y* in a NPV-MARR graph with projects *x* and *y* such that

$$[NPV_x]_{0\%} > [NPV_y]_{0\%}$$

Consequently, in a graph showing the relationship between INPV and IIRR, we have

$$[\Delta NPV_{x-y}]_{0\%} > 0$$

Two typical examples are shown in Figs. 6.6 and 6.7 in which the value of i_{x-y} corresponding to the intersection of the curves representing NPV_x and NPV_y in part (a) of each figure is identical to the value of i_{x-y} in part (b) showing the relationship between ΔNPV_{x-y} and MARR. Since MARR $= i_{x-y}$ for $\Delta NPV_{x-y} = 0$, the value of i_{x-y} can be obtained from Eq. (6.7). If $[NPV_x]_{0\%} = [NPV_y]_{0\%}$, indicating $[\Delta NPV_{x-y}]_{0\%} = 0$, then $i_{x-y} = 0\%$ is the root of *i* in Eq. (6.7).

Since the incremental cash flow profile $\Delta A_{t,x-y}$ is obtained from the difference of cash flow profiles $A_{t,x}$ and $A_{t,y}$, it is quite possible that there is no sign change in $\Delta A_{t,x-y}$ even if both $A_{t,x}$ and $A_{t,y}$ have only one sign change. Two typical examples are shown in Figs. 6.8 and 6.9, in which the curves representing NPV_x and NPV_y do not intersect in the half-plane of positive *i* in the NPV-MARR graph and therefore no positive i_{x-y} exists.

In general, either the cash flow profile of *x* or that of *y* or both may have two or more sign changes. For such cases, the incremental cash flow profile $\Delta A_{t,x-y}$ may lead to multiple roots of *i*, indicating multiple intersections between the curves representing NPV_x and NPV_y. When that happens, the relationship between INPV and IIRR should be examined in locating the multiple values of i_{x-y}. More detailed discussion of the solution for all possible cases is given in Chapter 8.

Example 6.4

For the three mutually exclusive alternatives in Example 6.2, verify that the curves representing the net present values of any two of these alternatives will not intersect in the half-plane of positive *i* in the NPV-MARR graph.

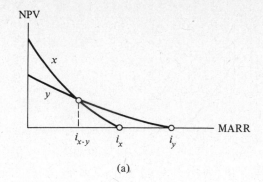

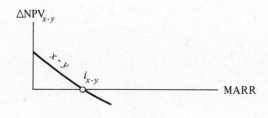

FIGURE 6.6

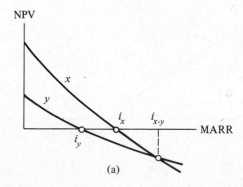

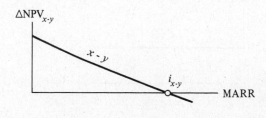

FIGURE 6.7

149

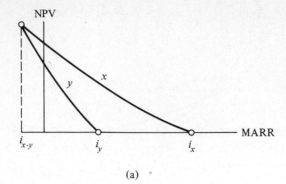

(a)

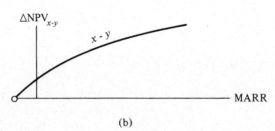

(b)

FIGURE 6.8

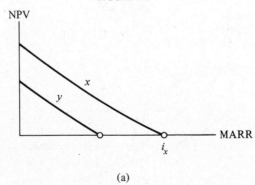

(a)

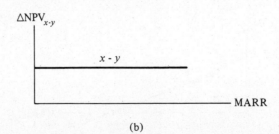

(b)

FIGURE 6.9

The cash flow profiles of these mutually exclusive alternatives are first netted out according to Eq. (5.1), and the results of $A_{t,x}$ for $x = 1, 2$, and 3 are shown in Table 6.5. For each of the alternatives, we can compute

$$[\text{NPV}_1]_{0\%} = -200 + (23)(40) = 720$$

$$[\text{NPV}_2]_{0\%} = -250 + (22)(40) = 630$$

$$[\text{NPV}_3]_{0\%} = -300 + (23)(40) = 580$$

In finding the incremental net present value for each pair of alternatives, we order the pair so that $[\Delta\text{NPV}_{x-y}]_{0\%} > 0$. Hence, the incremental cash flow profiles of $x = 2$ over $x = 3$, that of $x = 1$ over $x = 2$, and that of $x = 1$ over $x = 3$ are computed by Eq. (6.4), and the corresponding incremental net present values are computed by Eq. (6.5). These results for $i = 0\%$ are also shown in Table 6.5.

To find $\text{IIRR} = i_{x-y}$, we set $\Delta\text{NPV}_{x-y} = 0$ for each case. Thus, for $\Delta\text{NPV}_{2-3} = 0$,

$$+50 + (0)(P\,|\,U, i, 40) = 0 \qquad (P\,|\,U, i, 40) = -\infty$$

This result indicates that i_{x-y} does not exist. For $\Delta\text{NPV}_{1-2} = 0$,

$$+50 + (1)(P\,|\,U, i, 40) = 0 \qquad (P\,|\,U, i, 40) = -50$$

and for $\Delta\text{NPV}_{1-3} = 0$,

$$+100 + (1)(P\,|\,U, i, 40) = 0 \qquad (P\,|\,U, i, 40) = -100$$

In both of these cases, the result indicates that i_{x-y} does not exist in the half-plane of positive i of the NPV-MARR graph. Therefore, we can conclude that the NPV curves representing the three mutually exclusive alternatives will not intersect in the half-plane of positive i of the NPV-MARR graph without actually plotting such a graph.

Table 6.5

Cash Flows and Incremental Cash Flows for Example 6.2

t	$A_{t,1}$	$A_{t,2}$	$A_{t,3}$	$\Delta A_{t,2-3}$	$\Delta A_{t,1-2}$	$\Delta A_{t,1-3}$
0	-200	-250	-300	$+50$	$+50$	$+100$
1–40 (each)	$+23$	$+22$	$+22$	0	$+1$	$+1$
$[\text{NPV}]_{0\%}$	$+720$	$+630$	$+580$	$+50$	$+90$	$+140$

Example 6.5

The cash flow profiles of two mutually exclusive alternatives are given in Table 6.6. The incremental cash flow profile of $x = 2$ over $x = 1$ is also shown in the table. Find the points of intersection of the curves representing NPV_1 and NPV_2 in the NPV-MARR graph.

The cash flow profile of each of these two alternatives has two sign changes and may have up to two roots of i. For $x = 1$, the values of IRR are found to be 12.35% and 40.15% (see Example 4.10 in Chapter 4 for complete solution). Similarly for $x = 2$, the values of IRR are found to be 10.1% and 33.9%. To find the incremental internal rate of return IIRR $= i_{2-1}$, we set

$$\Delta NPV_{2-1} = 39.1 - (28)(P|U, i, 4) + (80)(P|F, i, 5) = 0$$

By trial solution, we get

i	$(P|U, i, 4)$	$(P|F, i, 5)$	ΔNPV_{2-1}
10%	3.1698	0.6209	−0.018
20%	2.5887	0.4019	−1.232
30%	2.1662	0.2693	+0.010
40%	1.8492	0.1859	+2.194

The value of ΔNPV_{2-1} is very close to zero at $i = 10\%$ and $i = 30\%$. Hence, the curves representing NPV_1 and NPV_2 intersect at these values as shown in Fig. 6.4.

Table 6.6

Cash Flows and Incremental Cash Flows
(in $ million)

t	$A_{t,1}$	$A_{t,2}$	$\Delta A_{t,2-1}$
0	+18	+57.1	+39.1
1	+10	−18	−28
2	−40	−68	−28
3	−60	−88	−28
4	+30	+2	−28
5	+50	+130	+80
$[NPV]_{0\%}$	+8	+15.1	+7.1

Table 6.7

Cash Flows and Incremental Cash Flows
(in $1,000)

t	$A_{t,1}$	$A_{t,2}$	$\Delta A_{t,2-1}$
0	-38.3	-79.9	-41.6
1	$+28$	$+28$	0
2	$+28$	$+28$	0
3	$+28$	$+28$	0
4	$+28$	$+28$	0
5	-80	0	$+80$
$[\text{NPV}]_{0\%}$	-6.3	$+32.1$	$+38.4$

Example 6.6

The cash flow profiles of two mutually exclusive alternatives are given in Table 6.7. The incremental cash flow profile of $x = 2$ over $x = 1$ is also shown in the table. Find the points of intersection of the curves representing NPV_1 and NPV_2 in the NPV-MARR graph.

The cash flow profile of $x = 1$ has two sign changes and the values of IRR for $x = 1$ are found to be 8% and 33.6%. The cash flow profile of $x = 2$ has only one sign change, and the value of IRR for $x = 2$ is found to be 15.0%. To find the incremental internal rate of return $\text{IIRR} = i_{2-1}$, we set

$$\Delta \text{NPV}_{2-1} = -41.6 + (80)(P\,|\,F,\,i,\,5) = 0$$

Hence,

$$(P\,|\,F,\,i,\,5) = \frac{41.6}{80} = 0.52$$

from which we find $i = 14.0\%$ by interpolation between 12% and 15%. Hence, the curves representing NPV_1 and NPV_2 intersect at $i_{2-1} = 14\%$ as shown in Fig. 6.5.

Example 6.7

The cash flow profiles for the three drilling machines in Example 6.1 and their incremental cash flows are shown in Table 6.8. Find the points of intersection of the curves representing NPV_1, NPV_2, and NPV_3 in the NPV-MARR graph.

Table 6.8

Cash Flows and Incremental Cash Flows (in $1,000)

t	$A_{t,1}$	$A_{t,2}$	$A_{t,3}$	$\Delta A_{t,2-1}$	$\Delta A_{t,1-3}$	$\Delta A_{t,2-3}$
0	−10,000	−10,000	−1,500	0	−8,500	−8,500
1–3 (each)	+3,000	+6,000	+1,000	+3,000	+2,000	+5,000
4–6 (each)	+3,000	0	+1,000	−3,000	+2,000	−1,000
$[\text{NPV}]_{0\%}$	8,000	8,000	4,500	0	3,500	3,500

Since $[\text{NPV}_1]_{0\%} = [\text{NPV}_2]_{0\%} = 0$, leading to $[\Delta\text{NPV}_{2-1}]_{0\%} = 0$, the curves representing NPV_1 and NPV_2 intersect at $i_{2-1} = 0\%$. For $x = 1$ and $x = 3$,

$$\text{NPV}_{1-3} = -8,500 + (2,000)(P \mid U, i, 6) = 0$$

from which we obtain $i_{1-3} = 10.86\%$. Similarly, for $x = 2$ and $x = 3$,

$$\text{NPV}_{2-3} = -8,500 + (5,000)(P \mid U, i, 3) - (1,000)(P \mid U, i, 3)(P \mid F, i, 3) = 0$$

from which we get $i_{2-3} = 27.8\%$. These points of intersection are shown in Fig. 6.10.

Example 6.8

The cash flow profiles of three mutually exclusive alternatives and their incremental cash flow profiles are shown in Table 6.9.

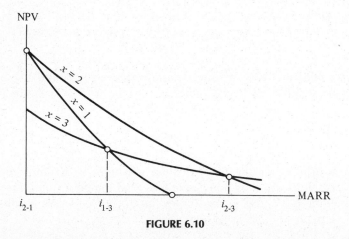

FIGURE 6.10

Table 6.9

Cash Flows and Incremental Cash Flows (in $1,000)

t	$A_{t,1}$	$A_{t,2}$	$A_{t,3}$	$\Delta A_{t,\,2-1}$	$\Delta A_{t,\,3-1}$	$\Delta A_{t,\,3-2}$
0	-205	-350	-295	-145	-90	$+55$
1	$+50$	$+100$	$+70$	$+50$	$+20$	-30
2	$+50$	$+90$	$+70$	$+40$	$+20$	-20
3	$+50$	$+80$	$+70$	$+30$	$+20$	-10
4	$+50$	$+70$	$+70$	$+20$	$+20$	0
5	$+50$	$+60$	$+70$	$+10$	$+20$	$+10$
$[\text{NPV}]_{0\%}$	$+45$	$+50$	$+55$	$+5$	$+10$	$+5$

1. Find the net present values at a **MARR** of 3%.
2. Find the points of intersection of the curves representing the net present values.

1. The net present values of the three alternatives at a **MARR** of 3% are as follows:

$$[\text{NPV}_1]_{3\%} = -205 + (50)(P\,|\,U, 3\%, 5) = 24.0$$

$$[\text{NPV}_2]_{3\%} = -350 + (100)(P\,|\,U, 3\%, 5) - (10)(P\,|\,G, 3\%, 5) = 19.1$$

$$[\text{NPV}_3]_{3\%} = -295 + (70)(P\,|\,U, 3\%, 5) = 25.6$$

Since $[\text{NPV}_3]_{3\%}$ has the maximum nonnegative value among the three mutually exclusive alternatives, the alternative $x = 3$ should be selected.

2. The intersections of the curves representing NPV_1, NPV_2, and NPV_3 can be obtained by considering the alternatives pairwise. Thus, for $x = 2$ and $x = 1$,

$$\Delta\text{NPV}_{2-1} = -145 + (50)(P\,|\,U, i, 5) - (10)(P\,|\,G, i, 5) = 0$$

from which we obtain $i_{2-1} = 1.47\%$. For $x = 3$ and $x = 1$,

$$\Delta\text{NPV}_{3-1} = -90 + (20)(P\,|\,U, i, 5) = 0$$

from which we get $i_{3-1} = 3.62\%$. For $x = 3$ and $x = 2$,

$$\Delta\text{NPV}_{3-2} = +55 - (30)(P\,|\,U, i, 5) + (10)(P\,|\,G, i, 5) = 0$$

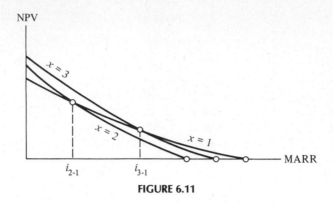

FIGURE 6.11

It is found from the last equation that i_{3-2} does not exist in the half-plane of positive i in the NPV-MARR graph. The intersections of the curves representing NPV_1, NPV_2, and NPV_3 are shown in Fig. 6.11.

6.5   Indirect Approaches for Comparison

The net present value not only is a convenient direct indicator of the profit potential of an individual proposal, but also is a valid basis for ranking the profits from a set of mutually exclusive proposals. Therefore, the net present value criterion is the most straightforward and reliable method in selecting the best among a set of mutually exclusive alternatives on the basis of profit maximization without capital rationing. Alternatively, a decision criterion based on the net future values or the net equivalent uniform annual values of mutually exclusive alternatives will have the same effects.

Other methods that have been used for analyzing the economic feasibility or acceptability of independent projects are not *directly* applicable to the selection of the best among mutually exclusive proposals and are therefore referred to as *indirect approaches*. It is important to recognize this fact and not to misuse other methods when they are not applicable.

Although the benefit-cost ratio is an indicator of the profit potential of an individual proposal, it is *not* a valid basis for profit maximization because the benefit-cost ratio does not reflect the absolute value of profit or net benefit. The internal rate of return is also an indicator of the merit of an individual proposal which is independent of the MARR, but it is *not* a valid basis for profit maximization. The payback period is *not* even an indicator of the profit potential, but it is a measure of how fast the initial outlay is repaid. None of these measures can be used as a criterion for ranking mutually exclusive proposals.

While the overall rate of return is derived from the same underlying assumptions of a specific planning horizon and a specified MARR as in the case of computing the NFV or the NPV, it provides only an indicator of the profit potential of an individual proposal. Generally, it is *not* a valid basis for ranking the profit potentials of mutually exclusive alternatives. Its usefulness as an indicator of the profit potential of a private capital investment is analogous to that of the benefit-cost ratio as an indicator of the net benefit of a public project.

Nevertheless, a method of analysis based on the *incremental benefit-cost ratios* can be developed to satisfy the net present value criterion for profit maximization in ranking mutually exclusive proposals, and this benefit-cost ratio method will be explained fully in Chapter 7. Similarly, a method of analysis based on the *incremental internal rates of return* can also be developed to satisfy the net present value criterion for profit maximazation in ranking mutually exclusive proposals, and this internal rate of return method will be treated extensively in Chapter 8. We shall therefore defer the detailed discussion of the meaning of incremental benefit-cost ratios and incremental internal rates of return.

6.6 Comparison of Measures of Merit

It is important to distinguish between the measures of merit and the methods of analysis when we deal with the benefit-cost ratios or the internal rates of return of mutually exclusive proposals. Some decision makers may want to know the benefit-cost ratio or the internal rate of return for the *best proposal selected* because they are more accustomed to gauge the profit potential of an investment on the basis of such a measure. If so, the mutually exclusive alternatives can be ranked according to the net present value criterion, and, after the best alternative is selected on this basis, other measures of merit for the selected proposal can be computed in accordance with the procedures which have been fully discussed in Chapters 4 and 5. Since various measures of merit of the selected proposal can be obtained directly by using well-established procedures which are independent of the methods of ranking mutually exclusive alternatives and selecting the best among them, we need to know and use only the simplest and most reliable method of analysis, which is the method based on the net present value criterion described in Section 6.2. This argument will be further explained in Chapters 7, 8, and 9.

It is also important to emphasize that although profit maximization is the primary objective in evaluating mutually exclusive proposals, some secondary objectives such as the payback period may be introduced by decision makers. In fact, an organization may be satisfied with selecting a reasonably profitable proposal without necessarily seeking the most profitable alternatives because of other considerations. A public agency may even wish to select a proposal with a negative net present value in order to achieve certain socially desirable goals. However, the use of profit maximization as a decision criterion will allow us to know the price of selecting an alternative other than the one that has the maximum nonnegative net present value.

Example 6.9

Compare the measures of merit of the six mutually exclusive projects whose cash flow profits are given in Table 6.10. Use three values of $i = 0\%$, 3%, and 6% for the MARR in computing the net present value, the overall rate of return, and the benefit-cost ratio. If $i = 3\%$ is the MARR specified for the selection of the project, and $i = 0\%$ and $i = 6\%$ are used for sensitivity analyses only, determine the correct ranking of this set of mutually exclusive projects.

Since the procedures for computing various measures of merit have been described previously in Chapters 4 and 5, only the results of computation are tabulated in Table 6.11.

In comparing the net present values of projects $x = 1, 2, \ldots, 6$, it is noted that ranking the projects at $i = 3\%$ is unambiguous, indicating that project $x = 3$ will produce the maximum profit or net benefit. However, ranking the projects is relatively sensitive within the limits of $\pm 3\%$ since it may be changed within the range of $i = 0\%$ to $i = 6\%$.

Although the values of B/C are consistent with the net present values insofar as the determination of the economic feasibility of individual projects is concerned, they do not give the correct ranking of the mutually exclusive projects. This observation also applies to the values of ORR.

On the other hand, the internal rate of return for each project is independent of the knowledge of the MARR. Although the cash flow profiles for projects $x = 4$, $x = 5$, and $x = 6$ are quite different, each of them has an internal rate of return of 8%. However, for project $x = 4$, neither value of the IRR provides any meaningful information. The IRR values cannot be used to determine the ranking of the mutually exclusive projects.

The payback period provides no useful information for determining the project with maximum profit. It can at best be used as a measure of the liquidity of the cash flow profile for the project selected on the basis of the net present value criterion.

Table 6.10

Cash Flow Profiles (in $1,000) of Six Mutually Exclusive Proposals

t	$A_{t,1}$	$A_{t,2}$	$A_{t,3}$	$A_{t,4}$	$A_{t,5}$	$A_{t,6}$
0	-205	-350	-295	-76.6	-185.5	0
1	$+50$	$+100$	$+70$	$+56$	$+56$	-50
2	$+50$	$+90$	$+70$	$+56$	$+56$	-50
3	$+50$	$+80$	$+70$	$+56$	$+56$	-50
4	$+50$	$+70$	$+70$	$+56$	$+56$	-50
5	$+50$	$+60$	$+70$	-160	0	$+243.3$

Table 6.11

Comparison of Measures of Merit for Six Mutually Exclusive Proposals

Project		$x = 1$	$x = 2$	$x = 3$	$x = 4$	$x = 5$	$x = 6$
NPV ($1,000)	$i = 0\%$	+45.0	+50.0	+55.0	−12.6	+38.5	+43.3
	$i = 3\%$	+24.0	+19.1	+25.6	−6.5	+22.7	+24.0
	$i = 6\%$	+5.6	−8.1	−0.1	−2.1	+8.5	+8.6
ORR	$i = 0\%$	4.0%	2.7%	3.5%	<0%	3.9%	4.0%
	$i = 3\%$	5.3%	4.1%	4.7%	2.4%	5.4%	5.5%
	$i = 6\%$	6.6%	5.5%	6.0%	5.4%	7.0%	7.0%
B/C	$i = 0\%$	1.22	1.14	1.19	0.95	1.21	1.22
	$i = 3\%$	1.12	1.05	1.09	0.97	1.12	1.13
	$i = 6\%$	1.03	0.98	1.00	0.99	1.05	1.05
IRR		7.0%	5.1%	6.0%	8.0% and 33.6%	8.0%	8.0%
PBP (years)		5	5	5	—	4	5
Correct ranking based on [NPV]$_{3\%}$		Second	Fifth	First	Sixth	Fourth	Second

6.7 Optimization of a Continuous Set of Alternatives

In some situations, the alternatives for a proposed project may represent a variation of the project size. Since the cost of an alternative depends on its size, the benefits for a set of mutually exclusive alternatives may be expressed in terms of varying costs. Then the optimal size of the project is the alternative which produces the maximum net benefit.

For the sake of simplicity, we shall consider the ideal case when the present value of the benefits of a project can be expressed as a continuous function of the present value of the costs. Let us introduce the following notation:

C = the present value of the costs in the cash flow profile of a proposed project
B = the present value of the benefits in the cash flow profile of the same project
N = the net present value

Then, the function representing the benefits of a set of alternatives with continuously increasing costs is given by

$$B = f(C) \tag{6.8}$$

For example, the relationship may be in the form of a polynomial

$$B = 1 + \frac{31}{32} C - \frac{1}{2C} \quad \text{for } C \geq 1$$

where both B and C are expressed in millions of dollars. If we wish to consider a set of eight alternatives with $C = 1, 2, \ldots, 8$, we can easily find the corresponding values of B.

The net present value of a set of alternatives may also be expressed as a continuous function of C as follows:

$$N = B - C = f(C) - C \tag{6.9}$$

The value of C that will produce an alternative with maxiumum net benefit may be obtained by taking the first derivative of N with respect to C and setting it equal to zero. That is, if a maximum N exists,

$$\frac{dN}{dC} = 0 \tag{6.10}$$

For $N = B - C$, we have

$$\frac{dN}{dC} = \frac{dB}{dC} - 1 = 0$$

or

$$\frac{dB}{dC} = 1 \tag{6.11}$$

The relationships in Eqs. (6.8) through (6.11) are graphically represented in Fig. 6.12. For any given $B = f(C)$, we can plot a graph of B versus C as shown schematically in part (a) of Fig. 6.12. Note that the inclined line $B/C = 1$ passes through the origin and has a slope of 1 : 1. Hence, the function $B = f(C)$ is above the inclined line when $B > C$. The difference between the curve $B = f(C)$ and the inclined line $B/C = 1$ represents the net present value N. We can also plot a graph of N versus C as shown schematically in part (b) of Fig. 6.12 if N is first obtained from Eq. (6.9). Note that the maximum net benefit $N_{\max}$ occurs at a value of C corresponding to $dN/dC = 0$ or $dB/dC = 1$, as indicated in Fig. 6.12.

Example 6.10

At a site upstream from a town, a dam is being proposed for flood protection. The benefit from the proposed dam is expected to increase with the increasing height of

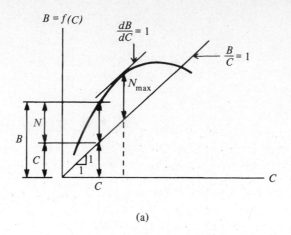

$B = f(C)$

$\dfrac{dB}{dC} = 1$

$\dfrac{B}{C} = 1$

N_{max}

N

B

C

C

C

(a)

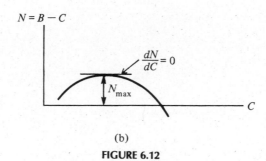

$N = B - C$

$\dfrac{dN}{dC} = 0$

N_{max}

C

(b)

FIGURE 6.12

the dam. The variation of the present value of benefits with respect to the present value of costs may be expressed by

$$B = 1 + \frac{31}{32} C - \frac{1}{2C} \qquad \text{for } C \geq 1$$

where both B and C are expresed in millions of dollars. Determine the value of C that will produce the maximum net benefit N and the value of this net benefit.

Since the maximum net benefit N occurs at the value of C when $dB/dC = 1$ or $dN/dC = 0$, we note that

$$N = B - C = 1 - \frac{1}{32} C - \frac{1}{2C}$$

$$\frac{dN}{dC} = -\frac{1}{32} - \left(\frac{1}{2}\right)(-1)(C^{-2}) = 0$$

Table 6.12

Total Benefits
and Net Benefits
Versus Costs (in 10^6)

C	B	N
1	1.469	0.469
2	2.688	0.688
3	3.740	0.740
4	4.750	0.750
5	5.744	0.744
6	6.729	0.729
7	7.710	0.710
8	8.688	0.688

Hence,

$$\tfrac{1}{2}C^{-2} = \tfrac{1}{32} \quad \text{or} \quad C = 4$$

The second derivative of N is given by

$$\frac{d^2N}{dC^2} = \left(\frac{1}{2}\right)(-2)(C^{-3}) = -C^{-3}$$

At $C = 4$, $d^2N/dC^2 = -1/64$, indicating a maximum N. Hence, the maximum net beneift at $C = 4$ is

$$N = 1 - \frac{4}{32} - \frac{1}{(2)(4)} = \frac{3}{4} = 0.75$$

If we compute the values of B and N for $C = 1, 2, \ldots, 8$, we obtain the results in Table 6.12. The plot of B versus C and that of N versus C will be similar to parts (a) and (b) of Fig. 6.12.

6.8   Minimum Cost and Maximum Benefit Criteria

Two variations of the net present value method are sometimes used to simplify the computation when conditions are warranted. The first is based on a fixed level of performance or effectiveness for all mutually exclusive proposals, and the objective is to select the alternative that requires the minimum cost. The second is based on a fixed or constant cost for all proposals and the objective is to select the alternative that produces the maximum benefit.

Let BPV_x and CPV_x be the present values and costs, respectively, of project x. If BPV_x is known to be constant for a set of m mutually exclusive proposals, then the criterion for selecting a particular proposal j is that it has the minimum discounted cost at present. That is, for $x = 1, 2, \ldots, m$,

$$CPV_j = \min_{x \in m} CPV_x \tag{6.12}$$

provided that

$$NPV_j = BPV_j - CPV_j \geq 0$$

Equation (6.12) is referred to as the *minimum cost criterion*.

On the other hand, if CPV_x is known to be constant for a set of m mutually exclusive proposals, then the criterion for selecting a particular project j is that it has the maximum discounted total benefit at present. That is, for $x = 1, 2, \ldots, m$,

$$BPV_j = \max_{x \in m} BPV_x \tag{6.13}$$

provided that

$$NPV_j = BPV_j - CPV_j \geq 0$$

Equation (6.13) is referred to as the *maximum benefit criterion*.

It is important to emphasize that both Eqs. (6.12) and (6.13) are based on the condition that $BPV_j - CPV_j \geq 0$. They should be used only if that condition can be fulfilled.

Example 6.11

A plant engineer is considering the purchase of one of the three lathes that can perform the intended functions equally well. The estimated service lives of the three alternatives ($x = 1, 2, 3$) as well as the cost streams over the service lives are given in Table 6.13. Assume that within a planning horizon of 20 years, each alternative will be perpetually replaced at the end of its service life and the cost stream of each replacement is identical to that of the original lathe. If MARR is 6%, select the alternative that requires the minimum cost.

Table 6.13

Cost Streams of Alternatives in Example 6.11

	$x = 1$	$x = 2$	$x = 3$
Service life (years)	20	10	5
Purchase cost ($1,000s)	25	20	10
Annual maintenance ($1,000s)	1	1.2	2
Salvage value at end ($1,000s)	5	3	1

The cost streams of the three alternatives are depicted in Fig. 6.13 in which the planning horizon coincides with the expiration of all three alternatives. The present values of the costs of these alternatives are computed as follows:

$$[CPV_1]_{6\%} = 25 + (1)(P \mid U, 6\%, 20) - (5)(P \mid F, 6\%, 20)$$
$$= 25 + (1)(11.4699) - (5)(0.3118) = 34.911$$

$$[CPV_2]_{6\%} = [20 + (1.2)(P \mid U, 6\%, 10) - (3)(P \mid F, 6\%, 10)][1 + (P \mid F, 6\%, 10)]$$
$$= [20 + (1.2)(7.3601) - (3)(0.5584)](+0.5584) = 42.321$$

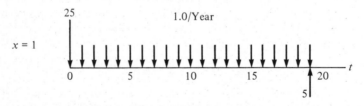

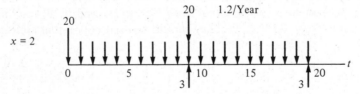

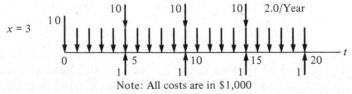

Note: All costs are in $1,000

FIGURE 6.13

$$[CPV_3]_{6\%} = [10 + (2)(P|U, 6\%, 5] - (1)(P|F, 6\%, 5)][1 + (P|F, 6\%, 5)$$
$$+ (P|F, 6\%, 10) + (P|F, 6\%, 15)]$$
$$= [10 + (2)(4.2124) - (1)(0.7473)](1 + 0.7473 + 0.5584 + 0.4173)$$
$$= 48.136$$

Since alternative $x = 1$ has the minimum cost, it should be selected.

For this particular problem in which the planning horizon coincides with the expiration of all three alternatives, the solution can be simplified by considering the equivalent uniform annual value of costs of the alternatives. Let CUV_x be the equivalent uniform annual value of costs of alternative x. Then,

$$[CUV_1]_{6\%} = (25)(U|P, 6\%, 20) + 1 - (5)(U|F, 6\%, 20)$$
$$= (25)(0.0872) + 1 - (5)(0.0272) = 3.044$$

$$[CUV_2]_{6\%} = (20)(U|P, 6\%, 10) + 1.2 - (3)(U|F, 6\%, 10)$$
$$= (20)(0.1359) + 1.2 - (3)(0.0759) = 3.690$$

$$[CUV_3]_{6\%} = (10)(U|P, 6\%, 5) + 2 - (1)(U|F, 6\%, 5)$$
$$= (10)(0.2374) + 2 - (1)(0.1774) = 4.197$$

Again, alternative $x = 1$ should be selected.

Note that the simplification by using the equivalent uniform annual values of costs is possible because of the assumption in the problem statement concerning the replacements in the planning horizon. Such an assumption should be used only if it is justified.

Example 6.12

A small community is expected to receive a revenue-sharing grant from the federal government and intends to spend the full amount on one of the two capital project improvements. The first project will generate a stream of benefits over a period of 5 years with $10,000 for the first year, $9,000 for the second year, $8,000 for the third year, $7,000 for the fourth year, and $6,000 for the fifth year. The second project will generate a stream of uniform benefits of $10,000 per year over a period of 4 years, and no replacement will be made in the fifth year. If the MARR is 10%, which project will provide greater benefits?

Using a planning horizon of 5 years, the present values of the benefits of these two mutually exclusive projects can be computed as follows:

$$[BPV_1]_{10\%} = (10,000)(P|U, 10\%, 5) - (1,000)(P|G, 10\%, 5)$$
$$(10,000)(3.7908) - (1,000)(6.8618) = 31,046$$

$$[BPV_2]_{10\%} = (10,000)(P|U, 10\%, 4) = (10,000)(3.1699) = 31,699$$

The second project produces the maximum benefit and should be selected.

The equivalent uniform annual values of benefits (BUV_x) of project x (for $x = 1$ and $x = 2$) over the 5-year period can also be obtained as follows:

$$[\mathrm{BUV}_1]_{10\%} = (31{,}046)(U\,|\,P,\ 10\%,\ 5) = (31{,}046)(0.2638) = 8{,}190$$

$$[\mathrm{BUV}_2]_{10\%} = (31{,}699)(U\,|\,P,\ 10\%,\ 5) = (31{,}699)(0.2638) = 8{,}362$$

Again, the second project yields the maximum benefit and is the preferred alternative.

6.9   Treatment of Relative Benefits and Costs

In some situations, certain components of benefits and/or costs are difficult to measure, but they are expected to be virtually identical for all mutually exclusive alternatives under consideration. For such cases, *relative* benefits and costs of the alternatives excluding the unmeasured components may be used in the evaluation of the *relative* merits of these alternatives. In other words, in using relative benefits and/or costs, we can correctly rank the mutually exclusive alternatives, but we cannot find out whether even the best alternative has a nonnegative net present value.

The minimum cost and maximum benefit criteria discussed in Section 6.7 represent two special cases often used in comparing the relative merits of mutually exclusive alternatives without determining the net present values of the alternatives. However, this concept has other applications in a broader context in investment decision making. For example, a capital investment project may be deemed very important in achieving certain socially desired goals whether or not it is economically acceptable, and the problem confronting the decision maker may then become the maximization of the net benefit subject to a given level of subsidy. In such a case, we will be primarily interested in the relative merits of different plans or designs in implementing this project.

In general, we may deal with relative benefits and/or costs of various projects in any periods over the planning horizon. Let us introduce the following notation:

L_t = benefit items in year t omitted from all alternatives
M_t = cost items in year t omitted from all alternatives
K_t = net benefits in year t omitted from all alternatives
$\bar{B}_{t,x}$ = relative annual benefits in year t for alternative x
$\bar{C}_{t,x}$ = relative annual costs in year t for alternative x
$\bar{A}_{t,x}$ = relative annual net benefits in period t for alternative x

Then, the actual benefits, costs, and net benefits in period t for alternative x are, respectively,

$$B_{t,x} = \bar{B}_{t,x} + L_t \tag{6.14}$$

$$C_{t,x} = \bar{C}_{t,x} + M_t \tag{6.15}$$

$$A_{t,x} = \bar{A}_{t,x} + K_t \tag{6.16}$$

where

$$K_t = L_t - M_t \tag{6.17}$$

$$\bar{A}_{t,x} = \bar{B}_{t,x} - \bar{C}_{t,x} \tag{6.18}$$

Consequently, from Eq. (5.2) in Chapter 5

$$\begin{aligned} \text{NPV}_x &= \sum_{t=0}^{n} A_{t,x}(1 + i)^{-t} \\ &= \sum_{t=0}^{n} \bar{A}_{t,x}(1 + i)^{-t} + \sum_{t=0}^{n} K_t(1 + i)^{-t} \end{aligned}$$

or

$$\text{NPV}_x = \overline{\text{NPV}}_x + \bar{K} \tag{6.19}$$

where

$$\overline{\text{NPV}}_x = \sum_{t=0}^{n} \bar{A}_{t,x}(1 + i)^{-t} \tag{6.20}$$

$$\bar{K} = \sum_{t=0}^{n} K_t(1 + i)^{-t} \tag{6.21}$$

Note that $\overline{\text{NPV}}_x$ is the present value of an alternative x when the relative values of some benefits and/or costs are used for all mutually exclusive alternatives, and $\bar{K}$ is the net present value of the benefits and/or cost items that have been omitted in assessing the relative benefits and/or costs of all alternatives. Since $\bar{K}$ is a constant which is independent of a particular alternative, $\overline{\text{NPV}}_x$ will be maximized whenever NPV_x is maximized, and vice versa.

When we make pairwise comparisons of two alternatives, say x and y, to determine their relative merits, it is convenient to consider the incremental cash flow profile of x over y and to find the incremental net present value of x over y. In view of Eq. (6.16), the incremental cash flow profile of x over y as represented by Eq. (6.4) becomes

$$\Delta A_{t,x-y} = (\bar{A}_{t,x} + K_t) - (\bar{A}_{t,y} + K_t)$$

or

$$\Delta A_{t,x-y} = \bar{A}_{t,x} - \bar{A}_{t,y} \tag{6.22}$$

Similarly, in view of Eq. (6.19), the incremental net present value of x over y as represented by Eq. (6.5) becomes

$$\Delta \text{NPV}_{x-y} = (\overline{\text{NPV}_x + \bar{K}}) - (\overline{\text{NPV}_y + \bar{K}})$$

or

$$\Delta \text{NPV}_{x-y} = \overline{\text{NPV}_x} - \overline{\text{NPV}_y} \tag{6.23}$$

In other words, the use of relative benefits and/or costs will not affect the pairwise comparison of mutually exclusive alternatives if the incremental net present value (INPV) of these alternatives is used as the criterion for making the choice. That is, alternative x is at least as good or better than alternative y if

$$\Delta \text{NPV}_{x-y} \geq 0 \tag{6.24}$$

Example 6.13

The Public Works Department of Alomos County plans either to rent or buy a special grader for repairing its access roads. The rental fee for the grader is $60 per day. The purchase price of the grader is $12,000 with an estimated useful life of 4 years and an estimated salvage value of $2,000 at the end of 4 years. The annual maintenance cost of the grader, if purchased, is estimated to be $1,200. All other benefits and expenses are otherwise identical. Based on MARR = 12%, how many working days per year must this grader be used in order to make the purchase worthwhile in comparison with renting?

Let W be the number of working days that the grader will be used during a year. Then, the cash flow profiles over 4 years for purchase (alternative x) and renting (alternative y) are given by $\bar{A}_{t,x}$ and $\bar{A}_{t,y}$ in Table 6.14, from which the incremental cash flow profile $\bar{A}_{t,x-y}$ is computed.

Table 6.14

Computation of the Incremental Cash Flow Profile

t	$\bar{A}_{t,x}$	$\bar{A}_{t,y}$	$\Delta \bar{A}_{t,x-y} = \bar{A}_{t,x} - \bar{A}_{t,y}$
0	$-12,000$	0	$-12,000$
1–4 (each)	$-1,200$	$-60W$	$-1,200 + 60W$
4	$+2,000$	0	$+2,000$

Hence,

$$\Delta NPV_{x-y} = -12,000 + (60W - 1,200)(P\,|\,U, 12\%, 4) + (2,000)(P\,|\,F, 12\%, 4)$$
$$= -12,000 + (60W - 1,200)(3.0373) + (2,000)(0.6355)$$
$$= -14,374 + 182.24W$$

For $\Delta NPV_{x-y} = 0$, we get $W = 79$. In other words, the alternative of purchasing the grader is preferred if it will be used for 79 days or more during each year.

6.10   Decisions on the Timing of Investments

Frequently, the choice of investment alternatives may involve decisions on the timing of investments. Examples of such considerations include multiple-stage acquisition, replacement, and capitalization of a physical asset.

In planning large-scale facilities, we are often confronted with the decision whether the project should be constructed for the "ultimate capacity" or constructed in multiple stages with limited capacities in the intermediate stages. The choice depends on the projected demand as well as the difference in costs between single-stage and multiple-stage construction. For some facilities, such as urban highways, the demand will grow rapidly as more facilities are added to reduce the congestion. Consequently, there is no such thing as the "ultimate capacity." On the other hand, in constructing a sewage treatment plant for a new community, it is reasonable to expect that the demand will grow gradually over the years until the community reaches its maturity in population growth. Consequently, each situation must be considered individually on the basis of the available information.

In the replacement of existing facilities, the question often raised is whether the facility should be replaced now or some time later if the facility can be maintained or overhauled to last until a later date. In such a situation, at least several important issues should be considered. First, assuming that the demand and/or the benefit of having the facility remains unchanged, what is the optimal period that the existing facility should be kept in order to minimize the equivalent uniform annual value of costs during this period? Second, under the same conditions, what is the likelihood of current advances in technology which may reduce drastically the costs of a new facility as replacement? Third, what is the projected demand and potential increase in benefits if a new facility is introduced as replacement? The answer to the first question is relatively simple and will be discussed later in Chapter 10. The remaining two questions are much more complex and must be dealt with according to the available information.

Since some public projects, particularly infrastructures in urban areas, are expected to provide service "forever," it is interesting to find out the difference in funding a project with a finite useful life and a project with an "infinite" useful life. Although no physical asset will last forever, it is possible to provide a sufficient fund at the beginning of the planning horizon so that a physical asset with finite useful life can be constructed and, at the end of its useful life, be replaced by an identical asset, and this process of replacement can be repeated forever. The fund required at the beginning of the planning horizon for achieving such purposes is referred to as the *capitalization cost* of a project. If U denotes the equivalent uniform annual value of costs of a project and P_c denotes its capitalizing cost, then from Eq. (3.16) in Chapter 3, we have for $n = \infty$

$$U = P_c(U \mid P, i, \infty)$$

Note that by carrying out the division in the compound interest factor,

$$(U \mid P, i, \infty) = \lim_{n \to \infty} \left[\frac{i(1 + i)^n}{(1 + i)^n - 1} \right] = \lim_{n \to \infty} \left[i + \frac{i}{(1 + i)^n - 1} \right] = i$$

Consequently, $U = P_c i$, or

$$P_c = \frac{U}{i} \qquad (6.25)$$

Example 6.14

In planning the water supply for a new community over the next 40 years, the City Water Authority is considering the following two plans. Using a MARR of 10%, determine which plan is preferable.

1. Build the complete system now at a cost of $220 million. The net revenues from supplying the local residents are expected to grow from $10 million in the first year to $48 million in the twentieth year, increasing at a rate of $2 million per year, and to reach a uniform amount of $50 million per year for the subsequent 20 years.
2. Build the system in two stages at a cost of $140 million now and another $140 million 20 years later. The net revenues from the plan are expected to grow from $10 million in the first year to $48.8 million in the twenty-fifth year, increasing at a rate of $1.6 million per year and to reach a uniform amount of $50 million per year for the subsequent 15 years.

The net present values of plans 1 and 2 (in millions of dollars) can be computed from the cash flow profiles shown in Fig. 6.14 as follows:

$$
\begin{aligned}
[\text{NPV}_1]_{10\%} &= -220 + (50)(P \mid U, 10\%, 40) - (50 - 10)(P \mid U, 10\%, 20) \\
&\quad + (2)(P \mid G, 10\%, 20) \\
&= -220 + (50)(9.7791) - (40)(8.5136) + (2)(55.4069) \\
&= \$39.225 \text{ million}
\end{aligned}
$$

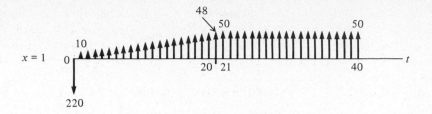

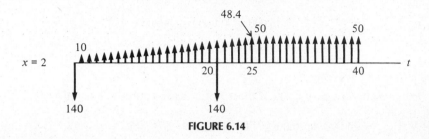

FIGURE 6.14

$$[\text{NPV}_2]_{10\%} = -140 - (140)(P\,|\,F,\,10\%,\,20) + (50)(P\,|\,U,\,10\%,\,40)$$
$$- (50 - 10)(P\,|\,U,\,10\%,\,25) + (1.6)(P\,|\,G,\,10\%,\,25)$$
$$= -(140)(1 + 0.1486) + (50)(9.7791) - (40)(9.0770) + (1.6)(67.6964)$$
$$= \$73.385 \text{ million}$$

Since plan 2 has a higher nonnegative net present value, it is preferable.

Example 6.15

A consulting firm is leasing a minicomputer from its manufacturer which offers three options with annual payments at the beginning of each year.

1. A 1-year lease at $24,000
2. A 3-year lease at $22,000 per year
3. A 5-year lease at $18,000 per year

The consulting firm expects that a new model of this minicomputer with the same capacity will be available for leasing next year at $16,000 per year if the firm waits until then to sign up for a 4-year lease. Furthermore, another new model with the same capacity will be ready for leasing 3 years from now at $11,000 per year with no time limit. The consulting firm is expected to be in business in the next 5 years and has a MARR of 10%. Which option should it choose?

Using a planning horizon of 5 years, the cash flow profiles for the three options are as shown in Table 6.15.

Table 6.15

Cash Flow Profiles for Three Options

t	$C_{t,1}$	$C_{t,2}$	$C_{t,3}$
0	24,000	22,000	18,000
1	16,000	22,000	18,000
2	16,000	22,000	18,000
3	16,000	11,000	18,000
4	16,000	11,000	18,000

The present values of costs of these options are computed as follows:

$$[CPV_1]_{10\%} = 24,000 + 16,000(P\,|\,U, 10\%, 4) = \$74,718$$

$$[CPV_2]_{10\%} = 22,000 + 11,000(P\,|\,U, 10\%, 2) + 11,000(P\,|\,U, 10\%, 4) = \$75,959$$

$$[CPV_3]_{10\%} = 18,000 + 18,000(P\,|\,U, 10\%, 4) = \$75,058$$

The first option has the minimum present value and is preferable.

Example 6.16

A city is spending \$10 million on a new sewage system with the expectation that it will last 50 years with no salvage value at the end of that period. If the MARR specified by the city is 8%, what is the capitalized cost of the system?

Since the cost of the system is \$10 million and it is expected to last 50 years with no salvage value at the end, the equivalent uniform annual value of costs is

$$U = P(U\,|\,P, 8\%, 50) = (10)(0.081743) = \$0.81743 \text{ million}$$

Note that the compound interest factor has been computed for more significant figures than that given in the table in Appendix A in order to provide the accuracy desired. The capitalized cost for the system can be obtained by Eq. (6.24):

$$P_c = \frac{U}{i} = \frac{0.81743}{0.08} = \$10.217875 \text{ million}$$

Thus, the additional amount to be raised now is

$$P_0 = 10.217875 - 10 = \$0.217875 \text{ million}$$

Since we are dealing with the difference between two numbers, the value of U must be carried to a sufficient number of digits in order to avoid serious truncation errors. Then, we can expect a present sum of $P_0 = 0.217875$ to produce a sum of $P_c = 10.217875$ at $n = 50$ so that the cycle can be repeated forever. That is,

$$P_c = P_0(F \mid P, 8\%, 50) = (0.217875)(46.9016) = \$10.218686 \text{ million}$$

The discrepancy between \$10.218686 million and \$10.217875 million is caused by the truncation of the digits in the computation.

6.11 Summary and Study Guide

This chapter has presented the basic principles in the economic evaluation of mutually exclusive proposals. It has emphasized the direct approaches by which the best among a set of mutually exclusive alternatives can be selected in a straightforward and unambiguous manner. Examples of solutions based on the net present value criterion are given throughout the entire chapter.

Since the minimum attractive rate of return is crucially important in the computation of the net present value but difficult to pinpoint exactly, the NPV-MARR graph for mutually exclusive alternatives can be used to examine the sensitivity of ranking the alternatives based on their net present values. Specifically, the relationship between the incremental net present value (INPV) and the incremental internal rate of return (IIRR) is considered in order to find the intersection of the curves representing the net present values of any two of the alternatives. Thus, the values of the MARR at which the ranking of various alternatives may change can be determined.

While the net present value is a convenient direct indicator of the profit potential of an investment proposal, other indicators may also be obtained for a proposal once it has been selected as the best among a set of mutually exclusive alternatives on the basis of the net present value criterion. However, it is important to distinguish among the measures of merit and the methods of analysis when we deal with the benefit-cost ratios or the internal rates of return. The methods of analysis based on these two measures will be discussed in Chapters 7 and 8, respectively.

When the present value of benefits of a project can be expressed as a continuous function of the present value of costs, the optimal alternative which produces the maximum net benefit can be obtained by differential calculus. If the proposed alternatives represent a continuous variation of the project size, then the optimal size of the project is the alternative with the maximum net benefit.

If the level of performance or effectiveness for all mutually exclusive proposals is fixed, the objective can be regarded as selecting the alternative which requires the minimum total cost. On the other hand, if the cost of all proposals is fixed or constant, the objective then is to select the alternative that produces the maximum benefits. The minimum cost and maximum benefit criteria represent two special cases used in comparing the relative merits of mutually exclusive alternatives without determining the net present values of the alternatives. In general, we may deal with relative benefits and/or costs of various projects when certain components of benefits and/or costs are difficult to measure. When we make pairwise comparisons of two alternatives to determine their relative merits, it is often convenient to consider the incremental cash flow profile of the alternatives and to use the incremental net present value as the criterion in selecting the better of the two alternatives.

Finally, the choice of investment alternatives may involve decisions on the timing of investments. Some examples are given to illustrate decisions related to multiple-phase acquisition, replacement, and capitalization of a physical asset.

REFERENCES

6.1 Hirschleifer, J., J. C. DeHaven, and J. W. Milliman, *Water Supply Economics, Technology and Policy.* Chicago, IL: University of Chicago Press, 1960.

6.2 Winfrey, R., *Economic Analysis for Highways.* Scranton, PA: International Textbook Co., 1969.

6.3 Wohl, M., and B. V. Martin, *Traffic Systems Analysis for Engineers and Planners.* New York: McGraw-Hill, 1967.

PROBLEMS

P6.1 Three mutually exclusive proposals, each with a life of 5 years, have cash flow profiles as follows. Using a MARR of 8%, select the best proposal.

t	$A_{t,1}$	$A_{t,2}$	$A_{t,3}$
0	$-\$1,597$	$-\$1,650$	$-\$1,500$
1	$+$ 400	$+$ 500	$+$ 300
2	$+$ 400	$+$ 450	$+$ 350
3	$+$ 400	$+$ 400	$+$ 400
4	$+$ 400	$+$ 350	$+$ 450
5	$+$ 400	$+$ 300	$+$ 500

P6.2 Three mutually exclusive proposals with cash flow profiles given below are being considered for a planning horizon of 5 years. Using a MARR of 6%, select the best proposal.

t	$A_{t,1}$	$A_{t,2}$	$A_{t,3}$
0	$-\$ 76.6$	$-\$185.5$	$\$ 0$
1	$+$ 56	$+$ 56	$-$ 50
2	$+$ 56	$+$ 56	$-$ 50
3	$+$ 56	$+$ 56	$-$ 50
4	$+$ 56	$+$ 56	$-$ 50
5	$-$ 160	0	$+$ 243.3

P6.3 Find the overall rates of return for all three proposals in Problem P6.1 and determine which proposal should be selected.

P6.4 Plot the NPV-MARR graph of the three proposals in Problem P6.1 for $i = 0\%$, 5%, and 10%.

P6.5 Two different oil pumps may be used for the extraction of oil from a well for 2 more years. The more expensive pump will permit the oil to be extracted quicker and slightly increase the total amount of oil extracted. After 2 years, the well is expected to be dry, and there is no salvage value for either pump. The benefit and cost streams of the two pumps are given below. Using a MARR of 15%, determine which pump should be selected. Also, compare the overall rates of return for both pumps.

t	$A_{t,1}$	$A_{t,2}$
0	$-\$100,000$	$-\$110,000$
1	$+\ \ \ 70,000$	$+\ \ 115,000$
2	$+\ \ \ 70,000$	$+\ \ \ \ 30,000$

P6.6 Two different designs of a heat exchanger for a chemical processing plant are being considered. Both heat exchangers are expected to last 10 years with no salvage value at the end of 10 years. The benefits and costs associated with these two designs are given below. Using a MARR of 12%, determine which design should be selected. Also compare the overall rates of return for both designs.

t	$A_{t,1}$	$A_{t,2}$
0	$-\$250,000$	$-\$200,000$
1–5 (each)	$+\ \ \ 50,000$	$+\ \ \ 30,000$
6–10 (each)	$+\ \ \ 40,000$	$+\ \ \ 40,000$

P6.7 The cash flow profiles of three mutually exclusive alternatives of 1-year's duration are given as follows:

t	$A_{t,1}$	$A_{t,2}$	$A_{t,3}$
0	$-\$100$	$-\$200$	$-\$300$
1	$+\ 150$	$+\ 280$	$+\ 395$

Find their net present values for the range of MARR with $i = 0\%$, 10%, 20%, 30%, 40%, and 50%, and plot the NPV-MARR graph. Determine the IRR for these projects, i.e., i_1, i_2, and i_3. Verify also that the values of IIRR are $i_{3-2} = 15\%$, $i_{3-1} = 22.5\%$, and $i_{2-1} = 30\%$.

P6.8 The cash flow profiles of three mutually exclusive alternatives of 2 years' duration are given as follows:

t	$A_{t,1}$	$A_{t,2}$	$A_{t,3}$
0	$-\$500$	$-\$1,000$	$-\$2,000$
1	0	$+\ \ \ 591.7$	$+\ 1,200$
2	$+\ 720$	$+\ \ \ 591.7$	$+\ 1,100$

Find their net present values for the range of MARR with $i = 0\%$, 5%, 10%, 15%, and 20%, and plot the NPV-MARR graph.

P6.9 Find the internal rates of return and the incremental internal rate of return where applicable for the three mutually exclusive projects in Problem P6.8.

P6.10 Plot the NPV-MARR graph of the three mutually exclusive projects in Problem P6.2 for $i = 0\%$, 4%, 8%, and 12%.

P6.11 The benefit for a set of alternative projects with continuously increasing costs may be expressed by the function

$$B = 2\sqrt{C}$$

where the cost C is the present value of costs and B is the present value of benefits, both expressed in millions of dollars.

(a) Determine the maximum net benefit N and the corresponding cost C.
(b) Plot a graph showing the relation of net benefit N versus cost C for the range of values of $C = 0$, 1, 2, 3, 4, and 5.

P6.12 The benefit for a set of alternative projects with continuously increasing costs may be expressed by the function

$$B = 3C - \tfrac{1}{4}(C^2 + 7) \quad C \geq 1$$

where B is the present value of benefits and C is the present value of costs over the planning horizon, both expressed in millions of dollars. Determine the value of C that will maximize the net benefit N and find the corresponding maximum value of N.

P6.13 Two different types of conveyers can be used to transport rocks to a rock crusher at a large construction site. The construction project is expected to last 5 years and the MARR of 6% is specified for the project. Determine which conveyer should be selected on the basis of the following information:

	Type I	Type II
Initial cost	$3,000	$4,000
Annual operating and maintenance cost	600	400
Salvage value after 5 years	500	800
Annual benefits for rocks transported	$1,500	$1,600

P6.14 An industrial firm is considering the purchase of a machine for the performance of a given task in the next 10 years. Two machines with different physical characteristics but performing equally well are available. Using a MARR of 8%, and assuming that the costs of replacements are identical to the originals, determine which alternative should be selected.

	Machine 1	Machine 2
Estimated useful life	5 years	7 years
Installed cost	$10,000	$13,000
Salvage value at the end of life	$1,000	$1,000
Salvage values after 3 years	$3,000	$6,000
Uniform annual operating cost	$1,200	$1,000

P6.15 A culvert of 4-foot diameter under an existing roadway for the runoff from a creek is causing flooding during heavy rains. To remedy the situation, two solutions have been proposed for consideration:

1. Remove the existing culvert and replace it with a 6-foot-diameter culvert at an installed cost of $8,000. This new culvert is expected to last 30 years and has no salvage value when abandoned.
2. Add a new 4-foot-diameter culvert alongside the existing culvert at an installed cost of $5,000. This new culvert is expected to last 30 years and has no salvage value when abandoned. However, the existing culvert will last only 15 more years, at which time it must be replaced by another 4-foot-diameter culvert at an installed cost of $5,000.

Assuming that the roadway will be abandoned 30 years from now and using a MARR of 12%, determine which alternative should be selected.

P6.16 A firm is considering the option of either purchasing or leasing a minicomputer that is estimated to have a useful life of 5 years and no salvage value at the end of 5 years. The initial cost for purchase is $200,000, and the maintenance cost charged to the firm at the end of each year is $20,000. For leasing, an annual payment must be made at the beginning of each year, and, in addition, the annual maintenance cost charged to the firm at the end of each year is $10,000 because only part of the maintenance is done under the lease agreement. Using a MARR of 10%, determine the annual payment for leasing that will make the two alternatives equally attractive.

P6.17 An irrigation project is proposed for the development of a rural area. Two alternatives in timing are under consideration:

1. If the project is constructed to full capacity now, the initial construction cost will be $1,000,000, and the benefit will be $100,000 per year in the next 40 years. There will be no salvage value at the end of 40 years.
2. If the project is constructed in two stages, the initial construction cost for the first stage will be $400,000 and the benefit will be $40,000 per year until the second stage will be added at the end of 20 years. The construction cost for the second stage will be $800,000 but the benefit will be $100,000 per year from the twenty-first through the fortieth year. There will be no salvage value.

If a MARR of 8% is specified, determine which alternative should be selected.

P6.18 A cable television company plans to construct a system of cable networks in a new community in two stages. The initial installation cost for the first stage will be $2 million and the benefit will be $300,000 per year until the second stage is completed. The installation cost for the second stage will also be $2 million but the benefit from the year after the installation of the second stage to the end of the planning horizon will be $400,000 per year. The system is planned for 30 years with no salvage value at the end. Assuming a MARR of 6%, determine the net present value for the range of timing of the second stage installation at the end of 10, 15, and 20 years.

CHAPTER

7

THE BENEFIT-COST
RATIO METHOD

7.1 A Historical Perspective

The idea that benefits of a capital investment project should be measured and that they should exceed costs in order for the project to be justified was institutionalized in the United States by the Flood Control Act of 1936, which established the principle of benefit-cost analysis for public projects.[1] As a result of this act and subsequent legislation, the principle of benefit-cost analysis was applied in the late 1930s to a number of programs under the jurisdiction of the Corps of Engineers, the Department of Agriculture, and the Bureau of Reclamation of the Department of Interior. By 1950, attempts had been made to standardize the practices for economic evaluation of water projects undertaken by these and other government agencies including the Federal Power Commission and the Department of Commerce. The report to the Federal Inter-Agency River Basin Committee,[2] prepared by the Subcommittee on Benefits and Costs, in May 1950, identifies the ratio of benefits to costs as the criterion to indicate the relative merits of different proposals. The report, which is frequently referred to as *the green book*, provides a rational basis for accepting and selecting public projects to be undertaken by these government agencies. Although the benefit-cost ratio is not necessarily the only measure used for the comparison of projects, the higher the ratio above unity, the more favorably a project is generally looked upon by the federal agency and the U. S. Congress. Consequently, the method of economic evaluation which uses the benefit-cost ratio as a decision criterion is referred to as the *benefit-cost ratio method*.

The use of the benefit-cost ratio as a measure of the worth of public projects is by no means confined to federal agencies or to water projects only. For example, the American Association of State Highway Officials describes only the benefit-cost ratio method in its information report by the Committee on Planning and Design

---

[1] See *United States Code* (Washington, D.C.: Government Printing Office, 1940), p. 2964.
[2] See Ref. [7.2], p. 14.

179

Policies on Road User Benefit Analyses for Highway Improvements.[3] This report, which is frequently referred to as *the red book*, has promoted the use of the benefit-cost ratio method almost exclusively for economic evaluation in the highway field from 1952 to 1977.

The benefit-cost ratio method is not as straightforward and unambiguous as the net present value method but, if applied correctly, should produce the same results as the net present value method. The pitfalls of using the benefit-cost ratio as a measure of merit or as a decision criterion in project evaluation are well known.[4] However, because the method has been used widely for half of a century, it is still preferred by those who are familiar with it.

Therefore, we shall treat the benefit-cost ratio method as completely as possible so that it will at least be correctly used if an analyst so chooses. We will go beyond the brief discussion in Chapters 5 and 6 and examine some causes of misunderstanding and misuse of the method. Specifically, we will discuss two aspects of its application in economic evaluation:

1. The use of the benefit-cost ratio method in the *direct analysis* of the acceptability of an independent project (in comparison with the null alternative).
2. The use of the benefit-cost ratio method in the *incremental analysis* through successive pairwise comparisons for the selection of the best among a set of mutually exclusive alternatives.

The application of the benefit-cost ratio method when capital rationing is imposed will be discussed in Chapter 9.

7.2   Independent Projects Versus Mutually Exclusive Projects

In order to understand clearly the necessity of using the direct analysis for evaluating independent projects and the incremental analysis for evaluating mutually exclusive projects when the benefit-cost ratio is used as a decision criterion, let us first examine the relationship between the *present value* of the benefits and the *present value* of the costs of a group of proposed projects on a benefit-cost graph. For the sake of simplicity, let us introduce the following abbreviations:

C = the present value of the costs (CPV) in the cash flow profile of a proposed project
B = the present value of the benefits (BPV) in the cash flow profile of the same project
N = the net present value (NPV)

---

[3] For an updated version of this report, which has corrected a number of erroneous concepts in its 1960 version, see Ref. [7.3], especially pp. 156–157.
[4] For a detailed explanation, see Ref. [7.1], especially pp. 113–116.

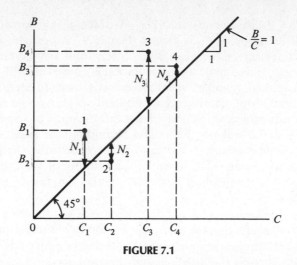

FIGURE 7.1

A typical benefit-cost graph showing four proposed projects is given in Fig. 7.1. Note that the inclined line $B/C = 1$ passes through the origin and has a slope of $1 : 1$, i.e., at a 45° angle with the horizontal axis C. Hence, the value B_x corresponding to the value C_x for project x should be above the inclined line $B/C = 1$ if $B_x > C_x$, and otherwise if $B_x < C_x$. The algebraic difference between B_x and the point on the inclined line $B/C = 1$ corresponding to C_x represents the net present value N_x for project x ($x = 1, 2, 3,$ or 4 for the four proposed projects.)

If the proposed projects are independent of each other and we are only interested in determining whether each of them is economically feasible, we can plot the benefit-cost ratios for all projects on the benefit-cost graph as shown in Fig. 7.2. The

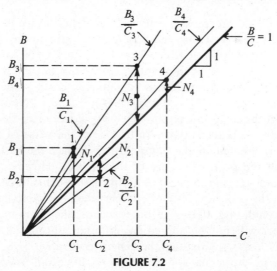

FIGURE 7.2

inclined line $B/C = 1$ corresponds to NPV $= 0$ since $B = C$ for all points on the line. Therefore, if the slope B_x/C_x is greater than 1, N_x is positive, as in the case of $x = 1, 3$, and 4; conversely, if the slope B_x/C_x is less than 1, N_x is negative, as in the case of $x = 2$. Hence, this graphical representation is consistent with the benefit-cost ratio criterion for evaluating independent projects discussed in Section 5.8.

However, if the proposed projects are mutually exclusive, we will be interested in determining which project is the best among this group of proposed projects. The ratios B_x/C_x in Fig. 7.2 will not be helpful in finding the best project since the project with the maximum benefit-cost ratio is not necessarily the project with the maximum net present value. Consequently, the ranking of the profit potentials of mutually exclusive projects cannot be based on the ranking of their benefit-cost ratios.

We shall therefore follow two different approaches in using the concept of benefit-cost ratio for evaluating the economic feasibility of independent projects and for selecting the best project among mutually exclusive proposals. These two approaches are referred to as the *direct analysis* and the *incremental analysis*, respectively.

7.3   Direct Analysis of Independent Projects

The direct analysis makes use of the criterion for accepting an independent project on the basis of the benefit-cost ratio, which has been developed in Section 5.9 and is restated as follows:

$$\frac{B_x}{C_x} = \frac{\text{BPV}_x}{\text{CPV}_x} \geq 1 \tag{7.1}$$

where BPV_x and CPV_x are present values of benefits and costs, respectively, of project x. It should be noted that the benefit-cost ratio in Eq. (7.1) may also be based on $\text{BFV}_x/\text{CFV}_x$ or $\text{BUV}_x/\text{CUV}_x$ where BFV_x and CFV_x are future values of benefits and costs, respectively, compounded to the future time n, while BUV_x and CUV_x are the equivalent uniform annual benefits and costs, respectively. Such substitutions are possible because NFV $= 0$ and NUV $= 0$ when NPV $= 0$.

Some items in the cash flow profile of a project can often be interpreted either as additional benefits or reduced costs. In that case, the value of B_x/C_x depends on how such items are treated in the computation; hence the ratio B_x/C_x is not a reliable measure of the profit potential of the project. However, if the project is acceptable when such items are treated as additional benefits in computing B_x/C_x, it can be shown that the project is also acceptable when the same items are treated as reduced costs in computing B_x/C_x. In other words, the economic feasibility of an independent project will not be altered by different interpretations of additional benefits or reduced costs in computing the benefit-cost ratio.

Consider, for example, that the cash flow profile of an investment project has been established except one item. Let the present value of this item be d, which may be interpreted either as an additional benefit or a reduced cost, while the present values of benefits and costs of the remaining items in the cash flow profile are denoted by b and c, respectively. Suppose that we consider the following two cases: (1) d is an additional benefit; (2) d is a reduced cost. By using Eq. (5.8) to compute the net present value, we get

$$(1) \ \text{NPV} = (b + d) - c = b - c + d$$

$$(2) \ \text{NPV} = b - (c - d) = b - c + d$$

On the other hand, by using Eq. (5.11) to compute the benefit-cost ratio we have

$$(1) \ \frac{B}{C} = \frac{b + d}{c}$$

$$(2) \ \frac{B}{C} = \frac{b}{c - d}$$

It can be seen that if d is identified either as an additional benefit or a reduced cost, Eq. (5.8) yields the same NPV for both cases (1) and (2) whereas Eq. (5.11) leads to different B/C ratios. However, if

$$\frac{b + d}{c} \geq 1 \qquad (\text{i.e., } b + d \geq c)$$

then

$$\frac{b}{c - d} \geq 1 \qquad (\text{i.e., } b \geq c - d)$$

That is, if a project is acceptable on the basis of the first ratio, it is also acceptable on the basis of the second ratio. Therefore, the economic feasibility of the project will not be altered.

The same reasoning can be applied to similar situations in which the value of the benefit-cost ratio can be changed by the relative values of benefits and costs used in the computation. For example, the cash flow profile of a project is often represented by the *net* annual cash flow A_t (for $t = 0, 1, 2, \ldots$) instead of separate time streams of benefits B_t of costs C_t (both for $t = 0, 1, 2, \ldots$). Furthermore, some items such as the salvage value of a physical asset may be treated either as benefits or negative costs. To the extent possible, it is consistent to treat all receipts in the time stream as benefits regardless of their sources and all disbursements in the time stream as costs regardless of their designated purposes. Then, the criterion based on the benefit-cost ratio can be used to determine the economic feasibility of a project, even though the ratio itself is not a good indicator of the size of the profit.

Example 7.1

A public agency is considering four independent projects which have different useful lives. The cash flow profile for each project x consists of an initial cost $C_{0,x}$, a stream of uniform annual operating and maintenance costs $\bar{C}_x$, and a stream of uniform annual benefits $\bar{B}_x$ for years $t = 1, 2, \ldots, N_x$ where N_x is the useful life of project x. The salvage value at $t = N_x$ for project x is $S_{N,x}$. There will be no replacement when the useful life of a project expires. The numerical data for these projects are given in Table 7.1. The agency intends to adopt a planning horizon of 10 years and specifies a MARR of 10%. Determine whether these projects are economically feasible on the basis of the benefit-cost ratio using

1. The given time streams of costs and benefits
2. The net annual cash flows resulting from the given data

Using the given time streams of costs and benefits, the present value of costs of each project x for case (1)

$$\text{CPV}_x = C_{0,x} + \sum_{t=1}^{n} C_{t,x}(P|F, 10\%, t)$$
$$= C_{0,x} + \bar{C}_x(P|F, 10\%, N_x)$$

The present value of benefits of the project is

$$\text{BPV}_x = \sum_{t=1}^{n} B_{t,x}(P|F, 10\%, t) + S_{N,x}(P|F, 10\%, N_x)$$
$$= \bar{B}_x(P|U, 10\%, N_x) + S_{N,x}(P|F, 10\%, N_x)$$

Table 7.1

Data for the Independent Projects in Example 7.1

Project No. x	Useful Life N_x	Initial Cost $C_{0,x}$	Uniform Annual Cost $\bar{C}_x$ for $t = 1, 2, \ldots, N_x$	Uniform Annual Benefit B_x for $t = 1, 2, \ldots, N_x$	Salvage Value $S_{N,x}$
1	10	$50,000	$6,000	$25,460	$14,000
2	4	45,000	3,000	13,280	5,000
3	10	40,000	4,000	17,040	10,000
4	6	30,000	3,500	15,120	0

Table 7.2

Benefit-Cost Ratios for Projects in Example 7.1

Project No. x	(1) Ratio Based on Gross Annual Benefits and Costs			(2) Ratio Based on Net Annual Benefits and Costs		
	BPV_x	CPV_x	B_x/C_x	BPV_x	CPV_x	B_x/C_x
1	$161,839	$86,868	1.86	$125,000	$50,000	2.50
2	45,511	54,510	0.83	36,000	45,000	0.80
3	108,559	64,578	1.68	84,000	40,000	2.10
4	65,852	45,244	1.46	50,600	30,000	1.69

On the other hand, if the net annual cash flow profile is first determined from the given data, we have $C_{0,x}$ at $t = 0$ and $U_x = \bar{B}_x - \bar{C}_x$ for $t = 1, 2, \ldots, N_x$. That is

$$U_1 = 25,460 - 6,000 = 19,460$$

$$U_2 = 13,280 - 3,000 = 10,280$$

$$U_3 = 17,040 - 4,000 = 13,040$$

$$U_4 = 15,120 - 3,500 = 11,620$$

Since the values U_1, U_2, U_3, and U_4 are positive, they represent net annual benefits. Then, for case (2)

$$CPV_x = C_{0,x}$$

$$BPV_x = U_x(P|U, 10\%, N_x) + S_{N,x}(P|F, 10\%, N_x)$$

The benefit-cost ratios for both cases (1) and (2) are computed according to Eq. (7.1) and the results are tabulated in Table 7.2. Thus, while projects 1, 3, and 4 should be accepted, project 2 should be rejected since $BPV_2/CPV_2 < 1$. Note that the acceptability of these projects is not affected by using the ratios B_x/C_x in case (1) or (2).

Example 7.2

Using the net annual cash flows in the previous example, recompute the benefit-cost ratios for all projects if the salvage value is treated as a negative cost instead of a benefit.

Table 7.3

Different Treatments of Salvage Values in Analysis

Project x	Salvage Value as Benefit		Salvage Value as Negative Cost			
	B_x/C_x	Acceptability	BPV_x	CPV_x	B_x/C_x	Acceptability
1	2.50	Yes	119,574	44,603	2.68	Yes
2	0.80	No	32,587	41,585	0.78	No
3	2.10	Yes	80,126	36,145	2.22	Yes
4	1.69	Yes	50,609	30,000	1.69	Yes

The present values of costs and benefits using the net cash flows can be obtained as follows:

$$CPV_x = C_{0,x} - S_{N,x}(P|F, 10\%, N_x)$$

$$BPV_x = \bar{B}_x(P|U, 10\%, N_x)$$

The results of the computation are shown in Table 7.3. Note again that acceptability of the projects is not altered by a different treatment of the salvage value in the analysis.

7.4   Incremental Analysis of Mutually Exclusive Proposals

The underlying principle of evaluating mutually exclusive proposals is to maximize the profit potential as measured by the discounted net benefit, i.e., net present value. When the net present value is used as the criterion for selecting the best proposal from a set of mutually exclusive alternatives, all we need to do is to select the one which has the maximum nonnegative value. When the benefit-cost ratio is used as the measure of the profit potential, the proposal with the maximum ratio generally does not lead to the maximum net benefit. Consequently, the direct analysis based on the net benefit cost ratios is not applicable to the evaluation of mutually exclusive alternatives.

For the four projects in Fig. 7.2, for example, it is seen that $N_3 > N_1 > N_4 > N_2$. From the slopes of the lines representing their benefit-cost ratios, however, it is noted that $B_1/C_1 > B_3/C_3 > B_4/C_4 > B_2/C_2$. If we follow the ranking of the benefit-cost ratios and select $x = 1$, which has the highest B/C value, we will deprive ourselves of the opportunity of investing an additional amount of money to realize a bigger net benefit (in terms of the net present value) as represented by N_3 for alternative $x = 3$. Therefore, we should make successive pairwise comparisons to determine whether the *additional* benefits generated by the higher cost alternative outweigh the *additional* costs in each comparison. Since the profit potential of the additional investment is expressed as the ratio of the incremental cost, this approach is referred to as the *incremental analysis* or *incremental benefit-cost ratio* analysis.

The incremental analysis can be carried out systematically by using successive pairwise comparisons as shown schematically in Fig. 7.3. Basically, the set of mutually exclusive proposals under consideration is arranged according to the ascending order of their *present values of costs*. Starting with the lowest cost alternative ($x = 1$), we compare it with the null alternative ($x = 0$) to determine whether this proposal ($x = 1$) is at least as profitable as the best foregone opportunity. If the answer is affirmative, we accept the lowest cost alternative as the tentative choice; otherwise we retain the null alternative. Next, compare this tentative choice with the next lowest cost alternative ($x = 2$) to determine whether the additional investment is profitable. If this answer is affirmative, we accept the latter over the former as the tentative choice; otherwise we retain the former. We can repeat the procedure until the complete set of alternatives is compared in this manner. Then, the final choice is the best among the set of alternatives. The rationale behind this approach is that as long as we can invest an additional amount of money at the MARR and receive a greater net benefit, we should accept the higher cost alternative (based on the present value of costs of a set of mutually exclusive alternatives computed at the specified MARR); otherwise the left-over amount will not earn a return as good as the specified MARR. Hence we must examine in each step whether the profit potential will be increased by changing from the lower cost alternative to the higher cost alternative, until all alternatives have been compared successively.

In order to develop an operating procedure for the incremental benefit-cost ratio analysis, let us introduce the following notation:

C_y = the present value of costs of the alternative y, which refers to the last lower cost alternative accepted prior to the comparison with the higher cost alternative x

ΔC_{x-y} = the incremental cost between the alternatives x and y

B_y = the present value of benefits of the alternative y

ΔB_{x-y} = the incremental benefit between the alternatives x and y

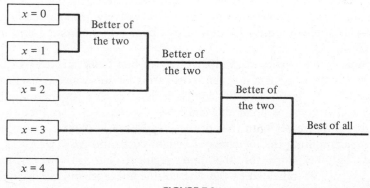

FIGURE 7.3

Then, the incremental benefit-cost ratio for a pair of alternative x and y is defined as follows:

$$\frac{\Delta B_{x-y}}{\Delta C_{x-y}} = \frac{B_x - B_y}{C_x - C_y} \tag{7.2}$$

If the alternatives are arranged in the ascending order of *the present values of their costs*, we can be sure that the denominator in Eq. (7.2) will always be positive. Then, in making a pairwise comparison between a lower cost alternative y and the higher cost alternative x, the higher cost alternative x is preferable if

$$\frac{\Delta B_{x-y}}{\Delta C_{x-y}} \geq 1 \tag{7.3}$$

Otherwise the lower cost alternative y is preferable. Note that the incremental benefit ΔB_{x-y} and consequently the ratio itself may be positive or negative, but Eq. (7.3) holds true even if the ratio is negative (less than zero). Therefore, Eq. (7.3) is the criterion for accepting the higher cost alternative x in the pairwise comparison between the alternatives y and x.

The successive pairwise comparisons of all alternatives will lead to the choice of the best alternative, but the choice is not necessarily economically acceptable since even the best may not be good enough. In order to make sure that the final choice is economically feasible as well as the best among all alternatives, we can always test each alternative for acceptability based on the benefit-cost ratio criterion in Section 5.9 and include only those which are economically feasible in the set of alternatives for selection. However, this extra work is unnecessary if we first compare the lowest cost alternative (say $x = 1$) with the null alternative ($x = 0$). In fact, we simply consider the benefit-cost ratio B_1/C_1 for testing the acceptability of alternative $x = 1$ as the incremental benefit-cost ratio $\Delta B_{1-0}/C_{1-0}$ for the pairwise comparison between $x = 0$ and $x = 1$. If $x = 1$ is preferable, we proceed to compare $x = 1$ with the next higher cost alternative $x = 2$; otherwise, we reject $x = 1$ and compare $x = 0$ with $x = 2$, and so on. We can therefore begin with the lowest cost alternative and conduct pairwise comparisons successively in the ascending order of the present values of costs until all alternatives have been compared and the choice is made from the last pair.

The procedure for pairwise comparisons can best be illustrated by referring to Fig. 7.4 in which the incremental benefit-cost ratios for successive pairwise comparisons are plotted. We begin with the comparison of $x = 1$ with the null alternative ($x = 0$) and accept $x = 1$ as preferable since $\Delta B_{1-0}/\Delta C_{1-0} > 1$, i.e., the slope of the line segment 0–1 is greater than that of the line $B/C = 1$. Next, we compare $x = 1$ and $x = 2$ by computing the incremental benefit-cost ratio $\Delta B_{2-1}/\Delta C_{2-1}$, which is represented by the slope of the line segment 1–2 in the figure. Since $\Delta B_{2-1}/\Delta C_{2-1} < 1$, as indicated by the slope of the line segment 1–2, we reject $x = 2$

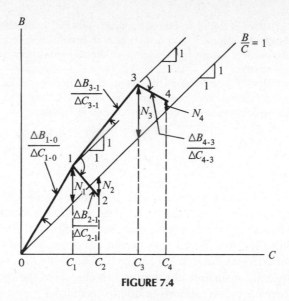

FIGURE 7.4

and next proceed to compare $x = 1$ and $x = 3$. Then we compute the incremental benefit-cost ratio $\Delta B_{3-1}/\Delta C_{3-1}$ because we are interested in knowing how good is $x = 3$ compared with $x = 1$. Thus, the comparison is always between a higher cost alternative x with the *last lower cost alternative accepted*, which is not necessarily the lower cost alternative immediately preceding x, i.e., $y \neq x - 1$ in this case. (In fact, the slope of the line segment 2–3 is irrelevant for the comparison between $x = 1$ and $x = 3$.) Since $\Delta B_{3-1}/\Delta C_{3-1} > 1$, we accept $x = 3$. Finally, we note that $\Delta B_{4-3}/\Delta C_{4-3} < 1$; hence the alternative $x = 3$ is the best among the four mutually exclusive alternatives.

7.5   Procedure for Incremental Analysis

The procedure for the incremental benefit-cost ratio analysis for selecting the best proposal among a set of mutually exclusive alternatives may therefore be summarized as follows:

1. Compute the present values of costs and benefits for the mutually exclusive alternatives, using the specified **MARR** as the discount rate.
2. Arrange the alternatives in the ascending order of the present values of their costs for the purpose of making pairwise comparisons. If the present values of costs of two or more alternatives are equal, it makes no difference how they are ordered among themselves.
3. Compare the lowest cost alternative ($x = 1$) with the null alternative ($x = 0$). If $\Delta B_{1-0}/\Delta C_{1-0} \geq 1$, accept $x = 1$; otherwise, compare $x = 0$ with the next higher cost alternative.

4. After an alternative is found to be economically feasible, compare it with the next higher cost alternative. If the incremental benefit-cost ratio is greater than or equal to one, accept the higher cost alternative; otherwise retain the lower cost alternative.
5. Repeat the pairwise comparisons by using the criterion in Eq. (7.3) successively until all alternatives have been compared; the alternative accepted in the last pairwise comparison is the best among all alternatives.

Example 7.3

Four mutually exclusive alternatives ($x = 1, 2, 3,$ and 4) are known to have the following benefits and costs discounted to the present values according to the specified MARR. The benefit-cost ratios have also been computed. Determine the best alternative by using the incremental cost-benefit ratio analysis if (1) the economically infeasible alternative as determined by the benefit-cost ratios is eliminated first, and (2) the economically infeasible alternative is included in the incremental analysis. All costs and benefits are in millions of dollars as follows:

x	CPV_x	BPV_x	BPV_x/CPV_x	Acceptability
1	2	3	1.50	Yes
2	5	4	0.80	No
3	7	11	1.57	Yes
4	9	12	1.33	Yes

In case (1), we eliminate alternative $x = 2$ before performing the incremental analysis. We arrange the remaining alternatives in the ascending order of the alternatives and begin with the comparison of $x = 1$ with the null alternative $x = 0$. The successive pairwise comparisons are as follows:

$$\frac{\Delta B_{1-0}}{\Delta C_{1-0}} = \frac{3-0}{2-0} = 1.50 \qquad (\text{choose } x = 1)$$

$$\frac{\Delta B_{3-1}}{\Delta C_{3-1}} = \frac{11-3}{7-2} = 1.60 \qquad (\text{choose } x = 3)$$

$$\frac{\Delta B_{4-3}}{\Delta C_{4-3}} = \frac{12-11}{9-7} = 0.50 \qquad (\text{choose } x = 3)$$

In case (2), we include alternative $x = 2$ in the incremental analysis. The computation leads to the same final choice. That is,

$$\frac{\Delta B_{1-0}}{\Delta C_{1-0}} = \frac{3-0}{2-0} = 1.50 \qquad (\text{choose } x = 1)$$

$$\frac{\Delta B_{2-1}}{\Delta C_{2-1}} = \frac{4-3}{5-2} = 0.33 \qquad \text{(choose } x = 1)$$

$$\frac{\Delta B_{3-1}}{\Delta C_{3-1}} = \frac{11-3}{7-2} = 1.60 \qquad \text{(choose } x = 3)$$

$$\frac{\Delta B_{4-3}}{\Delta C_{4-3}} = \frac{12-11}{9-7} = 0.50 \qquad \text{(choose } x = 3)$$

Example 7.4

Seven mutually exclusive building projects are considered for a site. Each building is expected to have a useful life of 40 years and there is no salvage value at the end of 40 years. The initial construction costs, the uniform annual operating and maintenance (O&M) costs, and the uniform annual benefits (in millions of dollars) for these alternatives for $x = 1, 2, \ldots, 7$ are given in Table 7.4. The MARR is specified to be 7%. Select the best among the seven mutually exclusive alternatives by using the incremental benefit-cost ratio analysis.

We first compute the present values of costs and benefits for each of the mutually exclusive projects by noting that, for any project x,

$$C_x = \text{CPV}_x = C_{x,0} + \bar{C}_x(P \mid U, 7\%, 40)$$

$$B_x = \text{BPV}_x = \bar{B}_x(P \mid U, 7\%, 40)$$

where $C_{x,0}$, $\bar{C}_x$, and $\bar{B}_x$ are given in Table 7.4. For example, we compute for $x = 1$,

$$C_1 = \text{CPV}_1 = 1.0 + (0.075)(13.3317) = 2.0$$

$$B_1 = \text{BPV}_1 = (0.202)(13.3317) = 2.693$$

Table 7.4

Cash Flow Profiles of the Mutually Exclusive Alternatives

Alternative x	Initial Cost $C_{0,x}$	Annual O&M Costs $C_{t,x} = \bar{C}_x$ for $t = 1, 2, \ldots, 40$	Annual Benefits $B_{t,x} = \bar{B}_x$ for $t = 1, 2, \ldots, 40$
1	1.000	0.075	0.202
2	2.000	0.075	0.270
3	1.867	0.160	0.356
4	3.800	0.090	0.420
5	4.600	0.105	0.504
6	5.600	0.105	0.600
7	5.600	0.180	0.666

The results of CPV_x and BPV_x for all alternatives are tabulated in Table 7.5 where the alternatives are arranged in the ascending order of CPV_x. Now we compare alternative $x = 1$ with the null alternative ($x = 0$) for which both CPV_0 and BPV_0 are zero. Consequently, we obtain

$$\frac{\Delta B_{1-0}}{\Delta C_{1-0}} = \frac{2.693 - 0}{2.000 - 0} = 1.347 \quad (>1)$$

According to the decision criterion in Eq. (7.3), $x = 1$ is preferable to $x = 0$. Note that the column $x - y$ refers to the pairwise comparison between the higher cost alternative x and the alternative y which is the last lower cost alternative accepted. Consequently, we must complete the computation for each line in Table 7.5 before we can decide which pair is to be compared in the next line. That is, because $x = 1$ is chosen at the end of the computation in the first line, we have $y = 1$ in the second line; similarly, because $x = 1$ is also chosen at the end of the computation in the second line, we have $y = 1$ again in the third line. Thus,

$$\frac{\Delta B_{2-1}}{\Delta C_{2-1}} = \frac{3.600 - 2.693}{3.000 - 2.000} = \frac{0.907}{1.000} = 0.907 \quad (<1)$$

Hence, $x = 2$ is unacceptable and $x = 1$ should be retained. Next, we compute

$$\frac{\Delta B_{3-1}}{\Delta C_{3-1}} = \frac{4.746 - 2.693}{4.000 - 2.000} = \frac{2.053}{2.000} = 1.027 \quad (>1)$$

which indicates that $x = 3$ is preferable. The same procedure is repeated until $x = 6$ is chosen as the best when all the alternatives have been compared.

We may note in passing that if the net present value method had been used,

Table 7.5

Incremental Benefit-Cost Analysis of Example 7.4

x	CPV_x	BPV_x	$x - y$	ΔC_{x-y}	ΔB_{x-y}	$\dfrac{\Delta B_{x-y}}{\Delta C_{x-y}}$	Decision
1	2.000	2.693	$1 - 0$	2.000	2.693	1.347	Choose 1
2	3.000	3.600	$2 - 1$	1.000	0.907	0.907	Choose 1
3	4.000	4.746	$3 - 1$	2.000	2.053	1.027	Choose 3
4	5.000	5.599	$4 - 3$	1.000	0.853	0.853	Choose 3
5	6.000	6.719	$5 - 3$	2.000	1.973	0.987	Choose 3
6	7.000	7.999	$6 - 3$	3.000	3.253	1.084	Choose 6
7	8.000	8.879	$7 - 6$	1.000	0.880	0.880	Choose 6

we only need to compute for each of the alternatives ($x = 1, 2, \ldots, 7$)

$$\mathrm{NPV}_x = \mathrm{BPV}_x - \mathrm{CPV}_x$$

and the alternative with the highest nonnegative value of NPV_x is the best among all mutually exclusive alternatives. For this particular example, the method also yields the alternative $x = 6$ as the best choice.

7.6   Treatment of Additional Benefits or Reduced Costs

It has been pointed out in Section 7.3 that in the course of assessing benefits and costs, some items may exist that can be interpreted either as additional benefits or reduced costs. The treatment of such an item as a *positive* benefit or a *negative* cost will affect the value of the benefit-cost ratio of a project in the direct analysis but will not affect the acceptability of the project. The same situation may also occur in the incremental benefit-cost ratio analysis. The treatment of such items one way or another will produce different incremental benefit-cost ratios but will not change the selection among the alternatives if the criterion in Eq. (7.3) is followed.

The same reasoning can be applied to similar situations in which the value of the incremental benefit-cost ratio can be changed by the relative values of benefits and costs used in the computation. For example, the cash flow profile of a project x is often represented by the *net* annual cash flows $A_{t,x}$ (for $t = 0, 1, 2, \ldots$) instead of separate time streams of benefits $B_{t,x}$ and costs $C_{t,x}$ (both for $t = 0, 1, 2, \ldots$). The use of $A_{t,x}$ for all mutually exclusive projects will produce the same selection among these alternatives as the use of a combination of $B_{t,x}$ and $C_{t,x}$ for all projects.

We shall introduce a simple example to illustrate that Eq. (7.3) is valid even though some items in each of the mutually exclusive projects may be regarded either as additional benefits or reduced costs. Let d_x be the present value of an item which may be interpreted either as an additional benefit or a reduced cost for the alternative x, while b_x and c_x are, respectively, the present values of benefits and costs of the remaining items in the cash flow profile of the alternative x. Let d_y, b_y, and c_y be similarly defined for the alternative y which refers to the last lower cost alternative accepted. Then, the incremental benefit-cost ratio $\Delta B_x / \Delta C_x$ may be computed for the following two cases: (1) d_x and d_y are treated as additional benefits, and (2) d_x and d_y are treated as reduced costs. Thus, from Eq. (7.2), we get

$$(1) \quad \frac{\Delta B_{x-y}}{\Delta C_{x-y}} = \frac{(b_x + d_x) - (b_y + d_y)}{c_x - c_y} = \frac{(b_x - b_y) + (d_x - d_y)}{c_x - c_y}$$

$$(2) \quad \frac{\Delta B_{x-y}}{\Delta C_{x-y}} = \frac{b_x - b_y}{(c_x - d_x) - (c_y - d_y)} = \frac{b_x - b_y}{(c_x - c_y) - (d_x - d_y)}$$

However, if

$$\frac{(b_x + d_x) - (b_y + d_y)}{c_x - c_y} \geq 1$$

it follows that

$$(b_x - b_y) + (d_x - d_y) \geq (c_x - c_y)$$

By transposing terms

$$(b_x - b_y) \geq (c_x - c_y) - (d_x - d_y)$$

Consequently,

$$\frac{b_x - b_y}{(c_x - c_y) - (d_x - d_y)} \geq 1$$

Thus, in a pairwise comparison, if the alternative x is preferable over the alternative y in the first case, the same condition also holds in the second case. Therefore, the criterion in Eq. (7.3) is valid for either case when the alternatives are arranged in the ascending order of the present values of their costs. However, such items should be treated consistently for all alternatives.

Example 7.5

Suppose that an extra item with a present value of d_x which can be treated either as an additional benefit or a reduced cost is discovered for each alternative in Example 7.3. The values of d_x and the present values of benefits and costs for these alternatives have been computed by treating (1) d_x as an added benefit, and (2) as a reduced cost as shown in Table 7.6. Determine the best alternative by using the incremental cost-benefit method for each case.

The incremental benefit-cost ratios for the two cases may be computed as shown in Table 7.7. Although the incremental benefit-cost ratios are different for the two cases, the decisions are identical.

Table 7.6

Treatment of Added Benefits or Reduced Costs in Example 7.5

		Case (1)		(Case (2))	
x	d_x	CPV_x	BPV_x	CPV_x	BPV_x
1	0.5	2	$3 + 0.5 = 3.5$	$2 - 0.5 = 1.5$	3
2	1.1	5	$4 + 1.1 = 5.1$	$5 - 1.1 = 3.9$	4
3	1.2	7	$11 + 1.2 = 12.2$	$7 - 1.2 = 5.8$	11
4	0.8	9	$12 + 0.8 = 12.8$	$9 - 0.8 = 8.2$	12

Table 7.7

Benefit-Cost Ratios Based on Both Cases in Example 7.5

$\Delta B_{x-y}/\Delta C_{x-y}$	Case (1)	Case (2)	Decision
$\dfrac{\Delta B_{1-0}}{\Delta C_{1-0}}$	$\dfrac{3.5-0}{2-0}=1.75$	$\dfrac{3-0}{1.5-0}=2.00$	Choose $x=1$
$\dfrac{\Delta B_{2-1}}{\Delta C_{2-1}}$	$\dfrac{5.1-3.5}{5-2}=0.53$	$\dfrac{4-3}{3.9-1.5}=0.42$	Choose $x=1$
$\dfrac{\Delta B_{3-1}}{\Delta C_{3-1}}$	$\dfrac{12.2-3.5}{7-2}=1.74$	$\dfrac{11-3}{5.8-1.5}=1.86$	Choose $x=3$
$\dfrac{\Delta B_{4-3}}{\Delta C_{4-3}}$	$\dfrac{12.8-12.2}{9-7}=-0.30$	$\dfrac{12-11}{8.2-5.8}=0.42$	Choose $x=3$

Example 7.6

Suppose that the net annual cash flows of the seven mutually exclusive projects in Example 7.4 are obtained first and used as the basis for computing the incremental benefit-cost ratios. Using a MARR of 7%, select the best alternative from the incremental analysis.

If the net annual cash flows U_x (for $t=1, 2, \ldots, 40$) are computed first from the given values of $\bar{B}_x$ and $\bar{C}_x$ for each project x in Example 7.4, we have

$$U_x = \bar{B}_x - \bar{C}_x$$

Since U_x (for $t=1, 2, \ldots, 40$) is positive for each of the seven projects, the only net cost is the initial cost $C_{0,x}$ for a project. Then,

$$CPV_x = C_{0,x}$$

$$BPV_x = U_x(P\,|\,U, 7\%, 40)$$

From the data in Table 7.4 of Example 7.4, we compute CPV_x and BPV_x according to these formulas and the results are arranged in the ascending order of CPV_x. Note that project $x=2$ follows project $x=3$ because $CPV_3 = 1.867$ and $CPV_2 = 2.000$. Note also that $CPV_6 = CPV_7 = 5.600$, and when a tie exists, it does not matter which project is listed first. However, under such circumstances, either ΔC_{7-6} or ΔC_{6-7} is zero; consequently, the incremental benefit-cost ratio is negative infinity (less than 1). However, we can also examine $\Delta B_{7-6} = -0.120$ or $\Delta B_{6-7} = 0.120$, which means that proposal $x=7$ is not as good a proposal as $x=6$. Hence, project $x=6$ is selected.

Table 7.8

Incremental Benefit-Cost Analysis of Example 7.6

x	CPV_x	BPV_x	$x - y$	ΔC_{x-y}	ΔB_{x-y}	$\dfrac{\Delta B_{x-y}}{\Delta C_{x-y}}$	Decision
1	1.000	1.693	1 − 0	1.000	1.693	1.693	Choose 1
3	1.867	2.613	3 − 1	0.867	0.920	1.061	Choose 3
2	2.000	2.600	2 − 3	0.133	−0.013	−0.098	Choose 3
4	3.800	4.400	4 − 3	1.267	1.787	1.410	Choose 4
5	4.600	5.319	5 − 4	0.800	0.919	1.149	Choose 5
6	5.600	6.599	6 − 5	1.000	1.280	1.280	Choose 6
7	5.600	6.479	7 − 6	0	−0.120	−∞	Choose 6

7.7 Ordering Alternatives on the Basis of Initial Costs

A common practice in the application of the incremental benefit-cost analysis for the selection of mutually exclusive alternatives is to arrange them in the ascending order of the *initial costs* (at year 0) of the alternatives. In general, however, there is no advantage in ordering the alternatives according to the initial costs, and its use may introduce some unnecessary complications.

Suppose that y refers to the lower cost alternative accepted and x refers to the next higher cost alternative on the basis of an ordering scheme in which the alternatives are arranged in the ascending order of the *initial costs*. Then the incremental cost $\Delta C_{x-y} = C_x - C_y$ used in Eq. (7.3) may be positive or negative since C_x and C_y are the respective *present values of the costs* of x and y, respectively, and their ranking is not necessarily the same as that based on the initial cost $C_{0,x}$ and $C_{0,y}$ of these alternatives. Therefore, we may have either $C_x > C_y$ or $C_x < C_y$ corresponding to ΔC_{x-y} greater than or less than zero, respectively.

If $C_x > C_y$ while $C_{0,x} > C_{0,y}$, $\Delta C_{x-y} = C_x - C_y$ is positive, and the criterion in Eq. (7.3) can be applied to the new ordering scheme based on initial costs. Note that when $\Delta B_{x-y} = B_x - B_y$ is positive, the incremental ratio $\Delta B_{x-y}/\Delta C_{x-y}$ may be greater than 1 or less than 1 (but greater than 0). When $B_{x-y} = B_x - B_y$ is negative, the incremental ratio is negative (less than 0 and hence less than 1).

If $C_x < C_y$ while $C_{0,x} > C_{0,y}$, $\Delta C_{x-y} = C_x - C_y$ is negative. Hence, the sign of the incremental ratio $\Delta B_{x-y}/\Delta C_{x-y}$ will be negative for a positive ΔB_{x-y}, and positive for a negative ΔB_{x-y}. Then, the criterion in Eq. (7.3) cannot be applied to the new ordering scheme based on initial costs and a different criterion reflecting this situation must be adopted. In that case, the alternative x with a higher initial cost $C_{0,x}$ is preferable if

$$\frac{\Delta B_{x-y}}{\Delta C_{x-y}} = \frac{B_x - B_y}{C_x - C_y} \leq 1 \qquad (7.4)$$

Otherwise, the alternative y with a lower initial cost $C_{0,y}$ is preferable. If the initial costs of two or more alternatives are equal, it does not matter how they are ordered among themselves.

The set of criteria used for selecting the alternatives when they are arranged in the ascending order of their *initial costs* can be stated as follows:

1. If $\Delta C_{x-y} > 0$ while $C_{0,x} - C_{0,y} > 0$, use the criterion in Eq. (7.3). That is, when the denominator of the incremental benefit-cost ratio is positive, the criterion is unambiguous, whether the numerator is positive or negative.
2. If $\Delta C_{x-y} < 0$ while $C_{0,x} - C_{0,y} > 0$, use the criterion in Eq. (7.4). When only the denominator ΔC_{x-y} is negative, the incremental benefit-cost ratio is also negative. Then, the alternative with a higher initial cost is always preferable. When both the numerator and denominator of the ratio are negative, the incremental benefit-cost ratio is positive. Then, the alternative with a higher initial cost is preferable if the ratio is *less than* or equal to 1; otherwise the alternative with a lower cost is preferable.

Example 7.7

The seven mutually exclusive projects in Example 7.4 have been rearranged according to the ascending order of the initial costs as shown in the first and second columns in Table 7.9. Furthermore, since the initial costs of alternatives $x = 7$ and $x = 6$ are equal, they can be ordered either way and $x = 7$ is listed ahead of $x = 6$ in the table. Select the best among the seven mutually exclusive alternatives by using

Table 7.9

Incremental Benefit-Cost Analysis of Example 7.7

x	$C_{0,x}$	CPV_x	BPV_x	$x - y$	ΔC_{x-y}	ΔB_{x-y}	$\dfrac{\Delta B_{x-y}}{\Delta C_{x-y}}$	Decision
1	1.000	2.000	2.693	1 − 0	2.000	2.693	1.347	Choose 1
3	1.867	4.000	4.746	3 − 1	2.000	2.053	1.027	Choose 3
2	2.000	3.000	3.600	2 − 3	−1.000	−1.146	1.146	Choose 3
4	3.800	5.000	5.599	4 − 3	1.000	0.853	0.853	Choose 3
5	4.600	6.000	6.719	5 − 3	2.000	1.973	0.987	Choose 3
7	5.600	8.000	8.879	7 − 3	4.000	4.133	1.033	Choose 7
6	5.600	7.000	7.999	6 − 7	−1.000	−0.880	0.880	Choose 6

the incremental benefit-cost ratio method and arranging the alternatives according to the ascending order of the initial costs.

The values of CPV_x and BPV_x have already been computed in Example 7.4. The other steps are also similar to those in Example 7.4, except when we encounter a negative sign in ΔC_{x-y}. In such situations, the criterion in Eq. (7.4) instead of the one in Eq. (7.3) should be used. Thus, in the pairwise comparison between $x = 3$ and $x = 2$, we choose $x = 3$ (the alternative with *lower initial cost*) when ΔB_{x-y} is also negative and the ratio is *greater* than 1. Similarly, in the pairwise comparison between $x = 7$ and $x = 6$, we choose $x = 6$ (the alternative with *higher order* even though its initial cost is the same as that of alternative $x = 7$) when ΔB_{x-y} is also negative and the ratio is *less* than 1.

7.8   Summary and Study Guide

In this chapter, we have considered the use of the benefit-cost ratio criteria in the direct analysis of the acceptability of an independent project and in the incremental analysis for selecting the best project among a set of mutually exclusive alternatives. Since the direct analysis of independent projects using the benefit-cost ratio criterion is based on the same principle as the net present value method, its application is relatively straightforward. However, the criterion for incremental benefit-cost ratio analysis is much more complicated than the net present value method for selecting the mutually exclusive alternatives. The incremental analysis may be further complicated if the projects are arranged in the ascending order of the initial costs instead of the present values of costs. Unfortunately, the benefit-cost ratio method is still regarded (in 1981) as the officially preferred method by some government agencies responsible for the planning of public projects such as water resource projects and transportation systems. Consequently, we should be familiar with the idiosyncrasies of this method until it is abandoned when its clumsiness is fully recognized by the practitioners.

The benefit-cost ratio is not a good measure of the profit of a project because it is influenced by some items which may be treated as additional benefits or reduced costs. This is true whether the projects under consideration are independent or mutually exclusive. However, the treatment of these items in either manner will not alter the acceptability of an independent project or the selection of the best project among a set of mutually exclusive projects.

REFERENCES

7.1 McKean, R. N., *Efficiency in Government Through Systems Analysis*. New York: John Wiley & Sons, 1958.

7.2 *Proposed Practices for Economic Analysis of River Basin Projects*, Report to the Federal Inter-Agency River Basin Committee, prepared by the Subcommittee on Benefits and Costs, Washington, DC, 1950.

7.3 *Manual on User Benefit Analysis of Highway and Bus-Transit Improvements*, American Association of State Highway and Transportation Officials (1977).

PROBLEMS

P7.1 Select the best proposal among the alternatives in Problem P6.1 (Chapter 6), using the benefit-cost ratio method.

P7.2 Select the best proposal among the alternatives in Problem P6.2 (Chapter 6), using the benefit-cost ratio method.

P7.3 Select the best proposal among the alternatives in Problem P6.7 (Chapter 6), using the benefit-cost ratio method for the following values of MARR: (a) 10%, (b) 20%, and (c) 30%.

P7.4 Select the best proposal among the alternatives in Problem P6.8 (Chapter 6), using the benefit-cost ratio method for the following values of MARR: (a) 5%, (b) 10%, and (c) 15%.

P7.5 Six mutually exclusive projects are considered as alternatives for a recreation facility. The present values of benefits and costs based on an appropriate interest rate over the entire planning period for all four alternatives are given below. Select the alternative with maximum net benefits, using the benefit-cost ratio method. Also sketch the net benefits of these alternatives on a *benefit versus cost graph* to show the relative desirability of these alternatives.

Project Alternative	CPV in 10^6	BPV in 10^6
1	2.0	2.688
2	3.1	3.300
3	4.2	4.550
4	5.2	5.610
5	6.0	6.724
6	7.1	7.975

P7.6 Three plans have been proposed for a small commercial building at a leased site. The building is expected to have a useful life of 40 years and no salvage value at the end of the period. The initial construction costs, the annual maintenance costs, and the annual benefits are shown below. The MARR is specified to be 6%. Select the best of three plans using the benefit-cost ratio method and computing the present values of benefits and costs in each of the following manners: (a) the benefit stream and the cost stream are treated as given, and (b) the net benefits for years 1 to 40 are first obtained from the difference between the given benefits and costs, and the net benefits are regarded as the benefit stream. All costs and benefits are expressed in thousands of dollars.

t	$x = 1$		$x = 2$		$x = 3$	
	$C_{t,1}$	$B_{t,1}$	$C_{t,2}$	$B_{t,2}$	$C_{t,3}$	$B_{t,3}$
0	200	0	250	0	300	0
1–40 (each)	40	63	30	52	55	77

P7.7 Repeat both (a) and (b) of Problem P7.6 if the alternatives are arranged according to the *initial costs* instead of the present values of costs for the incremental analysis in using the benefit-cost ratio method.

P7.8 A company is considering investing in a water purification system. Three alternatives are under consideration and their cash flow profiles are given below. The MARR specified is 10%. Select the best proposal among these alternatives, using the benefit-cost ratio method.

Year	System 1	System 2	System 3
0	− 80,000	− 120,000	− 100,000
1	+ 40,000	+ 60,000	+ 35,000
2	+ 35,000	+ 50,000	+ 35,000
3	+ 30,000	+ 40,000	+ 35,000
4	+ 25,000	+ 30,000	+ 35,000

CHAPTER

8

THE INTERNAL
RATE OF
RETURN METHOD

8.1 Nature and Scope of Current Usage

The concept of the internal rate of return and its computation have previously been discussed in detail in Chapter 4. However, the use of the internal rate of return as a method of economic evaluation for independent projects and mutually exclusive projects have been mentioned only briefly in Chapters 5 and 6 respectively. Basically, the internal rate of return method requires far more computation than the net present value method and, if applied correctly, should produce the same results as the net present value method. While the internal rate of return on a project can always be computed if desired, it would be unnecessary to consider the internal rate of return method for project evaluation if it weren't for the popularity of its usage by analysts in the industrial and financial world.

The term *internal rate of return method* (IRR) has been used by different analysts to mean somewhat different procedures for project evaluation. The method is often misunderstood and misused, and its popularity is undeserved even when the method is defined and interpreted in the most favorable light. According to a study published in 1980, many frequently cited arguments in favor of using the internal rate of return are incorrect, but several surveys of private corporations conducted in the 1970s indicate its widespread use in many countries.[1] A summary of these surveys showing the percentages of firms that used the internal rate of return is reproduced in Table 8.1. Another 1975 survey of the *Fortune* 500 firms indicated that about 40% of the 109 firms responding to the survey used the internal rate of return method as their primary economic evaluation technique.[2] Clearly, a method

---

[1] See Ref. [8.2].
[2] See Ref. [8.1].

Table 8.1

Summary of Recent Surveys on the Use of the IRR Method

Year of Publication	Author of Survey	Percentage of Firms Using the IRR Methods
1967	Renck (Sweden)	50%
1973	Abdelsamad (U.S.)	69%
1973	Fremgen (U.S.)	71%
1973	Rockley (England)	59%
1974	Berry and Tanner (England)	76%
1975	Honko and Virtanen (Finland)	78%
1977	Andersson (Sweden)	54%
1978	Tell (Sweden)	53%

Source: Rapp, B., "The Internal Rate of Return Method—A Critical Study," *Engineering Costs and Production Economics*, Vol. 5 (Amsterdam, The Netherlands: Elsevier Scientific Publishing Co., 1980), p. 44.

with such popularity cannot be ignored even though its value as a method of economic analysis is dubious.

We shall define the internal rate of return method as the method of economic evaluation which primarily uses the internal rate of return as the decision criterion. We shall treat it as completely as possible so that it will at least be correctly used if an analyst so chooses. We shall adopt a complete set of decision criteria that will include all possible conditions whether they occur often or rarely.[3] Specifically, we will discuss two major aspects of application in order to differentiate their characteristics.

1. The use of the internal rate of return method in the *direct analysis* of the acceptability of an independent project (in comparison with the null alternative)
2. The use of the internal rate of return method in the incremental analysis through successive pairwise comparisons for the selection of the best proposal among a set of mutually exclusive alternatives

These topics will be presented in sufficient detail to clarify the rationale of the method and to dispel some erroneous notions which are not intuitively obvious. The application of the internal rate of return method when capital rationing is imposed will be discussed in Chapter 9.

---

[3] A correct procedure covering virtually all possible conditions in application has been stated in [8.3]. The rationale of this procedure is developed further in this chapter. The authors are indebted to M. Wohl for sharing the idea about this procedure through private communication prior to its publication.

8.2   The Internal Rate of Return for Direct Analysis

The idea of using the internal rate of return as a measure of the profit potential is based on the premise that the internal rate of return of a project x must be greater than the minimum attractive rate of return specified by the organization. When there is only one sign change in the cash flow profile of an investment project, only one internal rate of return exists. Let the IRR for an independent project x be denoted by i'_x and the specified MARR be denoted by i^*. Then, the project x is economically feasible if

$$i^* \leq i'_x \tag{8.1}$$

Otherwise, it should be rejected. Such a decision criterion leads to the same result obtained on the basis of the net present value criterion, which can be verified by noting that NPV_x is positive at i^* when $i^* < i'_x$ as shown in the NPV-MARR graph in Fig. 8.1. In the case of borrowing or financing, the cash flow profile of a loan involving one or more receipts at the early year periods and one or more repayments at later periods also has only one sign change. Hence the criterion for accepting a loan x by the borrower is

$$i^* > i'_x \tag{8.2}$$

where i'_x is the IRR of the loan x to the lender. The meaning of this criterion is illustrated in the NPV-MARR graph in Fig. 8.2.

The situation becomes much more complicated when the cash flow profile consists of a mixed series of disbursements and receipts. Again, let us consider a relatively simple case for which the cash flow profile consists of only two sign changes; hence according to discussion in Section 4.3, we may find 0, 1, or 2 values for IRR. Let us assume further that we have found only one value of IRR after searching *exhaustively* within the practical range of the MARR. If NPV_x at $i = 0\%$

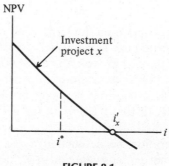

FIGURE 8.1

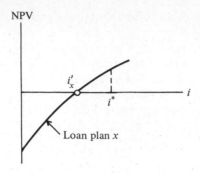

FIGURE 8.2

is positive, we can at least say that for the value of MARR that is likely to be specified by the organization, there will be a single value of $IRR_x = i_x$ for a project x. Then, the project x is economically feasible if $i^* \leq i'_x$.

However, even for this simple case, we must search the practical range of the MARR exhaustively; otherwise we may have missed a second value of IRR_x in the range. This means that we must compute the net present values at small intervals of i to make sure that we have not missed the point when $[NPV]_i = 0$. In effect, we need a NPV versus MARR graph for the practical range of the MARR when we use IRR_x as the basis for accepting the project x even in this simple case. If there are indeed two values of IRR_x instead of one, the situation will become far more complicated.

In the next section we shall discuss the possible situation that may arise from the general case of a cash flow profile consisting of mixed series of disbursements and receipts. It is sufficient to point out here that the use of internal rate of return as the basis for accepting an independent project involves a considerable amount of work if we want to avoid the ambiguity that may arise in connection with its application.

Example 8.1

Suppose that a strip-mining operation for soft coal requires an initial cost of $545,000, which will yield an annual net income of $150,000 from mining for the next 8 years. At the end of the eighth year, the cost of restoring the landscape for environmental protection is $490,000, resulting in a net cost of $340,000 after deducting the net income of $150,000 for the year. Is this operation economically feasible for a specified MARR of 10%? Use both the net present value method and the internal rate of return method.

Let the proposed operation be designated $x = 1$ ($x = 0$ for the null alternative). Then, by using the net present value method, we have at $i = 10\%$ (with all values in thousands of dollars)

$$[NPV_1]_{10\%} = -545 + 150(P|U, 10\%, 7) - 340(P|F, 10\%, 8) = 27$$

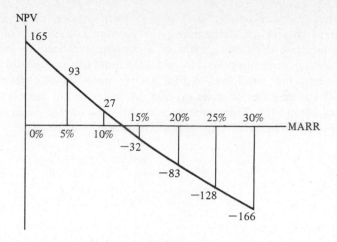

FIGURE 8.3

Hence, the proposed project is economically feasible. If we wish to check the sensitivity of this decision to the variation in the MARR, we can compute the NPV values for several MARR values and plot the NPV versus MARR graph as shown in Fig. 8.3.

By using the internal rate of return method, we must solve for the IRR_1 from the equation

$$[NPV_1]_{i_1} = -545 + 150(P \,|\, U, i_1, 7) - 340(P \,|\, F, i_1, 8) = 0$$

Since the cash flow profile for this project has two sign changes, it is possible to have 0, 1, or 2 values for IRR_1. By examining the NPV versus MARR graph, we expect to find a value of IRR_1 between $i = 10\%$ and $i = 15\%$. Thus, for $i = 15\%$

$$[NPV_1]_{15\%} = -545 + 150(P \,|\, U, 15\%, 7) - 340(P \,|\, F, 15\%, 8) = -32$$

An internal rate of return is found by linear interpolation as follows:

$$i_1' = 10\% + (15\% - 10\%) \, \frac{27}{27 + 32} = 12.3\%$$

If the range of MARR from 0% to 30% may be regarded as the practical limits for which we will ever specify any value of MARR for project evaluation, then and only then a NPV versus MARR graph as shown in Fig. 8.3 gives us some reasonable assurance that the proposed operation should be undertaken since the IRR of $i_1' = 12.3\%$ is greater than the MARR of $i^* = 10\%$.

8.3   Decision Criteria for Accepting Independent Projects

Because of the possibility of multiple internal rates of return for investment and financing projects, a set of criteria rather than a single criterion is needed to cover all possible conditions as shown in Fig. 8.4. Furthermore, the availability of a complete set of criteria for determining the economic feasibility of independent projects will facilitate the development of a consistent procedure for incremental analysis in selecting the best proposal from a set of mutually exclusive alternatives.

In examining the conditions in Fig. 8.4, we note that the net present value NPV at $i = 0\%$ is positive for cases (a) and (b), negative for cases (c) and (d), and zero for cases (e) and (f). Therefore, we use $[NPV]_{0\%}$ as the basis for classifying various conditions. When $[NPV]_{0\%}$ is positive or negative, we can examine the case

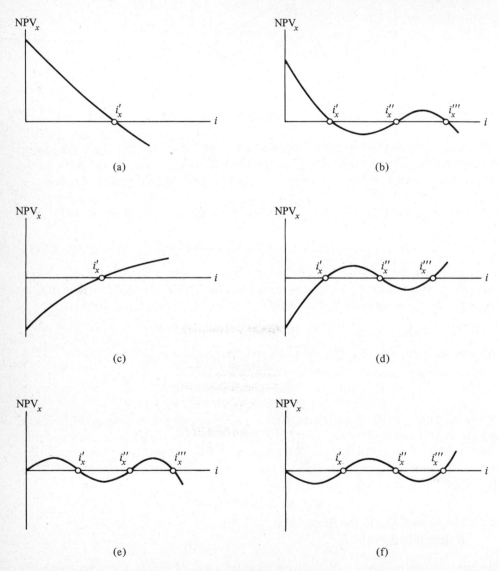

FIGURE 8.4

with a single value of IRR and that with multiple values of IRR separately. When $[NPV]_{0\%} = 0$, we divide the conditions into the case with a positive initial slope and one with a negative initial slope of the curve at $i = 0\%$. Since the slope of the curve can be represented by the derivative, $d(NPV)/di$, or simply dN/di, the sign of the initial slope will be indicated by $[dN/di]_{0\%}$. The calculation of this derivative from a given cash flow profile will be discussed later.

Theoretically, we may also encounter the case of a zero initial slope at $i = 0\%$ when $[NPV]_{0\%}$, i.e., we may have the situation that both $[NPV]_{0\%} = 0$ and $[dN/di]_{0\%} = 0$. The set of criteria can be extended to cover this situation by considering the higher derivatives at $i = 0\%$. The calculation of the second derivative from a given cash flow profile will also discussed later, and by using the same principle, higher derivatives can also be obtained if necessary. That is, we should consider whether the second derivative at $i = 0\%$ is positive, negative, or zero. If it is zero, we should test the third derivative, etc. Since the occurrence of such cases is very unlikely, they are not included here.

Basically, the decision criteria based on the internal rate(s) of return for all these conditions must be consistent with the net present value criterion represented by Eq. (5.10) in Chapter 5. Let IRR_x be the internal rate of return on a project x. If there is only a single value of IRR_x, it will be denoted as i'_x; if there are multiple values of IRR_x, they will be designated by i'_x, i''_x, etc., starting from the lowest to the highest value except when one of the values is zero. In that case, the zero value will not be counted in the designation. Since the MARR is used as the discount rate i in computing the NPV, the MARR specified for the proposed project x is denoted by i^*. Then, we may observe from Fig. 8.4 the following conditions based on the net present value criterion:

(a) When NPV_x is positive at $i = 0\%$ and there is only a single value of IRR_x, the project x is acceptable if $i^* \leq i'_x$.

(b) When NPV_x is positive at $i = 0\%$ and there are multiple values of IRR_x, the project x is acceptable if $i^* \leq i'_x$, unacceptable if $i'_x < i^* < i''_x$, and acceptable again if $i''_x \leq i^* \leq i'''_x$, etc.

(c) When NPV_x is negative at $i = 0\%$ and there is only a single value of IRR_x, the project x is acceptable if $i^* \geq i'_x$.

(d) When NPV_x is negative at $i = 0\%$ and there are multiple values of IRR_x, the project x is unacceptable if $i^* < i'_x$, acceptable if $i'_x \leq i^* \leq i''_x$, and unacceptable again if $i''_x < i^* < i'''_x$, etc.

(e) When $NPV_x = 0$ at $i = 0\%$ and the slope dN_x/di is positive at $i = 0\%$, the project x is acceptable if $i^* \leq i'_x$, unacceptable if $i'_x < i^* < i''_x$, acceptable again if $i''_x \leq i^* \leq i'''_x$, etc. The value of $IRR = 0\%$ will not be counted.

(f) When $NPV_x = 0$ at $i = 0\%$ and the slope dN_x/di is negative at $i = 0\%$, the project x is unacceptable if $i^* < i'_x$, acceptable if $i'_x \leq i^* \leq i''_x$, and unacceptable again if $i''_x < i^* < i'''_x$, etc. The value of $IRR = 0\%$ will not be counted.

It should be noted that for $i^* = i'_x, i''_x, \ldots$, we are really indifferent to accepting or rejecting project x. The equality signs associated with the acceptable limits in the above discussion merely reflect the fact that at $i^* = i'_x, i''_x, \ldots$ project x is at least as good as the best opportunity foregone and therefore is acceptable. These equality signs can be omitted if so desired. Furthermore, since we are primarily interested in the range of i^* that is nonnegative, the condition of $0 \leq i^*$ can be added to the above inequalities wherever appropriate. Thus, the decision criteria for accepting independent projects can be summarized as in Table 8.2.

The decision criteria based on Fig. 8.4 do not cover the special cases in which the case flow profile has no sign change. For such cases, the internal rate of return is either indeterminate or negative as shown in Fig. 8.5. When the IRR is indeterminate, the project x may lead to a positive NPV_x for all values of i_x as represented by the parallel line above the horizontal axis in Fig. 8.5(a), or to a negative NPV for all values of i_x, as represented by a parallel line below the horizontal axis. When the value(s) of the IRR are negative, the project x may lead to a $[NPV_x]_{0\%}$ greater than zero, as shown in Fig. 8.5(b), or to a $[NPV_x]_{0\%}$ less than zero, as represented by the mirror image of Fig. 8.5(b) with respect to the horizontal axis. Consequently, when all IRR are either indeterminate or negative, the decision criterion is to accept project x if $[NPV_x]_{0\%} \geq 0$ and to reject project x if $[NPV_x]_{0\%} < 0$.

The use of the decision criteria developed in this section will lead to the same results of project acceptance as determined by the net present value criterion. However, the amount of work involved is quite substantial since the determination of the internal rate(s) of return requires the numerical solution of a polynomial equation of the nth power where n is the number of years in the planning horizon.

Table 8.2

Decision Criteria for Accepting Independent Projects

Range of i^*	$[NPV_x]_{0\%} > 0$	$[NPV_x]_{0\%} < 0$	$[NPV_x]_{0\%} = 0$ ($i_x = 0$ is not counted)	
			$[dN_x/di]_{0\%} > 0$	$[dN_x/di]_{0\%} < 0$
$0 \leq i^* < i'_x$	Accept	Reject	Accept	Reject
$i'_x < i^* < i''_x$	Reject	Accept	Reject	Accept
$i''_x < i^* < i'''_x$	Accept	Reject	Accept	Reject
$i'''_x < i^* < i''''_x$	Reject	Accept	Reject	Accept
additional i_x	Alternate accept/reject	Alternate reject/accept	Alternate accept/reject	Alternate reject/accept
Negative or indeterminate	Accept	Reject		

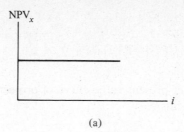

(a)

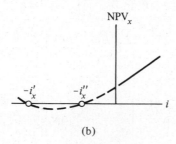

(b)

FIGURE 8.5

8.4   Computation of Net Present Value and and Its Derivatives at Zero Discount Rate

The decision criteria for direct analysis based on the internal rate(s) of return discussed in the previous section require the knowledge of $[\mathrm{NPV}_x]_{0\%}$ and, in some cases, $[dN_x/di]_{0\%}$ also in the ordering of independent projects. In order to compute these quantities without making reference to the NPV-MARR graph, we begin with Eq. (5.9) in Chapter 5, i.e.,

$$\mathrm{NPV}_x = \sum_{t=0}^{n} (B_{t,x} - C_{t,x})(1 + i)^{-t}$$

or

$$\mathrm{NPV}_x = \sum_{t=0}^{n} A_{t,x}(1 + i)^{-t}$$

Then, the net present value of project x at $i = 0\%$ is

$$[\mathrm{NPV}_x]_{0\%} = \sum_{t=0}^{n} (B_{t,x} - C_{t,x}) \tag{8.3}$$

or

$$[NPV_x]_{0\%} = \sum_{t=0}^{n} A_{t,x} \tag{8.4}$$

To find the slope of the net present value curve of project x at $i = 0\%$, we first find the derivative of NPV_x. Thus

$$\frac{dN_x}{di} = \frac{d}{di}\left[\sum_{t=0}^{n} (B_{t,x} - C_{t,x})(1 + i)^{-t} \right]$$

$$= -\sum_{t=1}^{n} t(B_{t,x} - C_{t,x})(1 + i)^{-(t+1)}$$

For $i = 0\%$,

$$\left[\frac{dN_x}{di}\right]_{0\%} = -\sum_{t=1}^{n} t(B_{t,x} - C_{t,x}) \tag{8.5}$$

or

$$\left[\frac{dN_x}{di}\right]_{0\%} = -\sum_{t=1}^{n} t A_{t,x} \tag{8.6}$$

If we want to find the second derivative of NPV_x for solving the case when both $[NPV_x]_{0\%} = 0$ and $[dN_x/di]_{0\%} = 0$, we get

$$\frac{d^2 N_x}{di^2} = +\sum_{t=1}^{n} t(t + 1)(B_{t,x} - C_{t,x})(1 + i)^{-(t+2)}$$

For $i = 0\%$,

$$\left[\frac{d^2 N_x}{di^2}\right]_{0\%} = \sum_{t=1}^{n} t(t + 1)(B_{t,x} - C_{t,x}) \tag{8.7}$$

or

$$\left[\frac{d^2 N_x}{di^2}\right]_{0\%} = \sum_{t=1}^{n} t(t + 1) A_{t,x} \tag{8.8}$$

Consequently, the computation of the net present value and its derivatives of a project can be carried out systematically by using these equations.

Table 8.3

Cash Flows (in $1000) for
Three Independent Projects

Year t	$A_{t,1}$	$A_{t,2}$	$A_{t,3}$
0	−545	−340	−340
1–7 (each)	+150	+150	+150
8	0	−830	−710

Example 8.2

The cash flow profiles of three independent projects are shown in Table 8.3. Using a MARR of 10%, apply the decision criteria based on the internal rate of return to determine if each of these projects is acceptable. (The data for projects $x = 1$, 2, and 3 correspond to those for Examples 5.4, 5.5, and 5.6 in Chapter 5, respectively. See these examples for a detailed explanation.)

For $x = 1$, there is only a single rate of return because of one sign change in the cash flow profile. It is seen that

$$[\text{NPV}_1]_{0\%} = -545 + (7)(150) = 505$$

The internal rate of return i_1 can be obtained by interpolation from $[\text{NPV}_1]_{15\%} = +79.1$ and $[\text{NPV}]_{20\%} = -4.3$. Thus,

$$i = 15\% + (20\% - 15\%) \frac{79.1}{79.1 + 4.3} = 19.7\%$$

Since the specified MARR is $i^* = 10\%$, we have 19.7% > 10%. Hence, the proposed project is acceptable.

For $x = 2$, $[\text{NPV}_2]_{0\%} = -120$, and two values of i_2 have been found (9.6% and 22.9%). For the specified MARR $i^* = 10\%$, we have 9.6% < 10% < 22.9%. Hence, the proposed project is again acceptable. However, it should be cautioned again that 10% is very close to 9.6%, and any slight change in the MARR to a lower value (say to 9%) would affect the acceptability of the proposed project.

For $x = 3$, $[\text{NPV}_3]_{0\%} = 0$, and two values of i_3 have been found (0% and 28.4%). We therefore will compute from Eq. (8.6) the following:

$$\left[\frac{dN_3}{di}\right]_{0\%} = -[(1 + 2 + 3 + 4 + 5 + 6 + 7)(150) + (8)(-710)]$$
$$= -[(28)(150) - (8)(710)] = +1{,}480$$

Ignore the value of 0% and consider 28.4% as the lowest value of i_3. Then, for the specified MARR $i^* = 10\%$, we have $28.4\% > 10\%$. Hence, the proposed project is acceptable.

8.5   The Concept of Incremental Internal Rate of Return Analysis

In the selection of the best proposal from a set of mutually exclusive alternatives, the alternative with the highest internal rate of return is not necessarily the alternative with the maximum net present value. This disagreement can easily be seen in the NPV versus MARR graph in Fig. 8.6(a). Let us assume that each of the three alternatives ($x = 1, 2, 3$) has only a single value of $IRR_x = i_x$. If we consider each project separately and note that $i^* < i_1$, $i^* < i_2$, and $i^* < i_3$, we conclude that all three alternatives are economically acceptable. However, since we are interested in selecting only the best one among these three alternatives, we have to rank them on the basis of their profit potential and select the one that has the greatest merit. At the specified MARR of i^*, the alternative $x = 2$ is clearly the best, $x = 3$ the second best, and $x = 1$ is the last in spite of the fact that $i_1 > i_2 > i_3$.

The reason why the ranking $i_1 > i_2 > i_3$ cannot be used as the ranking of the merits of alternatives $x = 1$, $x = 2$, and $x = 3$ is that the internal rate of return is not a *direct* measure of the profit potential expressed in the discounted cash flows at a specified time, e.g., the net present value. If we select $x = 1$ which has the highest $IRR = i_1$, we will deprive ourselves of the opportunity of investing an additional amount of money to realize a bigger profit or net benefit (in terms of the net present value) as represented by the alternative $x = 2$. Therefore, we should make successive pairwise comparisons to determine whether the incremental internal of return (IIRR) of the additional amount of investment is worthwhile. However, in using the IIRR analysis, we do not compute the present values of costs of the alternatives at the specified MARR $= i^*$ as we do in the incremental benefit-cost analysis. Consequently, we cannot arrange the alternatives in the ascending order of the present values of their costs for the purpose of making successive pairwise comparisons.

One way to overcome this problem is to arrange the alternatives in the ascending order of their net present valuse at MARR $= 0\%$, since $[NPV_x]_{0\%}$ for any alternative x can readily be obtained from its cash flow profile without discounting. Referring again to Fig. 8.6(a), the net present values at $i = 0\%$ for $x = 1, 2$, and 3 are in the ascending order. We shall defer the discussion of ordering the alternatives under special conditions, such as when the net present values at $i = 0\%$ for two alternatives are equal. In this section, we shall only examine the basic concept of the IIRR analysis for the example in Fig. 8.6(a).

Let us emphasize again that each of the three alternatives ($x = 1, 2$, and 3) in Fig. 8.6(a) is assumed to have only a single value of IRR_x. Then, we may consider the internal rate of return i_1 as the incremental internal rate of return i_{1-0} for the

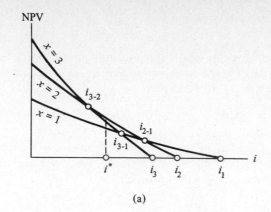

(a)

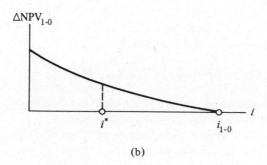

(b)

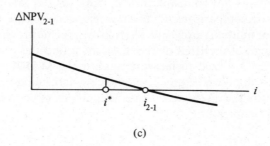

(c)

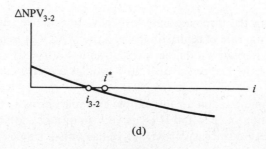

(d)

FIGURE 8.6

213

pairwise comparison between $x = 1$ and the null alternative $x = 0$. Thus, we can plot a ΔNPV_{1-0} versus i graph as shown in Fig. 8.6(b). Note that because $NPV_0 = 0$ for the null alternative $x = 0$, we have

$$\Delta NPV_{1-0} = NPV_1 - NPV_0 = NPV_1$$

Since $i_{1-0} > i^*$ as indicated in the figure, we choose $x = 1$ over $x = 0$. Next, we compare $x = 1$ with the next higher order alternative $x = 2$ and obtain a ΔNPV_{2-1} versus i graph as shown in Fig. 8.6(c) in which

$$\Delta NPV_{2-1} = NPV_2 - NPV_1$$

With $i_{2-1} > i^*$ as shown in the figure we choose $x = 2$ over $x = 1$. Finally, we compare $x = 2$ with the next higher order alternative $x = 3$ and obtain a ΔNPV_{3-2} versus i graph as shown in Fig. 8.6(d) in which

$$\Delta NPV_{3-2} = NPV_3 - NPV_2$$

Because $i_{3-2} < i^*$ as shown in the figure, we choose $x = 2$ over $x = 3$; hence $x = 2$ is the best among the three mutually exclusive alternatives.

Note that i_{1-0} in Fig. 8.6(b) is identical to i_1 in Fig. 8.6(a), and that i_{2-1} in Fig. 8.6(c) and i_{3-2} in Fig. 8.6(d) are identical to i_{2-1} and i_{3-2} in Fig. 8.6(a), respectively. Since we have not compared alternative $x = 1$ and $x = 3$ directly as a pair, i_{3-1} in Fig. 8.6(a) is not compared to i^*. Thus, for the example in Fig. 8.6(a), we have made pairwise comparisons in the ascending order of the net present values at $i = 0\%$ for a set of mutually exclusive alternatives, including the null alternative. At the successive stages of the IIRR analysis, we must find the values of i_{1-0}, i_{2-1}, and i_{3-1} because they are used to measure against the MARR $= i^*$. The computation of these IIRR values can be quite complicated, depending to a large extent on the cash flow profiles of the alternatives, but the methods of computation have been discussed in detail in Chapter 4.

Example 8.3

Select the best among the three mutually exclusive alternatives in Table 8.4, using the incremental internal rate of return analysis, if the MARR specified is 20%.

For the given alternatives, the net present values at $i = 0\%$ as represented by the algebraic sums of the respective cash flow profiles are also computed as shown in Table 8.4.

Since the planning horizon for this simple example consists of only one interest period, the computation of IRR and IIRR is very simple, i.e., to find the percentage gain over a 1-year period since each alternative has only a single value of IRR. The alternatives $x = 1$, 2, and 3 are arranged in the ascending order of $[NPV_x]_{0\%}$.

Table 8.4

Cash Flow Profiles of Three Alternatives

t	$A_{1,t}$ $(x = 1)$	$A_{2,t}$ $(x = 2)$	$A_{3,t}$ $(x = 3)$
0	-100	-200	-300
1	$+150$	$+280$	$+395$
$[NPV_x]_{0\%}$	$+\ 50$	$+\ 80$	$+\ 95$

Thus, we begin by comparing the lowest order alternative $x = 1$ with the null alternative $x = 0$. That is,

$$i_{1-0} = i_1 = \frac{150 - 100}{100} = \frac{50}{100} = 50\% \quad (>20\%)$$

Hence, the alternative $x = 1$ is preferable. Next we compare $x = 1$ with the next higher order alternative by computing

$$i_{2-1} = \frac{(280 - 150) - (200 - 100)}{200 - 100} = \frac{30}{100} = 30\% \quad (>20\%)$$

Hence, the alternative $x = 2$ is preferable. Finally, we compare $x = 2$ with the next higher ordered alternative by computing

$$i_{3-2} = \frac{(395 - 280) - (300 - 200)}{300 - 200} = \frac{15}{100} = 15\% \quad (<20\%)$$

Again, we choose the alternative $x = 2$, which is the best among the three mutually exclusive alternatives.

Note that by taking the first step to compare $x = 1$ with the null alternative, we are assured that the final choice is economically feasible as well as being the best among the set of mutually exclusive alternatives.

8.6 Ordering Mutually Exclusive Alternatives for Pairwise Comparisons

After introducing the basic concept of incremental internal rate of return analysis, we can now consider the ordering of a set of mutually exclusive alternatives for successive pairwise comparisons in detail. We shall adopt the following notation:

y = the lower order alternative previously accepted prior to the comparison with the higher order alternative x

i_{x-y} = the incremental internal rate of return for the pairwise comparison between the alternatives x and y

ΔNPV_{x-y} = the difference of the net present values of the cash flow profiles of alternatives x and y, i.e., $NPV_x - NPV_y$.

$d(\Delta N)/di$ = the first derivative of ΔNPV_{x-y} with respect to i

We recommend arranging the alternatives in the ascending order of their net present values at $i = 0\%$ because this arrangement is the basis of a correct and workable procedure covering all possible conditions for determining the economic acceptability of the alternatives as well as for selecting the best among all alternatives.

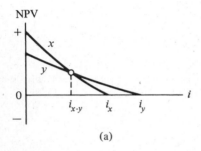

(a)

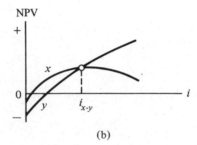

(b)

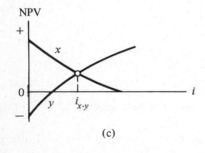

(c)

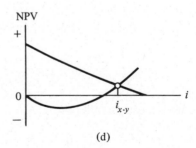

(d)

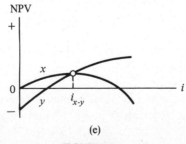

(e)

FIGURE 8.7

In arranging the mutually exclusive alternatives in the ascending order of $[NPV_x]_{0\%}$, we start with the alternative having the lowest *algebraic* value. This arrangement is always possible as long as the values of $[NPV_x]_{0\%}$ for all alternatives are distinct (unequal). Then, with a pairwise comparison between alternatives x and y, the alternative with the *lower algebraic value* of $[NPV_x]_{0\%}$ can be positive, negative, or zero. Figure 8.7 shows examples of pairwise combinations of the algebraic values of $[NPV_x]_{0\%}$ which are unequal. Figure 8.8 also shows cases with unequal $[NPV_x]_{0\%}$, but the NPV curves representing the two alternatives do not intersect in the positive range of i.

If the values of $[NPV_x]_{0\%}$ for two or more alternatives are equal, they may be all positive, all negative, or all zero. In either case, we must seek a way to break the tie in ordering them. We can first compute the values of $[dN_x/di]_{0\%}$ for these alternatives, using Eq. (8.5) or (8.6). Then, we arrange them according to the ascending order of $[dN_x/di]_{0\%}$, starting with the alternative having the *lowest* algebraic value. Recalling that dN_x/di represents the slope of the NPV-MARR curve, this arrangement will simply follow the ascending order of the *algebraic values of the initial slopes* of these curves. Figure 8.9 shows examples of pairwise combinations of

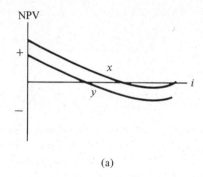

(a)

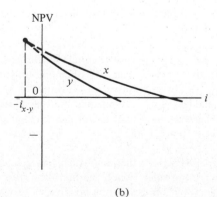

(b)

FIGURE 8.8

the algebraic values of $[NPV_x]_{0\%}$ that are equal, and hence the alternatives are arranged according to the algebraic values of the initial slopes $[dN_x/di]_{0\%}$.

To recapitulate, the ordering of a set of mutually exclusive alternatives can be based on the following rules:

1. Arrange the alternatives according to the ascending order of the *algebraic values* of $[NPV_x]_{0\%}$ if these values are unequal.
2. Among those whose algebraic values of $[NPV_x]_{0\%}$ are equal, arrange them in the ascending order of the *algebraic values* of $[dN_x/di]_{0\%}$.

These rules for ordering the alternatives will cover all possible conditions shown in Figs. 8.7, 8.8, and 8.9.

In order to compute i_{x-y} in a pairwise comparison between x and y, we note that the incremental benefit and the incremental cost at any time period t may be obtained from the cash flow profiles of alternatives x and y as follows:

$$\Delta B_{t,x-y} = B_{t,x} - B_{t,y} \tag{8.9}$$

$$\Delta C_{t,x-y} = C_{t,x} - C_{t,y} \tag{8.10}$$

Alternately, the incremental net value (between benefit and cost) at any time period is given by

$$\Delta A_{t,x-y} = A_{t,x} - A_{t,y} \tag{8.11}$$

Then, for a discount rate i,

$$[\Delta NPV_{x-y}]_i = [NPV_x]_i - [NPV_y]_i \tag{8.12}$$

The incremental internal rate of return i_{x-y} is the discount rate i at which ΔNPV_{x-y} is zero. To differentiate the multiple values of the incremental internal rate of return, they will be designated as i'_{x-y}, i''_{x-y}, etc., starting from the lowest and reaching the highest value except when one of the values is zero. In that case, the zero value will not be counted in the designation.

In making pairwise comparisons of two alternatives x and y, the following situations may be encountered:

1. When $[NPV_x]_{0\%}$ and $[NPV_y]_{0\%}$ are unequal, the former is greater than the latter according to the ordering rule. Whether one or more values of IIRR exists, $[\Delta NPV_{x-y}]_{0\%}$ is always positive, as shown in Fig. 8-10(a) or (b).
2. When $[NPV_x]_{0\%}$ and $[NPV_y]_{0\%}$ are unequal but the value(s) of IIRR is either indeterminate or negative, the former is still greater than the latter according to the ordering rule. Hence, $[NPV_{x-y}]_{0\%}$ is also positive, as shown in Fig. 8.10(c) or (d).
3. When $[NPV_x]_{0\%} = [NPV_y]_{0\%}$, then $[dN_x/di]_{0\%}$ is greater than $[dN_y/di]_{0\%}$ according to the ordering rule. Hence, the first derivative of the incremental net present value at $i = 0\%$ must also be positive, as shown in Fig. 8.10(e) or

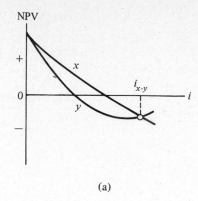

(a)

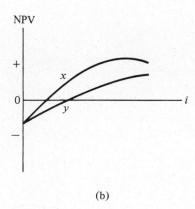

(b)

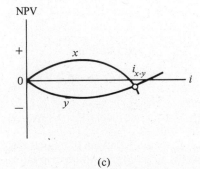

(c)

FIGURE 8.9

219

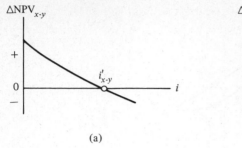

(a)

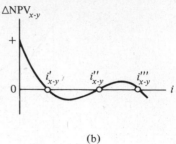

(b)

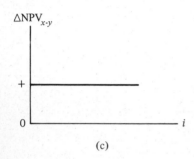

(c)

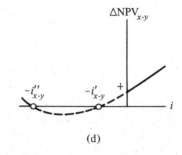

(d)

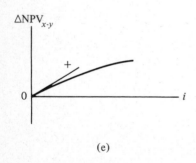

(e)

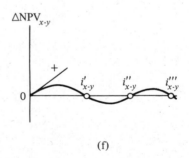

(f)

FIGURE 8.10

(f), because

$$[d(\Delta N)/di]_{0\%} = [dN_x/di]_{0\%} - [dN_y/di]_{0\%} > 0$$

4. When both $[\Delta NPV_{x-y}]_{0\%}$ and $[d(\Delta N)/di]_{0\%}$ equal zero, we can check whether the second derivative at $i = 0\%$ is positive, negative, or zero. If it is zero, we should test the third derivative, etc. However, the occurrence of such cases is very unlikely, and therefore their discussion is not included.

Consequently, we need a set of criteria instead of a single criterion for selecting the best among a set of mutually exclusive alternatives. This set of criteria may be stated as follows:

(a) When $[NPV_{x-y}]_{0\%}$ is positive and there is only a single value of i_{x-y}, the higher order alternative x is preferable if $i^* \leq i'_{x-y}$; otherwise the lower order alternative y is preferable.

(b) When $[NPV_{x-y}]_{0\%}$ is positive but there are multiple values of i (i'_{x-y}, i''_{x-y}, i'''_{x-y}, etc., starting from the lowest to the highest value), the following rules hold:

    (1) If the Marr i^* is less than i'_{x-y}, the project x is preferable.

    (2) If the MARR i^* is higher than i'_{x-y} but less than i''_{x-y}, the project y is preferable.

    (3) If the MARR i^* is higher than the i''_{x-y} but less than i'''_{x-y}, the project x is preferable.

    (4) The preference of x or y alternates with each successive value of i_{x-y}.

(c) When $[NPV_{x-y}]_{0\%}$ is positive but i_{x-y} is indeterminate, the higher order alternative x is preferable.

(d) When $[\Delta NPV_{x-y}]_{0\%}$ is positive but all values of i_{x-y} are negative, the higher order alternative is preferable.

(e) When $[\Delta NPV_{x-y}]_{0\%}$ is zero and there is only a single value of $i_{x-y} = 0$, the higher order alternative x is always preferable.

(f) When $[\Delta NPV_{x-y}]_{0\%}$ is zero but there are multiple values of i_{x-y}, use the same rule as (b) except ignore the value of $i_{x-y} = 0$. That is, the first i_{x-y} value which is greater than zero is defined as the lowest value.

8.7   Decision Criteria for Selection Among Mutually Exclusive Alternatives

The decision criteria for selecting an alternative in the successive pairwise comparisons can be summarized as in Table 8.5. The final choice will be the best among the mutually exclusive alternatives. If the null alternative is included in the successive pairwise comparisons, then the best alternative must necessarily be economically feasible without making a separate investigation.

Example 8.4

The cash flow profiles for the three mutually exclusive alternatives are shown in the top part of Table 8.6. The MARR is specified to be 12%. Using the incremental internal rate of return analysis, select the best alternative that is economically feasible.

For the purpose of ordering alternatives, we first compute $[NPV_x]_{0\%}$ for $x = 1, 2,$ and 3 using Eq. (8.4).

Table 8.5

Decision Criteria for Accepting or Rejecting
Higher Order Alternative *x*
in Successive Pairwise Comparisons

Range of $i*$	Condition: $[NPV_{x-y}]_{0\%} \geq 0$
$0 \leq i* \leq i'_{x-y}$	Accept *x*
$i'_{x-y} < i* < i''_{x-y}$	Reject *x*; accept *y*
$i''_{x-y} < i* < i'''_{x-y}$	Accept *x*
$i'''_{x-y} < i* < i''''_{x-y}$	Reject *x*; accept *y*
Additional i_{x-y}	Alternate accepting and rejecting *x*
Negative or indeterminate	Accept *x*

$$[NPV_1]_{0\%} = -10,000 + (6)(3,000) = 8,000$$

$$[NPV_2]_{0\%} = -10,000 + (3)(6,000) = 8,000$$

$$[NPV_3]_{0\%} = -1,500 + (6)(6,000) = 4,500$$

Thus, $x = 3$ is the lowest order alternative, but $x = 1$ and $x = 2$ are tied. Therefore, we proceed to compute $[dN_x/di]_{0\%}$ for $x = 1$ and $x = 2$, using Eq. (8.6).

$$[dN_1/di]_{0\%} = -(1 + 2 + 3 + 4 + 5 + 6)(3,000) = -63,000$$

$$[dN_2/di]_{0\%} = -(1 + 2 + 3)(6,000) = -36,000$$

Since the *algebraic value* of the slope for $x = 1$ is smaller (most negative), $x = 1$ is regarded as having a lower order. Hence, the ascending order of these alternatives is $x = 3$, $x = 1$, and $x = 2$. The results of the computation are tabulated in the bottom part of Table 8.6.

We therefore first compare $x = 3$ with the null alternative ($x = 0$) by computing $\Delta A_{t,3-0}$ as tabulated in Table 8.7. Since this incremental cash flow profile has only one sign change, we expect a single value for i_{3-0}. Noting that $[\Delta NPV_{3-0}]_{0\%}$ is positive, we proceed to solve for $i = i_{3-0}$ by letting $[\Delta NPV_{3-0}]_i = 0$. That is,

$$-1,500 + (1,000)(P \mid U, i, 6) = 0$$

Table 8.6

Cash Flow Profiles for
Three Mutually Exclusive Alternatives

t	$A_{t,1}$	$A_{t,2}$	$A_{t,3}$
0	−10,000	−10,000	−1,500
1	3,000	6,000	1,000
2	3,000	6,000	1,000
3	3,000	6,000	1,000
4	3,000	0	1,000
5	3,000	0	1,000
6	3,000	0	1,000
$[NPV_x]_{0\%}$	+ 8,000	+ 8,000	+4,500
$[dN_x/di]_{0\%}$	−63,000	−36,000	
Ascending order	Middle	Highest	Lowest

or

$$(P \mid U, i, 6) = \frac{1,500}{1,000} = 1.5$$

We know that i is greater than $i^* = 12\%$ since its value is outside the range of the discrete compound interest tables in Appendix A. It has been found by a pocket

Table 8.7

Incremental Cash Flow Profiles

t	$\Delta A_{t,3-0}$	$\Delta A_{t,1-3}$	$\Delta A_{t,2-3}$
0	−1,500	−8,500	−8,500
1	1,000	2,000	5,000
2	1,000	2,000	5,000
3	1,000	2,000	5,000
4	1,000	2,000	−1,000
5	1,000	2,000	−1,000
6	1,000	2,000	−1,000
$[\Delta NPV_{x-y}]_{0\%}$	+4,500	+3,500	+3,500
i_{x-y}	62.6%	10.86%	27.57%

calculator to be approximately 62.6%. Since this value of $i_{3-0} = 62.6\%$ is greater than $i^* = 12\%$, the alternative $x = 3$ is preferable over the null alternative ($x = 0$).

Next, we compare $x = 3$ with the next higher order alternative $x = 1$ by computing $\Delta A_{t,1-3}$ as tabulated in Table 8.7. Since this incremental cash flow profile has only one sign change, we expect a single value for i_{1-3}. Noting that $[\Delta NPV_{1-3}]_{0\%}$ is positive, we solve for $i = i_{1-3}$ by letting $[\Delta NPV_{1-3}]_i = 0$. That is,

$$-8,500 + (2,000)(P\,|\,U, i, 6) = 0$$

or

$$(P\,|\,U, i, 6) = \frac{8,500}{2,000} = 4.25$$

From the discrete compound interest tables in Appendix A, the value of i is found to lie between 10% and 12%; using interpolation

$$i = 10\% + (12\% - 10\%)\,\frac{4.3553 - 4.25}{4.3553 - 4.1114} = 10.86\%$$

Since $i_{1-3} = 10.86\%$ is less than $i^* = 12\%$, the alternative $x = 3$ is preferable.

Finally, we compare $x = 3$ with $x = 2$ by computing ΔA_{2-3} as tabulated in Table 8.7. Since this incremental cash flow profile has two sign changes, it is possible to have 0, 1, or 2 values for i_{2-3}. Noting that $[\Delta NPV_{2-3}]_{0\%}$ is positive, we solve for $i = i_{2-3}$ by letting $[\Delta NPV_{2-3}]_i = 0$. That is,

$$-8,500 + (6,000)(P\,|\,U, i, 3) - (1,000)(P\,|\,U, i, 6) = 0$$

Try $i = 25\%$:

$$-8,500 + (6,000)(1.9520) - (1,000)(2.9514) = +260.6$$

Try $i = 30\%$:

$$-8,500 + (6,000)(1.8161) - (1,000)(2.6427) = -246.1$$

By interpolation,

$$i = 25\% + (30\% - 25\%)\,\frac{260.6}{260.6 + 246.1} = 27.57\%$$

Since $i_{2-3} = 27.57\%$ is greater than $i^* = 12\%$, the alternative $x = 2$ is preferable. The final choice of $x = 2$ is not only the best among the three mutually exclusive alternatives but it must necessarily be economically feasible because $x = 1$ is proved to be economically feasible (compared to the null alternative $x = 0$) and $x = 2$ is proved to be better than $x = 1$ through successive pairwise comparisons.

Note that the pair in each column (except the pair of $x = 1$ and $x = 0$) cannot be determined until a choice has been made in the previous column. In other words, we select $x = 1$ over $x = 0$ and then compare $x = 1$ with the next higher order alternative $x = 3$; similarly, we select $x = 1$ over $x = 3$ before comparing it with the next higher alternative $x = 2$.

Example 8.5

Suppose that $x = 1$ and $x = 2$ in Example 8.4 are the only mutually exclusive alternatives. Rework the problem using the incremental internal rate of return analysis.

Since these two alternatives have the same value for $[NPV_x]_{0\%}$, they are ordered according to the algebraic value of $[dN_x/di]_{0\%}$. Thus, $x = 1$ is regarded as the lower order alternative and $x = 2$ the higher order one.

In comparing $x = 1$ with the null alternative $x = 0$, we find the incremental cash flow profile $\Delta A_{t,1-0}$ as shown in Table 8.8. With only one sign change and $[\Delta NPV_{1-0}]_{0\%}$ being positive, we can find $i = i_{1-0}$ by letting $[\Delta NPV_{1-0}]_{0\%} = 0$. That is,

$$-1,000 + (3,000)(P\,|\,U,\,i,\,6) = 0$$

or

$$(P\,|\,U,\,i,\,6) = \frac{10,000}{3,000} = 3.3333$$

Table 8.8

Incremental Cash Flow Profiles
for Two Alternatives

t	$\Delta A_{t,1-0}$	$\Delta A_{t,2-1}$
0	− 10,000	0
1	3,000	3,000
2	3,000	3,000
3	3,000	3,000
4	3,000	− 3,000
5	3,000	− 3,000
6	3,000	− 3,000
$[\Delta NPV_{x-y}]_{0\%}$	+ 8,000	0
i_{x-y}	20%	0%

From the discrete compound interest tables in Appendix A, we find that i equals 20% approximately. Since $i_{1-0} = 20\%$ is greater than $i^* = 12\%$, the alternative $x = 1$ is preferable.

Next, we compare $x = 1$ with $x = 2$ by finding the incremental cash flow profile $\Delta A_{t,2-1}$ as shown in Table 8.8. Since there is only one sign change in this cash flow profile and $[\Delta NPV_{2-1}]_{0\%} = 0$, $i_{2-1} = 0\%$. Then, the higher order alternative $x = 2$ is preferable without the necessity of making any further analysis. (The alternatives are arranged in the increasing order of the algebraic values of the initial slopes of the NPV versus MARR curve; hence the initial slope of the ΔNPV_{2-1} versus MARR curve is positive, indicating that $x = 2$ is preferable.)

Example 8.6

A small oil company is deciding between two different oil pumps for extracting oil from a well. The more expensive pump ($x = 1$) would permit the oil to be extracted more quickly and increase slightly the total amount of oil extracted than the less expensive pump ($x = 2$). The cash flow profiles of these two mutually exclusive alternatives (in thousands of dollars) are shown in Table 8.9. The MARR is specified to be 15%. Using the incremental internal rate of return analysis, determine which pump, if any, should be selected.

Based on the values of $[NPV_x]_{0\%}$ for $x = 1$ and $x = 2$ in Table 8.9, $x = 1$ is regarded as the lower order alternative and $x = 2$ the higher order one. Therefore, we first compare $x = 1$ with the null alternative ($x = 0$), using the cash flow profile $A_{t,1}$ which is identical to the incremental cash flow profile $A_{t,1-0}$. Since there is only one sign change in the cash flow profile, we can find $i = i_{1-0}$ by letting $[\Delta NPV_{1-0}]_i = 0$. That is,

$$-110,000 + 115,000 (1 + i)^{-1} + 30,000(1 + i)^{-2} = 0$$

Table 8.9

Cash Flow Profiles for Two Oil Pumps (in $1,000)

t	$B_{t,1}$	$C_{t,1}$	$A_{t,1}$	$B_{t,2}$	$C_{t,2}$	$A_{t,2}$	$\Delta A_{t,2-1}$ $= A_{t,2} - A_{t,1}$
	x = 1			x = 2			
0	0	110	−110	0	100	−100	+10
1	115	0	115	70	0	70	−45
2	30	0	30	70	0	70	+40
$[NPV_x]_{0\%}$			+ 35			+ 40	+ 5

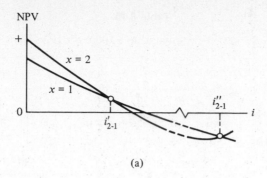

(a)

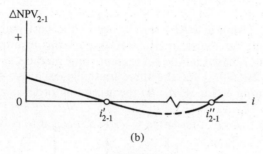

(b)

FIGURE 8.11

from which we get $i = 26.16\%$. Since $i_{1-0} = 26.16\%$ is greater than $i^* = 15\%$, the alternative 1 is preferable to the null alternative $x = 0$.

Next, we compare $x = 1$ with $x = 2$ by computing the incremental profile $A_{t,2-1}$ as shown in Table 8.9. Since there are two sign changes, we may have 0, 1, or 2 values of i which will satisfy $[\Delta NPV_{2-1}]_i = 0$. That is,

$$+10,000 - 45,000 (1 + i)^{-1} + 40,000 (1 + i)^{-2} = 0$$

from which we get $i = 21.92\%$ and 228.08%. Thus, for a positive value of $[\Delta NPV_{2-1}]_{0\%}$, the alternative 2 is preferable between $i = 0\%$ and 21.92%, but not between 21.92% and 228.08%. Hence, the alternative 2 is preferable since $i^* = 15\%$ is less than $i'_{2-1} = 21.92\%$. The relationships of NPV versus MARR and NPV_{2-1} versus MARR are shown in Fig. 8.11. Therefore, $x = 2$ is economically acceptable and is the better of the two alternatives.

Example 8.7

Three plans have been proposed for a small commercial building at a leased site, and the time streams of costs and benefits for these plans in the next 40 years are

Table 8.10

Cost and Benefit Streams (in $1,000) of Three Plans

	$x = 1$		$x = 2$		$x = 3$	
t	$C_{t,1}$	$B_{t,1}$	$C_{t,2}$	$B_{t,2}$	$C_{t,3}$	$B_{t,3}$
0	200	0	250	0	300	0
1–40 (each)	40	63	30	52	55	77
$[NPV_x]_{0\%}$	720		630		580	

shown in Table 8.10. Using a MARR of 6%, select the best plan on the basis of incremental internal rate of return analysis. (Compare this example with Example 6.2 in Chapter 6, which is based on the net present value method.)

The values of $[NPV_x]_{0\%}$ for the three mutually exclusive alternatives have been computed according to Eq. (8.4), and the ascending order of the alternatives is found to be $x = 3$, $x = 2$, and $x = 1$.

Comparing with the null alternative $x = 0$, we proceed to solve for $i = i_{3-0}$ by letting $[\Delta NPV_{3-0}]_i = 0$. That is,

$$-300 + (77 - 55)(P|U, i, 40) = 0$$

from which we find $i_{3-0} = 6.82\%$. Since this is greater than $i^* = 6\%$, the alternative $x = 3$ is preferable to the null alternative.

Next, we try to solve $i = i_{2-3}$ from the equation representing $[\Delta NPV_{2-3}]_i = 0$. We obtain

$$-(250 - 300) + [(52 - 77) - (30 - 55)](P|U, i, 40) = 0$$

or

$$(P|U, i, 40) = \frac{-50}{0} = -\infty$$

According to the criteria in Table 8.5, we accept the higher order alternative, which is $x = 2$ in this case.

Finally, we try to solve for $i = i_{1-2}$ from the equation representing $[\Delta NPV_{1-2}] = 0$. We find

$$-(200 - 250) + [(63 - 52) - (40 - 30)](P|U, i, 40) = 0$$

or

$$(P \mid U, i, 40) = -50$$

Therefore, we accept the higher order alternative $x = 1$, which is the best among the three plans.

8.8   The Application of the Internal Rate of Return Method

It is often argued by the advocates of the internal rate of return method that the multiple values of the internal rate of return seldom occur in practice. Let us examine whether this statement is correct.

In the direct analysis of independent projects, cash flow profiles with multiple sign changes may be found most often in the following situations:

1. Capital projects which require periodic rehabilitation as well as equipment replacement, such as highway resurfacing or bridge repair projects, over the entire planning horizon or life cycle
2. Capital projects which require large expenditures for restoring the natural environment at the end of their useful lives, such as the restoration of a strip-mining site after the removal of coals or the disposal of hazardous materials upon the termination of the operation of a chemical plant
3. Overseas construction projects or military equipment orders by foreign governments for which large partial payments are made in advance as well as at the end of the projects

The criteria presented in Table 8.2 are intended to cover all possible siutations in direct analysis.

However, the multiple sign changes in a cash flow profile occur most frequently in the incremental internal rate of return analysis for selecting the best among the mutually exclusive alternatives. The cash flow profiles used in Examples 8.4, and 8.6 are certainly quite conventional, but in each example, multiple sign changes appear in an incremental cash flow profile obtained from the given data. Furthermore, the existence of equal values of $[\mathrm{NPV}_x]_{0\%}$ for some or all of the alternatives is not at all uncommon, as in the case of Example 8.5. Consequently, the criteria presented in Table 8.5 are needed to cover different situations in the incremental analysis.

It is a common current practice to arrange the projects in the ascending order of the *initial costs* in the application of the internal rate of return method. However, such an ordering scheme is not generally applicable, particularly when some of the cash flow profiles of the mutually exclusive alternatives have multiple internal rates of return. Consequently, only the ordering scheme described in this chapter is recommended.

8.9   Summary and Study Guide

In this chapter, we have considered the use of the internal rate of return (IRR) criteria in the direct analysis of the acceptability of an independent project. In particular, we have considered a set of decision criteria needed to cover all possible conditions that may be encountered in the analysis. We can use $[NPV]_{0\%}$ as the basis for classifying various conditions, and when $[NPV]_{0\%} = 0$, we can further divide the conditions into the case with a positive initial slope and that of a negative initial slope of the NPV curve at $i = 0\%$. The cases in which the IRR is indeterminate or negative were also considered.

The concept of incremental internal rate of return (IIRR) was introduced for successive pairwise comparisons in selecting the best among a set of mutually exclusive alternatives. The alternatives were arranged in the ascending order of $[NPV_x]_{0\%}$ and, when there was a tie between two alternatives, in the ascending order of $[dN_x/di]_{0\%}$. A set of decision criteria has also been introduced to cover all possible conditions in the incremental analysis. If the null alternative is included in the successive pairwise comparisons, then the best alternative must necessarily be economically feasible without making a separate investigation.

The internal rate of return method for economic evaluation is cumbersome, whether it is applied to the direct analysis of independent projects or to the incremental analysis of mutually exclusive alternatives. The popularity of the IRR method can only be attributed to the ignorance of the shortcomings of the method. If the advocates of the method understand fully the complications which may be introduced in order to apply the method correctly, there is every reason to believe that this method will eventually be rejected. In the meantime, this chapter has presented a complete treatment of the method so that it can at least be used correctly for economic evaluation.

REFERENCES

8.1 Petty, J. Q., D. F. Scott, Jr., and M. M. Bird, "The Capital Expenditure Decision Maing Process of Large Corporations," *The Engineering Economist*, **20**, no. 3 (1975), 159–173.

8.2 Rapp, B., "The Internal Rate of Return Method—A Critical Study," *Engineering Costs and Production Economics*, Vol. 5. Amsterdam, The Netherlands: Elsevier Scientific Publishing Co., (1980), 43–52.

8.3 Wohl, M., "New Ranking Procedure and Set of Decision Rules for Method of Internal Rate of Return," *Transportation Research Record* no. 828 (1981), 3–5.

PROBLEMS

P8.1 Select the best proposal among the alternatives in Problem P6.1 (Chapter 6), using the internal rate of return method.

P8.2 Select the best proposal among the alternatives in Problem P6.2 (Chapter 6), using the internal rate of return method.

P8.3 Select the best proposal among the alternatives in Problem P6.6 (Chapter 6), using the internal rate of return method.

P8.4 Select the best proposal among the alternatives in Problem P6.8 (Chapter 6), using the internal rate of return method if MARR = 4%.

P8.5 Select the best proposal among the mutually exclusive alternatives given below, using the internal rate of return method. The MARR specified is 6%.

t	$A_{t,1}$	$A_{t,2}$	$A_{t,3}$
0	-200	-350	-300
1	$+50$	$+100$	$+70$
2	$+50$	$+90$	$+70$
3	$+50$	$+80$	$+70$
4	$+50$	$+70$	$+70$
5	$+50$	$+60$	$+70$

P8.6 The benefits and costs of the alternatives for a stagewise improvement of an existing bridge are given below (in thousands of dollars). Select the best proposal using the internal rate of return method. The MARR specified is 10%.

	$x = 1$		$x = 2$	
t	$C_{t,1}$	$B_{t,1}$	$C_{t,1}$	$B_{t,2}$
0	100	0	800	0
1–10 (each)	0	50	0	200
11	900	50	0	200
12–20 (each)	0	200	0	200
21	0	200	500	200
22–30 (each)	0	200	0	150

P8.7 The public works department of a city is considering three mutually exclusive proposals for a road-resurfacing program. The cash flow profiles for the benefits and costs of the program are given below. The MARR specified is 8%. Select the best proposal using the internal rate of return method.

t	$A_{t,1}$	$A_{t,2}$	$A_{t,3}$
0	− 40,000	− 20,000	− 70,000
1	+ 30,000	+ 25,000	+ 40,000
2	+ 30,000	+ 25,000	+ 35,000
3	+ 30,000	+ 25,000	+ 30,000
4	− 30,000	− 25,000	+ 25,000
5	+ 30,000	+ 25,000	+ 20,000
6	+ 30,000	+ 25,000	+ 15,000

P8.8 Select the best proposal among the alternatives in Problem P7.8 (Chapter 7), using the internal rate of return method.

9

CAPITAL RATIONING

9.1 Basic Concepts

In previous chapters, we have assumed that the MARR specified by an organization is the appropriate discount rate for computing the net present values of investment proposals. Thus, the measure of the profit potential of investment proposals and subsequently the decision for accepting or selecting investment projects are dependent on the specified MARR. The basic idea underlying the decision criteria for accepting and selecting investment projects is that if an organization can lend or borrow as much money as it wishes at the MARR, the goal of profit maximization of the organization is best served by accepting all independent projects whose net present values based on the MARR are nonnegative, or by selecting the project with the maximum nonnegative net present value among a set of mutually exclusive alternatives. When an organization can lend or borrow freely at the MARR, the acceptance and selection of investment projects does not depend on the amount of internal funds available in the organization since it can always finance worthwhile projects through borrowing if necessary.

As stated in Section 5.4, an organization may acquire the necessary funds for an investment project in a variety of ways, usually through a combination of internal funding, borrowing, and lending. The internal funds can be made available by using the working capital generated from its operations, by liquidating part of its business, or by selling its holdings in marketable securities such as government bonds. Borrowing refers to the acquisition of capital from outside sources such as issuing additional securities, e.g., long-term notes and bonds, or securing short-term loans from banks. Lending refers to investing the surplus funds in outside agents, such as acquiring the stock of other companies, purchasing certificates of deposit, or depositiong money in banks or money market funds. The borrowing rate refers to the interest rate at which investment capital can be acquired from outisde, and the lending rate refers to the interest rate at which a firm or an agency is willing to loan or invest its assets outside of the organization. In a perfectly competitive market, the borrowing rate and the lending rate are equal, and this market interest rate may be regarded as the MARR.

In reality, the lending rate and the borrowing rate are different because of market imperfections, and the divergence of these two rates may occur for a variety of reasons, such as financial transaction costs, brokerage fees, and the credit ratings of the firms. Consequently, the determination of the MARR by an organization is to some degree arbitrary. In the private sector, the MARR reflects the *opportunity cost of capital* of a firm, the market interest rates for lending and borrowing, and the risks associated with investment opportunities. In the public sector, the MARR is referred to as the *social discount rate* since it reflects social and economic welfare considerations in the public interest as well as the opportunity cost of capital. Although the discussion of major issues influencing the determination of the MARR for private firms and public agencies will be deferred until Chapters 16 and 17, it is possible to examine the effects of market imperfections on the use of the MARR in computing the discounted cash flows for economic evaluation. Furthermore, when the management of an organization arbitrarily uses a cut-off rate which is higher than the market interest rates, it may inadvertently reject some profitable investment opportunities and thus dilute the goal of profit maximization.

Both types of situations referred to above, which prevent the acquisition of investment funds to realize the goal of profit maximization for an organization, are referred to as *capital rationing*. The situation which prevents lending and borrowing at the same interest rate because of market imperfections is referred to as *external capital rationing*, and the constraint imposed by the management which prevents the accepting of profitable investment opportunities is referred to as *internal capital rationing*.[1]

9.2   Schedule of Cumulative Present Costs for Investments

Suppose that several independent projects are examined for possible investments in a budgeting period and are found to have positive net present values at a specified discount rate. If the discount rate is increased, their net present values generally tend to decrease as typified by the NPV-MARR graph for conventional investments, and some of the net present values become negative at higher discount rates. Consequently, as the discount rate is increased, the cumulative outlays for investments in the budgeting period are expected to decrease because fewer projects will be acceptable. Therefore, we can construct a schedule or curve indicating the relationship between the cumulative present costs of acceptable projects versus the discount rates used in computing the net present values as shown schematically in Fig. 9.1.

It is important to define the term *cumulative present costs acceptable* in con-

---

[1] This classification of capital rationing and the concept associated with its application were first introduced in Ref. [9.1].

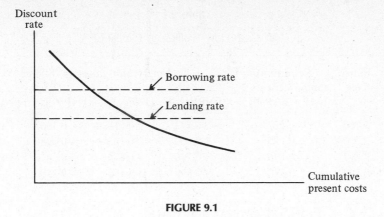

FIGURE 9.1

nection with capital rationing. Frequently, only the initial capital outlays in the current budgeting period are regarded as the present costs since the operation and maintenance costs in future years of these projects are budgeted separately. In reality, capital outlays may be required in future years, such as outlays for staged construction of a project or for periodic rehabilitations during the useful life of a project. Since the initial cost of a project by itself is not necessarily a good indicator of the total costs over the planning horizon, a more reasonable approach is to define the cumulative present cost as the *present values of costs* based on the *net cash flow profiles* of the projects. If the inflows in all future periods exceed the outflows beyond $t = 0$, then the persent values of costs will automatically reflect the initial costs of the projects only; otherwise, future outlays may be taken into consideration. While this approach offers only an approximate solution because the trade-offs between initial costs and subsequent rehabilitation costs are not systematically considered, it provides a useful framework for examining the effects of discount rates on the present values of costs of the accepted projects.

Example 9.1

Four independent projects, each having a useful life of 40 years and no salvage value at the end, are considered in the current budgeting period. The net cash flow profiles for each project x consists of an initial cost $C_{0,x}$ (at $t = 0$) and a stream of net uniform annual benefits U_x at $t = 0, 1, 2, \ldots, 40$ as shown in Table 9.1. The net present values of these projects are computed at the discount rates of $i = 7\%$, 8%, 9%, and 10%. Construct a schedule showing the relationship between the cumulative present costs and the discount rates.

Let the cumulative present costs of acceptable projects be denoted by Q. The present values of costs of the projects are the same as the initial costs in this case,

Table 9.1

Net Cash Flow Profiles (in $ million)

Project x	Initial cost $C_{0,x}$	Net uniform annual benefits U_x ($t = 1$ to 40)	Net present values at different i			
			$[NPV_x]_{7\%}$	$[NPV_x]_{8\%}$	$[NPV_x]_{9\%}$	$[NPV_x]_{10\%}$
1	1.000	0.127	+0.693	+0.514	+0.366	+0.242
2	2.000	0.195	+0.600	+0.325	+0.098	−0.093
3	1.867	0.196	+0.746	+0.470	+0.241	+0.050
4	3.800	0.330	+0.599	+0.135	−0.250	−0.573

i.e., $CPV_x = C_{0,x}$. From Table 9.1, we note that

$$[NPV_x]_{7\%} \geq 0 \text{ for all } x$$

$$[NPV_x]_{8\%} \geq 0 \text{ for all } x$$

$$[NPV_x]_{9\%} \geq 0 \text{ for } x = 1, 2, \text{ and } 3$$

$$[NPV_x]_{10\%} \geq 0 \text{ for } x = 1 \text{ and } 3$$

Consequently, the cumulative present costs Q of acceptable projects corresponding to different discount rates i are as follows:

$$[Q]_{7\%} = CPV_1 + CPV_2 + CPV_3 + CPV_4$$
$$= 1.000 + 2.000 + 1.867 + 3.800 = 8.667$$

$$[Q]_{8\%} = 8.667$$

$$[Q]_{9\%} = CPV_1 + CPV_2 + CPV_3 = 4.867$$

$$[Q]_{10\%} = CPV_1 + CPV_3 = 2.867$$

The schedule or curve representing the relationship between the cumulative present costs Q and discount rates i is shown in Fig. 9.2. Note that the curve becomes vertical below 8% because all four projects are acceptable for i values less than 8%.

9.3   External Capital Rationing

When the borrowing rate and the lending rate in the capital markets are significantly different, the effect of their difference on the investment and financial policies

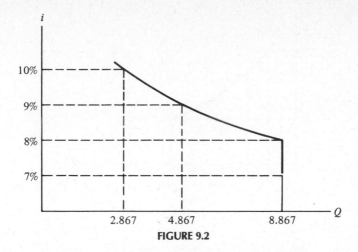

FIGURE 9.2

of a firm cannot be ignored. Under such circumstances, the firm must determine the internal funds available and the amount to be borrowed, if any, in financing capital projects. The portion of funding from internal sources is sometimes referred to as *equity funding*, and the portion obtained by borrowing from outside sources is referred to as *debt funding*.

It is important to note that a business firm periodically lends its idle funds to outside agents to earn interest as well as borrow from outside sources to finance available investment opportunities. Therefore, a firm may find itself in the lending as well as the borrowing situation during a budgeting period. The problems of financing capital projects and the choice of various debt instruments (stocks, bonds, etc.) require extensive knowledge of corporate finance and are left to the financial analysts. However, some simple policies may be examined here to illustrate when to borrow and when to lend, if at all, in the light of different borrowing and lending rates in the capital markets.

Let us consider three possible situations for which the MARR may be specified when the borrowing rate r_B is higher than the lending rate r_L as shown in the schedule of cumulative present costs in Fig. 9.3. Let the internal funds available for investment during the current budgeting period be denoted by the amount Q_I. In the first case, the discount rate corresponding to Q_I is seen to be r_I as shown in Fig. 9.3(a). Thus, at a discount rate r_I higher than the borrowing rate r_B, it would be profitable for the firm to borrow the amount $(Q_B - Q_I)$ to finance additional investments. In other words, by setting the MARR i^* equal to r_B, the procedures for economic evaluation described in previous chapters will not be affected. In the second case, the discount rate r_I corresponding to Q_I is lower than both the borrowing rate r_B and the lending rate r_L as shown in Fig. 9.3(b). Then, no borrowing will be necessary, and at a discount rate lower than the lending rate r_L, it would be profitable for the firm to loan the amount $(Q_I - Q_L)$ to outside agents. That is, by setting the MARR i^* equal to r_L, the procedures for economic evaluation described in previous chapters again will not be affected. In the third case, the discount rate r_I

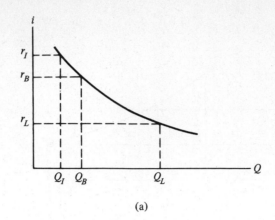

(a)

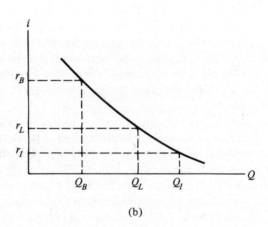

(b)

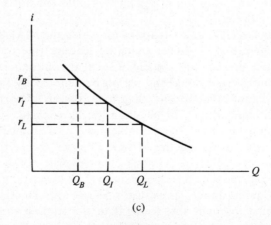

(c)

FIGURE 9.3

238

corresponding to the Q_I is lower than the borrowing rate r_B but higher than the lending rate r_L as shown in Fig. 9.3(c). Then, the firm would profit neither from borrowing any additional amount nor lending its available internal funds, and the MARR i^* will be set equal to r_I.

Consequently, the treatment of external capital rationing in budgeting can be summarized as follows:

1. If $i^* = r_B$, corresponding to the situation that $Q_I < Q_B$, it would be profitable to borrow up to the amount $(Q_B - Q_I)$.
2. If $i^* = r_L$, corresponding to the situation that $Q_I > Q_L$, it would be profitable to lend up to the amount $(Q_L - Q_I)$.
3. If $r_B < i^* < r_L$, neither borrowing nor lending would be profitable, and $i^* = r_I$.

9.4   Internal Capital Rationing

Internal capital rationing in budgeting often arises from the desire of the management of an organization to avoid borrowing for a variety of reasons. Hence, the cumulative present costs of all projects accepted for a budgeting period may be limited to a maximum amount C_q equal to the internal funds that can be made available. This approach is similar to the external capital rationing except that no upper limit is placed on the MARR so that some profitable projects may be rejected as a result of the budget constraint. Alternately, a cut-off rate i_q corresponding to the amount C_q may be specified as the MARR so that some projects with positive net present values at rates below i_q may also be rejected.

When budget constraints are imposed by an organization, the decision maker will be confronted with the problem of selecting the group of independent projects within the constraints which, taken together as a group, will produce the maximum net benefit. A theoretical approach to achieve this objective is to list all the possible combinations of grouping the independent projects and then select the group with the highest net present value after computing the net present values for all groups. Suppose that there are six feasible projects $(x = 1, 2, 3, 4, 5, 6)$ as well as the null alternative $(x = 0)$ under consideration. Let $\binom{m}{r}$ denote the number of combinations in selecting r projects from a set m projects. Since we can select 0, 1, 2, ..., 6 projects in a group, the total number of combinations in grouping the six projects is

$$N = \binom{6}{0} + \binom{6}{1} + \binom{6}{2} + \binom{6}{3} + \binom{6}{4} + \binom{6}{5} + \binom{6}{6}$$
$$= 1 + \frac{6!}{1!5!} + \frac{6!}{2!4!} + \frac{6!}{3!3!} + \frac{6!}{4!2!} + \frac{6!}{5!1!} + 1 = 64$$

In general, there are 2^m possible combinations for m projects. In this particular case, $2^6 = 64$. Because of the amount of work involved in computing the net present values for the combinations, this exhaustive search approach is not recommended in practice.

An approximate but practical approach is to rank all acceptable independent projects according to the benefit-cost ratios as computed by Eq. (5.11), using the specified MARR. If the budget constraint is reached *exactly* after a number of projects are selected according to the priority based on the highest benefit-cost ratios, then we have indeed accepted the group of projects which, taken together as a group, will produce the maximum net present value. However, if the budget constraint is not reached exactly after selecting a number of projects but it will be exceeded by the inclusion of the next highest ranked project, then it is not necessarily true that the group of projects under the budget constraint is the best selection. The reason for this outcome is that, given the possibility of not accepting one or more of the higher ranking projects, it is conceivable to find some combination of one with lower ranking projects to use up the budget completely such that, taken as a group, the new combination produces a larger net present value.

The indivisibility of acceptable projects is an important consideration in project selection under budget constraints. In general, if a relatively large number of independent projects of approximately the same size can be selected under a budget constraint, it is likely that selecting according to the priority based on the highest benefit-cost ratios leads to the best result, even though the actual investment is slightly under the budget constraint. On the other hand, if only a relatively small number of independent projects of different sizes can be selected under the budget constraint, then trial solutions may be necessary. These situations are depicted schematically in Figs. 9.4(a) and (b). Inasmuch as the mutually exclusive proposal may be made up of a number of projects, the problem of indivisibility of projects may also affect their selection.[2]

For simple situations in which the number of projects is small, some judgment can be exercised by the decision maker in picking the trial combinations, and the amount of work will usually be limited to a small number of trials. The examples in this chapter will be restricted to such cases.

Example 9.2

A public agency is considering six independent projects that have different useful lives. The cash flow profile for each project x consists of an initial cost $C_{0,x}$ and a stream of net uniform annual benefits U_x for years $t = 1, 2, \ldots, N_x$ where N_x is the useful life of project x. The salvage value at $t = N_x$ for project x is $S_{N,x}$. There will be no replacement when the useful life of a project expires. The numerical data for these projects are given in Table 9.2. The agency intends to adopt a planning horizon of 10 years and specifies a MARR of 10%. Which projects should be

---

[2] A more general formulation of this problem may be based on the mathematical programming approach. However, the discussion of such an approach and the technique for its solution are beyond the scope of this book.

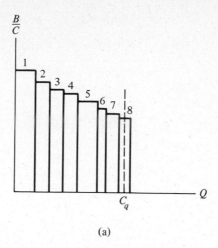

(a)

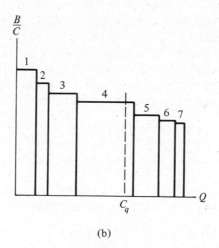

(b)

FIGURE 9.4

selected if the present value of the budget constraint is (a) $C_q = \$50$ million and (b) $C_q = \$100$ million?

The present values of benefits and costs (BPV_x and CPV_x, respectively) of these projects can be computed as follows:

$$\text{CPV}_x = C_{0,x}$$

$$\text{BPV}_x = U_x(P \mid U,\ 10\%,\ N_x) + S_{N,x}(P \mid F,\ 10\%,\ N_x)$$

Furthermore,

$$\text{NPV}_x = \text{BPV}_x - \text{CPV}_x$$

Table 9.2

Cash Flow Profiles of Six Independent Projects (in $1,000)

Project No. x	Life N_x	Initial Cost $C_{0,x}$	Net Uniform Annual Benefits U_x at $t = 1, 2, ..., N_x$	Salvage Value $S_{N,x}$
1	10	50	19.460	14
2	10	20	9.451	5
3	4	10	4.733	0
4	10	40	13.040	10
5	6	30	18.250	8
6	6	30	11.620	6

Using the priority based on the highest benefit-cost ratios in selecting these projects, we therefore compute first the benefit-cost ratios B_x/C_x. The results of the computation are shown in Table 9.3.

Under the given budget constraints, we select as many projects as possible according to the ranking of the benefit-cost ratios of these projects.

(a) For $C_q = 50$, we can select $x = 2$ and $x = 5$ according to the rank based on benefit-cost ratios. Thus, for this group of projects,

$$\text{Total CPV} = 20 + 30 = 50$$

$$\text{Total NPV} = 40 + 54 = 94 \quad \text{(maximum possible)}$$

(b) For $C_q = 100$, we can select $x = 2$, $x = 5$, and $x = 1$ according to the rank based on the benefit-cost ratios. Then, for this group of projects,

$$\text{Total CPV} = 20 + 30 + 50 = 100$$

$$\text{Total NPV} = 40 + 54 + 75 = 169 \quad \text{(maximum possible)}$$

Example 9.3

Rework Example 9.2 if the budget constraint is (a) $C_q = \$80$ million and (b) $C_q = \$90$ million.

For both constraints in this problem, we cannot find a group of independent projects with the highest ranking of benefit-cost ratios to invest up to the exact limit of the budget. Consequently, several trials are made for each case, following the order of ranking whenever possible, but switching to a heuristic search if necessary. For the relatively small number of projects in this problem, the optimal solution becomes obvious after several trials.

(a) For $C_q = 80$, we seek the combinations whose total cost is closer to the

Table 9.3

Benefits and Costs of Projects (in $1000)

x	BPV_x	CPV_x	NPV_x	B_x/C_x	Rank
1	125	50	75	2.5	3
2	60	20	40	3.0	1
3	15	10	5	1.5	6
4	84	40	44	2.1	4
5	84	30	54	2.8	2
6	54	30	24	1.8	5

budget constraint than 50 which results from selecting $x = 2$ and $x = 5$ only. (If $x = 1$ were also accepted, the total cost would exceed $C_q = 80$.)

Trial 1: $x = 2$, $x = 5$, and $x = 6$

$$\text{Total CPV} = 20 + 30 + 30 = 80$$

$$\text{Total NPV} = 40 + 54 + 24 = 118$$

Trial 2: $x = 2$, $x = 1$, and $x = 3$

$$\text{Total CPV} = 20 + 50 + 10 = 80$$

$$\text{Total NPV} = 40 + 75 + 5 = 120$$

Trial 3: $x = 5$ and $x = 1$

$$\text{Total CPV} = 30 + 50 = 80$$

$$\text{Total NPV} = 54 + 75 = 129 \quad \text{(observed maximum)}$$

(b) For $C_q = 90$, we seek other combinations on the same basis.

Trial 1: $x = 5$, $x = 1$, and $x = 3$

$$\text{Total CPV} = 30 + 50 + 10 = 90$$

$$\text{Total NPV} = 54 + 75 + 5 = 134$$

Trial 2: $x = 2$, $x = 5$, and $x = 4$

$$\text{Total CPV} = 20 + 30 + 40 = 90$$

$$\text{Total NPV} = 40 + 54 + 44 = 138 \quad \text{(observed maximum)}$$

9.5 Ranking Independent Projects Under Budget Constraints on the Basis of Overall Rates of Return

It is often stated in the literature that the internal rates of return on independent projects can be used to rank such projects when there is a budget constraint. Even if no multiple values of IRR exist for any of the projects, this statement is generally incorrect. The reason that the IRR should not be used as a basis for ranking independent projects is that the reinvestment rate for the early year returns from all projects will be based on the MARR of the organization rather than the internal rate of return for each of the individual projects. Hence, the overall rate of return (ORR) over the planning horizon rather than the IRR is the appropriate measure for ranking the profit potentials for a group of independent projects.

Let us illustrate this point by considering a group of m independent projects $(x = 1, 2, \ldots, m)$, each of which has a net cash flow profile consisting of an initial cost $C_{x,0}$, a net uniform annual return U_x over its useful life of N_x years, and a salvage value of $S_{N,x}$ at the end of N_x as shown in Fig. 9.5(a). The useful life N_x of some or all projects may be identical to the planning horizon of n years. Since there is only one sign change in each cash flow profile, there is a single internal rate of return i_x for each project. However, the early returns from all projects will be reinvested at MARR $= i^*$ specified by the organization until the end of n years, not at the IRR $= i_x$ for each individual project x. Since no replacement is made for project x when it expires at $N_x < n$, it is *incorrect* to assume that the early returns from a project x will be reinvested at its IRR $= i_x$ if $N_x < n$.

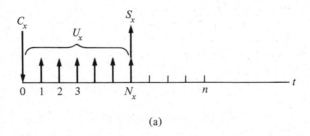

(a)

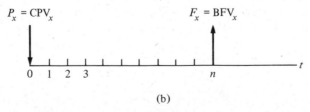

(b)

FIGURE 9.5

On the other hand, the overall rate of return $\text{ORR}_x = i_x^0$ for a project x can be computed on the basis of a single equivalent sum P_e at $t = 0$ and a single equivalent sum F_e at $t = n$ as shown in Fig. 9.5(b). The procedure of computation has been explained in detail in Chapter 4. It is sufficient to point out that the ranking of m independent projects ($x = 1, 2, \ldots, m$) based on ORR_x represents the correct measure of the profit potentials of the projects from the viewpoint of an organization. Thus, when there is no budget constraint, all projects for which ORR_x is greater than the specified MARR should be accepted.

When there is a budget constraint, the ranking of independent projects becomes very important since usually only some of the economically feasible projects will be selected. If the budget constraint is reached exactly after a number of projects are selected according to the priority based on the highest overall rates of return, then we have indeed selected the group of projects which, taken together as a group, will produce the maximum net present value. However, if the budget constraint is not reached exactly after a number of projects, but it will be exceeded by the inclusion of the next highest ranked project, then it is not necessarily true that the group of projects under the budget constraint is the best selection.

Example 9.4

For the six independent projects in Example 9.2, compute the internal rate of return for each project and compare the rank of these projects based on IRR_x with the rank based on B_x/C_x computed for Example 9.2.

Since the computation of the internal rate of return has been explained in detail in Chapter 4, it is sufficient to mention briefly the procedure of computation here. For any project x whose cash flow profile appears in Table 9.2, the net present value is given by

$$\text{NPV}_x = -C_{0,x} + U_x(P \mid U, i, N_x) + S_{N,x}(P \mid F, i, N_x)$$

Table 9.4

Ranks of Projects According to B/C and IRR

Project x	B_x/C_x	Rank of B_x/C_x	IRR_x	Rank of $\text{IRR}_x = i_x$
1	2.5	3	38.1%	3
2	3.0	1	46.9%	2
3	1.5	6	31.7%	5
4	2.2	4	31.1%	6
5	2.8	2	58.5%	1
6	1.8	5	33.0%	4

The internal rate of return, $IRR_x = i_x$, can be obtained by letting $NPV_x = 0$. Hence,

$$-C_{0,x} + U_x(P|U, i_x, N_x) + S_{N,x}(P|F, i_x, N_x) = 0$$

This equation can be solved either by interpolation from the discrete compound interest tables in Appendix A or by finding a numerical solution with the aid of a programmable calculator.

The results of the IRR_x for the six independent projects are tabulated in Table 9.4. In comparing the rank of these results with the rank of the projects based on B_x/C_x, it is obvious that they are different.

Example 9.5

Assuming that the reinvestment rate is the same as $MARR = 10\%$, determine the overall rate of return (ORR) for each of the six independent projects in Example 9.2.

The procedure for computing the ORR has been explained in detail in Chapter 4. It is sufficient to note that in this problem the single sum P_x at $t = 0$ is CPV_x, and the equivalent single sum F_x at $t = n$ is BFV_x as shown in Fig. 9.5. Part (a) of the figure represents the given cash flow profile of the project x while part (b) shows the equivalent sums for computing ORR_x as follows:

$$P_x = CPV_x = C_{x,0}$$

$$F_x = BFV_x = (BPV_x)(F|P, 10\%, 10)$$

where BFV_x can be conveniently computed from BPV_x of the cash flow profile. The $ORR_x = i_x^0$ can be obtained from the solution of the following equation:

$$NPV_x = -CPV_x + (BFV_x)(P|F, i_x^0, 10) = 0$$

or

$$(P|F, i_x^0, 10) = \frac{CPV_x}{BFV_x}$$

Hence, the value of i_x^0 can be obtained by interpolation from the discrete compound interest tables in Appendix A. The results of $ORR_x = i^0$ for all six independent projects are tabulated in Table 9.5.

Note that $(P|F, i^0, 10)$ is a monotonically decreasing function of i_x^0. That is, the value of $(P|F, i^0, 10)$ decreases as the value of i^0 increases. Conversely,

$$(F|P, i_x^0, 10) = \frac{1}{(P|F, i_x^0, 10)} = \frac{BFV_x}{CPV_x}$$

Table 9.5

Ranks of Projects According to ORR

Project x	BPV_x	CPV_x	BFV_x	$\dfrac{CPV_x}{BFV_x}$	ORR_x	Rank of $ORR^0_{xZ=i_x}$
1	125	50	324.213	0.1542	20.7%	3
2	60	20	155.622	0.1285	23.1%	1
3	15	10	38.906	0.2570	14.6%	6
4	84	40	217.871	0.1836	18.7%	4
5	84	30	217.871	0.1377	22.2%	2
6	54	30	140.060	0.2142	16.9%	5

is a monotonically increasing function of i_x^0. (See Fig. 4.2 in Chapter 4.) Since BFV_x/CPV_x differs from $B_x/C_x = BPV_x/CPV_x$ by a constant factor of $(F\,|\,P,\ 10\%, 10)$, the rank of i_x^0 for the independent projects, as shown in Table 9.5, should be the same as the rank of B_x/C_x shown in Table 9.4.

Example 9.6

For the projects in Example 9.2 whose ORR are computed in Example 9.5, determine which projects should be selected on the basis of the overall rate of return if the present value of the budget constraint is (a) $C_q = \$50$ million and (b) $C_q = \$100$ million.

   The solution of this problem is identical to that of Example 9.2 in which the projects are selected on the basis of the benefit-cost ratios. Hence the ranking based on the overall rates of return of the independent are identical to that based on their benefit-cost ratios.

   If the incorrect ranking based on the internal rates of return had been used, we would have selected some projects with profit potentials less than those of the rejected projects.

9.6   Selection Among Mutually Exclusive Alternatives Under Budget Constraints

When a budget constraint is imposed by an organization, the decision criteria based on the net present value for selecting the best proposal among a set of mutually exclusive alternatives will still be valid, provided that all alternatives with present values of costs exceeding the budget constraint are excluded from consideration.

   If the budget constraint is expressed in terms of the present value of costs based on the net cash flow profiles over the planning horizon, we first eliminate those alternatives on the basis of the present values of all costs and select the best among the remaining alternatives. The proposal thus selected should have the maximum positive net present value that does not exceed the budget constraint. Let CPV_q be the maximum present value of the costs that may be invested in any given project. Then, for a set of m mutually exclusive proposals ($x = 1, 2, \ldots, m$), the criterion for selecting a particular proposal j is as follows:

$$NPV_j = \max NPV_x \qquad (NPV_j \geq 0)$$

subject to

$$CPV_j \leq CPV_q \qquad\qquad (9.1)$$

If the budget constraint is based on the initial costs, some projects may be eliminated because of their high initial costs instead of high present values of costs over the planning horizon. Then, for the same group of m projects, the criterion for selecting a proposal j is as follows:

$$NPV_j = \max NPV_x \qquad (NPV_j \geq 0)$$

subject to

$$C_{0,j} \leq C_{0,q} \qquad\qquad (9.2)$$

where $C_{0,q}$ is the maximum initial cost permitted during the budgeting period $t = 0$, and $C_{0,j}$ is the initial cost of proposal j.

Example 9.7

Three mutually exclusive building projects are proposed for a given site. All have a useful life of 40 years and no salvage values at the end. The initial construction cost $C_{0,x}$, the net rehabilitation costs at each of year 10, 20, and 30 are $C_{t,x} = W_x$, and the net uniform annual benefits are $U_{t,x} = U_x$ for year $t = 1, 2, \ldots, 40$ except none for year $t = 10, 20,$ and 30. These values for alternatives $x = 1, 2,$ and 3 are given in Table 9.6. The MARR is specified to be 7%. Select the best alternative if there is a budget constraint of (a) \$7.0 million for the present value of costs based on the net cash flow profiles and (b) \$5.6 million for the initial cost.

The present values of costs CPV_x and benefits BPV_x for any alternative x are given by

$$CPV_x = C_{x,0} + W_x[(P \mid F, 7\%, 10) + (P \mid F, 7\%, 20) + (P \mid F, 7\%, 30)]$$

$$BPV_x = U_x(P \mid U, 7\%, 40) - U_x[(P \mid F, 7\%, 10) + (P \mid F, 7\%, 20) + (P \mid F, 7\%, 30)]$$

Table 9.6

Costs and Benefits of Projects (in $ million)

x	$C_{0,x}$	$C_{t,x} = W_x$ $t = 10, 20, 30$	$B_{t,x} = U_x$ $t = 1, 2, ..., 40$ Except 10, 20, 30	CPV_x	BPV_x	NPV_x
1	4.600	2.500	0.550	6.845	6.838	-0.007
2	5.600	1.500	0.666	6.947	8.281	1.334
3	6.400	0.500	0.700	6.849	8.704	1.855

Then,

$$NPV_x = BPV_x - CPV_x$$

These results for $x = 1$, 2, and 3 are tabulated in Table 9.6.

For case (a), we note that all values of CPV_x (for $x = 1$, 2, and 3) are below 7.0. Hence, $x = 3$ should be selected since $NPV_3 = 1.855$ is the maximum among the net present values for the three alternatives.

For case (b), $C_{0,3} = 6.4$ exceeds the constraint of 5.6 for the initial cost. Hence, $x = 3$ should be excluded and $x = 2$ is the better of the remaining two alternatives since $NPV_2 = 1.334$ is greater than $NPV_1 = -0.007$.

9.7 Effects of Financing Policies on Project Evaluation

Up to this chapter, we have tried to separate the economic evalution of investment projects and the financing of such projects whenever possible. However, financing policies are often introduced, if only implicitly, in specifying the MARR for project evaluation. With capital rationing the financing policies become more explicit.

In the case of external capital rationing, it is quite clear that the internal funds can be made available by using the working capital generated from its operations, by liquidating part of the business in the organization, or by selling its holdings in marketable securities. The decision of how to acquire the necessary funds will affect the determination of the MARR as explained in Section 9.3. Similarly, in the case of internal capital rationing, the organization simply decides to stop borrowing from outside sources even though it may forego some profitable investment opportunities. Ultimately the financial decisions affecting an organization must be made by its highest authority. We shall at this time consider only the consequences of various financing policies regarding the timing of providing the necessary funds.

In the context of economic evaluation, we will not discuss the advantages and disadvantages of financing policies which would require a good understanding of the capital markets. However, we must at least recognize the effects of financing policies on project evaluation and determine such effects when the financing policies of an organization are explicitly stated.

The financing policies implicit in the economic evaluation using the net present value criterion or equivalent criteria are:

1. The financing of a project begins and ends with the planning horizon.
2. A single sum at the beginning of the planning horizon ($t = 0$) which, if unused at $t = 0$ and being compounded at the MARR, will be just sufficient to provide all outlays in the net cash flow profile over the planning horizon.
3. The net returns for all periods are reinvested at the MARR until the end of the planning horizon ($t = n$) such that a single sum is accumulated at the end.
4. Depending on the criterion used in the evaluation, the single sum at $t = n$ is measured against the single sum at $t = 0$ to determine the profit potential of the project. For example, in the net present value method, the single sum at $t = n$ is discounted to $t = 0$ in computing the NPV; similarly, in the net future value method, the single sum at $t = 0$ is compounded to $t = n$ in computing the NFV. In the overall rate of return method, the single sum at $t = 0$ and the single sum at $t = n$ are used to compute the annual rate of return.

If the financing policies adopted by an organization are different from those implicit in the methods for project evaluation derived in earlier chapters, the technique of analysis should also be modified or adjusted. When such modifications are necessary, the resulting adjusted values will be so identified to avoid confusion.

9.8   Computation of the Adjusted Rate of Return

The overall rate of return can be affected by different financing policies when the cash flow profile of an investment project consists of a series of outlays and a series of returns at different time periods in the planning horizon, whether or not these outlays and returns are mixed in the profile. Consequently, the overall rate of return as defined in Section 4.7 is applicable only when all net returns in the cash flow profile are compounded at the MARR until the end of the planning horizon and all net outlays are discounted at the MARR to the beginning.

Suppose that the financing policy of such a project is to acquire the cash needed at any later time period (beyond the amounts generated by the project before that period) from the available internal funds at the time of need, and to reinvest the excess net returns (beyond the amounts required for the project after that period) externally at some specified rate until the end of the planning horizon. Then, the overall rate of return of the project based on such a policy can be expected to be different from that as defined previously and is therefore referred to as the *adjusted rate of return* (ARR). Since this policy is by no means the only possible alternative financing policy it is obvious that an adjusted rate of return is associated with a specific financing policy only.

Without broadening the discussion of this subject further, we shall illustrate with an example the computation of the adjusted rate of return of a project based on the above financing policy when the external rate of return for reinvestment is the MARR.

Example 9.8

The cash flow profile of a 5-year project (in millions of dollars) shows $A_0 = +18$, $A_1 = +10$, $A_2 = -40$, $A_3 = -60$, $A_4 = +30$, and $A_5 = +50$. Using the financing policy stated in this section and a MARR of 8% for reinvestment, determine the adjusted rate of return for this project.

The cash flows of the project are first adjusted according to the financing policy. Thus, A_0 and A_1 will be reinvested externally at 8% until $t = 2$ when they will be pooled with additional new money to provide the amount needed at $t = 2$. Similarly, A_4 will be reinvested externally at 8% until $t = 5$ when the project is completed. The adjusted new cash flows $\hat{A}_t$ together with their computation are shown in Table 9.7. Effectively, the organization spends a sum of 8.205 at $t = 2$ and a sum of 60 at $t = 3$ and receives a sum of 82.4 at $t = 5$ with no other expenditures or receipts.

Then, the adjusted rate of return $\hat{\imath}$ can be determined by considering NPV = 0 at $t = 0$ for the adjusted cash flows $\hat{A}_t$ and by using the trial solution. Thus,

$$NPV = -(8.205)(P \,|\, F, \hat{\imath}, 2) - (60)(P \,|\, F, \hat{\imath}, 3) \\ + (82.4)(P \,|\, F, \hat{\imath}, 5) = 0$$

For $\hat{\imath} = 0\%$,

$$NPV = -8.205 - 60 + 82.4 = 14.195$$

For $\hat{\imath} = 10\%$,

$$NPV = -(8.205)(0.8264) - (60)(0.7513) + (82.4)(0.6209) \\ = -6.781 - 45.078 + 51.162 = -0.697$$

Table 9.7

Adjusted Cash Flows Based on the Stated Financing Policy

t	A_t	$\hat{A}_t$	Adjustment Based on Reinvestment at MARR = 8%
0	+18	0	$(18)(F \,|\, P, 8\%, 1) = 19.44$
1	+10	0	$(19.44 + 10)(F \,|\, P, 8\%, 1) = 31.795$
2	−40	−8.205	$31.795 - 40 = -8.205$
3	−60	−60	No adjustment
4	+30	0	$(30)(F \,|\, P, 8\%, 1) = 32.4$
5	+50	+82.4	$32.4 + 50 = 82.4$

Obviously, there exists a positive real root $\hat{\imath}$ between 0% and 10% which sets $NPV = 0$. Trying $\hat{\imath} = 9\%$, we find $NPV = +0.313$. By using linear interpolation between 9% and 10%, we obtain $\hat{\imath} = 9.3\%$, which is the adjusted rate of return.

The computational procedure can be simplified by using $t = 2$ as a point of reference for the present time since $\hat{A}_0 = 0$ and $\hat{A}_1 = 0$. Then,

$$NPV = 8.205 - (60)(P|F, \hat{\imath}, 1) + (82.4)(P|F, \hat{\imath}, 3) = 0$$

For finding $NPV = 0$, we try several values of $\hat{\imath}$ as follows:

$$[NPV]_{i=8\%} = -8.05 - (60)(0.9259) + (82.4)(0.7938) = +1.805$$

$$[NPV]_{i=9\%} = -8.205 - (60)(0.9174) + (82.4)(0.7722) = +0.380$$

$$[NPV]_{i=10\%} = -8.205 - (60)(0.9091) + (82.4)(0.7513) = -0.844$$

Hence, the adjusted rate of return is between 9% and 10%. Upon interpolation, we get $\hat{\imath} = 9.3\%$ also.

9.9   Adjustments for Financing Policies Related to Capital Rationing

If the financing policies are related to capital rationing, we can make similar adjustments within the prescribed conditions. Again, we shall not cover a variety of possible financing policies but shall discuss only how the technique of project evaluation can be modified when a specific financing policy is adopted to impose capital rationing.

In Section 9.3, we have already discussed the general conditions under which it is profitable or unprofitable for a firm to borrow or lend. When the MARR is less than the borrowing rate, it is generally not profitable to borrow. However, under such circumstances, a firm may decide to become a lender rather than an investor. In other words, the firm can use the borrowing rate r_B as its MARR such that the firm will loan its funds to earn a rate of return of r_B from outside agents unless it can do better or at least equally well by investing in a proposed project. On the other hand, if the firm cannot or will not become a lender when the MARR is less than the market borrowing rate, then the technique of project evaluation must be modified.

We shall illustrate the technique required to handle such a rate situation when the firm is not allowed to become a lender even if the MARR or i^* is less than the borrowing rate r_B but must acquire the necessary investment capital only from outside sources to meet the requirements of the funding for a project with mixed cash flows.[3]

---

[3] This case is so unusual that it was deliberately concocted by the author of Ref. [9.3] to answer the critics of the treatment of mixed cash flows under capital rationing.

Example 9.9

The cash flow profile of a three-year project shows $A_0 = -\$1,000$, $A_1 = +\$3,700$, $A_2 = -\$4,520$, and $A_3 = +\$1,820$. The firm cannot act as a lender and can acquire the necessary investment only from outside sources at a borrowing rate of 35%, which is greater than the MARR of 32% specified by the firms. Determine whether the project is worthwhile on the basis of (a) the net present value approach and (b) the adjusted rate of return approach.

In Chapter 4, the relationship between A_t, the cash flow at the end of period t in the profile, and R_t, the unrecovered balance or cumulative surplus at the end of period t, is given by Eq. (4.24) as follows:

$$R_t = A_t + R_{t-1}(1 + i)$$

where i is the interest rate earned on the unrecovered balance for each time period, and $R_0 = A_0$ at period $t = 0$ for this recursive relationship for $t = 1, 2, \ldots$. However, for this particular problem in which the borrowing rate $r_B = 35\%$ is greater than the MARR of $i^* = 32\%$, we should use $i = 32\%$ for compounding the cumulative surplus (positive R_t) at the end of period t, and use $i = 35\%$ for compounding the unrecovered balance (negative R_t) at the end of period t as indicated by the computation in Table 9.8.

The value of R_t at $t = 3$ represents the net future value, i.e.,

$$\text{NFV} = R_3 = -94$$

Then, the net present value is given by

$$
\begin{aligned}
\text{NPV} &= -(94)(P\,|\,F, 32\%, 3) \\
&= -(94)[(0.4552) - (2/10)(0.4552 - 0.3644)] \\
&= -(94)(0.4370) = -41.1
\end{aligned}
$$

Table 9.8

Unrecovered Balance or Cumulative Surplus at the End of Time Periods

t	A_t	R_{t-1}	i	$R_{t-1}(1 + i)$	R_t
0	$-1,000$	—	—	—	$-1,000$
1	$+3,700$	$-1,000$	35%	$-1,350$	$+2,350$
2	$-4,520$	$+2,350$	32%	$+3,102$	$-1,418$
3	$+1,820$	$-1,418$	35%	$-1,914$	-94

Table 9.9

Adjusted Cash Flows Based on Capital Rationing

t	A_t	$\hat{A}_t$	Reinvestment at $i^* = 32\%$
0	$-1,000$	$-1,000$	No adjustment
1	$+3,700$	0	$3,700(1 + 0.32) = +4,884$
2	$-4,520$	0	$(4,884 - 4,520)(1 + 0.32) = 480$
3	$+1,820$	$+2,300$	$480 + 1,820 = 2,300$

The adjusted cash flows $\hat{A}_t$ based on a reinvestment rate of $i^* = 32\%$ for early period returns in this problem are computed in Table 9.9. Finally, we set NPV $= 0$ at $t = 0$ for the adjusted cash flows $\hat{A}_t$ such that

$$\text{NPV} = -1,000 + 2,300(P\,|\,F, \hat{\imath}, 3) = 0$$

or

$$(P\,|\,F, \hat{\imath}, 3) = \frac{1,000}{2,300} = 0.4348$$

By interpolation from the tables in Appendix A, we get $\hat{\imath} = 32.3\%$. Note that this adjusted rate of return should be compared with $r_B = 35\%$ because it is greater than the MARR of $i^* = 32\%$. That is, we should not borrow from outside sources to finance this project in view of $32.3\% < 35\%$. Hence, the project is not worthwhile under the stated condition of capital rationing.

9.10   Summary and Study Guide

This chapter has presented the basic concepts of external and internal capital rationing and their effects on the economic evaluation of investment projects. The determination of the MARR under various possible conditions of external capital rationing has been discussed. The selection of both independent projects and mutually exclusive projects under internal capital rationing has been explained.

It has been shown that the overall rates of return (ORR) as well as the benefit-cost ratios computed with the specified MARR can be used to rank independent projects under budget constraints. However, the internal rates of return (IRR) generally do not lead to the correct ranking of independent projects as often claimed in the literature.

Although the operation and maintenance costs in the future years of capital projects are usually budgeted separately, capital outlays may be required in future years, such as outlays for staged construction of a project or for periodic rehabilitations. Consequently, the present values of costs based on the net cash flow profiles of the projects should be used in computing the cumulative present costs of acceptable projects.

If the financing policies adopted by an organization are different from those implicit in the methods for project evaluation derived in earlier chapters, the technique of analysis should also be modified or adjusted. The computation of the adjusted rate of return and the net present values under various financing policies has been illustrated with examples.

REFERENCES

9.1 Bierman, H., Jr., and S. Smidt, *The Capital Budget Decision*, 4th ed., New York: Macmillan, 1975.

9.2 Teichroew, D., A. A. Robichek, and M. Montalbano, "An Analysis of Criteria for Investment and Financing Decisions under Certainty," *Management Service*, **12**, 3 (1965), 151–179.

9.3 Wohl, M., "Common Misunderstandings About the Internal Rate of Return and Net Present Value Economic Analysis," *Transportation Research Record*, 731 (with discussions) (1979), 1–19.

PROBLEMS

P9.1 The present values of benefits and costs in millions of dollars for six independent projects ($x = 1, 2, \ldots, 6$) are found to be as follows:

x	BPV_x	CPV_x
1	1.700	0.500
2	2.250	1.200
3	6.000	3.100
4	3.300	1.400
5	2.800	1.000
6	3.750	1.900

If the budget constraint on the total present value of costs is $3 million, which projects should be selected in order to maximize the net benefit? Use the trial method to obtain the most satisfactory answer.

P9.2 Rework Problem P9.1 if the budget constraint on the total present value of costs is (a) $5 million and (b) $6 million.

P9.3 The cash flow profiles of four *independent* projects (in millions of dollars) are given below. For a specified MARR of 8%, the overall rates of return (ORR) of the projects are also computed. Determine which projects should be selected if the budget constraint on the total present value of costs is (a) $170 million and (b) $250 million.

t	$A_{t,1}$	$A_{t,2}$	$A_{t,3}$	$A_{t,4}$
0	−77.0	−77.0	−75.3	0
1	0	+38.0	+28.0	−28.0
2	0	+32.0	+28.0	−28.0
3	0	+26.0	+28.0	−28.0
4	0	+20.0	+28.0	−28.0
5	+235.0	+14.0	+28.0	+201.9
ORR	25.0%	15.5%	17.0%	17.0%

P9.4 Compute the benefit-cost ratios in Problem P9.4 to verify that the ranking of the projects based on B/C is identical to that based on ORR.

P9.5 The cash flow profiles (in $1,000) of six *independent* projects are given below. For a specified MARR of 3%, the overall rates of return (ORR) of the projects are also computed. If the budget constraint on the present value of costs is $500,000, which alternatives should be selected? Also verify that the same projects would have been selected if the ranking were based on the benefit-cost ratios.

t	$A_{t,1}$	$A_{t,2}$	$A_{t,3}$	$A_{t,4}$	$A_{t,5}$	$A_{t,6}$
0	−205	−350	−295	−76.6	−185.5	0
1	+50	+100	+70	+56	+56	−50
2	+50	+90	+70	+56	+56	−50
3	+50	+80	+70	+56	+56	−50
4	+50	+70	+70	+56	+56	−50
5	+50	+60	+70	−160	0	+243.3
ORR	5.3%	4.1%	4.7%	2.4%	5.4%	5.5%

P9.6 Find the annual adjusted rate of return for the investment in Problem P4.6 (Chapter 4) if the MARR for the investor is 25%. Assume that all early year returns will be reinvested at MARR and that the money needed at various time periods (other than early year returns) is supplied at the time of need.

P9.7 Find the annual adjusted rate of return for the investment in Problem P4.7 (Chapter 4) if the MARR for the investor is 10%. Assume that all early year returns will be reinvested at MARR and that the money needed at various time periods (other than early year returns) is supplied at the time of need.

P9.8 Find the annual adjusted rate of return for the investment in Problem P4.8 (Chapter 4) if the MARR for the investor is 8%. Assume that all early year returns will be reinvested at MARR and that the money needed at various time periods (other than early year returns) is supplied at the time of need.

CHAPTER

10

Estimation of Costs
and Benefits

10.1 Problems Associated with Measuring
Benefits and Costs

Until now, we have concentrated on examining the concept of discounted cash flows and its application to the economic evaluation of proposed investment projects. When these techniques are used, the implicit assumption is that benefits and costs are measured by cash receipts and disbursements. Actually, the task of estimating costs and benefits is usually far more complex than it has appeared. It is now time to shift the focus from cash inflows and outflows to benefits and costs, which are the real measures in profit maximization.

Although we will consider both benefits and costs in this chapter, we will give a decidedly greater emphasis to costs for two reasons. First, costs are generally more measurable and easier to forecast than benefits. Second, the job of producing benefits is generally not the sole responsibility of the engineer, but also of such groups as sales and marketing personnel in the private sector, and social planners in the public sector. We will not be able to consider all the factors in detail but will merely attempt to identify some of them so that the reader may have an appreciation of the depth and intricacy of the problem.

A few examples will show why costs and benefits cannot always be conveniently represented by cash flows. For instance, a company employs labor, material, and machinery to produce and sell a certain quantity of fertilizer, and this production process causes pollution of the air and water near the factory. The company can measure its benefits by the amount of revenue generated by the sale of the fertilizer, and its costs by the outlays for the goods and services used in the production. However, the total costs to society of producing the fertilizer have not been computed, because the effect of the pollution has not been taken into account. The difficulties in estimating costs and benefits lie not only in the method and reliability of measurement, but on the responsibility of the private firm to the society. Many issues involving private initiatives versus governmental intervention in the public interest are continually debated in the U. S. Congress, and new legislation governing various aspects of industrial production often affect the inclusion or exclusion of various benefits and/or cost items in capital investment decisions.

The problems of estimating net benefits in the public sector are even greater. Aside from the method and reliability of measurement, the problem of responsibility or point of view is a serious and legitimate concern. Some projects have unfortunately been justified from the point of view of the local governments when the federal funds are not treated as costs since they are regarded as "free." Such problems with implications for distribution of national income will be left to Chapter 17.

Another reason why cash inflows and outflows differ from benefits and costs is because cash flows include the proceeds from financial transactions as well as real returns from the operation of physical assets. Depreciation allowance, interest, and taxes are related to financial transactions. Such considerations increase the difficulty in measuring benefits and costs in terms of cash flows.

In this chapter, we will briefly widen our previous analysis of cash flows to an examination of the benefits and costs associated with these factors. The theory behind cost, benefit, and output volume, and the optimization of net benefits by minimizing costs will be introduced. Then some applications of the theory to investment decisions will be considered. We will also mention some of the elements of cash flow that have financial origins, rather than being related to production or operation in order to lay the groundwork for a study of these financial considerations in subsequent chapters.

10.2 Variation of Costs and Benefits with Output Volume

The costs incurred in production are related both to the cost of the facilities and the volume of output produced. Within the capacity of the available facilities, inputs of labor and material required to manufacture a given number of units of product vary with the volume of output. The relationship between the inputs and outputs is called the *production function* and depends on the technology of production that is used. Naturally, a firm will want to choose the least-cost technology if suitable. Some determinants of the cost of various technologies, and thus the technology chosen, include the general state of technological development, the relative costs of various factors of production, the volume of output, and the interrelationship of the selected production process with the production of other products of the firm.

Once a facility for production has been installed, there are certain types of expenses called *fixed costs*, which cannot be changed substantially over the short run, regardless of the output volume; other types of expenses which do vary directly with output volume are called *variable costs*. The total cost of production over a specified period of time is the sum of the fixed cost and the variable cost. The relationship between the total cost and the output volume is called the *cost function.*

Fixed costs are constant over the useful life of the asset and must be taken as given over this relevant period of time. For instance, the cost of the plant is a fixed cost over its estimated useful life. Once the plant has been built, the costs associated with its use in the production of output will be almost the same within a certain level of production. The fixed costs of facilities with a useful life greater than 1 year may be amortized over the estimated useful life. The remuneration of salaried workers such as executives, manager, and engineers is generally considered to be a fixed cost over the short term because these salaries are definite amounts. However, over the long term these salaries can be controlled by employment policies.

Costs that are related directly or indirectly to the volume of output are called variable costs. The cost of raw materials is a variable cost: so many tons of raw material (and therefore an equivalent cost) *per unit* of product. The wages of hourly workers are generally considered variable costs, because a certain number of hours and hence a certain amount of pay are associated with each unit of input, and workers can be shifted to or from other products, given overtime, or laid off as output levels dictate. Some costs, such as telephones and electricity, have both fixed and variable components: a flat charge for the installation of the facilities and an hourly usage charge.

The main reason that we must be careful to distinguish between fixed and variable costs is because variable costs are reflected in day-to-day operations, while fixed costs are committed in capital investment decisions made at the *beginning* of the relevant time period. The decision to produce or not to produce, or to select an alternative over the method currently used, is made only on the basis of benefits versus variable costs, but the decision of whether or not to *invest* in a given production facility is made on the basis of benefits versus both fixed and variable costs.

This concept can be explained further as follows. Once a plant is built, the fixed costs have already been incurred and can no longer be controlled. If revenues on the sale of a product are less than the variable costs, the company is incurring additional costs (losses) on each unit produced and should stop producing and shut down the plant. Examples of this can be seen in the hard-hit steel and auto industries. If the revenues are greater than variable costs but less than the sum of variable and fixed costs, the company should continue to produce over the life of the plant to recover *part* of the fixed costs, unless it is more profitable to dispose of the plant. If the revenues are greater than the sum of variable and fixed costs, then all of the costs have been covered, and the company is making a profit.

Example 10.1

The cost accounting records of a university indicate that its Office Service Department is allocated an overhead cost of $50,000 per year on the basis of the floor space it occupies. The Office Service Department charges the use of its services for printing on the basis of the direct labor and material costs plus the indirect costs assigned to the job in proportion to its size in order to recover its overhead cost. The Registrar's Office plans to print 5,000 copies of a catalog, and, contrary to the past practice of routinely sending the work to the Office Service Department, it solicits a price quotation first from both a commercial printer and that department. The quotation from the outside printer is $4,500 and that from the Office Service Department is $4,600, with the following breakdowns:

Direct labor cost	$1,850
Direct material cost	750
Overhead cost	2,000
Total	$4,600

The business manager of the university decides that it is in the interest of the university to have the catalog printed in the Office Service Department. Why?

The Office Service Department has been counting on the printing of the catalog for the Registrar's Office as usual in its budget for the year. The overhead cost of $2,000 for printing the catalog is quite substantial (4% of the annual total of $50,000). The department does not expect other sources of revenues from which it can recover this amount of overhead, and it cannot adjust its operation to reduce its share of overhead allocated by the university this year. Consequently, it is in the interest of the university to have the catalog printed internally since the additional cost of $100 charged to the Registrar's Office will be compensated by the increase in overhead recovery of $2,000 by the Office Service Department.

Example 10.2

A contractor has the option of leasing or renting a power excavator which he uses infrequently in some of his jobs. He can lease and maintain the equipment himself for the entire year at a cost of $3,200, and the operating cost of the equipment is $80 per day when it is in use. On the other hand, he can rent the equipment at $160 per day including operating cost if he does not want to keep the equipment when it is not in use. What is the number of days in use in a year that the owner will be indifferent to leasing or renting?

If the contractor leases the power excavator for the entire year, he will incur a fixed expense of $3,200 for the year and a variable expense of $80 per day when it is in use. Let x be the number of days when the equipment is in use. Then, the cost function $C_1(x)$ for leasing is

$$C_1(x) = 3,200 + 80x$$

On the other hand, if he rents the equipment on a daily basis, he will incur only a variable expense of $160 per day when it is in use. The cost function $C_2(x)$ for renting is

$$C_2(x) = 160x$$

These two cost functions are represented by the solid lines in Fig. 10.1.
    The contractor will be indifferent to leasing or renting if $C_2(x) = C_1(x)$. That is,

$$160x = 3{,}200 + 80x$$

from which

$$x = 40 \text{ days}$$

Note that in this problem, we assume implicitly that the benefit of having a power excavator outweighs the cost of either leasing or renting, and that the benefit of using one arrangement is identical to that of using the other. Hence, the cost alone may be used as a measure of profitability. The value $x = 40$ is the point below which daily rental service will cost less and above which leasing for the year will cost less.

10.3   Pricing Strategies and Profit Maximization

A private firm which produces a product for sale expects to make a profit, which is the difference between the total revenue from sales and the total cost. The unit price of the product is determined by dividing the total revenue by the expected volume of

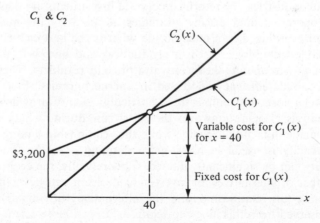

FIGURE 10.1

sales; the average total cost per unit is obtained by dividing the total cost by the volume of output. The size of the profit can be highly variable, depending on the price and the volume of sales. The firm may try to increase the total profit while maintaining the output volume and therefore increasing the unit price, or it may try to increase the output volume (within the capacity of its facilities) while maintaining the unit price, thus increasing the total profit because the fixed cost remains constant while the output volume is increased. Obviously raising the unit price is the simplest of all options, but the firm cannot do so without considering the competitive market. The relationship between the unit price of a product and the output volume reflecting certain pricing strategies is called the *price function* based on supply.

The total benefit to the firm as reflected by the total revenue from sales depends on the demand for the product, which is determined by its real or perceived value to the customers. The volume of sales in a competitive market also depends on the unit price of the product. At the unit price charged by the firm, the volume of sales realized represents the "equilibrium" volume between the supply and the demand. At the point of equilibrium, the volume of production equals the volume of sales. Thus, the total benefit to the firm varies with the volume of sales. The relationship between the total revenue and the volume of sales is referred to as the *revenue function*. In public projects, the total benefit is defined to cover user benefits not necessarily accrued to the producer, and hence the term *benefit function* reflects this broader connotation.

Thus, costs and benefits vary over the years and are dependent on the scale of initial investment, future expansion, operation and maintenance, and the market economy. The accounting system of a firm is an important source of historical data on costs and profits for similar projects. However, the estimated costs and targeted profits for future projects must be carefully scrutinized on the basis of current information.

For private industries, the returns on capital investments are dependent on the technological, operating, and pricing strategies adopted by the management. In order to maximize profits, a firm must decide what is the best capacity of a facility based on available technologies used in production, and once a facility is selected, what is the best way to operate the facility and price its products. These are familiar questions of economic efficiency addressed in microeconomics. Essentially, the relationship between costs and output for a particular facility provides a convenient tool for the analysis of operations over the short run, during which no substantial change can be made in facility capacity, while the relationship among costs, output, and facility capacity is useful in investment planning over the long run, during which the facility can be significantly altered. Theoretically, the economic efficiency of a large number of alternatives for investment decision can be examined by constructing the long-run relationship, and the alternative with maximum economic efficiency as observed from this long-run relationship can be selected. Once a particular facility is chosen, the profits in day-to-day operations can also be maximized on the basis of the short-run relationship. In practice, this analytical process is very complex, even if certain assumptions are introduced to simplify the analysis.

We shall not consider the full implications of these relationships on investment planning and operation of facilities. Instead of using the relationship among costs, output, and facility capacity over the long run, which can provide a much wider range of technological possibilities, we limit our discussion to the generation of a small set of promising technological alternatives on the basis of experience and judgment, and to the selection of the best among these alternatives according to their profit potentials. Nor are we interested in applying the short-run relationship between costs and output for a particular facility to its operation per se. However, we shall consider some simple elements of the short-run relationship commonly encountered in manufacturing industries in order to estimate more realistically the benefits as well as the costs for the cash flow profiles of proposed investment projects.

10.4   Linear Cost and Revenue Functions

If both the cost function $C(x)$ and the revenue function $B(x)$ are assumed to be linear with respect to the output volume x of a single product, the analysis of the profit under different levels of production and sales can be greatly simplified. The cost-volume-profit analysis based on linear cost and revenue functions over the short run is referred to as *linear break-even analysis*.

Let F denote the fixed cost over a time period that is constant for the given capacity of the facility, and $V(x)$ denote the variable cost that is proportional to x, i.e., $V(x) = Wx$ where W is the average variable cost per unit of production. Then, the total cost is the sum of F and $V(x)$, i.e.,

$$C(x) = F + Wx \qquad (10.1)$$

The total revenue from the volume x sold is represented by the revenue function

$$B(x) = Px \qquad (10.2)$$

where P is the unit price for the product. The profit or net income from the sales of volume x is the difference between $B(x)$ and $C(x)$, i.e.,

$$N(x) = (P - W)x - F \qquad (10.3)$$

Let x' be the output volume planned for the time period. Then, at $x = x'$, the fixed cost F, the variable cost $V(x')$, the total cost $C(x')$, the total revenue $B(x')$, and the profit $N(x')$ are as shown in Fig. 10.2.

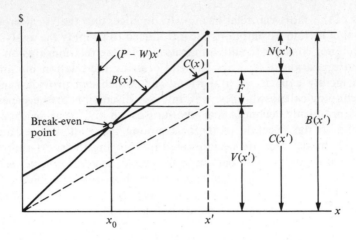

FIGURE 10.2

The term $(P - W)x$ in Eq. (10.3) is called the *contribution margin* and is denoted by

$$z = (P - W)x \qquad (10.4)$$

The term $(P - W)$ represents the *contribution margin per unit*. The *contribution margin ratio* as the percentage of the total revenue is defined by

$$r = \frac{(P - W)x}{Px} = 1 - \frac{W}{P} \qquad (10.5)$$

The intersection of $B(x)$ and $C(x)$ on the graph in Fig. 10.2, indicating that $B(x) = C(x)$ at $x = x_0$, is called the *break-even point*. The volume $x = x_0$ is called the *break-even volume*, since at $x = x_0$,

$$N(x_0) = B(x_0) - C(x_0) = 0$$

From Eq. (10.3), we find that for $N(x_0) = 0$,

$$x_0 = \frac{F}{P - W} \qquad (10.6)$$

and

$$F = (P - W)x_0 \qquad (10.7)$$

Thus, the contribution margin per unit beyond $x = x_0$ represents an increment of profit of $(P - W)$.

Example 10.3

A manufacturer of power garden tools is planning to introduce a new power shear that will sell for $20. The fixed cost for 1 year of operation is $96,000 and the variable cost per unit is $12. If the planned volume of sales is 15,000 units for the period, determine the break-even volume and the contribution margin and profit at both the planned volume and the break-even volume.

Since $P = \$20$, $W = \$12$, and $F = \$96,000$, we find from Eq. (10.6) that the break-even volume

$$x_0 = \frac{96,000}{20 - 12} = 12,000 \text{ units}$$

The remaining quantities may be obtained from Eqs. (10.1) through (10.4) and tabulated as follows:

	Planned Volume	Break-even Volume
Total revenue	$ 300,000	$ 240,000
Variable cost	180,000	144,000
Contribution margin	120,000	96,000
Fixed cost	96,000	96,000
Profit	24,000	0

Example 10.4

An import company buys foreign-made lawn mowers at $25 per unit. The fixed cost of the importing operation is $20,000 per year. The mowers are sold on commission by sales representatives who receive 30% of the selling price for each mower sold. At what price should the mowers be sold to allow the importer to break even on a total shipment of 4,000 lawn mowers per year? If the commission of the sales representatives is reduced to 15%, it is expected that $8,000 must be added to the fixed cost for advertising in order to sell all 4,000 units at the same price. Will this latter course of action produce a profit or loss?

On the basis of a 30% commission, the total revenue per year will be 70% of the total selling price. At the break-even volume $x_0 = 4,000$, we have

$$B(x_0) = (0.7P)(4,000) = 2,800P$$

$$C(x_0) = 40,000 + (25)(4,000) = 140,000$$

At the break-even point, $B(x_0) = C(x_0)$. Hence

$$2,800P = 140,000$$

from which we obtain $P = \$50$.

If the commission is reduced to 15%, then the total revenue per year will be 85% of the total price. On the other hand, the fixed cost is increased to $40,000 + 8,000 = \$48,000$. Hence at $x = 4,000$,

$$B(x) = (0.85)(50)(4,000) = 170,000$$

$$C(x) = 48,000 + (25)(4,000) = 148,000$$

Hence

$$N(x) = 170,000 - 148,000 = \$22,000$$

This action is obviously profitable.

10.5   Nonlinear Cost and Revenue Functions

Although the linear cost and revenue functions are realistic approximations of some industrial operations in the short run, the cost functions or revenue functions or both may be nonlinear in other operations. Consequently, we shall consider the more general case in which both the cost function $C(x)$ and the revenue function $B(x)$ are nonlinear with respect to the output volume x of a single product. Although we can also determine the break-even volumes in the cost-volume-profit analysis based on nonlinear cost and revenue functions, we are particularly interested in the output volume which produces the maximum profit since the profit does not necessarily increase with the increase of output volume in this case.

Let us illustrate the general case of the nonlinear cost and revenue functions as shown in Fig. 10.3(*a*). The profit or net income $N(x)$ is given by

$$N(x) = B(x) - C(x) \tag{10.8}$$

The total revenue $B(x)$ increases as the output volume x increases up to a point, and may or may not decline as x continues to increase. Without losing generality, let us simplify the discussion by considering only the situation that $B(x)$ increases with x at progressively lower rates. Then, the slope of $B(x)$ is positive but becomes progressively smaller. On the other hand, the total cost $C(x)$ increases with the output volume x at progressively higher rates, and its slope becomes progressively larger.

The variations in the slopes of $B(x)$ and $C(x)$ as represented by dB/dx and dC/dx, respectively, are shown schematically in Fig. 10.3(b). The derivative dB/dx is called the *marginal revenue* and dC/dx is called the *marginal cost*. The marginal revenue (or cost) represents the revenue (or cost) of producing one more unit of the product *at a specified output volume*. Characteristically, the marginal revenue (or

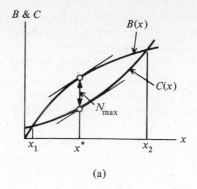

(a)

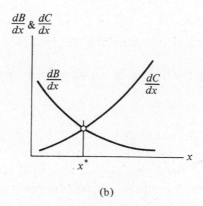

(b)

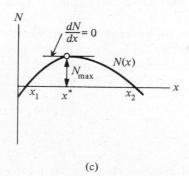

(c)

FIGURE 10.3

cost) changes at different level of production since the slope of the revenue (or cost) function changes with increase or decrease of x. The intersection of dB/dx and dC/dx indicates that

$$\frac{dB}{dx}\bigg|_{x=x*} = \frac{dC}{dx}\bigg|_{x=x*} \tag{10.9}$$

That is, the marginal revenue equals the marginal cost at the output volume x^*. Below x^*, the marginal revenue is greater than the marginal cost, and above x^*, the marginal revenue is less than the marginal cost.

In view of Eq. (10.9), we see that the slopes of $B(x)$ and $C(x)$ at $x = x^*$ in Fig. 10.3(a) are parallel to each other. Then, the value of $N(x)$ is maximized at $x = x^*$, i.e., $N_{max} = N(x^*)$, since the difference between $B(x)$ and $C(x)$ is at a maximum when the slopes of two tangents are parallel to each other. If we plot the values of $N(x) = B(x) - C(x)$ in Fig. 10.3(a) on a horizontal base as shown in Fig. 10.3(c), we note that the maximum value of $N(x)$ occurs at $x = x^*$ when the slope of the tangent is 0, i.e.,

$$\frac{dN}{dx}\bigg|_{x=x^*} = 0 \tag{10.10}$$

Note also that the sufficient condition for $N_{max} = N(x^*)$ is that $d^2N/dx^2 < 0$ at $x = x^*$.

The relation in Eq. (10.10) can be easily verified by differentiating Eq. (10.8) with respect to x. Then

$$\frac{dN}{dx}\bigg|_{x=x^*} = \frac{dB}{dx}\bigg|_{x=x^*} - \frac{dC}{dx}\bigg|_{x=x^*} = 0 \tag{10.11}$$

Since Eq. (10.11) leads to the same result as Eq. (10.9), we can conclude that the output volume $x = x^*$ which produces a maximum profit $N_{max} = N(x^*)$ is the same volume at which the marginal revenue equals the marginal cost. Note also that in both parts (a) and (c) of Fig. 10.3, $x = x_1$ and $x = x_2$ are break-even points where the profit $N(x)$ is zero.

Consequently, when the revenue and cost functions for the operation of a facility over a short run are nonlinear, we can determine the volume $x = x^*$ that will produce the maximum profit by using either Eq. (10.9) or Eq. (10.10). Then, the maximum profit $N_{max} = N(x^*)$ can be obtained by substituting the value $x = x^*$ into Eq. (10.8).

Example 10.5

A bicycle manufacturer is planning the production for next year and has found the cost and revenue functions, respectively, for the output volume x during this period:

$$C(x) = Dx^2 + E$$

$$B(x) = G - \frac{F}{x}$$

where D, E, F, and G are numerical constants. Determine the output volume which maximizes the profit of the operation and find the maximum profit in terms of D, E, F, and G. Specifically, if $D = 10^{-3}$, $E = 10^6$, $F = (16)(10^9)$, and $G = (3)(10^6)$ such that $B(x)$ and $C(x)$ are in dollars, determine the maximum profit, and the marginal revenue and marginal profit at the output volume which produces the maximum profit.

The profit function $N(x)$ for the planned operation is obtained by noting Eq. (10.8). Thus,

$$N(x) = G - \frac{F}{x} - Dx^2 - E$$

Taking the derivative of $N(x)$ and setting it equal 0,

$$\frac{dN}{dx} = \frac{F}{x^2} - 2Dx = 0$$

from which we obtain

$$x^3 = \frac{F}{2D} \quad \text{and} \quad x = \sqrt[3]{\frac{F}{2D}}$$

We substitute this value of x into $N(x)$ to obtain the maximum profit. Thus,

$$N_{max} = G - F\left(\sqrt[3]{\frac{2D}{F}}\right) - D\left(\sqrt[3]{\frac{F^2}{4D^2}}\right) - E$$

Simplifying, we get

$$N_{max} = G - E - (1.5)(\sqrt[3]{2DF^2})$$

For the numerical values of D, E, F, and G given for the problem, we obtain the optimal production volume and the maximum profit as follows:

$$x = \sqrt[3]{\frac{(16)(10^9)}{(2)(10^{-3})}} = 20,000 \text{ units}$$

$$N_{max} = (3)(10^6) - 10^6 - (1.5)[\sqrt[3]{(2)(10^{-3})(16)^2(10^9)^2}]$$
$$= \$800,000$$

The marginal cost and marginal revenue may be obtained from

$$\frac{dC}{dx} = 2Dx \qquad \frac{dB}{dx} = \frac{F}{x^2}$$

at $x = 20,000$,

$$\frac{dC}{dx} = (2)(10^{-3})(20,000) = \$40/\text{unit}$$

$$\frac{dB}{dx} = \frac{(16)(10^9)}{(20,000)^2} = \$40/\text{unit}$$

10.6   Average Cost and Marginal Cost

The *average cost* (AC) or *average total cost* of a product is defined as the total cost divided by the total number of units of production during a specified time period. In general, the average cost is given by

$$AC = \frac{C(x)}{x} \tag{10.12}$$

and the average variable cost (AVC) is given by

$$AVC = \frac{V(x)}{x} \tag{10.13}$$

For the linear cost function in Eq. (10.1), for example,

$$AC = \frac{F}{x} + W$$

where the average fixed cost F/x decreases as the output x increases, but the average variable cost is constant, i.e.,

$$AVC = W$$

The marginal cost (MC) is the cost of producing one more unit of the product at a specified level of production. Numerically, the marginal cost is approximately equal to the derivative of $C(x)$ with respect to x, i.e.,

$$MC = \frac{dC(x)}{dx}$$

For the linear cost function in Eq. (10.1),

$$MC = W$$

which is the same constant value as the average variable cost.

When the cost function is nonlinear, both the average total cost and the marginal cost vary with the volume x. In Example 10.5, for instance, the average cost of the bicycle is

$$AC = \frac{Dx^2 + E}{x} = \frac{x}{10^3} + \frac{10^6}{x}$$

and

$$MC = 2Dx = \frac{2x}{10^3}$$

The values of AC and MC at several values of x are shown below:

x	10,000	20,000	30,000	40,000	50,000
AC	$110	$ 70	$ 63	$ 65	$ 70
MC	$ 20	$ 40	$ 60	$ 80	$100

Note that for this example the value of AC first decreases and then increases with x while the value of MC increases with x. The variation of the average cost results from decreasing unit fixed cost and rising unit variable cost as the volume x increases. In fact, the output volume x which produces a minimum value of AC may be determined by setting the derivative of AC equal to zero, or

$$\frac{d}{dx}(AC) = \frac{1}{10^3} - \frac{10^6}{x^2} = 0$$

from which $x^2 = 10^9$ or $x = 31{,}622$. Hence, the minimum value of AC is obtained by back substitution, i.e.,

$$(AC)_{min} = \frac{31{,}622}{10^3} + \frac{10^6}{31{,}622} = 31.62 + 31.62 = \$63.24$$

It should be noted also that at $x = 31{,}622$,

$$MC = \frac{(2)(31{,}622)}{10^3} = \$63.24$$

If we plot the values of AC and MC versus x as shown in Fig. 10.4, we see that the AC and MC curves intersect at $x = x^*$ where AC is minimum and that $x = x_0$ where MC is minimum corresponds to the point of inflection of $C(x)$.

So far in this section, we have discussed only two examples of costs over the short run since both Sections 10.3 and 10.4 were introduced to illustrate the tech-

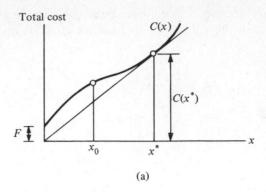

(a)

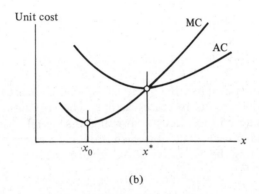

(b)

FIGURE 10.4

niques of estimating costs and benefits in the cash flow profiles of proposed projects, once the technologies and capacities of the projects are decided. We used the time period of 1 year in the examples in order to avoid the discussion of the treatment of interest payments which would be required if the time period exceeded the interest period of 1 year usually used in economic evaluations. No attempt was made to extend the application of these principles for the analysis of operations beyond 1 year.

However, it may be noteworthy that the concepts of average cost and marginal cost introduced in this section are applicable to long-run investment planning. Without going into detail, it is sufficient to point out that the cost function has the general shape as shown in Fig. 10.4(a), and the corresponding average cost curve and the marginal cost curves are shown in Fig. 10.4(b). Note that the marginal cost declines at the beginning due to the economics of large-scale production associated with the technology, but ultimately rises because of the diminishing returns. The input volume x_0 for the minimum marginal cost corresponds to that for the point of inflection on the total cost curve, while the input volume x^* leading to the minimum average cost, i.e., AC $= C(x^*)/x^*$, also yields MC $= C(x^*)/x^*$ as indicated by the slope of the total cost curve at $x = x^*$ in Fig. 10.4(a). Hence, the marginal cost curve and the average cost curve always intersect at the point of minimum average cost.

10.7 Minimization of Total Cost

Although the concept of profit maximization for nonlinear cost and revenue functions has been presented in the context of short-run operations in Section 10.4, it is applicable to a much wider range of problems. Let x be defined as an independent variable involving any quantity, such as output volume, time, amount of effort, etc. Let $C(x)$ and $B(x)$ be nonlinear cost and benefit functions of x, respectively, and $N(x)$ be the profit or net benefit function. Furthermore, $C(x)$, $B(x)$, and $N(x)$ are expressed in the current values of money (in dollars) for short-run problems but can be expressed in their present values or equivalent uniform annual values after discounting for the appropriate interest for long-run problems. Then, Eqs. (10.10) through (10.11) are applicable to the maximization of the net benefit for the class of problems just defined.

Since the benefits are more difficult to measure than costs in many situations, it is often tempting to minimize the cost over the relevant range of the variable, provided that the benefit is constant in the same range. If both cost and benefit functions are nonlinear, this condition cannot hold. However, we can often modify the problem so that we can determine the desired level of output by minimizing a modified form of the total cost without explicitly determining the total benefit.

Let $C(x)$ and $B(x)$ be the nonlinear cost and benefit functions of the variable x as previously defined. Let $\hat{B}$ be the maximum total benefit (a constant value) that can ever be achieved in the relevant range of the variable x, and let $L(x)$ be the loss function of x which represents the opportunity (or benefit) lost in achieving the ideal maximum total benefit. That is,

$$B(x) = \hat{B} - L(x) \tag{10.15}$$

where $\hat{B}$ is constant but $B(x)$ and $L(x)$ are nonlinear functions. Also let $T(x)$ be defined as the *grand total cost* such that

$$T(x) = C(x) + L(x) \tag{10.16}$$

Then, the net benefit can be expressed as follows:

$$N(x) = B(x) - C(x) = \hat{B} - L(x) - C(x)$$

Hence

$$N(x) = \hat{B} - [L(x) + C(x)] = \hat{B} - T(x) \tag{10.17}$$

It can be seen from Eq. (10.17) that the level of x which maximizes $N(x)$ also minimizes $T(x)$. That is,

$$\max N(x) = \max [\hat{B} - T(x)]$$
$$= \hat{B} + \max [-T(x)]$$

or

$$\max N(x) = \hat{B} - \min T(x) \tag{10.18}$$

Thus, we can modify the original problem of maximizing net benefit $N(x)$ to form a new problem of minimizing the grand total cost $N(x)$. If $\hat{B}$ is known, then the maximum value of $N(x)$ can be obtained from Eq. (10.18) after the minimum value of $T(x)$ is found. However, in many situations, we are only interested in the level of the variable x which maximizes $N(x)$ and not the maximum value of $N(x)$. Then, we can avoid the difficult task of determining $\hat{B}$ and simply try to find the optimal level

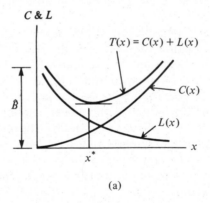

(a)

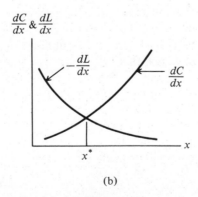

(b)

FIGURE 10.5

of the variable x by minimizing $T(x)$. Thus,

$$\min T(x) = \min [C(x) + L(x)] \tag{10.19}$$

The grand total cost functions $T(x)$, the cost function $C(x)$, and the loss function $L(x)$ are shown schematically in Fig. 10.5(a). Note that by differentiating Eq. (10.15), we have

$$\frac{dB}{dx} = -\frac{dL}{dx}$$

Thus, at $x = x^*$ where $T(x^*)$ is a minimum, we have

$$-\frac{dL}{dx} = \frac{dC}{dx} \tag{10.20}$$

as shown in Fig. 10.5(b). Note that dL/dx is negative because the slope of $L(x)$ is negative in the relevant range of x; hence $(-dL/dx)$ is a positive quantity.

Thus, when a problem is properly formulated to include the "loss" in total benefit which can theoretically be achieved as well as the actual expenses in the total cost, the minimization of the total cost will result in the optimal level of the variable which will also maximize the net benefit or profit.

Example 10.6

The level of detail in cost estimating for economic evaluation may be denoted by the variable x. The cost and benefit functions of cost estimating are, respectively,

$$C(x) = Dx^2 + E$$

$$B(x) = G - \frac{F}{x}$$

where D, E, F, and G are constants. The constant G represents the maximum total benefit that can ever be achieved ideally but cannot easily be determined. Noting that

$$N(x) = G - \frac{F}{x} - Dx^2 - E$$

find the level of x which minimizes the grand total cost

$$T(x) = E + Dx^2 + \frac{F}{x}$$

We can find the optimal level of x by setting the derivative of $T(x)$ equal to zero. Thus

$$\frac{dT}{dx} = -\frac{F}{x^2} + 2Dx = 0$$

from which we obtain

$$x^3 = \frac{F}{2D} \quad \text{and} \quad x = \sqrt[3]{\frac{F}{2D}}.$$

The same result may be obtained by maximizing $N(x)$.

If we examine the grand total cost $T(x)$ closely, we note that the term E represents the fixed cost, which does not change with x; the term Dx^2 represents the variable cost, which increases with x; and the term F/x represents the loss resulting from the inaccuracy of estimating, which decreases with x. The sum of the first two terms constitutes the amount paid for preparing the cost estimate. The last term is not an amount paid out but rather the loss in benefits that could have been received if the cost estimate were carried to perfection instead of stopping at the level x.

10.8   Optimal Economic Life of Physical Assets

The concept of minimization of total cost can be applied to assess the optimal economic life of a physical asset that is likely to be replaced by a similar asset when, because of physical deterioration, it can no longer perform the intended function. The category of physical assets includes equipment and facilities that are not subject to rapid technological obsolescence. In such a case, the benefit is considered to be identical whether the existing asset or its new replacement is in use if the existing asset is fully operational.

Let us consider the typical cash flow profile for a piece of equipment as shown in Fig. 10.6. The capital cost includes the initial acquisition cost P at year $t = 0$, less the salvage value S at year $t = N$. The operating and maintenance (O&M) cost consists of a uniform series of magnitude U_1 from year $t = 1$ to year $t = N$, and a linear gradient with a value of 0 at year $t = 1$ to a value of $(N - 1)G$ at year $t = N$. The O & M cost is expected to increase linearly with time because it will cost more to maintain the equipment in fully operable condition as it gets older. We can of course find the present value of the costs for operating and maintaining the equipment during N years and for disposing of it at the end. The cost expressed in the present value is given by

$$\text{CPV} = P - S(P\,|\,F, i, N) + U_1(P\,|\,U, i, N) + G(P\,|\,G, i, N) \tag{10.21}$$

However, we are more interested in the *equivalent uniform annual value of cost* because it will give us some idea of the annualized cost over a period of n years. Let

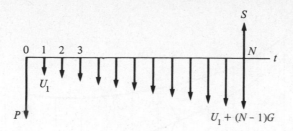

FIGURE 10.6

CUV denote the equivalent uniform annual value of cost. Then

$$CUV = P(U \mid P, i, N) - S(U \mid F, i, N) + U_1 - G(U \mid G, i, N)$$

Noting from Eqs. (3.15) and (3.17) in Chapter 3 that

$$(U \mid F, i, N) = (U \mid P, i, N) - i$$

we find

$$CUV = (P - S)(U \mid P, i, N) + Si + U_1 - G(U \mid G, i, N) \qquad (10.22)$$

Note also from Eq. (3.24)

$$(U \mid G, i, N) = (U \mid P, i, N)(P \mid G, i, N)$$

Thus, CUV can be computed by using the discrete compound interest tables in Appendix A if the values of P, S, U_1, G, i, and N are known.

We note that the CUV consists of two cost components: the CUV of capital recovery (CR) and the CUV of operating and maintenance (O&M). They are given by

$$CUV \text{ of } CR = (P - S)(U \mid P, I, N) + Si \qquad (10.23a)$$

$$CUV \text{ of } O \& M = U_1 + G(U \mid G, i, N) \qquad (10.23b)$$

We can compute these two components as well as the total value of CUV and plot the results of CUV versus N as shown schematically in Fig. 10.7. In general, for the range of N values under consideration, a particular value N^* exists at which the total value of CUV is a minimum. Note that the CUV of operating and maintenance increases with N, while the CUV of capital recovery decreases as N increases. If the planning horizon n coincides with N^*, then N^* is the optimal economic life of the equipment because the equipment, if acquired, should not be kept beyond N^* years.

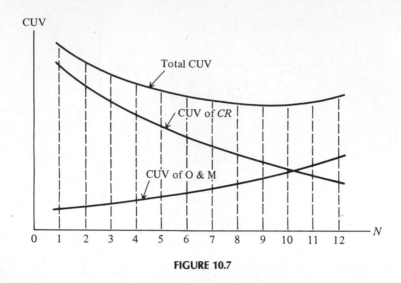

FIGURE 10.7

Let us examine further the underlying assumptions in the determination of the optimal economic life N^* of a piece of equipment. First, we have assumed that N^* coincides with the planning horizon n and that the technology remains essentially the same during these N^* years. Neither one of these assumptions is entirely realistic, but they do not negate some useful observations concerning the optimal economic life. Thus, the total CUV curve for most equipment is relatively flat after N takes on values greater than in the first few years when the capital recovery costs are relatively high. Consequently, if N^* is close to the planning horizon n, we can use n as the practical limit of the economic life of the equipment. Second, even if N^* coincides with n, new equipment with improved technology is expected to appear during the period of N^* years, and the current equipment may become technologically obsolete and/or economically unprofitable before the end of N^* years. Consequently, N^* may be regarded as the maximum number of years that the equipment should be kept, and the economic efficiency of this equipment should be reviewed periodically to determine if it should be replaced before the end of N^* years.

However, we must not extend this idea of finding the optimal economic life of equipment beyond the limits of its original assumptions. This approach should not be used when the assumptions do not reflect the actual conditions of technological obsolescence and therefore are no longer valid.

Example 10.7

A construction firm is considering the purchase of a heavy-duty tractor which costs $130,000. The salvage value S of the tractor, if it is sold after $1, 2, \ldots, 12$ years, and the annual O&M cost if it is kept over these years are given in Table 10.1. The

Table 10.1

Computation of CUV for a Range of N

N	S	O&M	CUV of CR	CUV of O&M	Total CUV
0	130,000				
1	90,000	4,000	43,200 + 7,200 = 50,400	4,000 + 0 = 4,000	54,400
2	60,000	7,000	39,260 + 4,800 = 44,060	4,000 + 1,440 = 5,440	49,500
3	40,000	10,000	34,920 + 3,200 = 38,120	4,000 + 2,850 = 6,850	44,970
4	30,000	13,000	30,190 + 2,400 = 32,590	4,000 + 4,210 = 8,210	40,800
5	20,000	16,000	27,560 + 1,600 = 29,160	4,000 + 5,540 = 9,540	38,700
6	10,000	19,000	25,960 + 800 = 26,760	4,000 + 6,830 = 10,830	37,590
7	10,000	22,000	23,050 + 800 = 23,850	4,000 + 8,080 = 12,080	35,930
8	10,000	25,000	20,880 + 800 = 21,680	4,000 + 9,290 = 13,290	34,970
9	10,000	28,000	19,210 + 800 = 20,010	4,000 + 10,470 = 14,470	34,480
10	10,000	31,000	17,880 + 800 = 18,680	4,000 + 11,610 = 15,610	34,290
11	10,000	34,000	16,810 + 800 = 17,610	4,000 + 12,720 = 16,720	34,330
12	10,000	37,000	15,920 + 800 = 16,720	4,000 + 13,790 = 17,790	34,510

tractor cannot be kept in serviceable condition after 12 years, regardless of the O&M cost. Determine the equivalent uniform annual cost if the tractor is kept for $N = 1, 2, \ldots$, or 12 years, if MARR = 8%.

For this problem, the initial cost $P = 130,000$ is the same as the salvage value S at $N = 0$, i.e., the tractor has not been used yet. The O&M cost can be broken up into a uniform series and a linear gradient with $U_1 = 4,000$ and $G = 3,000$, as indicated by the data in Table 10.1. Hence, the two components of CUV can be computed by Eqs. (10.23) and the total CUV computed from Eq. (10.22). The results of this problem follow the typical trends of thee CUV curves shown in Fig. 10.7.

10.9   Cash Flow Profiles in Replacement Analysis

It has been emphasized in Chapters 5 and 6 that we should specify a planning horizon to which we wish to look ahead. Hence, when we use the equivalent uniform annual costs for comparing and/or selecting investment proposals, we can consider the realistic cash flow profiles of these proposals instead of assuming that each proposed physical asset will be replaced by a similar asset until a period equal to the least common multiple of the useful lives of all physical assets has expired. The idea of replacing a physical asset by another similar new asset with an identical cash profile is appealing because of its simplicity, but it is very unrealistic in an age when technological advances often produce a significant increase in efficiency and decrease in price. The computer and biomedical technologies are only two dramatic examples of productivity improvements that have characterized many industries. Consequently, it is important to emphasize the meaning of the cash flow profiles in the replacement analysis, particularly when the equivalent uniform annual cost method is used. (See discussions in Section 6.10 of Chapter 6.)

Another possible pitfall in the use of the equivalent uniform annual cost method for comparing and/or selecting investment proposals is that we may be comparing alternatives whose benefits are quite different. For example, when we consider a physical asset which deteriorates with usage, we have consciously built in higher future O&M costs in the form of a linear gradient that increases with time. If the asset is eventually replaced by another similar new asset, we expect that similar benefit will continue, although both the capital recovery cost and the operating and maintenance cost may be different. However, because of technological improvements, the efficiency of the new asset may increase as the cost decreases. Consequently, by comparing only the cost, we may in fact "save" money by not replacing the asset and reducing the loss of an unprofitable operation. If we generate enough bad alternatives, even a poor proposal may look very attractive by comparison when we consider only the costs and not the net benefits of the proposals.

Example 10.8

Five years ago, a construction firm purchased a heavy-duty tractor which had an estimated cash flow profile like the one in Example 10.7 and decided at that time to keep the tractor for 10 years. In the past 5 years, the actual operating and maintenance costs were very close to the estimated values and the firm was quite satisfied with the choice of this tractor. The firm is expected to continue in the construction business for 5 more years and is now confronted with the decision whether to keep this tractor or to replace it with a new model which may be less expensive. Two new models available are expected to provide the same level of service as that of the existing tractor. The CR costs and O&M costs of the two new models (nos. 1 and 2) in contention for replacement of the old tractor (no. 3) are shown in Table 10.2. Should the existing tractor be replaced now if MARR = 8%?

In reviewing whether the existing tractor should be replaced by the new models available this year, we should use a planning horizon of 5 years since the firm originally intended to keep the existing tractor for 5 more years, even though the tractor may last longer than that. Note that the costs incurred in the past 5 years are sunk costs and therefore should not be considered; what matters is the costs for the next 5 years as duplicated in Table 10.2 from Table 10.1. If we had used a planning horizon of 10 years, we would have to forecast the costs of the replacement for the existing tractor after it is kept for 5 more years. While this is not impossible to do, the approach is unrealistic and is not recommended. Conse-

Table 10.2

Costs of the Two New Tractors and the Existing Tractor

	Tractor No. 1		Tractor No. 2		Tractor No. 3	
N	S	O&M	S	O&M	S	O&M
0	120,000		110,000		20,000	
1	85,000	3,000	80,000	4,000	10,000	19,000
2	55,000	6,000	55,000	7,000	10,000	22,000
3	35,000	9,000	30,000	10,000	10,000	25,000
4	25,000	12,000	20,000	13,000	10,000	28,000
5	15,000	15,000	10,000	16,000	10,000	31,000
6	10,000	18,000	5,000	19,000		
7	10,000	21,000	5,000	22,000		
8	10,000	24,000	5,000	25,000		
9	10,000	27,000	5,000	28,000		
10	10,000	30,000	5,000	31,000		

quently, we simply compare the three alternatives over the next 5 years by computing either their net present costs or the equivalent uniform annual costs over the 5-year period. Thus, from Eq. (10.21)

$$[CPV_1]_{8\%} = 120,000 - (15,000)(P \mid F, 8\%, 5) + (3,000)(P \mid U, 8\%, 5)$$
$$+ (3,000)(P \mid G, 8\%, 5)$$
$$= 120,000 - (15,000)(0.6806) + (3,000)(3.9927) + (3,000)(7.3724)$$
$$= 120,000 - 10,210 + 11,980 + 22,120 = 143,890$$

$$[CPV_2]_{8\%} = 110,000 - (10,000)(0.6806) + (4,000)(3.9927) + (3,000)(7.3724)$$
$$= 110,000 - 6,810 + 15,970 + 22,120 + 141,280$$

$$[CPV_3]_{8\%} = 20,000 - (10,000)(0.6806) + (19,000)(3.9927) + (3,000)(7.3724)$$
$$= 20,000 - 6,810 + 75,860 + 22,120 = 111,170$$

From this analysis, it is obvious that the existing tractor has the minimum cost and therefore should be kept.

It may be noted that in this case, the costs of new tractors have not been drastically reduced below the old one, while the efficiency of the existing tractor holds up well through extensive maintenance. This is usually not the case when the physical asset faces rapid technological obsolescence, as in the case of computer equipment.

If some dramatic technological breakthroughs are anticipated in the near future, a firm may sometimes defer the replacement of a physical asset even though the analysis favors such a replacement now. By delaying the replacement, the firm essentially looks at a long-range planning horizon and forecasts low costs beyond the expiration date of the existing asset. This point was illustrated by Example 6.15 in Chapter 6.

10.10 Cash Flows Related to Financial Transactions

We have so far discussed various analytical relationships in predicting benefit and cost items. However, we have covered only those items which are directly related to an economic activity, such as industrial production. There are other important items related to financing and income taxes which will be treated in later chapters.

Since the correct enumeration of benefits and costs in the cash flow profiles is very important in economic evaluation, we should carefully avoid omission or double counting of benefits and costs. Consequently, we shall provide a cursory view of some items related to financing and income taxes as a reminder that they have not been forgotten.

Many financing plans or strategies may be adopted in implementing each investment proposal. If the investment is financed entirely from internal funds, then no financing costs will appear in the cash flow profile of the proposal. However, if funds are borrowed from external sources, there will be a time stream of loans and repayments of principal and interest, depending on the interest rate, the method of repayment, and other factors in the financing plan. Consequently, the cash receipts and reimbursements in the time stream for financing must be superimposed on those in the time stream for operation in order to obtain the complete cash flow profile for an investment proposal.

For private firms, income taxes represent a significant cost of operation. Income taxes are computed on the basis of the tax rates and the taxable income as defined in the prevalent tax laws and regulations. Taxable income refers to the gross revenues less all expenses and allowable deductions. The most significant allowable deductions are depreciation and interest. Depreciation refers to the decline in value of physical assets in a given year and does not involve any cash outlay; however, it is an allowable deduction if one of the approved methods of depreciation is followed. Interest on debt (borrowed funds for financing) is also an allowable deduction. Thus, by selecting the method of depreciation and the financing plan which are most favorable, a firm can exert a certain degree of control on the taxable income and hence the income taxes.

We cannot possibly exhaust the complete list of benefits and costs for every conceivable situation in capital investment and financing. Nevertheless, we have pointed out the most significant items influencing the economic evaluation, some of which will be examined further in detail in Chapters 11 and 12.

10.11 Summary and Study Guide

In this chapter, we discussed the problems associated with the estimation of benefits and costs. We considered primarily the costs and benefits in connection with the operation of physical assets, with only a cursory treatment of other factors.

We examined briefly the theory behind the cost function and the optimization of net benefits by minimizing costs, and applied these principles to investment decisions. We started with the consideration of the variation of costs and benefits with output volume in production. Next, we considered the pricing strategies for maximizing the profits from sales. Thus, the basic concepts of production function, cost function, price function, and benefit function (or revenue function) were introduced in an intuitive manner.

We introduced a number of examples dealing with both linear and nonlinear cost and revenue functions. In particular, we applied the concept of profit maximization for nonlinear cost and revenue functions to determine the desired level of output by minimizing a modified form of the total cost without explicitly determining the total net benefit. The determination of the optimal life of physical assets was used as an example for applying this concept.

Although we discussed the computation of the equivalent uniform annual costs as a measure of the annualized cost of operating a physical asset, we warned against the use of such costs for comparing and/or selecting replacement proposals without considering realistically the projected cash flow profiles of various proposals. Some of the issues involved in replacement analysis were discussed and examples were given to illustrate their significance.

Finally, we considered the cash flows related to financial transactions, such as depreciation allowances and income taxes, as a reminder that they will be treated in detail in the next two chapters.

REFERENCES

10.1 Riggs, J. L., *Economic Decision Models for Engineers and Managers*, New York: McGraw-Hill, 1968.

10.2 Samuelson, P. A., *Economics*, 10th ed., New York: McGraw-Hill, 1976.

10.3 Wohl, M., *Transportation Investment Planning: An Introduction for Engineers and Planners*, Lexington, MA: D. C. Heath, 1972.

PROBLEMS

P10.1 Charles Manufacturing Company distributes overhead costs according to the number of employees in each department. Within a department the overhead is allocated according to direct labor-hours. According to the incomplete records, the monthly data for two departments A and B are as follows:

	Dept. *A*	Dept. *B*	Total *A* & *B*
Direct labor-hours	750	1200	1950
No. of employees	5	7	12
Overhead costs			$18,000

The company has just received a job order that requires a total of $800 for direct material, and 60 hours and 100 hours of direct labor from departments *A* and *B*, respectively. If the costs for direct labor in departments *A* and *B* are $10 per hour and $8 per hour, respectively, determine the total cost for the job order including direct material, direct labor, and overhead costs.

P10.2 Two methods for printing documents in a consulting office are being considered. The first method has an annual fixed cost of $10,000 and a variable cost of $0.12 per page. The second method has an annual fixed cost of $15,000 and a variable cost of $0.10 per page. What is the minimum number of pages to be processed during the year such that the second method will have a lower total cost?

P10.3 In a construction project involving the excavation of 50,000 m³ of earth, a mechanical excavator which can excavate 500 m³ per day was rented at $100 per day, plus a one-way shipping cost of $300 to the construction site. After 40 days of operation, the contractor discovers another similar excavator for rent which can also excavate 500 m³ per day, but will cost only $90 per day, plus a one-way shipping cost of $300 to the site. Assuming each excavator will be left on site until it is no longer needed and the return shipping cost must be borne by the contractor, is it cheaper to continue to rent the first excavator or to change to the second excavator?

P10.4 An intercity bus service between two communities requires a fixed cost of $36,000 per month and can handle a maximum of 2,000 passengers per month. The contribution margin per passenger is 60% of the $75 ticket price for a one-way trip. What is the number of passengers per month that the service must attract in order to break even?

P10.5 A subcontractor specializing in foundation excavation has estimated the cost and revenue functions with respect to the volume of excavation work (in units of 1,000 yd³) for the next year as follows:

$$C(x) = Dx + E$$

$$B(x) = G - \frac{F}{x}$$

where $D = 500$, $E = 20$, $F = 200,000$, and $G = 100,000$ such that both $C(x)$ and $B(x)$ are expressed in dollars. Determine the output volume x that will maximize the profit.

P10.6 For Problem P10.5, determine the marginal cost function and the marginal revenue functions, and find their values at the output volume for maximum profit.

P10.7 The building energy performance (BEP) can be expressed in an index x (which is inversely proportional to annual energy consumption in millions of BTU). Both the amortized uniform annual cost C for energy conservation measures and the annual cost for net energy consumption E are functions of the index x. Suppose that the annual energy conservation cost C (in dollars) for a building is expressed as

$$C = 50(x^2 + 1)$$

where x has a range of values from 1 to 10, and the annual net energy consumption cost E (in dollars) for that building is expressed as

$$E = -200 + \frac{21,600}{x}$$

The total equivalent uniform annual cost T to the owner of the building is the sum of E and C. Determine the index x that will minimize this total cost. Also plot the functions E, C, and T at $x = 1, 2, \ldots, 10$.

P10.8 For Problem P10.7, determine the functions for the marginal energy conservation cost and the marginal net energy consumption cost. If $B = \hat{B} - E$ where B is the benefit of energy conservation measures and $\hat{B}$ is a constant representing the theoretical maximum benefit that can be achieved when there is no net energy consumption, plot the values of the marginal benefit of energy conservation and those of the marginal cost of net energy consumption at $x = 1, 2, \ldots, 10$.

CHAPTER

11

DEPRECIATION AND
CORPORATE TAXATION

11.1   Depreciation as Tax Deduction

Depreciation is defined as the decline in value of physical assets, such as buildings and equipment, over their estimated useful lives. In the context of tax liability, depreciation is the amount allowed as a deduction in computing taxable income and, hence, income tax. It is a bookkeeping entry that does not involve an outlay of cash, and the amount of depreciation allowed by laws and regulations is referred to as the *depreciation allowance.*

It is important to differentiate between the *estimated useful life* used in depreciation computation and the *actual useful life* of a physical asset. The former is often an arbitrary length of time, specified in the regulations for computing federal income taxes, while the latter refers to the economic life of the physical asset which may be terminated because of deterioration or technological obsolescence. The estimated useful life used in depreciation computation is also referred to as *depreciable life.*

In order to understand the depreciation allowance, it is necessary to retrace the cycle of the acquisition, use, and disposal of a physical asset. When the physical asset is first purchased, an expenditure is made, but the expenditure cannot be deducted as an expense in computing federal income taxes because no expense is incurred when one asset is exchanged for another, e.g., cash for a physical asset. The outflow of resources comes at the end of the useful life of the physical asset when it is disposed of. The depreciation allowance is a way of recognizing that this outflow did not happen all at once but was in the process of taking place over a period of years. So, the depreciation allowance is a systematic allocation of the cost of a piece of equipment between the time it is acquired and the time it is disposed of.

The method and amount of taxation are matters of public policy. The methods of computing depreciation, as well as the estimated useful lives for various classes of equipment, represent a part of that public policy and are therefore specified by government regulations. The federal government plays an active role in

286

promulgating regulations to stimulate economic growth and to maintain stability. The regulations on depreciation computation are intended to encourage timely capital investments made by the private corporations.

The depreciation regulations form a part of the federal income tax laws which are revised periodically. In the past few decades, there have been no major changes in the methods of computing depreciation. However, a series of guidelines has been issued on the estimation of the useful life of various assets or groups of assets in order to standardize its application. The most dramatic change in such guidelines is embodied in the Economic Recovery Tax Act of 1981 which provides an *accelerated cost recovery system* to encourage capital investment.[1]

There are several methods of computing depreciation which are acceptable to the U.S. Internal Revenue Service. The different methods of computing depreciation have different effects on the streams of annual depreciation charges and, hence, on the stream of taxable income and taxes paid. These depreciation methods will be discussed in detail in this chapter.

11.2   Straight Line Depreciation

The cost of an asset less the salvage value is called the *net depreciable value*. The *annual depreciation allowance* refers to the amount of depreciation allowed for a given year. The sum of all the annual depreciation allowances from the current and previous years is called *accumulated depreciation*. The *book value* of an asset is the undepreciated value which is equal to the cost of the asset less accumulated depreciation up to the current year.

Let P be the cost of an asset, S its estimated salvage value, and N the estimated useful life (depreciable life) in years. Furthermore, let D_t denote the depreciation amount in year t, T_t denote the accumulated depreciation up to year t, and B_t denote the book value of the asset at the end of year t, where $t = 1, 2, \ldots,$ or N refers to the particular year under consideration. Then,

$$T_t = D_1 + D_2 + \cdots + D_t = \sum_{j=1}^{t} D_j \qquad (11.1)$$

where j is a dummy index for summation from 1 to t. Also,

$$B_t = P - T_t \qquad (11.2)$$

or

$$B_t = B_{t-1} - D_t \qquad (11.3)$$

---

[1] The Economic Recovery of Tax Act of 1981 was signed into law on August 13, 1981. However, some provisions of this act are being reconsidered by the U.S. Congress in 1982. Eventually, the act will be incorporated in the updated version in publications, such as those listed as Ref. [11.1] and Ref. [11.2].

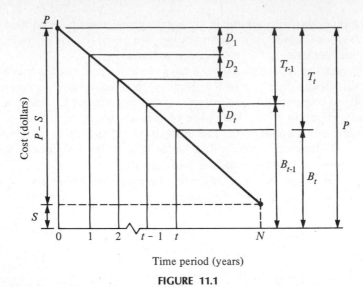

Time period (years)

FIGURE 11.1

The above relationships are completely general and are applicable to all depreciation methods. Such relationships for the case of straight line depreciation are shown in Fig. 11.1.

The most common form of depreciation, and the one easiest to comprehend, is *straight line depreciation*. Under straight line (SL) depreciation, the cost of a physical asset, less its estimated salvage value, is allocated uniformly to each year of the estimated useful life. Thus, D_t is constant for all values of t and is given by

$$D_t = \frac{P - S}{N} \tag{11.4}$$

From Eq. (11.2), the book value at the end of year t is

$$B_t = P - \left(\frac{P - S}{N}\right)t \tag{11.5}$$

Example 11.1

A compressor was purchased at a cost of $16,000 with an estimated salvage value of $2,000 and an estimated useful life of 7 years. Determine the depreciation allowance for each year and the book value at the end of each year, using straight line depreciation.

For $P = \$16,000$, $S = \$2,000$, and $N = 7$, we have for each year $(t = 1, 2, \ldots,$ or 7)

$$D_t = \frac{16,000 - 2,000}{7} = \$2,000$$

Furthermore,

$$B_t = 16,000 - 2,000t$$

Hence, $B_1 = \$14,000$, $B_2 = \$12,000$, $B_3 = \$10,000$, $B_4 = \$8,000$, $B_5 = \$6,000$, $B_6 = \$4,000$, and $B_7 = \$2,000$.

11.3   Sum-of-the-Years'-Digits Depreciation

Several other methods of depreciation are known as *accelerated depreciation methods*. Under an accelerated depreciation method, the depreciation allowance for an asset will be greater in the earlier years of its life and less in the later years of its life than under the straight line method. The total depreciation allowance would be the same under the accelerated method as under the straight line method, and, hence, total taxable income would be the same for the whole period; however, greater allowances in the earlier years also mean less tax in the earlier years. When the time value of money is taken into consideration, there is a substantial advantage in having the smaller amounts of taxable income in earlier years and larger amounts of taxable income in later years. Thus, using a method of accelerated depreciation amounts to getting an interest-free loan from the government.

One form of accelerated depreciation is the *sum-of-the-years'-digits (SOYD) method*. Under the SOYD method, the annual depreciation allowance is obtained by multiplying the net depreciable value $(P - S)$ by a fraction which has as its numerator the number of years of remaining useful life, and its denominator the sum of all the digits from 1 to N. Let S be the sum of the years' digits such that

$$Z = 1 + 2 + \cdots + (N - 1) + N = \frac{N(N + 1)}{2}$$

Then, the depreciation allowance for any year t is

$$D_t = \frac{N - (t - 1)}{Z} (P - S) \qquad (11.6)$$

Thus, for $t = 1, 2, \ldots, (N-1), N$, we have

$$D_1 = \frac{N}{Z}(P-S), \quad D_2 = \frac{(N-1)}{Z}(P-S), \ldots, D_{N-1} = \frac{2}{Z}(P-S),$$

$$D_N = \frac{1}{Z}(P-S)$$

Substituting the value of Z into Eq. (11.6),

$$D_t = \frac{N-(t-1)}{N(N+1)/2}(P-S) \tag{11.7}$$

The accumulated depreciation at the end of year t is

$$T_t = \frac{[N + (N-1) + \cdots + (N-t+1)]}{Z}(P-S)$$

$$= \frac{(2N-t+1)t}{2Z}(P-S) = \frac{(2N-t+1)t}{N(N+1)}(P-S)$$

Hence, the book value at the end of year t is given by

$$B_t = P - \frac{(2N-t+1)t}{N(N+1)}(P-S) \tag{11.8}$$

or from Eq. (11.3), we find

$$B_t = B_{t-1} - \frac{N-(t-1)}{Z}(P-S) \tag{11.9}$$

Example 11.2

Find the depreciation allowance for each year and the book value at the end of each year for the asset in Example 9.1, using the SOYD method.

In this problem, $Z = 1 + 2 + 3 + \cdots + 7 = 28$ and $P - S = 14{,}000$. From Eqs. (11.6) and (11.3), we get

$$D_1 = \tfrac{7}{28}(14{,}000) = \$3{,}500 \qquad B_1 = 16{,}000 - 3{,}500 = \$12{,}500$$

$$D_2 = \tfrac{6}{28}(14{,}000) = \$3{,}000 \qquad B_2 = 12{,}500 - 3{,}000 = \$9{,}500$$

$$D_3 = \tfrac{5}{28}(14{,}000) = \$2{,}500 \qquad B_3 = 9{,}500 - 2{,}500 = \$7{,}000$$

$$D_4 = \tfrac{4}{28}(14,000) = \$2,000 \qquad B_4 = 7,000 - 2,000 = \$5,000$$

$$D_5 = \tfrac{3}{28}(14,000) = \$1,500 \qquad B_5 = 5,000 - 1,500 = \$3,500$$

$$D_6 = \tfrac{2}{28}(14,000) = \$1,000 \qquad B_6 = 3,500 - 1,000 = \$2,500$$

$$D_7 = \tfrac{1}{28}(14,000) = \$500 \qquad B_7 = 2,500 - 500 = \$2,000$$

11.4 Declining Balance Depreciation

The *declining balance depreciation* is another form of accelerated depreciation in which the depreciation allowance for any year t is obtained by multiplying the book value of the previous year $(t-1)$ by a *constant depreciation rate* r. Since the book value at year 0 is the original cost of the asset, i.e., $B_0 = P$, we have

$$D_1 = B_0 r, \quad D_2 = B_1 r, \ldots, \quad D_{N-1} = B_{N-2} r, \quad D_N = B_{N-1} r$$

Thus, for year t,

$$D_t = B_{t-1} r \tag{11.10}$$

The book value at the end of any year t can be obtained by noting that, from Eqs. (11.2) and (11.3),

$$B_1 = B_0 - D_1 = P - Pr = P(1-r)$$

$$B_2 = B_1 - D_2 = B_1 - B_1 r = B_1(1-r) = P(1-r)^2$$

$$B_3 = B_2 - D_3 = B_2 - B_2 r = B_2(1-r) = P(1-r)^3$$

Hence, for year $t-1$,

$$B_{t-1} = P(1-r)^{t-1} \tag{11.11}$$

Substituting the value of B_{t-1} into Eq. (11.10), we get

$$D_t = Pr(1-r)^{t-1} \tag{11.12}$$

Also, from Eq. (11.3),

$$B_t = B_{t-1} - D_t = P(1-r)^t \tag{11.13}$$

The advantage of the declining balance depreciation method is that the salvage value S need not be estimated in the beginning years when the method is used for filing annual income tax returns. But there is no assurance that the accumulated depreciation at the end of year N will equal the net depreciable value $(P - S)$ if the constant depreciation factor r is arbitrarily chosen. In order to assure that $T_N = P - S$ or $B_N = S$ for $S > 0$, we find the value of B_N by letting $t = N$ in Eq. (11.13) such that

$$P(1 - r)^N = S$$

from which we obtain

$$r = 1 - \sqrt[N]{\frac{S}{P}} \tag{11.14}$$

Under the long-standing guidelines issued by the U.S. Internal Revenue Service, a factor $r = 2/N$ is allowed for all new depreciable property other than real estate (which includes buildings but excludes land, which is not depreciable). A smaller factor $r = 1.5/N$ is allowed for used machinery and equipment and for new buildings, and the smallest factor $r = 1.25/N$ is allowed for used buildings. Thus, Eq. (11.14) cannot be applied if r thus obtained exceeds the specified limits.

On the other hand, when the specified r does not satisfy Eq. (11.14), the book value B_N at the end of N years will either be less than or greater than S. In the former case, no further depreciation will be allowed when the accumulated depreciation reaches the net depreciation value $(P - S)$ before year N. In the latter case, larger depreciation is permitted in the latter years so that the accumulated depreciation at the end of year N will be adjusted to the net depreciable value $(P - S)$. The conditions of $B_N < S$, $B_N = S$, and $B_N > S$ are shown in Fig. 11.2. If $B_N = S$ at the specified r, no adjustment need be made. If $B_N < S$, then no further depreciation is allowed after t_2, and the accumulated depreciation at t_2 is $(P - S)$. If $B_N > S$, the regulations of the U.S. Internal Revenue Service allow the switching from the declining balance method to the straight line method after t_1 when the latter method leads to larger annual allowances.

Example 11.3

For the asset in Example 11.1, find the constant depreciation factor r such that $B_N = S$.

Using Eq. (11.14), we find that for $P = 16,000$, $S = 2,000$, and $N = 7$,

$$r = 1 - \sqrt[7]{\frac{2,000}{16,000}} = 1 - 0.743 = 0.257$$

Since $2/N = 0.286$, the value of $r = 0.257$ is below the specified factor for new

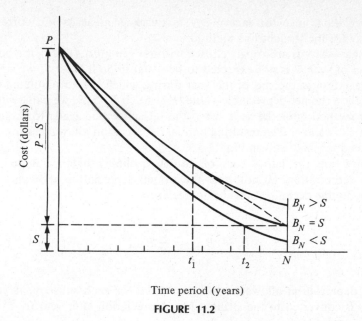

Time period (years)

FIGURE 11.2

equipment except real estate and is therefore acceptable. If $r = 0.257$ is used instead of $r = 2/N = 0.286$, we have not taken full advantage of the accelerated depreciation permitted by the regulations.

Example 11.4

If the salvage value of the asset in Example 11.1 is $500 instead of $2,000, find the constant depreciation factor of an asset r such that $B_N = S$.
   In this case, we have $P = 16,000$, $S = 500$, and $N = 7$. Hence

$$r = 1 - \sqrt[7]{\frac{500}{16,000}} = 1 - 0.610 = 0.390$$

Since this value of r is greater than $2/N = 0.286$, it is not permitted under the regulations of the U.S. Internal Revenue Service.

11.5 Double Declining Balance Depreciation

Since the constant depreciation factor $r = 2/N$ is applicable to many classes of assets except real estate, the declining balance depreciation based on $r = 2/N$ is a common form of accelerated depreciation and is referred to as the *double declining balance*

(DDB) *depreciation* since the factor $2/N$ is twice as great as the corresponding multiplier $1/N$ for the straight line method.

Because $r = 2/N$ is arbitrarily chosen without using Eq. (11.14), the book value B_N at the end of year N is not expected to be equal to S. If $B_N < S$, we simply stop further depreciation at the end of the year during which the accumulated depreciation has reached the net depreciable value $(P - S)$. If $B_N > S$, we can switch to the straight line method after the year when the latter method leads to larger annual depreciation allowances. The resulting annual depreciation allowances for these two cases are shown schematically in Fig. 11.3.

In converting the later years of double declining balance depreciation to straight line depreciation, we note that the annual depreciation allowance at year t based on the double declining balance depreciation is

$$D_t = rB_{t-1} = \frac{2}{N} B_{t-1}$$

The annual depreciation allowance for year t and for each subsequent year if the depreciation is converted to the straight line depreciation after year $(t - 1)$ is given by

$$D_t = \frac{1}{N - (t - 1)} (B_{t-1} - S)$$

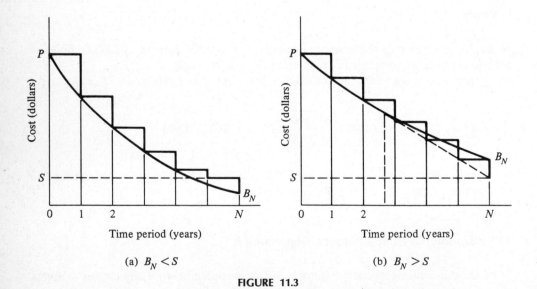

(a) $B_N < S$ (b) $B_N > S$

FIGURE 11.3

Thus, we should switch to straight line depreciation when the SL depreciation is greater than the DDB depreciation, i.e.,

$$\frac{B_{t-1} - S}{N - (t-1)} > \frac{2}{N} B_{t-1} \tag{11.15}$$

We can start with year N in the descending order of t, i.e., N, $(N-1)$, $(N-2)$, ..., until we reach a value of t at which the relationship in Eq. (11.15) no longer holds. For example, for $t = N$, $(N-1)$, $(N-2)$, Eq. (11.15) becomes, respectively,

$$\frac{B_{N-1} - S}{1} > \frac{2}{N} B_{N-1} \quad (\text{or } D_N \text{ based on DDB})$$

$$\frac{B_{N-2} - S}{2} > \frac{2}{N} B_{N-2} \quad (\text{or } D_{N-1} \text{ based on DDB})$$

$$\frac{B_{N-3} - S}{3} > \frac{2}{N} B_{N-3} \quad (\text{or } D_{N-2} \text{ based on DDB})$$

These relationships can easily be verified for the given values of P, S, and N.

Example 11.5

For the asset in Example 11.1, using the DDB method, find the depreciation allowance for each year and the book value at the end of each year. The accumulated depreciation must not exceed the limit allowed by the U.S. Internal Revenue Service.

Since $r = 2/N = 2/7$, we can use Eqs. (11.10) through (11.13) to compute D_t and B_t alternately as follows:

$$D_t = B_{t-1}(\tfrac{2}{7})$$

$$B_t = B_{t-1} - D_t$$

Thus, using the DDB method and noting that $B_0 = 16,000$, we get

$$D_1 = \$4,571.43 \qquad B_1 = \$11,428.57$$

$$D_2 = \$3,265.31 \qquad B_2 = \$8,163.26$$

$$D_3 = \$2,332.36 \qquad B_3 = \$5,830.90$$

$$D_4 = \$1,665.97 \qquad B_4 = \$4,164.93$$

$$D_5 = \$1,189.98 \qquad B_5 = \$2,974.95$$

$$D_6 = \$849.99 \qquad B_6 = \$2,124.96$$

$$D_7 = \$607.13 \qquad B_7 = \$1,517.83$$

Since B_7 is less than the salvage value $S = 2,000$, the full depreciation for that year is not allowed. Therefore, we must adjust the annual depreciation allowance for $N = 7$ by the amount

$$S - B_7 = 2,000 - 1,517.83 = 482.17$$

Then the adjusted values of D_7 and B_7 are

$$D_7' = 607.13 - 482.17 = \$124.96$$

$$B_7' = \$2,000$$

Since B_6 is greater than $S = 2,000$, no adjustment is needed for $N \le 6$.

Example 11.6

If the salvage value of the asset in Example 11.1 is $500 instead of $2,000, using the DDB method, find the depreciation allowance for each year and the book value at the end of each year. Convert to the SL method to take advantage of the full net depreciable value allowed by the U.S. Internal Revenue Service if appropriate.

    Since $P = 16,000$, $S = 500$, and $N = 7$, the results of D_t and B_t using the DDB method are exactly the same as those computed for Example 11.5. However $B_7 = 1,517.83$ thus obtained is greater than $S = 500$. Hence, the conversion to the SL method is carried out by finding out the year at which the conversion should begin. By using Eq. (11.15), we find

$$t = 7 \quad \frac{2,124.96 - 500}{1} = 1,624.96 \quad (>607.13)$$

$$t = 6 \quad \frac{2,974.95 - 500}{2} = 1,237.48 \quad (>849.99)$$

$$t = 5 \quad \frac{4,164.93 - 500}{3} = 1,221.64 \quad (>1,189.98)$$

$$t = 4 \quad \frac{5,830.90 - 500}{4} = 1,332.73 \quad (<1665.97)$$

Consequently, we should convert to SL for $t = 5$ through $t = 7$. Then, the adjusted values of D_t and B_t for $t = 5, 6$, and 7 are as follows:

$$D_5' = \$1,221.64 \qquad B_5' = 4,164.93 - 1,221.64 = \$2,943.29$$

$$D_6' = \$1,221.64 \qquad B_6' = 2,943.29 - 1,221.64 = \$1,721.65$$

$$D_7' = \$1,221.64 \qquad B_7' = 1,721.65 - 1,221.64 = \$\ \ 500.01$$

It can be seen that if $D_5' > D_5$ based on DDB as shown in the computation for $t = 5$, it follows that $D_6' > D_6$ and $D_7' > D_7$, where D_6 and D_7 are also based on DDB, since D_5', D_6', and D_7' are equal for straight line depreciation. Note also that $B_7' = 500.01$ is the same as the salvage value $S = 500$ except for the truncation error in the numerical computation.

11.6   Units of Production Depreciation

When the depreciation of an asset is more closely related to its use than to the length of time of ownership, it is permissible to determine the depreciation allowance on that basis under certain restricted conditions. Essentially, the unit of production may be expressed in terms of one of the following measures:

1. Production output, such as the volume or weight of material handled by a piece of equipment in any given year compared to the respective total volume or weight that may be handled during the useful life of the equipment
2. Operating days, indicating the number of days used in any given year compared to the expected total number of days in the useful life of the equipment
3. Projected income, which estimates the rental income from a rented property in any given year, compared to the expected total rental income from the property during its useful life

Under the *units of production (UP) depreciation*, the depreciation allowance is based on the principle that equal depreciation is allowed for each unit of production regardless of the lapse of time. The unit of production may be expressed in terms of one of the measures just described. Let U_t be the number of units of production during year t and U be the total number of units of production during the useful life of the asset. Then, the annual depreciation allowance D_t is equal to the net depreciable amount $(P - S)$ multiplied by the ratio U_t/U. That is,

$$D_t = \frac{U_t}{U}(P - S) \qquad\qquad (11.16)$$

Also, from Eq. (11.2), the book value at the end of year t is given by

$$B_t = P - \left(\frac{P - S}{U}\right)(U_1 + U_2 + \cdots + U_t) \qquad (11.17)$$

Example 11.7

A stone crusher is purchased at a cost of $12,000 with an estimated salvage value of $2,000 at the end of its useful life of 5 years. This stone crusher will be used for providing crushed stones for the construction of a large concrete dam over the next 5 years. The construction schedule calls for the following units of production (cubic yards of crushed stones) in the 5-year period: 8,000, 12,000, 18,000, 8,000, and 4,000 for years 1, 2, 3, 4, and 5, respectively. Using the units of production method, determine the annual depreciation allowance and the book value at the end of each year.

The total number of units of production over the useful life of 5 years is

$$U = 8,000 + 12,000 + 18,000 + 8,000 + 4,000 = 50,000$$

The net depreciable value over 5 years is

$$P - F = 12,000 - 2,000 = 10,000$$

Consequently, the values D_t and B_t can be obtained from Eqs. (11.16) and (11.17) as follows:

$$D_1 = (\tfrac{8}{50})(10,000) = \$1,600 \qquad B_1 = 12,000 - 1,600 = \$10,400$$

$$D_2 = (\tfrac{12}{50})(10,000) = \$2,400 \qquad B_2 = 10,400 - 2,400 = \$8,000$$

$$D_3 = (\tfrac{18}{50})(10,000) = \$3,600 \qquad B_3 = 8,000 - 3,600 = \$4,400$$

$$D_4 = (\tfrac{8}{50})(10,000) = \$1,600 \qquad B_4 = 4,400 - 1,600 = \$2,800$$

$$D_5 = (\tfrac{4}{50})(10,000) = \$800 \qquad B_5 = 2,800 - 800 = \$2,000$$

11.7   Comparison of Depreciation Methods

The depreciation methods for computing the depreciation allowance may be classified as follows:

1. Uniform depreciation
2. Accelerated depreciation
3. Units of production depreciation
4. Decelerated depreciation

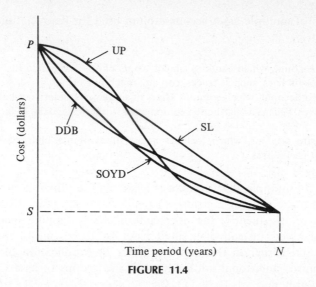

FIGURE 11.4

The straight line (SL) method leads to uniform depreciation and is the easiest to apply. Both the sum-of-the-years'-digits (SOYD) method and the double declining balance (DDB) method are accelerated methods of depreciation, with no decided advantage of either one over the other. In fact, any consistent method similar to the double declining balance method is acceptable.

The units of production method may produce accelerated or decelerated depreciation in certain periods of the useful life of the asset, depending on the timing of the production. When it is used properly within the restricted conditions, it may produce an overall schedule of depreciation with accelerated characteristics.

There is one other form of depreciation, called *sinking fund depreciation,* which is essentially a decelerated method of depreciation. Although it was used until some years ago, it has now been totally abandoned since no firm is interested in paying more tax in the earlier years of the life of an asset, thus adding interest to its tax liability. Consequently, we have not included this method in this chapter, and we mention it here only to warn against its use.

A schematic view of the comparison of various depreciation methods discussed in this chapter is shown in Fig. 11.4.

11.8   Multiple Asset Depreciation

In a large organization that owns many physical assets, it is permissible to combine a number of assets into a *multiple asset account* and to apply a single depreciation charge to the entire account.[2]

---

[2] Under the accelerated cost recovery system of the 1981 tax act, this approach becomes less significant for assets with short ranges of cost recovery, e.g., 3 years for cars, light-duty trucks, etc.

The types of multiple asset accounts often used for depreciation computation are:

1. Group account, which contains similar assets of approximately the same esti-mated useful lives, such as trucks, copying machines, etc.
2. Classified account, which contains assets of similar characteristics but different useful lives, such as construction equipment or other categories of large special assets
3. Composite account, which includes assets of dissimilar characteristics and different useful lives

The use of a multiple asset account is based on the principle that the mean life expectancy and dispersion for a group of assets can be determined statistically from historical data. Consequently, the depreciation charge can be made against the entire group of assets instead of a single asset by using one of the depreciation methods discussed earlier in this chapter. Since the application of multiple asset accounting requires additional information on the groups of assets, it will not be discussed in detail here.

11.9   Corporate Tax Rates and Depreciation Regulations

The government levies taxes on corporations and individuals in order to pay the costs of maintaining the government, to promote socially necessary services, such as defense and education, or to redistribute income among different segments of the society. Sometimes the government deliberately adopts a discriminatory policy of taxation in order to encourage certain actions or to discourage other actions to be taken by corporations and individuals. Although there are many kinds of taxes, the only kind that is particularly significant in economic analysis is the income tax. Federal and state income tax laws are intricate and subject to change over time. Consequently, only the general concepts and basic principles of the federal income tax laws as applied to private corporations are introduced here in order to illustrate their application to the economic evaluation of capital investment projects. The analyst should seek assistance from tax counselors on tax laws in effect at the specific locality and time.

Beginning in 1983, the tax rates on ordinary income of corporations are 15% for the first $25,000, 18% on the second $25,000 up to $50,000, 30% on the third $25,000 up to $75,000, 40% on the fourth $25,000 up to $100,000, and 46% on all income over $100,000. The lower graduated tax rates at the lower tax brackets were made as a concession to provide some measure of relief to small businesses.

Furthermore, there are other provisions in the federal income tax laws that offer special advantages to capital investment. For example, gains on the sale of machinery and equipment held for more than a year (long-term capital gains) are taxed at a lower rate than profits from ordinary operations. Another example is the investment tax credit which allows a deduction from the income tax of a small percentage of the value of certain newly acquired assets. This deduction affects income tax liability more directly than the depreciation allowance which is a reduction of the taxable income. These effects will be discussed further in later sections.

The 1981 tax act also liberalizes rules on tax benefits from equipment lease agreements. The purpose is to have some of the enhanced tax benefits available to the owner to be passed on to the renters.

The federal government has also established a set of guidelines for specifying the depreciable lives for various classes of assets, called the asset depreciation range (ADR), which is revised periodically in accordance with the prevailing tax laws. Before the 1981 tax act, the idea was to match annual depreciation allowances with the income produced by the assets during the year. Hence, under older laws, buildings were estimated to have a useful life of 40 years, machinery of various classifications from 10 to 30 years, and transportation equipment from 3 to 9 years. Under the 1981 tax act, an accelerated cost recovery system provides for much faster recovery of the costs of capital expenditures, although optional longer ranges for depreciation will be allowed under a flexibility provision of the system. Basically, the cost recovery periods allowed for various categories of assets are as follows:[3]

1. Three years for cars, light-duty trucks, research and development equipment, etc.
2. Five years for most equipment except long-lived properties
3. Ten years for railroad tank cars, mobile homes, amusement park structures, and certain special properties
4. Fifteen years for long-lived properties, including nonresidential buildings and public utility properties

11.10   Capital Gains and Losses

One source of income for a company is taxed at a lower rate than others. It is the gain on the sale of used equipment at a price higher than the book value. The difference in the sale value and the book value of a capital asset is known as the *capital gain.*

If an asset is sold for less than the book value, the difference is known as the *capital loss.* Capital losses can be offset against capital gains. Any excess capital loss can be a charge against capital gains in any of the 3 preceding years, and a tax

[3] The cost of recovery periods used in the examples do not necessarily correspond to the periods specified in the 1981 tax act because the use of different lengths for these periods in the examples permits a greater variety of numerical operations in illustrating the principles.

refund filed for the amount of capital loss, or it can be "carried forward" to offset capital gains in any of the following 5 years. If there are no capital gains during any of those 8 years, no capital deduction of any kind can be taken for capital losses.

Capital gains and losses can be either short-term or long-term. Short-term gains and losses are those on equipment held for a year or less. Long-term gains or losses are accrued on equipment held for more than a year before being sold. Long-term gains and losses are offset against each other to arrive at a net long-term gain or loss, and short-term gains and losses are offset against each other to arrive at a net short-term gain or loss.

Only net long-term capital gains are eligible for the special lower rate for capital gains. Net short-term capital gains must be included in ordinary income. The long-term capital gain may be offset by net short-term capital loss, if any. Net short-term capital gains may not offset net long-term capital losses. Any excess capital loss, either long-term or short-term, may be "carried back" to previous years or "carried forward" to future years and used to offset either short-term or long-term capital gains.

Net long-term capital gains (after being offset by long-term capital losses and net short-term capital losses) are taxed at the rate of 28% if the company so elects. This 28% tax rate is less than the 46% tax rate paid on ordinary income over $100,000 and normally represents a tax break. If the company is operating at a loss, or would be taxed at a rate lower than 46% even after the inclusion of the long-term capital gain, the company may instead elect to add the capital gain to ordinary operating income (or loss) if this yields a lower tax rate than the 28% capital gains tax.

11.11 The Investment Tax Credit

The *investment tax credit* (ITC) allows as a deduction from income taxes a small percentage of the value of certain newly acquired eligible assets. This provision was first established in 1962, suspended briefly later, and terminated in 1969. It was restored in 1971 with a 7% rate for qualified investment, and the rate for qualified investment was raised to 10% in 1975. Under the 1981 tax act, the classification of qualified investments has been simplified and the eligibility for the investment tax credit is based on the estimated useful life of the equipment.

Equipment with an estimated useful life of fewer than 3 years is not eligible for the ITC. For equipment with an estimated useful life of 3 to 5 years, 6% of the cost of the asset can be deducted from the income tax in the year when the asset is put in use; for equipment with an estimated useful life of more than 5 years, the percentage of the cost of the asset that can be deducted from the income tax is increased to 10%.

The estimated life of an asset for the purpose of claiming the ITC is calculated as of the time of purchase by the present owner or investor. For new equipment, the asset depreciation range can be used to estimate useful life. For used equipment, the *remaining* useful life can be estimated by the condition of the equipment or by subtracting the number of years of previous use from the ADR guideline life. Newly purchased used equipment is eligible for the ITC only to the extent of remaining useful life rather than the original useful life. Thus, an 8-year-old machine with an original estimated useful life of 10 years and a remaining useful life of 2 years when purchased is not eligible for the ITC. The laws governing the investment tax credit therefore favor the purchase of new equipment instead of used equipment, and they particularly favor the purchase of equipment with longer useful lives.

Example 11.8

During the current fiscal year, a construction company purchased a used fork-lift truck for $5,000 with a remaining useful life of 2 years, a new heavy truck with a useful life of 3 years for $15,000, a new bulldozer with an estimated useful life of 5 years for $24,000, and another piece of equipment with an estimated useful life of 10 years for $20,000. How much can the company claim for investment tax credit?

The used fork-lift truck is not eligible for the ITC. Both the heavy truck and the bulldozer are eligible for the ITC equivalent to 6% of their costs. The other equipment with an estimated life of 10 years is eligible for the ITC equivalent to 10% of its cost. Hence, the total investment tax credit is

$$(0.06)(15,000 + 24,000) + (0.10)(20,000) = \$4,340$$

11.12   Summary and Study Guide

In this chapter, the concept of depreciation of physical assets was introduced as a cost recovery scheme under the federal tax laws. Since depreciation regulations form a part of the federal income tax laws which are revised periodically, we emphasized the principles of computing depreciation allowances instead of the ever-changing guidelines which specify the allowable cost recovery periods for various categories of assets.

There are several methods for computing depreciation which are acceptable to the U.S. Internal Revenue Service, i.e., the straight-line method, the sum-of-the-years'-digits method, the double declining balance method, the units of production method, and others. The different methods of computing depreciation have different effects on the stream of taxable income and taxes paid. All these methods have been discussed in detail.

This chapter also covered some aspects of the tax laws and depreciation regulations, including the changes made in the tax act of 1981. The provisions of the 1981 tax act covering corporate tax rates, the accelerated cost recovery system, capital gains and losses, and the investment tax credits were discussed briefly in providing the background information for the computation of after-tax cash flows in Chapter 12.

REFERENCES

11.1 *Federal Tax Guide*, Englewood Cliffs, NJ: Prentice-Hall (annual publication).

11.2 *Federal Tax Reporter*, Chigaco, IL: Commerce Clearing House, (annual publication).

PROBLEMS

P11.1 A tractor costing $17,000 has a useful life of 5 years with a salvage value of $2,000 at the end of 5 years. Determine the annual depreciation allowance and the book value for each year by using

(a) The straight line method
(b) The sum-of-the-years'-digits method.

P11.2 A pressure vessel costing $70,000 has a useful life of 6 years with a salvage value of $10,000 at the end of 6 years. Determine the annual depreciation allowance and the book value for each year by using

(a) The straight line method
(b) The sum-of-the-years'-digits method.

P11.3 A concrete mixer costing $20,480 has a useful life of 6 years with a salvage value of $3,645 at the end of 6 years. Using a declining balance depreciation method with a constant depreciation rate $r = 1.5/N$, determine the annual depreciation allowance and the book value for each year.

P11.4 A remote-controlled small industrial robot costing $72,900 has a useful life of 6 years with a salvage value of $6,400 at the end of 6 years. Using the double declining balance depreciation method, determine the annual depreciation allowance and the book value for each year.

P11.5 A soldering machine costing $25,000 has a useful life of 5 years with a salvage value of $5,000. Using the double declining balance method, determine the annual depreciation allowance and the book value for each year until the maximum net depreciable value of $5,000 permitted by the U.S. Internal Revenue Service is reached.

P11.6 A pile-driving machine costing $250,000 has a useful life of 10 years with a salvage value of $25,000 at the end of 10 years. Using the double declining balance method with conversion to straight line, if necessary, determine the annual depreciation allowance and the book value for each year.

P11.7 A pump costing $2,400 has a useful life of 6 years with a salvage value of $300 at the end of 6 years. Determine the annual depreciation and the book value for each year by using the following methods:

(a) Straight line method
(b) Sum-of-years'-digits method
(c) Double declining balance method, with the maximum net depreciable value not to exceed $2,100

Tabulate the results systematically for comparison.

P11.8 The cost of an off-shore installation for oil-drilling is $5 million. The useful life of the installation for depreciation is 8 years. Its salvage value at the end of the useful life is estimated to be $300,000.

(a) Using the double declining balance method, determine the annual depreciation and book value for each year.
(b) If the book value at the end of 8 years does not equal $300,000 exactly, adjust the values of the annual depreciation allowance and book value for the best tax advantage such that the total depreciation will be $300,000.

P11.9 The Confederate Coal Co. bought a tract of land which has an estimated reserve of 2 million tons of coal underground. The cost of the property including the mineral rights was $22 million, of which $2 million was the value of the land and $20 million was the value of the coal reserve. During the first year of operation, 250,000 tons of coal was produced. What was the allowable depletion for the year on the basis of unit of production cost depletion method?

P11.10 A truck rental company purchases a heavy-duty truck at $20,000 with the intention of renting it on daily basis. The truck is expected to be used for 5 years with forecasted net annual revenues of $14,000 in the first year, and $2,000 less in each succeeding year (i.e., $6,000 in the fifth year). The company intends to depreciate this truck on the basis of the unit of production method until the book value reaches zero. Determine the annual depreciation allowances.

12

ANALYSIS OF
BEFORE-TAX AND
AFTER-TAX CASH FLOWS

12.1 Effects of Financing Plans on
Economic Evaluation

In the discussion of the economic evaluation of investment proposals in earlier chapters, we have deliberately attempted to separate the investment plans from the financing plans in order to emphasize the basic principles in analyzing the acceptability of investment projects. Actually, there may be significant interactions between investment and financing decisions because of the imperfections of the capital markets and possible tax shields on debt financing for private corporations.

Since many financing plans may be adopted in implementing each investment project, a stream of cash flows exists for financing corresponding to each financing plan. We shall not discuss here what financing plan will be most advantageous to an organization because such a treatment requires a knowledge and understanding of the financial structure of the organization. We shall simply examine the effects of some simple financing plans on economic evaluation without considering other financial side effects.

We shall therefore consider first the economic evaluation of investment projects for tax-exempt organizations for which the consideration of tax shields can be eliminated. We shall examine the effects of financing plans under different conditions of the capital markets. We are particularly interested in the conditions under which the investment decision and financing decision are independent of each other. Under such conditions, we need to be concerned only with the investment decision, as we have been up to this point, and leave the financing decision to the financial manager for consideration later.

For private corporations, the interest on debt financing is deductible from the income and thus provides an *interest tax shield*. We shall consider the effects of debt financing, given that the amount of debt for an investment project is known. In some cases, the amount of debt used to finance an investment project can be clearly identified, as in the case of a mortgage loan to finance a real estate project. In other cases, it is not easily identifiable because firms usually raise large sums of money through long-term debt for a number of investment projects over time and not for each project individually. Ultimately, we must look at the impact of accepting an investment proposal and its financing plan on the financial position of a firm, which will be discussed in detail in Chapter 16.

12.2 Before-Tax Cash Flows

Let us consider the general case when an investment is financed partly by internal funds and partly by borrowing from outside sources. Let us introduce the following notation which is applied to any year t in a planning horizon of n years:

B_t = total revenues and other benefits before tax from the operation of a physical asset, excluding cash receipts from loan for financing

C_t = total expenses before tax for the operation, including the costs of the acquisition and disposal of the asset but excluding cash disbursements (repayments of principal and interest on loans) for financing

A_t = net cash flow for operation before tax

$\bar{B}_t$ = cash receipt (from loan) for financing

$\bar{C}_t$ = cash disbursement (repayment of principal and interest on loan) for financing

$\bar{A}_t$ = net cash flow for financing before tax

$\hat{B}_t$ = total benefit from all sources before tax

$\hat{C}_t$ = total cost from all sources before tax

$\hat{A}_t$ = net cash flow from all sources before tax

Then, for the time stream $t = 0, 1, 2, \ldots, n,$

$$A_t = B_t - C_t \tag{12.1a}$$

$$\bar{A}_t = \bar{B}_t - \bar{C}_t \tag{12.1b}$$

$$\hat{A}_t = \hat{B}_t - \hat{C}_t \tag{12.1c}$$

and

$$\hat{A}_t = A_t + \bar{A}_t \tag{12.2}$$

If an investment project is financed entirely by internal funds, $\bar{A}_t = 0$ and $A_t = \hat{A}_t$ for $t = 0, 1, 2, \ldots, n$. Thus, if no money is borrowed to finance an investment project, the before-tax cash flow profile for the acquisition and operation of a physical asset is the before-tax cash flow profile that should be used for economic evaluation.

Often an investment project may be financed, in part at least, through borrowing. Then, we will consider the stream of cash flows for financing as well as that for acquisition and operation. However, if the borrowing interest rate for financing is identical to the minimum attractive rate of return, then the net present value for the before-tax stream of cash flows for acquisition and operation is identical to that for the combined before-tax cash flow profile.

Example 12.1

The stream of cash flows for the acquisition and operation of a piece of equipment is given by the values of A_t for $t = 0, 1, 2, \ldots, 5$ in Table 12.1. The acquisition cost at year 0 is $22,000 and the salvage cost at year 5 is $2,000, which is listed separately from the uniform annual net income of $6,000. There are four financing plans, each charging a borrowing rate of 8% but having a different method of repayment, as shown in Table 12.1. The minimum attractive rate of return specified is also 8%. Find the four before-tax cash flow profiles combining operation and financing. Also, determine the net present value for each of these four cash flow profiles.

The four financing plans shown in Table 12.1 illustrate some common methods of repayment:

(a) Repayment of principal and interest at the end of the planning horizon
(b) Uniform annual repayment covering both principal and interest
(c) Annual repayment of interest only, plus the repayment of the principal at the end
(d) Annual repayment of a constant fraction of principal and all accrued interest

Table 12.1

Streams of Cash Flows for Operation and Financing

t	A_t (Operation)	$\bar{A}_t$ Financing) (a)	(b)	(c)	(d)
0	−22,000	+10,000	+10,000	+10,000	+10,000
1	+6,000	0	−2,505	−800	−2,800
2	+6,000	0	−2,505	−800	−2,640
3	+6,000	0	−2,505	−800	−2,480
4	+6,000	0	−2,505	−800	−2,320
5	+6,000 / +2,000	−14,693	−2,505	−10,800	−2,160

Table 12.2

Before-Tax Cash Flow Profiles
with Different Financing Plans

t	$\hat{A}_t = A_t + \bar{A}$ (combined)			
	(a)	(b)	(c)	(d)
0	−12,000	−12,000	−12,000	−12,000
1	+6,000	+3,495	+5,200	+3,200
2	+6,000	+3,495	+5,200	+3,360
3	+6,000	+3,495	+5,200	+3,520
4	+6,000	+3,495	+5,200	+3,680
5	$\begin{cases} -8,693 \\ +2,000 \end{cases}$	$\begin{cases} +3,495 \\ +2,000 \end{cases}$	$\begin{cases} -4,800 \\ +2,000 \end{cases}$	$\begin{cases} +3,840 \\ +2,000 \end{cases}$

Note that for each financing plan, the net present value discounted at the borrowing interest rate of 8% is zero.

The before-tax cash flow profile combining operation and financing for each financing plan can be computed by Eq. (12.2) and the results for the four financing plans are shown in Table 12.2. For MARR = 8%, we find

(a) $[\text{NPV}]_{8\%} = -12,000 + (6,000)(P\,|\,U, 8\%, 4) + (-8,693 + 2,000)(P\,|\,F, 8\%, 5)$
   $= +3317$

(b) $[\text{NPV}]_{8\%} = -12,000 + (3,495)(P\,|\,U, 8\%, 5) + (2,000)(P\,|\,F, 8\%, 5)$
   $= +3,317$

(c) $[\text{NPV}]_{8\%} = -12,000 + (5,200)(P\,|\,U, 8\%, 4) + (-4,800 + 2,000)(P\,|\,F, 8\%, 5)$
   $= +3,317$

(d) $[\text{NPV}]_{8\%} = -12,000 + (3,200)(P\,|\,U, 8\%, 5) + (160)(P\,|\,G, 8\%, 5)$
   $+ (2,000)(P\,|\,F, 8\%, 5) = +3,317$

Since the MARR equals the borrowing interest rate for this problem, each financing plan contributes nothing (a net value of zero) to the net present value of the cash flow profile combining operation and financing. Consequently, the net present values for all four cases are identical.

12.3   Evaluation of Projects for Tax-Exempt Organizations

Government agencies and nonprofit organizations are tax-exempt. Consequently, we are only concerned with the before-tax cash flows in evaluating investment projects for such organizations. A government agency may finance an investment project through the appropriation of general or special funds obtained by taxation, or through long-term borrowing from bond issues. A nonprofit organization may raise the necessary funds for a capital project from donations or by borrowing.

If an investment project is in fact financed entirely by internal funds, the investment decision is completely independent from financing considerations. When an investment project is financed in whole or in part by debt, such as government bonds for financing a public project or a mortgage loan secured for a new building by a nonprofit private organization, it can be argued that the minimum attractive rate of return for the investment can be set equal to the borrowing interest rate. To the extent that this assumption is correct, the financing plans have no effect on the investment decision, although they are still important in scheduling the required working capital for the organization in order to implement the investment project. For this and other reasons to be discussed in a later chapter, the investment decision and financing decision are often regarded as independent by public agencies.

Example 12.2

An investment project proposed by a public agency has a cash flow profile for operation such as that represented by A_t $(t = 0, 1, 2, \ldots, 5)$ in Table 12.1. Four possible financing plans for borrowing \$10,000, each charging a borrowing rate of 8% but having a different method of repayment are also shown in Table 12.1. If the MARR specified by the agency is 8%, show that the investment decision is independent of any one of the four financing plans.

The net present value of the cash flow profile for operation, discounted at MARR = 8%, is

$$[\text{NPV}]_{8\%} = -22{,}000 + 6{,}000(P \,|\, U, 8\%, 5) + 2{,}000(P \,|\, F, 8\%, 5)$$
$$= +3{,}317$$

This result is identical to the net present value for each cash flow profile combining operation and a financing plan as computed in Example 12.1. It is obvious that the investment decision would have been the same if any one of the financing plans had been adopted. Consequently, we conclude that the investment decision is independent of the financing plan when the specified MARR = 8% is equal to the borrowing interest rate of 8%.

Example 12.3

For the same investment project and financing plans in Example 12.2, determine the effect of each of the financing plans if

1. The specified MARR is 10%
2. The specified MARR is 6%

In case 1, the specified MARR of 10% is greater than the borrowing interest rate of 8%. The net present value of the cash flow profile for operation, discounted at MARR = 10%, is

$$[NPV]_{10\%} = -22,000 + (6,000)(P\,|\,U, 10\%, 5) + (2,000)(P\,|\,F, 10\%, 5)$$
$$= +1,987$$

The net present value for each cash flow profile combining operation and a financing plan shown in Table 12.2 can be obtained as follows:

(a) $[NPV]_{10\%} = -12,000 + (6,000)(P\,|\,U, 10\%, 4) + (-8,693 + 2,000)(P\,|\,F, 10\%, 5)$
   $= +2,864$
(b) $[NPV]_{10\%} = -12,000 + (3,495)(P\,|\,U, 10\%, 5) + (2,000)(P\,|\,F, 10\%, 5)$
   $= +2,491$
(c) $[NPV]_{10\%} = -12,000 + (5,200)(P\,|\,U, 10\%, 4) + (-4,800 + 2,000)(P\,|\,F, 10\%, 5)$
   $= +2,745$
(d) $[NPV]_{10\%} = -12,000 + (3,200)(P\,|\,U, 10\% \ 5) + (160)(P\,|\,G, 10\%, 5)$
   $+ (2,000)(P\,|\,F, 10\%, 5)$
   $= +2,470$

Note that for all four financing plans, the net present value of the cash flow profile including debt financing is higher than that for operation alone. Thus, any of these four financing plans is more attractive than internal funding since the internal funds can be diverted to other opportunities to earn a return of 10%, which is higher than the borrowing interest rate of 8%. Furthermore, among the four financing plans, the one that makes the most use of the borrowed fund during the 5-year period is most desirable, as indicated by the highest NPV for plan (a).

In case 2, the specified MARR of 6% is less than the borrowing interest rate of 8%. The net present value of the cash flow profile for operation, discounted at MARR = 6%, is

$$[NPV]_{6\%} = -22,000 + (6,000)(P\,|\,U, 6\%, 5) + (2,000)(P\,|\,F, 6\%, 5)$$
$$= +4,767$$

The net present value for each cash flow profile combining operation and a financing plan shown in Table 12.2 can also be obtained:

(a) $[NPV]_{6\%} = -12,000 + (6,000)(P\,|\,U, 6\%, 4) + (-8,693 + 2,000)(P\,|\,F, 6\%, 5)$
   $= +3,789$
(b) $[NPV]_{6\%} = -12,000 + (3,495)(P\,|\,U, 6\%, 5) + (2,000)(P\,|\,F, 6\%, 5)$
   $= +4,217$
(c) $[NPV]_{6\%} = 12,000 + (5,200)(P\,|\,U, 6\%, 4) + (-4,800 + 2,000)(P\,|\,F, 6\%, 5)$
   $= +3,926$
(d) $[NPV]_{6\%} = -12,000 + (3,200)(P\,|\,U, 6\%, 5) + (160)(P\,|\,G, 6\%, 5)$
   $+ (2,000)(P\,|\,F, 6\%, 5) = +4,244$

Note that for this case, the net present value of each cash flow profile including debt financing is lower than that for operation alone, regardless of which financing plan is used. Thus, debt financing is not as attractive as internal funding, since any internal funds diverted to other opportunities can earn a return of only 6%, which is lower than the borrowing interest rate of 8%. As a result, the financing plan which keeps the largest amount of the loan over the borrowing period is least desirable, as indicated by the lowest NPV for plan (a).

Example 12.4

The Port Authority of a metropolitan area is planning an exclusive bus-lane expressway project to speed up the commuter traffic during rush hours. It is expected that the engineering design and construction will take 4 years before the project can be ready for service. However, the costs of engineering design and construction must be incurred before the project is ready for service. The Port Authority receives 80% of the funds for the project from the federal government and 20% from the state and local governments. How should the costs incurred during the period of engineering design and construction be treated in the cash flow profile for economic evaluation?

There are two ways by which the costs incurred during the period of engineering design and construction can be handled. First, we may consider the beginning of engineering design and construction as year 0 in the planning horizon. Thus, there will be heavy expenditures in the first 4 years with no benefits received during these years. Alternately, we can set up a separate accounting system for engineering design and construction such that all expenses related to engineering design and construction including financing *and* opportunity cost up to the completion date of the project will be regarded as the acquisition cost. Then, the planning horizon will begin with the time when the expressway is ready for service, and thus, only a single acquisition cost is charged at year 0. The latter approach may be thought of as a "turnkey" operation for which the owner of the project symbolically turns the key to open the facility for operation after paying the acquisition cost in a single sum.

12.4   Corporate Income Taxes

In Chapter 11, we discussed the most important aspects of federal income tax laws that offer special advantage to capital investment, including the regulations for depreciation allowance. Although the tax rates on the ordinary income of corporations are specified in several brackets for income up to $100,000, a tax rate of 46% is applied to all income over $100,000. For large corporations, the saving on the first $100,000 of taxable income represents a miniscule amount. Consequently, the marginal rate of 46% is applied to all taxable income after allowable deductions.

Furthermore, some states also levy a corporation tax. Consequently, a tax rate of 50% is often used as an approximate effective rate for all *taxable income*. Because of the high tax rate, firms try to find every opportunity to reduce the tax burden by taking deductions whenever possible. The depreciation allowance is a significant deduction for capital investments as discussed in Chapter 11. The net tax rate, after deductions, is usually considerably lower than 46%. Whenever the exact rate, the effect of income taxes is a major factor in evaluating the profitability of investment projects. The appropriate tax rate to be used in the calculation of cost and benefit streams is supplied by the firm's tax department.

In this chapter, we only emphasize the principles of analyzing the effects of corporate income taxes on the economic evaluation of investment proposals. We should certainly be aware of the assumptions imposed on the analysis and the limitations of the conclusions derived from such an analysis.

12.5 After-Tax Cash Flows

Except for small businesses for which the graduated tax rates represent a significant reduction in taxes, most corporations are primarily concerned with earnings above $100,000. Consequently, we shall consider only a single tax rate in the computation of after-tax cash flows.

Let us introduce further the following notation which is also applied to any year t in a planning horizon of n years:

D_t = depreciation allowance
I_t = interest accrued (positive on the unpaid balance of a loan and negative on the overpayment)
Q_t = amount available for reducing the unpaid balance on loan
W_t = taxable income
X_t = income tax rate
T_t = income tax
Y_t = net cash flow after tax

Then, for the time stream $t = 0, 1, 2, \ldots, n$

$$W_t = A_t - D_t - I_t \tag{12.3}$$

$$T_t = X_t W_t \tag{12.4}$$

Finally, the cash flow profile after tax (for $n = 0, 1, 2, \ldots, n$) is

$$Y_t = \hat{A}_t - X_t W_t \tag{12.5}$$

Note that the taxable income W_t is based on the net income A_t from operation before tax (for $t = 0, 1, 2, \ldots, n$), less the allowable deductions on depreciation D_t and interest I_t for $t = 1, 2, \ldots, n$. Note that Q_t representing the net increase (positive) or decrease (negative) of the repayment of principal does not enter into the calculation of the taxable income, but it is related to I_t for $t = 1, 2, \ldots, n$ according to Eq. (4.22) as follows:

$$\bar{A}_t = Q_t - I_t \qquad (12.6)$$

where $\bar{A}_t$ is positive for a receipt from a loan and the negative for the payment of principal and interest. The computation of the principal Q_t and interest I_t for $t = 1, 2, \ldots, n$ has been discussed in Section 4.5 of Chapter 4. Thus the cash flow profile after tax for $t = 0, 1, 2, \ldots, n$ may also be given by

$$Y_t = A_t + \bar{A}_t - X_t(A_t - D_t - I_t) \qquad (12.7)$$

When an investment project is financed by equity only, $Q_t = 0$, $I_t = 0$, and $\bar{A}_t = 0$. Then, Eq. (12.7) is simplified as follows:

$$Y_t = A_t - X_t(A_t - D_t) \qquad (12.8)$$

For private corporations, the financing of an investment project by equity or debt may influence the overall equity-debt mix of the entire corporation, depending on the size of the project and the risk involved. When a corporation decides to finance a particular investment project by borrowing, it incurs new obligations and risks, and thus affects its future capacity for additional borrowing. Hence, the internal funds of a corporation represent a common pool of resources from both equity and debt. If an investment project is financed through internal funds, it is difficult to determine the exact proportions of equity and debt for this particular investment project. Equity financing is only an idealized case for which the after-tax cash flow profile of an investment project is assumed to be independent of debt financing.

However, the most important question is how significant the interactions between investment proposals and financing plans really are under different corporate environments and tax laws. If the interactions are insignificant, then, we can either ignore or at most incorporate the effects of financing plans into the decision criteria for evaluating investment proposals. Then, the financing plans can be considered separately by the financial manager later. On the other hand, if the interactions between the two are strong, we cannot treat them separately. We shall discuss some of the factors that affect the interactions of investment decisions and financial decisions in Chapter 16. At present, we shall only consider the effects of some financing plans, given the equity-debt mix for a particular investment proposal, so that we can evaluate its acceptability on the basis of the after-tax minimum attractive rate of return specified by the corporation.

Example 12.5

A large firm received revenues of $500,000 and incurred expenses of $300,000 (not counting depreciation) in one of its divisions last year. The allowable depreciation on the equipment for the operation was $20,000. Assume that this division did not borrow money to finance the aquisition of the equipment or its operation and hence had no interest payment last year. For an income tax rate of 50%, what was the net cash inflow after tax from this division?

Assuming equity financing, the before-tax cash flow for last year was given by Eq. (12.1a):

$$A_t = 500,000 - 300,000 = 200,000$$

From Eq. (12.8), we obtain the after-tax cash flow as follows:

$$Y_t = 200,000 - (50\%)(200,000 - 20,000) = \$110,000$$

Example 12.6

The Rockwood Corporation is considering the installation of a mechanical device to facilitate the production of one of its products during the next 5 years. The device will cost $12,000 and will have a salvage value of $2,000 at the end of 5 years. The firm chooses to use the straight line depreciation method for the device and pays an annual income tax for its profits at a rate of 46%. If the minimum attractive rate of return after tax is 6%, what is the minimum uniform annual net benefit before tax that must be generated by this device in order to justify its installation? Assume that the purchase is financed by equity.

Let the uniform annual net benefit before tax be denoted by A_t (for $t = 0$, 1, 2, ... 5). The straight line depreciation for each year is given by Eq. (11.4).

$$D_t = (1/5)(12,000 - 2,000) = 2,000$$

The after-tax cash flow for each year is obtained by Eq. (12.8):

$$Y_t = A_t - (0.46)(A_t - 2,000)$$
$$= 0.54A_t + 920$$

The net present value of the cash flow profile for the investment discounted at the specified after-tax MARR of 6% is

$$[\text{NPV}]_{6\%} = -12,000 + (0.54A_t + 920)(P\,|\,U, 6\%, 5) + 2,000(P\,|\,F, 6\%, 5)$$
$$= -12,000 + 2.275A_t + 3,875 + 1,495 = 2.275A_t - 6,630$$

For the investment to be acceptable, NPV must at least be zero. Hence,

$$2.275A_t - 6,630 = 0$$

from which we find the minimum uniform annual net benefit to be

$$A_t = \$2,914$$

12.6   Effects of Allowable Deduction for Depreciation

The depreciation methods will produce different effects on the after-tax cash flow profile of an investment. The accelerated depreciation methods generate larger depreciation allowances during the early years and correspondingly smaller allowances in the later years of the "estimated useful life" of the asset. Hence, the tax liabilities in the early years will be lower and those in the later years will be higher. The total undiscounted amount of taxes on ordinary incomes throughout the life of an asset will be the same, regardless of the depreciation method used, if the asset is fully depreciated to its salvage value at the end of the estimated useful life. Consequently, the discounted value of the after-tax cash flow using any one of the accelerated depreciation methods is expected to be better than that obtained by using the straight line method.

The estimated useful life used in computing the depreciation allowance will also affect the after-tax cash flow profile of an investment. Under an accelerated cost recovery system in the 1981 tax law, the period for recovering the cost of an asset is generally much shorter than the actual useful life of the asset. A shorter recovery period for the cost of an asset will produce larger annual depreciation allowance and hence greater deductions in income taxes. Thus, the system provides a strong incentive for capital investment.

Example 12.7

Roper Manufacturing Corporation considers purchasing new automatic equipment to improve its production. An expenditure of \$46,000 on the equipment is expected to produce a before-tax benefit of \$15,000 in the first year and \$2,000 less in each succeeding year for a total of 6 years (i.e., before-tax benefit of \$13,000 in the second year, \$11,000 in the third year, until \$5,000 in the sixth year). The salvage value of the equipment will be \$4,000 at the end of 6 years. Assume that the purchase is financed by equity and that the income rate for the firm is 50%. If the minimum attractive rate of return after tax is 6%, determine whether the purchase is worthwhile, using each of the following depreciation methods:

1. Sum-of-the-years'-digits (SOYD) depreciation
2. Straight line (SL) depreciation

The annual depreciation allowances based on the SOYD method are obtained by Eq. (11.6). The computation of the after-tax cash flows using Eq. (12.8) is shown in part (a) of Table 12.3. Then, for the after-tax MARR of 6%, we get

$$[NPV]_{6\%} = -46,000 + (13,500)(P\,|\,U, 6\%, 6) - (2,000)(P\,|\,G, 6\%, 6)$$
$$+ (4,000)(P\,|\,F, 6\%, 6) = +285$$

Table 12.3

Computation of After-Tax Cash Flows

(a) SOYD Depreciation

Year t	Before-tax Cash Flow A_t	Depreciation (SOYD) D_t	Taxable Income W_t	Income Tax T_t	After-tax Cash Flow Y_t
0	−46,000				−46,000
1	+15,000	12,000	3,000	1,500	+13,500
2	+13,000	10,000	3,000	1,500	+11,500
3	+11,000	8,000	3,000	1,500	+9,500
4	+9,000	6,000	3,000	1,500	+7,500
5	+7,000	4,000	3,000	1,500	+5,500
6	{ +5,000 +4,000	2,000	3,000	1,500	{ +3,500 +4,000

(b) SL Depreciation

Year t	Before-tax A_t	Depreciation (SL) D_t	Taxable Income W_t	Income Tax T_t	After-tax Y_t
0	−46,000				−46,000
1	+15,000	7,000	8,000	4,000	+11,000
2	+13,000	7,000	6,000	3,000	+10,000
3	+11,000	7,000	4,000	2,000	+9,000
4	+9,000	7,000	2,000	1,000	+8,000
5	+7,000	7,000	0	0	+7,000
6	{ +5,000 +4,000	7,000	−2,000	−1,000	{ +6,000 +4,000

Similarly, the annual depreciation allowances based on the SL method are obtained by Eq. (11.6). The computation of the after-tax cash flows using Eq. (12.8) is shown in part (b) of Table 12.3. For after-tax MARR of 6%,

$$[\text{NPV}]_{6\%} = -46,000 + (11,000)(P\,|\,U,\,6\%,\,6) - (1,000)(P\,|\,G,\,6\%,\,6) \\ + (4,000)(P\,|\,F,\,6\%,\,6) = -549$$

This example illustrates how the choice of the depreciation method may affect the investment decision.

Example 12.8

A private firm is interested in the purchase of a minicomputer through equity financing. The before-tax cash flow profile for the acquisition and operation of this minicomputer is identical to that for the equipment in Example 12.1. The income tax rate is 50% and the after-tax MARR specified by the firm is 8%. Determine whether the purchase is worthwhile for each of the following depreciation methods:

1. Double declining balance (DDB) depreciation up to the limit
2. Sum-of-the-years'-digits (SOYD) depreciation

The annual depreciation allowances based on the DDB method are obtained by Eqs. (11.10) through (11.13) and tabulated in part (a) of Table 12.4. However, for $t = 5$, the computed depreciation allowance $D_5 = 1,140$ leads to a book value $B_5 = 1,711$. Since B_5 cannot be less than the salvage value $S = 2,000$, the adjusted depreciation allowance becomes

$$D_5' = 1,140 - (2,000 - 1,711) = 851$$

The computation of the after-tax cash flows using Eq. (12.8) is also shown in part (a) of Table 12.4. Then, for the after-tax MARR of 8%, we have

$$[\text{NPV}]_{8\%} = -22,000 + (7,400)(P\,|\,F,\,8\%,\,1) + (5,640)(P\,|\,F,\,8\%,\,2) \\ + (4,584)(P\,|\,F,\,8\%,\,3) + (3,950)(P\,|\,F,\,8\%,\,4) \\ + (3,425 + 2,000)(P\,|\,F,\,8\%,\,5) = -79$$

Similarly, the annual depreciation allowances based on the SOYD method are obtained by Eq. (11.6). The computation of the after-tax cash flows using Eq. (12.8) is shown in part (b) of Table 12.4. For the after-tax MARR of 8%, we get

$$[\text{NPV}]_{8\%} = -22,000 + 6,333(P\,|\,U,\,8\%,\,5) - 667(P\,|\,G,\,8\%,\,5) + 2,000(P\,|\,F,\,8\%,\,5) \\ = -270$$

Table 12.4

Effects of Depreciation Methods on After-Tax Analysis

(a) DDB Depreciation

Year t	Before-tax Cash Flow A_t	Depreciation (DDB) D_t	Taxable Income W_t	Income Tax T_t	After-tax Cash Flow Y_t
0	$-22,000$				$-22,000$
1	$+6,000$	8,800	$-2,800$	$-1,400$	$+7,400$
2	$+6,000$	5,280	720	360	$+5,640$
3	$+6,000$	3,168	2,832	1,416	$+4,584$
4	$+6,000$	1,901	4,099	2,050	$+3,950$
5	$\begin{cases} +6,000 \\ +2,000 \end{cases}$	851	5,149	2,575	$\begin{cases} +3,425 \\ +2,000 \end{cases}$

(b) SOYD Depreciation

Year t	Before-tax Cash Flow A_t	Depreciation (SOYD) D_t	Taxable Income W_t	Income Tax T_t	After-tax Cash Flow Y_t
0	$-22,000$				$-22,000$
1	$+6,000$	6,667	-667	-333	$+6,333$
2	$+6,000$	5,333	667	333	$+5,667$
3	$+6,000$	4,000	2,000	1,000	$+5,000$
4	$+6,000$	2,667	3,333	1,667	$+4,333$
5	$\begin{cases} +6,000 \\ +2,000 \end{cases}$	1,333	4,667	2,333	$\begin{cases} +3,667 \\ +2,000 \end{cases}$

Note that the purchase is not worthwhile, regardless of which depreciation method is used, although the DDB method is more advantageous.

12.7 Effects of Allowable Deduction for Interest

The interest on debt financing is deductible for income tax purposes. If a firm can borrow money at a borrowing interest rate equal to or less than its MARR, it is more profitable for the firm to finance an investment project by debt because of the allowable deduction for interest. However, this advantage is realized only if the borrowing does not alter the long-term financial position of the firm.

If a firm lacks the necessary funds to acquire a physical asset which is deemed desirable, it can often lease the asset by entering into a contract with another party which will obligate the firm legally to make payments for a well-defined period of time. The payments in leasing are expenses that can be deducted in full from the gross revenues in computing taxable income. On the other hand, if the firm borrows money to buy the asset, it can deduct the allowable depreciation and interest for financing. The decision to buy or to lease depends on a number of factors, such as the borrowing interest rate, the term of the lease, etc.

We can determine the effect of allowable deduction for interest in debt financing for a given amount of debt by comparing the net present value of the cash flow profile combining operation and financing against that based on equity financing. We can also evaluate the buy-or-lease alternatives by comparing the net present values.

Example 12.9

Suppose that the purchase of the minicomputer in Example 12.8 is financed partly by debt (for an amount of $10,000). Two financing plans are being considered, and the cash flow profiles for these financing plans are shown in the column $\bar{A}_t$ $(t = 0, 1, 2, \ldots, n)$ in parts (a) and (b) of Table 12.5. The double declining balance (DDB) depreciation up to the limit of allowable deduction will be used in computing depreciation allowance. The income tax rate is 50% and the after-tax MARR specified by the firm is 8%. Determine whether the purchase is worthwhile for each of the two financing plans.

The amount of interest I_t (for $t = 1, 2, \ldots, 5$) associated with each of the financing plans has been computed in Example 4.12 (Chapter 4), and the results for the two financing plans are tabulated in the column I_t in parts (a) and (b) of Table 12.5. The computation of the after-tax cash flows in part (a) of Table 12.5 discounted at the after-tax MARR of 8% is given by

$$[\text{NPV}]_{8\%} = -12{,}000 + (7{,}800)(P\,|\,F, 8\%, 1) + (6{,}072)(P\,|\,F, 8\%, 2)$$
$$+ (5{,}050)(P\,|\,F, 8\%, 3) + (4{,}454)(P\,|\,F, 8\%, 4)$$
$$+ (-10{,}724 + 2{,}000)(P\,|\,F, 8\%, 5) = +1{,}772$$

Similarly, by adopting the financing plan (b), the net present value for the combined after-tax cash flows in part (b) of Table 12.5 discounted at the after-tax MARR of 8% is

$$[\text{NPV}]_{8\%} = -12{,}000 + (5{,}295)(P\,|\,F, 8\%, 1) + (3{,}467)(P\,|\,F, 8\%, 2)$$
$$+ (2{,}337)(P\,|\,F, 8\%, 3) + (1{,}624)(P\,|\,F, 8\%, 4)$$
$$+ (1{,}013 + 2{,}000)(P\,|\,F, 8\%, 5) = +974$$

Table 12.5

Effects of Financing Plans on After-Tax Cash Flows

(a) Financing Plan with a Single Repayment at the End

t	A_t	$\bar{A}_t$	D_t	I_t	W_t	T_t	Y_t
0	−22,000	+10,000					−12,000
1	+6,000	0	8,800	800	−3,600	−1,800	+7,800
2	+6,000	0	5,280	864	−144	−72	+6,072
3	+6,000	0	3,168	933	1,899	950	+5,050
4	+6,000	0	1,901	1,008	3,091	1,546	+4,454
5	{ +6,000 +2,000	−14,693	851	1,088	4,061	2,031	{ −10,724 +2,000

(b) Financing Plan with Uniform Annual Repayments

t	A_t	$\bar{A}_t$	D_t	I_t	W_t	T_t	Y_t
0	−22,000	+10,000					−12,000
1	+6,000	−2,505	8,800	800	−3,600	−1,800	+5,295
2	+6,000	−2,505	5,280	664	56	28	+3,467
3	+6,000	−2,505	3,168	516	2,316	1,158	+2,337
4	+6,000	−2,505	1,901	357	3,742	1,871	+1,624
5	{ +6,000 +2,000	−2,505	851	185	4,964	2,482	{ +1,013 +2,000

Note that both financing plans will make the investment worthwhile, but plan (a) is superior to plan (b).

Example 12.10

Suppose that a firm is interested in acquiring the minicomputer in Example 12.8 but lacks the funds to purchase it through equity. However, it has two options: (1) borrowing the full amount at a borrowing rate of 8%, using a financing plan that requires a single repayment at the end of the 5 years; and (2) leasing the equipment with terms to pay $7,500, $6,500, $5,500, $4,500, and $3,500 at the end of years 1, 2, 3, 4, and 5, respectively. The income tax rate is 50% and the after-tax MARR specified by the firm is 8%. Should the firm buy or lease?

With the proposed financing plan and the DDB method of computing depreciation allowable, the computation of the after-tax cash flows combining operation and financing is obtained by Eq. (12.7) and the results are shown in part (a) of Table 12.6. The net present value discounted at the after-tax MARR of 8% is

$$[\text{NPV}]_{8\%} = (8,280)(P\,|\,F,\,8\%,\,1) + (6,591)(P\,|\,F,\,8\%,\,2)$$
$$+ (5,610)(P\,|\,F,\,8\%,\,3) + (5,059)(P\,|\,F,\,8\%,\,4)$$
$$+ (-27,703 + 2,000)(P\,|\,F,\,8\%,\,5)$$
$$= +3,995$$

For the leasing option, the after-tax cash flow at any year t can be obtained as follows:

$$A_t = B_t - C_t$$

$$Y_t = A_t - A_t X_t = A_t - T_t$$

The results of the computation are shown in part (b) of Table 12.6. Hence, the net

Table 12.6

After-Tax Cash Flows for Buy-or-Lease Alternatives

(a) The Buy Option

t	A_t	$\bar{A}_t$	D_t	I_t	W_t	T_t	Y_t
0	−22,000	+22,000					0
1	+6,000	0	8,800	1,760	−4,560	−2,280	+8,280
2	+6,000	0	5,280	1,901	−1,181	−591	+6,591
3	+6,000	0	3,168	2,053	779	390	+5,610
4	+6,000	0	1,901	2,217	1,881	941	+5,059
5	$\begin{cases} +6,000 \\ +2,000 \end{cases}$	−32,325	851	2,394	2,755	1,378	$\begin{cases} -27,703 \\ +2,000 \end{cases}$

(b) The Lease Option

t	B_t	C_t	A_t	T_t	Y_t
0	0	0	0	0	0
1	6,000	7,500	−1,500	−750	−750
2	6,000	6,500	−500	−250	−250
3	6,000	5,500	+500	250	+250
4	6,000	4,500	+1,500	750	+750
5	6,000	3,500	+2,500	1,250	+1,250

present value discounted at the after-tax MARR of 8% is

$$[NPV]_{8\%} = -(750)(P\,|\,U, 8\%, 5) + (500)(P\,|\,G, 8\%, 5)$$
$$= +691$$

Thus, both options are acceptable, but the buy option is preferable.

It is interesting to note from Examples 12.8, 12.9, and 12.10 that for the same conditions of depreciation and after-tax MARR, the investment plan coupled with different financing plans leads to different net present values as follows:

1. Equity financing   NPV =   −79
2. Borrowing $10,000   NPV = +1,772
3. Borrowing $22,000   NPV = +3,995

Since the borrowing rate is equal to the after-tax MARR in this case, the allowable deduction for interest produces beneficial effects. However, if the borrowing rate were higher, debt financing would produce a less favorable or even negative effect on the investment proposal.

12.8   Effects of Capital Gains

The provisions of the 1981 tax act concerning the treatment of capital gains and losses have already been discussed in Section 11.10 (Chapter 11). Among other possible tax savings, net long-term capital gains are eligible for the special lower rate of 28% instead of the marginal rate of 46% on ordinary income over $100,000 for corporations. Consequently, it simply represents a tax break when all the conditions of eligibility are fulfilled. The computation of the capital gain tax is straightforward and can be illustrated by a simple example.

Example 12.11

An office building which costs $1,500,000 for construction plus $100,000 for the land is planned as a rental property. The before-tax receipts in rent after the deduction of maintenance is expected to be $300,000 annually over the next 40 years. However, the 1981 tax law allows the depreciation of the entire construction cost (with no salvage value) over a period of 15 years, but the value of the land cannot be depreciated. The owner, a corporation, specifies a minimum attractive rate of return of 10% after tax and pays income tax at a rate of 46%. The owner plans to sell this building after 15 years and expects to receive an appreciated value of $2,100,000 for both the building and the land at the time. Determine the net present value of this investment for each of the following conditions:

1. Straight line depreciation over 15 years as permitted by the 1981 tax act and a net capital gain tax rate of 28% for corporations
2. Straight line depreciation over 40 years as required prior to the 1981 tax act and a net capital gain tax rate of 28%

Using the straight line depreciation over 15 years as permitted under the 1981 tax act, an allowance each year for the building is given by Eq. (11.4) as $D_t =$ $100,000. Hence, the after-tax receipts in rent each year can be obtained from Eq. (12.8) as follows:

$$Y_t = 300,000 - (46\%)(300,000 - 100,000)$$
$$= 300,000 - (46\%)(200,000) = 208,000$$

The capital gain tax for the sale of the building including the accumulated depreciation at the end of 15 years is

$$(2,100,000 - 1,600,000 + 1,500,000)(0.28) = 560,000$$

The net present value of the after-tax cash flow profile over the 15-year period under the 1981 tax act is

$$[NPV]_{10\%} = -1,600,000 + (208,000)(P\,|\,U,\ 10\%,\ 15)$$
$$+ (2,100,000 - 560,000)(P\,|\,F,\ 10\%,\ 15)$$
$$= -1,600,000 + (208,000)(7.6061) + (1,540,000)(0.2394)$$
$$= +350,745$$

Using the straight line depreciation over 40 years as required prior to the 1981 tax act, the depreciation allowance for the building is given by Eq. (11.4) as $37,500. Hence, the after-tax receipts in rent each year can be obtained from Eq. (12.8) as follows:

$$Y_t = 300,000 - (46\%)(300,000 - 37,500) = 179,250$$

The capital gain tax for the sale of the building including the accumulated appreciation at the end of 15 years is

$$[2,100,000 - 1,600,000 + (15)(37,500)](0.28) = 297,500$$

Then, the net present value of the after-tax cash flow profile over the 15-year period prior to the 1981 tax act would have been

$$[NPV]_{10\%} = -1,600,000 + (179,250)(P\,|\,U,\ 10\%,\ 15)$$
$$+ (2,100,000 - 297,500)(P\,|\,F,\ 10\%,\ 15)$$
$$= +194,912$$

Comparing cases 1 and 2, it is obvious that the 1981 tax act offers an advantage over the older laws for this investment because of the accelerated cost recovery system. However, there is no change in the capital gain tax rate for corporations such as that for individuals in the 1981 tax act. Hence, the rate of 28% is used for both cases.

12.9   Effects of Investment Tax Credit

The provisions of the 1981 tax act concerning the investment tax credit have already been discussed in Section 11.11 (Chapter 11). The amount of investment tax credit allowed under the law is deducted directly from income taxes. Consequently, for a profitable firm, the investment tax credit has the same effect as cash received from the government to pay for a small percentage of the value of certain eligible assets. The eligibility for the investment tax credit is based on the estimated life of the equipment, and the maximum rate is 10% of the cost of an asset with an estimated useful life of more than 5 years. The effect of the investment tax credit is illustrated by an example.

Example 12.12

Rocksberry Manufacturing Company has the opportunity to purchase a piece of equipment which costs $10,000 and is expected to generate an after-tax income of $1,500 per year over the next 10 years. The after-tax MARR of the company is 10%. Determine whether the company should make the investment

1. If there is no investment tax credit
2. If a 10% ITC is allowed at the time of purchase

If there is no investment tax credit, we get

$$[NPV]_{10\%} = -10,000 + (1,500)(P\,|\,U,\ 10\%,\ 10)$$
$$= -10,000 + (1,500)(6.1446) = -\$783$$

However, if there is a 10% investment tax credit,

$$[\text{NPV}]_{10\%} = -10,000(1 - 0.10) + (1,500)(P \mid U, 10\%, 10)$$
$$= \$217$$

Thus, the investment tax credit does make a difference in turning an unprofitable investment into a profitable one.

12.10   Summary and Study Guide

This chapter has discussed the effects of financing plans on the overall cash flows of an investment project. The primary purpose is to illustrate the methods of separating the streams of cash flows for operation and financing for some simple financing plans which are assumed to produce no other financial side effects to the organization.

We first considered the effects of financing plans on the evaluation of investment projects for tax-exempt organizations. Then, we examined the additional effects of depreciation deductions and income taxes on the evaluation of projects undertaken by private corporations. Appropriate formulas were derived for application to both situations.

Deferring the discussion of the possible impact of accepting an investment proposal and its financing plan on the financial position of a firm until Chapter 16, other effects of financial nature were illustrated by a variety of examples, including allowable deduction for depreciation, interest, capital gain, and investment tax credit. In some examples, all-equity financing is assumed in discounting the stream of cash flows for operation of the assets. In other cases, different financing plans are used to compare the advantage of tax deduction. Finally, an example is given to illustrate the use of investment tax credit in the economic evaluation.

REFERENCES

12.1 American Telephone and Telegraph Company, *Engineering Economy: Manager's Guide to Financial Decision Making*, 3rd ed., New York: McGraw-Hill, 1977.

12.2 White, J. A., M. H. Agee, and K. E. Case, *Principles of Engineering Economic Analysis*, New York: John Wiley, 1977.

PROBLEMS

P12.1 The stream of cash flows for the acquisition and operation of an earth excavator is given by A_t. There are three financing plans, each charging a borrowing rate of 10% but having a different method of repayment as represented by the stream of cash flows $\bar{A}_t$ for each financing plan. The values of A_t and $\bar{A}_t$ for $t = 0, 1, 2, 3, 4$ are given below. The MARR specified is also 10%. Find the three before-tax cash flow profiles combining operation and financing, and determine the net present value for each of these three cash flow profiles.

t	A_t	$\bar{A}_t$ (Financing) (a)	(b)	(c)
0	− 56,000	+ 20,000	+ 20,000	+ 20,000
1	+ 15,775	0	− 6,310	− 2,000
2	+ 15,775	0	− 6,310	− 2,000
3	+ 15,775	0	− 6,310	− 2,000
4	+ 15,775 +6,000	− 29,982	− 6,310	− 22,000

P12.2 A public agency is considering the purchase of the earth excavator in Problem P12.1 and the choice of one of the financing plans. Determine the effect of each of the financing plans if the MARR specified is (1) 6% and (2) 12%.

P12.3 An investment in an automatically controlled printing press will cost $50,000 and have a salvage value of $10,000 at the end of 5 years when it will be retired. The press will generate a gross income of $15,000 per year, but its operating cost will be $3,000 during the first year, increasing by $500 per year until it reaches $5,000 in the fifth year. The straight line depreciation method is used. The tax rate is 46% and the after-tax MARR is 10%. Determine the net present value of the proposal.

P12.4 The Acron Construction Company is considering the purchase of a diesel power shovel to improve its productivity. The shovel, which costs $77,000, is expected to produce a before-tax benefit of $38,000 in the first year, and $6,000 less in each succeeding year for a total of 5 years (i.e., before-tax benefit of $32,000 in the second year, $26,000 in the third year, until $14,000 in the fifth year). The salvage value of the equipment will be $5,000 at the end of 5 years. The firm chooses to use the sum-of-years'-digits depreciation for the equipment and pays an annual income tax for its profits at a rate of 50%. If the minimum attractive rate of return after tax is 10%, is the purchase worthwhile?

P12.5 The Sherman Corporation is considering the purchase of a numberof pipe-laying machines in order to facilitate the operation in a new pipeline project which is expected to last for 6 years. Each machine will cost $26,000 and will have a salvage value of $2,000 when the production under this contract is completed at the end of 6 years. The firm chooses to use the straight line depreciation method for the machine and pays annual federal and state income taxes for its profits at a rate of 50%. If the minimum attractive rate of return after tax is 10%, what is the minimum uniform annual benefit before tax that must be generated by this device in order to justify its installation?

P12.6 The Myron Corporation is planning to purchase a metal-forming machine which has an estimated useful life of 8 years. The machine costs $50,000 with no salvage value and is expected to generate a gross income of $12,000 per year before tax. The tax rate is 50% and the after-tax MARR is 10%. The straight line method is used in computing depreciation. Determine whether the investment is worthwhile if

(a) The depreciation is based on the useful life of 8 years.
(b) The machine is depreciated in 4 years with no salvage at the end of 4 years even though the machine can still be used to generate income for the remaining years. The company has other profitable projects to offset unused deductions for taxable income from this project.

P12.7 A branch office of Telesafe Bank is considering the installation of an automated "night-depositor" to increase its profits by $10,000 per year over the next 10 years. This installation will have no salvage value at the end of 10 years and is depreciated over the 10-year period using the straight line method. Based on a rate of 50% for federal and state income taxes and an after-tax MARR of 10%, what is the maximum amount that should be spent for the equipment in order to justify the investment?

P12.8 A heavy-duty lifting machine costing $70,000 will be depreciated to its salvage value of $7,000 at the end of 5 years by the straight line method. The machine will produce a gross income of $45,000 per year for 5 years and the operating expenses for years 1 through 5 are $15,000, $16,000, $17,000, $18,000, and $19,000, respectively. The income tax rate of the firm is 50%, and the after-tax MARR is 8%. Determine the net present value of the after-tax cash flows for the project.

P12.9 Sandhurst Electric Corporation is considering four mutually exclusive alternatives for a major capital investment project. All alternatives have a useful life of 10 years with no salvage value at the end. Straight line depreciation will be used. The corporation pays federal and state tax at a rate of 50%, and expects an after-tax MARR of 12%. Determine which alternative should be selected, using the NPV method.

Alternatives	Initial cost ($ million)	Before-tax uniform annual net benefits ($ million)
1	4.0	1.5
2	3.5	1.1
3	3.0	1.0
4	3.7	1.3

P12.10 The Cantor Company is considering either leasing or buying a computer for the next 5 years. The company pays federal and state income taxes at a rate of 50% and uses an after-tax MARR of 8%. The details of the two options are as follows:

(a) Under the lease agreement, the company will pay the lessor a uniform fee at the *beginning* of each of the 5 years, plus a cost of $10,000 per year at the *end* of each year under a maintenance contract which accompanies the lease agreement. Assume that the company does not receive any benefit from depreciation or investment tax credit.

(b) Under the purchase plan, the purchase price is $200,000, but the company can apply 10% of the purchase price for an investment tax credit in the year of the purchase (year 0). The computer will be depreciated by the straight line method with no salvage value at the end of 5 years. The maintenance cost is $20,000 per year charged at the end of each year.

Determine the uniform fee paid to the lessor at the beginning of each year which will make the lease agreement as attractive as the purchase plan.

P12.11 An automatic copier will cost $10,000 and have no salvage value at the end of 4 years. The sum-of-the-years'-digits method will be used for computing the depreciation allowance. The firm has an income tax rate of 50% and an after-tax MARR of 6%. What should be the before-tax uniform annual benefit generated by this copier in order to make the purchase worthwhile?

CHAPTER

13

PRICE LEVEL
CHANGES

13.1 Effects of Price Changes on
Economic Evaluation

Up to this chapter, we have not discussed the problem of price changes in estimating future benefits and costs. With the dynamic nature of the economy, the prices of goods and services change with time. It is, therefore, extremely important to consider the effects of price changes on the economic evaluation of investment proposals.

The cash flows in economic evaluation usually are estimates expressed in the base-year dollars for discount to a specific point in time; they are not the same as the obligated amounts for budgeting in the funding years if inflation or deflation is expected over the years. Consequently, depending on the overall environment of the economy and taxation, the evaluation of investment proposals may be based on one of the following two approaches:

1. Express all cash flows in terms of base-year dollars and use a discount rate which excludes the inflation or deflation rate.
2. Express all cash flows in terms of then-current dollars and use a discount rate which includes a component accounting for the inflation or deflation rate.

Before explaining in detail these two approaches for economic evaluation, we should first examine the nature of price changes and their possible effects on the estimates of cash flows, as well as on the discount rate used in the evaluation. Then, we can judge which approach is more appropriate for a given situation.

13.2 Price Indices and Rates of Price Changes

The prices of goods and services may rise or fall over a period of time, resulting in inflation or deflation of the value of the dollars. The best-known indicator of

330

general price changes is the consumer price index (CPI), compiled and published monthly by the Bureau of Labor Statistics, U. S. Department of Labor.[1] This index is a measure of the purchasing power of the average family for items deemed to be typical and essential. Consequently, it is widely used as a broad gauge of the change in the cost of living by the policy makers and by the general public.

There are other price indices developed for special purposes. However, it is important to understand what an index is intended to measure and how it is put together. A *price index* is a weighted aggregate measure of constant quantities of goods and services selected for the package. The price index in a subsequent year represents a proportionate change in the same weighted aggregate measure because of the changes in prices. Let I_t be the price index in year t, and I_{t+1} be the price index in the following year $t + 1$. Then, the percent change in price index for the 12-month period in year $t + 1$ is given by

$$j_{t+1} = \frac{I_{t+1} - I_t}{I_t} (100\%) \tag{13.1}$$

If j_{t+1} is positive, it represents the inflation rate in year $t + 1$ over year t, and if it is negative, it represents the deflation rate. Conversely, the price index I_{t+1} in year $t + 1$ is related to the price index I_t in year t by

$$I_{t+1} = I_t(1 + j_{t+1}) \tag{13.2}$$

If the price index at the base year $t = 0$ is set at a value of 100, then the price indices $I_1, I_2, \ldots, I_n$ for year 1, 2, $\ldots$, n beyond the base year can be computed successively by Eq. (13.2).

As a base, the consumer price index (CPI) is set at a value of 100 for the weighted aggregate measure of a selected package of goods and services for the average family in 1967. Although the CPI is sometimes criticized for overstating the inflation because some of its components, notably the home ownership component which accounts for about 6% of the families in computing the weighted aggregate measure of the average family, have outpaced other components disproportionately in price changes in recent years, it is still one of the most important price indices. The CPI and its annual rate of change (in percent) since 1967 are tabulated in Table 13.1. The same trend of changes in the consumer price index is shown in Fig. 13.1 to emphasize the compounded effects of the rates of price changes.

The need for special price indices has been highlighted by the fact that the price changes in some components of an investment project may outpace disproportionately those of the remaining components. For example, the outlays for plants and facilities often require new construction, the costs of which are affected by the prices of special materials and labor. Two special cost indices are compiled

---

[1] See *Monthly Labor Review*, Bureau of Labor Statistics, U.S. Department of Labor.

Table 13.1
Rates of Price Changes and Price Indices

Year	Consumer Price Index		Construction Cost Index		Building Cost Index	
	CPI	% Change	CCI	% Change	BCI	% Change
1967	100.0	—	100.0	—	100.0	—
1968	104.7	4.6%	107.9	7.9%	107.3	7.3%
1969	111.1	6.1%	118.6	9.9%	117.6	9.6%
1970	117.2	5.5%	129.4	9.1%	124.4	5.8%
1971	121.2	3.4%	147.8	14.2%	141.1	11.3%
1972	125.3	3.4%	163.8	10.8%	156.0	10.6%
1973	136.3	8.8%	177.1	8.1%	169.3	8.5%
1974	152.9	12.2%	188.8	6.6%	179.2	5.8%
1975	163.6	7.0%	296.7	9.5%	194.3	8.4%
1976	171.5	4.3%	224.4	8.6%	212.1	9.2%
1977	183.2	6.8%	240.8	7.3%	229.9	8.4%
1978	199.7	9.0%	259.6	7.8%	249.1	8.4%
1979	226.3	13.3%	279.5	7.7%	269.3	8.1%
1980	254.4	12.4%	301.9	8.0%	287.9	6.9%

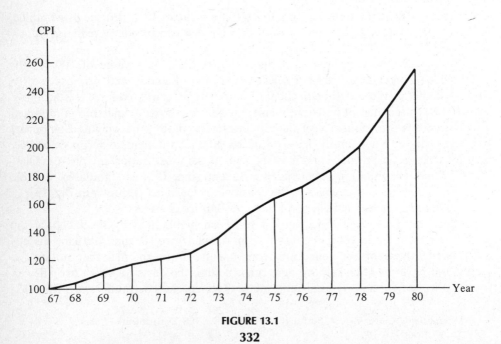

FIGURE 13.1

and reported periodically in the *Engineer News-Record* (ENR).[2] The construction cost index (CCI) was designed as a general-purpose construction cost index, which is a weighted aggregate measure of constant quantities of structural steel, portland cement, lumber, and common labor. The building cost index (BCI) was introduced to weigh the impact of skilled labor on construction cost by replacing the common labor component with the average wages of the carpenter, bricklayer, and structural iron worker. Both indices measure the effects of wage rate and material price trends, but they are not adjusted for productivity, efficiency, competitive conditions, or automation changes. Each of these indices has been converted to 100 for the year 1967 as the base, and the percent change over the 12-month period in each subsequent year has also been computed. The results are tabulated in Table 13.1, along with the consumer price index for comparison. It should be emphasized that the costs of construction have not risen as fast as either the CCI or CBI because of improvement in productivity and other factors. Consequently, they can only be used as a general guide in projecting construction costs for investment projects.

Example 13.1

Determine the percent changes in the consumer price index for 1978 and 1979 from the indices for 1977, 1978, and 1979 in Table 13.1.

Using Eq. (13.2), we can compute the percent changes in CPI for 1978 and 1979 as follows:

$$j(1978) = \frac{199.7 - 183.2}{183.2} = 0.090 = 9.0\%$$

$$j(1979) = \frac{226.3 - 199.7}{199.7} = 0.133 = 13.3\%$$

Example 13.2

Suppose that we wish to change the base of the construction cost index from 1967 to 1977 by setting the index for 1977 at 100. What will the CCI be for 1978 and 1979?

The new CCI for 1978 and 1979, using 1977 as the base year can be obtained as follows:

$$I(1978) = \frac{259.6}{240.8}(100) = 107.8$$

$$I(1979) = \frac{279.5}{240.8}(100) = 116.1$$

---

[2] See the fourth quarter summary of each year for both indices in *Engineering News-Record*. New York: McGraw-Hill.

13.3   General and Differential Price Change Rates

It can be seen from the price indices in Table 13.1 that the rate of price change varies from year to year. In order to convert an amount of cash expressed in base-year dollars to an equivalent amount expressed in the value of dollars in a later year, we must apply Eq. (13.2) successively. Let A_t be the cash flow in year t expressed in terms of base-year (year 0) dollars, and A_t' be the cash flow in year t expressed in terms of then-current dollars as shown in Fig. 13.2. Then,

$$A_t' = A_t(1 + j_1)(1 + j_2) \ldots (1 + j_{t-1})(1 + j_t) \tag{13.3}$$

Conversely,

$$A_t = A_t'(1 + j_t)^{-1}(1 + j_{t-1})^{-1} \ldots (1 + j_2)^{-1}(1 + j_1)^{-1} \tag{13.4}$$

For the purpose of economic evaluation, it is often sufficient to project the trend of future prices by using a constant rate of price change j for each year. Then,

$$A_t' = A_t(1 + j)^t \tag{13.5}$$

and

$$A_t = A_t'(1 + j)^{-t} \tag{13.6}$$

Note that the discrete compound interest tables in Appendix A may be used to evaluate the factors $(1 + j)^t$ and $(1 + j)^{-t}$ in Eqs. (13.5) and (13.6) by treating j as if it were a compound interest rate. In reality, of course, j is the compound rate of price change.

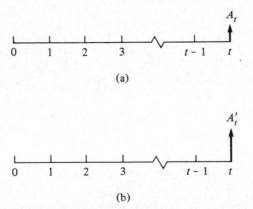

(a)

(b)

FIGURE 13.2

Although the rate of general price change j may be positive or negative, representing the general inflation rate or deflation rate respectively, we will consider primarily the case of inflation since this has been the general trend of price level changes in the last four decades. Thus, a positive j (in percent) denotes the *general inflation rate* which may be used to convert an amount A_t in year t, expressed in terms of base-year dollars to the inflated amount A'_t in year t, expressed in terms of then-current dollars according to Eq. (13.5). Conversely, A'_t may be converted to A_t by means of Eq. (13.6).

In some situations, the prices of certain key items affecting the estimates of future benefits and costs are expected to escalate faster than the general price levels. Then, it becomes necessary to consider the differential price changes over and above the general inflation in assessing the cash flows. Let k (in percent) denote the *differential inflation rate* for a specific item over and above the general inflation rate. Let A_t^0 be the cash flow in year t for the cost of that item based on base-year price level *and* expressed in base-year dollars; and let A_t be the corresponding cash flow in year t for the *relative* cost of that item compared to then-current general price level but expressed in base-year dollars as shown in Fig. 13.3. Then

$$A_t = A_t^0 (1 + k)^t \tag{13.7}$$

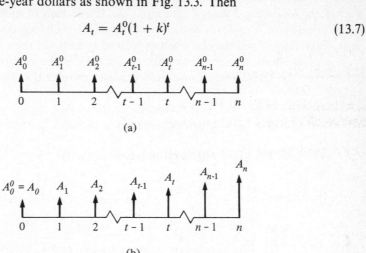

(a)

(b)

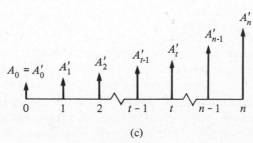

(c)

FIGURE 13.3

When none of the items for estimating future benefits and costs need be singled out for special attention, we have $k = 0$ and $A_t = A_t^0$. In other words, when k is positive, Eq. (13.5) becomes,

$$A_t' = A_t^0(1 + j + k)^t \qquad (13.8)$$

If the inflation rates (general or differential) can be predicted with a high degree of accuracy, then Eqs. (13.3) and (13.4) instead of Eqs. (13.5) and (13.6) can be used as the basis for developing additional relationships. However, in view of the uncertainty in economic forecasting, it is usually justified to assume a constant or "average" inflation rate over the planning horizon for the purpose of economic evaluation.

Example 13.3

Suppose that the annual inflation rate in the next 3 years is expected to be 10% and that in the following 2 years it slows to 8%. If a stream of cash flows for the next 5 years consists of a uniform annual amount of $10,000 expressed in terms of base-year dollars, what will they be when expressed in terms of then-current dollars?

For the first 3 years, then-current values can be computed directly by Eq. (13.5). For the last 2 years, however, we must consider the change of inflation rate. Hence,

$$A_1' = (10,000)(1 + 0.10) = 11,000$$

$$A_2' = (10,000)(1 + 0.10)^2 = 12,100$$

$$A_3' = (10,000)(1 + 0.10)^3 = 13,310$$

$$A_4' = (10,000)(1 + 0.10)^3(1 + 0.08) = 14,375$$

$$A_5' = (10,000)(1 + 0.10)^3(1 + 0.08)^2 = 15,525$$

Example 13.4

In considering the investment in an energy conservation project for an existing building, it is expected that the extra insulation will save the same amount of energy each year over the next 15 years. However, the cost of energy is expected to increase over and above the general inflation rate by 3%. If the energy saved each year costs $60,000 at today's prices, what would be the *relative* cost of the same amount of energy in year t, compared to the then-current general price level but expressed in base-year dollars?

Since the differential inflation rate k is 3%, the relative cost of the energy in year t is obtained by Eq. (13.7) for $n = 1, 2, \ldots, 15$,

$$A_t = (60{,}000)(1 + 0.03)^t$$

The value A_t can be obtained with the aid of the discrete compound interest tables in Appendix A since A_t can be expressed in the functional notation:

$$A_t = (60{,}000)(F \mid P, 3\%, t)$$

13.4   Explicit and Implicit Treatments of Inflation in Discounting

In the economic evaluation of investment proposals, two approaches may be used to offset the effects of future price changes. The differences between the two approaches are primarily philosophical and can be succinctly stated as follows:

1. *The explicit approach.* The investor wants a specified minimum attractive rate of return excluding inflation. Consequently, the cash flows should be expressed in terms of base-year dollars, and a discount rate excluding inflation should be used in computing the net present value.
2. *The implicit approach.* The investor includes an inflation component in the specified minimum attractive rate of return. Hence, the cash flows should be expressed in terms of then-current dollars, and a discount rate including inflation should be used in computing the net present value.

If these approaches are applied correctly, they should lead to identical results.

To demonstrate the equivalence of the two approaches, let us use the following notation:

A_t = cash flow in year t expressed in terms of base-year dollars
A_t' = cash flow in year t expressed in terms of then-current dollars
i = discount rate excluding inflation
i' = discount rate including inflation

We shall consider first the case with a cash flow in year t only, but the procedure can easily be extended to a series of cash flows at $t = 0, 1, 2, \ldots, n$ over the entire planning horizon.

For the explicit approach, the net present value of A_t is discounted at a rate i to year 0. Thus

$$NPV = A_t(1 + i)^{-t} \tag{13.9a}$$

In view of Eq. (13.6), we get

$$\text{NPV} = A'_t(1+j)^{-t}(1+i)^{-t} \tag{13.9b}$$

Hence,

$$\text{NPV} = A'_t[(1+j)(1+i)]^{-t}$$
$$= A'_t(1+i+j+ij)^{-t}$$

Let

$$i' = i + j + ij \tag{13.10}$$

Then

$$\text{NPV} = A'_t(1+i')^{-t} \tag{13.11a}$$

In other words, given i and j, the discount rate i' including inflation can be obtained by Eq. (13.10). If i and j are small, the product term is negligible. Hence, the discount rate including inflation is approximately equal to the discount rate i excluding inflation plus the inflation rate j.

For the implicit approach, the net present value of A'_t is discounted at a rate i' to year 0, resulting in Eq. (13.11a). From Eq. (13.5), we get

$$\text{NPV} = A_t(1+j)^t(1+i')^{-t} \tag{13.11b}$$

Hence

$$\text{NPV} = A_t\left(\frac{1+i'}{1+j}\right)^{-t} = A_t\left(1+\frac{i'-j}{1+j}\right)^{-t}$$

Note that from Eq. (13.10), we get $i' - j = i(1+j)$. Hence,

$$i = \frac{i'-j}{1+j} \tag{13.12}$$

Then, from Eq. (13.11b), we have

$$\text{NPV} = A_t(1+i)^{-t}$$

which is the same as Eq. (13.9a). Note also that given i' and j, the discount rate i excluding inflation can be obtained by Eq. (13.12). If j is small, the denominator $(1+j)$ can be approximated by 1. Then, the discount rate i excluding inflation is approximately equal to the discount rate i' including inflation minus the inflation rate j.

For a series of cash flows at $t = 0, 1, 2, \ldots, n$ over the planning horizon n as

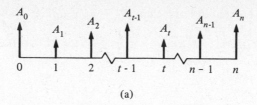

(a)

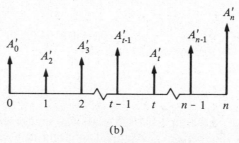

(b)

FIGURE 13.4

shown in Fig. 13.4, the NPV obtained by using the explicit approach is

$$\text{NPV} = A_0 + \sum_{t=1}^{n} A_t(1 + i)^{-t} \tag{13.13}$$

Similarly, the NPV obtained by using the implicit approach is

$$\text{NPV} = A_0 + \sum_{t=1}^{n} A_t'(1 + i')^{-t} \tag{13.14}$$

In both cases, A_0 (at $t = 0$) is not affected by the inflation. It can easily be verified that as long as Eqs. (13.9a) and (13.11a) hold, the results obtained from Eqs. (13.13) and (13.14) are identical.

Example 13.5

Mary Benson plans to invest \$1,200 for 5 years with the expectation of a minimum attractive rate of return of 4% excluding inflation. If the inflation rate will be 9% per year, what is the return (in then-current dollars) at the end of the 5 years that will make it worthwhile? What is the rate of return including inflation?

For the investment to be worthwhile, the NPV should at least be zero. Let A_5'

be the return in then-current dollars; then $A_5 = A_5'(1 + j)^{-5}$. Using Eq. (13.9b),

$$\text{NPV} = -1,200 + A_5'(1 + j)^{-5}(1 + i)^{-5} = 0$$

Hence, for $i = 4\%, j = 9\%,$

$$A_5' = (1,200)(1 + 0.09)^5(1 + 0.04)^5 = 2,246$$

Also, from Eq. (13.10)

$$i' = i + j + ij = 0.04 + 0.09 + (0.04)(0.09)$$
$$= 0.1336 = 13.36\%$$

Example 13.6

David Hearn deposited $1,000 in a bank 5 years ago and received a total return of $1,403 today. During this period, the annual inflation rate was 3%. What is the annual rate of return excluding inflation?

The interest rate i' paid by the bank which includes inflation can be obtained by Eq. (13.11a):

$$\text{NPV} = -1,000 + 1,403(1 + i')^{-5} = 0$$

Hence

$$(1 + i')^5 = \frac{1,403}{1,000} = 1.403 \quad \text{or} \quad (F \mid P, i', 5) = 1.403$$

from which we get $i' = 7\%$. Then, for $j = 3$, Eq. (13.12) yields

$$i = \frac{i' - j}{1 + j} = \frac{0.07 - 0.03}{1 + 0.03} = 3.88\%$$

Example 13.7

Harry Brown has recently inherited $30,000 and wants to set aside the equivalent of $20,000 in today's dollars to be available 10 years later when he will start his retirement. He expects the inflation rate to be 8% per year over the next 10 years. He wishes to consider only the opportunities available to him that are risk-free and has found the following two alternatives:

1. Depositing the money in a savings account in a bank that pays 6% interest compounded annually

2. Purchasing a 10-year certificate of deposit that pays 10% interest compounded annually

How much money must he now set aside in order to accomplish his goal for each of the two alternatives?

In both cases, the interest rate implicitly includes a component for inflation since no additional compensation to that effect will be paid by the bank if inflation does occur at a rate of $j = 8\%$ as anticipated by Harry. Consequently, he should first compute the cash flow A_t' at $t = 10$ in terms of then-current dollars, which is equivalent to $20,000 of base-year dollars. Thus,

$$A_{10}' = A_{10}(1 + j)^{10} = (20,000)(1 + 0.08)^{10} = 43,178$$

For case (1), $i' = 6\%$,

$$[\text{NPV}]_{6\%} = A_{10}'(1 + i')^{-10} = (43,178)(1 + 0.06)^{-10} = 24,110$$

For case (2), $i' = 10\%$,

$$[\text{NPV}]_{10\%} = A_{10}'(1 + i')^{-10} = (43,178)(1 + 0.10)^{-10} = 16,647$$

Although Harry can afford to choose either plan, it is obvious that the second plan is superior. In the first plan, the interest cannot even keep up with the inflation; consequently, he has to set aside more than $20,000 now in order to maintain the same purchasing power 10 years from now.

13.5 The Use of a Discount Rate Excluding Inflation

The explicit approach has the distinct advantage of estimating future benefits and costs in base-year dollars without speculating on the inflation rate except in the cases when differential price changes exist for certain items that affect the estimates significantly. However, since income taxes are paid on the basis of then-current dollars, the simplicity of this approach is more appealing to tax-exempt organizations that do not pay income taxes.

The Office of Management and Budget (OMB) requires that, except for certain exemptions, federal agencies must use this approach for evaluating public investment projects.[3] Only the differential price changes for critical items over and above the expected general price changes can be included in the estimates of future cash flows. The future energy prices are among those few categories allowed for inclusion

---

[3] OMB Circular A-94, "Discount Rates to be Used in Evaluating Time-Distributed Costs and Benefits," Executive Office of the President, March 27, 1972.

in projecting different price changes. The OMB also specifies that, with certain exceptions, federal agencies should use a discount rate of 10% excluding inflation to evaluate investment projects under its jurisdiction.

In evaluating public projects, this approach is a direct application of Eq. (13.13). For projects which involve critical items with differential inflation rates, Eq. (13.7) can be applied by each of them, and the relative costs of those items will then be used in Eq. (13.13).

For private firms, the taxable income in each future year will be based on the then-current value, but the depreciation allowance will still be based on the purchase price at the time of acquisition. Consequently, we must perform a double conversion of the cash flows if the discount rate excluding inflation rate is used in computing the net present value. Let us recapitulate the following notation introduced in Chapter 12 with modifications for application to any year t over a planning horizon of n years:

A_t = before-tax cash flow in terms of base-year dollars
A_t' = before-tax cash flow in terms of then-current dollars
D_t = depreciation allowance based on one of the acceptable methods
X_t = income tax rate
T_t' = income taxes in terms of then-current dollars
Y_t' = after-tax cash flow in terms of then-current dollars
Y_t = after-tax cash flow in terms of base-year dollars

To simplify the presentation, we shall consider the case of equity financing. Then Eq. (12.8) in Chapter 12 can be modified for inflation consideration as follows:

$$A_t' = A_t(1 + j)^t \tag{13.15a}$$

$$T_t' = X_t(A_t' - D_t) \tag{13.15b}$$

$$Y_t' = A_t' - T_t' = A_t' - X_t(A_t' - D_t) \tag{13.15c}$$

$$Y_t = Y_t'(1 + j)^{-t} \tag{13.15d}$$

Equation (13.15a) is identical to Eq. (13.5), and Eq. (13.15d) is analogous to Eq. (13.6) except that the after-tax cash flow Y_t instead of the before-tax cash flow A_t is considered, as shown in Fig. 13.5. Consequently, Eq. (13.13) is applicable to after-tax computation if A_t is replaced by Y_t, i.e.,

$$\text{NPV} = Y_0 + \sum_{t=1}^{n} Y_t(1 + i)^{-t} \tag{13.16}$$

where i is the after-tax MARR excluding inflation.

If differential inflation rates should be applied to some critical items in evaluating investment projects for private firms, the relation in Eq. (13.7) can be substitu-

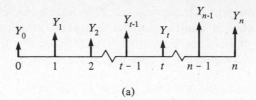

(a)

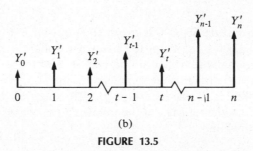

(b)

FIGURE 13.5

ted into the pertinent terms in Eqs. (13.15). Hence, the same procedure can be used for the evaluation of such projects.

Example 13.8

An office building owned by the federal government is being retrofitted at a cost of \$500,000 for the purpose of energy conservation. It is expected that as a result of retrofitting, the consumption of electricity for heating and cooling the building will be reduced each year for the next 15 years by an amount which costs \$60,000 at today's prices. If the cost of electricity is expected to escalate 3% per year over and above the general inflation rate, determine whether the retrofitting project is worthwhile. The MARR excluding the general inflation rate is specified to be 10%.

The cash flow A_t for $t = 1, 2, \ldots, 15$ representing the savings in base-year dollars including additional savings from the differential rate of $k = 3\%$ is given by

$$A_t = A_t^0 (1 + k)^t = (60,000)(1.03)^t$$

Then, at the specified MARR of 10%, we have

$$[\text{NPV}]_{10\%} = -500,000 + \sum_{t=1}^{15} (60,000)(1.03)^t (1.10)^{-t}$$

$$= -500,000 + (60,000) \sum_{t=1}^{15} (F \,|\, P, 3\%, t)(P \,|\, F, 10\%, t)$$

$$= -500,000 + (60,000)(9.2263) = +53,578$$

Hence, the project is worthwhile.

It is easy to show that if there were no *differential* price change between the rate increase in the cost of electricity and the general inflation rate, the project would not be worthwhile. That is, with $A_t = 60{,}000$ for $t = 1, 2, \ldots, 15$, the net present value discounted at MARR = 10% is

$$[\text{NPV}]_{10\%} = -500{,}000 + (60{,}000)(P \mid U, 10\%, 15) = -43{,}634$$

Example 13.9

A piece of equipment costing $10,000 is expected to produce a uniform annual net benefit before tax of $3,000 in terms of the base-year dollars over the next 5 years. The equipment has no salvage value at the end of 5 years and the depreciation allowance is based on the straight line depreciation method. The federal and state income tax rate is 48%, and the after-tax MARR specified by the firm is 8% excluding inflation. Considering each of the following two cases, determine whether the investment is worthwhile.

(a) There will be no inflation during the next 5 years.
(b) There will be an annual inflation rate of 5%.

The computations of the after-tax cash flows for both cases are shown in parts (a) and (b) of Table 13.2. For case (a), the net present value discounted at the

Table 13.2

After-Tax Cash Flows for Investment in the Equipment

(a) No Inflation

Year t	Before-tax Cash Flow A_t	Straight-line Depreciation D_t	Taxable Income $A_t - D_t$	Income Tax T_t	After-tax Cash Flow Y_t
0	− 10,000				− 10,000
1–5 (each)	+ 3,000	2,000	1,000	480	+ 2,520

(b) Inflation Rate $j = 5\%$

t	A_t	A_t'	D_t	$A_t' - D_t$	T_t'	Y_t'	Y_t
0	− 10,000					− 10,000	− 10,000
1	+ 3,000	+ 3,150	2,000	1,150	552	+ 2,598	+ 2,474
2	+ 3,000	+ 3,308	2,000	1,308	628	+ 2,680	+ 2,431
3	+ 3,000	+ 3,473	2,000	1,473	707	+ 2,766	+ 2,389
4	+ 3,000	+ 3,647	2,000	1,647	791	+ 2,856	+ 2,350
5	+ 3,000	+ 3,829	2,000	1,829	878	+ 2,951	+ 2,312

after-tax MARR = 8% is

$$[\text{NPV}]_{8\%} = -10,000 + (2,520)(P\,|\,U,\,8\%,\,5) = +62$$

Consequently, without inflation, the investment is worthwhile.

For case (b), the before-tax cash flow A_t in terms of base-year dollars is first inflated at $j = 5\%$ to then-current dollars for the computation of the taxable income and income taxes. The resulting after-tax cash flow Y'_t in terms of then-current dollars is converted back to base-year dollars. Using Eqs. (13.15), we get

$$A'_t = A_t(1 + 0.05)^t$$

$$T'_t = (48\%)(A'_t - 2,000)$$

$$Y'_t = A'_t - (48\%)(A'_t - 2,000)$$

$$Y_t = Y'_t(1 + 0.05)^{-t}$$

The net present value discounted at the after-tax MARR = 8% excluding inflation is obtained from Eq. (13.16) as follows:

$$\begin{aligned}
[\text{NPV}]_{8\%} = {} & -10,000 + (2,474)(P\,|\,F,\,8\%,\,1) + (2,431)(P\,|\,F,\,8\%,\,2) + (2,389)(P\,|\,F,\,8\%,\,3) \\
& + (2,350)(P\,|\,F,\,8\%,\,4) + (2,312)(P\,|\,F,\,8\%,\,5) \\
= {} & -428
\end{aligned}$$

With 5% inflation, the investment is no longer worthwhile because higher income taxes are paid on the taxable incomes based on then-current dollars.

13.6   The Use of a Discount Rate Including Inflation

In some situations, the minimum attractive rate of return for an investor is restricted by a fixed lending or borrowing interest rate set for a relatively long period of time, irrespective of the general inflation trend during this period. For example, under some state laws, the interest rate on a mortgage loan for the purchase of real estate must remain constant for the duration of the loan, which is usually 20 or 30 years. Under such circumstances, it may be more convenient to use a discount rate which includes a component accounting for the inflation rate. In that case, the implicit approach can be used to offset the effects of inflation on the economic evalution of investment proposals.

For public projects, the before-tax cash flows A'_t (for $t = 1, 2, \ldots, n$) expressed in terms of then-current dollars are discounted to time $t = 0$ according to Eq. (13.14), using the before-tax discount rate i' which includes inflation. For private investment projects, the after-tax cash flows can be obtained by using Eqs. (13.15a) through (13.15c). Equation (13.5d) is not needed since Y_t' (not Y_t) is needed to replace A_t' in Eq. (13.14) for computing the net present value, i.e.,

$$\text{NPV} = Y_0 + \sum_{t=1}^{n} Y_t'(1 + i')^{-t} \tag{13.17}$$

where i' is the after-tax MARR including inflation.

Example 13.10

Perrymont Corporation plans to finance the purchase of a sheet metal punching machine through borrowing. The machine costs $20,000 and has no salvage value after 4 years. It is expected to produce a uniform annual net benefit before tax of $7,000 in terms of base-year dollars in the next 4 years. The machine will be depreciated by the straight line method. The borrowing interest rate is set at a fixed rate of 10% per year, but the inflation rate is expected to be 5% per year. The tax rate of the corporation is 50%. Is this purchase worthwhile?

Since the corporation must earn a profit after tax to pay off the debt, its after-tax MARR including inflation is 10%, which is fixed irrespective of the inflation rate. Thus the before-tax cash flows A_t ($t = 1$, 2, 3, and 4) in terms of base-year dollars are converted to then-current dollars for computing the taxable income and income taxes. The after-tax cash flows Y_t' ($t = 1$, 2, 3, and 4) in terms of then-current dollars are obtained and tabulated in Table 13.3. Note that the after-tax cash flows Y_t in base-year dollars are not needed, although they have also been tabulated in the last column of Table 13.3. The net present value of this investment is based on Y_t' ($t = 1$, 2, 3, 4) discounted at 10%, using Eq. (13.17). Hence,

$$\text{NPV} = -20,000 + (6,175)(P\,|\,F,\ 10\%,\ 1) + (6,359)(P\,|\,F,\ 10\%,\ 2)$$
$$+ (6,551)(P\,|\,F,\ 10\%,\ 3) + (6,754)(P\,|\,F,\ 10\%,\ 4) = +404$$

Consequently, the investment is worthwhile.

Table 13.3

After-Tax Cash Flows for Investment in the Machine

t	A_t	A_t'	D_t	$A_t' - D_t$	T_t'	Y_t'	Y_t
0	−20,000	−20,000				−20,000	−20,000
1	+7,000	7,350	5,000	2,350	1,175	6,175	+5,881
2	+7,000	7,718	5,000	2,718	1,359	6,359	+5,768
3	+7,000	8,103	5,000	3,103	1,552	6,551	+5,659
4	+7,000	8,509	5,000	3,509	1,755	6,754	+5,557

Alternately, we can compute first the discount rate i excluding inflation by Eq. (13.12). Noting that $i' = 10\%$ and $j = 5\%$,

$$i = \frac{i' - j}{1 + j} = \frac{0.10 - 0.05}{1 + 0.05} = 0.476 = 4.76\%$$

Then, the after-tax cash flows Y_t in terms of base-year dollars in the last column of Table 13.3 can be discounted at the rate i by using Eq. (13.16). Then

$$[NPV]_{4.76\%} = -20,000 + \frac{5,881}{1.0476} + \frac{5,768}{(1.0476)^2} + \frac{5,659}{(1.0476)^3} + \frac{5,557}{(1.0476)^4}$$
$$= +405$$

This result is the same as that obtained previously.

13.7 Obligated Cash Flows in Budgeting for Capital Projects

It was noted in Section 13.1 that the estimates of costs and benefits in economic evaluation are not obligated amounts for budgeting in future years. However, for the purpose of capital budgeting, both private corporations and public agencies must apply inflation factors in projecting revenues (or benefits) and costs for proposed capital projects. Hence, accurate forecasting of inflation rates for specific labor, material, and energy costs as well as anticipated sales prices of goods and services (or user charges) becomes very important. The differential inflation rates of these factors may be decisive in both the evaluation and financing of capital projects.

Because the accounting costs for a project are recorded on an "as spent" and "as received" basis, the high inflation rates in the 1970s and 1980s have had an extremely important effect on the obligated amounts in budgeting for a capital project. An accurate projection of the starting date and completion date of a project is essential in maintaining the budgeted amounts of the then-current dollars. Any delay in a project, whether it is the delay of the starting date or the extension of the project duration, will automatically increase the accounting costs because of inflation.

Consequently, we must be fully aware of the distinction between the analysis of inflation in economic evaluation of capital projects and that in budgeting obligated cash flows for their implementation. The separation of the two will enable us to use either the explicit or implicit treatments for inflation in evaluating capital projects correctly.

13.8   Summary and Study Guide

In this chapter, we discussed the price indices and the rates of price changes at times of inflation or deflation in general and the differential price change rates for special items in particular. With such conditions in mind, we examined the effects of price changes on economic evaluation of capital investment projects.

We emphasized two approaches that may be used in economic evaluation to offset the effects of future price changes. In the *explicit approach*, the investor wants a specified minimum attractive rate of return excluding inflation. Consequently, the cash flows should be expressed in terms of base-year dollars, and a discount rate *excluding* inflation should be used in computing the net present value. On the other hand, in the *implicit approach*, the investor includes an inflation component in the specified minimum attractive rate of return. Hence, the cash flows should be expressed in terms of then-current dollars, and a discount rate *including* inflation should be used in computing the net present value. If these approaches are applied correctly, they should lead to identical results.

The equivalence of these two approaches was demonstrated first by deriving the equations needed for treating the effects of price changes and then by tracing the similar effects resulting from the two approaches. Numerical examples were given to illustrate the application of both approaches.

The explicit approach has the distinct advantage of simplicity when no income tax is involved and is favored by the public agencies. In fact, the Office of Management and Budget requires that, except for certain exemptions, federal agencies must use this approach for evaluating public investment projects. For private firms which pay income taxes on the basis of then-current value, the implicit approach is often preferred. If differential rates must be applied to some critical items in evaluating investment projects, then such modifications will be included in the evaluation regardless of which approach is used.

REFERENCES

13.1 *Engineering News-Record.* New York: McGraw-Hill (weekly publication).

13.2 Ibbotson, R. G., and R. A. Sinquefield, *Stocks, Bonds, Bills, and Inflation: The Past (1926–1976) and the Future (1977–2000).* Charlottesville, VA: Financial Analysts Research Foundation, 1977.

PROBLEMS

P13.1 A hydraulic machine for laying pipes valued at $25,000 now must be replaced 7 years later. Suppose that the annual inflation rate during the next 4 years is expected to be 9% and that in the following 3 years it is to be reduced to 5%.

The real cost of this machine would remain unchanged if there were no inflation. What is the then-current value of the machine at the end of 7 years?

P13.2 A corporation plans to set aside the equivalent of $100,000 in today's dollars for its chief executive when she retires 10 years from today. The inflation rate is expected to be 10% per year during the next 4 years and 8% per year thereafter. If the corporation can invest the money at 6% rate of return excluding inflation,

   (a) How much should it invest now in order to obtain the equivalent of $100,000 in today's dollars 10 years from now?
   (b) How many dollars (in the value of dollars 10 years later) will the executive receive 10 years from now?

P13.3 An investment of $80,000 in a new underwater bulldozer is expected to produce a before-tax net uniform revenue of $30,000 per year in base-year value over the next 5 years. Using a before-tax MARR of 12% including inflation, determine whether the investment is worthwhile if the annual inflation rate is 6% during the next 5 years.

P13.4 An investment of $60,000 in a diesel truck is expected to produce a before-tax net uniform revenue of $20,000 per year in then-current value during the next 5 years. Using a before-tax MARR of 10% excluding inflation, determine whether the investment is worthwhile if the annual inflation rate is 10% during the next 3 years and 8% during the subsequent 2 years.

P13.5 The energy cost of conventional home heating is expected to have an inflation rate of 6% per year above the general inflation rate during the next 10 years and 3% above the general inflation rate for the following 15 years. A solar heating system for a typical home costs $3,000 with no salvage value at the end of the 25 years of service. The annual saving in energy cost in terms of base-year price levels and expressed in base-year dollars is $500 per year for 25 years to the owner after considering all tax benefits. Determine whether this investment is worthwhile if the after-tax MARR excluding inflation is 10%.

P13.6 A new model of electric clothes dryer is advertised as saving 5% of electricity compared to an existing model which is sold for $100 less. Both dryers last for 5 years with no salvage value at the end. A family which spends an estimated $80 per year at the base-year value on electricity for drying clothes with the existing model needs to replace its dryer and is comparing the new and the existing models. The annual differential inflation rate of electricity is expected to be 2% above the general inflation. If the MARR of this family excluding inflation is 6%, which model is a better choice?

P13.7 Joyce McNeil has just invested $10,000 in a 6-year certificate of deposit which pays an annual compound interest rate of 12%. If the annual inflation rate during this period is expected to be 8%, what is the annual rate of return excluding inflation? What is the value in base-year dollars for the amount she gets back when she cashes in the certificate at the end of 6 years?

P13.8 Edward Johnson has agreed to loan a sum of $1,000 to a friend for 4 years at a 5% annual compound interest rate excluding inflation. If the annual inflation rate during the next 4 years is 10%, what is the annual compound interest rate including inflation? What will be the sum in then-current dollars which will be repaid to him at the end of 4 years?

P13.9 In an investment proposal for a 4-year project, the cash flows expressed in base-year dollars are $A_0 = -\$20,000$, $A_1 = +\$4,000$, $A_2 = +\$6,000$, $A_3 = +\$8,000$, and $A_4 = +\$12,000$. The MARR specified for the project is 20% irrespective of whether there will be inflation. Determine whether the project is worthwhile assuming that

(a) There will be no inflation.
(b) The inflation rate will be 5% per year.

P13.10 An investment of $40,000 in a vibratory hammer is expected to produce a net uniform annual cash flow of $15,000 per year in base-year dollars before tax. The depreciation allowance is based on the straight line method with a salvage value of $5,000 at the end of 5 years. A MARR of 12% after tax excluding inflation is specified. The income tax rate is 50%. Determine whether the project is worthwhile assuming that

(a) There will be no inflation.
(b) The inflation rate will be 6% per year.

P13.11 An investment of $40,000 in a delivery truck is expected to produce net annual benefits in base-year dollars for the next 3 years as follows: +18,000 for year 1, +16,000 for year 2, +14,000 for year 3. The equipment is depreciated by the straight line method with a salvage value of $10,000. The inflation rate is expected to be 10% per year. The specified MARR excluding inflation is 8%. The corporate income tax rate is 50%. Is this investment worthwhile?

P13.12 The Ternadem Corporation plans to purchase a demolition and wrecking machine to save labor costs. The machine costs $50,000 and has a salvage value of $10,800 at the end of 5 years. The machine is expected to be in operation for 5 years, and it will be depreciated by the double declining balance method up to the salvage value. The corporation specifies an after-tax MARR excluding inflation of 20% and has an income tax rate of 50%. The annual inflation rate is expected to be 10% during the next 5 years. If the uniform annual net benefit before tax in terms of base-year dollars for the next 5 years is $20,000, is the investment worthwhile?

P13.13 Macmillion Chemical Company plans to invest $2 million in a new plant which is expected to produce a uniform annual net benefit before tax of $600,000 in terms of the base-year dollars over the next 6 years. The plant has a salvage value of $200,000 at the end of 6 years and the depreciation allowance is based on the straight line depreciation method. The corporate tax rate is 46%, and the after-tax MARR specified by the firm is 12% excluding inflation. If the annual inflation rate during the next 6 years is expected to be 8%, determine whether the investment is worthwhile.

P13.14 A company is considering investing in a water purification system. Three alternatives are under consideraton and their before-tax cash flow profiles in base-year dollars are given, and all three have no salvage values after 4 years.

Year	System *A*	System *B*	System *C*
0	−80,000	−120,000	−100,000
1	+40,000	+60,000	+35,000
2	+35,000	+50,000	+35,000
3	+30,000	+40,000	+35,000
4	+25,000	+30,000	+35,000

The depreciation allowance is based on the straight line method. The general inflation rate is expected to be 6% per year during the next 4 years. The tax rate is 46%, and the after-tax MARR excluding inflation is 8%. Determine which alternative, if any, should be adopted.

CHAPTER

14

FINANCIAL STATEMENTS

14.1 The Importance of Financial Reports of a Firm

The decision to undertake any capital investment project cannot be made on the basis of the profitability of the project alone but must be considered in the context of its impact on the financial strength and position of the firm that is proposing to undertake the project. A firm that is currently in a strong financial position will be more willing and able to undertake projects than the same firm would be when it is weaker. The purpose of this chapter is to provide an overview of the major determinants of the financial position of a firm as reflected periodically in its financial statements. This chapter also provides a general background in preparation of later discussions on the return in capital markets and the financial structure of private firms in Chapters 15 and 16.

The financial statements are contained in the annual report of a corporation, which includes the *balance sheet*, the *income statement*, the *statement of changes in financial position*, and the *auditors' report*. These statements are usually preceded in the annual report by a brief description of the corporation and its operations. The balance sheet summarizes the financial position of the corporation and lists the values of its assets and financial obligations or liabilities. The income statement itemizes revenues and expenses for the year and provides an overview of the operations for the year. The statement of changes in financial position lists the sources and application of funds. The auditors' report is an independent appraisal of the financial statements of the corporation by a team of professional accountants.

Financial statements are prepared on an annual basis because the year is a standard unit of time and because the year is a good period of time for evaluating the activities of a firm. It is long enough to provide a meaningful measure of the operations, but short enough so that statements do not become outdated. It includes all four seasons and thus eliminates the effect of trends that are purely seasonal. It normally includes several cycles of production and sale of goods (except for a handful of industries such as the tobacco industry where the growing period is longer than a year). Publicly held corporations are also required to prepare financial statements on a quarterly basis, and all corporations must prepare financial statements when they wish to raise capital by either borrowing money or selling stock.

14.2   Balance Sheets

The balance sheet is a statement of the financial position of a firm. It balances the assets and the claims against those assets of a firm. The assets and claims are, by definition, equal. Claims against those assets include both liability and stockholders' equity. According to convention, the balance sheet has a standard form which lists *assets* on the left side and *liabilities and stockholders' equity* on the right side. Other formats are sometimes used but they are less common. Usually, a balance sheet presenting the information for the year just ended and the previous year is given in the annual report for the purpose of comparison. An example is shown in Table 14.1.

Assets are listed on the balance sheet in descending order of liquidity. At the top of the list, under *current assets*, is *cash*, which represents the ultimate degree of liquidity because it can be used to acquire assets or pay off debts. The term *cash* refers to monies held on company premises and in banks. The next item after cash is usually *marketable securities*, which include such items as stocks, bonds, and Treasury bills, which are held to earn interest but may be sold at any time to raise the funds needed for operations. Next is *accounts receivable*, which are amounts owed by customers on credit sales, but not yet paid. Since cash is soon collected on accounts receivable, they are considered a near-cash item.

Inventory refers to goods produced or purchased and held for sale or used in the production of services. It does not represent a definite commitment that will generate cash and income for the firm; nevertheless, it is held with the expectation that it will be sold within the year. Revenue is accrued when an order is placed by a customer for inventory, and the order is charged to accounts receivable. When the cash is collected from the accounts receivable, it is either used to purchase more inventory or set aside for other investment purposes. Thus, the operating cycle begins with the production or purchase of inventory, continues with the sale of inventory and the accumulation of accounts receivable, and is completed with the liquidation of these accounts for cash.

Other items commonly listed as current assets on the balance sheet may include *prepaid expenses*, such as rent and insurance. Prepaid expenses are payments made in advance to satisfy certain necessary expenses. Such payments are sometimes made several years in advance, but if the portion beyond the current year may be reclaimed, that portion is included as a current asset.

Noncurrent assets consist largely of *fixed assets* such as land, buildings, machinery, and equipment. Sometimes these items are included under the one heading, but usually one or more of these items are listed separately. Other noncurrent assets

Table 14.1

Balance Sheet
G. Fitzgerald Corporation

December 31	1980	1979
ASSETS		
Current assets		
Cash	$ 100,000	$ 90,000
Marketable securities	50,000	50,000
Accounts receivable	150,000	115,000
Inventories	290,000	250,000
Prepaid expenses	10,000	20,000
Total current assets	$ 600,000	$525,000
Fixed assets		
Land and buildings	350,000	350,000
Machinery and equipment	200,000	180,000
Total cost of fixed assets	550,000	530,000
Less accumulated depreciation	150,000	110,000
Total fixed assets net of depreciation	400,000	420,000
TOTAL ASSETS	$1,000,000	$945,000

include the value of such *intangible items* as *patents, trademarks,* and *goodwill.* Non-current assets are used by the firm in the production of goods and services and are expected to generate revenues on a long-term basis.

The *market value* of most assets fluctuates greatly over a period of time. The values of all assets except cash on the balance sheet are only *estimates* of the true value of the assets. Assets are subject to declines in value due to risk, use, technological obsolescence, and other factors. When it occurs, the decline in value for an asset is estimated and subtracted from the original value to arrive at a revised lower estimate.

On the same balance sheet, the asset may be shown at its original value, minus an allowance for the decline in value in an offsetting account called a *contra account.* Thus, *accounts receivable* will be offset by an account called *allowance for doubtful accounts* (estimated uncollectible receivables). The *original value of machinery and equipment* will be offset by an account for the *depreciation accumulated to date.* The offsetting account for intangible assets such as patents is called *allowance for amortization.* Although some firms state their assets at the original values together with

Table 14.1 (continued)

December 31	1980	1979
LIABILITIES AND STOCKHOLDERS' EQUITY		
Current liabilities		
Accounts payable	$ 125,000	$110,000
Salaries payable	20,000	20,000
Taxes payable	20,000	15,000
Dividends payable	10,000	7,500
Unsecured short-term notes payable	10,000	5,000
Mortgage notes payable, current maturities	20,000	20,000
Interest payable	15,000	12,500
Total current liabilities	$ 220,000	$190,000
Long-term liabilities		
Long-term mortgage notes payable, net of current maturities	$ 180,000	$220,000
Stockholders' equity		
Preferred stock, 10%, $1 par value 50,000 shares issued and outstanding	$ 50,000	$ 50,000
Common stock, $2 par value, 200,000 shares authorized; 100,000 shares issued and outstanding in 1980 and 1979	200,000	200,000
Additional paid-in capital	25,000	25,000
Retained earnings	325,000	260,000
Total stockholders' equity	$ 600,000	$535,000
TOTAL LIABILITIES AND EQUITY	$1,000,000	$945,000

the related contra account, other firms may state only the net values on the balance sheets.

The examination of the contra accounts, if they exist, can give an indication of the firm's financial position. Allowance for doubtful accounts should be only a small percentage of the accounts receivable, and if this figure exceeds 5%, there is cause for concern that the firm is making a substantial proportion of credit sales to customers with questionable credit ratings. Accumulated depreciation can range anywhere from 0% on equipment just put into service to 100% on equipment that has been in service longer than its estimated useful life. If the accumulated depreciation of the equipment is a high proportion of the original value, it may be a sign that the firm is using obsolete equipment. A high percentage of amortization of the original value of patents may also indicate that the patent is not as valuable as it once was, due to its possible obsolescence or the development of similar processes by competitors.

Inventory poses a special problem in valuation. It can have any one of several stated values: original cost to purchase or produce, present cost to purchase or produce, or resale value at market retail prices. The most conservative practice is to record the inventory at the original cost of acquisition, except that when the current retail market value is less than the original cost, the inventory is revalued at the market price. The loss in the revaluation is reflected on the income statement, not the balance sheet, and is referred to as valuing inventory at the *lower of cost or market*.

Liabilities are the debts incurred to acquire assets and therefore are obligations for definite amounts of money. Like assets, liabilities are classified as current or noncurrent. Liabilities are listed in descending order of priority or urgency on the balance sheet.

At the top of the *current liabilities* are obligations that are due within a few days or weeks. *Accounts payable* are the debts that the firm owes to suppliers of goods and services, and are usually due within 30 days. *Wages and salaries payable* are amounts due to the employees of the firm that have been earned during the pay period of 2 weeks or a month. *Taxes payable* are taxes that are due to federal, state, and local governments, with the taxes being due at the end of each quarter. *Dividends payable* are dividends that have been declared, but not yet paid. *Short-term debt* to bank and other lending institutions are, by definition, current liabilities. The *current portion of long-term debt* refers to the principal portion of the long-term debt that is due in the upcoming year. Closely related to debt liability is *interest payable* which is accrued on a current basis.

Long-term liabilities include notes payable and bonds payable. *Notes payable* are written contracts for the incurrence and repayments of indebtness, signed by both borrower and lender. This contrasts with accounts payable which is an informal debt arrangement evidenced only by a seller's invoice. Notes may either be unsecured or secured by collateral such as inventory or accounts receivable. *Mortgage notes* are a special kind of note payable that is secured by real property, i.e., the fixed assets of the firm. A *bond* is a long-term debt instrument that commits the firm to make periodic interest payments and to repay the principal sum stated on the face of the instrument at the maturity date. Schedules of the terms of long-term debt, disclosing the interest rate and the maturity dates, are included in the financial statement. Such information indicates whether the company is in a comfortable financial situation, with low interest rates and dispersed maturity dates of liabilities, or is in an upcoming financial bind, with high interest rates and a large amount of shortly maturing liability. Under the long-term liabilities section of the balance sheet, the value of notes payable is stated "less current portion," i.e., less the part that is listed under current liabilities.

The *stockholders' equity* is the portion of capital that belongs to the investors. There are several classes of stock which entitle their holders to varying degrees of rights regarding income and participation in the affairs of management. There are three major types of stock: preferred stock, common stock, and treasury stock. Preferred stock is a privileged class of stock that gives its holders the right to annual dividends at a stated rate and to receive such payments before other classes of share-holders if the management declares dividends. Preferred stock does not give its holders the right to receive dividends above this rate unless it is *participating*, and it is not normally accompanied by the right to vote for the members of the board of directors. Common stock is the general class of stock that entitles its holders to receive dividends and to vote for directors and on certain issues at the rate of one vote per share of stock. Treasury stock is stock repurchased by the firm and removed from the market.

Under stockholders' equity, the number of shares of each class of stocks authorized and/or issued as well as the *par value* for each share are listed separately. The par values for each share of preferred stock and common stock are values designated arbitrarily by the management, including the option of not designating any par value. The total value of the stocks issued in excess of par value is recorded in an account called *additional paid-in capital*. Retained earnings is the sum of all net income, less dividends of the corporation, that has been retained or plowed back into the business since its beginning.

The stockholders' equity section is important both in analyzing the structure of the firm and in providing investment opportunities. This section poses some of the most critical and complex problems in finance, but we are only concerned with stockholders' equity in terms of the structure of ownership and therefore will not discuss these problems here in detail.

Example 14.1

Verify the contra account for accumulated depreciation (under fixed assets) of the G. Fitzgerald Corporation from the following data:

	Land & Buildings	Machinery & Equipment
Costs of items purchased before 1980	$350,000	$180,000
Costs of addition in 1980	0	20,000
Accumulated depreciation before 1980	75,000	35,000
Depreciation allowance in 1980	25,000	15,000

For the given data, we can compute the contra account for accumulated depreciation as follows:

	1980	1979
(1) Land and buildings		
Costs of acquisition	$350,000	$350,000
Less accumulated depreciation	100,000	75,000
Amount net of depreciation	250,000	275,000
(2) Machinery and equipment		
Costs of acquisition	200,000	180,000
Less accumulated depreciation	50,000	35,000
Amount net of depreciation	150,000	145,000
(3) Total fixed assets, (1) + (2)		
Costs of acquisition	550,000	530,000
Less accumulated depreciation	150,000	110,000
Total net of depreciation	$400,000	$420,000

Example 14.2

The G. Fitzgerald Corporation issued 100,000 shares of common stock with a par value of $2 per share. The total market value of these shares is $225,000. How would this total value be recorded on the balance sheet?

Of this total amount, $200,000 would be recorded under common stock (100,000 shares outstanding at $2 par value per share), and $25,000 would be credited to additional paid-in capital under the stockholders' equity on the balance sheet.

14.3   Income Statements

The income statement lists the revenues and expenses during the year, together with the net income and retained earnings at the end of the year. It is sometimes referred to as the statement of income and reinvested earnings. The income statement usually includes the information for the year just ended and the previous year for the purpose of comparison. An example is shown in Table 14.2.

At the top of the income statement is the *gross income*, which may include both operating and nonoperating income. *Operating income* refers to the *revenues from sales* and other operations of the firm; *nonoperating income* refers to revenues from other sources such as dividends received from marketable securities held by the firm, or gains and losses on the sale of equipment. The gross income is one measure of the size and financial strength of the firm.

Table 14.2

Income Statement
G. Fitzgerald Corporation

For years ended December 31	1980	1979
REVENUES		
Sales and other operating revenues	$1,100,000	$940,000
COSTS AND EXPENSES		
Production and operating expenses	600,000	545,000
General and administrative expenses	235,000	215,000
Depreciation	40,000	30,000
Total	875,000	790,000
REVENUES LESS COSTS AND EXPENSES	225,000	150,000
OTHER DEDUCTIONS		
Interest expense, net of interest income	15,000	10,000
INCOME BEFORE TAXES	$ 210,000	$140,000
TAXES ON INCOME	105,000	75,000
NET INCOME	$ 105,000	$ 65,000
CASH DIVIDENDS		
Preferred stock (per share, $0.10)	5,000	5,000
Common stock (per share, 1980, $0.35; 1979, $0.25)	35,000	25,000
	40,000	30,000
RETAINED EARNINGS		
Beginning of year	260,000	225,000
Current year	65,000	35,000
End of year	$ 325,000	$260,000
EARNINGS PER SHARE OF COMMON STOCK	$1.00	$0.80

The expenses may also be classified as *operating* and *nonoperating*. The production and other operating expenses generally include the *cost of goods sold* and *cost of selling*. The cost of goods sold refers to the costs incurred in the production, including materials, wages of workers, and certain overhead items. The cost of selling covers the cost of advertising and the remuneration of sales persons. The *general and administrative expenses* include the salaries of managers and the administrative personnel who are not directly engaged in production, and other items of expenditure not directly related to production. Although the depreciation allowance is a deduction and not a "charge" because it does not involve an outlay of cash, it is usually considered an operating expense. Hence, the amount of depreciation allowance is a part of the costs and expenses which are deducted from revenues of the current year to arrive at net income. Other deductions for nonoperating expenses include *interest* paid, but income taxes are usually listed separately.

Extraordinary items are financial gains and losses due to unusual and nonrecurring events such as mergers or natural disasters and are usually shown separately to emphasize the unusual nature of the transaction. After all income before taxes is computed, the applicable tax rate is used to compute the tax expense, which is deducted from before-tax income to arrive at after-tax income. The after-tax income is referred to as *net income* or *net earnings*.

Cash dividends declared for various classes of stock are listed next. They are deducted from the net income to obtain the retained earnings for the current year, which in turn are added to the retained earnings at the beginning of the year to arrive at the retained earnings at the end of the year.

At the bottom of the income statement is a required computation of *earnings per share*: net income after taxes divided by the number of shares of common stock or common stock *equivalent*. This is a figure of great interest to investors with holdings of stock because it is one measure of the value of their stock. The computation of equivalent shares of common stock is a very complicated one for some firms because of the number and types of outstanding convertible securities. It is sufficient to point out that there are two types of figures for earnings per share that are usually presented: primary earnings per share, which assumes that only certain types of securities would be converted into common stock, and a lower figure for fully diluted earnings per share, which assumes that all convertible securities will be converted. The fully diluted figure is lower because of the larger number in the denominator representing more equivalent shares of common stock.

There is a close connection between the items listed on the balance sheet and the transactions summarized in the income statement. This is due to the fact that the balance sheet consists of the assets used to produce income, and the income statement reflects the addition to the firm's capital, and eventually its assets, from net earnings generated and retained each year. For this reason, the two statements are said to *articulate* with each other.

Income statements in modified forms are also presented for the previous 5 or 10 years in the annual report of a firm. They often represent a financial and statistical summary emphasizing special features such as the revenue, income, and asset composition of the firm. Earnings per share data are also presented on a year-to-year basis. The historical presentation of income statements shows the trend of revenues and income over a period of time. It allows prospective investors to see the growth (or decline) of a firm, and assists them in forming an opinion about the firm's future prospects.

14.4   Statements of Changes in Financial Position

The sources of revenues and expenses are often indicators of the strengths and weaknesses of the operations of a firm. In addition, the inflow and outflow of income usually have a differential effect on the various balance sheet accounts of the firm. These effects are summarized in the *statement of changes in financial position.* This statement details how the firm acquired funds and how the funds were used. In the words of the Accounting Principles Board, such a statement "summarizes the financing and investing activities of the firm."[1] Because it makes the analysis of the flow of funds so much more convenient, as well as providing greater insight into the results of the firm's operations, the inclusion of the statement of changes in financial position in a firm's financial report is required. An example of such a statement is shown in Table 14.3.

The term *funds* has been variously defined as cash, monetary assets such as cash plus marketable securities, and working capital. *Working capital refers to the difference between current assets and current liabilities. It is the most generally accepted definition for the term funds in the statements of large corporations,* because it is a measure of liquidity. However, it has the disadvantage of including certain relatively nonliquid items such as inventory. For *small firms* that do business on a cash rather than an accrual basis, *cash* may be a better definition of funds than working capital.

The statement of changes in financial position is divided into two parts. The upper portion of the statement lists the sources and uses of funds. If the conventional definition (working capital) is used to denote funds, then the change of working capital refers to funds added to or subtracted from working capital which arise from transactions involving nonworking capital items. Specifically, *sources of funds* include increases in equity through the issuance of new stock, increases in long-term liabilities through the issuance of new debt and decreases in long-term assets through sales or depreciation. *Uses of funds* refer to expenditures for nonworking capital items such as the acquisition of fixed assets or repayment of debt. They are composed of decreases in equity or long-term liabilities, and increases in long-term assets. The difference between the total of funds from all sources and the total uses of funds is the change (increase or decrease) in working capital.

In the second part of the statement, the changes in the individual working capital accounts, such as cash, inventory, or accounts payable, are itemized. The changes in the various accounts are then added (with increases and decreases in liabilities inversely related to increases and decreases in assets). The sum of all

[1] American Institute of Certified Public Accountants, Accounting Principles Board (APB) Opinion No. 19, "Reporting Changes in Financial Position." New York: AICPA, 1971.

Table 14.3

Statement of Changes in Financial Position
G. Fitzgerald Corporation

For years ending December 31	1980	1979
SOURCES OF FUNDS		
Operations		
Net Income	$105,000	$ 65,000
Depreciation	40,000	30,000
Total from operations	145,000	95,000
Additions to long-term debt	0	35,000
Total source of funds	145,000	130,000
USES OF FUNDS		
Additions to land, buildings, and equipment	20,000	15,000
Cash dividends	40,000	30,000
Reduction of long-term debt	40,000	15,000
Other	0	20,000
Total application of funds	100,000	80,000
INCREASE (DECREASE) IN WORKING CAPITAL	$ 45,000	$ 50,000
INCREASE (DECREASE) IN COMPONENTS OF WORKING CAPITAL		
Cash and short-term investments	10,000	20,000
Accounts receivable	35,000	30,000
Inventories and prepaid expenses	30,000	15,000
Accounts payable	(15,000)	(10,000)
Federal and other taxes	(5,000)	(5,000)
Other payables	(10,000)	0
Increase (decrease) in working capital	45,000	50,000
Working capital, beginning of year	335,000	285,000
Working capital, end of year	$380,000	$335,000

working capital accounts equals the changes in working capital and should match the figure arrived at by taking the difference between sources and uses of funds.

In analyzing the change in working capital as sources and uses of funds during a specified period (usually one year), as shown in the first part of Table 14.3, we adopt the following notation:

ΔW = change in working capital, with a positive value indicating an increase, and a negative value a decrease

ΔA_s = decrease in long-term assets through sales or depreciation for the period

ΔL_s = increase in equity (including net income for the period) or increase in long-term debt

ΔA_u = increase in long-term assets through acquisition

ΔL_u = decrease in equity (including the use of retained earnings during the period) or decrease in long-term debt

S = sources of funds, always expressed as a positive quantity

U = uses of funds, always expressed as a positive quantity

Then,

$$S = \Delta A_s + \Delta L_s \tag{14.1}$$

$$U = \Delta A_u{}^{\bullet} + \Delta L_u \tag{14.2}$$

$$\Delta W = S - U \tag{14.3}$$

The change in components of working capital, as shown in the second part of Table 14.3, can be analyzed by considering the components of current assets and liabilities. We adopt the following notation:

$\Delta W'$ = change in working capital, with a positive value indicating an increase and a negative value indicating a decrease

$\Delta A'_x$ = increase (positive) or decrease (negative) in each current asset account x, such as cash, accounts receivable, and inventory

$\Delta L'_y$ = increase (positive) or decrease (negative) in each current liability account y, such as accounts payable, salaries, and taxes payable

$\Delta A'$ = total change in current assets (positive for an increase and negative for a decrease)

$\Delta L'$ = total change in current liabilities (positive for an increase and negative for a decrease)

Thus, the change in current assets represents the value of all the current asset accounts ($x = 1, 2, \ldots, m$):

$$\Delta A' = \sum_{x=1}^{m} \Delta A'_x \tag{14.4}$$

and the change in current liabilities represents the value of all the current liability accounts $(y = 1, 2, \ldots, n)$:

$$\Delta L' = \sum_{y=1}^{n} \Delta L'_y \qquad (14.5)$$

Hence the change in working capital equals the difference between the change in current assets and the change in current liabilities:

$$\Delta W' = \Delta A' - \Delta L' \qquad (14.6)$$

Since the first and second parts of the statement of changes in financial position must show the same increase or decrease in working capital, it is obvious that

$$\Delta W = \Delta W' \qquad (14.7)$$

Thus, the statement reveals the change in the firm's liquidity by highlighting the components that are affected the most in the change of working capital.

Besides summarizing the changes on the balance sheet, the statement of changes in financial position reveals transactions that would otherwise have been hidden. Items that affect both sources and uses of funds must be listed separately rather than netted out. For instance, the increase in retained earnings is the difference between net income and dividend payments. Net income is a source of funds and dividend payments are a use of funds; and the two items are listed under their respective categories instead of under a single entry for increase in retained earnings. Similarly, the actual amount of new debt taken out during the year is shown under sources of funds, and the actual amount of repayment of previous loans is listed separately under uses of funds.

Finally, the statement provides an insight into the operations of the firm by including the results of operations under sources of funds. The first and most obvious source of funds is net income. Then, items such as depreciation and amortization are added back to net income to arrive at working capital generated from operations. This is because depreciation and amortization are *accounting* deductions that reduce gross income but do not involve an outflow of working capital. Hence, they must be added back to income to arrive at working capital generated from operations. Then, other sources of funds caused by changes in nonworking capital balance sheet items are added to funds provided by operations to arrive at total sources of funds. Uses of funds represent investments made by the firm in the current year to benefit future years and are therefore subtracted from sources of funds to arrive at the changes in working capital.

The strength of the financial position of a firm cannot be judged by the increase or decrease of working capital alone. A decrease in working capital may reflect the use of available resources to fund a major expansion of capital investment. On the other hand, improved management of inventory, receivables, and payables may contribute to the increase of working capital. Consequently, an evaluation of the changes in the financial position of the firm must include a detailed analysis of the inflow and outflow of funds and an itemization of changes in components of working capital in comparison to the previous year. It is imperative that the statement of changes in financial position be viewed within the larger context of the firm's overall operations. However, a steady decrease in working capital year after year is an indication that the firm may be in financial trouble, and a steady increase in working capital accompanying the growth of the firm as a whole is a good sign.

Example 14.3

Derive the increases and decreases in the components of working capital of the G. Fitzgerald Corporation for 1980 in Table 14.3 on the basis of the information on the balance sheet in Table 14.1.

The working capital for 1980 can be computed by noting the pertinent items on sources and uses of funds in Table 14.1 and by using Eqs. (14.1) through (14.3). Thus,

$$S = 40{,}000 + 105{,}000 = 145{,}000$$

$$U = 20{,}000 + (40{,}000 + 40{,}000) = 100{,}000$$

$$\Delta W = 145{,}000 - 100{,}000 = 45{,}000$$

From the list of current assets in Table 14.1, we can compute the increase or decrease in each component of working capital in 1980 in comparison with the corresponding component in 1979 as follows:

1. Cash and short-term investments (marketable securities):

$$\Delta A_1' = (100{,}000 + 50{,}000) - (90{,}000 + 50{,}000) = 10{,}000$$

2. Accounts receivable:

$$\Delta A_2' = 150{,}000 - 115{,}000 = 35{,}000$$

3. Inventories and other (prepaid expenses):

$$\Delta A_3' = (290{,}000 + 10{,}000) - (250{,}000 + 20{,}000) = 30{,}000$$

From the list of current liabilities in Table 14.3, we can do likewise.

  1. Accounts payable:

$$\Delta L_1' = 125{,}000 - 110{,}000 = 15{,}000$$

  2. Federal and other taxes (taxes payable):

$$\Delta L_2' = 20{,}000 - 15{,}000 = 5{,}000$$

  3. Other, net (referring to all other current liabilities):

$$\Delta L_3' = (220{,}000 - 125{,}000 - 20{,}000) - (190{,}000 - 110{,}000 - 15{,}000) = 10{,}000$$

Consequently, the total changes in current assets and current liabilities are obtained from Eqs. (14.4) and (14.5), respectively, as follows:

$$\Delta A' = 10{,}000 + 35{,}000 + 30{,}000 = 75{,}000$$

$$\Delta L' = 15{,}000 + 5{,}000 + 10{,}000 = 30{,}000$$

Then, from Eq. (14.6),

$$\Delta W' = 75{,}000 - 30{,}000 = 45{,}000$$

As a final check, we can compare the total working capital in the current year (1980) with that in the previous year (1979), as shown in Table 14.3. Hence,

$$\Delta W = 380{,}000 - 335{,}000 = 45{,}000$$

14.5   Analysis of the Financial Position of a Firm

The analysis of financial statements has so far been limited to a line-by-line examination of all the categories under a firm's balance sheet and income statement, and the possible implications of certain items. However, the figures shown on the financial statements do not stand alone; they are meaningful only in the context of their relationships to the other figures in the financial statements. A handful of key relationships can tell a great deal about the firm's financial position. A much more effective analysis can be accomplished by examining these relationships.

   The financial areas of a firm that concern a prospective investor the most are liquidity, solvency, and profitability. *Liquidity* is the ability of a firm to raise enough cash to pay its liabilities as they become due. *Solvency* refers to the long-term ability of a firm to meet its obligations, based on the structure of its debt in relationship to its assets. *Profitability* is the ability of the firm to generate profits. Managers, investors, and lenders watch these areas closely to make sure that the firm is able both to stay afloat and to provide a return on investment.

Liquidity can be determined from the relationship between current assets and current liabilities. One measure of liquidity is the difference between the two, which is the working capital. However, this measure is often misleading because a firm with $200,000 in current assets and $100,000 in current liabilities and another firm with $1,100,000 in current assets and $1,000,000 in current liabilities have the same amount of working capital, i.e., $100,000, but it is intuitively obvious that the first firm is more liquid percentage-wise.

A better measure of liquidity than net working capital is the *current ratio,* which is defined as the ratio between current assets and current liabilities. In the above example, the current ratio for the first firm is 2, while the current ratio for the second firm is only 1.1. Generally, the current ratio should range between 2 and 3.5. If the current ratio is much below 2, the firm may have some trouble generating enough cash in the short term to meet its short-term obligations, because some of its accounts receivable and inventories included under current assets may not be converted into cash quickly. If the current ratio is much beyond 3.5, the firm is maintaining overly large balances of liquid assets relative to its current needs. Inventories may be sitting idle and not earning a profit while storage costs mount, or the payments on accounts receivable may be slow, increasing both the lost interest and the risk of default. If it is substantial in amount, excess cash should be invested in more fixed assets to generate more income.

The liquidity of certain current asset items leads to another test of liquidity. Cash or near-cash assets, such as marketable securities and accounts receivable, are called *quick assets.* In general, current assets minus inventories represent quick assets which can be mobilized quickly enough to pay off current liabilities. The ratio of quick assets to current liabilities is called the quick ratio or *acid-test ratio.* For this reason, the quick ratio should not be less than 1 and in fact, should be slightly higher. A quick ratio of greater than 2, however, may indicate the presence of unused funds.

Closely related to the problem of liquidity is solvency, the ability to pay off long-term debt commitments. The two measures of solvency are the ability to meet interest (and principal) payments, and the proportion of debt financing of the firm. The income statement gives an indication of the ability to pay interest, while the balance sheet is the indicator of the proportion of debt.

The ratio of income *before* taxes to interest expense is generally taken as a sign of "ability to pay." (Interest payments are deductible from income before tax and are therefore paid out of "before-tax" income.) Normally, a firm with an income-to-interest ratio of less than 3 is in financial trouble, because it has little money left over after making its current debt repayments. Not only is the ability to pay dividends on equity or purchase new assets impaired, but the firm will get into an even tighter situation if its income should decline further or if it needs to borrow even more money. A more comfortable income-to-interest ratio is 7. A much higher income-to-interest ratio may be an indication of the ability to expand by borrowing more money.

The ratio of debt to stockholders' equity is another measure of ability to absorb more borrowed capital. Lenders are very risk conscious and do not look favorably on a firm that has an unduly high proportion of debt and does not have a sizeable amount of equity capital. Since lenders have first priority over stockholders for repayment of debt in the event of a failure and can in fact appropriate invested capital (or assets purchased with invested capital) in repayment of the debt, invested capital is a financial "cushion" for lenders. American bankers and bond purchasers normally do not like to see a debt-to-equity ratio of much more than 1 when a firm "owes what it owns." A higher ratio will make it difficult to borrow more money, but borrowing money is usually easy with a debt equity of less than 1 : 1. However, banks in certain foreign countries, notably Japan, where loans are guaranteed by the government, are willing to finance higher debt-to-equity ratios.

The measures of profitability of an investment may be based on two criteria: capital gains through increases in the price of the stock or through dividend payments. The profitability of a firm will affect both the desirability of the stock (and hence its price) and the ability of the firm to pay out dividends. Naturally, it is in the interest of the firm to maximize earnings, but the question of whether to attract capital by paying out earnings in the form of dividends or by reinvesting the earnings in the company is often a tricky one.

The attractiveness of stock to an investor is based on both the profitability of the firm as a whole and the profitability to the stockholders. Sometimes a firm that is profitably operated will not be particularly attractive to a stockholder due to an unfavorable equity structure, such as a large amount of preferred stock, or a large number of shares already issued and outstanding; and sometimes a firm that is only moderately profitable may be attractive to stockholders because of the returns paid to stockholders. Therefore, measures of both the operating profitability of a firm and the return on stockholders' equity will be discussed.

The two most important measures of operating profitability are return on sales and return on assets, expressed in percentages. *Return on sales* is defined as the ratio of income after taxes to sales and other operating revenues. It varies from industry to industry and may range from as low as 2% in certain high-volume retail industries to 15% or more on low-volume, high-quality goods. The only way to judge a firm by return on sales is to compare it with other firms in the industry. A year-to-year comparison of the same firm's profitability will also show whether its financial position is improving or declining.

Return on assets, otherwise known as *return on investment*, is another widely used method of measuring profitability. It is defined as the ratio of income after taxes to total assets. Its advantage is its simplicity, because a certain rule of thumb may be used to gauge the profitability. For example, some business people consider a return on assets of 3% or less as poor, 5% as fair, and 10% or more as outstanding. Its disadvantage as a measure is that it does not take into account the asset structure of the firm. A firm that is currently building up its assets, especially fixed assets, may show a low return on assets temporarily but may have good long-term prospects. In a time of high inflation, however, a firm with a large proportion of fixed assets acquired at times of lower prices and/or highly depreciated assets may show high rates of return on assets based on high current earnings in inflated dollars generated by older or even obsolete assets.

Stockholders, however, are even more interested in what company earnings mean to them. The most important measure of return to common stockholders is the *earnings per share of common stock*. The earnings accrued to common stock refers to the net income (after tax) minus the dividends paid to the holders of preferred stock. Thus, a firm with a low return on assets may have a high earnings per share of common stock because it is largely financed with debt and there are relatively few shares of common stock. An alternate measure is the *dividend pay-out ratio* which expresses the percentage of dividends paid out on common stock to the earnings accrued to common stock.

The conventional measures for liquidity, solvency, and profitability discussed in this section can be summarized in the following equations:

1. For liquidity:

$$\text{Current ratio} = \frac{\text{current assets}}{\text{current liabilities}} \tag{14.8}$$

$$\text{Quick ratio} = \frac{\text{current assets} - \text{inventories}}{\text{current liabilities}} \tag{14.9}$$

2. For solvency:

$$\text{Income to interest ratio} = \frac{\text{income before tax}}{\text{interest expense}} \tag{14.10}$$

$$\text{Debt to equity ratio} = \frac{\text{current liabilities} + \text{long-term liabilities}}{\text{stockholders' equity}} \tag{14.11}$$

3. For profitability:

$$\text{Return on sales} = \frac{\text{income after taxes}}{\text{sales and other operating revenues}} \tag{14.12}$$

$$\text{Return on assets} = \frac{\text{income after taxes}}{\text{total assets}} \tag{14.13}$$

$$\text{Earnings per common share} = \frac{\text{net income} - \text{preferred dividends}}{\text{number of common shares}} \tag{14.14}$$

$$\text{Dividend pay-out ratio} = \frac{\text{dividend paid out to common stock}}{\text{net earnings} - \text{preferred dividends}} \tag{14.15}$$

Example 14.4

On the basis of the information for 1980, determine the liquidity, solvency, and profitability of the G. Fitzgerald Corporation, using the conventional measures.

Using the information on the balance sheet and the income statement in Tables 14.1 and 14.2, respectively, we get

$$\text{Current ratio} = \frac{600,000}{220,000} = 2.73$$

$$\text{Quick ratio} = \frac{600,000 - 290,000}{220,000} = 1.41$$

$$\text{Income-to-interest ratio} = \frac{210,000}{15,000} = 14$$

$$\text{Debt-to-equity ratio} = \frac{220,000 + 180,000}{600,000} = 0.67$$

$$\text{Return on sales} = \frac{105,000}{1,100,000} = 9.5\%$$

$$\text{Return on assets} = \frac{105,000}{1,000,000} = 10.5\%$$

$$\text{Earnings per common share} = \frac{105,000 - 5,000}{100,000} = \$1.00$$

$$\text{Dividend pay-out ratio} = \frac{35,000}{105,000 - 5,000} = 35\%$$

It can be concluded that the G. Fitzgerald Corporation is in a sound financial position. It has probably retained too much cash on hand that should be invested; it also has a tremendous capacity for expansion through borrowing. The firm is extremely profitable from the viewpoints of both the management and investors.

14.6   Auditors' Report

Before making a decision on the financial position of a firm from its financial statements, readers must satisfy themselves that the statements are reliable. What is to prevent a firm from unintentionally misrecording, or worse, intentionally falsifying the record of its transactions, thus giving a misleading impression of its strength?

The financial statements of most firms, except those of a small number of closely held firms, include a report from a team of independent certified public accountants who are not connected with the firm. Thus, the veracity of the records is attested to by an outside source.

Before rendering their opinion, accountants *audit* the firm in order to obtain "reasonable assurance" that the firm's records are reasonably accurate. The audit examination usually includes at least the following:

1. Checking the accuracy of the computations in the accounting records and the appropriateness of the accounting methods used
2. Verifying by inspection the physical existence and the company's ownership of the items listed under property, plant, equipment, and inventory, and making independent estimates of the value of such items
3. Confirming the amounts and condition of outside transactions with the outside sources involved, such as customers and bankers

After the team of accountants has formed an estimate of the reliability of the firm's financial statements and satisfied itself that the estimate is supported by its findings, it issues one of several types of opinions:

1. The unqualified opinion
2. The "subject to" qualified opinion
3. The "except for" qualified opinion
4. A disclaimer of opinion
5. An adverse opinion

The type of opinion rendered indicates the state of the firm's financial statements.

Although a typical auditors' report contains a preamble about "generally accepted auditing standards" and "generally accepted accounting principles," the heart of the report lies in the opinion. The most common type of opinion is the unqualified or "clean" opinion, which states that "In our opinion, the financial statements referred to above *present fairly* the financial position of XYZ Company as of ...". The unqualified opinion asserts the accuracy of the financial statements as presented by management but does not pass judgment on the results of operations, which is up to the reader. Thus, a set of financial statements showing losses from operations may have a clean opinion if these results are accurately reported.

If the auditors have less than full confidence in the accuracy and fairness of the financial statements, a qualifying phrase such as "subject to," or "except for" after the words "In our opinion" may be added. A "subject to" qualification is less serious because it refers only to uncertainty rather than inaccuracy in the firm's financial statements. Such an uncertainty might arise from a possible loss contingency such as a pending or ongoing lawsuit or adverse government ruling, where the probable amount of damage cannot be reasonably estimated or accounted for. The reader is thus placed on notice of a major contingency that might affect the financial position of the firm and make it less attractive than it appears in the financial statements. The "except for" qualification following "In our opinion" means that the financial statements are misleading in one or more major respects because of management accounting and reporting policies. A report with the "except for" opinion will both list the specific deficiencies in the financial statements and alert the reader to be suspicious of management's overall intentions.

Many companies, especially small, closely held companies will have outside accountants prepare their financial statements, without auditing the company, and issue a report. Such statements are considerably more reliable than those issued by the company alone, but considerably less reliable than audited statements. The auditors' report will contain a *disclaimer of opinion* which reads: "We *have not audited* the statements of XYZ Company and accordingly, do not express an opinion on them."

If the financial statements of a firm are totally misleading, the auditors' report will issue an adverse opinion which states: "In our opinion, the financial statements above *do not present fairly* the financial position of XYZ Company ... etc." Thus, the reader is warned not to place any trust in its financial statements.

14.7   Inflation Accounting

The effects of price level changes have caused difficulties in measuring and comparing the performance of business and industrial firms over the years. In periods of inflation, the net earnings in the financial statements may not be indicative of actual performance due to the increasing costs of replacing existing inventories and operating assets.

In an effort to help readers of financial reports to understand the effects of price level changes, the historical cost financial data are supplemented by the inflation-adjusted financial information. Two approaches to disclosing the effects of price level changes have been suggested by the Financial Accounting Standards Board (FASB).[2] The *constant dollar method* measures the effects of general inflation by restating certain historical cost financial data to the average dollar value for the year just ending by use of a suitable price index. The *current cost method* measures the effects of changes in specific prices by taking into consideration the differential price changes.

According to the theory prescribed by FASB no. 33, the effects of inflation are greatest on property, plant and equipment, and inventories. This result occurs because fixed assets and inventory tend to rise or fall in nominal value with the changes in price levels while maintaining relatively constant real values. In times of rising prices, the historical values recorded for such assets on the balance sheet tend to understate the monetary values. On the other hand, liquid assets such as cash, marketable securities, and receivables have constant nominal values on the balance but decline in real values due to the effects of inflation.

---

[2] American Institute of Certified Public Accountants, Financial Accounting Standards Board (FASB) Statement No. 33, "Financial Reporting and Changing Prices," New York: AICPA, 1979.

Although inflation affects balance sheet values, the effect of price level changes is greatest on the income statement because past costs are matched against current revenues. As a result, a number of companies have prepared inflation-adjusted income statements for the purpose of comparison with nonadjusted income statements. This recent practice reflects general concern that expenses in real terms are understated, and thus income is overstated on the traditional income statement.

Table 14.4 gives an example of comparative income statements (as reported and adjusted for changing prices) and shows why real income must be adjusted downward for the effects of inflation. As shown in the table, out-of-pocket expenses incurred currently, such as general administrative expenses, and interest expense are the same on both sets of statements. Expense for production (cost of goods sold) and depreciation, however, are higher under the inflation adjusted statement. This is because the cost of goods sold and depreciation are related to inventory and plant and equipment purchased in *previous years*. In order to reflect more accurately their current costs, these expenses (and their related assets) must be adjusted for price level changes to reflect the rise in value from the time of acquisition to the time of disposal.

The rising costs of maintaining productive capacity in inflationary periods lead to a reduction in real net income. However, even though pretax income on a constant dollar basis is lower compared to the historical dollar amount, the provision for income taxes is unchanged, thus increasing the firm's effective tax rate.

Table 14.4

Consolidated Income Statement
Adjusted for Changing Prices
Year Ended December 31, 1980

	As Reported (No Adjustment)	Adjusted for Changing Prices (In average 1980 dollars)
Revenues	$1,100,000	$1,100,000
Cost and expenses		
Production and operating	600,000	625,000
General and administrative	235,000	235,000
Depreciation	40,000	55,000
Interest expense, net	15,000	15,000
	890,000	930,000
Income before taxes	210,000	170,000
Taxes on income	105,000	105,000
Net income	$ 105,000	$ 65,000
Gain from decline in purchasing power of net amounts owed		$ 12,400

To offset or aggravate the results of real income decline, the firm may realize a holding gain or loss on balance sheet items. On the theoretical assumption that fixed assets and inventory values keep up with inflation, only the firm's monetary assets such as cash, securities, and receivables are exposed to decline in purchasing power due to inflation. This exposure is offset by monetary liabilities such as current liabilities and long-term debt that will be repaid in cheaper dollars. If these monetary liabilities exceed monetary assets, there will be a net holding gain; otherwise there will be a net holding loss. In the case of G. Fitzgerald Corporation in Table 14.4, the holding gain or loss can be estimated approximately from the information in the financial statements in Tables 14.1 and 14.2. Since monetary liabilities of $400,000 exceed monetary assets of $300,000 for the corporation, there will be a holding gain on the net liabilities of $100,000. The amount of holding gain is estimated approximately by multiplying the $100,000 net liability by the inflation rate for the year, which is assumed to be 12.4% as indicated by the Consumer Price Index for 1980. Thus, inflation affects a firm's income directly by reducing its value and a firm's financial structure indirectly by encouraging smaller holdings of assets and large holdings of debt.

14.8   Summary and Study Guide

The chapter presented an overview of the major determinants of the financial position of a firm as reflected periodically in its financial statements. The financial statements are contained in the annual report of a corporation, which includes the balance sheet, the income statement, the statement of changes in financial position, and the auditors' report. Each of these statements was explained in detail in order to offer some insights into the financial position of a firm as well as to provide a general background for the discussions in Chapters 15 and 16.

The possible implications of the financial statements of a firm that concern a prospective investor the most are liquidity, solvency, and profitability. An effective analysis of the financial position of a firm can be obtained by examining a set of measures related to such areas. We have therefore considered the definitions of the following quantitative measures: current ratio, quick ratio, income-to-interest ratio, return on sales, return on assets, earnings per common share, and dividend pay-out ratio.

The financial statements of most firms include an auditors' report indicating that the veracity of the records is attested to by an outside independent source. The significance of different types of opinions that may be expressed in the auditors' report has been explained.

Finally, we have considered briefly the effects of price level changes on the measurement and comparison of business and industrial firms over the years. An example has been given to illustrate the methods of disclosing such effects as suggested by the Financial Accounting Standards Board.

REFERENCES

14.1 Bernstein, L. A., *Financial Statement Analysis: Theory, Application and Interpretation*, rev. ed. Homewood, IL: Richard D. Irwin, 1978.

14.2 Chippindale, W., and P. L. Defliese (eds.), *Current Value Accounting: A Practical Guide For Business*. Englewood Cliffs, NJ: AMACOM (A Division of American Mangement Association), 1977.

14.3 Dearden, J., *Cost Accounting and Financial Control Systems*. Reading, MA: Addision-Wesley, 1973.

14.4 Horngren, C. T., *Accounting for Management Control: An Introduction*, 3rd ed., Englewood Cliffs, NJ: Prentice-Hall, 1974.

PROBLEMS

P14.1 From the balance sheet and the income statement of Company *A*, calculate the appropriate ratios in evaluating the company's liquidity, solvency, and profitability. Comment on these ratios and indicate what additional information you wish to have in order to render a better judgment.

P14.2 If the auditors' report for Company *A* was qualified by a "subject to" opinion regarding a contingency liability of $100,000 due to a pending lawsuit, how would this affect your evaluation of the company's prospects?

P14.3 From the balance sheet and the income statement of Company *B*, calculate the appropriate ratios in evaluating the company's liquidity, solvency, and profitability. Comment on these ratios and indicate what additional information you wish to have in order to render a better judgment.

P14.4 If the auditors' report for Company *B* was qualified by an "except for" opinion indicating a possible additional liability of $30,000 for taxes, how would this affect your evaluation of the company's prospects?

P14.5 From the balance sheet and the income statement of Company *C*, calculate the appropriate ratios in evaluating the company's liquidity, solvency, and profitability for the year ending December 31, 1982.

P14.6 Rework Problem P14.5 for the year ending December 31, 1981.

P14.7 From the financial statements of Company *C*, compute the sources of funds, uses of funds, and the changes in working capital for the year ending December 31, 1982.

P14.8 From the financial statements of Company *C*, compute the increase or decrease in each component of working capital for the year ending December 31, 1982.

Balance Sheet
Company A

December 31, 1982

ASSETS

Current assets

Cash	$ 10,000
Marketable securities	35,000
Accounts receivable	80,000
Inventories	75,000
Total	$200,000

Fixed assets

Land	20,000
Plant and equipment less accumulated depreciation (400,000 − 120,000) =	280,000
Total	$280,000

TOTAL ASSETS $500,000

LIABILITIES AND STOCKHOLDERS' EQUITY

Current liabilities

Accounts payable	$ 60,000
Wages payable	5,000
Dividends payable	10,000
Notes payable	15,000
Income taxes payable	15,000
Long-term debt, current	5,000
Total	$110,000

Long-term liabilities

Long-term debt, less current portion	60,000
Bonds payable	100,000
Total	$160,000

Stockholders' equity

Capital stock, $10 par value	30,000
Additional paid-in capital	20,000
Retained earnings	180,000
Total	$230,000

TOTAL LIABILITIES AND EQUITY $500,000

376

Income Statement
Company *A*

For year ending December 31, 1982

REVENUES

Sales and operating revenues	$850,000

COSTS AND EXPENSES

Cost of goods sold	450,000
Selling expenses	200,000
General and administrative expenses	90,000
Depreciation	30,000
Total	770,000

REVENUES LESS COSTS AND EXPENSES	80,000

OTHER DEDUCTIONS

Interest expense, net of interest income	20,000

INCOME AFTER TAXES	60,000
PROVISION FOR INCOME TAXES	30,000
NET INCOME AFTER TAX	30,000
CASH DIVIDENDS	10,000

RETAINED EARNINGS

Current year	20,000
Beginning of the year	160,000
End of the year	180,000

EARNINGS PER SHARE OF STOCK	$10.00

Balance Sheet
Company *B*

December 31, 1982

ASSETS

Current assets

Cash	$ 200,000	
Marketable securities	350,000	
Accounts receivable	940,000	
Inventories	850,000	
Total		2,340,000

Fixed assets

Land	360,000	
Buildings less accumulated depreciation (500,000 − 100,000) =	400,000	
Machinery less accumulated depreciation (700,000 − 200,000) =	500,000	
Total		1,260,000

TOTAL ASSETS	$3,600,000

LIABILITIES AND STOCKHOLDERS' EQUITY

Current liabilities

Accounts payable	$1,000,000	
Accrued taxes payable	50,000	
Notes payable, current	10,000	
Total		1,060,000

Long-term liabilities

Mortgage notes, net of current portion		100,000

Stockholders' equity

Common stock, $1 par value	400,000	
Retained earnings	2,040,000	
Total		2,440,000

TOTAL LIABILITIES AND EQUITY	$3,600,000

Income Statement
Company *B*

For year ending December 31, 1982

REVENUES

Sales and operating revenues	$6,500,000

COSTS AND EXPENSES

Cost of goods sold	3,000,000
Selling expenses	1,500,000
General and administrative expenses	950,000
Depreciation	40,000
Total	5,490,000

REVENUES LESS COSTS AND EXPENSES	1,010,000

OTHER DEDUCTIONS

Interest expense, net of interest income	10,000

INCOME AFTER TAXES	1,000,000
PROVISION FOR INCOME TAXES	500,000
NET INCOME AFTER TAX	500,000
CASH DIVIDENDS	0

RETAINED EARNINGS

Current year	500,000
Beginning of the year	1,540,000
End of the year	2,040,000

EARNINGS PER SHARE OF COMMON STOCK	$1.25

Balance Sheet
Company C

ASSETS

December 31	1982	1981
Current assets		
Cash	$ 15,000	$ 14,000
Marketable securities	36,000	30,000
Accounts receivable	82,000	60,000
Inventories	143,000	115,000
Total current assets	276,000	219,000
Fixed assets		
Land	48,000	46,000
Plant and equipment	360,000	360,000
Total cost of fixed assets	408,000	406,000
Less accumulated depreciation	84,000	54,000
Total cost net of depreciation	324,000	352,000
TOTAL ASSETS	$600,000	$571,000

LIABILITIES AND STOCKHOLDERS' EQUITY

December 31	1982	1981
Current liabilities		
Accounts payable	$ 90,000	$ 76,000
Wages payable	20,000	15,000
Taxes payable	25,000	20,000
Notes payable, current portion	15,000	15,000
Total current liabilities	150,000	126,000
Long-term liabilities		
Notes payable, net of current portion	150,000	160,000
Bonds payable	75,000	80,000
Total long-term liabilities	225,000	240,000
Stockholders' equity		
Common stock, $2 par value (40,000 shares)	80,000	80,000
Paid-in surplus	0	0
Retained earnings	145,000	125,000
Total stockholders' equity	225,000	205,000
TOTAL LIABILITIES AND EQUITY	$600,000	$571,000

Income Statement
Company C

For year ending December 31	1982	1981
REVENUES		
Sales and operation revenues	$1,000,000	$800,000
COSTS AND EXPENSES		
Cost of goods sold	700,000	500,000
Selling expenses	150,000	140,000
General and administrative expenses	60,000	50,000
Depreciation	30,000	40,000
Total	940,000	730,000
REVENUES LESS COSTS AND EXPENSES	60,000	70,000
OTHER DEDUCTIONS		
Interest expenses, less interest income	20,000	10,000
INCOME BEFORE TAXES	$40,000	$60,000
PROVISION FOR INCOME TAXES	20,000	30,000
NET INCOME AFTER TAX	$20,000	$30,000
RETAINED EARNINGS		
Current year	20,000	30,000
Beginning of the year	125,000	95,000
End of the year	$145,000	$125,000
EARNINGS PER SHARE COMMON STOCK	$0.50	$0.75

15

UNCERTAINTY
AND RISK

15.1 Decisions Under Uncertainty

In our discussion of capital investment up to this point, we have assumed that an investment can be represented by a unique stream of cash flows. In reality, the cash flow profile of an investment will be affected by future events, the outcomes of which are uncertain and cannot be controlled by the decision maker. Such events can be international or national in scope, or of an industrywide or local character. For example, the international political situation affects the price of oil, and the monetary and fiscal policies of the federal government affect the level of business activities. On the other hand, the steel and automobile industries are confronted with problems that are characteristic of the particular industry. At the level of a firm, a change of its management or a natural disaster may produce profound changes in the viability of the firm. No one can predict exactly in advance the outcome of any of these events, let alone every event that may be relevant to an investment decision.

Let us consider specifically a simplified situation. Suppose that two prospective investments of 1-year duration will produce net benefits a year later under different conditions of the economy as shown in Table 15.1, and the chance of having each of these conditions is equally likely. Which investment is more profitable?

Intuitively, we may attempt to find the average of the net benefits for each investment. Having found that the averages of the two investments are equal ($1,000 for each case), however, we are no closer to an answer because we are unlikely to be indifferent in accepting either one of the two investments in view of the difference in the spreads of the net benefit for the two cases. In other words, the dispersion of net benefits is smaller for the investment in household goods than that in recreational supplies under varying conditions of the economy. If the economy is expanding, the investment in recreational supplies is more profitable, but if the economy is contracting, the investment in recreational supplies produces a loss.

382

Table 15.1

Forecasts of Net Benefits

Condition of Economy	Net Benefits of Prospective Investments	
	Household Goods	Recreational Supplies
Expanding	$1,200	$2,050
Stable	$1,000	$1,000
Contracting	$ 800	−$ 50

Therefore, the uncertainty associated with the net benefit for the first investment is visibly smaller than that associated with the second one. Even if the degree of uncertainty can be determined for each case, the choice depends to a large extent on our attitude toward risk. There is empirical evidence to indicate that most investors are averse to risk, and they demand higher expected returns from more uncertain investments to compensate for the higher levels of risk.

Under the conditions of uncertainty, we can no longer simply ask which investment produces the maximum net benefit because other factors must also be considered. The criterion of profit maximization, which has been used to evaluate prospective investments when the cash flows are assumed to be unique and certain, is not necessarily applicable when the cash flows are uncertain. We shall therefore examine the basic concepts and measures related to uncertainty and risk in order to determine the conditions under which the criteria of maximizing expected profits are applicable, and to examine other factors which are pertinent. Because of the complexities of the underlying issues, we shall attempt to introduce the key ideas with a minimum amount of detail.

15.2   Expected Values and Variances

We shall first introduce mathematical descriptions of expected returns and the uncertainty associated with these returns on the basis of probability theory. We shall confine our discussion to the most elementary level since no prior knowledge of probability theory is assumed.

Let $x_1, x_2, \ldots, x_n$ be n mutually exclusive possible outcomes of an uncertain event X, and let $p_1, p_2, \ldots, p_n$ be the probabilities of their occurrence, respectively, such that

$$p_1 + p_2 + \cdots + p_n = 1.$$

The *expected value* of event X is denoted by $E[X] = \mu$ and is defined as

$$\mu = p_1 x_1 + p_2 x_2 + \cdots + p_n x_n \tag{15.1}$$

In order to see that $E[X] = \mu$ represents a forecast of an average, suppose that m observations of the event X have been recorded in the past, with values x'_1, $x'_2, \ldots, x'_m$. The average of these observations is given by

$$\mu = \frac{1}{m} (x'_1 + x'_2 + \cdots + x'_m)$$

Suppose that among these values, x_1 occurs m_1 times, x_2 occurs m_2 times, $\ldots$, and x_n occurs m_n times where n is the number of distinct observed values $x_1, x_2, \ldots, x_n$. Then, we can combine the common values to get

$$\bar{x} = \frac{1}{m} (m_1 x_1 + m_2 x_2 + \cdots + m_n x_n)$$

$$= \frac{m_1}{m} x_1 + \frac{m_2}{m} x_2 + \cdots + \frac{m_n}{m} x_n$$

If m is large, the relative frequencies m_1/m, m_2/m, $\ldots$, m_n/m approach the probabilities $p_1, p_2, \ldots, p_n$, respectively. Hence, the expected value of uncertain event X may be interpreted as the weighted average of the relative frequencies of the occurrence of the outcomes $x_1, x_2, \ldots, x_n$. The expected value μ is identical to the *mean* value of the outcomes.

The *variance* of an uncertain event X is defined as the expected value of the function $(X - \mu)^2$, whose possible outcomes are $(x_1 - \mu)^2$, $(x_2 - \mu)^2$, $\ldots$, and $(x_n - \mu)^2$ with probabilities of occurence $p_1, p_2, \ldots, p_n$, respectively. The variance of event X is denoted by $V[X] = \sigma^2$ which is numerically equal to

$$\begin{aligned}
\sigma^2 &= p_1 (x_1 - \mu)^2 + p_2 (x_2 - \mu)^2 + \cdots + p_n (x_n - \mu)^2 \\
&= p_1 (x_1^2 - 2x_1 \mu + \mu^2) + p_2 (x_2^2 - 2x_2 \mu + \mu^2) + \cdots + p_n (x_n^2 - 2x_n \mu + \mu^2) \\
&= (p_1 x_1^2 + p_2 x_2^2 + \cdots + p_n x_n^2) - 2\mu (p_1 x_1 + p_2 x_2 + \cdots + p_n x_n) \\
&\quad + \mu^2 (p_1 + p_2 + \cdots + p_n) \\
&= (p_1 x_1^2 + p_2 x_2^2 + \cdots + p_n x_n^2) - 2\mu^2 + \mu^2
\end{aligned}$$

Hence

$$\sigma^2 = \sum_{i=1}^{n} p_i x_i^2 - \mu^2 \tag{15.2}$$

Note that the variance of the uncertain event may be interpreted as the weighted average of $(x_1 - \mu)^2$, $(x_2 - \mu)^2$, $\ldots$, and $(x_n - \mu)^2$. The values $(x_1 - \mu)$, $(x_2 - \mu)$, $\ldots$, and $(x_n - \mu)$ represent the deviations of the possible outcomes $x_1, x_2, \ldots,$ and x_n from the expected value μ. Although the deviations may be positive or negative and thus cancel each other if they are added algebraically, the squares of these quantities are always positive and the sum of the squares is an indication of the magnitudes of the deviations. Consequently, the variance σ^2 is a measure of the dispersion of the outcomes but by no means the only measure of all the characteristics of uncertainty.

The quantity σ is referred to as the *standard deviation* and has the same unit as μ. Thus, it is a more convenient measure of the dispersion and its value is given by

$$\sigma = \sqrt{\sum_{i=1}^{n} p_i x_i^2 - \mu^2} \tag{15.3}$$

Since x_i can be expressed in any unit, but p_i is dimensionless, σ always has the same unit as μ. For example, if $x_1, x_2, \ldots,$ and x_n represent the predicted net benefits in dollars under different conditions of the economy, both μ and σ will be expressed in terms of dollars.

Another quantity for measuring dispersion is the *coefficient of variation* which is defined as

$$C = \frac{\sigma}{\mu} \tag{15.4}$$

This coefficient gives the variability of event X in dimensionless form and indicates the dispersion relative to the expected value.

Therefore, an uncertain event X with a number of possible outcomes is referred to as a *random variable*. The probabilistic description of a random variable X is defined by all possible outcomes $x_1, x_2, \ldots, x_n$ and the corresponding probabilities of their occurrence $p_1, p_2, \ldots, p_n$. The function $p_i = f(x_i)$, as schematically shown in Fig. 15.1, is called the probability distribution of X. When the outcomes of X represent a set of discrete values, X is said to be a *discrete random variable*, and the probability distribution of X is referred to as the *probability mass function* of X.

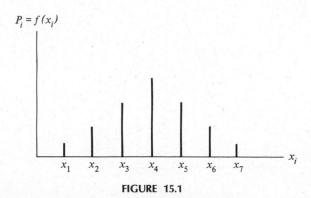

FIGURE 15.1

In some situations, X may be idealized as a *continuous random variable* which can assume all values of x within a specified interval. Then, the probability distribution of X can be represented by the function $p = f(x)$, which is referred to as the *probability density function*. The *normal probability distribution* shown in Fig. 15.2 is an example of a continuous probability distribution in which the ordinate $f(x)$ represents the *probability density* for a given value of x and the *probability* is defined only for an interval of x.

The normal distribution is characterized by a bell-shaped curve which is symmetical with respect to $x = \mu$ and has points of inflection at $x = \mu \pm \sigma$. Mathematically, it is represented by

$$f(x) = \frac{1}{\sqrt{2\pi}\sigma} \exp\left[-\frac{1}{2}\left(\frac{x - \mu}{\sigma}\right)^2 \right] \tag{15.5}$$

where exp is an exponential function of the natural base e of the logarithm, and x covers the range from $-\infty$ to $+\infty$. The probabilities of occurrence at intervals of σ are represented by the respective areas under the curve for such intervals. Hence, the probabilities that a normally distributed random variable X will have a value with σ, 2σ, or 3σ on either side of the expected value μ are approximately 68.3%, 95.5%, and 99.7%, respectively.

The expected value and the standard deviation are the two most important parameters describing the central tendency and the dispersion of a probability distribution, respectively. In comparing random variables with different expected values, the coefficients of variation of the variables indicate the relative dispersions of their probability distributions. We shall limit our discussion to these parameters.

In statistics, we often conduct observations on a small sample of outcomes of a random variable and make statistical inferences about its probability distribution as

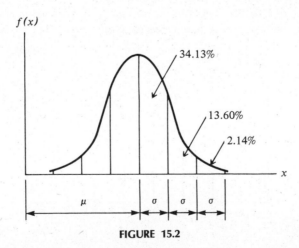

FIGURE 15.2

if we were able to observe all possible outcomes. We shall not consider the implications of statistical sampling. Hence, Eqs. (15.1) and (15.2) will be used for computing the expected value and the variance regardless of the number of observations. Then, the standard deviation and the coefficient of variation can also be computed from Eqs. (15.3) and (15.4) accordingly.

Example 15.1

Find the expected value and the standard deviation of each investment in Table 15.1 if the occurrence of each outcome is equally likely, i.e., $p_1 = p_2 = p_3 = \frac{1}{3}$.

For the investment in household goods, $x_1 = \$1,200$, $x_2 = \$1,000$, and $x_3 = \$800$. Hence

$$\mu = (\tfrac{1}{3})(1,200 + 1,000 + 800) = \$1,000$$

and

$$\sigma = \sqrt{(\tfrac{1}{3})[(1,200)^2 + (1,000)^2 + (800)^2] - (1,000)^2}$$
$$= \sqrt{26,667} = \$163$$

For the investment in recreational supplies, $x_1 = \$2,000$, $x_2 = \$1,050$, and $x_3 = -\$50$. Then

$$\mu = (\tfrac{1}{3})(2,050 + 1,000 - 50) = \$1,000$$

and

$$\sigma = \sqrt{(\tfrac{1}{3})[(2,050)^2 + (1,000)^2 + (-50)^2] - (1,000)^2}$$
$$= \sqrt{735,000} = \$857$$

It can be seen that while μ is identical for both cases, the value of σ for the second case is greater than that for the first case. Consequently, the uncertainty concerning the second investment is greater than that of the first.

15.3 Individual Attitudes Toward Uncertainty and Risk

The return from an investment under uncertainty may be regarded as a *random variable* with a number of possible outcomes whose probabilities of occurrence may be determined on the basis of historical observations or subjective judgment. The expected value of the return is a measure of its *expected profitability*, whether the return is expressed in a dollar amount or in an annual percentage rate. The dispersion of the return reflects the *degree of uncertainty* to the investor and is a measure of the *risk*, since the return of an investment proposal with a small standard deviation indicates a high degree of confidence in its outcome and a high standard deviation indicates otherwise. The coefficient of variation, which is the ratio of the standard deviation and the expected value of the probability distribution for the return, is a measure of the *variability* in dimensionless form.

Other things being equal, investors prefer higher returns to lower returns; they will attempt to reduce risk without reducing the expected returns. In the absence of special reasons, it would appear that investors will be better off in the long run if investment projects with positive expected returns are accepted. Actually, it cannot be stated that this will definitely be the case, but the probability that investors are better off increases as the number of projects accepted on this basis increases because the long-run average will approach the expected value.

However, the expected value cannot be applied universally as a decision criterion because of the difference of individual attitudes toward risk. Investors are known to have different degrees of propensity for or aversion to risk. A risk-averse investor will be unwilling to accept an investment with a positive expected return if the magnitude of possible loss is large or if the probability of any loss is large. This risk-averse attitude among most investors is evidenced by the large number of persons who are eager and willing to buy insurance to avoid the possibility of financial disaster.

Since the standard deviation is a measure of risk, it is desirable to reduce the magnitude of the risk through diversification. That is, instead of investing a sum of money in a single project, we may invest the same amount in a group of smaller projects whose returns are not affected by the return from any other project in the group. Because of risk sharing, the standard deviation of all of the projects in the group theoretically tends to decrease as the number of projects in the group is increased. In practical terms, it can be seen that if the returns from a group of projects are independent of each other, any adverse or beneficial effect to one of the projects generally will not affect the others. Thus, by undertaking a large number of independent projects of relatively small risk, the total expected return resulting from all the projects is fairly close to certainty since the variability of the outcomes is greatly reduced.

In general, it is useful to break down the risk from a group of projects undertaken by an organization into two components: *unsystematic* risk and *systematic* risk. The unsystematic risk refers to the risk that is caused by some unique and uncontrollable factors such as a technological breakthrough or a natural disaster which is independent of other projects and can be eliminated by diversification. The systematic risk refers to the risk that is still present after the elimination of unsystematic risk because the returns from different projects are correlated with one another to some extent and tend to fluctuate more or less in unison under the influence of environmental factors. Unsystematic risk and systematic risk are also referred to as *diversifiable* risk and *nondiversifiable* risk, respectively. The reduction

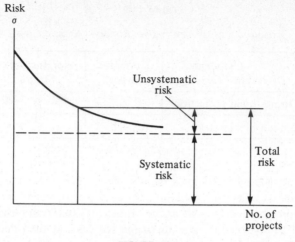

FIGURE 15.3

of unsystematic risk through diversification is shown schematically in Fig. 15.3. Thus, the individual preference for projects with different degrees of systematic risk reflects the decision maker's propensity for or the aversion to risk.

15.4 Expected Value Decision Criterion

Under conditions of uncertainty where the systematic risk is negligibly small and the unsystematic risk is well diversified, the criterion of maximizing the expected profit or net benefit is applicable. This criterion is based on the rationale that under such circumstances, the expected value of an investment project is a reasonable measure of the profit or net benefit over a large number of decisions.

Suppose that a government agency is considering building a number of break-water projects at different locations along the Gulf Coast as havens for small boats during hurricanes. Without a breakwater, the total damage at a particular location during a hurricane season is estimated to be D dollars if it is struck by hurricanes. With the protection of a breakwater, the total damage due to hurricanes is reduced to qD dollars where q is a fraction less than unity, i.e., $0 < q < 1$. If no hurricane occurs, then of course there is no loss, whether or not a breakwater is constructed. The initial cost of constructing a breakwater to provide the required protection is C_0 dollars and will be amortized to an equivalent uniform annual cost of C_u over its useful life of n years at a discount rate i. Hence $C_u = C_0(U \mid P, i, n)$. The problem confronting the government agency is to decide whether a breakwater should be built at this particular location.

The difficulty of this decision problem lies in the uncertainty of whether the

Table 15.2

Consequences of Alternative Actions (Annual Costs)

Decision〳Outcome	Hurricane Strikes	No Hurricane Strikes
Do not build protection	D	0
Build a breakwater	$C_u + qD$	C_u

location will be struck by hurricanes in any given year. The consequences of the alternative actions can be expressed in annual costs as shown in Table 15.2. In reaching a decision, the government agency must first determine the likelihood that this location will be struck during a hurricane season and then decide what action to take in the light of this likelihood.

Because the government agency has diversified the unsystematic risk through the construction of a large number of breakwater projects, and the systematic risk is negligibly small, the problem of uncertainty can be resolved through the prediction of the average results of all projects even though predicting the consequences of individual decisions is not possible. Since hurricanes in each season can be assumed to be independent events, the average annual cost incurred over the large number of projects will be approximately equal to the expected value if the statistical regularity of the hurricane strikes at various locations can be determined from historical data. Suppose that the probability of a particular location being struck by hurricanes in a season is p and the probability of no strike is $(1 - p)$. Furthermore, let the cost associated with a decision be denoted by a random variable X and the expected annual cost be denoted by $E[X]$. Then, the government agency should choose the alternative that will minimize the expected annual cost. The decision criterion based on the minimization of costs (or the maximization of net benefits) is referred to as the *expected value decision criterion*.[1]

The basic structure of a decision problem under uncertainty can be represented by a decision tree which is made up of nodes and branches. A typical decision tree includes three types of nodes: the decision nodes, the chance nodes, and the consequence nodes. At each decision node, the emerging branches represent the possible courses of action that can be selected by the decision maker. At each chance node, the emerging branches represent the chance outcomes that cannot be controlled by the decision maker. A consequence node is the end point of a sequence of branches representing a combination of a possible action and a chance outcome arranged in the proper chronological order. Although a decision tree can

---

[1] The theoretical basis for this criterion and its application is discussed in detail in Ref. [15.1], pp. 164–197.

be constructed for fairly complex problems, we shall confine our discussion to trees with a very simple structure.

A decision tree showing the combinations of actions and outcomes in deciding whether to construct a breakwater is shown in Fig. 15.4. The decision node is indicated by a square, the chance nodes are denoted by circles, and the consequence nodes are represented by the rectangular boxes which contain the annual costs resulting from various possible combinations of decisions and chances. The relative merits of the consequences from various combinations in Fig. 15.4 are identical to those shown in Table 15.2. The probability of occurrence or nonoccurrence of the hurricane strikes is also noted on the appropriate branch of the decision tree.

Then, according to the definition of expected values, the expected annual costs for the two alternatives in the decision tree can be computed as follows:

1. No protective action

$$E_1[X] = pD$$

2. Constructing a breakwater

$$E_2[X] = p(C_u + qD) + (1 - p)C_u = pqD + C_u$$

The relationship between p and $E[X]$ for these two alternatives is plotted in Fig. 15.5. It is apparent from the figure that if $p < \hat{p}$, $E_1[X] < E_2[X]$; and if $p > \hat{p}$, $E_1[X] > E_2[X]$. In other words, if $p < \hat{p}$, the construction of a breakwater is not

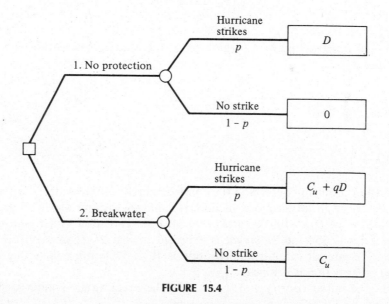

FIGURE 15.4

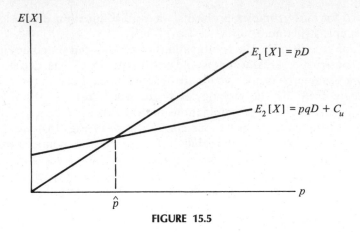

FIGURE 15.5

justified since the expected annual cost with no protective action is smaller; otherwise, it is justified. Since $\hat{p}$ is the value of p at the intersection of the two straight lines, we can find p by equating $E_1[X]$ and $E_2[X]$ as follows:

$$pD = pqD + C_u$$

Hence, the result becomes

$$\hat{p} = \frac{C_u}{D(1 - q)} \qquad (15.6)$$

Therefore, the construction of a breakwater at this particular location is economically justified if

$$p > \frac{C_u}{D(1 - q)}$$

Example 15.2

In the decision problem concerning the construction of a breakwater at a particular location described in this section, the annual damages without and with protection are estimated to be $D = \$100,000$ and $qD = \$40,000$. The initial construction cost of the breakwater is $54,446.50, which is expected to last 25 years with no salvage value, and the interest rate for amortization is 10%. Determine the value p above which the construction is justified.

Since the initial construction cost C_0 of the breakwater is amortized for 25 years at an interest rate of 10%, we have

$$C_u = C_0(U \mid P, 10\%, 25)$$
$$= (54,446.50)(0.1102) = 6,000$$

Also, $q = 40,000/100,000 = 0.4$. Then, from Eq. (15.6)

$$\hat{p} = \frac{6,000}{(100,000)(1 - 0.4)} = 0.1$$

Hence, the construction is justified if $p > 0.1$.

15.5 Regret or Opportunity Loss

Since a decision maker cannot predict exactly outcomes related to chance in advance, the decision based on the available information involving chance outcomes may turn out to be less than perfect when the decision is reconsidered in retrospect after the chance outcomes are unfolded. The *regret* or *opportunity loss* for each combination of action and outcome is defined as the difference between value of the consequence for that combination and the best that could have been achieved by considering all possible actions and the same outcome.

To illustrate this definition, let us consider the previous example concerning the construction of a breakwater for hurricane protection as represented by the decision tree in Fig. 15.4. Since the regret depends on the occurrence or nonoccurrence of hurricane strikes in retrospect, we shall first determine the best value that could have been achieved for each of the possible chance outcomes. Thus, if we can be certain before the decision that there will be hurricane strikes, the best action is to construct the breakwater and the cost corresponding to that action is C_u; on the other hand, if we are certain that there will be no hurricane strike, the best action is to provide no protection and the cost corresponding to that action is 0. Thus, the regret L for each combination of action and outcome can be determined as follows:

1. If no protection is provided and the hurricane strikes,

$$L = D - (C_u + qD) = D(1 - q) - C_u$$

   That is, this amount could have been saved if the decision maker had the foresight of knowing that the hurricane would strike.
2. If no protection is provided and there is no hurricane strike,

$$L = 0 - 0 = 0$$

   In this case, the decision maker has made the right choice with no regret.

3. If a breakwater is constructed and hurricanes strike,

$$L = (C_u + qD) - (C_u + qD) = 0$$

Again, the decision maker has made the right choice with no regret.

4. If a breakwater is constructed and no hurricane strikes,

$$L = C_u - 0 = C_u$$

In this case, the amount C_u could have been saved if it had been known in advance that there would be no hurricane strike.

Consequently, the regret or opportunity loss can be summarized in Table 15.3.

Note that the regret L is a random variable because it depends on the occurrence or nonoccurrence of hurricane strikes. That is, if no protection is provided,

$$L = \begin{cases} D(1-q) - C_u & \text{with probability } p \\ 0 & \text{with probability } (1-p) \end{cases}$$

and if a breakwater is constructed,

$$L = \begin{cases} 0 & \text{with probability } p \\ C_u & \text{with probability } (1-p) \end{cases}$$

The expected value of L is called the *cost of uncertainty* because it represents the long-run average cost which results from having less than perfect information. Thus, if there is no protection which will be justified for $0 \le p \le \hat{p}$, the expected value of L is given by

$$E[L] = [D(1-q) - C_u]p + (0)(1-p) = [D(1-q) - C_u]p \qquad (15.7a)$$

and if there is a protective breakwater which is justified for $\hat{p} \le p \le 1$,

$$E[L] = (0)(p) + C_u(1-p) = C_u(1-p) \qquad (15.7b)$$

Table 15.3

Regret or Opportunity Loss

Decision \ Outcome	Hurricane Strikes	No Hurricane Strikes
Do not build protection	$D(1-q) - C_u$	0
Build a breakwater	0	C_u

Example 15.3

Using the numerical data in Example 15.2, determine the regret and the cost of uncertainty for the decision problem concerning the construction of a breakwater for hurricane protection.

The regret L for each combination of action and outcome can be obtained as follows:

1. If no protection is provided $(0 \leq p \leq 0.1)$

$$L = \begin{cases} (100,000)(1 - 0.4) - 6,000 = 54,000 & \text{with probability } p \\ 0 & \text{with probability } (1 - p) \end{cases}$$

2. If a breakwater is constructed $(0.1 \leq p \leq 1)$

$$L = \begin{cases} 0 & \text{with probability } p \\ 6,000 & \text{with probability } (1 - p) \end{cases}$$

Hence, the cost of uncertainty can be obtained from Eqs. (15.7). That is, for $0 \leq p \leq 0.1$,

$$E[L] = 54,000p$$

and for $0.1 \leq p \leq 1$,

$$E[L] = 6,000(1 - p)$$

The decision tree is shown together with the regrets in Fig. 15.6.

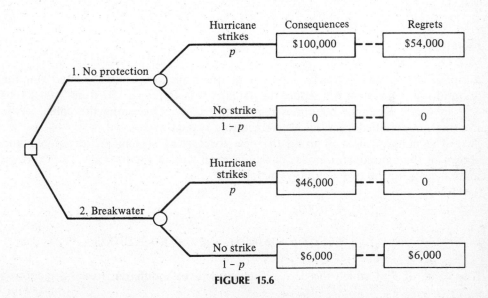

FIGURE 15.6

15.6   Value of Information for Reducing Uncertainty

The cost of uncertainty or expected regret provides a useful basis for evaluating the value of information developed to reduce uncertainty. Suppose that a new technology has been developed to provide a better forecast of hurricane strikes. If the cost of uncertainty can be reduced from $E[L]$ to $E'[L]$ because of the use of the new forecasting technology, then the average benefit derived from using the information in the long run can be expressed by the expected benefit $E[B]$ as follows:

$$E[B] = E[L] - E'[L] \qquad (15.8)$$

Suppose that the new technology can forecast exactly the locations of hurricane strikes several days in advance. Then the boats in the areas anticipating hurricane strikes can be removed to other havens where no strike will occur, and the cost of uncertainty or expected regret will be reduced to zero. Thus, for $E'[L] = 0$,

$$E[B] = E[L]$$

However, if the new technology can produce the same forecast only several hours in advance, then it is likely that only some of the damages can be avoided, and $E'[L]$ will be less than $E[L]$ but not equal to zero.

The expected benefit $E[B]$ is a useful measure against which a decision maker may judge the value of information to reduce uncertainty. A decision maker would be willing to pay for such information only if the cost does not exceed the expected benefit.

Example 15.4

Suppose that a new forecasting system of hurricane strikes is available and the adoption of this system will reduce the damage D in Example 15.2 from \$100,000 to \$50,000 while all other quantities remain the same. Determine the value of the information obtained from this new forecasting system.

The consequences of using the new forecasting system are computed and shown in the consequence nodes of the decision tree in Figure 15.7. The expected annual costs for the two alternative actions are

$$E_1[X] = 50,000p$$

$$E_2[X] = 26,000p + (6,000)(1 - p) = 6,000 + 20,000p$$

The value of $\hat{p}$ at which the decision maker will be indifferent to either action is

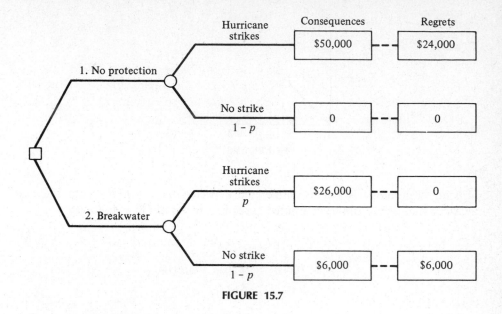

FIGURE 15.7

obtained from Eq. (15.6) as

$$\hat{p} = \frac{6,000}{(50,000)(1 - 0.4)} = 0.2$$

The regret L for each combination of action and outcome for using the new forecasting system can be obtained by using Eqs. (15.7). Thus, if there is no protection, which should be the case for $0 \leq p \leq 0.2$,

$$L = \begin{cases} 24,000 & \text{with probability } p \\ 0 & \text{with probability } (1 - p) \end{cases}$$

and if there is a protective breakwater, which would be for $0.2 \leq p \leq 1$,

$$L = \begin{cases} 0 & \text{with probability } p \\ 6,000 & \text{with probability } (1 - p) \end{cases}$$

Hence, the cost of uncertainty with the new forecasting system is reduced to

$$E'[L] = \begin{cases} 24,000p & \text{for } 0 \leq p \leq 0.2 \\ 6,000(1 - p) & \text{for } 0.2 \leq p \leq 1 \end{cases}$$

In view of the value of the cost of uncertainty in Example 15.3 when the new

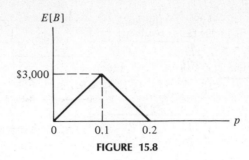

FIGURE 15.8

forecasting technology is not available, the expected benefit $E[B]$ from the new forecasting technology can be computed according to Eq. (15.8) as follows:

1. For $0 \le p \le 0.1$,

$$E[B] = 54,000p - 24,000p = 30,000p$$

2. For $0.1 \le p \le 0.2$,

$$E[B] = (6,000)(1 - p) - 24,000p = 6,000 - 30,000p$$

3. For $0.2 \le p \le 1$,

$$E[B] = (6,000)(1 - p) - (6,000)(1 - p) = 0$$

The relationship between $E[B]$ and p is shown in Fig. 15.8. It can be seen that the value of the information obtained from the new forecasting system is dependent upon p, which is a measure of the statistical regularity of the occurrence of hurricane strikes based on the historical record.

15.7 Risk Measurements in Capital Markets

The risk characteristics of a collection of financial assets may be examined in the context of expected returns. The collection of financial assets amassed by an investor is referred to as an *investment portfolio*. Investors who set prices in capital markets will take risky investments only if they are compensated for the risk they bear. Consequently, the greater the perceived risk, the higher must be the expected return. The collective action of investors in capital markets provides a standard in measuring the trade-off between expected return and risk.

For example, if an investor puts all his or her money in default-free government bonds, the expected return from the portfolio can be regarded as risk-free. On the other hand, if he or she puts the money in the stock of only one firm, the portfolio reflects both the expected return and risk associated with the stock of this firm. Generally, an investor chooses a variety of financial assets in the portfolio for the purpose of diversification.

The risk of a portfolio is measured by the standard deviation of its expected return. It is useful to break down the risk of a portfolio into *unsystematic* risk and *systematic* risk. Unsystematic risk is unique to a particular security and can be reduced by holding a large number of diversified securities. Systematic risk is related to the overall market risk caused by factors such as changes in the state of economy and energy prices, since most securities are affected by these factors to some degree. Since the unsystematic risk of a security can be reduced through diversification of the holdings in the portfolio, only the systematic risk is significant in the analysis of the risk characteristics of a security.

Suppose that an investor includes in her or his portfolio every common stock or its equivalent available in the market and that she or he buys the same proportion of each stock based on its current market value. Then the resulting portfolio will be a miniature of the capital market and is referred to as the *market portfolio*. For example, a portfolio which includes all of the stocks in the Standard and Poor's 500 stock average and in the same proportion is a close approximation of the market portfolio. Because of the diversification of the market portfolio, unsystematic risk has been reduced to a minimum and only systematic risk remains.

For a risk-free portfolio consisting entirely of default-free government bonds, there is no systematic risk associated with its expected return. For the market portfolio, the systematic risk associated with its expected return is measured by its standard deviation and is referred to as the *market risk*. The market risk is regarded as the standard against which the systematic risk of an individual security or portfolio is measured.

The systematic risk of a security can be compared to the systematic risk of the market portfolio by examining available historical data. For example, the rates of return based on Standard and Poor's 500 stock index versus those for a security over a large number of time periods may be plotted against each other as shown schematically in Fig. 15.9. Then, a theoretical line, referred to as the *regression line*, can be fitted to the scattered points by statistical techniques. The dispersion of the scattered points about the regression line is a measure of the unsystematic risk of the security. The intercept of the regression line with the vertical axis, denoted by α, is the average value of the rates of return of the security due to unsystematic risk over time and in theory tends to approach zero. The slope of the regression line, denoted by β, is called the *beta coefficient*, which represents the systematic risk of a security *relative to* that of the market portfolio. A value of $\beta = 1$ indicates that both have the same risk, $\beta > 1$ indicates that the security is riskier, and $\beta < 1$ indicates that it is less risky.

The type of stock with $\beta > 1$ is often referred to as an aggressive investment, and the type with $\beta < 1$ is called a defensive investment. Several financial organizations regularly publish beta values for actively traded stocks in the financial

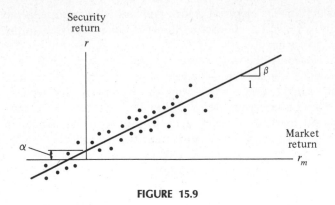

FIGURE 15.9

markets.[2] The beta coefficients of most stocks range from 0.7 to 1.4, although they may fall outside of this range for some stocks.

Although there is a tendency for stocks with large systematic risk to have large unsystematic risk, it is not always the case. It is possible for a stock with a high total risk to have a very high unsystematic risk but a relatively low systematic risk because the firm is engaged in some risky new ventures that are not closely tied to the overall economy. For example, the stock of a gold mining company may have a high unsystematic risk but a low systematic risk. The reverse is also true. The stock of an electronic components manufacturer may have a low unsystematic risk but a high systematic risk. If an individual stock is a part of a well-diversified portfolio, the unsystematic risk is unimportant and only the systematic risk need be considered in the return-risk trade-off.

15.8   The Capital Asset Pricing Model

Since securities can readily be exchanged in organized capital markets with relatively small transaction costs, there is clearly a criterion based on which values of the securities are evaluated by the financial community. Aside from short-run fluctuations of the prices of stocks and bonds which can be caused by a variety of factors, the value of a security is recognized and reflected by its market price in a long run. Given the risk-averse attitude of most investors in a competitive financial market, the price of a security reflects both its expected return and its risk.

The relationship between the expected return and the systematic risk of a security can be established by the *capital asset pricing model* (CAPM) which is based on simple economic principles.[3] The underlying theory is that assets with the same

---

[2] The beta and alpha values and their standard errors for actively traded stocks are published monthly in *Security Risk Evaluation* by Merrill Lynch, Pierce, Fenner, and Smith, Inc.
[3] This was developed during the mid 1960s simultaneously by several researchers. See Ref. [15.4] and Ref. [15.8] for their original contributions.

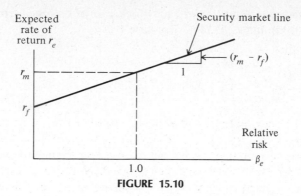

FIGURE 15.10

risk should have the same rate of return. Thus, the prices of assets in the capital markets should be adjusted until equivalent risk assets have identical expected returns. We shall not examine the theoretical basis of the CAPM but will only discuss briefly its practical implications.

The capital asset pricing model states that the expected rate of return on a portfolio should exceed the risk-free rate by an amount which is proportional to the beta coefficient of the portfolio. Supposing that an investor selects only a single security, the relationship between return and risk is given by

$$r_e = r_f + \beta_e(r_m - r_f) \tag{15.9}$$

where r_f = the risk-free rate of return
r_m = the expected rate of return on the market portfolio
r_e = the expected rate of return on a security
β_e = the beta coefficient for that security

The linear relationship between r_e and β_e in Eq. (15.9) is referred to as the *security market line*, which is graphically represented in Fig. 15.10. It is noted that $r_e = r_m$ for $\beta_e = 1$, and that $r_e > r_m$ for $\beta_e > 1$, and $r_e < r_m$ for $\beta_e < 1$. The factor $(r_m - r_f)$ represents the market's return-risk trade-off rate in determining the relative risk.

Example 15.5

The expected rate of return on U.S. Treasury bills is currently 10%, and the expected rate of return on the market portfolio is 14%. We are interested in following two stocks which have beta coefficients as indicated:

1. An airline stock with $\beta = 1.5$
2. A gold mining stock with $\beta = 0.5$

Determine the expected rate of return for each of these stocks.

The expected rate of return for each stock can be obtained from Eq. (15.9) by noting that $r_f = 10\%$ and $r_m = 14\%$. For case 1

$$r_e = 10\% + (1.5)(14\% - 10\%) = 16\%$$

For case 2

$$r_e = 10\% + (0.5)(14\% - 10\%) = 12\%$$

Since case 1 represents an aggressive stock with a high systematic risk, $r_e = 16\%$ is higher than that for the market portfolio. Conversely, because case 2 is a defensive stock with a low systematic risk, $r_e = 12\%$ is lower than that for the market portfolio.

15.9 Risk Premium

The expected rate of return r_e for a security in Eq. (15.9) may be interpreted as the sum of a risk-free rate r_f reflecting the time value of money and a risk component r_p representing an adjustment of the rate of return for the risk of the security. That is,

$$r_e = r_f + r_p \tag{15.10}$$

where r_e is referred to as the *risk-adjusted rate of return* for a security, and r_p is called the *risk premium*.

In comparing Eq. (15.10) with Eq. (15.9), it is obvious that the risk premium is given by

$$r_p = \beta_e(r_m - r_f) \tag{15.11}$$

The beta coefficient of the security in Eq. (15.11) represents the systematic risk of the company relative to the market risk. Since this coefficient generally depends on the financial leverage of the company's assets, i.e., the company's mix of equity and debt, it is referred to as the *levered beta* of the company. Thus, the beta coefficient β_e for the security of the company reflects both the operating risk of the type of business and the financial risk of the capital structure (as represented by the debt-to-equity ratio) of the company.

Since there are many types of debt instruments by which a company can borrow money, not all debt instruments are risk-free. Let β_a denote the beta of the firm's assets with all-equity financing to reflect operating risk only, and let β_d be the beta reflecting the risk of the debt instrument. Then, if there is no corporate income tax

$$\beta_a = \beta_e \left(\frac{E}{E + D}\right) + \beta_d \left(\frac{D}{E + D}\right) \tag{15.12}$$

where E and D are the market values of equity and debt of the company, respectively. Since the interest payment on debt is tax-deductible, Eq. (15.12) can be modified to include the effect of a tax rate of X as follows:

$$\beta_a = \beta_e \left[\frac{E}{E + D(1 - X)} \right] + \beta_d \left[\frac{D(1 - X)}{E + D(1 - X)} \right]$$

Simplifying, we get

$$\beta_a = \beta_e \left[\frac{1}{1 + (1 - X)D/E} \right] + \beta_d \left[\frac{(1 - X)D/E}{1 + (1 - X)D/E} \right] \qquad (15.13)$$

where D/E is the debt-to-equity ratio. The expected rates of return corresponding to β_d, β_e, and β_a are shown schematically in Fig. 15.11.

If the debt instruments can be assumed to be risk-free, e.g., U.S. Treasury bills, for which $\beta_d = 0$ and $r_d = r_f$. Then

$$\beta_a = \frac{\beta_e}{1 + (1 - X)D/E} \qquad (15.14)$$

or

$$\beta_e = \beta_a[1 + (1 - X)D/E] \qquad (15.15)$$

Generally, corporate debts are financed by bonds which are relatively risk free. Hence, Eqs. (15.14) and (15.15) instead of Eq. (15.13) are usually used to simplify the analysis. Thus, the risk premium r_p in Eq. (15.11) for a security can be broken into two components:

$$r_p = \beta_a(r_m - r_f) + \beta_c(r_m - r_f) \qquad (15.16)$$

where β_a is referred to as the *unlevered* beta and $\beta_c = \beta_e - \beta_a$ represents the beta

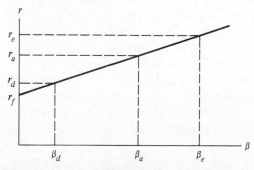

FIGURE 15.11

contributed by the financial risk resulting from D/E of the company. In the absence of debt, it is seen that $\beta_c = 0$ and $\beta_e = \beta_a$. The expected rate of return for a security which excludes the component of risk premium reflecting the financial risk is called the *unlevered* risk adjusted rate and is defined as

$$r_a = r_f + \beta_a(r_m - r_f) \tag{15.17}$$

Substituting Eq. (15.14) into this equation, we get

$$r_a = r_f + \frac{\beta_e(r_m - r_f)}{[1 + (1 - X)D/E]} \tag{15.18}$$

Example 15.6

The risk characteristic of the Kantaka Company which has a debt-to-equity ratio of 0.2 is reflected by a beta value of 1.1. The tax rate of the company is 50%. Determine the unlevered beta of this company.

Using Eq. (15.14), we obtain the unlevered beta of Kantaka Company as follows:

$$\beta_a = \frac{1.1}{[1 + (1 - 0.50)(0.2)]} = 1.0$$

15.10   Estimation of Expected Market Rates of Return

The capital asset pricing model provides the theoretical framework for the analysis of historical data on expected market rates of return. However, the use of historical information requires proper interpretation. The market rates of return for portfolios of common stocks, high-grade bonds, and other securities over long periods of time are available,[4] and the information pertinent to this discussion is cited in Table 15.4. The rates of return on common stocks include both dividends and market appreciation or depreciation (resulting in capital gain or loss). These rates are derived from returns with financial leverage because of the presence of debt in the capital structures of these firms.

The first column in Table 15.4 shows the average rates of annual returns over the period 1926–1976, and the second column shows the differential rates of common stocks relative to high-grade corporate bonds. Both the government bonds and Treasury bills are default-free and may be regarded as risk-free rates. However, the average rate on U.S. Treasury bills reflect more closely the short-term risk-free rate. High-grade corporate bonds are not default-free but they are considered less

---

[4] See Ref. [15.3], particularly p. 10.

Table 15.4

Rates of Return and Risk Premiums, 1926–1976

Category of Securities	Average Rate of Annual Returns	Differential Rates (Composite Stocks Relative to Others)
1. Common stocks	11.6%	—
2. Long-term corporate bonds	4.2%	7.4%
3. Long-term U.S. government bonds	3.5%	8.1%
4. U.S. Treasury bills	2.4%	9.2%

Source: Ibbotson, R., and R. Sinquefield, *Stocks, Bonds, Bills and Inflation: The Past (1926–1976) and the Future (1977–2000)*. Charlottesville, VA: Financial Analysts Research Foundation, 1977.

risky than common stocks because the holders of bonds have a prior claim on assets of a corporation before the stockholders.

The historical data in Table 15.4 cover a long period of time (1926–1976), during which deflation occurred in the 1930s and inflation was evident since the 1940s. Deflation and inflation offset each other to some extent but not completely, since there were more years with inflation than years with deflation. Therefore, the current risk rate r_f and the current expected rate of return on the market portfolio r_m in Eq. (15.9) must be based on current market data. However, the differential rate of composite stocks from risk-free assets $(r_m - r_f)$ may be assumed to be constant over a long period of time if the inflation components of r_f and r_m are regarded as being equal at any given time. As an approximate estimate, we take the average of the differential rate of common stocks to long-term government bonds and that of common stocks to U.S. Treasury bills, i.e., $(8.1\% + 9.2)/2 = 8.7\%$.

However, the historical risk premium based on levered returns is not necessarily a suitable standard for risk measurement because of the financial leverage. Therefore, the market risk premium based on the average value from unlevered returns is usually used as the market rate corresponding to the level of average risk. The downward adjustment of the market risk to account for the unlevered returns can be made by using Eq. (15.14), and the unlevered risk-adjusted rate can be obtained by Eq. (15.17) or (15.18). On the other hand, if the unlevered beta as well as the debt-to-equity ratio and the tax rate of a firm are known, its levered risk-adjusted rate can be obtained from Eq. (15.15).

Example 15.7

Suppose that the market risk-free rate r_f in 1980 is 12.2% and the differential rate of the market portfolio $(r_m - r_f)$ may be assumed to be 8.7% according to the historical data in Table 15.4. Determine the unlevered risk-adjusted rate of return for the Kantaka Company whose risk characteristics are given in Example 15.6.

Since the unlevered beta of the Kantaka Company has been found to be 1.0, the unlevered risk-adjusted rate of return of the company for 1980 is obtained by Eq. (15.17) as follows:

$$r_a = 12.2 + (1.0)(8.7) = 20.9\%$$

15.11 The Approximate Nature of the CAPM

Since the capital asset pricing model (CAPM) is based on a set of simplified assumptions, it is important to recognize the approximate nature of the quantities derived and/or estimated on the basis of the CAPM.

First of all, the systematic risk β of a security relative to that of the market portfolio is the value of the slope of the regression line which can best be fitted to the data points over a large number of time periods. Suppose that the points in Fig. 15.9 represent monthly data compiled over a period of 5 years. How would this beta value compare with another one obtained by using twice as many points over a period of 10 years? The answer depends on a number of factors. If a company is engaged in the same type of business with the same systematic risk (both operating and financial risks) over the 10-year period from which the data were taken, the beta value tends to be more reliable as the number of data points increases. On the other hand, if a company is engaged in one type of business using a specific capital structure in the first 5 years but suddenly changes its business risk characteristics and/or its capital structure in the second 5 years, then the data for the two periods should not even be mixed together. In other words, a beta value should be determined for each of the two 5-year periods to reflect different risk characteristics of the company during these two periods. What happens if the company changes its risk characteristics gradually by replacing its assets periodically? In that case, not only the beta value representing the slope of the regression line will change as new monthly data are added to replace the oldest ones, but the intercept of the regression line on the vertical axis also will not tend to be zero. This intercept, denoted by alpha (α), represents the rate of price appreciation of the security per time period of change, i.e., per month if the regression line is recomputed monthly. A positive alpha value indicates the rate of price appreciation earned by the holders of this security while the investors in the market portfolio receive no price appreciation at all. In general, a large alpha value indicates that the beta value of the company is unstable during the period.

Furthermore, different companies in the same industry have different capital structures. In order to compare the risk characteristics of various companies in an industry, we must first compute the *unlevered beta* for each company used for comparison. With some exceptions, which can often be explained by special circumstances, companies specializing in each type of business are found to have similar values of unlevered beta, which can be used to determine the relative systematic risk in operating each type of business. Generally, businesses with a high ratio of fixed costs to total production costs tend to have high systematic risk.

Finally, there are many types of debt instruments by which a company can borrow money. Not all of these debt instruments are risk-free, and their expected rates of return are different as indicated in Table 15.4. If the expected rate of return of Treasury bills is regarded as the risk-free rate r_f, then the expected rates of return for other types of debt instruments, such as high-grade corporate bonds, are expected to be higher than the risk-free rate. Consequently, the expected rate of return r_d from debt is related to the financial risk β_d of the particular debt instrument chosen, as shown in Fig. 15.11, which also shows the levered beta β_e and the unlevered beta β_a of a company. However, in the discussion of the capital structure of a company, we often speak of its debts in a general sense and treat all debts as risk-free for the sake of simplicity.

15.12   Application to the Evaluation of Capital Projects

Since the capital asset pricing model is based on a single-period investment, many attempts have been made to apply the methodology to long-lived capital assets.[5] It is possible to derive suitable formulas for the evaluation of capital investment projects on the basis of the CAPM, provided that further assumptions are introduced. We will not consider the mathematical derivations of these approaches but will only discuss their implications on the evaluation criteria.

In a world of certainty with perfect capital markets, the criteria for evaluating investment projects are well understood. In a world of uncertainty, it is plausible enough to replace the known cash flows with expected cash flows and to add a risk premium to the discount rate, but these modificatons lack vigorous support. Since time and risk are logically separate variables, two possible approaches have been suggested.

If the uncertainty is realistically tied to a constant rate over time only, then the risk-adjusted rate of return r_a for an all-equity financed project can be used as the discount rate to take into account the effects of time and operating risk on the present value of a stream of uncertain returns. Let Y_t (for $t = 0, 1, 2, \ldots, n$) be a stream of expected cash flows of an investment; then

$$[\text{NPV}]_{r_a} = Y_0 + \frac{Y_1}{1 + r_a} + \frac{Y_2}{(1 + r_a)^2} + \cdots + \frac{Y_n}{(1 + r_a)^n} \tag{15.19}$$

In this approach, it is assumed that our estimates of cash flows become progres-

[5] See Ref. [15.6] and Ref. [15.7] for detailed discussions.

sively more uncertain as we look further into the future. Since we have no other knowledge about the uncertainty, this approach is reasonable although its outlook is conservative.

However, there are many situations in which the uncertainty of events is not related to the passage of time at a constant rate. Then, an attempt may be made to determine the "certainty equivalent" of the cash flow at each period according to situations known to the decision maker. The idea is that at a given period t, the decision maker is willing to exchange an uncertain return with several possible outcomes for a certain return of $a_t Y_t$ where a_t is a factor less than one. If we know how to determine a_t (for $t = 1, 2, \ldots, n$), then we can essentially remove the uncertainty and use the risk-free rate for discounting. That is,[6]

$$[\text{NPV}]_{r_f} = Y_0 + \frac{a_1 Y_1}{1 + r_f} + \frac{a_2 Y_2}{(1 + r_f)^2} + \cdots + \frac{a_n Y_n}{(1 + r_f)^n} \qquad (15.20)$$

The difficulty in using this approach is that the factors a_t (for $t = 1, 2, \ldots, n$) cannot be determined easily except for relatively simple situations.

If some of the assumptions of the capital asset pricing model do not hold, the total risk of a firm may be important in the evaluation of investment proposals. For example, the probability that a firm will become insolvent depends on the total risk, not just the systematic risk. When the costs of insolvency and bankruptcy are insignificant, it is important to consider the effects of new investment proposals on the total risk of the firm. Therefore, in evaluating risky investment proposals, it is only prudent to check their effects on the total risk of the firm. Some aspects of this problem will be examined in the next chapter.

15.13   Summary and Study Guide

In this chapter, we have discussed the concepts of uncertainty and risk and how they affect investment decisions. We have introduced a bare minimum of terms in probability and statistics and have avoided the mathematical proofs of various methods and procedures in dealing with uncertainty and risk. However, we have placed great emphasis on the development of useful insights through the logical presentation of topics leading to the resolution of the dilemma of uncertainty and risk confronting a decision maker.

We have examined individual attitudes toward uncertainty and risk, and possible actions to be taken so that the unsystematic risk is diversified while only the

---

[6] The concept of a certainty equivalent has not been discussed in detail since it requires the consideration of individual situations, particularly in the evaluation of long-lived assets. In Ref. [15.2], it is argued that the CAPM implies untenable estimates of the rates of return on assets which are risk-free or virtually so, and thus the best and safest method to formulate the risk-return trade-off is to estimate it empirically over the class of assets and the period of interest.

systematic risk remains. We introduced the use of the decision tree and the expected value decision criterion where applicable. We discussed the meaning of regret or opportunity loss under uncertainty and the value of information for reducing uncertainty.

Then, we turned to the risk measurements in capital markets because they are of great importance in laying the groundwork for determining the minimum attractive rate of return in project evaluation. We introduced the capital asset pricing model (CAPM) for assessing systematic risk and examined the risk premium for both operating risk and financial risk. Using CAPM as a theoretical framework, we considered the estimation of expected market rates of returns of securities of companies and the various problems associated with the estimation because of the approximate nature of the CAPM. Finally, we considered the application of the idea of the CAPM and the "certainty equivalent" approach to the evaluation of capital projects.

REFERENCES

15.1 Au, T., R. M. Shane, and L. A. Hoel, *Fundamentals of Systems Engineering, Probabilistic Models.* Reading, MA: Addison-Wesley, 1972, pp. 164–197.

15.2 Blume, M. E., and I. Friend, "A New Look at the Capital Asset Pricing Model," *Journal of Finance,* **28** (March 1973), 19–33.

15.3 Ibbotson, R. G., and R. A. Sinquefield, *Stocks, Bonds, Bills, and Inflation: The Past (1926–1976) and the Future (1977–2000).* Charlottesville, VA: Financial Analysts' Research Foundation, 1977.

15.4 Lintner, J., "The Evaluation of Risk Assets and the Selection of Risky Investments in Stock Portfolios and Capital Budgets," *Review of Economics and Statistics,* **47** (February 1965), 13–77.

15.5 Modigliani, F., and G. A. Pogue, "An Introduction to Risk and Return," *Financial Analysts' Journal,* **30** (March–April 1974), 68–80 and (May–June 1974), 69–86.

15.6 Myers, S. C., and S. M. Turnbull, "Capital Budgeting and the Capital Asset Pricing Model: Good News and Bad News," *Journal of Finance,* **32,** (May 1977), 321–333.

15.7 Robichek, A. A., and S. C. Myers, "Conceptual Problems in the Use of Risk Adjusted Discount Rates," *Journal of Finance,* **21** (1966), 727–730.

15.8 Sharpe, W. F., "Capital Asset Prices: A Theory of Market Equilibrium under Conditions of Risk," *Journal of Finance,* **19** (1964), 425–442.

PROBLEMS

P15.1 Suppose that four possible outcomes of the uncertain return to an investment are $5,000, $6,000, $7,000 and $9,000, with the probabilities of their occurrence being 0.2, 0.3, 0.3, and 0.2, respectively. Determine the expected value and the standard deviation of the return.

P15.2 The possible damages to an area due to seasonal flooding are estimated to be $8,000, $4,000, and $3,000 with probabilities of 0.2, 0.3, and 0.5, respectively. Find the expected value and the standard deviation of the damage.

P15.3 A contractor having a sizable capital, equipment, and labor force is confronted with the decision whether it should submit a bid for a new construction project. In order to have a chance of getting the contract for this project, it must submit a detailed bid document which costs C_1 dollars. If it submits a bid and wins the contract, it will make a net profit of C_2 after deducting the bid cost as well as other costs. If it submits a bid and loses the contract, it will suffer a loss by incurring the bidding cost. On the other hand, if it makes no attempt to bid for the contract, it will neither gain a profit nor incur a loss. Construct a decision tree for this situation.

P15.4 A stretch of the parkway in the downtown area of a city is located on a flood plain. Each spring, there is the possibility that a flood may force the closing of the parkway for several days, and the costs of inconvenience to the travelers are estimated to be $100,000 when it occurs. If a protective wall is built, the probability of flooding for this stretch of parkway is reduced from 0.4 to 0.1, and the costs will also be reduced to $60,000 because a smaller area will be involved. The amortized uniform annual cost for building the protective wall is $10,000. Draw the decision tree for this situation and determine whether the protective wall should be build on the basis of the expected value criterion.

P15.5 A contractor specializing in the construction of highway bridges is confronted repeatedly with the problem of building a cofferdam for the protection of the working space at sites for bridge piers at river crossings. If it builds a very high cofferdam at an amortized uniform annual cost of $5,000, it is certain that there will be no possibility of flooding during the construction period. If it builds a low cofferdam at an amortized uniform annual cost of $4,000, flooding may occur with a probabililty p; and the total annual cost including the original construction and the restoration of the damaged site to working conditions due to flooding is $14,000.

(a) Using an expected value decision criterion, determine the probability p such that the contractor will be indifferent between building a high cofferdam and a low cofferdam.

(b) If perfect information about floods is available before the construction of each cofferdam so that the state of flooding for the low cofferdam can be ascertained in advance, what is the expected value of the benefit of this information?

P15.6 If the expected rate of return on U.S. Treasury bills is currently 12.2% and the expected rate of return on the market portfolio is 18%, determine the expected rate of a security which has a beta coefficient of 1.2.

P15.7 The security of Alfred Corporation has a beta coefficient of 1.2 which reflects a debt-to-equity ratio of 0.4. The tax rate of the company is 46%. Suppose the market risk-free rate r_f is 8% and the differential rate of the market portfolio and the risk-free bonds $(r_m - r_f)$ is 8.7%. Determine the unlevered beta and the unlevered risk-adjusted rate of return of the company.

P15.8 The Benjamin Company has a debt-to-equity ratio of 0.25 and has a company beta value of 1.15 according to the latest published reports. The market risk-free rate is 12%, and the differential rate of the market portfolio and the risk-free securities $(r_m - r_f)$ is 8.7%. Assuming perfect capital markets and a tax rate of 50% for the company, determine the expected rate of return on the stock of this levered firm and its unlevered risk-adjusted rate of return.

CHAPTER

16

CAPITAL INVESTMENT
DECISIONS IN
PRIVATE FIRMS

16.1 Impact of Capital Investment Projects on a Firm

So far we have devoted most of our efforts to the evaluation of investment projects without paying much attention to the impact of these projects to a firm. It is tacitly assumed that if a project is economically worthwhile, it will contribute to the long-range objectives of the firm. Actually, the acceptance of a project may change both the risk characteristics and the financial structure of the firm, either favorably or adversely. From the standpoint of the stockholders of a firm, the crucial question for accepting a proposed project is whether the project, as financed, will increase the market value of shares of the firm to the maximum extent possible, given the available investment opportunities.

It is impossible to address this question fully without considering some very complex and sometimes still unresolved issues in finance. For example, what should be the minimum attractive rate of return specified for an investment project? How are we going to treat projects that have different levels of risk? How do the financial policies change the risk characteristics of a firm? The detailed discussion of such topics rightfully belongs to a separate course in financial management. However, it is possible to consider some aspects of these basic issues in order to understand fully the criterion for accepting or rejecting an investment project which is consistent with the objective of maximizing the value of a firm. We shall therefore consider the pertinent issues in general terms in order to highlight the basic principles often used to guide the actions of decision makers.

16.2 Market Valuation of a Firm

The market value of a firm is represented by the package consisting of its assets, liabilities, and stockholders' equity. When a firm accepts a new investment project,

412

new value is created by the net benefit resulting from the higher value of goods and services produced by the investment over the cost of producing them. The new investment may be financed by using available working capital, by issuing new stock, or by incurring new debt. Hence, the acceptance of an investment project and its concomitant financing plan changes the value of the firm, and this change will be reflected in the market price of the firm over the long run when it is recognized by the investors.

We can look at the market value of a firm as if we were looking at both sides of the balance sheet of the firm. This is purely an analogy since the book value in accounting is different from the market value of the firm. However, such an analogy is desirable in order to examine some of the most important issues in corporate finance. On the left-hand side of the balance sheet is a collection of assets from which the value of the firm can be determined, regardless of the nature of the claims against it. On the right-hand side is a mix of debt and equity which represents the capital structure of the firm and the claims of its debtholders and stockholders.

Let us first consider the market value of the firm from its assets without worrying about where the money for acquiring these assets comes from. Then, the market value of a firm can be represented by the net present value of a stream of expected cash flows which may be negative or positive over the planning horizon of the firm. The net present value of the firm can also be obtained by summing up the net present values of the expected cash flow profiles of all ongoing projects over the same planning horizon, plus the present value of intangible assets if applicable. Intangible assets may include items such as patent rights or well-recognized management talents which are sought after in the market for a price. A new investment project is profitable if its expected cash flow profile will increase the net present value of the firm. The most critical questions in determining the market value of a firm from its assets are (1) what discount rate should be used if the NPV is computed directly from the stream of the expected cash flows of the firm, and (2) should different discount rates be used for different projects if the NPV is obtained by the superposition of the net present values of the expected cash flow profiles of all ongoing projects in the firm. The key to these answers clearly lies in knowing the systematic risks of the projects undertaken by the firms.

On the other hand, the stream of expected cash flows of a firm may be thought of as being split into two streams on the basis of debt and equity. Thus, the stream of expected cash flows for debt will be claimed by the debtholders, and the stream for equity will be claimed by the stockholders. By borrowing money, a firm can acquire more assets and thus increase its value. Since the debtholders have the first claim to the assets in case of financial distress, the expected rate of return to the debtholders is smaller than that for the shareholders because of the difference in their risks. In addition, the interest payment on debt is tax-deductible, an advantage resulting from debt financing that is referred to as the *tax shield*. Thus, the expected rate of return for the stockholders increases as the firm borrows more money to acquire profitable assets, provided that the firm does not encounter any costly financial distress which will negate the increase in profit from operation. Consequently, there appear to be significant interactions between corporate finance and investment decisions because the acceptance of an investment project and its concomitant financing plan generally will change the financial structure of a firm. The crucial question is whether an optimum debt-to-equity ratio exists that will maximize the market value of the firm.

Before answering these questions in practical terms, let us first consider a theoretical framework which provides an insight to some important issues in corporate finance and investment.

16.3   The MM Model of Corporate Finance and Investment

Based on the assumption of perfect capital markets, Modigliani and Miller[1] derived two basic propositions with respect to the valuation of the securities of companies with different capital structures, and their theory is often referred to as the *MM model*. In spite of their assumptions which cause some discrepancies between the theory and real-world observations, it is important to understand the conditions under which the MM model is valid so that we know what to expect under different conditions of market imperfections.

Proposition I of the MM model states that *the market value of a firm is independent of its capital structure and is given by the expected return from its assets at a rate* r_a *appropriate to its risk class*. This proposition allows the complete separation of the capital investment decision and the use of financial leverage. In the MM model, the firms are divided into "equivalent return classes" with similar operating characteristics, meaning that firms having similar unlevered relative systematic risks belong to the same risk class. As long as the rate of return r_a used to compute the net present value of the assets of a firm corresponds to that of other firms belonging to the same risk class, then we can ignore the financing decisions because no single combination of debt and equity is better than any other combination. If the MM model's proposition I holds, the simplest financing plan is to use all-equity financing. Hence, the market value of the firm can be determined by the net present value of the stream of cash flows from operations using the firm's assets.

With the hindsight of the capital asset pricing model (CAPM), it is easy to understand why firms belonging to the different risk classes would have different expected rates of return in capital markets. Therefore, we shall defer the discussion of the selection of the appropriate rate in capitalizing the expected return of a firm until a later section. At present, we shall concentrate on the discussion of the conditions under which the market value of any firm is independent of its capital structure.

[1] See Ref. [16.5] and Ref. [16.6] for the original presentation of the theory.

Although borrowing by a firm increases the expected rate of return on share-holders' investment, it also increases the firm's risk. The MM model postulates that the increase in the expected return by holding shares of a levered firm is offset exactly by the increase in its financial risk. In perfect capital markets, an investor can borrow as freely and at the same rate as a firm. Therefore, if an investor wishes to assume a higher risk through financial leverage in order to get a higher expected return, she or he can obtain a personal loan and buy more shares of an unlevered firm to achieve the same result since the expected return of an unlevered firm is lower than that of a levered firm in the same risk class. Thus, it makes no difference whether the investor assumes the financial risk indirectly by holding the shares of a levered firm or directly by obtaining a personal loan to buy more shares of an unlevered firm. However, because of market imperfections, it has been argued that personal borrowing may be more costly or inconvenient for some investors than corporate borrowing; consequently, the stockholders will be better off if firms use financial leverage to increase their expected returns. Except for isolated instances of market imperfections which have placed small investors at a disadvantage, there is no substantial evidence to indicate that the terms for corporate borrowing are generally more favorable than those for personal borrowing. Hence, the effects of market imperfections on investment decisions can indeed be considered separately from the financing decisions.

Proposition II of the MM model states that the *expected rate of return* r_e *on the stock of a levered firm is equal to the expected rate of return* r_a *on a firm's assets corresponding to the firm's risk class with all-equity financing, plus a financial risk premium equal to the debt-to-equity ratio times the spread between* r_a *and* r_d, *where* r_d *is the expected rate of return on debt.* That is,

$$r_e = r_a + \frac{D}{E}(r_a - r_d) \tag{16.1}$$

where D and E are market values of debt and equity, respectively. The above equation is based on the assumption of no tax as well as the assumption of perfect capital markets. This proposition indicates that the expected rate of return on the stock of a levered firm increases in proportion to the debt-to-equity ratio, as shown in Fig. 16.1.

Solving for r_a from Eq. (16.1), the expected return on a firm's assets with all-equity financing is seen to be

$$r_a = \frac{E}{D+E}r_e + \frac{D}{D+E}r_d \tag{16.2}$$

If an investor's portfolio consists of all of a firm's stock and debt, he or she is entitled to all of the firm's operating income generated by its assets. Then, the expected return on the portfolio is equal to the weighted average of the expected

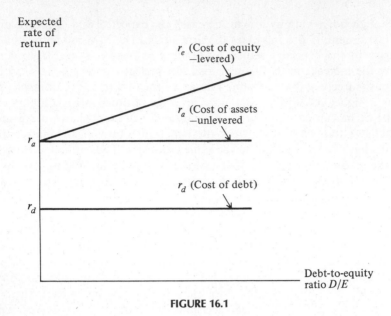

FIGURE 16.1

rate of return on its stock r_e and the expected rate of return on its debt, with the proportions of equity and debt respectively as weights. Consequently, r_a is sometimes referred to as the *weighted average cost of capital.*

The MM model does include a provision to account for tax shields which are related to the "target proportion of debt" of a firm. If the tax rate of the firm is X and the target proportion of the debt L is expressed as the ratio of the firm's debt D to its total assets $(E + D)$, i.e., $L = D/(E + D)$, then the expected rate of return on the firm's assets including its financial leverage and tax shields is given by

$$r_0 = r_a(1 - XL) = r_a\left[1 - \frac{X(D/E)}{1 + D/E}\right] \qquad (16.3)$$

The expected rate of return r_0 is referred to as the *adjusted cost of capital of a firm.* If $X = 0$, then of course $r_0 = r_a$. If $D/E = 0$, then from Eq. (16.1), $r_e = r_a$ also. Because of federal taxation on personal incomes of investors as well as on corporate incomes, the significance of tax shields to investors is still an unsettled question.[2] Nevertheless, the tax shields of a levered firm may be regarded as a government subsidy to the firm for the use of debt financing since debtholders are paid from the before-tax operating income and stockholders are paid from the after-tax operating income. Thus, within a safe debt-to-equity ratio which does not cause financial distress to a

_____

[2] See Ref. [16.3] and Ref. [16.4] for detailed discussions on dividend policies and taxes.

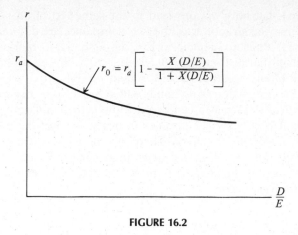

$$r_0 = r_a\left[1 - \frac{X\,(D/E)}{1 + X(D/E)}\right]$$

FIGURE 16.2

firm, the greater the debt-to-equity ratio, the lower the adjusted cost of capital of a firm, as indicated by Eq. (16.3). This relationship is shown schematically in Fig. 16.2.

It should be emphasized that the MM model is conceptually significant because it captures the major determinants of the opportunity cost of the capital of a firm. However, because of the assumptions used in its derivation, the model is not perfect because the conditions of the real world differ from the assumptions of the model.

Example 16.1

Company A, which has a market value of $50,000 for its equity and no debt, is expected to yield a rate of return of 20%. Company B, which has a market value of $40,000 for its equity and $10,000 for its debt, is expected to yield a rate of return of 22%. In a perfect capital market, the borrowing rate is 12% and there is no tax on the return. Suppose that you have $5,000 and are considering one of the following two options: (a) buy 10% of the stock of Company A, and (b) buy 10% of the stock and 10% of the bonds (a debt instrument) of Company B. Which option is better?

If you buy 10% of the stock of Company A as represented by its equity of $50,000, which has a market rate of return of 20%, your return from the stock is

$$(0.10)(50,000)(0.20) = \$1,000$$

If you buy 10% of both the stock and the bonds of Company B, your return is

From stock: $(0.10)(40,000)(0.22) = \$880$
From bonds: $(0.10)(10,000)(0.12) = \$120$
Total return: $880 + 120 = \$1,000$

It can be seen that both options lead to the same return on your investment, even though the financial structures of the two companies are different. Since Company *A* is unlevered, it has no financial risk. Consequently, its market rate of return of 20% is lower than that of Company *B*, which is 22%. If you do not want to take the additional risk of buying the stock of Company *B* only, you can protect yourself by buying a suitable proportion of its bonds which has a lower risk and also a lower market rate of return. In fact, you can invest $1,000 (10% of Company *B*'s debt) in any debt instrument which pays 12% return in order to offset the additional risk of investing $4,000 in Company *B*'s stock. Therefore, an investor can exercise the same method to accomplish what a firm can do in increasing or decreasing the financial leverage and its associated financial risk, provided that he or she can borrow freely and on the same terms as a firm.

Example 16.2

Determine the expected rate of return r_a for a firm under all-equity financing which has the same operating risk as Company *B* in Example 16.1.

For $D = \$10,000$, $E = \$40,000$, $r_d = 12\%$, and $r_e = 22\%$, we obtain from Eq. (16.12)

$$r_a = \frac{40,000}{50,000}(22\%) + \frac{10,000}{50,000}(12\%) = 20\%$$

It can be seen that Company *B* has the same operating risk as Company *A* in Example 16.1 since $r_a = 20\%$ for both companies.

16.4 Interactions of Investment and Financing Decisions

After examining the MM model which provides a theoretical framework for our subsequent discussions, we shall first examine the effects of financial leverage on the valuation of a firm in a world with market imperfections and corporate taxes. Since we do not intend to dwell on many issues in corporate finance, for which even financial experts do not have complete answers or often disagree, we shall only attempt to gain some understanding of the problems that are ultimately related to the economic evaluation of investment projects.

Proposition I of the MM model allows the complete separation of the valuation of the assets of a firm from its financial structure. To simplify the illustration further, suppose that a firm holds capital assets, all of which have the same operating risk. Under the capital asset pricing model discussed in Chapter 15, we can determine the expected market rate of return r_a for an unlevered firm having the

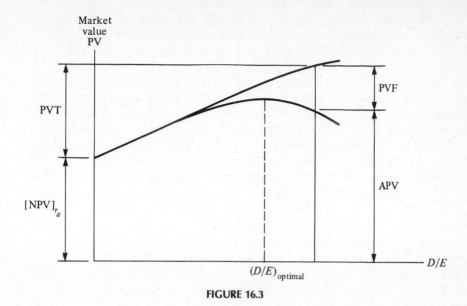

FIGURE 16.3

same unlevered risk β_a as this firm. In order to attract investors, the expected rate of return on the firm's assets with all-equity financing must be at least as high as r_a. Thus, the net present value of a stream of the after-tax cash flows from the operating income can be discounted at r_a if the firm is all-equity financed. However, the value of the firm increases through the use of the financial leverage because of the advantages of tax shields which increase linearly with the debt-to-equity ratio for a time but slow down as the cost of borrowing becomes greater. Furthermore, the possibility of financial distress increases as the debt-to-equity ratio approaches a certain limit. Thus, the "conventional wisdom" seems to indicate that there is an optimal debt-to-equity ratio at which the market value of a firm is maximum as indicated in Fig. 16.3.

The market value of a firm under the conditions of market imperfections and corporate taxes may therefore be represented by the adjusted net present value as follows:[3]

$$\text{APV} = [\text{NPV}]_{r_a} + \text{PVT} - \text{PVF} \tag{16.4}$$

where APV = adjusted net present value of a firm taking into account tax shields and costs of possible financial transactions
$[\text{NPV}]_{r_a}$ = net present value of a stream of after-tax cash flows discounted at the unlevered risk-adjusted rate of return r_a

[3] This approach was first suggested in Ref. [16.7] and further expanded in Ref. [16.2].

PVT = the present value of tax shields and other possible advantages of financing arrangement such as government subsidy on loans

PVF = the present value of all possible costs of financial transactions

Because of the great variety of debt instruments available in capital markets, the determination of PVT and PVF can best be left to the financial managers. Since capital investment analysis and financial analysis are often handled by two different groups of persons in a firm, their separate actions can be superimposed on one another in the final stage according to Eq. (16.4). This approach for determining the market value of a firm is referred to as the *adjusted present value approach*.

Proposition II of the MM model suggests another approach for considering the interactions of investment and financial decisions. To simplify the illustration, we again suppose that a firm holds capital assets, all of which have the same operating risk. Then, the expected rate of return r_a on a firm's assets with all-equity financing can be obtained from Eq. (16.2), and the adjusted cost of capital r_0 which takes into account tax shields within a safe debt-to-equity ratio is given by Eq. (16.3). However, as the debt-to-equity ratio increases, the risk of default increases, and therefore the expected market rate of return of r_d also increases even though the cost of debt to the firm is reduced by a factor of $(1 - X)$ where X is the tax rate of the firm.[4] With the possibility of financial distress when the debt-to-equity ratio approaches a certain limit, the expected rate of return r_e of a levered firm will probably increase faster than the linear relationship in Eq. (16.1). Thus, under the conditions of market imperfections and corporate taxes, the "conventional wisdom" also seems to suggest that there is an optimal debt-to-equity ratio at which the adjusted cost of capital r_0 of a firm is minimum, as indicated in Fig. 16.4.

If the adjusted cost of capital r_0 can be accurately determined, then the market value of a firm, taking into account tax shields and possible financial distress in one step, is as follows:

$$APV = [NPV]_{r_0} \qquad\qquad (16.5)$$

where $[NPV]_{r_0}$ is the net present value of a stream of after-tax cash flows discounted at the adjusted rate of capital r_0 of the firm. Such an approach in determining the market value of a firm is referred to as the *adjusted cost of capital approach*.

Note that in Eq. (16.5), the smaller the value adjusted rate r_0 used in discounting, the larger the market value of the firm as represented by the adjusted net present value APV. Consequently, it is often argued that if an optimal D/E exists

---

[4] Because of the complexity of the relationship between personal and corporate income taxes, this liberal interpretation as well as the simplified assumptions used to obtain Eq. (16.3) at best represent an approximation only. Without considering corporate income tax, the expected return on equity r_e increases linearly with D/E. As a firm borrows more, the risk of default increases, and the firm is required to pay higher interest r_d for debt. Hence, the rate of increase in r_e can be expected to slow down on the basis of Eq. (16.1). However, considering the deductibility of corporate income taxes and other financial side effects, r_e may actually decrease first but then increase faster with increasing D/E.

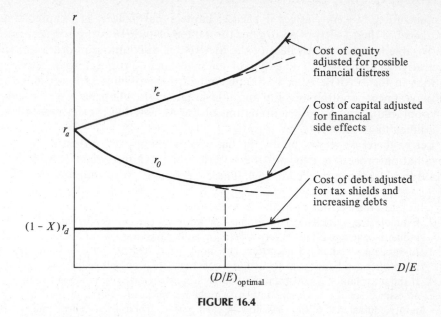

FIGURE 16.4

which maximizes the market value of a firm, then there should be an optimal D/E which minimizes its adjusted cost of capital. However, there is no convincing proof that such an optimal D/E exists.

Whether or not an optimal financing structure of a firm exists, the greatest difficulty in using Eq. (16.5) is the interlocking of investment and financing decisions. Since the financing of a new project may change the financial structure of a firm, its adjusted cost of capital, including the side effects of tax shields and the cost of possible financial distress, cannot be determined until the project is selected. On the other hand, without knowing the opportunity cost of capital including all side effects, there is no rational basis for selecting the new project.

Recalling that we have deliberately chosen a firm which holds only capital assets of the same operating risk to simplify our discussions in this section, we can anticipate additional questions which must be answered in order to get to the heart of the problem for selecting the appropriate rate of return in the economic evaluation of investment projects.

16.5 Evaluation of Capital Investment Opportunities

In the economic evaluation of capital investment opportunities, the minimum attractive rate of return (MARR) specified by an organization is critically important in determining whether an investment proposal is worthwhile from the standpoint of the organization. We emphasized in earlier chapters (particularly in Chapters 5 and 6) that because the MARR of an organization often cannot be measured accurately, it is advisable to use several values of the MARR for discounting in order to assess the sensitivity of the profit potential of an investment proposal with respect to variations in the MARR. After having examined the problems of uncertainty and risk in investments and the use of financial leverage by private firms, we now have a better appreciation why the determination of the MARR for project evaluation is such a difficult and inexact task.

Let us therefore review briefly the basic steps for project evaluation and how the evaluation process is tied into the selection of the appropriate MARR in the idealized firm described in Section 16.4. These basic steps are as follows:

1. Forecast the after-tax cash flows from the operation of the firm's assets.
2. Estimate the systematic risk in the operation of the project based on the industrial average of the *unlevered beta* for similar business operations.
3. Investigate whether the uncertain cash flows generated by the operations of the project can be realistically tied to a constant rate over time only.
4. If the uncertainty is not primarily tied to a constant rate over time, a careful assessment of the uncertain returns should be made to determine the "certainty equivalent" of the cash flow in each period. Then, the risk-free rate r_f should be used as the MARR *in connection with the certainty equivalents of the uncertain returns* in computing the net present value of the project.
5. If the uncertain cash flows of the project can be tied approximately to a constant rate, then the risk-adjusted rate of return r_a can be used as the MARR for discounting the expected after-tax cash flows in obtaining the net present value of the stream of cash flows as if the project were all-equity financed.
6. The effect of tax shields and the cost of possible financial distress due to the use of financial leverage can be determined and superimposed on the net present value obtained in step 5 to compute the adjusted net present value.
7. Instead of steps 5 and 6, we can first find the adjusted cost of capital r_0 of a proposed project which includes the impact of the project on the financial structure of the firm as well as the operating risk of the project. Then, the adjusted cost of capital r_0 can be used as the MARR to compute the net present value of the after-tax cash flows directly.
8. In using any one of these approaches, the effects of inflation or deflation must be treated consistently as explained in Chapter 13.

It cannot be overemphasized that the computational procedure which appears to be the simplest in theory may turn out to be the most difficult in practice. The difficulties in determining the "certainty equivalents" of future cash flows are well known to the analysts but have only been briefly alluded to in Chapter 15. Therefore, we have emphasized procedures which are based on the risk-adjusted rate of return, imperfect as such procedures may be. Furthermore, we have expressed a strong preference for the adjusted present value approach over the adjusted cost of capital approach because the investment and financing decisions are separable in the former, but they are interlocked intractably in the latter. The advantage of the adjusted present value approach is particularly significant for evaluating large-scale projects, each of which may refer to the entire division of a giant corporation. The financing decisions for such projects must be left to professional financial managers. However, the adjusted cost of capital approach has a long historical tradition and is still used extensively for evaluating small-scale routine projects, the financing of which has little or no effect on the financial structure of the firm. Consequently, we shall discuss both approaches in detail.

16.6   The Adjusted Present Value Approach

Although the acceptance of a new project may have a long-term impact on the operating risk and/or the financial risk of a firm, each project should generally be evaluated on the basis of the *opportunity cost of capital for the project* and not on the basis of the cost of capital to the firm. Consequently, the MARR is defined as the opportunity cost of capital which reflects the expected rate of return that can be earned from the best opportunity foregone. The opportunity cost of capital for a project is identical to the cost of the capital of a firm if and only if the systematic risk (both operating and financial) is identical to that of the average of the firm's existing projects.

For the adjusted present value approach, we shall confine our discussion to the determination of the net present value based on the MARR reflecting the operating risk only. Not only do the effects of tax shields and cost of possible financial distress depend on the debt instruments selected by the financial managers, but also any financing plan can be changed during the life of the capital assets through refinancing. Consequently, we shall concentrate on the evaluation of investment projects as if they are all-equity financed and leave the complex financing problems to the financial managers.

The opportunity cost of capital of an all-equity financed project x depends on the operating risk or the *unlevered* beta of project x, which is denoted as $\beta_{a,x}$. Using the CAPM, we can determine the expected market rate of return according to Eq. (15.17) as follows:

$$r_{a,x} = r_f + \beta_{a,x} (r_m - r_f) \tag{16.6}$$

The relationship in Eq. (16.6) is also shown in Fig. 16.5. The rate $r_{a,x}$ means that for a project with an operating risk of $\beta_{a,x}$, the expected rate of return from operating the firm's assets should be at least as high as $r_{a,x}$. Otherwise, the firm will be better off to invest its money in assets with similar operating risks that are available in the capital markets. Thus, the net present value of the project x can be obtained by

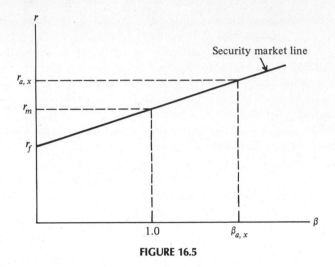

FIGURE 16.5

discounting the after-tax cash flows $Y_{t,x}$ (for $t = 0, 1, 2, \ldots, n$) at the rate $r_{a,x}$ as follows:

$$[\text{NPV}]_{r_{a,x}} = Y_0 + \frac{Y_{1,x}}{1 + r_{a,x}} + \frac{Y_{2,x}}{(1 + r_{a,x})^2} + \cdots + \frac{Y_{n,x}}{(1 + r_{a,x})^n} \qquad (16.7)$$

where n is the number of years representing the planning horizon adopted by the firm.

Since the opportunity cost of capital $r_{a,x}$ for a project x does not depend on the cost of capital to a firm, it does not matter whether the stock of the firm is publicly traded in the stock market. As long as we can identify firms in public trading which are engaged in business with a similar operating risk $\beta_{a,x}$, we can determine $r_{a,x}$ by using Eq. (16.6). On the other hand, the unlevered beta β_a of a firm must be obtained from the levered beta β_e of the firm which is the systematic risk of the security of the firm relative to that of the market portfolio. If the stock of the firm is actively traded, the levered beta value of the firm can be found from sources publishing such information. Then, the unlevered beta β_a of the firm can be computed by using Eq. (15.14). However, if the stock of the firm is not publicly traded, we cannot determine either beta value because the market value of the firm is not known. The *book values* or *accounting data* cannot be used in computing the *beta* value of a firm since the concept of risk premium in the CAPM is based on the risk of a security *relative* to the risk of the *market portfolio*.

In practice, it is not convenient to determine the expected market rate of return from the *unlevered* beta of an industry engaged in a similar business. Therefore, some firms attempt to divide the potential investment opportunities into several risk categories, e.g., very safe, safe, average, risky, and very risky. Then, an expected market rate of return $r_{a,x}$ is assigned to projects in each risk category corresponding to its operating risk β_a on the basis of the CAPM. For example, a value of $\beta_a = 0.9$ may be regarded as average, a value of $\beta_a = 0.3$ as very safe, and a value of $\beta_a = 1.5$ as very risky. For a corporation with several divisions engaging in different types of businesses with different operating risks, the expected market rates of return for investment projects may be divided along divisional lines. Consequently, the opportunity cost of capital for evaluating a new project in a division is based on the expected market rate of return of projects with similar operating risk. It is incorrect to demand the same rate of return from a very safe project as from a very risky project.

Returning to the theme of evaluating investment projects, the adjusted net present value of a proposed project x is conceptually similar to that for a firm expressed in Eq. (16.4) and can be stated as follows:

$$APV_x = [NPV_x]_{r_{a,x}} + PVT_x - PVF_x \tag{16.8}$$

We have already explained how the first term on the right-hand side of Eq. (16.8) can be obtained from Eq. (16.7). The second term takes into account the desirable effects of various forms of tax shields that are allowed by the government as incentives for making the proposed investment. The third term includes the transaction costs of issuing new securities (either new stock or bonds) to finance the proposed project and other additional costs that are attributable to the acceptance of the proposed projects.

Consequently, the criterion for accepting a proposed project is that project x should be accepted if

$$APV_x \geq 0 \tag{16.9}$$

Similarly, the criterion for selecting the best project from a set of m mutually exclusive projects is to select project j if

$$APV_j = \max_{x \in m} APV_x \tag{16.10}$$

provided that

$$APV_j \geq 0.$$

Example 16.3

A pilot plant for coal gasification requires an initial investment of $800 million and is expected to generate a uniform after-tax cash income of $150 million per year for 15 years, and there is no salvage value at the end. The opportunity cost of capital for the project based on its operating risk is 18%. The firm undertaking this project intends to secure a loan of $200 million, which will be repaid at the end of 15 years but the interest at a rate of 12% will be paid annually. The tax rate of this firm is 46%. The firm also plans to issue new stock to obtain another $300 million, and the transaction costs amount to 6% of the gross proceeds of the stock. Is this project worthwhile?

In using the adjusted net present value approach, the terms on the right-hand side of Eq. (16.7) can be obtained separately as follows: The net present value of the project from all-equity financing in millions of dollars is

$$[\text{NPV}]_{18\%} = -800 + (150)(P\,|\,U, 18\%, 15)$$
$$= -800 + (150)(5.0916) = -36.26$$

The present value of tax shields for the annual interest in millions of dollars over 15 years is

$$[\text{PVT}]_{12\%} = (200)(0.12)(0.46)(P\,|\,U, 12\%, 15)$$
$$= (11.04)(6.8109) = 75.19$$

The transaction costs of issuing the new stock are paid to underwriters, lawyers, and others at the time of initiating the project, and are obtained in millions of dollars as

$$\text{PVF} = \frac{300}{(1 - 0.06)} - 300 = 19.15$$

Consequently, according to Eq. (16.7), the adjusted net present value in millions of dollars is

$$\text{APV} = -36.26 + 75.19 - 19.15 = +19.78$$

Thus, the project is worthwhile since the APV is $19.78 million after the inclusion of the tax shields.

Example 16.4

A company has three divisions, each of which is assigned to operate a different class of project. Division A handles "safe" projects with well-established production processes and consumer markets. Division B handles relatively routine projects with "average" risk. Division C handles projects which are highly innovative and are regarded as risky. The company has decided to use the values of unlevered beta β_a of 0.3, 0.9, and 1.5 for divisions A, B, and C respectively. If the risk-free rate r_f is 12% and the differential rate of the market portfolio and the risk-free securities $(r_m - r_f)$ is 8.7%, determine the MARR for evaluating the projects with all-equity financing for each of these three divisions.

The opportunity cost of capital $r_{a,x}$ for each division x is based on the expected market rate of return on projects with operating risk similar to that of the divisional unlevered $\beta_{a,x}$. Hence, the MARR for each division can be obtained from Eq. (16.6). Let $x = A$, B, and C denote divisions A, B, and C, respectively. Then, the MARR for each of these divisions is given by

$$r_{a,A} = 12\% + (0.3)(8.7\%) = 14.61\%$$

$$r_{a,B} = 12\% + (0.9)(8.7\%) = 19.83\%$$

$$r_{a,C} = 12\% + (1.5)(8.7\%) = 25.05\%$$

16.7 The Adjusted Cost of Capital Approach

The adjusted cost of capital approach is a conceptually attractive method for project evaluation since the computational procedure can be carried out in one step. Unfortunately, the assumptions leading to the simplified computational procedure also produce severe limitations in practice. Consequently, this approach is not recommended except for the evaluation of small-scale routine projects whose systematic risk (both operating and financial) is essentially identical to that of the average of the firm's existing projects. Then, and only then, the adjusted cost of capital of the firm may be used as the MARR in the evaluation of new projects.

Historically, there are two different versions of the interpretation of the adjusted cost of capital. One is the MM model as represented by Eqs. (16.2) and (16.3); the other precedes the MM model and is often referred to as the *traditional* weighted average of cost of capital formula. We shall examine briefly their similarities and differences.

The MM model separates the computation of the adjusted cost of capital of the firm's assets including its financial leverage and tax shields into two steps. The first step, as represented by Eq. (16.2), determines the expected return r_a of a firm's • asset with *all-equity financing* as the *weighted average* of the expected rate of return r_e on the *equity of a levered firm* and the expected rate of return r_d on the firm's debt, with the proportions of equity and debt as weights, respectively. The second step, as represented by Eq. (16.3), takes into consideration the effects of the financial leverage and tax shields. Since r_a represents the opportunity cost of capital for the *firm* under all-equity financing and L is the target proportion of the debt of the *firm*, the MM model should be applied only to projects which have the same risk characteristics as a firm's existing assets and which will not shift the target proportion of debt of the firm. Theoretically, Eq. (16.3) can be generalized to obtain the opportunity cost of capital for a project, and therefore it is considered to be more flexible than it appears. However, because of the subtlety involved in this generalization, we shall not go beyond the original MM model.[5]

[5] The generalization of the MM model for determining the opportunity of cost of capital for evaluating projects has been mentioned in both Ref. [16.2] and Ref. [16.7].

The traditional weighted average of cost of capital formula determines the adjusted cost of capital including the effects of tax shields and financial leverage in one step as follows:

$$r_w = \frac{E}{D + E} r_e + \frac{D}{D + E} (1 - X)r_d \qquad (16.11)$$

Except for the term r_w, which represents the adjusted cost of capital obtained by this traditional formula, all other terms have the same meaning as their counterparts in Eqs. (16.2) and (16.3). The premise of Eq. (16.11) is based more on intuition than on any profound theory. Since the proportions of equity and debt in the financial structure of a firm are $E/(D + E)$ and $D/(D + E)$, respectively, and since the expected rate of return of equity is r_e and the equivalent expected rate of return on debt including tax shields is $(1 - X)r_d$, the adjusted cost of capital of a firm is therefore the weighted average of r_e and r_d using the proportions of equity and debt as weights. This traditional formula takes into account several factors simultaneously, namely (1) the risk level of the firm as reflected by the market rates r_e and r_d, (2) the financial leverage of the firm as represented by the proportions of equity and debt, and (3) the effects of the corporate income tax indicated by the factor $(1 - X)$. Consequently, the adjusted cost of capital r_w can be used as the minimum attractive rate of return for project evaluation when the projects conform with, at least approximately, the assumptions of constant risk characteristics and constant financial leverage. Then,

$$APV = [NPV]_{r_w} \qquad (16.12)$$

which is a variation of Eq. (16.5).

We have not examined carefully all the assumptions based on which r_0 and r_w are derived. However, it can be said that the MM model has been derived from a theoretical framework which is verified at least in part by empirical observations. Furthermore, the formula for r_0 based on the MM model can be generalized to determine the opportunity cost of capital for a project. On the other hand, the "traditional" formula for computing r_w has hardly anything else to stand on except the historical tradition.[6] Therefore, the MM model is definitely preferred over the traditional weighted average of cost of capital formula, if the adjusted cost of capital approach is used at all.

However, the most serious limitation for further generalization of the MM model is its assumption that the tax shield for interest payments is the only side effect of accepting a proposed project. In view of the recent surge of new forms of debt instruments and new types of government tax incentives for capital investments, the side effects of both tax shields and costs of financing will be increasingly

---

[6] An elegant derivation of this formula is given in Ref. [16.1], but that does not remove the limitations of its application because of the restrictive assumptions.

important for large-scale projects. Consequently, the use of the adjusted cost of capital approach is expected to be limited only to cases where it is applicable.

Example 16.5

The expected rate of return r_a on a firm with all-equity financing is 20%, and the expected rate of return r_d on its debt is 10%. The tax rate X of the firm is 50%. Determine (1) r_0 using the MM model and (2) r_w using the traditional weighted average cost of capital formula, for a range of debt-to-equity ratios $D/E = 0, \frac{1}{4}, \frac{1}{2}, 1, 2$, and 3. The expected rate of return r_e for the traditional formula can be obtained from the MM model.

The computation of both r_0 and r_w is straightforward through direct substitution of the given values in the equations. At $D/E = 0$, both $r_0 = r_a = 20\%$, and $r_w = r_e = r_a = 20\%$. For $D/E = \frac{1}{4}$, we get directly from Eq. (16.3)

$$r_0 = (20\%)\left[1 - (0.5)\left(\frac{0.25}{1 + 0.25}\right)\right] = 18\%$$

Similarly, from Eq. (16.11)

$$r_w = \frac{1}{1 + D/E}\, r_e + \frac{D/E}{1 + D/E}\,(1 - X)r_d$$

where, according to Eq. (16.1),

$$r_e = r_a + \frac{D}{E}\,(r_a - r_d)$$

Hence, for $D/E = \frac{1}{4}$, we get

$$r_e = 20\% + (0.25)(20\% - 10\%) = 22.5\%$$

and

$$r_w = \frac{1}{1 + 0.25}\,(22.5\%) + \frac{0.25}{1 + 0.25}\,(1 - 0.5)(10\%) = 19\%$$

The results of the computation of r_0 and r_w for various values of D/E are summarized as follows:

D/E	0	0.25	0.5	1	2	3
r_0	20%	18%	16.6%	15.0%	13.3%	12.5%
r_w	20%	19%	18.3%	17.5%	16.7%	16.3%

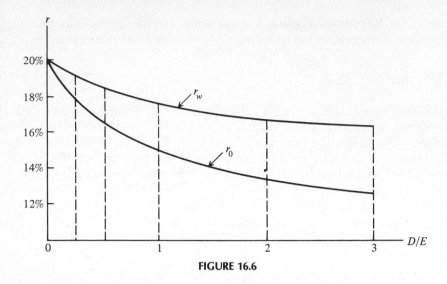

FIGURE 16.6

These results are also plotted in Fig. 16.6. Note that both the r_0 curve and the r_w curve tend to decrease asymptotically to a horizontal line. These curves do not imply the existence of an optimal ratio of D/E which will maximize the adjusted cost of capital since no side effect other than tax shields has been considered in the formulas for computing either r_0 or r_w.

Example 16.6

The sources of capital of a firm together with their expected market rates of return before tax are shown in Table 16.1. If the tax rate of the firm is 46%, determine the cost of capital of the firm, using the traditional weighted average of cost of capital formula.

The first two items in Table 16.1 represent the equity and the last two repre-

Table 16.1

Sources of Capital and Expected Rates of Return

Sources of capital	Market Value ($ million)	Before-Tax Expected Rate of Return
Common stock	8	25%
Retained earnings	4	18%
Bonds	6	10%
Long-term notes	2	14%

sent the debt of the firm. The total market value of debt and equity of the firm is $20 million. Hence,

$$r_w = \frac{8}{20}\,(25\%) + \frac{4}{20}\,(18\%) + \left[\frac{6}{20}\,(10\%) + \frac{2}{20}\,(14\%)\right](1 - 0.46)$$
$$= 10\% + 3.6\% + (3\% + 1.4\%)(0.54) = 16\%$$

16.8   Implications for the Choice of Investment Opportunities

After considering the interactions of investment and financing decisions for private firms and various methods for determining these interactions, we are in a position to examine rationally some practical implications in incorporating these interactions in the decision-making process. Although different firms have different characteristics which may defy generalization, we can nevertheless draw certain conclusions which are applicable to a large number of private firms.

First, the cost of capital of a firm, more commonly known as the weighted average cost of capital of a firm, should not be used as the MARR or hurdle rate in the evaluation of a new project unless the risk characteristics (both operational and financial) of the new project are an exact duplicate of that of a firm. Projects undertaken in the past by some companies supplying public utilities under government regulation probably came as close to an approximation of this condition as ever existed. However, even for public utilities companies, the situation is changing as new technologies are introduced at a rapidly increasing rate. Therefore, the cost of capital of a firm should not be adopted as the MARR for project evaluation unless there is a compelling reason to justify its use. As a matter of general principle, the MARR or hurdle rate for evaluating a new project should be based on the opportunity cost of capital which, in most cases, can best be determined from the expected market rate of return on investment with risk characteristics similar to those of the new project. The difference between using the cost of capital of a firm as the MARR for all new projects and adopting a different expected market risk-adjusted rate of return as the MARR for each new project is illustrated in Fig. 16.7. The use of a single cost of capital of a firm as the MARR for project evaluation has the same effect as selecting a decision criterion as represented by the horizontal line, whereas the adoption of the expected market risk-adjusted rates of return for different levels of risk corresponds to a decision criterion as represented by the inclined line.[7] For projects A and B, both criteria give the same signal of acceptance or rejection of the projects, i.e., the expected rate of return on A is higher than the MARR specified, and the expected rate of return on B is lower than the MARR specified. For projects C and D, however, the two criteria give different signals, i.e.,

[7] See Ref. [16.9] for further discussions.

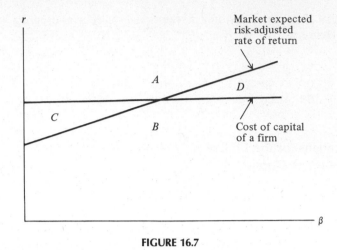

FIGURE 16.7

project C should be accepted according to the expected market risk-adjusted rate of return but rejected according to the cost of capital of the firm, and the situation is reversed for project D. Therefore, the use of the cost of capital as the decision criterion will lead to the wrong decisions to reject C and accept D.

Recognizing the approximate nature of the CAPM, we should keep in mind the factors which may require some modifications in using the expected market risk-adjusted rate of return for project evaluation. Because of the wide variety investment opportunities with different levels of systematic risk available, a firm can adopt a policy reflecting the risk propensity or aversion of its stockholders and/or management. For example, a fledgling firm may desire to expand rapidly by selecting new risky projects with a high expected market risk-adjusted rate of return. However, such a policy must be tempered by considering the possibility of bankruptcy if it goes too far in risk taking, thus creating an unsystematic risk which cannot be diversified away. On the other hand, a well-established company which has been engaged in a single line of business for decades may wish to examine periodically whether it may have lived too long on its past glory in a business whose expected market rate of return relative to its operating risk has shifted from a favorable position to an unfavorable position over the years.

For large multidivisional firms, different minimum attractive rates of return or hurdle rates are often selected along divisional lines. Such selections make good sense if the divisions are segmented along product lines with different levels of operating risk. However, in some firms, the divisions are nothing more than autonomous profit centers artificially segmented on the basis of marketing strategies rather than operating risk characteristics. Furthermore, the management may assess the prospects for each division based on market, cost, and competitive trends, and apply tight controls to monitor the performance of the divisions according to their projected financial return, growth, and capital requirements. Thus, the variable expected market risk-adjusted rates of return for evaluating projects with different levels of risk are used to justify the preconceptions of the management on the performance of various divisions, which are sometimes identified by labels such as "stars," "cash cows," or "dogs." A strict adherence to the CAPM as a management policy, even if applied correctly, tends to encourage each division to respond to customer needs in existing markets in order to improve short-run performance, but creates disincentives for research and development to advance the technological base of products which are the lifelines for long-run survival. Consequently, it is only prudent to consider these practical implications to a firm in the selection of the MARR or hurdle rate in the evaluation of investment opportunities.

16.9 Computational Techniques

In this chapter, we have emphasized the basic concepts concerning the impact of capital investment projects and their concomitant financing policies to a firm. We have used some elementary examples to illustrate these concepts without getting into detailed computations. However, the computational technique for more realistic situations were discussed in Chapter 12, except for cases involving costs of financial transactions (e.g., issuance of various types of securities) and costs of financial distress (e.g., bankruptcy).

In Chapter 12, we introduced the idea of separation between the operating stream of cash flows and the financing stream of cash flows without discussing their impact on the financial structure of a firm. Consequently, the financing plans discussed in Chapter 12 are those which are not expected to generate any financial transaction costs. Within that context, several examples are given for the computation of after-tax cash flows, and the cost of assets with all-equity financing has been used as the MARR for discounting (see Examples 12.4, 12.5, 12.6, and 12.7). Examples using different financing plans to take advantage of tax shields have also been given (see Examples 12.9 and 12.10). Reference is made to Chapter 12 for computational techniques related to such problems.

We do not intend to discuss in detail the calculation of costs of financial transactions and financial distress since they can best be handled separately by finanical managers. In this chapter, we have only alluded to their existence as implied by Eq. (16.4) for the adjusted present value approach and by the qualitative discussion of the optimal financial structure of a firm as shown in Figs. 16.3 and 16.4.

Example 16.7

Using the computational techniques of treating the financial stream of cash flows described in Chapter 12, recompute the present value of tax shields (PVT) in Example 16.3.

Let $\bar{A}_t$ (for $t = 0, 1, 2, \ldots, 15$) denote the financial stream of cash flows before tax. Also, let X_t be the tax rate and I_t be the interest (for $t = 1, 2, \ldots, 15$). Since we are only interested in the financial stream of cash flows, Eq. (12.7) becomes

$$\bar{Y}_t = \bar{A}_t + X_t I_t$$

where $\bar{Y}_t$ (for $t = 0, 1, 2, \ldots, 15$) is the financial stream of cash after tax.

In Example 16.3, $A_0 = \$200$ million, $\bar{A}_1, \bar{A}_2, \ldots, \bar{A}_{14}$ are the annual interest payments, each of which is numerically equal to

$$I_t = (200)(0.12) = \$24 \text{ million (for } t = 1, 2, \ldots, 14)$$

For $t = 15$, the before-tax cash flow A_{15} includes both the interest payment and the repayment of the principal. Since the tax rate X_t is assumed to be 46% for all years,

$$X_t I_x = (0.46)(24) = \$11.04 \text{ million}$$

Hence, the after-tax financial stream $\bar{Y}_t$ can be obtained from the before-tax financial stream $\bar{A}_t$ as shown in Table 16.2.

Using the expected market rate of return of 12% for risk-free debt as the MARR, the NPV of the before-tax financial stream $\bar{A}_t$ (in millions of dollars) is

$$\begin{aligned}[\text{NPV}]_{12\%} &= +200 - (24)(P\,|\,U,\, 12\%,\, 15) - (200)(P\,|\,F,\, 12\%,\, 15)\\ &= +200 - 163.46 - 36.54 = 0\end{aligned}$$

The NPV of the after-tax financial stream $\bar{Y}_t$ (in millions of dollars) is

$$\begin{aligned}[\text{NPV}]_{12\%} &= +200 - (12.96)(P\,|\,U,\, 12\%,\, 15) - 200(P\,|\,F,\, 12\%,\, 15)\\ &= 200 - 88.27 - 36.54 = \$75.19 \text{ million}\end{aligned}$$

The difference between the net present values for $\bar{Y}_t$ and for $\bar{A}_t$ is $75.19 - 0 = \$75.19$ million, which is the present value of tax shields for the interest payments. The

Table 16.2

After-Tax Financial Stream of Cash Flows

t	$\bar{A}_t$	$X_t I_t$	$\bar{Y}_t = \bar{A}_t + X_t I_t$
0	+200	0	+200
1–14	−24	11.04	−12.96
15	$\begin{cases} -24 \\ -200 \end{cases}$	11.04	$\begin{cases} -12.96 \\ -200 \end{cases}$

number agrees with the value obtained by a simplified procedure in Example 16.3 which is applicable to this simple case of a loan with annual interest payments only.

Example 16.8

Suppose that the pilot plant for coal gasification in Example 16.3 is qualified for a low-interest loan from a federal government program for encouraging the development of synthetic fuel projects. The loan of $200 million is subsidized at an interest rate of 3%, repayable in a series of uniform annual payments of $16.76 million each year over 15 years, covering both principal and interest. Hence, the firm will no longer try to obtain a commercial loan at 12% in the capital markets. What is the adjusted net present value of this project?

The only difference between this example and Example 16.3 is the term PVT in the computation of the adjusted net present value APV because of the government loan of $200 million at a subsidized interest rate of 3%. We must first determine the portions of principal and interest payments in each year from the uniform annual payments in order to assess the tax shield. Using Eqs. (4.21), (4.22), and (4.23) from Chapter 4, we obtain

$$I_t = R_{t-1}i$$

$$Q_t = \bar{A}_t + I_t$$

$$R_t = R_{t-1} + Q_t$$

where, as noted in Section 4.5,

i = specified interest rate per time period for borrowing

$\bar{A}_t$ = cash flow at the end of period t (positive for a receipt from loan and negative for payment of principal and/or interest)

R_t = principal amount of loan remaining at the end of period t (positive for an unpaid balance and negative for an overpayment beyond the principal and interest owed)

I_t = interest accrued during period t on R_{t-1} (positive for interest on an unpaid balance and negative for interest on an overpayment)

Q_t = amount to be added to the unpaid balance or the amount to be used to reduce the unpaid balance on loan during period t (positive for a net increase and negative for a net decrease).

The subsidized low-interest rate of 3% is reflected in the uniform annual payment since

$$(200)(U \,|\, P, 3\%, 15) = (200)(0.0838) = 16.76.$$

Table 16.3

Principals and Interests in Annual Payments

t	$\bar{A}_t$	R_{t-1}	I_t	Q_t	R_t
0	200	0			200
1	−16.76	200	6.00	−10.76	189.24
2	−16.76	189.24	5.68	−11.08	178.16
3	−16.76	178.16	5.34	−11.42	166.74
4	−16.76	166.74	5.00	−11.76	154.98
5	−16.76	154.98	4.65	−12.11	142.87
6	−16.76	142.87	4.29	−12.47	130.40
7	−16.76	130.40	3.91	−12.85	117.55
8	−16.76	117.55	3.53	−13.23	104.32
9	−16.76	104.32	3.13	−13.63	90.69
10	−16.76	90.69	2.72	−14.04	76.65
11	−16.76	76.65	2.30	−14.46	62.13
12	−16.76	62.19	1.87	−14.89	47.30
13	−16.76	47.30	1.42	−15.34	31.96
14	−16.76	31.96	0.96	−15.80	16.16
15	−16.76	16.16	0.48	−16.28	−0.12

The portions of principal and interest payments for the 15 years as computed by Eqs. (4.21), (4.22), and (4.23) are shown in Table 16.3. Note that the loan of $200 million received in year 0 is positive and the uniform annual payments to retire the loan are negative. Following the sign conventions defined in Section 4.5 (Chapter 4), the interest I_t on the unpaid balance for each year t is positive and the net increase Q_t for the unpaid balance in each year t is negative.

Therefore, the after-tax financial stream of cash flows can be obtained from Table 16.3 as follows:

At $t = 0$, $\bar{Y}_0 = \bar{A}_0 = A_0$

At $t = 1$ to 15, $\bar{Y}_t = \bar{A}_t + X_t I_t$
$$= (Q_t - I_t) + X_t I_t$$
$$= Q_t - (1 - X_t)I_t$$

where $X = 46\%$ is the income tax rate. Consequently,

$$\text{PVT} = A_0 + \sum_{t=1}^{15} [Q_t - (1 - X_t)I_t](P\,|\,F, 12\%, 5)$$

Note that the discount rate of 12% is used to obtain the present value because the

Table 16.4

Computation of Quantities Leading to PVT

t	$\bar{Y}_t = Q_t - (1 - X_t)I_t$	$(P\vert F, 12\%, t)$	$\bar{Y}_t(P\vert F, 12\%, t)$
1	-14	0.8929	-12.5006
2	-14.15	0.7972	-11.2804
3	-14.30	0.7118	-10.1787
4	-14.46	0.6355	-9.1893
5	-14.62	0.5674	-8.2954
6	-14.79	0.5066	-7.4926
7	-14.96	0.4523	-6.7664
8	-15.14	0.4039	-6.1150
9	-15.32	0.3606	-5.5244
10	-15.51	0.3220	-4.9942
11	-15.70	0.2875	-4.5138
12	-15.90	0.2567	-4.0815
13	-16.11	0.2292	-3.6924
14	-16.32	0.2046	-3.3391
15	-16.54	0.1827	-3.0219

Total $= -100.9857$

company can earn 12% at the capital markets even though it only pays a subsidized interest rate of 3% to the government. The computation of PVT can be simplified by tabulating the results of the product terms as shown in Table 16.4. Noting that $A_0 = 200$, we obtain

$$PVT = 200 - 100.99 = 99.01$$

The remaining terms for computing APV can be taken from Example 16.3. That is,

$$APV = [NPV]_{12\%} + PVT - PVF$$
$$= -36.26 + 99.01 - 19.15 = +\$43.60 \text{ million}$$

Hence, the project is worthwhile if this financing scheme is used.

16.10 Summary and Study Guide

This chapter has presented an overview of the impact of capital investment decisions on the long-range objectives of private firms. It has highlighted some pertinent issues in corporate finance in order to understand the criterion for accepting or rejecting an investment project which is consistent with the objective of maximizing the value of a firm.

We first looked at the market value of a firm from its assets without worrying about where the money for acquiring these assests comes from. Then, we looked separately at the stream of expected cash flows for debt which will be claimed by the debtholders and at the stream for equity which will be claimed by the stockholders. On the basis of this understanding, we considered the MM model of corporate finance and investment as a theoretical framework to provide useful insights into some important issues related to the interactions of investment and financing decisions. We also discussed some practical aspects of corporate finance and investment beyond the theoretical framework and examined qualitatively the "conventional wisdom" concerning the optimal financial structure of a firm.

We then addressed the crucial issue of selecting the appropriate minimum attractive rate of return (MARR) or hurdle rate for the evaluation of proposed investment projects. We have presented both the adjusted present value approach and the adjusted cost of capital approach in sufficient detail to appreciate their advantages and disadvantages. We also introduced the traditional weighted average of cost of capital formula in addition to the MM model for computing the cost of capital for a firm. However, we did not cover many aspects of corporate finance which are expected to be handled by financial managers.

Finally, we examined some practical implications for the choice of investment opportunities. We emphasized that the cost of capital of a firm generally should not be used as the MARR in the evaluation of new projects. Instead, the MARR for evaluating a new project should be based on the opportunity cost of capital which, in most cases, can best be determined from the expected market rate of return on investments with risk characteristics similar to those of the new projects. However, recognizing the approximate nature of the capital asset pricing model, we discussed various factors which may require some modifications in using the expected market risk-adjusted rate of return for project evaluation.

REFERENCES

16.1 Bar-Yosef, S., "Interactions of Corporate Financing and Investment Decisions—Implication for Capital Budgeting: Comment," and S. C. Myers, "Reply," *Journal of Finance*, **32**, (1977), 211–220.

16.2 Brealey, R., and S. Myers, *Principles of Corporate Finance*. New York: McGraw-Hill, 1981.

16.3 Miller, M. H., and F. Modigliani, "Dividend Policy, Growth and the Valuation of Shares," *Journal of Business*, **34**, (1961), 411–433.

16.4 Miller, M. H., "Debt and Taxes," *Journal of Finance*, **32** (1977), 261–275.

16.5 Modigliani, F., and M. H. Miller, "The Cost of Capital, Corporate Finance and Theory of Investment," *American Economic Review*, **48** (1958), 261–297.

16.6 Modigliani, F., and M. H. Miller, "Corporate Income Taxes and the Cost of Capital: A Correction, "*American Economic Review*, **43** (1963), 433–443.

16.7 Myers, S. C., "Interactions of Corporate Financing and Investment Decisions—Implications for Capital Budgeting," *Journal of Finance*, **29** (1974), 1–25.

16.8 Myers, S. C., "Determinants of Corporate Borrowing," *Journal of Financial Economics*, **5** (1977), 147–175.

16.9 Rubinstein, M. E., "A Mean-Variance Synthesis of Corporate Financial Theory," *Journal of Finance*, **28** (1973), 167–181.

16.10 Solomon, E., and J. J. Pringle, *An introduction to Financial Management*, 2nd ed. Santa Monica, CA: Goodyear Publishing Co., 1980.

16.11 Van Horne, J. C., *Financial Management and Policy*, 5th ed. Englewood Cliffs, NJ: Prentice-Hall, 1980.

PROBLEMS

P16.1 Redspot Company has a market value of $60,000 for its equity and $40,000 for its debt. Its stock has an expected rate of return of 20%, and its bonds (for the debt) have an expected return of 12.5%. The sole owner of the company, Ms. Redspot, can afford to pay off the debt of $40,000 by withdrawing the amount from deposits which currently earn a market interest rate of 12.5%. The expected rate of return of the stock of the company is 17% when the market value of its equity becomes $100,000 without debt. Assuming no income tax, compare the annual returns for Ms. Redspot in the following situations: (a) Do not pay off the debt and keep the cash in deposits. (b) Pay off the debt with the cash.

P16.2 Green Manufacturing Company has a 20% expected return on its assets which are currently valued at $1 million of equity and no debt. However, the company plans to borrow another $1 million for expansion at the market interest rate of 15%. What is the expected rate of return on the stock after incurring this debt? If the beta of the assets (with all-equity financing) is 0.9, what is the beta of the stock after the expansion? Assume that there is no income tax.

P16.3 Given that $r_a = 15\%$, $r_d = 10\%$, $D/E = 0.4$, and $X = 46\%$ for a firm, find the adjusted average cost of capital of the firm according to the MM model.

P16.4 Given that $r_e = 17\%$, $r_d = 10\%$, $D/E = 0.4$, and $X = 46\%$ for a firm, find the weighted average cost of capital of the firm. Use the traditional formula.

P16.5 The expected rate of return r_a on a firm with all-equity financing is 25% and the expected rate of return r_d of its debt is 12%. The tax rate X of the firm is 46%. Determine (a) r_0 using the MM model and (b) r_w using the traditional weighted average cost of capital formula, for a range of values of D/E including 0, 0.5, 1.0, 1.5, and 2.0. The expected rate of return r_e for the traditional formula can be obtained from the MM model.

P16.6 The cost of equity capital r_e of a firm adjusted for possible financial distress is assumed to be a function of the ratio D/E as follows:

$$r_e = 18 + 6 \left(\frac{D}{E} \right)^2 \quad \text{for } 0 \le D/E$$

where r_e is expressed as a percentage. The cost of debt r_d adjusted for financial side effects of the firm is assumed to be

$$r_d = \begin{cases} 10 & \text{for } 0 \le D/E \le 0.5 \\ 10 + 4 \left(\frac{D}{E} - 0.5 \right)^2 & \text{for } 0.5 \le D/E \end{cases}$$

where r_d is also expressed in percentage. The corporate income tax rate for the firm is 50%. Determine the weighted average cost of capital of the firm including taxes for the range of D/E at 0.1, 0.2, 0.3, ..., 1.0. Sketch the functions r_e, r_d, and r_w to determine if there is an optimal equity-to-debt ratio.

P16.7 The Wexford Corporation has four divisions, each of which is assigned to operate projects with different risk characteristics. The divisions A, B, C, and D are estimated to have unlevered beta values 0.5, 0.8, 1.1, and 1.4, respectively. The market risk-free rate r_f is 8% and the differential rate $(r_m - r_f)$ is 8.7%. Determine the MARR for evaluating capital projects with all-equity financing for each of these divisions.

P16.8 Company A which specializes in electronics has a debt-to-equity ratio of 0.2 and a levered beta value of 1.2. Company B which specializes in electric appliances has a debt-to-equity ratio of 0.8 and a levered beta value of 1.6. Company C has a division for electronics and another division for electric appliances, among other divisions. Company C believes that Company A and Company B are more representative of its corresponding divisions than the industry wide averages. All three companies have a tax rate of 46%. The market risk-free rate r_f is 12% and the differential rate $(r_m - r_f)$ is 8.7%. What should be the MARR selected for each of these two divisions of Company C for evaluating capital projects with all-equity financing?

P16.9 A manufacturer of solar energy collectors is considering an investment in a new plant which requires an initial amount of $3 million and is expected to generate a uniform stream of after-tax cash incomes of $1 million per year for the next 5 years with no salvage value at the end. The opportunity cost of capital for the project based on its operating risk is 15%. The company is assured of a government-subsidized loan of $1 million for which annual interest is charged at a rate of 4% at the end of each year with the repayment of principal at the end of 5 years. The market interest rate for borrowing and lending is 8%. The income tax rate of this company is 50%. The company will also issue a new stock to obtain another $1 million, and the transaction costs of the new issue amount to 5% of the proceeds of stock. Is this new plant worthwhile?

P16.10 Suppose that the pilot plant for the coal gasification in Example 16.3 in this chapter cannot get a government-subsidized loan and decides to secure a commercial loan of $300 million at 12% interest. The loan will be repaid in a series of uniform annual payments of $44.04 million per year over 15 years, covering both principal and interest. On the other hand, it will issue new stock to obtain another $200 million, and the transaction costs of issuing the new stock amount to 7% of the gross proceeds of the stock. Is the project worthwhile under the new financing plan?

CHAPTER

17

RESOURCE ALLOCATION
DECISIONS FOR
PUBLIC PROJECTS

17.1 Important Factors for Consideration

In the evaluation of public investment projects, we are often confronted with broad
social and political issues which we have avoided thus far. Significant interactions
among economic, social, and political concerns are tacitly, if not explicitly, considered in the acceptance and selection of public projects. The allocation of scarce
resources among alternative uses is said to be *economically efficient* when the total
amount of benefits received by members of society is maximized under the prevailing income distribution. In a mixed economy where the private market is subject to
government intervention, the crucial question is how to assess properly that a
proposed public project will maximize the improvement of social welfare.

In order to address this question adequately, we cannot ignore the reasons for
government intervention in the market economy. Some of the issues involving
government intervention are complex and controversial, and they rightfully belong
to more advanced courses in benefit-cost analysis, regulatory economics, and public
finance. We are only interested in bridging the gap between the engineers and social
planners in a decentralized capital budgeting process.

Some of the most important factors which often cause debates on the allocation of resources between private and public sectors are:

1. The inefficient allocation of resources because of private market failures
2. The determination of the minimum attractive rate of return for public projects, referred to as the *social discount rate*
3. The estimation of costs and benefits of public projects, particularly benefits
   which usually accrue to the public in general.

We shall consider these factors in general terms in order to understand some of the basic issues which cause much of the controversies. We cannot expect to discuss in detail many of the subtle points supporting various positions. Because government intervention in the private market economy may be based on a number of factors, it is advisable to consider briefly the role of government as reflected in its fiscal policy objectives.

17.2 Fiscal Policy Objectives
   for the Public Sector

The fiscal policy objectives for the public sector generally include the following major functions: (1) the allocation function, (2) the distribution function, and (3) the stabilization function.[1] Regulatory policies, which may be regarded as a part of the allocation function, are not directly related to the fiscal policy.

The allocation function refers to the process by which total resource use is divided between private and public goods, and by which the mix of public goods is chosen. The objective is to achieve an economically efficient allocation of resources where *economic efficiency* is defined as the maximum improvement in social welfare available under the prevailing income distribution. It does not address the basic social issues of income distribution and redistribution.

The question of fair distribution of wealth involves considerations of social philosophy and value judgments. Economists have increasingly held that a theory of fair or equitable distribution is not within the purview of economics. However, distribution problems are and will continue to be a vital factor in public policy formulation. Even though policy measures may not be concerned primarily with distributional objectives, they often have distributional repercussions. For example, in reducing expenditures on various types of public projects, the reductions for some types of projects have more effects on the urban poor while others will have more effects on rural and farming populations. On the other hand, different distributional changes may also distort economic efficiency in different ways. Finally, a standard of distributive justice or fairness should be applied in making distributional changes. Among various fiscal devices, redistribution is implemented most directly by (1) a tax scheme combining progressive income taxes for high-income households with a subsidy to low-income households, (2) publicly financed programs which benefit low-income households, and (3) taxes on luxury goods and subsidies of other goods which are used chiefly by low-income consumers. Because expenditures on public projects are related to the tax revenues, the distributional function is an important issue in public policy.

Another objective of budget policy is to achieve the goals of high employment

---

[1] This classification follows that suggested in Ref. [17.6], pp. 1–21.

and price stability. The overall level of employment and prices in the market economy depends upon the level of aggregate demand of millions of consumers whose decisions in turn depend on many factors such as income, wealth, credit availability, and expectations. At any given time, the level of expenditures may be insufficient to maintain full employment, and stimulating policies to raise aggregate demand may be introduced. On the other hand, expenditures may exceed the available output under conditions of high employment and then cause inflation, and restrictive conditions are needed to reduce demand. Thus, the stabilization function is often a part of the budget policy.

Public policy must also be introduced to influence the rate of growth of potential output as determined by market forces. Since growth depends on the rate of capital formation, the division of output between present consumption and future consumption is crucial in the choice of a rate of growth. Thus, the decisions affecting the rate of growth serve the allocation function more than the stabilization function.

In the United States, public expenditures and revenues are divided among the various levels of government. The basic functions of budget policy may not be well coordinated at different levels of government. Furthermore, at each level, budget planning often does not permit evaluation of various objectives on their own merits, and one objective may be achieved at the expense of another. Nevertheless, it is important to realize the conflicts of these objectives which eventually shape the investments in both public and private sectors of the economy.

17.3 The Provision of Public Projects

A normative view of a market economy is based on the premise that the composition of output should satisfy the preferences of individual consumers and that a market system which establishes prices competitively according to consumer preferences is the most efficient way of allocating resources. What then are the reasons for government intervention in the market economy?

One of the reasons for government invervention is the provision of *pure public goods*, as distinguished from private goods. They refer to commodities which provide benefits not only to the consumers who wish to purchase them, but also to others who do not. The consumption of such products by various individuals is not "rival" in the sense that accruing of benefits to an individual does not reduce the benefits available to others. Furthermore, it is often impossible or impractical to exclude others from deriving benefits provided by such goods, or it is undesirable to exclude others even if it can be done. National defense and weather forecasting are examples of pure public goods. Hence, pure public goods refer only to those commodities which are nonrival and nonexcludable, and the government has an obligation to provide them for the benefit of society since individual consumers have no reason to offer voluntary payments for them.

Aside from the provision of pure public goods, government intervention may take many forms, depending on the circumstances under which the private market mechanism fails. For example, because of *imperfect competition* in the private market (e.g., monopoly), the government may choose to invoke the antitrust laws to break up the monopoly, or to grant the exclusive right to a "natural monopoly" under the government regulation as it has been done for most public utilities. Another example of private market failure concerning *externalities* (e.g., benefits accruing to or costs inflicted on society instead of the producer of goods) can be dealt with either through government regulation of the private enterprise or by government takeover of that enterprise. The form of government intervention sometimes depends on historical precedence as well as economic efficiency. Hence, the political process may become a substitute for preferences of the individuals of the community.

It is important to distinguish the provision of *public projects* and the *public production*. These two concepts are different and should not be confused with each other. Public projects may be undertaken by private firms and paid for by the government, or carried out directly under public management. Private goods may also be produced either by private firms or by public enterprises. Thus, public projects refer to government investments on goods and services in the public sector. In the United States, most public projects and practically all private goods are produced by private firms; only a small fraction of public projects are produced by public agencies and managed by civil servants or public enterprises under the auspices of local governments and independent authorities. For example, a very large percentage of the gross national product is allocated annually for national defense by the federal government; however, the contractors which produce the defense equipment are private corporations. At the state and local levels, most public projects utilize the expertise of private firms under the supervision or control of the appropriate government units. Hence, in a mixed economy, a large share of resources may be allocated for the public sector even though the private firms may be heavily engaged in activities related to the provision of public projects.

17.4   Economic Efficiency and Externalities

Since economic efficiency is defined as the maximum improvement of social welfare under the prevailing income distribution, the allocation of available resources is said to be efficient when the total amount of benefits received by members of society from the consumption of all commodities produced from the resources is maximized. It is important to realize that when a decision is made to produce more of a commodity, less resources are available for the production of others. Hence, the *social benefits* gained from the production of the former are accompanied by the loss of potential benefits in foregoing the opportunity of producing the latter. The benefits thus foregone are often referred to as opportunity costs, which represent the *social costs*.

Given society's limited resources, the criterion of economic efficiency in the production of a commodity may be stated as the maximization of its *net social benefit* (NSB), which refers to the *difference* between *social benefits* (SB) and *social costs* (SC) resulting from the allocation of resources for producing this commodity. Alternately, the criterion of economic efficiency may be restated in terms of *marginal social benefit* (MSB) and *marginal social cost* (MSC) as follows: resources are efficiently allocated to the production of a commodity when the marginal social benefit equals the marginal social cost. In analogy to the discussions in Section 10.5 (Chapter 10), the relationship between these two different representations of the economic efficiency criterion is shown in Fig. 17.1.

In the private market system, individual consumers base their choice of com-

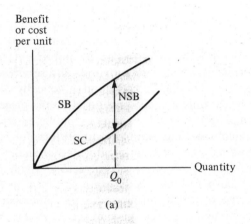

(a)

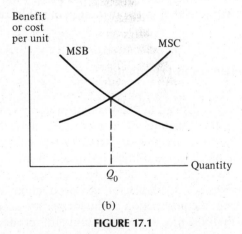

(b)

FIGURE 17.1

modities on the benefits they expect from consuming these commodities and the costs of these commodities as determined by their market prices. The benefits of consumption to individuals who purchase these commodities are said to be "internalized" because their consumption excludes the consumption by others. Hence, the benefits of consuming privately purchased goods are referred to as *private benefits* (PB) and the costs of purchasing such goods are referred to as *private costs* (PC). If the private market mechanism is perfect, the market price of a commodity is determined by a demand schedule and a supply schedule of the commodity under the prevailing income distribution of the consumers. Hence, the marginal private benefit (MPB) is equivalent to the demand for a commodity and the marginal private cost (MPC) is equivalent to the supply for a commodity as the consumers tend to maximize their net private benefits and the producers to maximize their profits. Because the private market system reaches the equilibrium when the quantity demanded equals the quantity supplied, this quantity also represents the amount at which the marginal private benefit equals the marginal private cost as shown in Fig. 17.2. Hence, resources are efficiently allocated to the production of a commodity in a perfectly competitive private market system since under such conditions, the marginal private benefit equals the marginal social benefit (MPB = MSB) and the marginal private cost equals the marginal social cost (MPC = MSC) as shown in Fig. 17.3

However, because of market imperfections, the goal of achieving economic efficiency is often elusive. Of all types of market failure, externality is most directly related to economic inefficiency of capital investment projects and therefore will be examined in this context.

Externality is defined as a benefit or cost in production or consumption that does not accrue to the producer or consumer of the commodity. It is an indirect benefit or cost to society. The marginal indirect benefit (MIB) is the difference between the marginal social benefit (MSB) and the marginal private benefit (MPB), and the marginal indirect cost (MIC) is the difference between the marginal social cost (MSC) and marginal private cost (MPC). That is, given MSC = MPC,

$$MIB = MSB - MPB \qquad (17.1)$$

Similarly, given MSB = MPB,

$$MIC = MSC - MPC \qquad (17.2)$$

The indirect benefit is referred to as a *positive externality* and the indirect cost is referred to as a *negative externality*. The terms MIB and MIC are referred to as *positive marginal externality* and *negative marginal externality*, respectively. Thus, a positive externality exists when the social benefit exceeds the private benefit, and a negative externality exists when the social cost exceeds the private cost. For example, homeowners who improve their buildings and grounds periodically contribute a

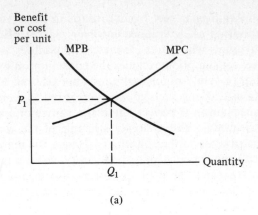

(a)

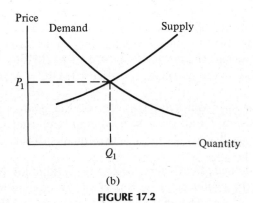

(b)

FIGURE 17.2

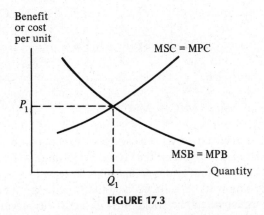

FIGURE 17.3

448

positive externality to the neighborhood while a factory which pollutes the air produces a negative externality to the community nearby.

Externalities cause problems in achieving economic efficiency when indirect benefits and costs are excluded in making resource allocation decisions. If MIB = 0 in Eq. (17.1) and MIC = 0 in Eq. (17.2), it can be seen that MSB = MPB and MSC = MPC as for the case of a perfectly competitive private market system shown earlier in Fig. 17.3. However, if MIB > 0, it means that MSB > MPB, and there is a tendency for underproduction under such circumstances. But if MIC > 0, it means that MSC > MPC, and there is an incentive for overproduction. In either case, the net social benefit is not maximized.

Since positive or negative externalities often have widespread geographic effects far beyond the sources from which they are generated, these effects are referred to as *spillovers*. The allocation function of the fiscal policy established by the government can provide a criterion for resolving the inefficiency problems of externalities. For example, positive externalities may be encouraged and negative externalities discouraged by regulations and/or by economic incentives and disincentives. The externalities may also be internalized if the indirect benefit (or cost) is accrued (or charged) to consumers. In the case of neighborhood improvement, for example, the local government may pass an ordinance requiring that all buildings and grounds in the neighborhood be maintained following certain standards; or in the case of air pollution from a plant, the factory may be required to spend a considerable amount of money for air pollution abatement, and it may charge this expense to customers who purchase its products. The difficulty in implementing such policies is to determine the appropriate level of government regulation so that the cure will not be worse than the problem. We shall illustrate qualitatively how the problem can be tackled with two examples.

Example 17.1

The private market for low-cost new housing units in a city is represented by the demand schedule (same as the MPB curve) and the supply schedule (same as the MPC curve) in Fig. 17.4. The market price and the quantity produced at the market equilibrium point 1 are P_1 and Q_1, respectively. However, the city council desires to encourage the construction of a larger new housing stock to the level of Q_2 in order to maximize the social benefits to low-income families. What professional advice can you offer to the city council?

In the private market system, the net private benefit is maximized at the market equilibrium point 1. Given that MSC = MPC, the net social benefit will be maximized at point 3 for which the quantity produced will be Q_2. However, in order to produce the quantity Q_2, the price of each housing unit will go up to P_3 because higher costs must be paid to bid for additional resources that are committed to other uses. On the other hand, in order to find enough buyers for the

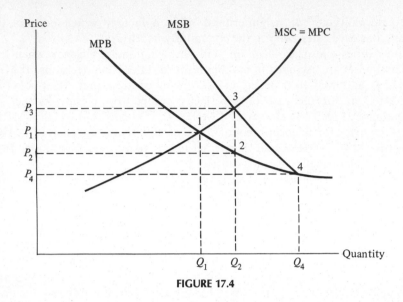

FIGURE 17.4

quantity Q_2, the market price must be set at P_2. Thus, the city council must be prepared to raise funds to pay a subsidy of $(P_3 - P_2)$ per unit either to the producer or to the buyer if it considers the construction of Q_2 new housing units is a socially desirable goal.

Note that $(P_3 - P_2)$ represents the positive marginal externality to the city when Q_2 units of new housing are produced. If a quantity greater than Q_2 is produced, not only the price of each unit must be reduced below P_2 in order to find sufficient buyers, but the positive marginal externality also becomes smaller. If the quantity produced exceeds Q_4, no positive externality exists since the marginal social benefit cannot be less than the marginal private benefit.

Example 17.2

Suppose that the curves in Fig. 17.4 for Example 17.1 can be approximated by straight lines. The values corresponding to the intersections of these straight lines are given as follows: $P_1 = \$70{,}000$, $P_3 = \$80{,}000$, $P_4 = \$50{,}000$, $Q_1 = 500$ units, $Q_2 = 600$ units, and $Q_4 = 1{,}000$ units. Determine the subsidy per unit that the city must provide in order to encourage the construction of 600 new housing units.

The straight line approximation of Fig. 17.4 is shown in Fig. 17.5 from which we find

$$P_1 = 70{,}000$$

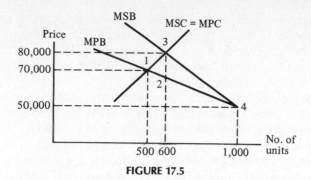

FIGURE 17.5

$$P_2 = 50,000 + (70,000 - 50,000) \frac{(1,000 - 600)}{(1,000 - 500)} = 66,000$$

$$P_3 - P_2 = 80,000 - 66,000 = 14,000$$

Thus, the city must provide a subsidy of $14,000 per housing unit.

Example 17.3

A cement factory which supplies its products to many builders in the region discharges its industrial waste into a river, causing pollution downstream. The private market for cement is represented by the demand schedule (same as the MPB curve) and the supply schedule (same as the MPC curve) in Fig. 17.6. The market price

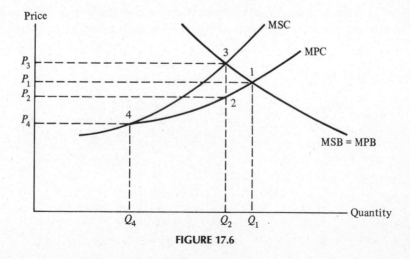

FIGURE 17.6

and the quantity produced at the market equilibrium point 1 are P_1 and Q_1, respectively. In order to reduce the level of water pollution, the state government is considering levying a tax for each sack of cement produced beyond the quantity Q_2, which is considered the quantity necessary for satisfying the needs of the builders in the state. What is a reasonable amount for this tax?

In the private market system, the net private benefit is maximized at the market equilibrium point 1. Given that MSB = MPB, the net social benefit will be maximized at point 3 for which the quantity produced will be Q_2. In order to limit the quantity produced to Q_2, the price per sack can be lowered to P_2 because of the reduction in costs for bidding the resources needed for the production. On the other hand, the consumers will bid up the price to P_3 because of scarcity. Consequently, if the state government levies a tax of $(P_3 - P_2)$ for each sack of cement produced beyond the quantity Q_2, the company may comply with the limit of production voluntarily rather than pay the tax imposed by the government.

Note that $(P_3 - P_2)$ represents the negative marginal externality to users of the river water downstream. If a quantity less than Q_2 is produced, not only the negative marginal externality becomes smaller but the price per sack also becomes lower. If the quantity produced is below Q_4, no negative externality exists since the marginal social cost cannot be less than the marginal private cost.

Example 17.4

Suppose that the curves in Fig. 17.6 for Example 17.3 can be approximated by straight lines. The values corresponding to the intersections of these straight lines are given as follows: $P_1 = \$10$, $P_3 = \$12$, $P_4 = \$6$, $Q_1 = 10,000$ sacks, $Q_2 = 9,000$ sacks, and $Q_4 = 6,000$ sacks. Determine the tax per sack of cement that the state should levy in order to discourage the production beyond the level of 9,000 sacks.

The straight line approximation of Fig. 17.6 is shown in Fig. 17.7 from which

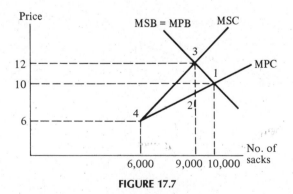

FIGURE 17.7

we find:

$$P_1 = 10$$

$$P_2 = 10 - (10 - 6)\frac{(10,000 - 9,000)}{(10,000 - 6,000)} = 9$$

$$P_3 - P_2 = 12 - 9 = 3$$

Hence, the state should levy a tax of $3 per sack of cement.

17.5   Consumers' Surplus

Let the market price and the quantity produced at the market equilibrium point 1 be represented by P_1 and Q_1, respectively, as shown in Fig. 17.8(a). The area under the demand curve up to the point Q_1 represents the amount that the consumers would be willing to pay for Q_1 units, and the total revenue R_1 to producers is the product P_1Q_1 as represented by the rectangular area. The shaded area S_1 which represents the difference between the area under the demand curve up to Q_1 and the rectangular area P_1Q_1, is referred to as the *consumers' surplus.*

Suppose that the producers produce Q_2 units and sell them at a price P_2 as shown in Fig. 17.8(b), which is analogous to the case of positive externality in Fig. 17.4. Then the total revenue to the producers is $R_2 = P_2Q_2$, and the consumer's surplus is S_2. By increasing the production from Q_1 to Q_2 units, the increase in private benefits to the producers is

$$R_2 - R_1 = P_2Q_2 - P_1Q_1 \tag{17.3}$$

and the increase in the consumers' surplus is

$$S_2 - S_1 = (P_1 - P_2)Q_1 + \tfrac{1}{2}(P_1 - P_2)(Q_2 - Q_1) \tag{17.4}$$

The last term in Eq. (17.4) is an approximation of the area 1–2–3 in Fig. 17.8(b) by a triangle. Since this term is very small when $(Q_2 - Q_1)$ is small, it is negligible compared to $(P_1 - P_2)Q_1$.

If the production is increased by one unit above Q_1, $(R_2 - R_1)$ represents the marginal private benefit to the producers, i.e.,

$$\text{MPB} = P_2Q_2 - P_1Q_1 \tag{17.5}$$

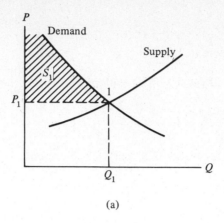

(a)

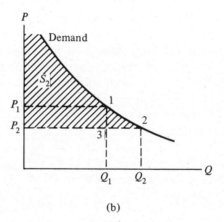

(b)

FIGURE 17.8

The sum of $(R_2 - R_1)$ and $(S_2 - S_1)$ represents the marginal social benefit to society (both producers and consumers), i.e.,

$$\text{MSB} = (P_2 Q_2 - P_1 Q_1) + (P_1 - P_2)Q_1 \qquad (17.6)$$

What is the implication of the consumers' surplus? First, if the producer is a monopolist, it will stop production at a quantity Q_2 when $R_2 - R_1$ becomes zero, thus creating the situation of underproduction. Second, in making decisions on a public project, the consumers' surplus is an indication of the benefits to a group of potential users of the proposed public project. In each situation, a knowledge of the consumers' surplus helps to analyze the consequences of the action.

Example 17.5

Suppose that for the demand curve in Figs. 17.8(a) and (b), it is known that an increase of production from $Q_1 = 100$ units to $Q_2 = 101$ units will cause $P_1 = \$10.00$ to drop to $P_2 = \$9.95$. Determine the marginal private benefit and the marginal social benefit.

Using Eqs. (17.5) and (17.6), we obtain

$$MPB = (9.95)(101) - (10.00)(100) = \$4.95$$

$$MSB = 4.95 + (10.00 - 9.95)(100) = \$9.95$$

17.6 Social Equity and Income Distribution

There are social and political as well as economic considerations in public investment decisions, even if the private market functions efficiently. A competitive market can respond only to the effective demand of consumers under the existing income distribution. However, a society may judge whether the prevailing income distribution is fair, and such a judgment is a matter for social and political debate rather than economic analysis.

Through taxation and fiscal policies, the government performs the distributive function of both costs and benefits in administering government programs among individuals. The general principles of fairness for taxation and social welfare programs are *horizontal equity* and *vertical equity*. In simple terms, horizontal equity means equal treatment of equals, and vertical equity means unequal treatment of unequals. Most frequently, personal incomes are used as the scale in classifying the "equal" and "unequal" groups.

Historically, these principles were first applied to taxation, thus requiring those in the same income group to pay the same tax and those belonging to higher income groups to pay higher taxes. When these principles were later applied to recipients of social welfare programs, they were extended to mean that those in the same income group receive the same benefits and those belonging to higher income groups receive less benefits.

Theoretically, it is desirable to provide a precise accounting of the groups who ultimately bear the burden of a tax or who are the eventual beneficiaries of a social program. Then, the general principles can be applied to measure the net benefits of both taxes and social programs to different groups of individuals. However, this concept is difficult to carry out in practice.

There are certain goods which are regarded as meritorious and their production is encouraged since they tend to produce positive externality to society. Such goods are referred to as *merit wants*. However, the distribution of merit wants often raises the question of fairness because they can be provided either through *supply-based* or *demand-based subsidies*. An example of merit want in the form of supply-based subsidy is the public housing for low-income families. Housing has long been singled out for government action because of the general belief that every person is entitled to a decent home. However, public housing units are rival and excludable in consumption, and not all low-income families can receive such benefits if they want to. Consequently, the provision of such merit wants violates the principles of social equity. On the other hand, merit wants in the form of demand-based subsidy, such as food stamps or any transfer payment in kind of goods and services (other than cash), can be distributed more fairly. Whether the merit wants are provided in the form of supply-based subsidy or demand-based subsidy, the government exercises the value judgment that these merit wants are good for the recipients who cannot legally exchange such goods for something else they prefer. Hence, the provision of merit wants is not justified on the ground of economic efficiency, nor even necessarily on the ground of social equity.

17.7 Different Views on Social Discount Rates

There are many factors affecting the choice of social discount rates, and these factors are often related to the fiscal policy objectives. However, the strongest arguments are centered on the issues of decision under uncertainty and the proper way in dealing with the time-risk adjustments in the public sector in order to avoid misallocation of resources. The substantially different views on the determination of the social discount rates have profound implications for the evaluation of public projects. Consequently, the basic arguments supporting different views are summarized for consideration:

1. The first position is to treat risk in the public sector in the same way as that in the private sector in order to avoid overinvestment in the public sector at the expense of private investments. Since investments are discounted with respect to both time and risk in perfect capital markets, the market-determined rates of return should be used to evaluate public investment opportunities.[2] This position suffers from the presupposition of the existence of perfect markets, and the conclusion also needs to be modified for the consideration of corporate income tax.

2. The second position is developed along the same approach as the first one but with added refinements.[3] It is demonstrated that when the risks associated with a public investment are publicly borne, the total cost of risk bearing is insignificant. Therefore, the government should ignore uncertainty in evaluating public investments, and the choice of the rate of discount should in this case be independent of considerations of risk. However, many of the risks

---

[2] See Ref. [17.9] and Ref. [17.10].
[3] See Ref. [17.1].

associated with public investments are borne by private individuals, and in such cases it is appropriate to discount for risk as would these individuals. This position seems more defensible than the argument that the government should ignore uncertainty and behave as if it were indifferent to risk because the government invests in a greater number of diverse projects and is able to pool risks to a much greater extent than private investors.[4]

3. The third position asserts that time and risk preferences relevant for government action should be established as a matter of policy.[5] This position is based on the arguments that the government has a broader responsibility than those of its individual members and that capital markets are so imperfect that they do not reflect the time and risk preferences of individuals. Therefore, the appropriate discount rate should be inferred from the national objectives. The weakness of this position is that the adoption of an artificially low discount rate for public investments as a national policy constitutes a redistribution of income from present to future generations as well as misallocation of resources between the public and private sectors.

It appears that the second position advanced by Arrow and Lind[6] is most attractive from the theoretical viewpoint. We shall therefore explore this approach further in its application. If the uncertain returns from a given public investment are independent of other components of national income, and if the size of the share of investment borne by each taxpayer is a negligible component of income, then the cost of risk bearing associated with holding it will be small. Under these conditions, the total cost of risk bearing is also small, since the risk associated with any investment is distributed among a large number of people, not because the government is able to pool investments. Therefore, the choice of social discount rate should be independent of risk. If private investments are replaced by public investments yielding a lower return as a result of the choice, the government should serve the role of a supplier of insurance by subsidizing private investments where appropriate. Although the philosophical foundation of this approach is by no means universally accepted, more economists seem to agree with the recommendation that *public investments should be evaluated according to their net present values computed on the basis of expected net returns, using a social discount rate equivalent to the market-determined risk-free rate for private investments.*

Another important aspect of the position suggested by Arrow and Lind has received less attention than it deserves, perhaps because of potential difficulties in its application. However, it provides some useful insights on cases where the risks of public investments are borne by private individuals. Under such circumstances, some benefits and costs will accrue to the government and the uncertainties involved will be publicly borne; other benefits and costs will accrue to individuals and the attendant uncertainties will be borne privately. Hence, two different streams of

[4] See Ref. [17.16].
[5] See Ref. [17.14].
[6] See Ref. [17.1].

benefits and costs should be treated differently with respect to uncertainty, using a risk-free rate for discounting the stream of benefits and costs accruing to government and higher rates reflecting the risk for the stream accruing directly to individuals. Such a procedure causes some difficulties in making the distinction between private and public benefits and costs, but the problem does not appear to be insurmountable. For the typical case where costs are borne publicly and benefits accrue privately, this procedure calls for the use of a risk-free discount rate for the costs but higher discount rates for the benefits, depending on the nature of the uncertainty and time-risk preferences of the individuals who receive these benefits.

The practical implications of the cases where the risks of public investments are borne by private individuals can easily be understood with some simple illustrations. For example, the public education system in the United States has been viewed as an investment in human capital where the social costs include the provision of physical facilities and staffing and the social benefits include the improvement of the character and ability of its citizens. It is generally agreed that the benefits and costs which accrue to the society should be discounted at a low social discount rate. However, the benefits and costs that accrue to individual students will be viewed differently by them and their parents. For those who value their future highly will use a low discount rate for future expected returns in computing their net present values and thus regard high school education as the key to upward mobility; whereas those who value present as being far more important than future will choose a high discount rate for future expected returns in computing their net present values and thus conclude that it is to their own advantage to drop out from high school. It has been argued by Banfield[7] that the division of social groups according to their attitudes toward present and future, i.e., their choice of social discount rates, is far more significant than other forms of grouping in order to understand the persistence of poverty in society.

It is ironic that for the typical case where costs are borne publicly and benefits accrue privately, the procedure of adopting a lower discount rate for public costs and a higher discount rate for private benefits will lead to a lower total net present value than a procedure using a single rate (either the higher or the lower) to discount both benefits and costs. However, the concept of treating cases in which risks associated with public investment differently from those cases where the risks are publicly borne is still an ideal which is seldom put into practice.

17.8 Multiobjectives in the Choice of Social Discount Rates

There are strong arguments that the private market will not make adequate provision for public investment because of problems of externalities and other market

[7] See Ref. [17.2], pp. 46–54.

imperfections. The classical arguments in favor of a larger share of the national wealth for the public sectors are familiar ones. In the words of Galbraith,[8]

> ... we must find a way to remedy the poverty which afflicts us in public services and which is in such increasingly bizarre contrast with our affluence in private goods. This is necessary to temper and, more hopefully, to eliminate the social disorders which are the counterpart of the present imbalance. It is necessary in the long run for promoting the growth of private output itself. Such balance is a matter of elementary common sense in a country in which need is becoming so exiguous that it must be cherished where it exists and nurtured where it does not.

However, the proponents of this view often regard the choice of lower social discount rates as a substitute for public subsidies in serving the distribution and stabilization functions of the fiscal policy objectives. Hence, the choice of social discount rates has created an unnecessary issue in favor of public projects with long-term commitments.

In the discussion of social discount rate for public projects, Marglin[9] has inadvertently also raised the question of investment for present versus future generations. Simply put: "why do governments require citizens to sacrifice current consumption in order to undertake investments that will not yield their benefits until those called upon to make the sacrifice are all dead?" Thus, we are confronted with the ethical issues as well as the economic issues in considering long-term versus short term public projects. Both of these issues have been examined by a number of economists who have clarified the nature of the problems.[10]

A balanced view toward the allocation of investment for the public sector between long-term and short-term projects has been presented by Baumol.[11] Citing the argument of Tullock[12] that the next generation is likely going to be wealthier than this generation and that we may want to redistribute income in favor of the present poor rather than the future poor, he correctly points out that an argument against a lower social discount rate is not necessarily an argument against activities in the public sector. It may well be in society's interest to spend more on short-term projects in solving today's problems and less on the long-term projects that will bring more wealth to future generations, given the total amount for the public sector. Such spending may serve the stabilization function of the fiscal policy by expanding employment and social order. Baumol summarizes his view succinctly:[13]

> However, this does not mean that the future should in every respect be left to the mercy of the free market. There are important externalities and investments of the public goods variety which cry for special attention. Irreversibilities consti-

---

[8] See Ref. [17.6], p. 271.
[9] See Ref. [17.14], p. 95.
[10] See Ref. [17.4], Ref. [17.11] and Ref. [17.18].
[11] See Ref. [17.4].
[12] See Ref. [17.18].
[13] See Ref. [17.4], p. 801.

tute a prime example. If we poison our soil so that never again will it be the same, if we destroy the Grand Canyon and turn it into a hydroelectric plant, we give up assets which like Goldsmith's bold peasantry, "...their country's pride, when once destroy'd can never be supplied." All the wealth and resources of future generations will not suffice to restore them. Investment in the preservation of such items then seems perfectly proper, but for this purpose the appropriate instrument would appear to be a set of selective subsidies rather than a low general discount rate that encourages indiscriminately all sorts of investment programs whether or not they are relevant.

Moreover, one can envision circumstances in which a more general program of encouragement to investment commends itself to us. In a country which is stagnating and where only a major restriction of current consumption can put life into its development program, one may well wish to make the sacrifice for tomorrow, for in such a case, without it the future generation will be as impoverished as the present.

So far, we have considered the fiscal policy for the public sector strictly from the national point of view. Actually, the fiscal system is decentralized among federal, state, and local governments. Fiscal decentralization permits adaptation of budget patterns to the preferences of the residents of particular jurisdictions. Ideally, the decentralized fiscal system encourages national services provided collectively on a nationwide basis, regional services provided for regionally, and local services accounted for locally. Except for national defense and other items which benefit the entire population in the nation, most public projects generate benefits which are spatially limited. However, because of the power of the federal government to levy tax, many public projects are provided for at the local level even though the funding may be supplied fully or partially by state and federal appropriations. This practice often produces the net effect of promoting stabilization of employment in some localities and regions at the expense of economic efficiency for resource allocation.

17.9   The Choice of Social Discount Rates in Practice

In recent years, there has been a greater recognition of the importance of social discount rate in the allocation function of government. Consequently, the minimum attractive rates of return on the public investments have been adjusted upward in order to avoid misallocation of resources.

The Office of Management and Budget (OMB) requires since 1972 that, with certain exceptions, federal agencies must use a real discount rate of 10% to evaluate federal investment decisions.[14] This real rate of 10%, excluding inflation, is comparable to the opportunity of cost of capital in the private sector.

---

[14] OMB Circular A-94, "Discount Rates to be used in Evaluating Time-Distributed Costs and Benefits," Executive Office of the President, March 27, 1972.

In order to avoid misallocation of resources among different federal agencies, a consistent policy should be applied uniformly to all government programs. However, for various reasons, some of which are political, certain programs are exempt from the OMB requirements. An example of the exception to the OMB requirements is the discount rate used for water projects which was set by the U.S. Congress over the years. A brief review of the history of the discount rates established for water projects will give some insight into the controversy that arises from the choice of social discount rates.[15]

Prior to 1968, the discount rate for water projects was set at the coupon rate of interest on U.S. government securities that had *original* terms of maturity of 15 years or more. This rule resulted in the low discount rate of $2\frac{5}{8}\%$ in the 1950s and early 1960s. By the late 1960s the yields on government securities were considerably higher than the average of the original coupon rates on outstanding government securities. In 1968, the rule for computing discount rates was changed to the yield during the preceding fiscal year on interest-bearing marketable securities of the United States, which at the time the computation is made have terms of 15 years or more remaining to maturity. This change had the effect of rapidly increasing the discount rate. To dampen this effect, a ceiling was introduced in 1974 such that "in no event shall the rate be raised or lowered more than one-quarter of one percent for any year." A grandfather clause in the Water Resources Development Act of 1974 also specifies that the discount rate used at the time of a project's authorization is binding, even though economic conditions at the time a project finally receives funding may have changed. Since many years may elapse between project authorization and appropriations for a project, the official discount rate at the time of appropriations is often higher than that at the time of projection authorization. The grandfather clause has the net effect of keeping the discount rate lower.

17.10 Estimation of Costs and Benefits for Public Projects

As pointed out in Chapter 10, the estimation of costs and benefits involves forecasting future events. We have given more emphasis to the estimation of costs since they are more tractable than benefits. This is particularly true in the case of public projects because it is often difficult to place monetary values on social benefits.

The problems associated with the estimation of costs are well known, and the accuracy of an estimate is affected more by variations in design decisions than in estimating methods. Since the decision-making process for selecting public projects often requires several iterations through public discussions, there is a strong possibility that the original basis for design of the project is revised, more often with additional requirements or sophistications. Consequently, the preliminary cost esti-

---

[15] See Ref. [17.8].

mates of many public projects turn out to be considerably below the final costs of the completed projects even when inflation is excluded. Such outcomes have the unfortunate effects of undermining the confidence of the public, which is unaware of the major cause of the variations in the cost estimates.

However, the estimation of benefits poses far more serious problems of great significance. Basically, there are different types of benefits that may be included in the evaluation. The most obvious are benefits which accrue directly to the users of the project who would be willing to pay as indicated by the consumers' surplus. Benefits may also accrue indirectly to nonusers because of the positive externality produced by a project. There are also possible secondary benefits such as economic growth, technological expansion, and increase in employment; however, these effects are difficult to measure and the techniques for estimating them are too imperfect to produce unmistakable results.

Because of the difficulties in the estimation of benefits and costs in the evaluation of public projects, the benefit-cost analysis is often open to challenge by its critics. Hence the final decision on selecting a public project may well be based on consensus through the political process.

17.11   Summary and Study Guide

This chapter has presented a cursory treatment of the broad social and political issues which often enter into the evaluation of public projects and has provided some understanding of the most important factors affecting public investment decisions.

We began with a discussion of the provision of public projects and pointed out the distinction between the provision of public projects and public production. We also mentioned briefly the types of market failure that have prompted government regulation and the types of goods and services which are the reasons for government action.

We then examined the fiscal policy objectives for the public sector, including the allocation function, the distribution function, and the stabilization function. We emphasized the significance of economic efficiency and the effects of externalities, and rationale for dealing with such problems is illustrated qualitatively with examples.

We also discussed the general principles of horizontal equity and vertical equity for taxation and social welfare programs, particularly with respect to income distribution. Furthermore, we considered the supply-based and demand-based subsidies in providing merit wants.

The problems of selecting the appropriate social discount rates and their significance in public investment decisions were examined. The multiobjectives in the choice of social discount rates were also discussed. Finally, the problems associated with the choice of social discount rates in practice as well as the problems in connection with the estimation of costs and benefits for public projects were also reviewed briefly.

REFERENCES

17.1 Arrow, K. J., and R. C. Lind, "Uncertainty and the Evaluation of Public Investment Decisions," *American Economic Review*, **60** (June 1970), 364–378.

17.2 Banfield, E. C., *The Unheavenly City*. Boston, MA: Little, Brown, 1970.

17.3 Baumol, W. J., *Welfare Economics and the Theory of the State*, 2nd ed. Cambridge, MA: Harvard University Press, 1965.

17.4 Baumol, W. J., "On the Social Rate of Discount," *American Economic Review*, **58** (September 1968), 788–802.

17.5 Eckstein, O., *Water-Resource Development, the Economics of Project Evaluation*, Cambridge, MA: Harvard University Press, 1958.

17.6 Galbraith, J. K., *The Affluent Society*, 2nd ed. Boston, MA: Houghton Mifflin, 1969.

17.7 Galbraith, J. K., *Economics and the Public Purpose*. Boston, MA: Houghton Mifflin, 1973.

17.8 Hanke, S. H., and J. B. Anwyll, "On the Discount Rate Controversy," *Public Policy*, **29** (Spring 1980), 171–183.

17.9 Hirshliefer, J., "Investment Decision Under Uncertainty: Choice-Theoretic Approaches," *Quarterly Journal of Economics*, **79** (November 1965), 509–536.

17.10 Hirshliefer, J., "Investment Decision Under Uncertainty: Applications of the State-Preference Approach," *Quarterly Journal of Economics*, **80** (May 1966), 252–277.

17.11 Lind, R. C., "Further Comments," *Quarterly Journal of Economics*, **78** (May 1964), 336–345.

17.12 Little, I. M. D., and J. A. Mirrless, *Project Appraisal and Planning for Developing Countries*. London, England: Heinemann Educational Books, 1974.

17.13 Margolis, J., "The Economic Evaluation of Federal Water Resource Development," *American Economic Review*, **49** (March 1959), 96–111.

17.14 Marglin, S. A., "The Social Rate of Discount and the Optimal Rate of Investment," *Quarterly Journal of Economics*, **77** (February 1963), 95–112.

17.15 Musgrave, R. A., and P. B. Musgrave, *Public Finance in Theory and Practice*, 2nd ed. New York: McGraw-Hill, 1976.

17.16 Samuelson, P. A., "Principles of Efficiency: Discussion," *American Economic Review*, **54** (May 1964), 93–96.

17.17 Schreiber, A. F., P. K. Gatons, and R. B. Clemmer, *Economics of Urban Problems: An Introduction*, 2nd ed. Boston, MA: Houghton Mifflin, 1976.

17.18 Tullock, G., "The Social Rate of Discount and the Optimal Rate of Investment: Comment," *Quarterly Journal of Economics*, **78** (May 1964), 331–336.

PROBLEMS

P17.1 A private caterer which provides lunch service for a university cafeteria offers a standard menu at $2 per person and has attracted 1,000 students to contract for the meal. In order to supply the same meal to 2,000 students, the caterer would have to raise the price to $2.50 per person because it has to forego other outside commitments. However, the university likes to encourage more students to participate in the lunch for social and other benefits and is willing to provide subsidy to 2,000 students. If it wants to subsidize the meal for all of its 4,000 students, the price per person would have to be $0.50 to find all takers. What amount should the university be willing to subsidize the price per student in order to produce the maximum social benefits? Assume that the MSB, MSC, MPB, and MPC curves can be approximated by straight lines.

P17.2 A sewage treatment plant which processes large quantities of sewage materials from local communities emits an unpleasant odor in its surrounding area. The maximum capacity of the plant for efficient operation is 250 mgd (million gallons per day), and its charges the customers a fee of $0.30 per gallon of discharge. If the plant operates at 100 mgd, there will be no emission of unpleasant odor, and it can charge $0.12 per gallon of discharge. A reasonable compromise is to process 200 mgd and charge the customers a fee of $0.42 per gallon of discharge. What fee per gallon of discharge should the local government assess the sewage plant for maintaining the desirable level of 200 mgd in order to minimize the social costs? Assume that the MSB, MSC, MPB, and MPC curves can be approximated by straight lines.

P17.3 Referring to Fig. 17.8 in this chapter, determine the increase in private benefits to the producers and the increase in consumers' surplus for a product if $P_1 = \$20$, $P_2 = 15, Q_1 = 200$ units, and $Q_2 = 300$ units.

P17.4 Referring to Fig. 17.8 in this chapter, determine the marginal private benefit to the producers and the marginal social benefit to society if $P_1 = \$80$, $P_2 = \$75$, $Q_1 = 15$ units, and $Q_2 = 16$ units. If the producer is a monopolist, is there any incentive for him or her to produce more than 15 units?

P17.5 A public project that requires an initial investment of $180,000 and a uniform annual operating cost of $40,000 in the next 40 years is expected to generate a uniform annual benefit of $63,000 over the planning horizon of 40 years. There will be no salvage value. The opportunity cost for similar projects in the private sector is approximately 12%, allowing for the difference in taxes. The social discount rate for similar projects has been set at 6% in the past. Determine the benefit cost ratio of this project on the basis of each of the following conditions: (1) both costs and benefits are discounted at 12%, (2) both are discounted at 6%, and (3) costs that will be borne by the public are discounted at 6% and benefits that will accrue to individuals are discounted at 12%.

P17.6 The cost of a college education to an average student attending a state-supported university is estimated to be as shown in the following table. Upon graduation, an average student is expected to earn $5,000 more per year in the next 45 years in comparison with what his or her earnings would be if he or she chooses not to attend college. Determine the net present value of the cash flows depicting the costs and benefits of this college education if the MARR of the student is (1) 6% and (2) 12%.

| Year | Private Cost | | | | Private Benefit (Increased Earning) |
	Tuition	Expenses	Foregone Earning	Total	
0	$2,000	$4,000	0	$6,000	0
1–3 (each)	$2,000	$4,000	$9,000	$15,000	0
4	0	0	$9,000	$9,000	0
5–49 (each)	0	0	0	0	$5,000

P17.7 In allocating state funds to state-supported colleges, the state legislature considers the social costs and benefits of this human capital investment and comes up with the data shown in the following table. The public subsidy per student is $8,000 per year above the total private cost, which includes tuition, expenses, and foregone earnings of the student. The benefit to the state is better educated citizens who, among other things, can generate more job opportunities for others as well as increase their own private gains. If the MARR used by the state legislature is 6%, determine the net present value of social benefit over social cost per student supported by the state.

| Year | Social Cost per Student | | | Social Benefit per Student | | |
	Private Cost	State Subsidy	Total	Private	Benefit to State	Total
0	$6,000	$8,000	$14,000	0	0	0
1–3 (each)	$15,000	$8,000	$23,000	0	0	0
4	$9,000	0	9,000	0	0	0
5–49 (each)	0	0	0	$5,000	$2,000	$7,000

APPENDIX

A

DISCRETE COMPOUND
INTEREST TABLES

Table A.1   Discrete Compound Interest Table $i = 0.5\%$

n	COMPOUND AMOUNT FACTOR (F|P,i,n)	DISCOUNT AMOUNT FACTOR (P|F,i,n)	COMPOUND UNIFORM SERIES FACTOR (F|U,i,n)	SINKING FUND FACTOR (U|F,i,n)	DISCOUNT UNIFORM SERIES FACTOR (P|U,i,n)	CAPITAL RECOVERY FACTOR (U|P,i,n)	DISCOUNT GRADIENT FACTOR (P|G,i,n)
1	1.0050	0.9950	1.0000	1.0000	0.9950	1.0050	0.0000
2	1.0100	0.9901	2.0050	0.4988	1.9851	0.5038	0.9893
3	1.0151	0.9851	3.0150	0.3317	2.9702	0.3367	2.9589
4	1.0202	0.9802	4.0301	0.2481	3.9505	0.2531	5.8992
5	1.0253	0.9754	5.0502	0.1980	4.9259	0.2030	9.8003
6	1.0304	0.9705	6.0755	0.1646	5.8964	0.1696	14.6522
7	1.0355	0.9657	7.1059	0.1407	6.8621	0.1457	20.4456
8	1.0407	0.9609	8.1414	0.1228	7.8229	0.1278	27.1712
9	1.0459	0.9561	9.1821	0.1089	8.7790	0.1139	34.8193
10	1.0511	0.9513	10.2280	0.0978	9.7304	0.1028	43.3813
11	1.0564	0.9466	11.2791	0.0887	10.6770	0.0937	52.8469
12	1.0617	0.9419	12.3355	0.0811	11.6189	0.0861	63.2069
13	1.0670	0.9372	13.3972	0.0746	12.5561	0.0796	74.4536
14	1.0723	0.9326	14.4642	0.0691	13.4887	0.0741	86.5757
15	1.0777	0.9279	15.5365	0.0644	14.4166	0.0694	99.5659
16	1.0831	0.9233	16.6142	0.0602	15.3399	0.0652	113.4152
17	1.0885	0.9187	17.6973	0.0565	16.2586	0.0615	128.1139
18	1.0939	0.9141	18.7857	0.0532	17.1727	0.0582	143.6539
19	1.0994	0.9096	19.8797	0.0503	18.0823	0.0553	160.0257
20	1.1049	0.9051	20.9791	0.0477	18.9874	0.0527	177.2214
21	1.1104	0.9006	22.0840	0.0453	19.8879	0.0503	195.2325
22	1.1160	0.8961	23.1944	0.0431	20.7840	0.0481	214.0491
23	1.1216	0.8916	24.3103	0.0411	21.6756	0.0461	233.6642
24	1.1272	0.8872	25.4319	0.0393	22.5628	0.0443	254.0688
25	1.1328	0.8828	26.5590	0.0377	23.4456	0.0427	275.2549
26	1.1385	0.8784	27.6918	0.0361	24.3240	0.0411	297.2139
27	1.1442	0.8740	28.8303	0.0347	25.1980	0.0397	319.9378
28	1.1499	0.8697	29.9744	0.0334	26.0676	0.0384	343.4179
29	1.1556	0.8653	31.1243	0.0321	26.9330	0.0371	367.6473
30	1.1614	0.8610	32.2799	0.0310	27.7940	0.0360	392.6160
35	1.1907	0.8398	38.1453	0.0262	32.0353	0.0312	528.2935
40	1.2208	0.8191	44.1587	0.0226	36.1721	0.0276	681.3133
45	1.2516	0.7990	50.3240	0.0199	40.2071	0.0249	850.7396
50	1.2832	0.7793	56.6450	0.0177	44.1427	0.0227	1035.6700
55	1.3156	0.7601	63.1256	0.0158	47.9813	0.0208	1235.2395
60	1.3488	0.7414	69.7698	0.0143	51.7254	0.0193	1448.6141
70	1.4178	0.7053	83.5658	0.0120	58.9393	0.0170	1913.6063
80	1.4903	0.6710	98.0674	0.0102	65.8022	0.0152	2424.6044
90	1.5666	0.6383	113.3105	0.0088	72.3311	0.0138	2976.0311
100	1.6467	0.6073	129.3333	0.0077	78.5425	0.0127	3562.7440

Table A.2 Discrete Compound Interest Table $\quad i = 1.0\%$

n	COMPOUND AMOUNT FACTOR (F|P,i,n)	DISCOUNT AMOUNT FACTOR (P|F,i,n)	COMPOUND UNIFORM SERIES FACTOR (F|U,i,n)	SINKING FUND FACTOR (U|F,i,n)	DISCOUNT UNIFORM SERIES FACTOR (P|U,i,n)	CAPITAL RECOVERY FACTOR (U|P,i,n)	DISCOUNT GRADIENT FACTOR (P|G,i,n)
1	1.0100	0.9901	1.0000	1.0000	0.9901	1.0100	0.0000
2	1.0201	0.9803	2.0100	0.4975	1.9704	0.5075	0.9803
3	1.0303	0.9706	3.0301	0.3300	2.9410	0.3400	2.9214
4	1.0406	0.9610	4.0604	0.2463	3.9020	0.2563	5.8043
5	1.0510	0.9515	5.1010	0.1960	4.8534	0.2060	9.6101
6	1.0615	0.9420	6.1520	0.1625	5.7955	0.1725	14.3203
7	1.0721	0.9327	7.2135	0.1386	6.7282	0.1486	19.9165
8	1.0829	0.9235	8.2857	0.1207	7.6517	0.1307	26.3809
9	1.0937	0.9143	9.3685	0.1067	8.5660	0.1167	33.6956
10	1.1046	0.9053	10.4622	0.0956	9.4713	0.1056	41.8431
11	1.1157	0.8963	11.5668	0.0865	10.3676	0.0965	50.8063
12	1.1268	0.8874	12.6825	0.0788	11.2551	0.0888	60.5682
13	1.1381	0.8787	13.8093	0.0724	12.1337	0.0824	71.1121
14	1.1495	0.8700	14.9474	0.0669	13.0037	0.0769	82.4215
15	1.1610	0.8613	16.0969	0.0621	13.8650	0.0721	94.4803
16	1.1726	0.8528	17.2579	0.0579	14.7179	0.0679	107.2726
17	1.1843	0.8444	18.4304	0.0543	15.5622	0.0643	120.7827
18	1.1961	0.8360	19.6147	0.0510	16.3983	0.0610	134.9949
19	1.2081	0.8277	20.8109	0.0481	17.2260	0.0581	149.8941
20	1.2202	0.8195	22.0190	0.0454	18.0455	0.0554	165.4655
21	1.2324	0.8114	23.2392	0.0430	18.8570	0.0530	181.6940
22	1.2447	0.8034	24.4716	0.0409	19.6604	0.0509	198.5653
23	1.2572	0.7954	25.7163	0.0389	20.4558	0.0489	216.0648
24	1.2697	0.7876	26.9735	0.0371	21.2434	0.0471	234.1789
25	1.2824	0.7798	28.2432	0.0354	22.0231	0.0454	252.8934
26	1.2953	0.7720	29.5256	0.0339	22.7952	0.0439	272.1944
27	1.3082	0.7644	30.8209	0.0324	23.5596	0.0424	292.0690
28	1.3213	0.7568	32.1291	0.0311	24.3164	0.0411	312.5034
29	1.3345	0.7493	33.4504	0.0299	25.0658	0.0399	333.4850
30	1.3478	0.7419	34.7849	0.0287	25.8077	0.0387	355.0007
35	1.4166	0.7059	41.6603	0.0240	29.4086	0.0340	470.1567
40	1.4889	0.6717	48.8863	0.0205	32.8347	0.0305	596.8543
45	1.5648	0.6391	56.4810	0.0177	36.0945	0.0277	733.7017
50	1.6446	0.6080	64.4631	0.0155	39.1961	0.0255	879.4155
55	1.7285	0.5785	72.8524	0.0137	42.1472	0.0237	1032.8123
60	1.8167	0.5504	81.6696	0.0122	44.9550	0.0222	1192.8036
70	2.0068	0.4983	100.6763	0.0099	50.1685	0.0199	1528.6446
80	2.2167	0.4511	121.6714	0.0082	54.8882	0.0182	1879.8739
90	2.4486	0.4084	144.8632	0.0069	59.1609	0.0169	2240.5641
100	2.7048	0.3697	170.4812	0.0059	63.0289	0.0159	2605.7721

Table A.3 Discrete Compound Interest Table $i = 2.0\%$

	COMPOUND AMOUNT FACTOR	DISCOUNT AMOUNT FACTOR	COMPOUND UNIFORM SERIES FACTOR	SINKING FUND FACTOR	DISCOUNT UNIFORM SERIES FACTOR	CAPITAL RECOVERY FACTOR	DISCOUNT GRADIENT FACTOR
n	(F|P,i,n)	(P|F,i,n)	(F|U,i,n)	(U|F,i,n)	(P|U,i,n)	(U|P,i,n)	(P|G,i,n)
1	1.0200	0.9804	1.0000	1.0000	0.9804	1.0200	0.0000
2	1.0404	0.9612	2.0200	0.4950	1.9416	0.5150	0.9611
3	1.0612	0.9423	3.0604	0.3268	2.8839	0.3468	2.8457
4	1.0824	0.9238	4.1216	0.2426	3.8077	0.2626	5.6173
5	1.1041	0.9057	5.2040	0.1922	4.7135	0.2122	9.2402
6	1.1262	0.8880	6.3081	0.1585	5.6014	0.1785	13.6800
7	1.1487	0.8706	7.4343	0.1345	6.4720	0.1545	18.9033
8	1.1717	0.8535	8.5830	0.1165	7.3255	0.1365	24.8777
9	1.1951	0.8368	9.7546	0.1025	8.1622	0.1225	31.5718
10	1.2190	0.8203	10.9497	0.0913	8.9826	0.1113	38.9549
11	1.2434	0.8043	12.1687	0.0822	9.7868	0.1022	46.9975
12	1.2682	0.7885	13.4121	0.0746	10.5753	0.0946	55.6709
13	1.2936	0.7730	14.6803	0.0681	11.3484	0.0881	64.9472
14	1.3195	0.7579	15.9739	0.0626	12.1062	0.0826	74.7996
15	1.3459	0.7430	17.2934	0.0578	12.8493	0.0778	85.2017
16	1.3728	0.7284	18.6393	0.0537	13.5777	0.0737	96.1284
17	1.4002	0.7142	20.0121	0.0500	14.2919	0.0700	107.5550
18	1.4282	0.7002	21.4123	0.0467	14.9920	0.0667	119.4577
19	1.4568	0.6864	22.8405	0.0438	15.6785	0.0638	131.8134
20	1.4859	0.6730	24.2974	0.0412	16.3514	0.0612	144.5998
21	1.5157	0.6598	25.7833	0.0388	17.0112	0.0588	157.7954
22	1.5460	0.6468	27.2990	0.0366	17.6580	0.0566	171.3789
23	1.5769	0.6342	28.8449	0.0347	18.2922	0.0547	185.3303
24	1.6084	0.6217	30.4218	0.0329	18.9139	0.0529	199.6299
25	1.6406	0.6095	32.0303	0.0312	19.5234	0.0512	214.2587
26	1.6734	0.5976	33.6709	0.0297	20.1210	0.0497	229.1981
27	1.7069	0.5859	35.3443	0.0283	20.7069	0.0483	244.4305
28	1.7410	0.5744	37.0512	0.0270	21.2813	0.0470	259.9386
29	1.7758	0.5631	38.7922	0.0258	21.8444	0.0458	275.7057
30	1.8114	0.5521	40.5681	0.0246	22.3964	0.0446	291.7158
35	1.9999	0.5000	49.9944	0.0200	24.9986	0.0400	374.8819
40	2.2080	0.4529	60.4019	0.0166	27.3555	0.0366	461.9923
45	2.4379	0.4102	71.8927	0.0139	29.4902	0.0339	551.5643
50	2.6916	0.3715	84.5793	0.0118	31.4236	0.0318	642.3596
55	2.9717	0.3365	98.5864	0.0101	33.1748	0.0301	733.3516
60	3.2810	0.3048	114.0514	0.0088	34.7609	0.0288	823.6965
70	3.9996	0.2500	149.9778	0.0067	37.4986	0.0267	999.8332
80	4.8754	0.2051	193.7718	0.0052	39.7445	0.0252	1166.7856
90	5.9431	0.1683	247.1564	0.0040	41.5869	0.0240	1322.1690
100	7.2446	0.1380	312.2319	0.0032	43.0983	0.0232	1464.7516

Table A.4   Discrete Compound Interest Table $i = 3.0\%$

n	COMPOUND AMOUNT FACTOR (F|P,i,n)	DISCOUNT AMOUNT FACTOR (P|F,i,n)	COMPOUND UNIFORM SERIES FACTOR (F|U,i,n)	SINKING FUND FACTOR (U|F,i,n)	DISCOUNT UNIFORM SERIES FACTOR (P|U,i,n)	CAPITAL RECOVERY FACTOR (U|P,i,n)	DISCOUNT GRADIENT FACTOR (P|G,i,n)
1	1.0300	0.9709	1.0000	1.0000	0.9709	1.0300	0.0000
2	1.0609	0.9426	2.0300	0.4926	1.9135	0.5226	0.9426
3	1.0927	0.9151	3.0909	0.3235	2.8286	0.3535	2.7729
4	1.1255	0.8885	4.1836	0.2390	3.7171	0.2690	5.4383
5	1.1593	0.8626	5.3091	0.1884	4.5797	0.2184	8.8887
6	1.1941	0.8375	6.4684	0.1546	5.4172	0.1846	13.0761
7	1.2299	0.8131	7.6625	0.1305	6.2303	0.1605	17.9547
8	1.2668	0.7894	8.8923	0.1125	7.0197	0.1425	23.4805
9	1.3048	0.7664	10.1591	0.0984	7.7861	0.1284	29.6119
10	1.3439	0.7441	11.4639	0.0872	8.5302	0.1172	36.3087
11	1.3842	0.7224	12.8078	0.0781	9.2526	0.1081	43.5329
12	1.4258	0.7014	14.1920	0.0705	9.9540	0.1005	51.2481
13	1.4685	0.6810	15.6178	0.0640	10.6350	0.0940	59.4195
14	1.5126	0.6611	17.0863	0.0585	11.2961	0.0885	68.0140
15	1.5580	0.6419	18.5989	0.0538	11.9379	0.0838	77.0001
16	1.6047	0.6232	20.1569	0.0496	12.5611	0.0796	86.3475
17	1.6528	0.6050	21.7616	0.0460	13.1661	0.0760	96.0278
18	1.7024	0.5874	23.4144	0.0427	13.7535	0.0727	106.0135
19	1.7535	0.5703	25.1169	0.0398	14.3238	0.0698	116.2786
20	1.8061	0.5537	26.8704	0.0372	14.8775	0.0672	126.7985
21	1.8603	0.5375	28.6765	0.0349	15.4150	0.0649	137.5495
22	1.9161	0.5219	30.5368	0.0327	15.9369	0.0627	148.5092
23	1.9736	0.5067	32.4529	0.0308	16.4436	0.0608	159.6564
24	2.0328	0.4919	34.4265	0.0290	16.9355	0.0590	170.9709
25	2.0938	0.4776	36.4592	0.0274	17.4131	0.0574	182.4334
26	2.1566	0.4637	38.5530	0.0259	17.8768	0.0559	194.0258
27	2.2213	0.4502	40.7096	0.0246	18.3270	0.0546	205.7307
28	2.2879	0.4371	42.9309	0.0233	18.7641	0.0533	217.5317
29	2.3566	0.4243	45.2188	0.0221	19.1885	0.0521	229.4134
30	2.4273	0.4120	47.5754	0.0210	19.6004	0.0510	241.3610
35	2.8139	0.3554	60.4621	0.0165	21.4872	0.0465	301.6264
40	3.2620	0.3066	75.4012	0.0133	23.1148	0.0433	361.7497
45	3.7816	0.2644	92.7198	0.0108	24.5187	0.0408	420.6322
50	4.3839	0.2281	112.7968	0.0089	25.7298	0.0389	477.4800
55	5.0821	0.1968	136.0715	0.0073	26.7744	0.0373	531.7408
60	5.8916	0.1697	163.0533	0.0061	27.6756	0.0361	583.0523
70	7.9178	0.1263	230.5939	0.0043	29.1234	0.0343	676.0866
80	10.6409	0.0940	321.3627	0.0031	30.2008	0.0331	756.0863
90	14.3005	0.0699	443.3485	0.0023	31.0024	0.0323	823.6300
100	19.2186	0.0520	607.2871	0.0016	31.5989	0.0316	879.8538

Table A.5   Discrete Compound Interest Table $i = 4.0\%$

n	COMPOUND AMOUNT FACTOR (F|P,i,n)	DISCOUNT AMOUNT FACTOR (P|F,i,n)	COMPOUND UNIFORM SERIES FACTOR (F|U,i,n)	SINKING FUND FACTOR (U|F,i,n)	DISCOUNT UNIFORM SERIES FACTOR (P|U,i,n)	CAPITAL RECOVERY FACTOR (U|P,i,n)	DISCOUNT GRADIENT FACTOR (P|G,i,n)
1	1.0400	0.9615	1.0000	1.0000	0.9615	1.0400	0.0000
2	1.0816	0.9246	2.0400	0.4902	1.8861	0.5302	0.9246
3	1.1249	0.8890	3.1216	0.3203	2.7751	0.3603	2.7026
4	1.1699	0.8548	4.2465	0.2355	3.6299	0.2755	5.2670
5	1.2167	0.8219	5.4163	0.1846	4.4518	0.2246	8.5547
6	1.2653	0.7903	6.6330	0.1508	5.2421	0.1908	12.5063
7	1.3159	0.7599	7.8983	0.1266	6.0021	0.1666	17.0658
8	1.3686	0.7307	9.2142	0.1085	6.7327	0.1485	22.1806
9	1.4233	0.7026	10.5828	0.0945	7.4353	0.1345	27.8013
10	1.4802	0.6756	12.0061	0.0833	8.1109	0.1233	33.8814
11	1.5395	0.6496	13.4864	0.0741	8.7605	0.1141	40.3772
12	1.6010	0.6246	15.0258	0.0666	9.3851	0.1066	47.2477
13	1.6651	0.6006	16.6268	0.0601	9.9856	0.1001	54.4546
14	1.7317	0.5775	18.2919	0.0547	10.5631	0.0947	61.9618
15	1.8009	0.5553	20.0236	0.0499	11.1184	0.0899	69.7355
16	1.8730	0.5339	21.8245	0.0458	11.6523	0.0858	77.7441
17	1.9479	0.5134	23.6975	0.0422	12.1657	0.0822	85.9581
18	2.0258	0.4936	25.6454	0.0390	12.6593	0.0790	94.3498
19	2.1068	0.4746	27.6712	0.0361	13.1339	0.0761	102.8934
20	2.1911	0.4564	29.7781	0.0336	13.5903	0.0736	111.5647
21	2.2788	0.4388	31.9692	0.0313	14.0292	0.0713	120.3414
22	2.3699	0.4220	34.2480	0.0292	14.4511	0.0692	129.2024
23	2.4647	0.4057	36.6179	0.0273	14.8568	0.0673	138.1284
24	2.5633	0.3901	39.0826	0.0256	15.2470	0.0656	147.1012
25	2.6658	0.3751	41.6459	0.0240	15.6221	0.0640	156.1040
26	2.7725	0.3607	44.3117	0.0226	15.9828	0.0626	165.1213
27	2.8834	0.3468	47.0842	0.0212	16.3296	0.0612	174.1385
28	2.9987	0.3335	49.9676	0.0200	16.6631	0.0600	183.1424
29	3.1187	0.3207	52.9663	0.0189	16.9837	0.0589	192.1206
30	3.2434	0.3083	56.0849	0.0178	17.2920	0.0578	201.0619
35	3.9461	0.2534	73.6522	0.0136	18.6646	0.0536	244.8768
40	4.8010	0.2083	95.0255	0.0105	19.7928	0.0505	286.5303
45	5.8412	0.1712	121.0294	0.0083	20.7200	0.0483	325.4028
50	7.1067	0.1407	152.6671	0.0066	21.4822	0.0466	361.1639
55	8.6464	0.1157	191.1592	0.0052	22.1086	0.0452	393.6890
60	10.5196	0.0951	237.9907	0.0042	22.6235	0.0442	422.9967
70	15.5716	0.0642	364.2905	0.0027	23.3945	0.0427	472.4789
80	23.0498	0.0434	551.2451	0.0018	23.9154	0.0418	511.1162
90	34.1193	0.0293	827.9835	0.0012	24.2673	0.0412	540.7369
100	50.5050	0.0198	1237.6239	0.0008	24.5050	0.0408	563.1249

Table A.6 Discrete Compound Interest Table $i = 5.0\%$

n	COMPOUND AMOUNT FACTOR (F|P,i,n)	DISCOUNT AMOUNT FACTOR (P|F,i,n)	COMPOUND UNIFORM SERIES FACTOR (F|U,i,n)	SINKING FUND FACTOR (U|F,i,n)	DISCOUNT UNIFORM SERIES FACTOR (P|U,i,n)	CAPITAL RECOVERY FACTOR (U|P,i,n)	DISCOUNT GRADIENT FACTOR (P|G,i,n)
1	1.0500	0.9524	1.0000	1.0000	0.9524	1.0500	0.0000
2	1.1025	0.9070	2.0500	0.4878	1.8594	0.5378	0.9070
3	1.1576	0.8638	3.1525	0.3172	2.7232	0.3672	2.6347
4	1.2155	0.8227	4.3101	0.2320	3.5460	0.2820	5.1028
5	1.2763	0.7835	5.5256	0.1810	4.3295	0.2310	8.2369
6	1.3401	0.7462	6.8019	0.1470	5.0757	0.1970	11.9680
7	1.4071	0.7107	8.1420	0.1228	5.7864	0.1728	16.2321
8	1.4775	0.6768	9.5491	0.1047	6.4632	0.1547	20.9699
9	1.5513	0.6446	11.0266	0.0907	7.1078	0.1407	26.1268
10	1.6289	0.6139	12.5779	0.0795	7.7217	0.1295	31.6520
11	1.7103	0.5847	14.2068	0.0704	8.3064	0.1204	37.4988
12	1.7959	0.5568	15.9171	0.0628	8.8633	0.1128	43.6240
13	1.8856	0.5303	17.7130	0.0565	9.3936	0.1065	49.9879
14	1.9799	0.5051	19.5986	0.0510	9.8986	0.1010	56.5538
15	2.0789	0.4810	21.5786	0.0463	10.3797	0.0963	63.2880
16	2.1829	0.4581	23.6575	0.0423	10.8378	0.0923	70.1597
17	2.2920	0.4363	25.8404	0.0387	11.2741	0.0887	77.1404
18	2.4066	0.4155	28.1324	0.0355	11.6896	0.0855	84.2043
19	2.5269	0.3957	30.5390	0.0327	12.0853	0.0827	91.3275
20	2.6533	0.3769	33.0659	0.0302	12.4622	0.0802	98.4884
21	2.7860	0.3589	35.7192	0.0280	12.8212	0.0780	105.6672
22	2.9253	0.3418	38.5052	0.0260	13.1630	0.0760	112.8461
23	3.0715	0.3256	41.4305	0.0241	13.4886	0.0741	120.0086
24	3.2251	0.3101	44.5020	0.0225	13.7986	0.0725	127.1402
25	3.3864	0.2953	47.7271	0.0210	14.0939	0.0710	134.2275
26	3.5557	0.2812	51.1134	0.0196	14.3752	0.0696	141.2585
27	3.7335	0.2678	54.6691	0.0183	14.6430	0.0683	148.2225
28	3.9201	0.2551	58.4026	0.0171	14.8981	0.0671	155.1101
29	4.1161	0.2429	62.3227	0.0160	15.1411	0.0660	161.9126
30	4.3219	0.2314	66.4388	0.0151	15.3725	0.0651	168.6225
35	5.5160	0.1813	90.3203	0.0111	16.3742	0.0611	200.5806
40	7.0400	0.1420	120.7997	0.0083	17.1591	0.0583	229.5451
45	8.9850	0.1113	159.7001	0.0063	17.7741	0.0563	255.3145
50	11.4674	0.0872	209.3479	0.0048	18.2559	0.0548	277.9147
55	14.6356	0.0683	272.7125	0.0037	18.6335	0.0537	297.5104
60	18.6792	0.0535	353.5836	0.0028	18.9293	0.0528	314.3431
70	30.4264	0.0329	588.5283	0.0017	19.3427	0.0517	340.8409
80	49.5614	0.0202	971.2283	0.0010	19.5965	0.0510	359.6460
90	80.7303	0.0124	1594.6064	0.0006	19.7523	0.0506	372.7488
100	131.5012	0.0076	2610.0236	0.0004	19.8479	0.0504	381.7492

Discrete Compound Interest Table $i = 6.0\%$

n	COMPOUND AMOUNT FACTOR (F|P,i,n)	DISCOUNT AMOUNT FACTOR (P|F,i,n)	COMPOUND UNIFORM SERIES FACTOR (F|U,i,n)	SINKING FUND FACTOR (U|F,i,n)	DISCOUNT UNIFORM SERIES FACTOR (P|U,i,n)	CAPITAL RECOVERY FACTOR (U|P,i,n)	DISCOUNT GRADIENT FACTOR (P|G,i,n)
1	1.0600	0.9434	1.0000	1.0000	0.9434	1.0600	0.0000
2	1.1236	0.8900	2.0600	0.4854	1.8334	0.5454	0.8900
3	1.1910	0.8396	3.1836	0.3141	2.6730	0.3741	2.5692
4	1.2625	0.7921	4.3746	0.2286	3.4651	0.2886	4.9455
5	1.3382	0.7473	5.6371	0.1774	4.2124	0.2374	7.9345
6	1.4185	0.7050	6.9753	0.1434	4.9173	0.2034	11.4593
7	1.5036	0.6651	8.3938	0.1191	5.5824	0.1791	15.4497
8	1.5938	0.6274	9.8975	0.1010	6.2098	0.1610	19.8416
9	1.6895	0.5919	11.4913	0.0870	6.8017	0.1470	24.5768
10	1.7908	0.5584	13.1808	0.0759	7.3601	0.1359	29.6023
11	1.8983	0.5268	14.9716	0.0668	7.8869	0.1268	34.8702
12	2.0122	0.4970	16.8699	0.0593	8.3838	0.1193	40.3368
13	2.1329	0.4688	18.8821	0.0530	8.8527	0.1130	45.9629
14	2.2609	0.4423	21.0151	0.0476	9.2950	0.1076	51.7128
15	2.3966	0.4173	23.2760	0.0430	9.7122	0.1030	57.5545
16	2.5404	0.3936	25.6725	0.0390	10.1059	0.0990	63.4592
17	2.6928	0.3714	28.2129	0.0354	10.4773	0.0954	69.4011
18	2.8543	0.3503	30.9056	0.0324	10.8276	0.0924	75.3569
19	3.0256	0.3305	33.7600	0.0296	11.1581	0.0896	81.3061
20	3.2071	0.3118	36.7856	0.0272	11.4699	0.0872	87.2304
21	3.3996	0.2942	39.9927	0.0250	11.7641	0.0850	93.1135
22	3.6035	0.2775	43.3923	0.0230	12.0416	0.0830	98.9411
23	3.8197	0.2618	46.9958	0.0213	12.3034	0.0813	104.7007
24	4.0489	0.2470	50.8156	0.0197	12.5504	0.0797	110.3812
25	4.2919	0.2330	54.8645	0.0182	12.7834	0.0782	115.9731
26	4.5494	0.2198	59.1564	0.0169	13.0032	0.0769	121.4684
27	4.8223	0.2074	63.7058	0.0157	13.2105	0.0757	126.8600
28	5.1117	0.1956	68.5281	0.0146	13.4062	0.0746	132.1420
29	5.4184	0.1846	73.6398	0.0136	13.5907	0.0736	137.3096
30	5.7435	0.1741	79.0582	0.0126	13.7648	0.0726	142.3588
35	7.6861	0.1301	111.4348	0.0090	14.4982	0.0690	165.7427
40	10.2857	0.0972	154.7619	0.0065	15.0463	0.0665	185.9568
45	13.7646	0.0727	212.7435	0.0047	15.4558	0.0647	203.1096
50	18.4201	0.0543	290.3358	0.0034	15.7619	0.0634	217.4574
55	24.6503	0.0406	394.1719	0.0025	15.9905	0.0625	229.3222
60	32.9877	0.0303	533.1280	0.0019	16.1614	0.0619	239.0428
70	59.0759	0.0169	967.9318	0.0010	16.3845	0.0610	253.3271
80	105.7959	0.0095	1746.5991	0.0006	16.5091	0.0606	262.5493
90	189.4644	0.0053	3141.0735	0.0003	16.5787	0.0603	268.3946
100	339.3019	0.0029	5638.3647	0.0002	16.6175	0.0602	272.0471

n	COMPOUND AMOUNT FACTOR (F|P,i,n)	DISCOUNT AMOUNT FACTOR (P|F,i,n)	COMPOUND UNIFORM SERIES FACTOR (F|U,i,n)	SINKING FUND FACTOR (U|F,i,n)	DISCOUNT UNIFORM SERIES FACTOR (P|U,i,n)	CAPITAL RECOVERY FACTOR (U|P,i,n)	DISCOUNT GRADIENT FACTOR (P|G,i,n)
1	1.0700	0.9346	1.0000	1.0000	0.9346	1.0700	0.0000
2	1.1449	0.8734	2.0700	0.4831	1.8080	0.5531	0.8734
3	1.2250	0.8163	3.2149	0.3111	2.6243	0.3811	2.5060
4	1.3108	0.7629	4.4399	0.2252	3.3872	0.2952	4.7947
5	1.4026	0.7130	5.7507	0.1739	4.1002	0.2439	7.6467
6	1.5007	0.6663	7.1533	0.1398	4.7665	0.2098	10.9784
7	1.6058	0.6227	8.6540	0.1156	5.3893	0.1856	14.7149
8	1.7182	0.5820	10.2598	0.0975	5.9713	0.1675	18.7889
9	1.8385	0.5439	11.9780	0.0835	6.5152	0.1535	23.1404
10	1.9672	0.5083	13.8164	0.0724	7.0236	0.1424	27.7156
11	2.1049	0.4751	15.7836	0.0634	7.4987	0.1334	32.4665
12	2.2522	0.4440	17.8885	0.0559	7.9427	0.1259	37.3506
13	2.4098	0.4150	20.1406	0.0497	8.3577	0.1197	42.3302
14	2.5785	0.3878	22.5505	0.0443	8.7455	0.1143	47.3718
15	2.7590	0.3624	25.1290	0.0398	9.1079	0.1098	52.4461
16	2.9522	0.3387	27.8881	0.0359	9.4466	0.1059	57.5271
17	3.1588	0.3166	30.8402	0.0324	9.7632	0.1024	62.5923
18	3.3799	0.2959	33.9990	0.0294	10.0591	0.0994	67.6220
19	3.6165	0.2765	37.3790	0.0268	10.3356	0.0968	72.5991
20	3.8697	0.2584	40.9955	0.0244	10.5940	0.0944	77.5091
21	4.1406	0.2415	44.8652	0.0223	10.8355	0.0923	82.3393
22	4.4304	0.2257	49.0057	0.0204	11.0612	0.0904	87.0793
23	4.7405	0.2109	53.4361	0.0187	11.2722	0.0887	91.7201
24	5.0724	0.1971	58.1767	0.0172	11.4693	0.0872	96.2545
25	5.4274	0.1842	63.2490	0.0158	11.6536	0.0858	100.6765
26	5.8074	0.1722	68.6765	0.0146	11.8258	0.0846	104.9814
27	6.2139	0.1609	74.4838	0.0134	11.9867	0.0834	109.1656
28	6.6488	0.1504	80.6977	0.0124	12.1371	0.0824	113.2264
29	7.1143	0.1406	87.3465	0.0114	12.2777	0.0814	117.1622
30	7.6123	0.1314	94.4608	0.0106	12.4090	0.0806	120.9718
35	10.6766	0.0937	138.2369	0.0072	12.9477	0.0772	138.1353
40	14.9745	0.0668	199.6351	0.0050	13.3317	0.0750	152.2928
45	21.0025	0.0476	285.7493	0.0035	13.6055	0.0735	163.7559
50	29.4570	0.0339	406.5290	0.0025	13.8007	0.0725	172.9051
55	41.3150	0.0242	575.9286	0.0017	13.9399	0.0717	180.1243
60	57.9464	0.0173	813.5204	0.0012	14.0392	0.0712	185.7677
65	81.2729	0.0123	1146.7552	0.0009	14.1099	0.0709	190.1452
70	113.9894	0.0088	1614.1343	0.0006	14.1604	0.0706	193.5185
75	159.8760	0.0063	2269.6576	0.0004	14.1964	0.0704	196.1035
80	224.2344	0.0045	3189.0629	0.0003	14.2220	0.0703	198.0748

Table A.9 Discrete Compound Interest Table $i = 8.0\%$

n	COMPOUND AMOUNT FACTOR $(F|P,i,n)$	DISCOUNT AMOUNT FACTOR $(P|F,i,n)$	COMPOUND UNIFORM SERIES FACTOR $(F|U,i,n)$	SINKING FUND FACTOR $(U|F,i,n)$	DISCOUNT UNIFORM SERIES FACTOR $(P|U,i,n)$	CAPITAL RECOVERY FACTOR $(U|P,i,n)$	DISCOUNT GRADIENT FACTOR $(P|G,i,n)$
1	1.0800	0.9259	1.0000	1.0000	0.9259	1.0800	0.0000
2	1.1664	0.8573	2.0800	0.4808	1.7833	0.5608	0.8573
3	1.2597	0.7938	3.2464	0.3080	2.5771	0.3880	2.4450
4	1.3605	0.7350	4.5061	0.2219	3.3121	0.3019	4.6501
5	1.4693	0.6806	5.8666	0.1705	3.9927	0.2505	7.3724
6	1.5869	0.6302	7.3359	0.1363	4.6229	0.2163	10.5233
7	1.7138	0.5835	8.9228	0.1121	5.2064	0.1921	14.0242
8	1.8509	0.5403	10.6366	0.0940	5.7466	0.1740	17.8061
9	1.9990	0.5002	12.4876	0.0801	6.2469	0.1601	21.8081
10	2.1589	0.4632	14.4866	0.0690	6.7101	0.1490	25.9768
11	2.3316	0.4289	16.6455	0.0601	7.1390	0.1401	30.2657
12	2.5182	0.3971	18.9771	0.0527	7.5361	0.1327	34.6339
13	2.7196	0.3677	21.4953	0.0465	7.9038	0.1265	39.0463
14	2.9372	0.3405	24.2149	0.0413	8.2442	0.1213	43.4723
15	3.1722	0.3152	27.1521	0.0368	8.5595	0.1168	47.8857
16	3.4259	0.2919	30.3243	0.0330	8.8514	0.1130	52.2640
17	3.7000	0.2703	33.7502	0.0296	9.1216	0.1096	56.5883
18	3.9960	0.2502	37.4502	0.0267	9.3719	0.1067	60.8425
19	4.3157	0.2317	41.4463	0.0241	9.6036	0.1041	65.0134
20	4.6610	0.2145	45.7620	0.0219	9.8181	0.1019	69.0898
21	5.0338	0.1987	50.4229	0.0198	10.0168	0.0998	73.0629
22	5.4365	0.1839	55.4567	0.0180	10.2007	0.0980	76.9256
23	5.8715	0.1703	60.8933	0.0164	10.3711	0.0964	80.6726
24	6.3412	0.1577	66.7647	0.0150	10.5288	0.0950	84.2997
25	6.8485	0.1460	73.1059	0.0137	10.6748	0.0937	87.8041
26	7.3964	0.1352	79.9544	0.0125	10.8100	0.0925	91.1841
27	7.9881	0.1252	87.3507	0.0114	10.9352	0.0914	94.4390
28	8.6271	0.1159	95.3388	0.0105	11.0511	0.0905	97.5687
29	9.3173	0.1073	103.9659	0.0096	11.1584	0.0896	100.5738
30	10.0627	0.0994	113.2832	0.0088	11.2578	0.0888	103.4558
35	14.7853	0.0676	172.3168	0.0058	11.6546	0.0858	116.0920
40	21.7245	0.0460	259.0564	0.0039	11.9246	0.0839	126.0422
45	31.9204	0.0313	386.5055	0.0026	12.1084	0.0826	133.7331
50	46.9016	0.0213	573.7699	0.0017	12.2335	0.0817	139.5928
55	68.9138	0.0145	848.9228	0.0012	12.3186	0.0812	144.0064
60	101.2570	0.0099	1253.2127	0.0008	12.3766	0.0808	147.3000
65	148.7798	0.0067	1847.2471	0.0005	12.4160	0.0805	149.7387
70	218.6063	0.0046	2720.0785	0.0004	12.4428	0.0804	151.5326
75	321.2043	0.0031	4002.5542	0.0002	12.4611	0.0802	152.8448
80	471.9545	0.0021	5886.9316	0.0002	12.4735	0.0802	153.8001

Table A.10 Discrete Compound Interest Table $i = 9.0\%$

n	COMPOUND AMOUNT FACTOR (F|P,i,n)	DISCOUNT AMOUNT FACTOR (P|F,i,n)	COMPOUND UNIFORM SERIES FACTOR (F|U,i,n)	SINKING FUND FACTOR (U|F,i,n)	DISCOUNT UNIFORM SERIES FACTOR (P|U,i,n)	CAPITAL RECOVERY FACTOR (U|P,i,n)	DISCOUNT GRADIENT FACTOR (P|G,i,n)
1	1.0900	0.9174	1.0000	1.0000	0.9174	1.0900	0.0000
2	1.1881	0.8417	2.0900	0.4785	1.7591	0.5685	0.8417
3	1.2950	0.7722	3.2781	0.3051	2.5313	0.3951	2.3860
4	1.4116	0.7084	4.5731	0.2187	3.2397	0.3087	4.5113
5	1.5386	0.6499	5.9847	0.1671	3.8897	0.2571	7.1110
6	1.6771	0.5963	7.5233	0.1329	4.4859	0.2229	10.0924
7	1.8280	0.5470	9.2004	0.1087	5.0330	0.1987	13.3746
8	1.9926	0.5019	11.0285	0.0907	5.5348	0.1807	16.8877
9	2.1719	0.4604	13.0210	0.0768	5.9952	0.1668	20.5711
10	2.3674	0.4224	15.1929	0.0658	6.4177	0.1558	24.3728
11	2.5804	0.3875	17.5603	0.0569	6.8052	0.1469	28.2481
12	2.8127	0.3555	20.1407	0.0497	7.1607	0.1397	32.1590
13	3.0658	0.3262	22.9534	0.0436	7.4869	0.1336	36.0731
14	3.3417	0.2992	26.0192	0.0384	7.7862	0.1284	39.9633
15	3.6425	0.2745	29.3609	0.0341	8.0607	0.1241	43.8069
16	3.9703	0.2519	33.0034	0.0303	8.3126	0.1203	47.5849
17	4.3276	0.2311	36.9737	0.0270	8.5436	0.1170	51.2821
18	4.7171	0.2120	41.3013	0.0242	8.7556	0.1142	54.8860
19	5.1417	0.1945	46.0185	0.0217	8.9501	0.1117	58.3868
20	5.6044	0.1784	51.1601	0.0195	9.1285	0.1095	61.7770
21	6.1088	0.1637	56.7645	0.0176	9.2922	0.1076	65.0509
22	6.6586	0.1502	62.8733	0.0159	9.4424	0.1059	68.2048
23	7.2579	0.1378	69.5319	0.0144	9.5802	0.1044	71.2359
24	7.9111	0.1264	76.7898	0.0130	9.7066	0.1030	74.1433
25	8.6231	0.1160	84.7009	0.0118	9.8226	0.1018	76.9265
26	9.3992	0.1064	93.3240	0.0107	9.9290	0.1007	79.5863
27	10.2451	0.0976	102.7231	0.0097	10.0266	0.0997	82.1241
28	11.1671	0.0895	112.9682	0.0089	10.1161	0.0989	84.5419
29	12.1722	0.0822	124.1353	0.0081	10.1983	0.0981	86.8422
30	13.2677	0.0754	136.3075	0.0073	10.2737	0.0973	89.0280
35	20.4140	0.0490	215.7107	0.0046	10.5668	0.0946	98.3590
40	31.4094	0.0318	337.8824	0.0030	10.7574	0.0930	105.3762
45	48.3273	0.0207	525.8586	0.0019	10.8812	0.0919	110.5561
50	74.3575	0.0134	815.0834	0.0012	10.9617	0.0912	114.3251
55	114.4082	0.0087	1260.0915	0.0008	11.0140	0.0908	117.0362

Table A.11 Discrete Compound Interest Table $\qquad i = 10.0\%$

	COMPOUND AMOUNT FACTOR	DISCOUNT AMOUNT FACTOR	COMPOUND UNIFORM SERIES FACTOR	SINKING FUND FACTOR	DISCOUNT UNIFORM SERIES FACTOR	CAPITAL RECOVERY FACTOR	DISCOUNT GRADIENT FACTOR
n	(F|P,i,n)	(P|F,i,n)	(F|U,i,n)	(U|F,i,n)	(P|U,i,n)	(U|P,i,n)	(P|G,i,n)
1	1.1000	0.9091	1.0000	1.0000	0.9091	1.1000	0.0000
2	1.2100	0.8264	2.1000	0.4762	1.7355	0.5762	0.8264
3	1.3310	0.7513	3.3100	0.3021	2.4869	0.4021	2.3291
4	1.4641	0.6830	4.6410	0.2155	3.1699	0.3155	4.3781
5	1.6105	0.6209	6.1051	0.1638	3.7908	0.2638	6.8618
6	1.7716	0.5645	7.7156	0.1296	4.3553	0.2296	9.6842
7	1.9487	0.5132	9.4872	0.1054	4.8684	0.2054	12.7631
8	2.1436	0.4665	11.4359	0.0874	5.3349	0.1874	16.0287
9	2.3579	0.4241	13.5795	0.0736	5.7590	0.1736	19.4214
10	2.5937	0.3855	15.9374	0.0627	6.1446	0.1627	22.8913
11	2.8531	0.3505	18.5312	0.0540	6.4951	0.1540	26.3963
12	3.1384	0.3186	21.3843	0.0468	6.8137	0.1468	29.9012
13	3.4523	0.2897	24.5227	0.0408	7.1034	0.1408	33.3772
14	3.7975	0.2633	27.9750	0.0357	7.3667	0.1357	36.8005
15	4.1772	0.2394	31.7725	0.0315	7.6061	0.1315	40.1520
16	4.5950	0.2176	35.9497	0.0278	7.8237	0.1278	43.4164
17	5.0545	0.1978	40.5447	0.0247	8.0216	0.1247	46.5819
18	5.5599	0.1799	45.5992	0.0219	8.2014	0.1219	49.6395
19	6.1159	0.1635	51.1591	0.0195	8.3649	0.1195	52.5827
20	6.7275	0.1486	57.2750	0.0175	8.5136	0.1175	55.4069
21	7.4002	0.1351	64.0025	0.0156	8.6487	0.1156	58.1095
22	8.1403	0.1228	71.4027	0.0140	8.7715	0.1140	60.6893
23	8.9543	0.1117	79.5430	0.0126	8.8832	0.1126	63.1462
24	9.8497	0.1015	88.4973	0.0113	8.9847	0.1113	65.4813
25	10.8347	0.0923	98.3470	0.0102	9.0770	0.1102	67.6964
26	11.9182	0.0839	109.1817	0.0092	9.1609	0.1092	69.7940
27	13.1100	0.0763	121.0999	0.0083	9.2372	0.1083	71.7772
28	14.4210	0.0693	134.2099	0.0075	9.3066	0.1075	73.6495
29	15.8631	0.0630	148.6309	0.0067	9.3696	0.1067	75.4146
30	17.4494	0.0573	164.4940	0.0061	9.4269	0.1061	77.0766
35	28.1024	0.0356	271.0243	0.0037	9.6442	0.1037	83.9871
40	45.2592	0.0221	442.5924	0.0023	9.7791	0.1023	88.9525
45	72.8904	0.0137	718.9045	0.0014	9.8628	0.1014	92.4544
50	117.3908	0.0085	1163.9079	0.0009	9.9148	0.1009	94.8889
55	189.0590	0.0053	1880.5903	0.0005	9.9471	0.1005	96.5619

Table A.12 Discrete Compound Interest Table $i = 11.0\%$

n	COMPOUND AMOUNT FACTOR $(F\|P,i,n)$	DISCOUNT AMOUNT FACTOR $(P\|F,i,n)$	COMPOUND UNIFORM SERIES FACTOR $(F\|U,i,n)$	SINKING FUND FACTOR $(U\|F,i,n)$	DISCOUNT UNIFORM SERIES FACTOR $(P\|U,i,n)$	CAPITAL RECOVERY FACTOR $(U\|P,i,n)$	DISCOUNT GRADIENT FACTOR $(P\|G,i,n)$
1	1.1100	0.9009	1.0000	1.0000	0.9009	1.1100	0.0000
2	1.2321	0.8116	2.1100	0.4739	1.7125	0.5839	0.8116
3	1.3676	0.7312	3.3421	0.2992	2.4437	0.4092	2.2740
4	1.5181	0.6587	4.7097	0.2123	3.1024	0.3223	4.2502
5	1.6851	0.5935	6.2278	0.1606	3.6959	0.2706	6.6240
6	1.8704	0.5346	7.9129	0.1264	4.2305	0.2364	9.2972
7	2.0762	0.4817	9.7833	0.1022	4.7122	0.2122	12.1872
8	2.3045	0.4339	11.8594	0.0843	5.1461	0.1943	15.2246
9	2.5580	0.3909	14.1640	0.0706	5.5370	0.1806	18.3520
10	2.8394	0.3522	16.7220	0.0598	5.8892	0.1698	21.5217
11	3.1518	0.3173	19.5614	0.0511	6.2065	0.1611	24.6945
12	3.4985	0.2858	22.7132	0.0440	6.4924	0.1540	27.8388
13	3.8833	0.2575	26.2116	0.0382	6.7499	0.1482	30.9290
14	4.3104	0.2320	30.0949	0.0332	6.9819	0.1432	33.9449
15	4.7846	0.2090	34.4054	0.0291	7.1909	0.1391	36.8709
16	5.3109	0.1883	39.1899	0.0255	7.3792	0.1355	39.6953
17	5.8951	0.1696	44.5008	0.0225	7.5488	0.1325	42.4094
18	6.5436	0.1528	50.3959	0.0198	7.7016	0.1298	45.0074
19	7.2633	0.1377	56.9395	0.0176	7.8393	0.1276	47.4856
20	8.0623	0.1240	64.2028	0.0156	7.9633	0.1256	49.8423
21	8.9492	0.1117	72.2651	0.0138	8.0751	0.1238	52.0771
22	9.9336	0.1007	81.2143	0.0123	8.1757	0.1223	54.1912
23	11.0263	0.0907	91.1479	0.0110	8.2664	0.1210	56.1864
24	12.2392	0.0817	102.1741	0.0098	8.3481	0.1198	58.0656
25	13.5855	0.0736	114.4133	0.0087	8.4217	0.1187	59.8322
26	15.0799	0.0663	127.9988	0.0078	8.4881	0.1178	61.4900
27	16.7386	0.0597	143.0786	0.0070	8.5478	0.1170	63.0433
28	18.5799	0.0538	159.8173	0.0063	8.6016	0.1163	64.4965
29	20.6237	0.0485	178.3972	0.0056	8.6501	0.1156	65.8542
30	22.8923	0.0437	199.0208	0.0050	8.6938	0.1150	67.1210
35	38.5748	0.0259	341.5895	0.0029	8.8552	0.1129	72.2538
40	65.0009	0.0154	581.8259	0.0017	8.9511	0.1117	75.7789
45	109.5302	0.0091	986.6383	0.0010	9.0079	0.1110	78.1551
50	184.5648	0.0054	1668.7707	0.0006	9.0417	0.1106	79.7340
55	311.0024	0.0032	2818.2034	0.0004	9.0617	0.1104	80.7712

Table A.13 Discrete Compound Interest Table $i = 12.0\%$

n	COMPOUND AMOUNT FACTOR $(F|P,i,n)$	DISCOUNT AMOUNT FACTOR $(P|F,i,n)$	COMPOUND UNIFORM SERIES FACTOR $(F|U,i,n)$	SINKING FUND FACTOR $(U|F,i,n)$	DISCOUNT UNIFORM SERIES FACTOR $(P|U,i,n)$	CAPITAL RECOVERY FACTOR $(U|P,i,n)$	DISCOUNT GRADIENT FACTOR $(P|G,i,n)$
1	1.1200	0.8929	1.0000	1.0000	0.8929	1.1200	0.0000
2	1.2544	0.7972	2.1200	0.4717	1.6901	0.5917	0.7972
3	1.4049	0.7118	3.3744	0.2963	2.4018	0.4163	2.2208
4	1.5735	0.6355	4.7793	0.2092	3.0373	0.3292	4.1273
5	1.7623	0.5674	6.3528	0.1574	3.6048	0.2774	6.3970
6	1.9738	0.5066	8.1152	0.1232	4.1114	0.2432	8.9302
7	2.2107	0.4523	10.0890	0.0991	4.5638	0.2191	11.6443
8	2.4760	0.4039	12.2997	0.0813	4.9676	0.2013	14.4714
9	2.7731	0.3606	14.7757	0.0677	5.3282	0.1877	17.3563
10	3.1058	0.3220	17.5487	0.0570	5.6502	0.1770	20.2541
11	3.4785	0.2875	20.6546	0.0484	5.9377	0.1684	23.1288
12	3.8960	0.2567	24.1331	0.0414	6.1944	0.1614	25.9523
13	4.3635	0.2292	28.0291	0.0357	6.4235	0.1557	28.7024
14	4.8871	0.2046	32.3926	0.0309	6.6282	0.1509	31.3624
15	5.4736	0.1827	37.2797	0.0268	6.8109	0.1468	33.9202
16	6.1304	0.1631	42.7533	0.0234	6.9740	0.1434	36.3670
17	6.8660	0.1456	48.8837	0.0205	7.1196	0.1405	38.6973
18	7.6900	0.1300	55.7497	0.0179	7.2497	0.1379	40.9080
19	8.6128	0.1161	63.4397	0.0158	7.3658	0.1358	42.9979
20	9.6463	0.1037	72.0524	0.0139	7.4694	0.1339	44.9676
21	10.8038	0.0926	81.6987	0.0122	7.5620	0.1322	46.8188
22	12.1003	0.0826	92.5026	0.0108	7.6446	0.1308	48.5543
23	13.5523	0.0738	104.6029	0.0096	7.7184	0.1296	50.1776
24	15.1786	0.0659	118.1552	0.0085	7.7843	0.1285	51.6929
25	17.0001	0.0588	133.3339	0.0075	7.8431	0.1275	53.1046
26	19.0401	0.0525	150.3339	0.0067	7.8957	0.1267	54.4177
27	21.3249	0.0469	169.3740	0.0059	7.9426	0.1259	55.6369
28	23.8839	0.0419	190.6989	0.0052	7.9844	0.1252	56.7674
29	26.7499	0.0374	214.5827	0.0047	8.0218	0.1247	57.8141
30	29.9599	0.0334	241.3327	0.0041	8.0552	0.1241	58.7821
35	52.7996	0.0189	431.6634	0.0023	8.1755	0.1223	62.6052
40	93.0510	0.0107	767.0913	0.0013	8.2438	0.1213	65.1159
45	163.9876	0.0061	1358.2298	0.0007	8.2825	0.1207	66.7342
50	289.0021	0.0035	2400.0178	0.0004	8.3045	0.1204	67.7624
55	509.3205	0.0020	4236.0043	0.0002	8.3170	0.1202	68.4082

Table A.14 Discrete Compound Interest Table $i = 15.0\%$

n	COMPOUND AMOUNT FACTOR (F|P,i,n)	DISCOUNT AMOUNT FACTOR (P|F,i,n)	COMPOUND UNIFORM SERIES FACTOR (F|U,i,n)	SINKING FUND FACTOR (U|F,i,n)	DISCOUNT UNIFORM SERIES FACTOR (P|U,i,n)	CAPITAL RECOVERY FACTOR (U|P,i,n)	DISCOUNT GRADIENT FACTOR (P|G,i,n)
1	1.1500	0.8696	1.0000	1.0000	0.8696	1.1500	0.0000
2	1.3225	0.7561	2.1500	0.4651	1.6257	0.6151	0.7561
3	1.5209	0.6575	3.4725	0.2880	2.2832	0.4380	2.0712
4	1.7490	0.5718	4.9934	0.2003	2.8550	0.3503	3.7864
5	2.0114	0.4972	6.7424	0.1483	3.3522	0.2983	5.7751
6	2.3131	0.4323	8.7537	0.1142	3.7845	0.2642	7.9368
7	2.6600	0.3759	11.0668	0.0904	4.1604	0.2404	10.1924
8	3.0590	0.3269	13.7268	0.0729	4.4873	0.2229	12.4807
9	3.5179	0.2843	16.7858	0.0596	4.7716	0.2096	14.7548
10	4.0456	0.2472	20.3037	0.0493	5.0188	0.1993	16.9795
11	4.6524	0.2149	24.3493	0.0411	5.2337	0.1911	19.1289
12	5.3503	0.1869	29.0017	0.0345	5.4206	0.1845	21.1849
13	6.1528	0.1625	34.3519	0.0291	5.5831	0.1791	23.1352
14	7.0757	0.1413	40.5047	0.0247	5.7245	0.1747	24.9725
15	8.1371	0.1229	47.5804	0.0210	5.8474	0.1710	26.6930
16	9.3576	0.1069	55.7175	0.0179	5.9542	0.1679	28.2960
17	10.7613	0.0929	65.0751	0.0154	6.0472	0.1654	29.7828
18	12.3755	0.0808	75.8364	0.0132	6.1280	0.1632	31.1565
19	14.2318	0.0703	88.2118	0.0113	6.1982	0.1613	32.4213
20	16.3665	0.0611	102.4436	0.0098	6.2593	0.1598	33.5822
21	18.8215	0.0531	118.8101	0.0084	6.3125	0.1584	34.6448
22	21.6447	0.0462	137.6316	0.0073	6.3587	0.1573	35.6150
23	24.8915	0.0402	159.2764	0.0063	6.3988	0.1563	36.4988
24	28.6252	0.0349	184.1678	0.0054	6.4338	0.1554	37.3023
25	32.9190	0.0304	212.7930	0.0047	6.4641	0.1547	38.0314
26	37.8568	0.0264	245.7120	0.0041	6.4906	0.1541	38.6918
27	43.5353	0.0230	283.5688	0.0035	6.5135	0.1535	39.2890
28	50.0656	0.0200	327.1041	0.0031	6.5335	0.1531	39.8283
29	57.5755	0.0174	377.1697	0.0027	6.5509	0.1527	40.3146
30	66.2118	0.0151	434.7451	0.0023	6.5660	0.1523	40.7526

Table A.15   Discrete Compound Interest Table $i = 18.0\%$

	COMPOUND AMOUNT FACTOR	DISCOUNT AMOUNT FACTOR	COMPOUND UNIFORM SERIES FACTOR	SINKING FUND FACTOR	DISCOUNT UNIFORM SERIES FACTOR	CAPITAL RECOVERY FACTOR	DISCOUNT GRADIENT FACTOR
n	(F|P,i,n)	(P|F,i,n)	(F|U,i,n)	(U|F,i,n)	(P|U,i,n)	(U|P,i,n)	(P|G,i,n)
1	1.1800	0.8475	1.0000	1.0000	0.8475	1.1800	0.0000
2	1.3924	0.7182	2.1800	0.4587	1.5656	0.6387	0.7182
3	1.6430	0.6086	3.5724	0.2799	2.1743	0.4599	1.9354
4	1.9388	0.5158	5.2154	0.1917	2.6901	0.3717	3.4828
5	2.2878	0.4371	7.1542	0.1398	3.1272	0.3198	5.2312
6	2.6996	0.3704	9.4420	0.1059	3.4976	0.2859	7.0834
7	3.1855	0.3139	12.1415	0.0824	3.8115	0.2624	8.9670
8	3.7589	0.2660	15.3270	0.0652	4.0776	0.2452	10.8292
9	4.4355	0.2255	19.0859	0.0524	4.3030	0.2324	12.6329
10	5.2338	0.1911	23.5213	0.0425	4.4941	0.2225	14.3525
11	6.1759	0.1619	28.7551	0.0348	4.6560	0.2148	15.9716
12	7.2876	0.1372	34.9311	0.0286	4.7932	0.2086	17.4811
13	8.5994	0.1163	42.2187	0.0237	4.9095	0.2037	18.8765
14	10.1472	0.0985	50.8180	0.0197	5.0081	0.1997	20.1576
15	11.9737	0.0835	60.9653	0.0164	5.0916	0.1964	21.3269
16	14.1290	0.0708	72.9390	0.0137	5.1624	0.1937	22.3885
17	16.6722	0.0600	87.0680	0.0115	5.2223	0.1915	23.3482
18	19.6733	0.0508	103.7403	0.0096	5.2732	0.1896	24.2123
19	23.2144	0.0431	123.4135	0.0081	5.3162	0.1881	24.9877
20	27.3930	0.0365	146.6280	0.0068	5.3527	0.1868	25.6813
21	32.3238	0.0309	174.0210	0.0057	5.3837	0.1857	26.3000
22	38.1421	0.0262	206.3448	0.0048	5.4099	0.1848	26.8506
23	45.0076	0.0222	244.4869	0.0041	5.4321	0.1841	27.3394
24	53.1090	0.0188	289.4945	0.0035	5.4509	0.1835	27.7725
25	62.6686	0.0160	342.6035	0.0029	5.4669	0.1829	28.1555
26	73.9490	0.0135	405.2721	0.0025	5.4804	0.1825	28.4935
27	87.2598	0.0115	479.2211	0.0021	5.4919	0.1821	28.7915
28	102.9666	0.0097	566.4809	0.0018	5.5016	0.1818	29.0537
29	121.5006	0.0082	669.4475	0.0015	5.5098	0.1815	29.2842
30	143.3706	0.0070	790.9481	0.0013	5.5168	0.1813	29.4864

Table A.16   Discrete Compound Interest Table $i = 20.0\%$

n	COMPOUND AMOUNT FACTOR (F|P,i,n)	DISCOUNT AMOUNT FACTOR (P|F,i,n)	COMPOUND UNIFORM SERIES FACTOR (F|U,i,n)	SINKING FUND FACTOR (U|F,i,n)	DISCOUNT UNIFORM SERIES FACTOR (P|U,i,n)	CAPITAL RECOVERY FACTOR (U|P,i,n)	DISCOUNT GRADIENT FACTOR (P|G,i,n)
1	1.2000	0.8333	1.0000	1.0000	0.8333	1.2000	0.0000
2	1.4400	0.6944	2.2000	0.4545	1.5278	0.6545	0.6944
3	1.7280	0.5787	3.6400	0.2747	2.1065	0.4747	1.8519
4	2.0736	0.4823	5.3680	0.1863	2.5887	0.3863	3.2986
5	2.4883	0.4019	7.4416	0.1344	2.9906	0.3344	4.9061
6	2.9860	0.3349	9.9299	0.1007	3.3255	0.3007	6.5806
7	3.5832	0.2791	12.9159	0.0774	3.6046	0.2774	8.2551
8	4.2998	0.2326	16.4991	0.0606	3.8372	0.2606	9.8831
9	5.1598	0.1938	20.7989	0.0481	4.0310	0.2481	11.4335
10	6.1917	0.1615	25.9587	0.0385	4.1925	0.2385	12.8871
11	7.4301	0.1346	32.1504	0.0311	4.3271	0.2311	14.2330
12	8.9161	0.1122	39.5805	0.0253	4.4392	0.2253	15.4667
13	10.6993	0.0935	48.4966	0.0206	4.5327	0.2206	16.5883
14	12.8392	0.0779	59.1959	0.0169	4.6106	0.2169	17.6008
15	15.4070	0.0649	72.0351	0.0139	4.6755	0.2139	18.5095
16	18.4884	0.0541	87.4421	0.0114	4.7296	0.2114	19.3208
17	22.1861	0.0451	105.9305	0.0094	4.7746	0.2094	20.0419
18	26.6233	0.0376	128.1167	0.0078	4.8122	0.2078	20.6805
19	31.9480	0.0313	154.7400	0.0065	4.8435	0.2065	21.2439
20	38.3376	0.0261	186.6880	0.0054	4.8696	0.2054	21.7395
21	46.0051	0.0217	225.0256	0.0044	4.8913	0.2044	22.1742
22	55.2061	0.0181	271.0307	0.0037	4.9094	0.2037	22.5546
23	66.2474	0.0151	326.2368	0.0031	4.9245	0.2031	22.8867
24	79.4968	0.0126	392.4842	0.0025	4.9371	0.2025	23.1760
25	95.3962	0.0105	471.9810	0.0021	4.9476	0.2021	23.4276
26	114.4754	0.0087	567.3772	0.0018	4.9563	0.2018	23.6460
27	137.3705	0.0073	681.8527	0.0015	4.9636	0.2015	23.8353
28	164.8446	0.0061	819.2232	0.0012	4.9697	0.2012	23.9991
29	197.8136	0.0051	984.0678	0.0010	4.9747	0.2010	24.1406
30	237.3763	0.0042	1181.8814	0.0008	4.9789	0.2008	24.2628

Table A.17   Discrete Compound Interest Table $i = 25.0\%$

n	COMPOUND AMOUNT FACTOR (F|P,i,n)	DISCOUNT AMOUNT FACTOR (P|F,i,n)	COMPOUND UNIFORM SERIES FACTOR (F|U,i,n)	SINKING FUND FACTOR (U|F,i,n)	DISCOUNT UNIFORM SERIES FACTOR (P|U,i,n)	CAPITAL RECOVERY FACTOR (U|P,i,n)	DISCOUNT GRADIENT FACTOR (P|G,i,n)
1	1.2500	0.8000	1.0000	1.0000	0.8000	1.2500	0.0000
2	1.5625	0.6400	2.2500	0.4444	1.4400	0.6944	0.6400
3	1.9531	0.5120	3.8125	0.2623	1.9520	0.5123	1.6640
4	2.4414	0.4096	5.7656	0.1734	2.3616	0.4234	2.8928
5	3.0518	0.3277	8.2070	0.1218	2.6893	0.3718	4.2035
6	3.8147	0.2621	11.2588	0.0888	2.9514	0.3388	5.5142
7	4.7684	0.2097	15.0735	0.0663	3.1611	0.3163	6.7725
8	5.9605	0.1678	19.8419	0.0504	3.3289	0.3004	7.9469
9	7.4506	0.1342	25.8023	0.0388	3.4631	0.2888	9.0207
10	9.3132	0.1074	33.2529	0.0301	3.5705	0.2801	9.9870
11	11.6415	0.0859	42.5661	0.0235	3.6564	0.2735	10.8460
12	14.5519	0.0687	54.2077	0.0184	3.7251	0.2684	11.6020
13	18.1899	0.0550	68.7596	0.0145	3.7801	0.2645	12.2617
14	22.7374	0.0440	86.9495	0.0115	3.8241	0.2615	12.8334
15	28.4217	0.0352	109.6868	0.0091	3.8593	0.2591	13.3260
16	35.5271	0.0281	138.1085	0.0072	3.8874	0.2572	13.7482
17	44.4089	0.0225	173.6357	0.0058	3.9099	0.2558	14.1085
18	55.5112	0.0180	218.0446	0.0046	3.9279	0.2546	14.4147
19	69.3889	0.0144	273.5558	0.0037	3.9424	0.2537	14.6741
20	86.7362	0.0115	342.9447	0.0029	3.9539	0.2529	14.8932
21	108.4202	0.0092	429.6809	0.0023	3.9631	0.2523	15.0777
22	135.5253	0.0074	538.1011	0.0019	3.9705	0.2519	15.2326
23	169.4066	0.0059	673.6263	0.0015	3.9764	0.2515	15.3625
24	211.7582	0.0047	843.0329	0.0012	3.9811	0.2512	15.4711
25	264.6978	0.0038	1054.7912	0.0009	3.9849	0.2509	15.5618
26	330.8722	0.0030	1319.4890	0.0008	3.9879	0.2508	15.6373
27	413.5903	0.0024	1650.3612	0.0006	3.9903	0.2506	15.7002
28	516.9879	0.0019	2063.9515	0.0005	3.9923	0.2505	15.7524
29	646.2348	0.0015	2580.9394	0.0004	3.9938	0.2504	15.7957
30	807.7935	0.0012	3227.1742	0.0003	3.9950	0.2503	15.8316

Table A.18   Discrete Compound Interest Table $i = 30.0\%$

n	COMPOUND AMOUNT FACTOR (F|P,i,n)	DISCOUNT AMOUNT FACTOR (P|F,i,n)	COMPOUND UNIFORM SERIES FACTOR (F|U,i,n)	SINKING FUND FACTOR (U|F,i,n)	DISCOUNT UNIFORM SERIES FACTOR (P|U,i,n)	CAPITAL RECOVERY FACTOR (U|P,i,n)	DISCOUNT GRADIENT FACTOR (P|G,i,n)
1	1.3000	0.7692	1.0000	1.0000	0.7692	1.3000	0.0000
2	1.6900	0.5917	2.3000	0.4348	1.3609	0.7348	0.5917
3	2.1970	0.4552	3.9900	0.2506	1.8161	0.5506	1.5020
4	2.8561	0.3501	6.1870	0.1616	2.1662	0.4616	2.5524
5	3.7129	0.2693	9.0431	0.1106	2.4356	0.4106	3.6297
6	4.8268	0.2072	12.7560	0.0784	2.6427	0.3784	4.6656
7	6.2749	0.1594	17.5828	0.0569	2.8021	0.3569	5.6218
8	8.1573	0.1226	23.8577	0.0419	2.9247	0.3419	6.4800
9	10.6045	0.0943	32.0150	0.0312	3.0190	0.3312	7.2343
10	13.7858	0.0725	42.6195	0.0235	3.0915	0.3235	7.8872
11	17.9216	0.0558	56.4053	0.0177	3.1473	0.3177	8.4452
12	23.2981	0.0429	74.3269	0.0135	3.1903	0.3135	8.9173
13	30.2875	0.0330	97.6250	0.0102	3.2233	0.3102	9.3135
14	39.3738	0.0254	127.9125	0.0078	3.2487	0.3078	9.6437
15	51.1859	0.0195	167.2863	0.0060	3.2682	0.3060	9.9172
16	66.5417	0.0150	218.4722	0.0046	3.2832	0.3046	10.1426
17	86.5041	0.0116	285.0138	0.0035	3.2948	0.3035	10.3276
18	112.4554	0.0089	371.5180	0.0027	3.3037	0.3027	10.4788
19	146.1920	0.0068	483.9734	0.0021	3.3105	0.3021	10.6019
20	190.0496	0.0053	630.1654	0.0016	3.3158	0.3016	10.7019
21	247.0645	0.0040	820.2150	0.0012	3.3198	0.3012	10.7828
22	321.1838	0.0031	1067.2794	0.0009	3.3230	0.3009	10.8482
23	417.5390	0.0024	1388.4633	0.0007	3.3254	0.3007	10.9009
24	542.8007	0.0018	1806.0023	0.0006	3.3272	0.3006	10.9433
25	705.6409	0.0014	2348.8029	0.0004	3.3286	0.3004	10.9773
26	917.3331	0.0011	3054.4438	0.0003	3.3297	0.3003	11.0045
27	1192.5331	0.0008	3971.7769	0.0003	3.3305	0.3003	11.0263
28	1550.2930	0.0006	5164.3099	0.0002	3.3312	0.3002	11.0437
29	2015.3809	0.0005	6714.6029	0.0001	3.3317	0.3001	11.0576
30	2619.9951	0.0004	8729.9836	0.0001	3.3321	0.3001	11.0687

Table A.19 Discrete Compound Interest Table $i = 40.0\%$

n	COMPOUND AMOUNT FACTOR (F|P,i,n)	DISCOUNT AMOUNT FACTOR (P|F,i,n)	COMPOUND UNIFORM SERIES FACTOR (F|U,i,n)	SINKING FUND FACTOR (U|F,i,n)	DISCOUNT UNIFORM SERIES FACTOR (P|U,i,n)	CAPITAL RECOVERY FACTOR (U|P,i,n)	DISCOUNT GRADIENT FACTOR (P|G,i,n)
1	1.4000	0.7143	1.0000	1.0000	0.7143	1.4000	0.0000
2	1.9600	0.5102	2.4000	0.4167	1.2245	0.8167	0.5102
3	2.7440	0.3644	4.3600	0.2294	1.5889	0.6294	1.2391
4	3.8416	0.2603	7.1040	0.1408	1.8492	0.5408	2.0200
5	5.3782	0.1859	10.9456	0.0914	2.0352	0.4914	2.7637
6	7.5295	0.1328	16.3238	0.0613	2.1680	0.4613	3.4278
7	10.5414	0.0949	23.8534	0.0419	2.2628	0.4419	3.9970
8	14.7579	0.0678	34.3947	0.0291	2.3306	0.4291	4.4713
9	20.6610	0.0484	49.1526	0.0203	2.3790	0.4203	4.8585
10	28.9255	0.0346	69.8137	0.0143	2.4136	0.4143	5.1696
11	40.4957	0.0247	98.7391	0.0101	2.4383	0.4101	5.4166
12	56.6939	0.0176	139.2348	0.0072	2.4559	0.4072	5.6106
13	79.3715	0.0126	195.9287	0.0051	2.4685	0.4051	5.7618
14	111.1201	0.0090	275.3002	0.0036	2.4775	0.4036	5.8788
15	155.5681	0.0064	386.4202	0.0026	2.4839	0.4026	5.9688
16	217.7953	0.0046	541.9883	0.0018	2.4885	0.4018	6.0376
17	304.9135	0.0033	759.7837	0.0013	2.4918	0.4013	6.0901
18	426.8789	0.0023	1064.6972	0.0009	2.4941	0.4009	6.1299
19	597.6304	0.0017	1491.5760	0.0007	2.4958	0.4007	6.1601
20	836.6826	0.0012	2089.2065	0.0005	2.4970	0.4005	6.1828

Table A.20   Discrete Compound Interest Table $i = 50.0\%$

n	COMPOUND AMOUNT FACTOR (F|P,i,n)	DISCOUNT AMOUNT FACTOR (P|F,i,n)	COMPOUND UNIFORM SERIES FACTOR (F|U,i,n)	SINKING FUND FACTOR (U|F,i,n)	DISCOUNT UNIFORM SERIES FACTOR (P|U,i,n)	CAPITAL RECOVERY FACTOR (U|P,i,n)	DISCOUNT GRADIENT FACTOR (P|G,i,n)
1	1.5000	0.6667	1.0000	1.0000	0.6667	1.5000	0.0000
2	2.2500	0.4444	2.5000	0.4000	1.1111	0.9000	0.4444
3	3.3750	0.2963	4.7500	0.2105	1.4074	0.7105	1.0370
4	5.0625	0.1975	8.1250	0.1231	1.6049	0.6231	1.6296
5	7.5938	0.1317	13.1875	0.0758	1.7366	0.5758	2.1564
6	11.3906	0.0878	20.7813	0.0481	1.8244	0.5481	2.5953
7	17.0859	0.0585	32.1719	0.0311	1.8829	0.5311	2.9465
8	25.6289	0.0390	49.2578	0.0203	1.9220	0.5203	3.2196
9	38.4434	0.0260	74.8867	0.0134	1.9480	0.5134	3.4277
10	57.6650	0.0173	113.3301	0.0088	1.9653	0.5088	3.5838
11	86.4976	0.0116	170.9951	0.0058	1.9769	0.5058	3.6994
12	129.7463	0.0077	257.4927	0.0039	1.9846	0.5039	3.7842
13	194.6195	0.0051	387.2390	0.0026	1.9897	0.5026	3.8459
14	291.9293	0.0034	581.8585	0.0017	1.9931	0.5017	3.8904
15	437.8939	0.0023	873.7878	0.0011	1.9954	0.5011	3.9224
16	656.8408	0.0015	1311.6817	0.0008	1.9970	0.5008	3.9452
17	985.2613	0.0010	1968.5225	0.0005	1.9980	0.5005	3.9614
18	1477.8919	0.0007	2953.7838	0.0003	1.9986	0.5003	3.9729
19	2216.8378	0.0005	4431.6756	0.0002	1.9991	0.5002	3.9811
20	3325.2567	0.0003	6648.5134	0.0002	1.9994	0.5002	3.9868

BASIC FACTORS FOR
CONTINUOUS COMPOUNDING

Table B Basic Factors For Continuous Compounding

rn	e^{rn}	e^{-rn}	rn	e^{rn}	e^{-rn}
.01	1.0101	.9900	.51	1.6653	.6005
.02	1.0202	.9802	.52	1.6820	.5945
.03	1.0305	.9704	.53	1.6989	.5886
.04	1.0408	.9608	.54	1.7160	.5827
.05	1.0513	.9512	.55	1.7333	.5769
.06	1.0618	.9418	.56	1.7507	.5712
.07	1.0725	.9324	.57	1.7683	.5655
.08	1.0833	.9231	.58	1.7860	.5599
.09	1.0942	.9139	.59	1.8040	.5543
.10	1.1052	.9048	.60	1.8221	.5488
.11	1.1163	.8958	.61	1.8404	.5434
.12	1.1275	.8869	.62	1.8589	.5379
.13	1.1388	.8781	.63	1.8776	.5326
.14	1.1503	.8694	.64	1.8965	.5273
.15	1.1618	.8607	.65	1.9155	.5220
.16	1.1735	.8521	.66	1.9348	.5169
.17	1.1853	.8437	.67	1.9542	.5117
.18	1.1972	.8353	.68	1.9739	.5066
.19	1.2092	.8270	.69	1.9937	.5016
.20	1.2214	.8187	.70	2.0138	.4966
.21	1.2337	.8106	.71	2.0340	.4916
.22	1.2461	.8025	.72	2.0544	.4868
.23	1.2586	.7945	.73	2.0751	.4819
.24	1.2712	.7866	.74	2.0959	.4771
.25	1.2840	.7788	.75	2.1170	.4724
.26	1.2969	.7711	.76	2.1383	.4677
.27	1.3100	.7634	.77	2.1598	.4630
.28	1.3231	.7558	.78	2.1815	.4584
.29	1.3364	.7483	.79	2.2034	.4538
.30	1.3499	.7408	.80	2.2255	.4493
.31	1.3634	.7334	.81	2.2479	.4449
.32	1.3771	.7261	.82	2.2705	.4404
.33	1.3910	.7189	.83	2.2933	.4360
.34	1.4049	.7118	.84	2.3164	.4317
.35	1.4191	.7047	.85	2.3396	.4274
.36	1.4333	.6977	.86	2.3632	.4232
.37	1.4477	.6907	.87	2.3869	.4190
.38	1.4623	.6839	.88	2.4109	.4148
.39	1.4770	.6771	.89	2.4351	.4107
.40	1.4918	.6703	.90	2.4596	.4066
.41	1.5068	.6637	.91	2.4843	.4025
.42	1.5220	.6570	.92	2.5093	.3985
.43	1.5373	.6505	.93	2.5345	.3946
.44	1.5527	.6440	.94	2.5600	.3906
.45	1.5683	.6376	.95	2.5857	.3867
.46	1.5841	.6313	.96	2.6117	.3829
.47	1.6000	.6250	.97	2.6379	.3791
.48	1.6161	.6188	.98	2.6645	.3753
.49	1.6323	.6126	.99	2.6912	.3716
.50	1.6487	.6065	1.00	2.7183	.3679

C

CONTINUOUS COMPOUND
INTEREST TABLES

Table C.1   Continuous Compound Interest Table $r = 2.0\%$

	COMPOUND AMOUNT FACTOR	DISCOUNT AMOUNT FACTOR	COMPOUND UNIFORM SERIES FACTOR	SINKING FUND FACTOR	DISCOUNT UNIFORM SERIES FACTOR	CAPITAL RECOVERY FACTOR	DISCOUNT GRADIENT FACTOR
n	(F|P,r,n)	(P|F,r,n)	(F|U,r,n)	(U|F,r,n)	(P|U,r,n)	(U|P,r,n)	(P|G,r,n)
1	1.0202	0.9802	1.0000	1.0000	0.9802	1.0202	0.0000
2	1.0408	0.9608	2.0202	0.4950	1.9410	0.5152	0.9609
3	1.0618	0.9418	3.0610	0.3267	2.8828	0.3469	2.8444
4	1.0833	0.9231	4.1229	0.2426	3.8059	0.2628	5.6138
5	1.1052	0.9048	5.2061	0.1921	4.7107	0.2123	9.2332
6	1.1275	0.8869	6.3113	0.1584	5.5976	0.1786	13.6678
7	1.1503	0.8694	7.4388	0.1344	6.4670	0.1546	18.8840
8	1.1735	0.8521	8.5891	0.1164	7.3191	0.1366	24.8491
9	1.1972	0.8353	9.7626	0.1024	8.1544	0.1226	31.5313
10	1.2214	0.8187	10.9598	0.0912	8.9731	0.1114	38.8999
11	1.2461	0.8025	12.1812	0.0821	9.7757	0.1023	46.9251
12	1.2712	0.7866	13.4273	0.0745	10.5623	0.0947	55.5780
13	1.2969	0.7711	14.6985	0.0680	11.3333	0.0882	64.8307
14	1.3231	0.7558	15.9955	0.0625	12.0891	0.0827	74.6559
15	1.3499	0.7408	17.3186	0.0577	12.8299	0.0779	85.0274
16	1.3771	0.7261	18.6685	0.0536	13.5561	0.0738	95.9197
17	1.4049	0.7118	20.0456	0.0499	14.2679	0.0701	107.3080
18	1.4333	0.6977	21.4505	0.0466	14.9655	0.0668	119.1686
19	1.4623	0.6839	22.8839	0.0437	15.6494	0.0639	131.4781
20	1.4918	0.6703	24.3462	0.0411	16.3197	0.0613	144.2142
21	1.5220	0.6570	25.8380	0.0387	16.9768	0.0589	157.3552
22	1.5527	0.6440	27.3599	0.0365	17.6208	0.0568	170.8800
23	1.5841	0.6313	28.9127	0.0346	18.2521	0.0548	184.7683
24	1.6161	0.6188	30.4967	0.0328	18.8709	0.0530	199.0003
25	1.6487	0.6065	32.1128	0.0311	19.4774	0.0513	213.5570
26	1.6820	0.5945	33.7615	0.0296	20.0719	0.0498	228.4201
27	1.7160	0.5827	35.4436	0.0282	20.6547	0.0484	243.5716
28	1.7507	0.5712	37.1596	0.0269	21.2259	0.0471	258.9943
29	1.7860	0.5599	38.9102	0.0257	21.7858	0.0459	274.6714
30	1.8221	0.5488	40.6963	0.0246	22.3346	0.0448	290.5871
35	2.0138	0.4966	50.1825	0.0199	24.9199	0.0401	373.2131
40	2.2255	0.4493	60.6664	0.0165	27.2592	0.0367	459.6726
45	2.4596	0.4066	72.2528	0.0138	29.3758	0.0340	548.4876
50	2.7183	0.3679	85.0579	0.0118	31.2910	0.0320	638.4270
55	3.0042	0.3329	99.2096	0.0101	33.0240	0.0303	728.4724
60	3.3201	0.3012	114.8497	0.0087	34.5921	0.0289	817.7891
70	4.0552	0.2466	151.2376	0.0066	37.2947	0.0268	991.6649
80	4.9530	0.2019	195.6818	0.0051	39.5075	0.0253	1156.1499
90	6.0496	0.1653	249.9661	0.0040	41.3191	0.0242	1308.9352
100	7.3891	0.1353	316.2691	0.0032	42.8024	0.0234	1448.8578

Table C.2 Continuous Compound Interest Table $r = 4.0\%$

	COMPOUND AMOUNT FACTOR	DISCOUNT AMOUNT FACTOR	COMPOUND UNIFORM SERIES FACTOR	SINKING FUND FACTOR	DISCOUNT UNIFORM SERIES FACTOR	CAPITAL RECOVERY FACTOR	DISCOUNT GRADIENT FACTOR
n	(F|P,r,n)	(P|F,r,n)	(F|U,r,n)	(U|F,r,n)	(P|U,r,n)	(U|P,r,n)	(P|G,r,n)
1	1.0408	0.9608	1.0000	1.0000	0.9608	1.0408	0.0000
2	1.0833	0.9231	2.0408	0.4900	1.8839	0.5308	0.9231
3	1.1275	0.8869	3.1241	0.3201	2.7708	0.3609	2.6970
4	1.1735	0.8521	4.2516	0.2352	3.6230	0.2760	5.2534
5	1.2214	0.8187	5.4251	0.1843	4.4417	0.2251	8.5283
6	1.2712	0.7866	6.6465	0.1505	5.2283	0.1913	12.4615
7	1.3231	0.7558	7.9178	0.1263	5.9841	0.1671	16.9962
8	1.3771	0.7261	9.2409	0.1082	6.7103	0.1490	22.0792
9	1.4333	0.6977	10.6180	0.0942	7.4079	0.1350	27.6607
10	1.4918	0.6703	12.0513	0.0830	8.0783	0.1238	33.6936
11	1.5527	0.6440	13.5432	0.0738	8.7223	0.1146	40.1339
12	1.6161	0.6188	15.0959	0.0662	9.3411	0.1071	46.9405
13	1.6820	0.5945	16.7120	0.0598	9.9356	0.1006	54.0748
14	1.7507	0.5712	18.3940	0.0544	10.5068	0.0952	61.5005
15	1.8221	0.5488	20.1447	0.0496	11.0556	0.0905	69.1839
16	1.8965	0.5273	21.9668	0.0455	11.5829	0.0863	77.0933
17	1.9739	0.5066	23.8633	0.0419	12.0895	0.0827	85.1992
18	2.0544	0.4868	25.8371	0.0387	12.5763	0.0795	93.4739
19	2.1383	0.4677	27.8916	0.0359	13.0440	0.0767	101.8919
20	2.2255	0.4493	30.0298	0.0333	13.4933	0.0741	110.4292
21	2.3164	0.4317	32.2554	0.0310	13.9250	0.0718	119.0634
22	2.4109	0.4148	34.5718	0.0289	14.3398	0.0697	127.7739
23	2.5093	0.3985	36.9827	0.0270	14.7383	0.0679	136.5413
24	2.6117	0.3829	39.4919	0.0253	15.1212	0.0661	145.3478
25	2.7183	0.3679	42.1036	0.0238	15.4891	0.0646	154.1769
26	2.8292	0.3535	44.8219	0.0223	15.8425	0.0631	163.0133
27	2.9447	0.3396	47.6511	0.0210	16.1821	0.0618	171.8428
28	3.0649	0.3263	50.5958	0.0198	16.5084	0.0606	180.6524
29	3.1899	0.3135	53.6607	0.0186	16.8219	0.0594	189.4300
30	3.3201	0.3012	56.8506	0.0176	17.1231	0.0584	198.1646
35	4.0552	0.2466	74.8626	0.0134	18.4609	0.0542	240.8677
40	4.9530	0.2019	96.8625	0.0103	19.5562	0.0511	281.3067
45	6.0496	0.1653	123.7332	0.0081	20.4530	0.0489	318.8991
50	7.3891	0.1353	156.5532	0.0064	21.1872	0.0472	353.3482
55	9.0250	0.1108	196.6396	0.0051	21.7883	0.0459	384.5583
60	11.0232	0.0907	245.6013	0.0041	22.2804	0.0449	412.5718
70	16.4446	0.0608	378.4454	0.0026	23.0133	0.0435	459.5990
80	24.5325	0.0408	576.6256	0.0017	23.5045	0.0425	496.0347
90	36.5982	0.0273	872.2756	0.0011	23.8338	0.0420	523.7511
100	54.5981	0.0183	1313.3336	0.0008	24.0545	0.0416	544.5373

Table C.3 Continuous Compound Interest Table $r = 6.0\%$

	COMPOUND AMOUNT FACTOR	DISCOUNT AMOUNT FACTOR	COMPOUND UNIFORM SERIES FACTOR	SINKING FUND FACTOR	DISCOUNT UNIFORM SERIES FACTOR	CAPITAL RECOVERY FACTOR	DISCOUNT GRADIENT FACTOR
n	(F|P,r,n)	(P|F,r,n)	(F|U,r,n)	(U|F,r,n)	(P|U,r,n)	(U|P,r,n)	(P|G,r,n)
1	1.0618	0.9418	1.0000	1.0000	0.9418	1.0618	0.0000
2	1.1275	0.8869	2.0618	0.4850	1.8287	0.5468	0.8869
3	1.1972	0.8353	3.1893	0.3135	2.6640	0.3754	2.5575
4	1.2712	0.7866	4.3866	0.2280	3.4506	0.2898	4.9174
5	1.3499	0.7408	5.6578	0.1767	4.1914	0.2386	7.8806
6	1.4333	0.6977	7.0077	0.1427	4.8891	0.2045	11.3690
7	1.5220	0.6570	8.4410	0.1185	5.5461	0.1803	15.3113
8	1.6161	0.6188	9.9630	0.1004	6.1649	0.1622	19.6428
9	1.7160	0.5827	11.5790	0.0864	6.7477	0.1482	24.3048
10	1.8221	0.5488	13.2950	0.0752	7.2965	0.1371	29.2441
11	1.9348	0.5169	15.1172	0.0662	7.8133	0.1280	34.4126
12	2.0544	0.4868	17.0519	0.0586	8.3001	0.1205	39.7669
13	2.1815	0.4584	19.1064	0.0523	8.7585	0.1142	45.2677
14	2.3164	0.4317	21.2878	0.0470	9.1902	0.1088	50.8800
15	2.4596	0.4066	23.6042	0.0424	9.5968	0.1042	56.5719
16	2.6117	0.3829	26.0638	0.0384	9.9797	0.1002	62.3153
17	2.7732	0.3606	28.6755	0.0349	10.3402	0.0967	68.0849
18	2.9447	0.3396	31.4487	0.0318	10.6798	0.0936	73.8580
19	3.1268	0.3198	34.3934	0.0291	10.9997	0.0909	79.6147
20	3.3201	0.3012	37.5202	0.0267	11.3009	0.0885	85.3374
21	3.5254	0.2837	40.8403	0.0245	11.5845	0.0863	91.0105
22	3.7434	0.2671	44.3657	0.0225	11.8516	0.0844	96.6203
23	3.9749	0.2516	48.1091	0.0208	12.1032	0.0826	102.1551
24	4.2207	0.2369	52.0840	0.0192	12.3402	0.0810	107.6044
25	4.4817	0.2231	56.3047	0.0178	12.5633	0.0796	112.9595
26	4.7588	0.2101	60.7864	0.0165	12.7734	0.0783	118.2129
27	5.0531	0.1979	65.5452	0.0153	12.9713	0.0771	123.3583
28	5.3656	0.1864	70.5983	0.0142	13.1577	0.0760	128.3904
29	5.6973	0.1755	75.9639	0.0132	13.3332	0.0750	133.3050
30	6.0496	0.1653	81.6612	0.0122	13.4985	0.0741	138.0986
35	8.1662	0.1225	115.8889	0.0086	14.1913	0.0705	160.1863
40	11.0232	0.0907	162.0915	0.0062	14.7046	0.0680	179.1156
45	14.8797	0.0672	224.4584	0.0045	15.0848	0.0663	195.0399
50	20.0855	0.0498	308.6450	0.0032	15.3665	0.0651	208.2454
55	27.1126	0.0369	422.2849	0.0024	15.5752	0.0642	219.0716
60	36.5982	0.0273	575.6828	0.0017	15.7298	0.0636	227.8649
70	66.6863	0.0150	1062.2575	0.0009	15.9292	0.0628	240.6259
80	121.5104	0.0082	1948.8545	0.0005	16.0386	0.0623	248.7235
90	221.4064	0.0045	3564.3392	0.0003	16.0986	0.0621	253.7680
100	403.4288	0.0025	6507.9447	0.0002	16.1316	0.0620	256.8660

Table C.4   Continuous Compound Interest Table $r = 8.0\%$

n	COMPOUND AMOUNT FACTOR (F|P,r,n)	DISCOUNT AMOUNT FACTOR (P|F,r,n)	COMPOUND UNIFORM SERIES FACTOR (F|U,r,n)	SINKING FUND FACTOR (U|F,r,n)	DISCOUNT UNIFORM SERIES FACTOR (P|U,r,n)	CAPITAL RECOVERY FACTOR (U|P,r,n)	DISCOUNT GRADIENT FACTOR (P|G,r,n)
1	1.0833	0.9231	1.0000	1.0000	0.9231	1.0833	0.0000
2	1.1735	0.8521	2.0833	0.4800	1.7753	0.5633	0.8521
3	1.2712	0.7866	3.2568	0.3071	2.5619	0.3903	2.4254
4	1.3771	0.7261	4.5280	0.2208	3.2880	0.3041	4.6039
5	1.4918	0.6703	5.9052	0.1693	3.9584	0.2526	7.2851
6	1.6161	0.6188	7.3970	0.1352	4.5771	0.2185	10.3791
7	1.7507	0.5712	9.0131	0.1109	5.1484	0.1942	13.8063
8	1.8965	0.5273	10.7637	0.0929	5.6756	0.1762	17.4974
9	2.0544	0.4868	12.6602	0.0790	6.1624	0.1623	21.3914
10	2.2255	0.4493	14.7147	0.0680	6.6117	0.1512	25.4353
11	2.4109	0.4148	16.9402	0.0590	7.0265	0.1423	29.5832
12	2.6117	0.3829	19.3511	0.0517	7.4094	0.1350	33.7950
13	2.8292	0.3535	21.9628	0.0455	7.7629	0.1288	38.0364
14	3.0649	0.3263	24.7920	0.0403	8.0891	0.1236	42.2781
15	3.3201	0.3012	27.8569	0.0359	8.3903	0.1192	46.4948
16	3.5966	0.2780	31.1770	0.0321	8.6684	0.1154	50.6654
17	3.8962	0.2567	34.7736	0.0288	8.9250	0.1120	54.7719
18	4.2207	0.2369	38.6698	0.0259	9.1620	0.1091	58.7997
19	4.5722	0.2187	42.8905	0.0233	9.3807	0.1066	62.7365
20	4.9530	0.2019	47.4627	0.0211	9.5826	0.1044	66.5726
21	5.3656	0.1864	52.4158	0.0191	9.7689	0.1024	70.3000
22	5.8124	0.1720	57.7813	0.0173	9.9410	0.1006	73.9130
23	6.2965	0.1588	63.5938	0.0157	10.0998	0.0990	77.4070
24	6.8210	0.1466	69.8903	0.0143	10.2464	0.0976	80.7789
25	7.3891	0.1353	76.7113	0.0130	10.3817	0.0963	84.0270
26	8.0045	0.1249	84.1003	0.0119	10.5067	0.0952	87.1502
27	8.6711	0.1153	92.1048	0.0109	10.6220	0.0941	90.1487
28	9.3933	0.1065	100.7759	0.0099	10.7285	0.0932	93.0231
29	10.1757	0.0983	110.1693	0.0091	10.8267	0.0924	95.7747
30	11.0232	0.0907	120.3449	0.0083	10.9174	0.0916	98.4055
35	16.4446	0.0608	185.4387	0.0054	11.2765	0.0887	109.8393
40	24.5325	0.0408	282.5473	0.0035	11.5172	0.0868	118.7070
45	36.5982	0.0273	427.4161	0.0023	11.6786	0.0856	125.4581
50	54.5981	0.0183	643.5351	0.0016	11.7868	0.0848	130.5242
55	81.4509	0.0123	965.9468	0.0010	11.8593	0.0843	134.2826

Table C.5 Continuous Compound Interest Table $r = 10.0\%$

n	COMPOUND AMOUNT FACTOR (F|P,r,n)	DISCOUNT AMOUNT FACTOR (P|F,r,n)	COMPOUND UNIFORM SERIES FACTOR (F|U,r,n)	SINKING FUND FACTOR (U|F,r,n)	DISCOUNT UNIFORM SERIES FACTOR (P|U,r,n)	CAPITAL RECOVERY FACTOR (U|P,r,n)	DISCOUNT GRADIENT FACTOR (P|G,r,n)
1	1.1052	0.9048	1.0000	1.0000	0.9048	1.1052	0.0000
2	1.2214	0.8187	2.1052	0.4750	1.7236	0.5802	0.8187
3	1.3499	0.7408	3.3266	0.3006	2.4644	0.4058	2.3004
4	1.4918	0.6703	4.6764	0.2138	3.1347	0.3190	4.3113
5	1.6487	0.6065	6.1683	0.1621	3.7412	0.2673	6.7375
6	1.8221	0.5488	7.8170	0.1279	4.2900	0.2331	9.4815
7	2.0138	0.4966	9.6391	0.1037	4.7866	0.2089	12.4610
8	2.2255	0.4493	11.6529	0.0858	5.2360	0.1910	15.6063
9	2.4596	0.4066	13.8784	0.0721	5.6425	0.1772	18.8589
10	2.7183	0.3679	16.3380	0.0612	6.0104	0.1664	22.1698
11	3.0042	0.3329	19.0563	0.0525	6.3433	0.1576	25.4985
12	3.3201	0.3012	22.0604	0.0453	6.6445	0.1505	28.8117
13	3.6693	0.2725	25.3806	0.0394	6.9170	0.1446	32.0820
14	4.0552	0.2466	29.0499	0.0344	7.1636	0.1396	35.2878
15	4.4817	0.2231	33.1051	0.0302	7.3867	0.1354	38.4116
16	4.9530	0.2019	37.5867	0.0266	7.5886	0.1318	41.4401
17	5.4739	0.1827	42.5398	0.0235	7.7713	0.1287	44.3630
18	6.0496	0.1653	48.0137	0.0208	7.9366	0.1260	47.1731
19	6.6859	0.1496	54.0634	0.0185	8.0862	0.1237	49.8653
20	7.3891	0.1353	60.7493	0.0165	8.2215	0.1216	52.4367
21	8.1662	0.1225	68.1383	0.0147	8.3440	0.1198	54.8858
22	9.0250	0.1108	76.3045	0.0131	8.4548	0.1183	57.2127
23	9.9742	0.1003	85.3295	0.0117	8.5550	0.1169	59.4184
24	11.0232	0.0907	95.3037	0.0105	8.6458	0.1157	61.5049
25	12.1825	0.0821	106.3269	0.0094	8.7278	0.1146	63.4749
26	13.4637	0.0743	118.5094	0.0084	8.8021	0.1136	65.3318
27	14.8797	0.0672	131.9731	0.0076	8.8693	0.1127	67.0791
28	16.4446	0.0608	146.8528	0.0068	8.9301	0.1120	68.7210
29	18.1741	0.0550	163.2975	0.0061	8.9852	0.1113	70.2616
30	20.0855	0.0498	181.4716	0.0055	9.0349	0.1107	71.7055
35	33.1155	0.0302	305.3644	0.0033	9.2212	0.1084	77.6289
40	54.5981	0.0183	509.6291	0.0020	9.3342	0.1071	81.7865
45	90.0171	0.0111	846.4045	0.0012	9.4027	0.1064	84.6508
50	148.4132	0.0067	1401.6534	0.0007	9.4443	0.1059	86.5959
55	244.6919	0.0041	2317.1041	0.0004	9.4695	0.1056	87.9017

ANSWERS
TO
PROBLEMS

Chapter 1

P1.1 and **P1.2**   No specific answers.

Chapter 2

P2.1   − $950 at beginning, $60 each for periods 1 to 19, $1,060 for period 20.

P2.2   − $9,800 for year 0, $800 each for years 1 to 24, $10,800 for year 25.

P2.3 $110.25 and $120.50.

P2.4 $112.36 and $123.

P2.5   3,000 units for a maximum profit $6 million.

P2.6   Public park with a maximum net benefit of $7 million.

P2.7   (a) Plan 2; (b) plan 1.

P2.8   U.S. Treasury notes with $31,523.89 at end of year.

P2.9   11.51%.

P2.10   Alternative 2 with NPV = $1,666.67.

Chapter 3

P3.1 $9594.

P3.2 $63,096.

P3.3 $14,737 (< $15,000).

P3.4 $70.5

P3.5 $6,145 (> $5,000).

P3.6 $562.2.

P3.7 $3,057.

P3.8 $9,959.

P3.9 $2,210.

P3.10 $176,966.

P3.11 $4,630.

P3.12 $2,696.

P3.13 $1,829,631.

P3.14 $39,739.

P3.15 $197,736.

P3.16 $1,989.

P3.17 $18,635.

P3.18 $17,908 and $17,333, respectively.

P3.19 $1,885 and $1,822, respectively.

P3.20   (a) 7.25%; (b)$750.70.

P3.21 $1,997.

P3.22   6.45%.

P3.23   34.01%.

P3.24 $2,220.

P3.25 $1,759,185.

P3.26 $18,817.

Chapter 4

P4.1   8.15%.

P4.2   9%.

P4.3   4.66%.

P4.4   11.93%.

P4.5   9.2%.

P4.6   20% and 80%.

P4.7   NPV = 0 for $i = 0\%$, 30%, and 40%.

P4.8   NPV = 0 for i = 10%, 20%, 30%, and 40%.

P4.9   7.46% for Ms. Sand.

P4.10   4.42% for Mr. Jackson; 9.46% for the new buyer.

P4.11   5.29%.

P4.12 i = 6%. Annual interests: $540, $370, and $191.

P4.13 i = 7.44%. Annual interests: $409, $380, $327, $247, and $139.

P4.14   (a) Annual interests: $2000, $2200, $2420, and $2662; (b) Annual interests: $2000, $1569, $1095, and $573.

P4.15   24.45%.

P4.16   9.20%.

P4.17   (a) IRR = 8% and 33.7%; (b) ORR = 20.8%.

P4.18   (a) IRR = 10.8% and 33.8%; (b) ORR = 25.6%.

Chapter 5

P5.1   NPV = 2334; NFV = 4608; NUV = 568.

P5.2   NFV = 18,741; NUV = 2309.

P5.3   IRR = 19.92%; ORR = 16.1%.

P5.4   IRR = 50%; ORR = 25.88%.

P5.5   NUV = $70.4.

P5.6   NPV = −$2,935; ORR = 7.67%.

P5.7   NPV = $239.

P5.8   NPV = −$7,828.

P5.9 $82.9, $30.5, $36.5, $44.7, −$1.6, and $1.4 (all in millions).

P5.10 $20.8, $7.6, $9.1, $11.2, −$0.4, and $0.4 (all in millions).

P5.11   2.08, 1.40, 1.48, 1.48, 0.98, and 1.02.

P5.12   (a) $26,454; (b) $27,014; (c) $27,854.

P5.13   Project no. 2 with NPV = $235.

P5.14   (a) NPV = $0.3864, (b) NPV = −$0.6522, (c) NPV = $1,4250, all in millions.

P5.15   NPV = −$24.

Chapter 6

P6.1   Proposal 3 with NPV = $67.

P6.2   Proposal 2 or 3, both with NPV = $8.5.

P6.3   (1) 8%, (2) 7.7%, (3) 8.94%.

P6.4 x = 3 best, x = 1 next, and x = 2 last for all specified values of MARR.

P6.5   First pump with NPV = $13,799. ORR = 22.75% and 21.5% for x = 1 and x = 2, respectively.

P6.6   First design with NPV = $12,056. ORR = 12.6% and 11.5% for x = 1 and x = 2, respectively.

P6.7 i_{3-2} = 15%, i_{3-1} = 22.5%, and i_{2-1} = 30%.

P6.8 $[\text{NPV}]_{10\%}$ = $95, $26.9, and 0 for x = 1, 2, and 3 respectively.

P6.9   IRR = 20%, 12%, and 10% for x = 1, 2, and 3, respectively. i_{3-1} = 4.29%, i_{3-2} = 7.93%, i_{2-1} < 0.

P6.10 $[\text{NPV}]_{8\%}$ = 0 for all three alternatives.

P6.11   Maximum N = 1 at C = 1, both in $ million.

P6.12   Maximum N = 2.25 at C = 4, both in $ million

P6.13   Select type II with NPV = $1,653.

P6.14   Select machine 1 with CPV = $23,714.

P6.15   Select the second alternative with CPV = $5,914.

P6.16 $57,054.

P6.17   Single-stage construction with NPV = $192,460.

P6.18   NPV = $1.6531, $1.7002, and $1.7353, all in millions, for starting the second stage in 10, 15, and 20 years, respectively.

Chapter 7

P7.1   Proposal 3 with $\Delta B_{3-0}/\Delta C_{3-0}$ = 1.04.

P7.2 Proposal 3 or 2, with $\Delta B_{3-0}/\Delta C_{3-0} = 1.05$ and $\Delta B_{2-3}/\Delta C_{2-3} = 1.0$.

P7.3 (a) Proposal 3, (b) proposal 2, and (c) proposal 1 or 2.

P7.4 Proposal 1 with $\Delta B_{1-0}/\Delta C_{1-0} = 1.31$, (b) proposal 1 with $\Delta B_{1-0}/\Delta C_{1-0} = 1.19$, and (c) proposal 1 with $\Delta B_{1-0}/\Delta C_{1-0} = 1.09$.

P7.5 $x = 6$ with $\Delta B_{6-5}/\Delta C_{6-5} = 1.14$.

P7.6 (a) Select $x = 1$ with $\Delta B_{1-2}/\Delta C_{1-2} = 1.65$; (b) select $x = 1$ with $\Delta B_{1-0}/\Delta C_{1-0} = 1.73$.

P7.7 (a) Select $x = 1$ with $\Delta B_{1-0}/\Delta C_{1-0} = 1.18$; (b) same as Problem P7.6.

P7.8 Select $x = 2$ with $\Delta B_{2-1}/\Delta C_{2-1} = 1.04$.

Chapter 8

P8.1 Proposal 3, using ascending order of $x = 2$, $x = 1$, and $x = 3$ in incremental analysis.

P8.2 Proposal 3, using ascending order of $x = 1$, $x = 2$, and $x = 3$ in incremental analysis.

P8.3 Proposal 1, using ascending order of $x = 2$ and $x = 1$ in incremental analysis.

P8.4 Proposal 3, using ascending order of $x = 2$, $x = 1$, and $x = 3$ in incremental analysis.

P8.5 Proposal 1, using ascending order of $x = 2$, $x = 3$, and $x = 1$ in incremental analysis, with $[dN_x/di]_{0\%}$ to break the tie for ordering all alternatives.

P8.6 Proposal 2, using ascending order of $x = 1$ and $x = 2$ in incremental analysis.

P8.7 Proposal 3, using ascending order of $x = 1$, $x = 2$, and $x = 3$ in incremental analysis, with

$[dN_x/di]_{0\%}$ to break the tie for ordering $x = 1$ and $x = 2$.

P8.8 Proposal 2, using ascending order of $x = 3$, $x = 1$, and $x = 2$ in incremental analysis.

Chapter 9

P9.1 $x = 1$, $x = 5$, and $x = 4$, with CPV = \$2.9 million and NPV = \$4.9 million.

P9.2 (a) $x = 1$, $x = 5$, $x = 4$, and $x = 6$, with CPV = \$4.8 million and NPV = 6.7 million; (b) two combinations are tied for CPV = \$6.0 million and NPV = \$7.8 million.

P9.3 (a) $x = 1$ and $x = 4$ with CPV = \$169.7 million and NPV = \$127.6 million; (b) $x = 1$, $x = 4$, and $x = 3$ with CPV = \$245 million and NPV = \$164.1 million.

P9.4 $B/C = 2.08$, 1.40, 1.48, and 1.48 for alternatives 1, 2, 3, and 4, respectively.

P9.5 $x = 6$ and $x = 3$, with CPV = \$480,900 and NPV = \$496,000.

P9.6 26.15%.

P9.7 9.86%.

P9.8 8%.

Chapter 10

P10.1 \$3,675.

P10.2 250,000.

P10.3 Both will cost the same.

P10.4 800.

P10.5 20.

P10.6 $dC/dx = 500$ and $dB/dx = 500$ at $x = 20$.

P10.7 Minimum total cost of \$5,250 at $x = 6$.

P10.8 $dC/dx = 600$ and $dB/dx = 600$ at $x = 6$.

Chapter 11

P11.1 (a) $D_1 = \$3,000, B_1 = \$14,000$; (b) $D_1 = \$5,000, B_1 = \$12,000$.

P11.2 (a) $D_1 = \$10,000, B_1 = \$60,000$; (b) $D_1 = \$17,143, B_1 = \$52,857$.

P11.3 $D_1 = \$5,120, B_1 = \$15,360$; $D_2 = \$3,840, B_2 = \$11,520$.

P11.4 $D_1 = \$24,300, B_1 = \$48,600$; $D_2 = \$16,200, B_2 = \$32,400$.

P11.5 $D_1 = \$10,000, B_1 = \$15,000$; $D_4 = \$400, B_4 = \$5,000$.

P11.6 $D_1 = \$50,000, B_1 = \$200,000$; $D_9' = \$8471.5, B_9' = \$33,471.5$.

P11.7 (a) $D_2 = \$350, B_2 = \$1,700$; (b) $D_3 = \$400, B_3 = \$900$; (c) $D_4 = \$237, B_4 = \$474$.

P11.8 $D_6 = \$297,000, B_6 = \$889,000$; $D_7' = \$295,000, B_7' = \$595,000$.

P11.9 $D_1 = \$2,500,000$.

P11.10 $D_5 = \$2,400$.

Chapter 12

P12.1 NPV $= -\$2,374$ for (a), (b), and (c).

P12.2 (1) NPV $= -\$334, \$1,550$, and $\$643$ for (a), (b), and (c), respectively; (2) NPV $= -\$3,323, -\$3,439$, and $-\$3,058$ for (a), (b), and (c), respectively.

P12.3 NPV $= -\$7,129$.

P12.4 NPV $= \$6,566$.

P12.5 $\$7,421$.

P12.6 (a) NPV $= -\$1,319$; (b) NPV $= \$236$.

P12.7 $\$44,348$.

P12.8 NPV $= \$16,123$.

P12.9 Alternative 1 with NPV $= \$1.368$ million.

P12.10 $\$54,267$.

P12.11 $\$3198$.

Chapter 13

P13.1 $\$40,852$.

P13.2 (a) $\$55,840$; (b) $\$232,334$.

P13.3 NPV $= \$47,547$.

P13.4 NPV $= -\$1,021$.

P13.5 NPV $= \$4,287$.

P13.6 Existing model with $\$82.16$ saving.

P13.7 (a) 3.7%; (b) $\$12,439$.

P13.8 (a) 15.5%; (b) $\$1,780$.

P13.9 (a) NPV $= -\$2,083$; (b) NPV $= \$487$.

P13.10 (a) NPV $= \$2,489$; (b) $\$641$.

P13.11 NPV $= -\$581$.

P13.12 NPV $= -\$3,169$.

P13.13 NPV $= -\$118,000$.

P13.14 System A with NPV $= \$5,527$.

Chapter 14

P14.1 (a) 1.82 and 1.14; (b) 3 and 1.17; (c) 3.5%, 6%, $\$10$ per share and 0.33.

P14.2 A contingent legal liability will make the firm less attractive.

P14.3 (a) 2.21 and 1.41; (b) 100 and 0.48; (c) 7.7%, 13.9, $\$1.25$ per share and 0%.

P14.4 Indication of company's inability or unwillingness to keep accurate records, or both.

P14.5 (a) 1.84 and 0.89; (b) 2 and 1.67; (c) 2%, 3.3%, $\$0.50$ per share and 0%.

P14.6 (a) 1.74 and 0.83; (b) 6 and 1.79; (c) 3.75%, 5.3%, $\$0.75$ per share and 0%.

P14.7 Sources of funds, $\$50,000$; uses of funds, $\$17,000$; increase in working capital, $\$33,000$.

P14.8 Net changes in components $\$33,000$.

Chapter 15

P15.1 $\mu = \$6,700$; $\sigma = \$1,350$.

P15.2 $\mu = \$4,300$; $\sigma = \$1,900$.

P15.3 Chance factor for the "to bid" branch; no uncertainty in the "not to bid" branch.

P15.4 Protective wall leading to minimum expected cost of $16,000.

P15.5 (a) $p = 0.1$; (b) 9,000 p for $0 \leq p \leq 0.1$, and 0 for $0.1 \leq p \leq 1$.

P15.6 19.16%.

P15.7 $\beta_a = 0.99$; $r_a = 16.61\%$.

P15.8 $r_e = 22.0$; $r_a = 22.88\%$.

Chapter 16

P16.1 $17,000 for both (a) and (b).

P16.2 $r_e = 25\%$; $\beta_e = 1.8\%$.

P16.3 $r_0 = 13.03\%$.

P16.4 $r_w = 13.69\%$.

P16.5 (a) $r_0 = 19.3\%$, and (b) $r_w = 22.2\%$, $r_e = 38.0\%$ for $D/E = 1.0$.

P16.6 $r_e = 20.9\%$, $r_d = 10.2\%$, and $r_w = 14.4\%$ for $D/E = 0.7$.

P16.7 Division A: MARR = 12.35%.

Division B: MARR = 14.96%.
Division C: MARR = 17.57%.
Division D: MARR = 20.18%.

P16.8 21.40% for electronics division; 21.74% for appliance division.

P16.9 APV = $0.5391 million.

P16.10 APV = $37.2 million.

Chapter 17

P17.1 $1.00 per person.

P17.2 $0.24 per gallon of discharge.

P17.3 $R_2 - R_1 = \$500$; $S_2 - S_1 = \$1,250$.

P17.4 MBP = 0; MPS = $75.

P17.5 (1) 1.02; (2) 1.21; (3) 0.66.

P17.6 (1) $7,989; (2) −$21,429.

P17.7 $3,090.

INDEX